Production Control: Systems and Decisions

THE IRWIN SERIES IN MANAGEMENT

Consulting Editor **John F. Mee** Indiana University

MOORE *Manufacturing Management* 4th ed.
NIEBEL *Motion and Time Study* 4th ed.
ROSCOE *Organization for Production* 4th ed.
JUCIUS *Personnel Management* 6th ed.
CRUICKSHANK & DAVIS *Cases in Management* 3d ed.
FILIPETTI *Industrial Management in Transition* rev. ed.
SPRIEGEL & MYERS (Editors) *The Writings of the Gilbreths*
TERRY *Principles of Management* 4th ed.
VORIS *Production Control: Text and Cases* 3d ed.
SIMONDS & GRIMALDI *Safety Management: Accident Cost and Control* rev. ed.
JONES *Executive Decision Making* rev. ed.
NIEBEL & BALDWIN *Designing for Production* rev. ed.
PATTON, LITTLEFIELD, & SELF *Job Evaluation: Text and Cases* 3d ed.
SHULL & DELBECQ (Editors) *Selected Readings in Management: Extensions and Modifications* Second Series
BRENNAN *Wage Administration: Plans, Practices, and Principles* rev. ed.
JUCIUS & SCHLENDER *Elements of Managerial Action* rev. ed.
HANEY *Communication and Organizational Behavior: Text and Cases* rev. ed.
JOHNSON *Personnel and Industrial Relations*
DEPHILLIPS, BERLINER, & CRIBBIN *Management of Training Programs*
MORRIS *The Analysis of Management Decisions* rev. ed.
THAYER *Administrative Communication*
ROSCOE *Project Economy*
EELLS & WALTON *Conceptual Foundations of Business*
HOUSTON *Manager Development: Principles and Perspectives*
SEIMER *Cases in Industrial Management*
REED *Plant Layout: Factors, Principles, and Techniques*
AMMER *Materials Management*
BROOM *Production Management* rev. ed.
SCOTT *Organization Theory: A Behavioral Analysis for Management*
SIEGEL *Industrial Psychology*
TIMMS *The Production Function in Business: Fundamentals and Analysis for Management* rev. ed.
NADLER *Work Design*
FOX *The Management Process: An Integrated Functional Approach*
CHAMPION & BRIDGES *Critical Incidents in Management*
MOORE & KIBBEY *Manufacturing: Materials and Processes*
MCDONOUGH & GARRETT *Management Systems: Working Concepts and Practices*
GREENE *Production Control: Systems and Decisions*
FARMER & RICHMAN *Comparative Management and Economic Progress*
LING *The Management of Personnel Relations: History and Origins*
RICHARDS & GREENLAW *Management Decision Making*
PRINCE *Information Systems for Management Planning and Control*
MEGGINSON *Personnel: A Behavioral Approach to Administration*

Production Control
SYSTEMS and DECISIONS

James H. Greene, Ph.D.
School of Industrial Engineering
Purdue University

1965
RICHARD D. IRWIN, INC.
HOMEWOOD, ILLINOIS

First Printing, June, 1965

Second Printing, January, 1967

Third Printing, February, 1968

Library of Congress Catalog Card No. 65–20524

PRINTED IN THE UNITED STATES OF AMERICA

To

Barbara, Robin and Tim

Preface

This text attempts to bridge the gap between the descriptive approach to production control which has prevailed for many years and the more recent theoretical and specialized approaches to inventory control theory, servo theory, linear programming, computers and other more or less exotic subjects.

I have tried my utmost to put subjects in their proper perspective. Little can be gained by a company installing extensive computer systems if the data have not been put in order first. It would be just as foolish to attempt elaborate linear programming models if the required accounting information is not to be had. It is a wise man who puts first things first, and every opportunity has been taken to develop perspective for the reader.

It is assumed that he is more interested in understanding system designing and decision making for production planning and control than he is in day-to-day operations of a production control office. It is for this reason that the theme throughout is a logical system designing approach, rather than descriptions of present systems.

For those of you who are actually engaged in the operation of a control system, there is a fresh view which should help solve many of your pressing problems. If the stress of daily operations has prevented you from remaining abreast of developments, then this text should offer you the opportunity to update yourself with a minimum of difficulty.

While prior knowledge of the subjects discussed in this text is not essential, the college student will find a background of mathematics through algebra and perhaps calculus useful. A basic course in production management will also enhance his appreciation of some of the subjects included in the text. Although basic statistics is included, an earlier exposure to this subject will increase understanding of the applications of statistics which are presented. All the subjects start at an elementary level, building knowledge upon knowledge, until the point is reached where actual and useful applications can be made with little hesitation.

The material herein is developed in five sections with the first serving as an introduction to system designing, the logic which is used for system designing, and an introduction to production control concepts. Emphasis has been placed on analogies for solving systems problems. In particular the input, output, and feedback concepts of the servo system.

Section two develops the input of information required for production control systems, while the third section includes a discussion of the various tools, such as card-data-processing and computer processing used in the design of systems.

Section four is given to decision-making techniques for control, including graphical techniques such as the Gantt Chart and PERT, as well as the mathematical techniques of linear programming.

In section five, the input, output, and feedback concepts are shown in some real-world case studies. A number of control systems are illustrated to show how companies with widely varying problems have solved them.

Man is a mosaic of his innumerable experiences. How can he recognize, let alone credit, all those who have influenced him? I recognize a debt of gratitude to too many people to list them all here.

I am deeply grateful to those at the State University of Iowa who assisted me toward my educational goals. Also, to those colleagues at Purdue who have been a constant stimulation during my teaching career. Above all, I probably owe the greatest debt for the development of this text to the graduate students whom I have supervised. I had the pleasure of being not only their teacher but also their student. In particular I would like to thank Mamdouh Bakr, Thomas Rehg, Chandry Rao, Christian Neve, and Captain Neil Saling who checked parts of this book.

Dr. Aaron Glickstein has kindly contributed the results of some of his research to the text, for which I would like to express my gratitude. Betty and Joseph Havlicek have graciously shared their knowledge in some of the technical fields.

To my wife, Barbara, goes my deepest gratitude. She had the courage to encourage me in this venture and had the foresight to prepare herself in home economics and journalism. No author could ask more.

My objective with this book is to communicate some ideas as simply and painlessly as possible. In trying to do this, I have adhered to one of the lesser theories of Albert Einstein: Matters of elegance ought to be left to the tailor and the cobbler.

JAMES H. GREENE

LAFAYETTE, INDIANA
April, 1965

Table of Contents

SECTION ONE

Introduction

CHAPTER 1

System Designing

This book is written for those interested in the design of systems and in the decision-making techniques for controlling the manufacturing of goods. It is not intended for those who are looking for a case-study approach of how control systems work, although a number of examples will be found in the book.

To make this point more clear, an analogy can be made between the person who operates a power plant and the person who designed it and supervised its construction. The operating engineer is involved with the day-to-day operations of this particular plant and will have to know the performance of its equipment from every angle. He probably wouldn't feel at home in any other plant and would find that the information he had obtained in one plant would be of very little use in another.

On the other hand, the designer must know a great deal about all aspects of building a power plant. This means he must know what load is expected to be placed on the machines, what energy inputs are available, and how they can be brought together to build a power plant system at an optimum cost.

The power plant operator, although highly skilled, does not have the breadth or depth of knowledge that the power plant designer has. While the operator might eventually be able to design and build good power plants (if he worked in enough such situations), he will never design as good a plant as the power plant design engineer.

This analogy can be carried into practically any profession. The businessman, the banker, the lawyer can all become competent technicians by working in their respective fields, but they will never be able to make important contributions until they understand the logic and principles of their subjects.

This book is written from the design approach for those who wish to develop systems for the control of manufacturing operations. Because of this, we will dwell upon basic information and how this information can be assimilated into the design of a system.

As a bridge designer learns from a study of many bridges, so does a manufacturing control systems designer learn from studying a number of control systems, but he had first better study the components and principles which make up the system.

THE MEANING OF SYSTEM DESIGNING

Since the words *system, design, production,* and *control* have significant meanings in this text, it is desirable to define them. Later on we shall combine the definitions to emphasize the objective of this book: system designing for production control. As a foundation, however, we will start with accepted definitions. For example, a system is defined as ". . . a complex unity formed of many often diverse parts subject to a common plan or serving a common purpose."[1]

It is apparent that this definition can be extended to many engineering projects, such as buildings, bridges, electrical networks, and hydraulic circuits. As we shall see, it will very easily include production control. Certainly all of these are complex unities of parts that serve a common purpose.

The second word of importance is *design.* It may be of interest to note here that the material written on design has to do with either the very broad concepts of design, as considered in art, or the very narrow use of the word, as used in machine design. Here we need a different concept of the word, and so we shall start again with an accepted definition of design ". . . to conceive and plan out in the mind."[2]

It should be recognized that a design exists even though it never passes the mental projection phase. However, it would be much more systematic if the designs, at least the important ones, were recorded in one way or another. Combining the two definitions, system and design, we might come up with this definition for system designing: Conceiving and planning in the mind a complex unit of many diverse parts.

The term "parts" should not imply a static quality, for such parts might consist of manufacturing facilities, materials-handling equipment, and other factors of production.

SYSTEM DESIGN FOR PRODUCTION CONTROL

We are not interested in just any system design but only in one which is used for the control of production. And *control,* which is the next word of concern to us, means ". . . to exercise restraining or directing influence over something."[3] The something we are concerned with is production, which

---

[1] By permission; from Webster's *Third New International Dictionary,* copyright 1961, G. & C. Merriam Co., publishers of the Merriam-Webster dictionaries.

[2] *Ibid.*

[3] *Ibid.*

is ". . . the making of goods available for human wants."[4] So, to put it briefly, production control means: To exercise restraining or directing influence over the making of goods.

System designing for production control, the major objective of this book, can now be stated as:

Conceiving and planning in the mind a complex unity of many diverse parts to exercise restraining or directing influence over the making of goods.

(The reader will forgive this delay in his pursuit because he must recognize that by starting with definitions which are generally accepted we have a far greater chance of coming to a common understanding.)

The primary concern in this book, either stated or implied, is to develop the thought processes necessary to make the system design. Consequently, a number of systems will be discussed and the similarities among systems will be pointed out. Later in this section, principles for system designing will be laid down.

SYSTEMS AND ANALOGIES

A system has been defined as a complex unity formed of many often diverse parts, subject to a common plan or serving a common purpose. And, as has been pointed out, this is primarily what engineers (as well as businessmen, doctors, and others) are concerned with. The professional divisions have come about by the type of system which is being emphasized. In engineering, the electrical engineer works with electrical systems, the mechanical engineer with mechanical systems, etc., and, of course, the production engineer works with production systems.

It is part of an engineer's background and education to solve the problems in one field by forming an analogy with another. For example, the mechanical engineer may solve vibrations problems by forming an analogy with an electrical system. In turn, the electrical engineer might find it much easier to think of his problem in terms of hydraulics. Although it has not been exploited to any extent, it seems quite possible that the analogy will serve an increasingly important means of solving production problems.

One important aspect of the analogy is the possibility of producing models of systems which are much smaller and cheaper than a full-scale design. This technique is used extensively in the design of ship hulls, plane wings, and hydraulic systems. Since many of the relationships between the model and full-scale structure are not in direct proportion to size, an extensive knowledge of scaling has been developed. It is not difficult to imagine how important this kind of knowledge would be to the designer of manufacturing systems. By studying a small scale operation he could predict what

---

[4] *Ibid.*

would happen when the operation was expanded. This technique, *simulation,* is only now becoming important in production.

Engineers, in general, have a very good knowledge of the materials with which they work, and therefore they can quite readily design their systems. Structural engineers have gathered years of experience and information about various materials, and they can predict very closely what the responses will be to any given condition. The same is true of the electrical engineer, for he can obtain the resistance, or the capacitance, or any other characteristic of a component. If he cannot find the accumulation of this information in handbooks, he can turn to the testing laboratory to get the design information he needs. But this is not true of the designer of the industrial system, for he works with a system that includes the unpredictable behavior of human beings and many other unpredictable interactions. If the designer of industrial systems is slow in advancing the techniques of design, it can be attributed to the extreme complexity of the problems he faces compared to the design problems of others.

There are a number of ways of classifying systems, but for a quick insight into some of the problems of system design let us consider three different types: a static model, a dynamic model, and one with feedback (called a servo-system model).

Static Model

A bridge, or a part of a building structure, is a good example of a static system. In the case of a bridge the designer must know the distance to be bridged, the load which must be carried, and other important facts. Calling on his knowledge of statics, he knows that the sum of the forces acting parallel to an axis must be equal to zero. With this knowledge the design engineer can select the materials of the proper characteristics, and design accordingly.

The industrial system designer is faced with a more or less static design when he designs an organization. The conditions under which the system is to perform are first decided, as in the bridge design, then, following certain principles of organizational design—such as the division of command, exception principles, and others—the components and the way they are to be put together are determined.

It is interesting to note the similarity of the simplifications made for the designs of the two systems. The bridge is not affected only by dead loads but also by dynamic loads, and there are some movements in the components. The organization chart also is far from static, and probably some important advances could be made in organizational designs if they were considered as being dynamic.

Dynamic Model

Many examples might be used in the study of dynamic systems, but let us select a mechanical system with which we are acquainted, the internal combustion engine. The designer wishes to know the useful output of an engine for any given input. Knowing this, he must determine how the components should be designed and how they should be put together to resist the forces and wear, all at a minimum cost. The designer does this by a well developed theory of vector analysis, coupled with volumes of information concerning the available materials and their characteristics.

Similarly, the designer of a production system knows the input and output expected of the system, and then sets forth to make the design. He is hampered, however, by the lack of consistent knowledge of the components. He must make the best evaluation he can within the limits of his knowledge.

One can carry these analogies on to electrical systems, or fluid systems, and make some interesting observations. For example, it is known that the total resistance of a circuit connected in series, as in Figure 1–1, is the summation of the individual resistances (which can be expressed in equation form, as shown).

Figure 1–1

Electrical-Manufacturing Analogy

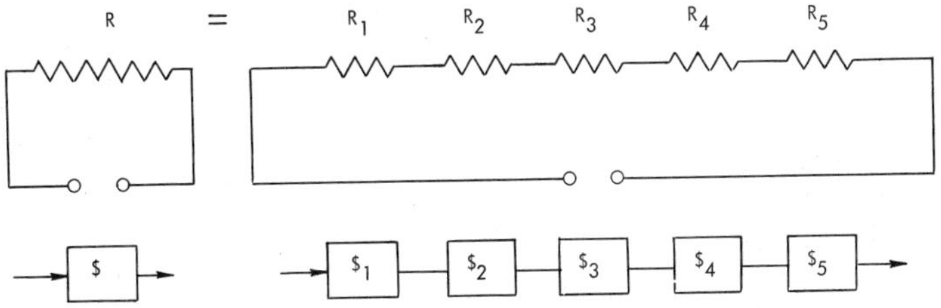

Similarly, the industrial systems designer might consider the cost of individual processes as "profit resistances" and add them up to find the total loss compared to profit.

It should not be overlooked that the person responsible for manufacturing system designs is as much concerned with the relationship of input to output as is any other designer. The designer is used to discussing the ratio of output to input as "efficiency," and, as we all know, the production managers have a long history of improving the efficiency of manufacturing organizations.

Servo-System Model

One of the most important and useful analogies for the industrial system designer is the servo-system.[5] The servo-system is a control system with two features, amplification and feedback. A little imagination will show that the

[5] "An automatic device for controlling large amounts of power by means of very small amounts of power and correcting performance of a mechanism to a desired standard by an error sensing feedback." By permission; from Webster's *Third New International Dictionary*, copyright 1961, G. & C. Merriam Co., publishers of the Merriam-Webster dictionaries.

industrial system, if properly designed, also includes these two features. The classical pyramid structure of the industrial organization, with its flow of authority—or *power of command*—flowing from the top to the bottom, shows the nature of power amplification. The output of an industrial system is evaluated by comparing it to a certain standard or objective. This serves as a motive for corrective action and reflects the feedback in the system.

Consider, for example, the steering gear of an early automobile. Probably the torque applied to the steering wheel to turn the wheels of the car is equal to the torque that reaches the wheels, causing them to turn. Power steering would be an example of amplification, while the driver's vision is comparable to the feedback.

We can simplify this illustration by using a set of conventional block diagrams, as shown in Figure 1–2. The position of the steering wheel represents the input, the gears and levers the control system, and, of course, the direction of the wheels the output. Mathematically, such a block diagram can be represented by an equation, k being a constant for the system. This illustration uses the angular change as the input and the output, but it could just as well have been voltage, current, or another value.

When we talk about manufacturing systems we are frequently at a loss to quantify the values of the inputs and outputs, but for the moment let us call them *effective input* and *effective output* so that we have a complete analogy.

Figure 1–2

Analogies

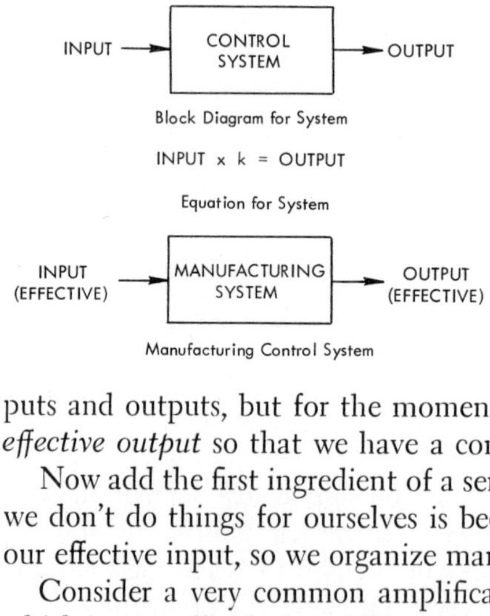

Now add the first ingredient of a servo-system to the analogy. The reason we don't do things for ourselves is because we want some amplification of our effective input, so we organize manufacturing industries.

Consider a very common amplification system where we have a motor which is controlled by a variable resistor, as shown in Figure 1–3. For certain types of motors there will be a fixed relationship between the position of the resistor dial and the torque of the motor. Here it should be observed that the power available from the system is not supplied by the controlling element.

An analogy of a control system and power amplification which is a little closer to home is you and the shower you used when you got up this morning. The input is indicated by the position of the control valve, similar to that of the resistor dial; the power amplification is afforded by the water system; and the output is the water. The body's response to the temperature, which results in adjusting the controls, is the feedback link.

Figure 1–3

Amplification Added to System

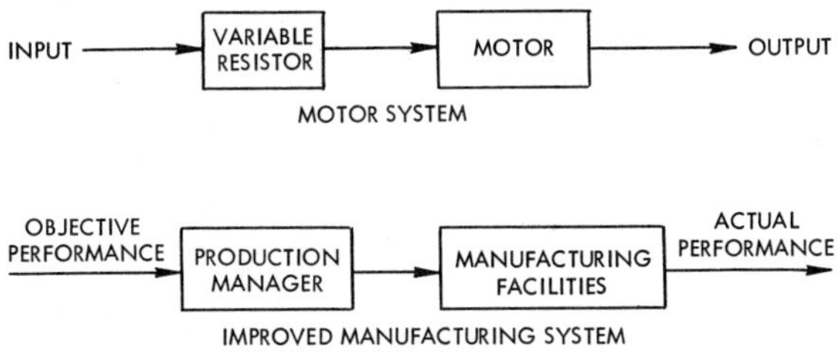

In the manufacturing system the input might be considered as the sales which need to be satisfied. The output would be the production, and the deviation would serve as the feedback in the system. Amplification will exist when the feedback induces the production manager to take some action to satisfy the objectives of the system.

It would be an oversimplification of our manufacturing system if we considered only one input, for there are many secondary inputs. It is the lack of understanding or recognition of these secondary inputs that causes all sorts of difficulties.

Consider our previous analogy of the car. Who is naive enough to believe that the car exactly obeys the driver's request? We know that the direction of the car is also influenced by the inertia of the mass, the wind pressure on the sides of the car, and the uneven friction exerted on the tires by ice, mud, and snow.

Or, considering the shower analogy, one cannot forget stepping quickly out of the shower when a disturbance to the temperature of the water was brought about by someone's turning on a faucet in another part of the house.

The secondary inputs are also in effect in the manufacturing system. The forces exerted by the supply of materials, the availability of outside capital, customers' demands, requirements by labor unions, and many others, are examples of secondary inputs.

So far we have talked only about power amplification, which is one of the important attributes of the servo-system, and the effect of secondary inputs. Now let us consider the important aspect of feedback, which gives us a *closed loop* from the output to the input.

Because of the secondary inputs mentioned above we never know what the actual output is without feedback. If you don't believe this, try driving down the street with your eyes closed when the street is covered with ice and the wind is blowing in heavy gusts. You cannot drive well because you don't have any feedback. Open your eyes and the closed loop is completed, as your eyes sense the way your car is going as opposed to the way you want it to go.

You are well acquainted with this feedback concept. The human body uses it in guiding the hands to pick up objects, and to maintain equilibrium. In fact, the common household furnace uses this concept. The controls turn on the furnace, which puts out hot air, which in turn travels to the living room and actuates the thermostat, which feeds back information to the furnace and either lets it continue to run or shuts it off.

Figure 1–4

Manufacturing Feedback System

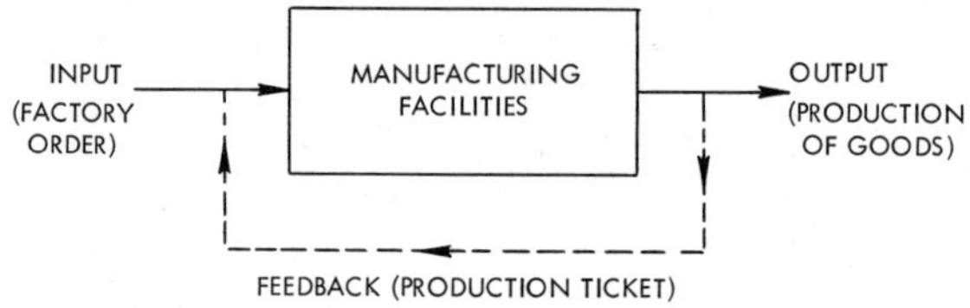

The same thing occurs in the manufacturing system (Figure 1–4). If we don't get a feedback of some sort, we will lose control. The feedback in a factory takes the form of reports, production cards, suggestions, and the like.

With this information about the servo-system and its analogies in industry, we can go ahead and discuss some of the performance characteristics of this system.

When the input and the output of a system are constant, the system is said to be in a *steady state*, or static. But when a system receives a new input, it generally takes time to achieve a new permanent condition or steady state. During this time, the system is said to be in a *transient* condition. The various transient conditions are more conveniently shown in a graphical form (see Figure 1–5).

To make the concept of the transient a little more meaningful, let us go back to the analogy of the shower system. If you get into the shower when it is too hot or too cold, you will wish to make the proper adjustment. But suppose the plumber has tightened the packing so that you can hardly turn the knobs; then you will have a condition similar to the first graph, and the system will be slow to respond and you will scald—or freeze.

Carrying the same situation over into the industrial system would be comparable to having a production center with a very slow response. The time it would take actual output to come up to the expected output would be long, and, since it is common to pay for time expended, the cost would be prohibitive. It should be noted that this curve is somewhat comparable to a learning curve, and the slope is of critical importance. Our system is not giving the desired results.

The second graph shows that we have overcompensated. In our analogy, we have tried to get the hot water cooled off too soon, causing us to go too far. In our concern to get the temperature we want, we tend to overcompensate. All of us have experienced this sort of thing while in a shower, driving

Figure 1–5

Transient Conditions

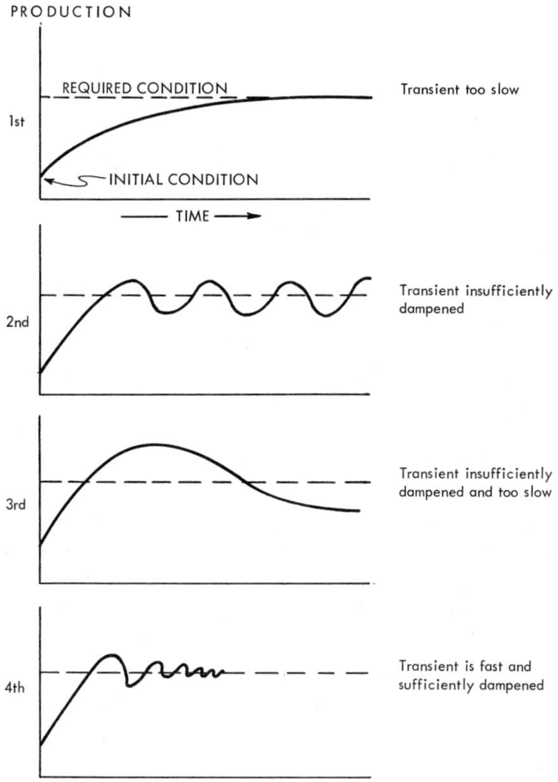

a car, bidding a bridge hand, and so on. In the industrial situation, this might be comparable to adding and removing work shifts in some production situation.

The third graph shows slowing down of the periodicity, something to be deplored. It is no doubt representative of a work system which is not properly disciplined, thus the output is erratic.

The best solution is of course in the last curve, in which the response is rapid, and although there is an effect of overcompensation, it is quickly dampened out. Doesn't this follow in an industrial system? You tell someone what is expected, how you wish him to comply; he does it immediately, and continues to do it with little variation from the norm.

This concept of the servo-model is not far removed from the typical organization chart hanging in many offices. Taking a typical chart, let us make the comparison. In Figure 1–6, the line leading through the boxes is the same as the input and output we have discussed. The boxes refer to the components of the system just as before, but the thing that is left out of the picture is the feedback, for it is implied. It is assumed that this is a two-way

Figure 1–6

Feedback Links Applied to the Organization

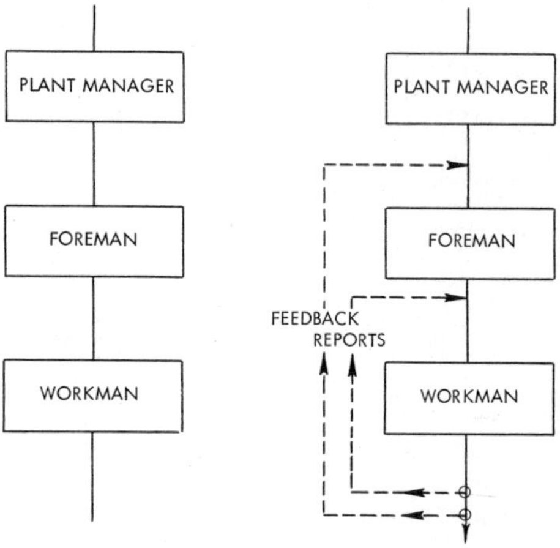

flow rather than our concept of feedback. How much better sense a chart would make if it showed the feedback lines as well. It would emphasize the necessity of communications being passed back up the line for corrective action.

One can go ahead and develop this analogy in all of its complexities. Blueprints, procedure manuals, office memos, production orders, time and quality standards are just a few examples of communication inputs in a factory system.

The feedback can take the form of time cards, quality control reports, machine downtime reports, and many other communications established upon a formal basis. On the less formal basis would be feedback in the form of general complaints, suggestion system entries, labor grievances, etc.

We will find many useful applications of the servo-system analogy, as well as the analogy of the static and dynamic systems.

THE DIFFERENCE BETWEEN SYSTEM DESIGN AND DECISION MAKING

A sharp distinction must be drawn between system design and decision making. The decision making has to do with the signal which is imposed upon the system, and the system is the structure that carries the signal. No one should get confused between the network of telephone lines and components that carry the voice across many miles, and the voice signals (suggesting decision making) that are carried along the line.

This analogy can be carried still farther if we consider the internal combustion engine referred to earlier. The decision that was made and impressed upon the system was how much gas should be given to the combustion chamber by the throttle. The impulse was carried through the system more or less efficiently to the crankshaft. There is no confusion here between the signal of the decision being carried and the system that serves as the medium. Your decision to turn on a light, and flipping the switch, is certainly never confused with the switch, lines, sockets, etc., which carry your decision.

This distinction between design and decision making may appear to be so obvious as to be hardly worth mentioning. However, as we progress through the text there will be times when the distinction will be difficult to make. This confusion has caused the delay in the science of system design and decision making for production control.

IMPEDIMENTS IN THE SCIENCE OF SYSTEM DESIGN AND DECISION MAKING

One of the most difficult obstructions to overcome in the development of a science of system design and decision making is the extreme complexity of the problem. This is easy to see when one considers a medium size manufacturing plant of about 500 direct-labor workers operating in a plant with perhaps 100 indirect laborers. Each laborer may be working in a group to operate one machine, or he may be responsible for working just one machine —or even a dozen or more machines. The indirect laborers may be responsible for moving materials within the plant, keeping the work progressing, supervising, and many other jobs. All of this is influenced by unpredictable outside forces such as customer demands, labor union demands, capital available, material shipments, etc. It should be obvious that we have a situation which is vastly complex and innumerable interactions that are nearly impossible to isolate. Such a complex design problem would be appalling to designers of constructions, mechanical devices, and electrical networks. It is a challenge to the production engineer who realizes the importance and potential of his task.

One thing which will probably delay the science of system designing and decision making is the lack of a consistent system of units. This problem has been overcome in most fields of engineering and science. Because of the physical relationship, all of the mechanical units of measure can be derived from the three fundamental units of mass, length, and time. The thermal quantities are conveniently derived from these units, plus the units of temperature. Electrical and magnetic quantities are derived from the three fundamental mechanical units and one fundamental electrical or magnetic unit. The system of units for the industrial system should be built up in this same way with modifications necessary to make the system consistent.

The convenience of using an analogy for solving problems has been pointed out and it is apparent that the analogy gives new insights to old problems. By changing physical media it is often possible to destroy mental blocks which are delaying a solution. These similarities are pointed out in Figure 1–7.

Figure 1–7

Units of Measure

Mechanical Units		*Electrical Units*		*Production Units*
F	Force	E	Voltage	?
x	Displacement	q	Charge	?
dx/dt	Velocity	i	Current	?
d^2x/dt^2	Acceleration	di/dt	Derivative of Current	?
M	Mass	L	Inductance	?
D	Damping	R	Resistance	?
K	Spring Force	$1/C$	Reciprocal of Capacitance	?

If we can add the information for the production units, we will have made a long stride toward a system design method which will make it possible to solve many of the complex problems we have discussed.

SUMMARY

This book is written for the designer of industrial systems and is not the customary casebook of system designs. System designing has been defined as: *Conceiving and planning in the mind a complex unity of many diverse parts to exercise restraining or directing influence over the making of goods.*

There are a number of ways to catalog systems, but—for convenience—the static, dynamic, and servo-systems have been discussed. The engineer will often attempt to get an insight to a particular problem by using analogies. In fact, the mathematical model is a form of analogy which is used to solve the system design problems. The production engineer is hampered in developing a science of system designing by the lack of a convenient system of units and by the extreme complexity of his problems.

Questions

1. Describe three distinct systems to be found in your normal activities. Why do these fit the definition of a system? Which ones are static and which ones are dynamic?
2. Give an example of a problem which you have solved by an analogy.
3. What advantages are there in solving problems with analogies?
4. Why are systems which include people especially difficult to analyze?
5. What are the two features of the servo-system?
6. What are some of the important secondary inputs for a factory system?
7. What are some of the feedback links in a factory system?

8. Define servo-system, transient, secondary input, and steady state.
9. Discuss, in terms of cost, the effect of a slow response in a dynamic factory system. Could a slow response be desirable?
10. What will be the important factors which will delay the full development of system designing as applied to the factory?
11. Explain the difference between system designing and decision making. Why do you think these concepts become confused?
12. List a set of units, such as length, time, and weight, which are consistent and could be useful in the design of systems and decision making for industry.

References

BUKSTEIN, EDWARD J. *Basic Servomechanisms.* New York: Holt, Rinehart & Winston, Inc., 1963.

CARNAHAN, BRICE; LUTHER, H. A.; and WILKES, JAMES O. *Applied Numerical Methods.* New York: John Wiley & Sons, Inc., 1964.

FLAGLE, CHARLES D.; HUGGINS, WILLIAM H.; and ROY, ROBERT H. *Operations Research and Systems Engineering.* Baltimore: Johns Hopkins Press, 1960.

FORRESTER, JAY WRIGHT. *Industrial Dynamics.* Cambridge, Mass.: M.I.T. Press, 1961.

GOODE, HENRY H., and MACHOL, ROBERT E. *System Engineering.* New York: McGraw-Hill Book Co., Inc., 1957.

GRABBE, EUGENE MUNTER; RAMO, SIMON; and WOOLDRIDGE, DEAN E. *Handbook of Automation, Computation, and Control.* New York: John Wiley & Sons, Inc., 1958–61.

GREENE, JAMES H. "Industrial Communications—An Engineering Approach," *The Tool Engineer,* Vol. 44, No. 3 (March, 1960), p. 75.

JOHNSON, RICHARD A.; KAST, FREMONT E.; and ROSENZWEIG, JAMES E. *The Theory and Management of Systems.* New York: McGraw-Hill Book Co., Inc., 1963.

LYNCH, WILLIAM A., and TRUXAL, JOHN G. *Introductory System Analysis.* New York: McGraw-Hill Book Co., Inc., 1961.

MCDONAUGH, ADRIAN M. *Information Economics and Management Systems.* New York: McGraw-Hill Book Co., Inc., 1963.

MURPHY, GLENN. *Similitude in Engineering.* New York: Ronald Press Co., 1950.

PAYNTER, HENRY M. *Analysis and Design of Engineering Systems.* Cambridge, Mass.: M.I.T. Press, 1961.

RHEGG, THOMAS. "A Servo System Analysis of an Industrial Organization." Unpublished Masters Thesis, Purdue University, 1963.

SAVANT, C. J. *Control System Design.* 2d ed. New York: McGraw-Hill Book Co., Inc, 1964.

SUTHERLAND, ROBERT L. *Engineering Systems Analysis.* Reading, Mass.: Addison-Wesley Publishing Co., 1958.

TRUXAL, JOHN G. *Control Engineers' Handbook.* New York: McGraw-Hill Book Co., Inc., 1958.

TUSTIN, ARNOLD. *The Mechanism of Economic Systems.* Cambridge, Mass.: Harvard University Press, 1953.

CHAPTER 2

The Logic of System Designing and Decision Making

The previous chapter defined the meaning of system designing for production control and it illustrated some useful design concepts, as well as pointed up the difference between system design and decision making. No attempt was made to delineate the thought processes referred to as designing.

It is surprising to note the paucity of material available on the subject of designing as it concerns the mental processes used in system designing. True, numerous books have been written on the subject of machine design, but they are primarily concerned with the application of mathematical and graphical techniques for solving specific design problems rather than with developing a technique for approaching all problems of design. But because little has been written on the thought process for designing does not mean that nothing has been done. The thought process for designing is found under such captions as Scientific Method, Engineering Mode of Analysis, Method of Inquiry, Methods, Thinking, Reasoning, and others.

The physiologist has tackled the problem from the mechanics of the thought process while the psychologist has approached the problem from the learning experiments of the laboratory. Philosophers have made their important contributions by going at the problem through the discipline of logic.

PHYSIOLOGISTS' CONTRIBUTION TO SYSTEM DESIGNING

There is probably little light that the physiologist can shed on the subject of system designing at this time. Physiologists have made some macroscopic experiments into the way the brain works by deliberate removal of parts of the brains of animal subjects to determine how they respond. They have been able to get similar information from human beings who have had brain damage as part of an accident or illness. This has produced information concerning the function of various parts of the brain, but it leads nowhere in the study of how the brain solves problems.

The most interesting property of the nervous system is that it enables us to learn and to think, but what happens to the neurons or their synaptic connections is little more than a surmise. Many gaps in what is known about the mechanics of thinking will have to be closed before we can make any use of physiological knowledge in deliberately setting up a technique for thinking suitable for everyone.

PSYCHOLOGISTS' CONTRIBUTION TO SYSTEM DESIGNING

The term "thinking" is often applied indiscriminately to a great many different kinds of psychological activities, and not just to problem solving or system designing. The restricted subject we are interested in is frequently spoken of as "reasoning" by the psychologists.

To highlight the difference between "reasoning" and "thinking," let us point out some of the concepts that can be considered as thinking activities. One is said to be thinking when he recollects some past experience such as a travel experience, a party experience, or similar memory. One is also said to be thinking when he instantaneously recalls tables of numbers or formulas.

Imagining things which have never been brought to pass is also considered a thinking process, as when one creates in his mind a house he plans to build or a picture he plans to paint. The daydreamer is also thinking as he purposefully constructs in his mind a world which is more satisfying than the real one in which he lives.

These different types of thinking contribute to the solving of problems but they certainly cannot be construed as reasoning, problem solving, or system designing as used in this text.

What is thinking for system designing? A system design problem is a particular type of problem. A problem exists for a person when he has a definite objective or goal which he cannot reach by the behavior pattern he already has available. Problem solving comes about when there is an obstruction of some sort to the attainment of an objective. No problem exists if the path to the solution is straight and open. Only when one has to discover a means of circumventing an obstacle is the stage set for problem solving.

When one solves a problem, it is necessary to select from previous experiences those which are relevant and to organize these parts of previous experiences into the correct answer.

Thinking for problem solving has the following features:

1. It is *directed* by the goal and a perception of the essential relationships in the situation.
2. It is *selective*, for one of the keys to successful solution is the ability to recall relevant experiences.
3. It is *insightful*, for it involves the reorganization of relevant experiences into a complete solution, with particular reference to means-end relations.
4. It is *creative*, for it results in an essentially new construct, a reorganization of ideas or movements, or both.
5. It is *critical*, for it is necessary to evaluate the adequacy of hypotheses or tentative solutions.[1]

While the psychologists have been slow in developing a structured technique for solving design problems, they have certainly made some invaluable contributions through their insights to the reasoning process. Ryan has stated that: ". . . the progress of thinking consists of a series of manipulations of objects and other 'tools of thinking.' "[2] Some of the tools of thinking he refers to are:

1. Perceived, Recollected, and Imagined Objects.
   a) Concrete or specific objects.
      You understand things by association. For example, friction is understood by a design engineer because he has rubbed two surfaces together and not necessarily through the understanding of the equation of $F = Wf$.
   b) Objects as examples; generalized objects.
      As in problems of geometry, one solves the general problems of a kind by using a specific example.
   c) Objects with dynamic properties.
      In solving many concrete problems, objects are seen as tools for doing certain things. For example, an engineer might see an "I" beam as a lever rather than as a piece of cold rolled steel, having so much weight per foot and a certain cross-section.
2. Concepts.
   A concept is a "general idea," an item in thinking that stands for a general class. As an experience, the concept may seem to be nothing more than an ordinary image, but as a concept it has acquired, through learning, various potentialities which give it much more general meaning.
3. Symbols and Signs.
   a) Thinking gains economy by making use of symbols and signs. Since every symbol is potentially a sign and every sign a symbol, they should be considered together.
   b) A symbol is a concrete particular item in thinking that stands for something more general. A concept is generally represented in thinking by symbols.
   c) Symbols tend to become signs. They act as signals for thinking or

[1] Arthur I. Gates, A. T. Jersild, T. R. McConnell, and T. Challman, *Educational Psychology* (New York: The Macmillan Company, 1948).

[2] Edwin Garrigues Boring, H. S. Langfeld, and H. P. Weld, *Foundations of Psychology* (New York: John Wiley & Sons, Inc., 1948).

> action, as stimuli for conscious or motor responses. The engineer is well aware that he uses signs as tools for thinking, especially in the mathematics.[3]

The language that we use every day is nothing but symbols, and as a man thinks he uses these symbols, whether verbal or not, as tools for the thinking process.

Other deterrents and assistances to problem solving have been explored by the psychologists. One of these is *motivation*. Although little is known about how motivation is obtained, it is well known that those most productive in creating new things are highly motivated by the desire to solve challenging problems.

Habit or *set* of thinking can be helpful in solving problems, and can also often delay the solution. When one practices the solving of problems, he is inclined to develop a set which makes him approach all problems in the same way. This is helpful in solving familiar problems rapidly, but when the time comes to solve new problems, the problem-solver frequently finds that it is difficult to take a new look at the situation.

Although the phenomenon of *incubation* is not well understood, many people who have been faced with problem solving are well aware of its existence. After a concentrated effort has been made to solve a problem, and a person lays it aside, the answer will frequently come to him at a time when he least expects it. Many great developments have come about in this way, and some of our greatest scientists have experienced the phenomenon of incubation to bring forth the most important developments. Incubation is no substitute for hard work, and one cannot expect to "hatch" a solution without previous sweat.

Each individual attempts to solve problems in his own particular fashion. A person well acquainted with graphical solutions will try that method rather than a mathematical approach. One should not be bound by the pseudosophistry of certain methods of solving problems, for the solution is the important thing regardless of how it is obtained.

As can be seen here, the psychologist has made some important contributions to the knowledge of how man solves problems, but there is little evidence of a methodology suitable for all. The philosopher in his study of logic has devised methodologies; some are useful and others have outlived their purpose and are of use only to the historian of logic.

PHILOSOPHY'S CONTRIBUTION TO SYSTEM DESIGNING

The study of control systems design is in reality a study of man controlling a small part of his environment; that part which is given to the production of goods to satisfy his needs.

---

[3] *Ibid.*

Man's first attempt to control his environment was given the very general name of magic. Thus magic was for early man what the scientific method is for man today. Through the use of magical rites, man attempted (with the same sincerity of purpose as the scientist of today) to control the forces that run through nature. The second stage of man's attempt to control his environment has been referred to as uncontrolled speculation, whereby problems were solved and explanations given in terms of phenomena in the world of common sense experience. The supernatural forces were no longer the influencing factors, but the elements of nature such as fire, air, and water became the common denominators. Explanations were accomplished not by definitely arranging experimental conditions for testing hypotheses, but by plausibility of argument alone. The flight of imagination alone was the limit, as long as the explanation seemed reasonable.

The third stage was marked by the introduction of the syllogism, a remarkable technique for testing arguments. This Aristotelian device is a common and useful thought process, although not always recognized in all its formality. The syllogism is an argument with two premises and a conclusion. To quote the classic example: "All men are mortal; Socrates is a man: Therefore Socrates is mortal."

The syllogism is frequently used today in daily discourse, but the pattern goes unnoticed because the reasoning is frequently incompletely stated. As an example: "This change in Company A's processing made a better product. Therefore this same change in Company B's processing will make a better product." Left out is that whatever processing change Company A uses can also be used in Company B's processing as an improvement.

The fourth stage utilized the syllogism for harmonizing knowledge with religious concepts. Of importance to us here is the fifth stage, which brought forth the experimental approach and the scientific method.

THE MODERN LOGIC

An understanding of some of the more important terms in the field of logic should be useful to further study of the subject. Logic itself comes from the Greek word *logos*, which means reason or discourse, and it occurs as the suffix of such words in science as geo-*logy*, bio-*logy*, and psycho-*logy*. It defines the systematic search for universal laws and principles in accordance with sound rational criteria and experimental procedures. In no facetious sense, the field of factory operations might be called industrology, for its purpose is (in part) a systematic search for universal laws and principles of industry.

The "hypothesis," which will be referred to again, is a tentative and provisional thesis put forward upon the basis of accumulated knowledge for the guidance of further investigation and research. The word is derived from the Greek word *hypo*, meaning under, and the word *tethenai*, meaning to place; and it suggests that when the hypothesis is placed under the evidence as a foundation, it will support it.

This gives some insight to the study of logic which has made important contributions to the knowledge of how people solve problems and design systems. A completely historical approach to preparing a methodology breaks down, for as Dewey states:

> Logic is a progressive discipline. The reason for this is that logic rests upon analysis of the best method of inquiry that exists at a given time. As the methods of sciences improve, corresponding changes take place in logic.[4]

Perhaps an entirely satisfactory methodology can never be devised, for someone has compared the process of thinking to a ballgame. One can describe the game in a general way, and in considerable detail can tell how the ball should be thrown, caught, and the proper position that should be taken to bat, but one can't tell in detail the way to *play* the game. Only by experiencing the game can one really know how to play, and the same may be true of the processes of thinking. However, we will proceed to introduce a systematic method of solving problems which will serve as a useful guide.

A GUIDE TO LOGICAL SYSTEM DESIGNING

Probably the most comprehensive analysis of the thought process (and frequently referred to by writers in the field) has been made by Dewey. The step-by-step procedure is given and should be studied extensively by anyone interested in improving his thought processes for system designing and decision making.

Step 1. Become Aware of the Problem

Although we are surrounded by problems that are unsolved, they do not become problems until we become aware of them as such. The number of problems we see, and their seriousness, depends upon our experience. The sensitivity to problems is perhaps one of the most important characteristics of the production engineer in his working with system designs.

Step 2. Define the Problem

A vague notion about the problem will lead a person nowhere, but if an effort is made to bracket the problem accurately, useful suggestions will come to mind. Often this is the most difficult part of the problem-solving procedure for the young system designer, for he is customarily given the problem—defined as such—in his academic work.

Step 3. Locate, Evaluate, and Organize Information

To prepare a hypothesis or tentative solution to a problem, it is first necessary to assemble information. This might be the information that an

---

[4] John Dewey, *How We Think* (Boston: D. C. Heath & Company, 1933).

experienced problem-solver has at hand, or it may require the collection of additional information. No solution can be better than the facts upon which it is based, and this lack has probably been the cause of many unsuccessful system designs.

Step 4. Discover Relationships and Formulate Hypotheses

From the data obtained, hypotheses and inferences are formed. In the actual process of thinking, however, one does not complete the definition of the problem or the location of information before he starts forming hunches, or tentative hypotheses. These two processes go on at the same time. This process of hypothesis-forming is the one about which the least is known in the process of thinking.

Although little can be said about the methodology of this step, it is known that there are certain conditions which help produce a fruitful inference. One of these is the persistence with which one attacks a problem. And, of course, this means one must be well saturated with the facts. One must be flexible in his approach and avoid the stereotyped answers which lead nowhere. The open mind, which is sensitive to all suggestions, is essential to the formulation of hypotheses.

Step 5. Evaluation of Hypotheses

The tentative solution must be rigorously tested in a systematic fashion. First, it should be determined whether or not the answer completely satisfies the requirements of the problem. Next, it should be determined whether or not the solution is consistent with all other facts and principles which are well established and accepted. And third, one should make a systematic search for negative exceptions which might throw some doubt upon the conclusion reached. If the hypothesis does not stand up, we must return to the hypothesis-formulating step and develop a new one, or perhaps return to the step of obtaining more information about the problem. Problem solving is not a straight-line procedure which leads directly to the answer; it is a continuously cycling procedure that requires an active mind to prevent the movement from stopping on dead center.

Step 6. Applying the Solution

The application step is not always readily seen in some purely intellectual problems, and it is possible that it won't always be seen in the solution of a system design. However, in many important cases, the solution will be quite evident and may change the course of a whole manufacturing organization. Applying the solution in some system designs may require the expenditure of thousands and thousands of dollars, and may require the cooperation of hundreds and hundreds of people. This is not the sort of thing that can be taken lightly, and one must develop his skill not only in obtaining the correct answers but also his skill in introducing the solutions. This is such an important part of system design that a whole chapter of this book is devoted to the subject; and it probably justifies even more space.

LOGIC APPLIED TO SYSTEM DESIGNING AND DECISION MAKING

The distinction between system designing and decision making was stressed in the first chapter. However, you should recognize that the logic used is the same. The system decisions are made more infrequently than are the decisions which are imposed upon the system.

Since this book is dedicated to the subjects of system designing and decision making, it is essential that you have some knowledge of the logic which is used. You should make a practice of using the steps of logic described in this chapter whenever you are faced with a system design or decision-making problem.

1. Become aware of the problem.
2. Define the problem.
3. Locate, evaluate, and organize information.
4. Discover relationships and formulate hypotheses.
5. Evaluate the hypotheses.
6. Apply the solution.

SUMMARY

Students are seldom exposed to a formal study of how thinking occurs or how they can improve their thinking by a systematic process. They obtain their insight to the proper method of solving problems by the process of doing problems. In fact, the technique of learning how to solve problems is frequently the justification for many courses. But it would probably be far better for a student to first understand what is to be known about the thinking process of problem solving early in his education. He could then be aware of the process and do what he could to systematically practice the methods.

Questions

1. What professional group has done the most in developing a procedure for thinking? Why is this true?
2. Compare the thought processes used by any two of the following professional groups: medicine, architecture, law, physics, business, accounting.
3. Examine your own problem-solving methods. Do you believe they can be enumerated as so many steps of a procedure? Explain your answer.
4. What are some of the obstructions to further development in how man thinks? Will these obstructions be overcome in the future?
5. How important is *incubation* to your thought processes? Give an example of an *incubation* experience.

6. How do you use *set* in solving problems? Give a specific example. How can *set* obstruct the thought processes in solving problems?
7. Does the college experience teach a person to "think"? Explain.
8. Who, in your professional field, has contributed to an understanding of the "thinking" process? If you know of none, choose one from another field but explain why you know of no one in your own field.
9. Relate system designing to what you have learned about logic.
10. Relate decision making to what you have learned about logic.
11. Is there any real distinction between the logic used in system designing and that used in the decision making which is transmitted on the system?
12. What can you do to further your understanding of the thought processes?

References

ACKOFF, RUSSELL L. *Scientific Method.* New York: John Wiley & Sons, Inc., 1962.

ALEXANDER, J. EUGENE, and BAILEY, J. MILTON. *Systems Engineering Mathematics.* Englewood Cliffs, N.J.: Prentice-Hall, Inc., 1962.

BLACK, MAX. *Critical Thinking, An Introduction to Logic and Scientific Method.* 2d ed. Englewood Cliffs, N.J.: Prentice-Hall, Inc., 1955.

BORING, EDWIN GARRIGUES; LANGFELD, H. S.; and WELD, H. P. *Foundations of Psychology.* New York: John Wiley & Sons, Inc, 1948.

CHURCHMAN, CHARLES W., and ACKOFF, RUSSELL L. *Methods of Inquiry, An Introduction to Philosophy and Scientific Method.* St. Louis: Educational Publishers, 1950.

DEWEY, JOHN. *How We Think.* Boston: D. C. Heath & Co., 1933.

DIMNET, ERNEST. *The Art of Thinking.* New York: Simon & Schuster, 1955.

GATES, ARTHUR I.; JERSILD, A. T.; MCCONNELL, T. R.; and CHALLMAN, T. *Educational Psychology.* New York: Macmillan Co., 1948.

HALL, ARTHUR D. *A Methodology for Systems Engineering.* Princeton, N.J.: D. Van Nostrand Co., 1962.

HAWKINS, G. A.; BOELTER, L. M. K. "Engineering Mode of Analysis," *Mechanical Engineering,* Vol. 75, No. 10 (October, 1953), pp. 799, 800, 808.

HODNETT, EDWARD. *The Art of Problem Solving: How to Improve Your Methods.* New York: Harper & Bros., 1955.

MURPHY, GLENN. *Similitude in Engineering.* New York: Ronald Press Co., 1950.

PETERSON, MARTIN S. *Scientific Thinking and Scientific Writing.* New York: Reinhold Pub. Corp., 1961.

SUPPES, PATRICK. *Introduction to Logic.* Princeton, N.J.: D. Van Nostrand Co., 1959.

VINACKE, W. EDGAR. *The Psychology of Thinking.* New York: McGraw-Hill Book Co., Inc., 1952.

CHAPTER 3

Production Control Concepts

A trend toward enlarging the subject of control is well established. In this text, emphasis is placed on the control problems directly related to production in a factory, but we must never forget that the methods to be discussed are equally suitable for many control problems.

Traditionally, production control texts emphasize the metal trade industries and give little consideration to the manufacture of other products, which, however, also require production control. Control problems also occur in other factory activities besides the production of goods. For example, the tooling, maintenance, materials handling, cost accounting, and personnel departments encounter control problems which are analogous to those found in the manufacture of a product.

The concepts of control can be expanded to include projects such as highways, dams, and buildings. It takes very little more imagination to apply these concepts to the design and operation of an airline ticket service, a hotel room reservation service, or to the efficient utilization of hospital operating rooms. The methods used in designing control systems are identical, and many of the decision-making techniques are interchangeable.

Be aware of the broad spectrum of system designing and decision making for control, and apply your knowledge to any suitable problem.

OBJECTIVES OF PRODUCTION CONTROL

Universally acceptable objectives for production control cannot be stated in a few words, for they are seen in the reflection of one's background. Experience with different products, markets, and plants will give different shades of meaning to the objectives.

Objectives of production control, which should at least meet the minimum requirements, might be stated in this way: *The coordination of the production facilities to produce a product on schedule at an optimum cost.*

Those who would like more extensive objectives might be better satisfied with the definition of production control found in the *Dictionary of Production and Inventory Control Terms:*

> The function of directing or regulating the orderly movement of goods through the entire manufacturing cycle, from the requisitions of raw material to the delivery of the finished product, by means of the systematic release of subsidiary orders under a routine plan which utilizes the plant facilities most economically.[1]

The literature abounds with other definitions and objectives for production control. An analysis of a few of these would illustrate the difficulty of establishing universally acceptable objectives.

In defining production control it is not uncommon to find it compared to the nervous system of the human body. This is an interesting and realistic comparison, for as the nervous system pervades the whole body, so does production control pervade the whole manufacturing organization as a comprehensive communications network. The nerve network assures conformance by many feedback links, as does the production control system. This will be illustrated before this chapter is completed.

Production planning is frequently spoken of (and in the same breath) as production control. The distinction, if one is made, is that *planning* refers to establishing the requirements while production control refers to keeping production within these requirements; but most frequently production control refers to both of these activities. Recognition of the difference will be made when we discuss the *planning stage*, the *action stage*, and the *compliance stage* of production control.

MAJOR TYPES OF PRODUCTION

One type of production control system would not be sufficient for all manufacturing situations. The control system needed for an automobile assembly plant is entirely different than the one needed for a plant producing one-of-a-kind punch presses. The type of control system depends upon the type of production, so it is imperative to know something about these.

In organizing some subjects it is best to first define the two extremes and then to classify the shades of meaning in between. Things are not always black or white, but only by comprehending black and white can we sense the many shades of gray which lie between. This is the way it is in discussing types of production.

---

[1] Clifford M. Baumback, *APICS-Dictionary of Production and Inventory Control Terms*, American Production and Inventory Control Society, 330 South Wells St., Chicago 6, Illinois. *Note:* This was compiled by the Language and Technique Committee, chairmaned by Clifford M. Baumback.

The two extremes which are well defined and understood in industry are:

Job Shop: A factory in which machines are grouped by the kind of work they perform.

Production Line: A factory in which machines are located by the sequence of operations required to produce the product.

The comparison between the job shop and the production line is readily made (see Figure 3–1).

Figure 3–1

Comparisons between the Two Major Types of Production

Job Shop	*Production Line*
1. Similar machines are grouped with common supervision.	1. Machines are located according to the sequence of operations required to produce a product.
2. The manufacturing cycles are long.	2. Manufacturing cycles are short and delivery dates are early.
3. Work loads are unbalanced, so that machines may be idle for days.	3. Work loads tend to be more balanced and every effort is made to keep the machines functioning all of the time.
4. Machine operators have extensive skills, frequently setting up their own machines.	4. Machine operators are highly skilled, but in only one type of operation.
5. Raw materials inventories may be high because of the many kinds of materials kept on hand.	5. Raw materials inventories may be high because of the quantities of material consumed. Ideally, the material is scheduled to be delivered as used.
6. Because of the long manufacturing cycle, in-process inventories are high. They are also high because the material is handled in batches.	6. In-process inventories are generally small in comparison to the large quantities produced.
7. Materials handling is more extensive in a job shop.	7. The purpose of the production line is to reduce the materials-handling costs.
8. Because there is more material handling, there must be wider aisles and other provisions for ready access to the machines.	8. Space may be utilized more efficiently.
9. Production control tends to be more complex because many jobs are in process at one time. This requires many instructions, time cards, and other forms needed to maintain schedules.	9. Production control will not be as complex because emphasis will be placed on supplying the lines with materials.
10. The output of the job shop is more flexible than that of the production line.	10. Unit costs for the production line will be lower if the production is maintained near the optimum level.

Although job shop and production line classifications are generally understood in industry, synonyms are occasionally found in the literature. For example, the job shop is referred to as a *process shop* because the machines are grouped by the processes they perform. That is, all turret lathes are together and all presses are together, and so forth. They are also called *intermittent shops* because the durations of the operations are short and the machines operate intermittently. The production line is referred to at times as a *product shop* because the machines are placed in the sequence needed to produce a product.

The length of time machines are set up for a particular job is the primary reason why one arrangement of machines is chosen over another. If the processing time is short, it is usually more efficient to use the job shop, although this rule does not hold for all situations. Sometimes similar machines are grouped together because they are noisy, dirty, require special foundations, electrical facilities, or supervision.

It has been said that manufacturing to customers' orders dictates the use of the job shop layout, and manufacturing to inventory dictates the use of the production line. This is not a sufficient criterion because many factories producing to stock use the job shop layout.

In actual practice we find plants operating between the two extremes (in the gray area) as a combination of the job shop and production line. Parts are commonly made in a job shop while the assembly of parts is done on a production line. Some common types of production between these two extremes are worthy of their own distinct classifications, but since these are not as important, they will be discussed as minor types of production.

MINOR TYPES OF PRODUCTION

Erection Shop

This type of manufacturing consists of taking material and parts to one central location where the product is assembled. Usually the quantity is small and the product is not easily transported. This is the way large transformers, turbines, and similar products are produced. The production is done in accordance with blueprints, but operation sheets—common to other metal fabricating plants—are not used.

Repair Shop

This kind of manufacturing is common in the electrical equipment and appliance industry. It may be part of a large production facility or part of the service function. It can even be operated in conjunction with a district sales office. Typical repair shops are found in the railroad industry, where freight car shops approach the production line concept. Automobile generators and starters are repaired in huge quantities in shops which may be similar to job shops or to production lines, depending upon how the management chooses to operate.

Model Shops

Since these shops customarily produce small quantities, they can serve several purposes. They are used for product research and are also called upon to produce small quantities of a product for market research. In the radio business it is common to submit transformers to the radio manufacturers to test compatability with the rest of the assembly. This calls for producing small quantities of transformers in a model shop. The model shops are informal job shops and the instructions to the workers are generally verbal because the workers are highly skilled.

TYPES OF CONTROL SYSTEMS

The type of control system reflects the type of production. In a job shop one can expect to find the *order control system*, but in the production line one can expect to find some form of the *flow control system*. These control systems are self-explanatory, but for a more explicit definition let us submit to the authority of the American Production and Inventory Control Society Dictionary.

Order Control: Control of the progress of each customer order or stock order through the successive operations in its production cycle.

Flow Control: Control of the rate or flow of production from one work station to another. (Appropriate to the continuous or line type of manufacture.)[2]

It is only implied in the definitions that the material in the job shop is separated into batches or lots, while in flow control this segregation is not attempted. This leads to an intermediate situation where the material flows through the process as in a production line, but for some reason regulating it in batch quantities is desirable. This condition calls for *block control.*

Block Control: Control of the production progress of groups or blocks of shop orders for products undergoing the same basic processes. (Appropriate to the repetitive type of manufacture.)[3]

In the clothing industry, block control may be required because of the necessity to separate different shades of cloth. In the aircraft industry, the lots must be recorded for quality control purposes. In some situations, block control is used during the transition between order control and flow control.

The size of the block is often determined by the process. For example, the block may consist of sufficient material to fill the heat treating furnace, or perhaps it may be the maximum amount which can be handled by a

[2] *Ibid.*
[3] *Ibid.*

materials-handling truck. The block size is also determined on the basis of time, such as the quantity which can pass through the process in a half day.

One might expect job shops to use flow control, and to a degree this is true. In some job shops the flow is so standardized that, even though instruction sheets are available, the flow of the product from operation to operation is common knowledge and the routing sheets are seldom used.

THE PRODUCTION CONTROL ORGANIZATION

The place of the production control department in the organization will depend on many factors, but a typical structure is illustrated in Figure 3–2.

Figure 3–2

Typical Organization Chart

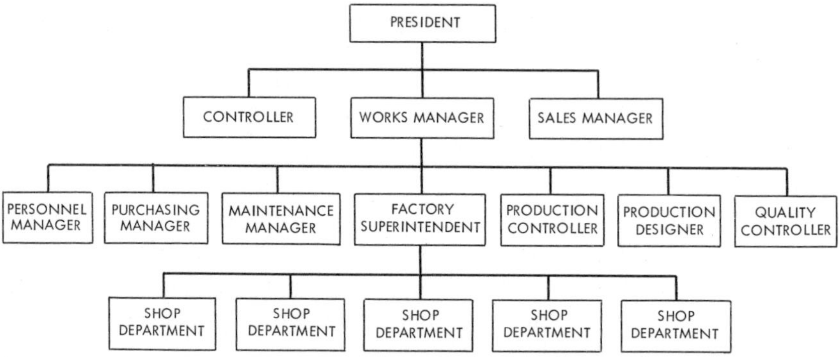

Ultimately, of course, the president of the manufacturing concern is responsible for the production control, but production control is actually the responsibility of whoever is directly charged with production: the works manager, the plant manager, or the manufacturing vice president. Except in a very small organization, this individual has many problems and therefore delegates his responsibility for the coordination of the production facilities to produce a product on schedule at an optimum cost. These responsibilities are gathered under one function under the Production Controller as shown on the organization chart.

Since this is a text on production control, it will be worthwhile to dwell on this part of the organization and to scrutinize the responsibilities. These responsibilities for control consist of three stages: the planning, action, and compliance stages; and each production activity is subject to these three stages of control. When an activity does not comply with the plan, the planning and action stages must be repeated; so the stages continually cycle until the activity is completed.

Traditionally, the subject of production control has been so stylized that a student is led to believe that all organizations for production control are identical. The terms for the classical divisions of production control have been *routing, scheduling, dispatching,* and *expediting.* Routing and scheduling activities are contained in the planning stage, dispatching is the action stage, and expediting is part of the compliance stage.

The Planning Stage: Routing

Routing determines where the work is to be done. At times this function starts with the representation of the product as a blueprint, and every detail of how the product is to be made is decided right down to the point of designating specific machines and tools. At other times all the processing is determined by some other group, and the routing decides only which specific machine is to be used.

The Planning Stage: Scheduling

Scheduling determines when the work is to be done. It sets the timing of production control, and is not unlike the establishment of schedules for railroads, theaters, and other similar activities.

The Action Stage: Dispatching

Dispatching is the function of issuing the orders at the correct time, a function similar to the dispatching of trains in the railroad industry. In flow control, dispatching consists of notifying the production facilities of the quantity needed, while in order control it becomes a complex procedure of issuing numerous production orders to direct and indirect workers.

The Compliance Stage: Expediting

Expediting is the function of determining whether or not the work is progressing as planned. In earlier industrial history this function was called by more descriptive terms, *stock chasing* or *follow-up,* and sometimes still goes under these older names. The expeditor serves as the feedback link between the performance of work and the scheduling and routing functions of production control. In a more modern context, the work of the expeditor is minimized because it is replaced by formal progress reports which are collected and processed by automatic data processing. An excessive number of expeditors probably indicates an inefficient operation. While the expeditor can serve an important purpose in production control, he must be selected with care, because if he exceeds his authority, instead of smoothing out production, he becomes an agitating agent in what would otherwise be an efficient work situation.

THE FOUR STAGES FROM TWO PERSPECTIVES

Because these four functions of production control—routing, scheduling, dispatching, and expediting—are referred to so frequently in the literature, the student often gets a picture something like this: There is a production control office which is centrally located in the factory, like the hub of a wheel. On the door of this office (of course) is the sign Production Control. Open this door and behind it you will find four doors leading to four equal-sized offices, each entirely divorced from the other, and inscribed Routing, Scheduling, Dispatching, and Expediting, respectively. Nothing could be further from the truth. As we shall see, in a small organization, one man, working part-time, might be doing the whole production control function. In a larger organization, we will find many people involved in one function and people handling more than one of the functions. Where specialization occurs there will have to be a great deal of communication among the groups.

The significant point is that these four activities occur in any pursuit, regardless of its importance. Even a person pursuing a hobby will go through these four steps. For example, the man who collects and refinishes antiques might progress on the restoring of a piece bought at auction as follows. First, he will plan how he is going to do the work and the tools he is going to use. This is routing. He may cut a repair part to size in his own shop, take it to his neighbor's to turn on a lathe, and return home to use his wife's vacuum cleaner to drive a paint sprayer for finishing. When the man plans to use the lathe on Saturday morning while his friend is home from work, and plans to do the painting on Sunday morning while his wife is at church (and can't object to the use of the vacuum), this is scheduling. And when he urges himself out of bed on Saturday and Sunday mornings to do the work, this is dispatching. And when the man's wife checks up to see if the refinishing will be complete by the time her sewing circle meets, this is expediting. A homely example, perhaps, and facetious, but it points up how elementary the whole production control function is and may help you to approach it with the proper perspective.

SCOPE OF PRODUCTION CONTROL

One difficulty in spelling out the objectives of production control occurs because different activities are combined in different organizations. These differences are caused by tradition, variations in products and markets, and by numerous other reasons. Here is a list of activities (many overlapping) which might be included in the production control department:

Receive and record orders from the sales department.
Estimate the cost of new jobs.
Serve as a liaison between the factory and sales department or customer.
Forecast sales.
Issue purchase requisitions.
Make decisions to make or buy.
Maintain control over raw materials and finished products.
Maintain stock rooms for raw materials and finished products.

Establish inventory levels.
Determine routing of purchased material.
Determine routing of finished goods.
Determine internal transportation of material.
Control stock in branch warehouses.
Estimate manpower and machine requirements from schedules.
Make schedules and maintain production throughout plant.
Replan schedules and minimize replanning failures.
Assign jobs to men and machines.
Make product "explosions."
Dispatch production orders.
Expedite orders.
Evaluate performance.
Issue and maintain engineering prints.
Issue and maintain engineering changes.
Print and duplicate manufacturing forms.
Design and redesign data-processing systems.
Data processing.
Install data-processing systems.
Program computers.
Evaluate data-processing systems.

PRODUCTION CONTROL AND THE ORGANIZATION

The objective of production control is to coordinate production facilities, and consequently numerous communication interfaces occur with the other departments. They all have a common interest in making a product on schedule at an optimum cost, but the method of doing it is at times a source of disagreement.

The sales department is interested in sales, and repeated sales. This can be accomplished only if the customer is satisfied, and he is usually satisfied if he obtains the product quality he desires at a reasonable cost and on schedule. Usually the delivery date becomes the point of conflict between production control and the sales department. To the sales department, the schedule is more important than living within the budget because a record of poor delivery can damage customer relations beyond repair.

The purchasing department wants requisitions placed well in advance of the time the material is needed. It also wants to purchase all material in large quantities, and to have freedom to substitute whenever this is desired.

Engineering would like to have designs accepted by the factory, regardless of the manufacturing difficulties. It would like to have any design changes made instantaneously, no matter how difficult.

The tool department wants time to design and build tools, and, if necessary, to experiment with production methods. The tool department itself is a small production facility, having many of the scheduling problems which exist in the factory as a whole.

Quality control and inspection are concerned with meeting the product standards, regardless of the production schedules to be met. This sometimes leads to open conflict, but most often production and quality control recognize their common interests and work harmoniously.

The personnel department would like to maintain a constant labor force and supply the skills from the available labor pool. Factory management is interested in long production runs with infrequent changes. They would like to keep inventories low, but at the same time keep the factory busy.

INDUSTRIAL RELATIONS AND PRODUCTION CONTROL

Production control impinges upon practically every other department, and its personnel are in contact with other people inside and outside the factory. Thus it is understandable that industrial relations are considered of utmost importance.

An organization with few disturbances reaches a state of "equilibrium" in which each person knows what is expected of him. Personnel become familiar with their surroundings and know how their fellow workers are going to react under certain conditions. When changes occur, the individual must make adjustments, and these adjustments may involve many distressing decisions. Production control is responsible for making many of these changes which the factory personnel may find so distressing. Every change in production quantity or methods may upset the organizational equilibrium. Members of the production control department must be aware of this possible problem and strive to alleviate the difficulties.

Because industrial relations are so important, the staff of the production control department should be selected with care:

1. They should know the work they are directing and be well acquainted with advanced methods.
2. Production control personnel operate in a no-man's-land between staff and line authority. Consequently, they should be aware of their position and of the source of their authority. They must exercise, but not usurp, authority.
3. Since production control personnel are often in direct contact with customers, they must present a good company image.
4. They must be friendly and enthusiastic.
5. They should have perseverance, but not be stubborn.
6. They have many opportunities to show favoritism; this, however, is not permissible, and they must be fair and unbiased.
7. They should be tactful and cooperative.
8. They should have excellent personal habits so that they will not offend those with whom they have contact.
9. They should be educated and trained in the subjects related to production control: statistics, economics, data processing, and others.

These are only a few of the important characteristics that should be looked for when hiring personnel for the production control department.

A TYPICAL PRODUCTION CONTROL SYSTEM

Now that the place of production control in the organization has been shown, this is a good point at which to introduce a typical production control system ("typical" because it would take the remainder of this text to discuss each of the variations to be found in industry). The system discussed here, and shown in Figure 3–3, is typical of an order control system to be found in the ordinary job shop that produces relatively small lots of a variety of products. Detail is purposefully left off the diagram so that it does not become too specific and so that you can observe the framework of a typical system.

The production control functions of routing, scheduling, dispatching, and expediting are shown as a box on the diagram, with the essential information inputs shown on the left. These inputs consist of the authority to manufacture the product, processing descriptions, time information, and information about the tools and machines used for production. This last input is seldom written down, but is part of the knowledge of the production control personnel.

The routing section not only determines the *route* but often prepares the numerous papers necessary for production control. The accumulation of paper forms is often referred to as the *route file*. In the route file will be at least some of the numerous forms listed to the right of the chart, and often there be many other kinds of forms. The number and kinds of forms depend upon the type and size of the manufacturing organization.

The *stores issue* order is the authority to remove the materials from stores. It eventually will be sent to inventory control records to make the necessary adjustments, and then to cost accounting where the product costs are accumulated.

The flow of the typical forms is shown in the diagram, and it is well worth your time to follow them through carefully. The route sheet, blueprints, and manufacturing order may follow the product as it goes through the plant. When this is done, some of the other forms may be eliminated. In fact, some industries (such as manufacturers of garments and shoes) reduce their paper work to a single form designed around the route sheet. You may wish to try, as an exercise, to reduce the number of forms given in the illustration. This has been only an introduction to production control systems, and you will find a number of other typical systems in the last section of this text.

THE WORK AUTHORIZATION

The production control department assumes the authority over production and takes the responsibility of issuing the *work authorization*. For a

Figure 3–3

Typical Production Control System

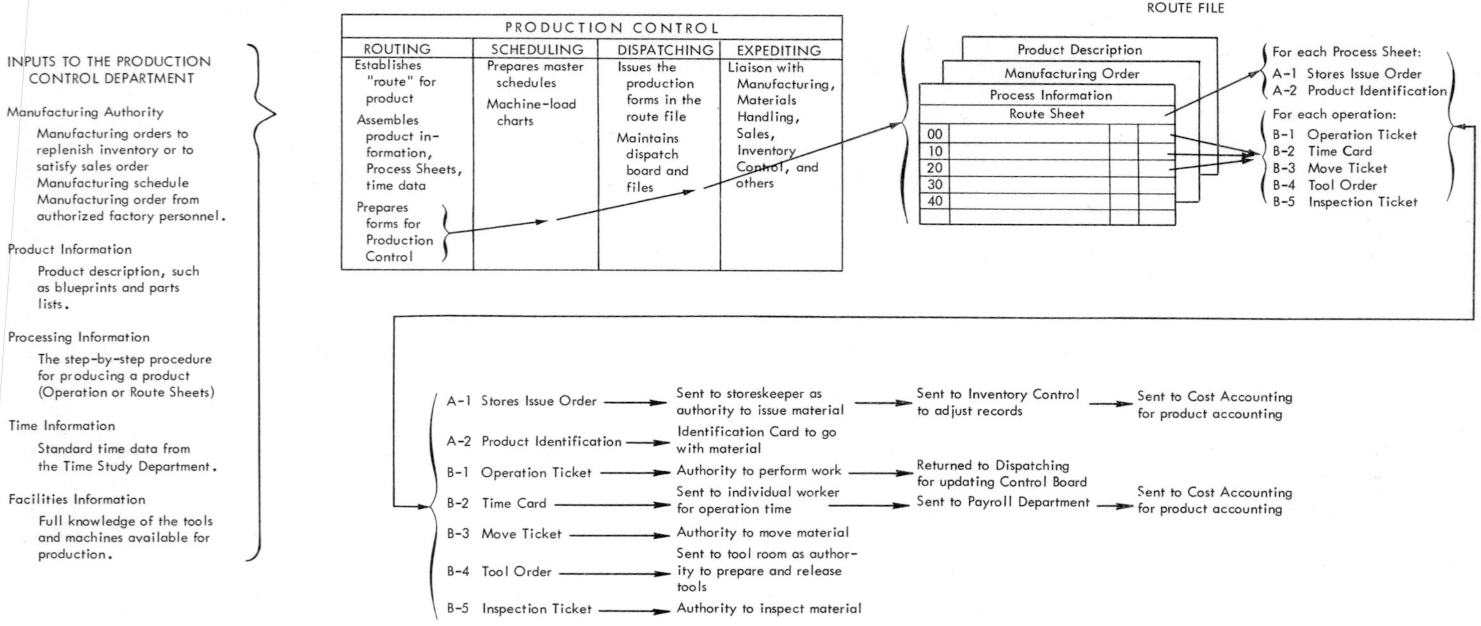

production line, this may not be issued daily, and will probably consist of a schedule of production for some future period of time. In a job shop it is usually necessary to issue work authorizations daily, or even more frequently. The work authorization may have many different names: job ticket, operation ticket, work ticket, shop order, work order, or some other appropriate term.

SYSTEM DESIGNING AND DECISION MAKING APPLIED TO PRODUCTION CONTROL

In the first chapter a definition for system designing for production control was given as "Conceiving and planning in the mind a complex unity of many diverse parts to exercise restraining or directing influence over the making of goods."

The logic used in solving any system-design and decision-making problem was discussed in the second chapter, but the system designing and decision making we are interested in has as its objective the coordination of production facilities to produce a product on time at an optimum cost.

Production control can be considered analogous to the servo-system which was discussed in Chapter 1. It is very complex, with numerous interacting secondary systems which are difficult to segregate. As a start, envision it as shown in Figure 3–4, with the manufacturing facilities in the block and

Figure 3–4

Factory Analogy

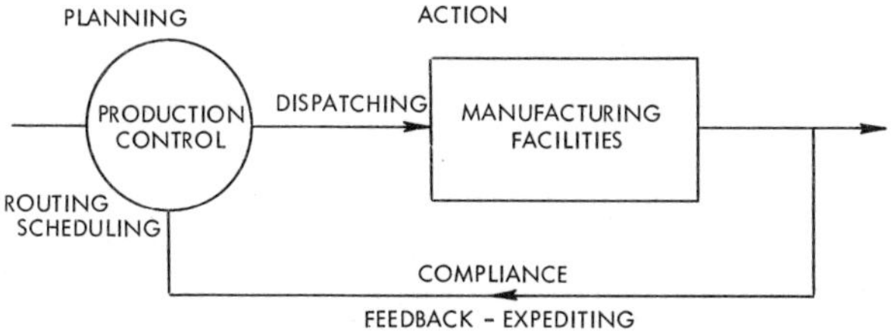

production control regulating the system. If everything worked perfectly, the output would be exactly as determined by production control. The difficulty is that many secondary inputs upset the system. The perturbations consist of such common production disturbances as material shortages, errors in machining, broken machine tools, absent workers, and hundreds of other problems which make it impossible for production to meet schedules. It is only by the feedback links in the system that corrective action can be taken to attain the desired schedule.

During the planning stage the production control personnel are interested in the inputs of materials, machine capacities, available labor and other factors which are expressed in the routing and scheduling of the product.

The action stage occurs when the authorization for production is dispatched to the factory. Finally, the compliance stage is encountered when information is fed back to readjust the schedule and possibly change the routing. Expediting serves as the feedback link, but the numerous forms, such as scrap reports, time cards, and finished materials reports, are also important feedback links. Notice that the planning, action, and compliance stages are operating for many different products. It is this overlap of activities which makes production control complicated.

UNIQUE PERTURBATIONS OF THE SYSTEM

Throughout the text some of the more common disturbances to the factory system will be discussed. For a moment, however, it is worth turning our attention to a few unique perturbations to the system.

Manufacturing a product which is to be sold in foreign markets can cause difficulties for production control. The product may require special metric fittings and instructions written in a foreign language. Even the packing may have to be more rugged to withstand the rigors of a sea voyage.

When a new part is designed, which is not interchangeable with the older one, a record of the date or serial number will have to be kept of the last assembly. The lack of this information has caused more than one customer to despair when he has had to order a repair part.

Often it is difficult to predict exactly how much of the product will go through the production cycle without being spoiled. This causes companies to start the manufacture of more products than are needed. If an excess is completed, it will either have to be stored until another order is received or be lost as scrap. If enough material to fill the order is not completed, more will have to be started, which will increase preparation costs.

Production control procedures can be especially difficult during the changeover of product lines. Often one line must make up part of the production which is being lost during the changeover. There is also the problem of stockpiling finished goods prior to closing down the line. Production control must be concerned with completing as many products as possible without having excess parts at the changeover which can never be used. During the run-in period, there is the constant problem of interruptions, often reflected in difficult storage conditions as materials continue to be received from the vendors.

Often production control must concern itself with minor production problems within the primary manufacturing system. Products are returned for repair or alteration, and these jobs must find their way through production. If special facilities for producing short runs for repairs are not available, parts must be scheduled through the factory, thereby complicating the situation. Often models of new products are also included in the production system.

Production control at times must be sensitive to the external market conditions. This is true in the meat-packing industry, where there are choices in the way the meat is cut or processed. Production control must reflect these changes in demand.

This is a sampling of the perturbations which can occur to the production system; only actual experience in production control can emphasize the frequent and unusual disturbances which actually occur.

THE EXCEPTION PRINCIPLE

Students of organizational theory will recognize the application of the *exception principle* in the feedback concept. In this principle, routine decisions are made without reference to higher authority. Those decisions which are not routine are an exception, and require further attention. The same idea is applied in the feedback concept, because it is only necessary to take action when information fed back indicates that the system is not conforming to what is desired.

The fact that routine decisions are handled automatically does not mean that no decision has been made. It *has* been made, but, since it works for a number of repetitious problems, it can be used over and over again. This is analogous to a gauge which is used for checking parts. The gauge itself is used repeatedly to check parts, but the gauge dimensions were decided only once. If the parts are outside the gauge tolerance, a higher authority must make the decision as to whether or not the parts are acceptable.

CENTRALIZED VS. DECENTRALIZED CONTROL

All of the production control activities operate out of one office in a *centralized production control system*. Decentralized control—in its purest sense—probably doesn't exist because it would lead to anarchy; but there are situations where all of the control activities are not centralized, and this is referred to as a *decentralized production control system*. Typical of such a situation would be a department which is given a schedule for completing work orders but where the foreman is left to work out the details of how the schedule is to be met.

There are both advantages and disadvantages in centralized control. Tighter schedules can be maintained with centralized control and more information is available for the customer on short notice. It has the disadvantage, however, of increasing the cost because more communications are required, more paper work is produced, and more people are needed to process it.

Perhaps the chief objection to centralized control is that supervisors lose their initiative. The foremen are not permitted to plan their work, and it is nearly an inborn instinct to want to. Because of this, the schedules are inflexible and inefficient plant operations result.

MULTIPLANT OPERATIONS

The problem of centralization and decentralization exists in multiplant operations. In some organizations, some centralization is imperative; in others it would be a needless waste. You will find an example of a successful centralized production control system in Chapter 21.

THE IMPACT OF AUTOMATION ON PRODUCTION CONTROL

Controlling production in a plant of any size requires a stupendous amount of data. The data must be produced, gathered, compiled in various ways, and evaluated, and action must be taken. This action often spawns more data. As factories become more progressive, more data must be handled and more rapidly. These and other reasons have put an emphasis upon automatic data handling. New methods of duplicating data are being developed daily and the manufacturers of card-data processing equipment and computers are constantly improving the designs of their equipment.

Since production control depends upon data handling, it is logical that production control systems designers must know more and more about the subjects of duplicating, card-data processing, and computers.

The trend is to incorporate the production control function within the data-processing organization. Even where this is not happening, it is important that the production control personnel be able to talk intelligently with those responsible for data processing. They should know the potentials and limitations of the equipment, for only by a thorough understanding of the principles can they expect to progress in the organization.

You should not be afraid to accept this challenge of more efficient data processing. The principles are relatively simple and are to be found in this text. It is no excuse to consider data processing as a technician's task, for only after a strong foundation in the fundamentals can you ever expect to rise above the status of technician.

ORGANIZATION OF THE PRODUCTION CONTROL SUBJECTS

The introduction to Production Control Concepts presented in this chapter concludes the introductory material. This included an introduction to system designing and decision making for production control, system designing, and the logic of system designing. Now we will turn our attention to new material.

The analogy has been stressed as a suitable way of presenting the production control systems. In the next section will be found the information needed as an input to the system. This consists of information about the product and process, information about costs, information about quantity (derived either from the forecast or the inventory), and information about time (which is essential to scheduling).

The third section is given to techniques for designing the systems. As the design of a suitable organization is of primary importance, it is discussed first. The following chapters move into progressively sophisticated data processing. First the techniques for designing a manual system are discussed, then card-data processing, and next computer processing.

The fourth section of the book discusses the various decision-making techniques which have found, or promise to find, their places in the production control procedures.

The last section is devoted to examples of control systems. They, too, go from the simplest to the most sophisticated, and a number of examples of unique applications is given. Hopefully, upon completion of the last chapter you will feel confident enough not only to operate a production control system but also to design and redesign systems.

COST OF CONTROL

More than one company has "controlled itself" out of existence. Therefore one of the most important considerations is how much control is necessary. Poor control can ruin a company by causing unnecessary set-up costs, excessive delivery times, excessive overtime costs, and many other unnecessary expenses. These expenses must be weighed against the cost of tighter control, which might lead to hiring more people and buying additional equipment. Part of this text is dedicated to decision making and one of the most important decisions is just how much control is desirable.

SUMMARY

The objective of production control is the coordination of production facilities to produce a product on schedule at an optimum cost. How this objective is met depends in part upon whether a factory is organized as a job shop or as a production line.

In the job shop, order control is used; in the production line we find flow control or block control. In many respects the production line is easier to control than the job shops, where many different types of products are made at one time, requiring numerous job instructions with attending scheduling difficulties.

Production control has three stages: the planning stage, the action stage, and the compliance stage. These stages can incorporate the traditional functions of routing, scheduling, dispatching, and expediting which are associated with production control.

The feedback concept is a useful model for considering the production control system, and we find that the three stages are analogous to the block diagram describing the servo-model.

Feedback is necessary as long as there are secondary inputs to the system which cannot be controlled. Although these perturbations take many forms, only a few could be described in the limits of this chapter.

Questions

1. Draw a typical organization chart for a factory. Number the points of control on the chart and discuss the purpose and scope of each.
2. Give an example of a business control system other than the production control system. Discuss it in detail, pointing out the similarity or dissimilarity with the production control function.
3. Search the literature for three definitions of production control. Write a critical analysis of these definitions and then write your own definition.
4. Classify each of the following industries as representing job shops or production lines. What type of control would you expect to find in each? (*a*) Packing plant. (*b*) Garment factory. (*c*) Radio cabinet factory. (*d*) Bakery. (*e*) Brewery.
5. What are the four traditional divisions of the production control function? Discuss how these are included in your activities.
6. How do the interests of the accounting department, purchasing department, and maintenance department respectively, conflict with the interests of the production control department?
7. How well equipped are you to work in a production control department? What personality strengths and weaknesses do you have for such a job?
8. List and discuss several of the more important secondary inputs of a production system.
9. Explain the exception principle and how it can be applied in an industrial situation.
10. Select an industry in which centralized control is desirable. What effect has this on the efficiency of the plant? What effect has this on the management and other employees?
11. What is the effect of automation on the production control function?
12. Discuss how automatic data processing affects the organizational structure.

References

AMERICAN MANAGEMENT ASSOCIATION. *Guides to Effective Production Management*. New York, 1954.

——— (M. S. DOOHER, ed.). *Successful Production Planning and Control from Forecast to Final Delivery*. New York, 1955.

AMERICAN PRODUCTION AND INVENTORY CONTROL SOCIETY (CHARLES W. DEBUS, JR., ed.). *APICS Bibliography*. 2d ed. Chicago, 1963.

——— (Clifford M. Baumback, ed.). *Dictionary of Production and Inventory Control Terms.* Chicago, 1963.

American Society of Tool and Manufacturing Engineers (Frank W. Wilson, ed.). *Tool Engineers Handbook.* 2d ed. New York: McGraw-Hill Book Co., Inc., 1959.

Bethel, Lawrence L.; Tann, Walter L.; Atwater, Franklin S.; and Rung, Edward E. *Production Control.* New York and London: McGraw-Hill Book Co., Inc., 1942.

Biegel, John E. *Production Control: A Quantitative Approach.* Englewood Cliffs, N.J.: Prentice-Hall, Inc., 1963.

Bock, Robert H., and Holstein, William K. *Production Planning and Control, Text and Readings.* Columbus, Ohio: Charles E. Merrill Books, Inc., 1963.

Carson, Gordon B. *Production Handbook.* New York: Ronald Press Co., 1958.

Dooley, Arch R.; McGarrah, Robert E.; McKenney, James L.; Rosenbloom, Richard S.; Skinner, C. Wickham; and Thurston, Philip H. *Casebooks in Production Management Operations Planning and Control.* New York: John Wiley & Sons, Inc., 1964.

Eilon, Samuel. *Elements of Production Planning and Control.* New York: Macmillan Co., 1962.

Fuller, Don. *Organizing, Planning, and Scheduling for Engineering Operations.* Boston: Industrial Education Institute, 1962.

Ireson, William Grant, and Grant, Eugene L. *Handbook of Industrial Engineering and Management.* Englewood Cliffs, N.J.: Prentice-Hall, Inc., 1955.

Koepke, Charles A. *Plant Production Control.* 3rd ed. New York: John Wiley & Sons, Inc., 1961.

Landy, Thomas M. *Production Planning and Control.* New York: McGraw-Hill Book Co., Inc., 1950.

Lewis, Ronello B. *Management Control Techniques for Improving Profits.* Englewood Cliffs, N.J.: Prentice-Hall, Inc., 1962.

MacNiece, E. H. *Production Forecasting, Planning and Control.* 3rd ed. New York: John Wiley & Sons, Inc., 1961.

Magee, John F. *Production Planning and Inventory Control.* New York: McGraw-Hill Book Co., Inc., 1958.

Maynard, Harold B. *Industrial Engineering Handbook.* New York: McGraw-Hill Book Co., Inc., 1956.

McMillan, Claude, and Gonzalez, Richard F. *Systems Analysis: a Computer Approach to Decision Models.* Homewood, Ill., Richard D. Irwin, Inc., 1965.

Moore, Franklin G. *Production Control.* New York: McGraw-Hill Book Co., Inc., 1959.

O'Donnell, Paul D. *Production Control.* Englewood Cliffs, N.J.: Prentice-Hall, Inc., 1952.

Parton, James Allan, Jr., and Steres, Chris P. *Production Control Manual.* New York: Conover-Mast Publications, 1955.

Pritzker, Robert A., and Gring, Robert A. *Modern Approaches to Production Planning and Control.* New York: American Management Association, Inc., 1960.

RAGO, LOUIS J. *Production Analysis and Control.* Scranton, Pa.: International Textbook Co., 1963.

REINFELD, NYLES V. *Production Control.* Englewood Cliffs, N.J.: Prentice-Hall, Inc., 1959.

RITCHIE, WILLIAM E. *Production and Inventory Control.* New York: Ronald Press Co., 1951.

SCHEELE, EVAN D.; WESTERMAN, WILLIAM L.; and WIMMERT, ROBERT J. *Principles and Design of Production Control Systems.* Englewood Cliffs, N.J.: Prentice-Hall, Inc., 1960.

STARR, MARTIN K. *Production Management, Systems and Synthesis.* Englewood Cliffs, N.J.: Prentice-Hall, Inc., 1964.

TIMMS, HOWARD L. *The Production Function in Business.* Homewood, Ill.: Richard D. Irwin, Inc., 1962.

TIRANTI, D. *Introduction to Production Control.* London: Chapman & Hall, 1946.

VAN DE MARK, ROBERT L. *Production Control Techniques.* Grand Rapids, Mich.: Gilson Press, 1964.

———. *Production and Inventory Control Case Studies.* Grand Rapids, Mich.: Gilson Press, 1963.

VORIS, WILLIAM. *The Management of Production.* New York: Ronald Press Co., 1960.

———. *Production Control.* Rev. ed. Homewood, Ill.: Richard D. Irwin, Inc., 1961.

YATES, MORRIS LORD. *Production Control in an Engineering Factory.* Manchester, England: Emmott, 1946.

YOUNGER, JOHN, and GESCHELIN, JOSEPH. *Work Routing, Scheduling and Dispatching in Production.* New York: Ronald Press Co., 1947.

SECTION TWO

Production System Inputs

CHAPTER 4

Product and Process Information

An essential input to the production control system is the *product information*, for by what other means would it be known how to produce a product? The first thing that comes to mind when we consider product information is the engineering drawing used to describe metal, plastic, and some wood products. But this would be a very narrow interpretation because many products cannot be adequately described by a drawing. For example, how can one describe, by an engineering print, such a thing as a lady's garment, a pair of shoes, a can of paint, or a drug?

PRODUCT AND PROCESS DESCRIPTION

The product information is an instruction, to the worker and others, of how a product is to be produced; and it takes two basic forms:

The *product description* tells how the product will appear in some stage of production. It may be a drawing, a picture, a model, or a sample of the product.

The *process description* does not describe the product; it describes the steps needed to attain the end product. This is the method used in the production of paint, dairy products, bakery goods, pharmaceuticals, etc.

To make the distinction clearer between the product description and the process description, consider the manufacture of an ice cream bar. The tasty slab of ice cream can be depicted as to size, flavor, and even porosity. The chocolate coating can be described, and we could say the stick is placed so it won't gag the unsuspecting customer, but all of this product description would be of little help if we wanted to produce ice cream bars. What we need is a step-by-step process description of how to make the product.

Ice cream bars are relatively simple, but consider a product such as a pharmaceutical. The description, even a chemical description, would be of little assistance in manufacturing the product. Such products require step-by-step information as to how the product is compounded, how long it is kept at a certain temperature, how it is filtered, and other necessary information.

Many industries use both the product description and the process description. In the metal trades it is common to have an engineering print and an operation sheet, which are, respectively, the product description and the process description. To bring some order to this discussion, the product description will come first, then the process description. Other information will be added along the way which may be useful to you some time in your career.

PRODUCT DESCRIPTION

Often the product description is conveyed verbally. The engineers in a model shop may confer directly with the operators, discussing what needs to be done to produce the model. This is the way exclusive garment makers work. It calls for a close liaison between designer and seamstress.

On assembly lines, the placement of a wire on a radio chassis or the location of a weldment on an automobile body might be passed on from foreman to worker or even from worker to worker. Some place there is probably a master print of the assembly, but it is not used by the individual operator to produce his part of the product. It would be far better, of course, if each operator had his own print showing how the task should be performed.

Formal product descriptions may be either pictorial or nonpictorial. Most important of the nonpictorial descriptions is the *specification*. Frequently the specification is associated only with the purchasing function, but the purchasing specification for one company may be the production specification for the vendor. A typical specification developed by an association is shown in Figure 4–1.

A good product specification for purchasing should conform to a general plan or format so those who use it may become accustomed to finding information in a familiar and orderly sequence. The important parts of the product specification, and their characteristics, are:

Heading. This should contain the specification number, the date it was issued, and an issue number. The specification number might be keyed to some established system of product numbers used for accounting purposes and shipping identification.

General Requirements. This section should give a brief description of the product and explain its uses. Of course, at times it may be desirable not to divulge the usage, especially if a product is part of a newly developed machine or has military significance.

Detail Requirements. This section lists all the necessary physical, chemical, electrical and other properties of the product specified. Everything about the

Figure 4–1

Product Specification

AEROSPACE MATERIAL SPECIFICATIONS — **AMS 5609**

SOCIETY OF AUTOMOTIVE ENGINEERS, Inc. 485 Lexington Ave., New York 17, N.Y.

Issued 1-31-64
Revised

STEEL BARS, FORGINGS, AND TUBING, CORROSION AND MODERATE HEAT RESISTANT
12.5Cr - 0.12Cb (SAE 51410 Cb Modified)
Ferrite Controlled

1. ACKNOWLEDGMENT: A vendor shall mention this specification number in all quotations and when acknowledging purchase orders.

2. FORM: Bars, forgings, mechanical tubing, and forging stock.

3. APPLICATION: Primarily for parts and assemblies requiring uniformly high room temperature properties and uniform response to tempering along with oxidation resistance up to 1000 F (540 C) where control of ferrite content is necessary.

4. COMPOSITION:

	min	max
Carbon	0.12 -	0.15
Manganese	--	0.60
Silicon	--	0.50
Phosphorus	--	0.025
Sulfur	--	0.025
Chromium	11.50 -	12.50
Nickel	--	0.75
Molybdenum	--	0.20
Columbium	0.05 -	0.20
Aluminum	--	0.05
Copper	--	0.50
Tin	--	0.05
Nitrogen	--	0.08

product should be listed, such as the tolerance permitted on the dimensions. The performance and sale of the product should be stressed, and all extraneous characteristics should be eliminated.

Methods for Testing. For each specification of a property there should be an accompanying test for compliance. These test methods should be fully explained to avoid any errors in interpretation. If a sampling procedure is used, it should be fully explained.

Packing and Packaging. Since the method of packing is so important in the distribution and sale of goods, it should be described in detail in this section of the specification.

Another nonpictorial product description is the *standard parts index.* Frequently a company uses common parts, such as bolts, pins, and washers, so often that it is desirable to standardize on certain sizes, catalog them under part numbers, and have them available to design engineers for their selection. In this situation a company can take advantage of the simplification and standardization of products. Parts indexed may be either purchased from the outside or produced in the factory. Often there is an incentive to produce special parts by modifying standard parts, if the standard parts are readily available.

A pictorial product description may consist of nothing more than a model which shows how the product is to be produced. In the dress industry, the

Figure 4–2

Product Description for the Garment Industry

finished garment is available for workers to examine, and, in addition, dress patterns (Figure 4–2) illustrate how paper models are used as patterns for cutting the material. There are numerous other instances where a model is used for describing how the product is made.

By far the most common pictorial product description is the engineering drawing, or a copy of it, made by one of the various techniques: the blueprint, ozalid, or spirit duplicating process. There are numerous books on the techniques of drawing, and not much can be added here except to reacquaint you with the basic concepts.

THE ENGINEERING DRAWING

The purpose of the engineering drawing is to convey, in the most efficient method possible, information concerning a part or an assemblage of parts. The engineering drawing is the language by which designers converse with each other and with people in the factory. It is such a common language in the factory that it is highly desirable that almost everyone be somewhat acquainted with the techniques used.

Since a drawing is a language, certain symbols and conventions are followed. While there are several standardized ways of selecting the views and projecting them, the one most common in ordinary engineering practice is the orthographic. For many, this means of envisioning an object is through an imaginary glass box. Imagine a part (Figure 4–3) encased in a glass box

Figure 4–3

The Engineering Drawing

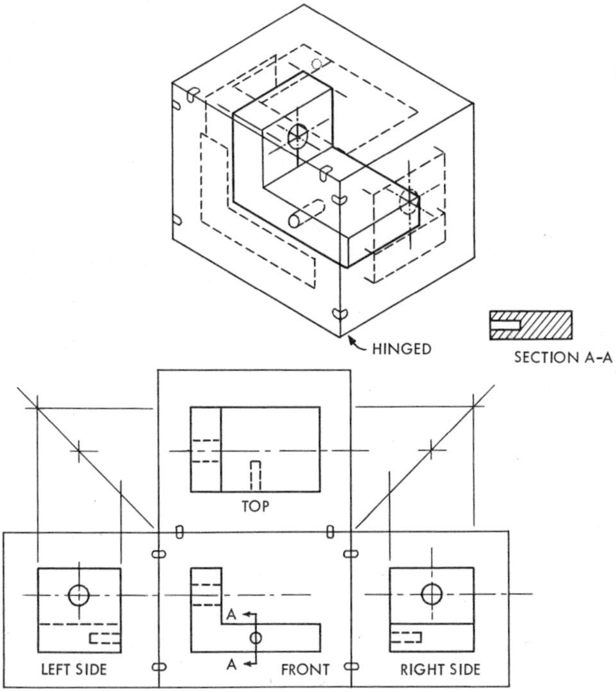

which forms planes. Now imagine looking at the part through these planes from a great distance, so that the rays of vision are parallel lines which would produce images on the glass in the true dimension. The objective, of course, is to show the three dimensions of the product on a flat sheet of paper. To do this requires the unfolding of the imaginary glass box. The standard way of unfolding the box is shown, with the top view above and the bottom view below the front view. Any face of the part can be shown as the front view, but usually that view is chosen which will reveal the most information with the least amount of drawing.

Notice that the part is the same length in the front, top, and bottom view—as you might expect. The views also agree in depth and height so that they are aligned, making it easy to move from one view to another. Auxiliary views and sectional views are frequently used to reveal some characteristics which are not shown by the projections just discussed. The sectional view is cross-hatched to make it stand out and show that this view represents a slice through the object. The point at which the cross-section is taken is indicated, as shown, by a dashed line with arrowheads at either end. The view is shown as if you were looking in the direction in which the arrows are pointing. Center lines are indicated by a dash-dot-dash line.

Good drawing practices permit making presentable product descriptions which will not be confusing to those who have to read them. In the past, drawing techniques emphasized more than the bare essentials needed for understanding. While the artistic engineering drawings are commendable, art should not be emphasized to the detriment of profits. Recently there have been several publications which emphasize simplified drawing practices which many companies could use to advantage. Drawings should be produced economically, but it should also be kept in mind that they leave an impression on the worker which may give him a clue to how he is to perform. If the drawings are slipshod, so may be the worker's interpretations.

It is often unnecessary to have a new drawing made for each product if the configuration remains the same from product to product. A standard drawing, with fill-in dimensions (Figure 4–4), can be used with considerable savings. One word of caution: factory personnel should not scale dimensions from a print, neither on the standard print nor on any other.

Figure 4–4

Part Drawings Using Fill-in Dimensions

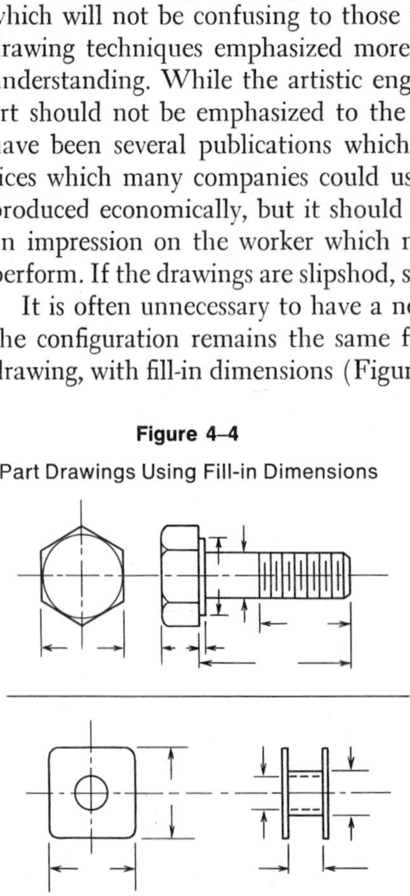

An engineering drawing may contain one part or more per sheet. The *one-part system* is favored by many companies, and for good reasons. The part number and print number can be the same, simplifying the indexing system. Drawings which have been superseded can be kept out of the files. The one-part system is simpler when a drawing change has to be made; one drawing can be rectified without disturbing a large drawing. This also simplifies drafting when several people are making changes on one large assembly. The one-part drawing will be easier to use in production as the drawings of concern to an individual need be issued only to him. This helps prevent confusion in the shop. The cost of reproduction is kept to a minimum because the prints are small, and only that part which has been changed must be reproduced. With this background in the product description, let us turn to the process description.

PROCESS DESCRIPTION

The process description is a step-by-step set of instructions that indicates how a product is to be produced. This contrasts with the product description, just discussed, telling what the end product should be. Often the process description and the product description are used together, but sometimes the product defies description, in which case the process description must be used alone.

Many different industries use the process description, but the example here is in the metal working industry. From this you can understand the process description as used in other industries. The objective here is not only to acquaint you with a typical process description but also to make you aware of a logical method of developing this description.

Responsibility for the process description can be that of the production department, the design engineers, tool engineers, a special process-planning group, estimators, sales engineers, or others, depending upon the product being produced and the personnel available in the various functions mentioned. Developing the process description is often called *process planning* or *process designing*. The end product is the set of instructions, which will go by such titles as *instruction sheets, operation sheets, route sheets,* etc.

Process planning is the technique of predetermining the most suitable materials and methods to produce a product of required quality at a minimum cost. This results in a set of written instructions for the production personnel.

Scrap heaps and profit-and-loss statements bear witness to the importance of process planning, an importance which cannot be overemphasized. This means that manufacturing management should choose process planners with the greatest care. Ideally, they should have the equivalent of a college education and a number of years working on the factory floor. In addition, it is imperative that they are endowed with ingenuity and respect for cost.

The logic of process planning can be developed more concisely if some of the terms are defined.[1]

The *process* is all the work done on a product from the time it leaves a controlled storage point until the time it returns to a controlled storage. The process, a comprehensive term, is made up of building blocks which are generally called operations.

An *operation* is all the work done at one location. This applies to a single worker on an engine lathe, several workers on a press, or one worker operating several automatic screw machines. The key to whether it is an operation or not is to determine if just one instruction is needed. If so, it is an operation. To think of it another way, can it be handled by just one set of time-card entries? If

---

[1] The following material first appeared in an article written by the author and published in the April, 1958, issue of *The Tool Engineer*. It is used with the permission of that publication (American Society of Tool and Manufacturing Engineers, Detroit, Mich.).

so, it is an operation. As the process can be broken down into operations, so can the operations be subdivided into suboperations.

The *suboperation* is defined as work which is done without interruption. For example, drill, paint, burr, broach, and mill are all common suboperations.

The logic of process planning can be stated as a step-by-step procedure:

First Step: Determine, by a systematic method, all the suboperations required to produce a product.

Second Step: Group the suboperations into logical operations.

Third Step: Place the operations in their proper sequence for the process.

To illustrate how this method works in actual practice, a common part—such as the fuel pin illustrated in Figure 4–5—will be used. The first step is to list every building block suboperation. It is important that every suboperation is included in this analysis because this process plan is the basis upon which costs are estimated and time studies are established. Should you miss one, it might make the difference between a profit or a loss.

Listing the suboperations could be on a hit-or-miss basis, but it is wise to use some systematic scheme. For example, all the cylindrical surfaces might be listed first—or maybe all the facing suboperations—from left to right. Here, we will work systematically from left to right, numbering the suboperations as we go.

There should be no difficulty in understanding the instructions: drill, turn, and the others. Other industries have similar terms which are just as easily understood by the experienced worker. The man in the woodworking plant knows the suboperations of rabbet and dado, and the operator in the garment plant knows the suboperations sew, buttonhole, and hemstitch.

Early in the process design, some considerations must be given to the characteristics of the material and to how it will be held while being processed. The obvious choice for the product illustrated, the fuel pin, is to make it from square bar stock of the dimension required. This material can be worked in a turret lathe or automatic screw machine by passing it through a collet in the head stock. It is held in a rack and turns freely as the suboperations are performed. The last suboperation must be the cut-off. Because of the concentric holes, it is apparent that the bar must be held as is shown on the diagram.

It is desirable to identify the suboperations by referring to the dimensions of the blueprint. This method has one inherent danger: shop personnel may produce the product to the specifications written on the instruction sheet, but this may not agree with the latest design change shown on the engineering print. Ideally, dimensions should not be used, but often this is the only practical method of identifying surfaces.

The next step is to group the suboperations into operations. There is no need to place the suboperations into any sequence order. Placing them in order would be meaningless where several suboperations are to be done

Figure 4–5

The Logic of Process Planning

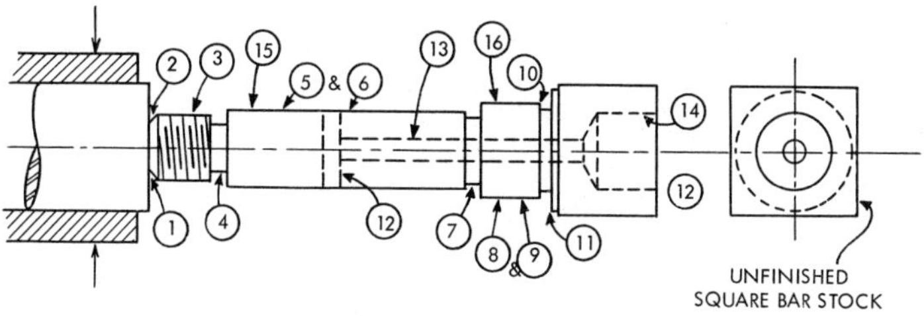

FIRST STEP

List of Suboperations:

1. Face and cut-off
2. Chamfer
3. Thread
4. Neck
5. Rough turn
6. Finish turn
7. Neck
8. Rough turn
9. Finish turn
10. Neck
11. Washer face
12. Drill lateral hole
13. Drill concentric hole (small)
14. Drill concentric hole (large)
15. Grind small diameter
16. Grind large diameter

SECOND STEP

Operation Groupings:

Drill lateral hole

Grind small diameter

Grind large diameter

Face and cut-off, chamfer,
neck, rough turn,
finish turn, neck, rough turn,
neck, washer face,
drill concentric hole (small)
drill concentric hole (large)
Thread

THIRD STEP

OPERATION SHEET

PRODUCT NAME *Fuel Pin* PRODUCT NO. *12-562*

MATERIAL *1020 C.R.S.* PRINT NO. *1-A-391*

PLANNER *T. I. M.* DATE *6/5/64* REVISIONS *R. G.*

OPERATION NO.	OPERATION DESCRIPTION		OPERATION	TOOLS
10	Face and cut-off, chamfer, neck, rough turn, finish turn, neck, rough turn, neck, washer face, drill large concentric hold, drill small concentric hole.	--	T.L.	*For special tools only*
15	Thread		T.L.	
20	Drill lateral hole	--	D.	
30	Grind small diameter	--	Gr.	
40	Grind large diameter	--	Gr.	

simultaneously. Also, the sequence can be determined by the operator or set-up man.

Next comes placing the operations in sequence for the process. This is an important step because there are many factors that must be taken into consideration. Some of these general factors, or *sequence criteria*, will be considered briefly to point up their importance.

Plant Layout. The process should generally cause the product to travel the shortest possible distance. Therefore the operations sequence should adhere to the layout of the equipment.

Reference Surfaces. Where dimensions are interrelated, it is necessary to place the operations in proper sequence to attain the requirements specified on the blueprints. For example, a part may have to be milled on one surface first in order that all measurements can be made from this reference surface.

Physical Requirements. First things must come first. For example, holes must be drilled before they are tapped.

Cost of Operations. If a product is likely to be scrapped during the process, then all costly operations should be deferred to the last.

Finishing. The finish should be put on a product near the last of the process so as to prevent marring.

There are other sequencing criteria, but the preceding gives an idea of what must be kept in mind while determining the operations sequence.

The final arrangement of the operations in a process is shown as a sequence of operations on the instruction (Operation) sheet. The operations are often numbered in sequence: 10, 20, 30, etc. The reason for numbering them by tens is so that other numbers may be inserted between operations in case an operation has been left out. Some factories use the operation number to designate what department is to do the work, such as 10 for drilling and 20 for milling, but this can lead to confusion if a product has to be processed in a department more than once. Maybe a part has to be drilled, milled, then drilled again, giving operation numbers 10, 20, 10. The question may come up, Which operation 10 are you talking about, the first or second?

Process planning has been discussed as a design procedure. This should not imply that all process planners follow the logic illustrated here. Many older, experienced planners go directly to the operation sequence, but they are often guilty of making costly errors which could have been minimized by the step-by-step procedure discussed herein.

To illustrate the process plan for other industries, an example is given for the manufacture of a pharmaceutical (Figure 4–6) and the manufacture of paint (Figure 4–7).

UNDERSTANDING THE PRODUCT INFORMATION

Some aspects of product descriptions included in many products are worthy of inclusion here. You should have some acquaintance with this information, if for no other reason than to have a broader understanding and to reduce the chance of embarrassment.

Two of these concepts are *tolerances* and *allowances*. At the risk of being facetious, or being criticized for using a word to define the word itself, tolerance can be defined as that which is tolerated and allowance as that which is allowed. These are not sophisticated definitions, but they should help you keep them straight.

Figure 4–6

Process Plan for Pharmaceutical Industry

MANUFACTURING DEPARTMENT
WORK SHEET

PRODUCT Aspirin Capsules
FOR Inventory

CONTROL NUMBER 397783

FORMULA: /Capsule

1. Aspirin 5 gr.
2.
3. Starch 1 gr.
4.
5. Talc 1/8 gr.
6.
7. Magnesium Stearate 1/8 gr.
8.
9. Red & Blue Capsules
10.
11.
12.
13.
14.

DATE BEGAN: ______
COMPLETED: ______
YIELD:
THEORETICAL 102,000
ACTUAL
BULK WEIGHT:
THEORETICAL ______
ACTUAL ______ BY ______
CONTROL CHECKED:
BY ______ DATE ______
BY ______ DATE ______
MIXING CHECKED:
WEIGHTS ______ DATE ______
INGRED'S ______ DATE ______

CHK	INGREDIENTS	INV	SOURCE	LPI LOT NOS	POUNDS	OUNCES	GRAINS	CAPSULES
1	Aspirin	✓	Mall.		72.86			
2	Starch	✓	✓		14.57			
3	Talc		✓		1.82			
4	Mag. Stearate		✓		1.82			
5	Blue & Red Cap.		✓					102,000
6								
7								
8								
9								
10								
11								
12								
13								
14								

PROCEDURE:
1) Weigh powders
2) Mix for 20 minutes in Ribbon blender
3) Grind mix thru "Fitz" #2A sieve (No mesh)
4) Label bulk powder
5) Check bulk wt.
6) Move to encapsulation

DELIVERY DATE ______

Tolerance: The total variation permitted for some characteristic of a product. It could be a weight variation, resistance, dimension, or other.

Allowance: An intentional difference between the maximum size of mating parts.

To illustrate these two concepts from a dimensional viewpoint, consider the shaft that fits in a bearing, as illustrated in Figure 4–8. In the first illus-

Figure 4–7

Process Plan for the Manufacture of Paint

XY-L347	#2	AMALGAMATED MACHINE TOOL CO., INC.	SMITHSVILLE, WISCONSIN
CODE	CARD NO.	CUSTOMER	ADDRESS

CODE	LBS/100 GALS	% BY WT.	N.V.% BY WT.	APPLICATION	CONTROL DATA--STANDARD	BATCH
				METHOD Spray	CLAIRTY	
				SURFACE Primed Steel	COLOR Gray	
					SOLIDS 53.70%	
				COATS	WT.PG. 8.75	
				THINNER RT-L257	HP. 925	
				VOL.MAT. 3	VISCOSITY 62 - 64 KU	
				VOL.TH. 1		
				A.D.TOUCH	GLOSS 48-52% on steel	
				A.D.HANDLE		
				A.D.TACK	SMOOTHNESS 6-6 1/2 NS	
				A.D.HARD	ADHESION	
				FLASHOFF 10 minutes	HARDNESS	
				TYPE OVEN	APPEARANCE	
				TYPE HEAT		
				BAKE SCHED. 20'@ 300°F	COLOR NO. ZYN-L2107	
				ARTICLE Machine Tools	SAMPLE NO.	
RM COST				MADE OF Steel	CNTRL.-CHEM.	
FB COST						
DATE						

	LOADING	GRINDING	UNLOADING	MIXING	TINTING	FILLING	MATERIAL STOCK
MACH.NO.							CONDITION
START							CONTAINERS
STOP							AMOUNT
OPERATOR							LOCATION
OK'D BY							

FORMULA CODE	COLOR	GLOSS	APPLY	CURE	SUBSTRATE	END USE
XY-L347	GRY	50	1	300	3 - 2	24 - 76

CARD NO. #2 MATERIAL 32L6 MACHINE TOOL GRAY BATCH NO. 12
FORMULATOR G.W. ORDER NO. L-69543 STOCK 4 gal. SECTION 31 PROD. DATE Feb. 19, 1946
DATE 6-3-61 COLOR NO. ZYN-L2107 MAKE 276 gal. THEO.YIELD 280 gal. ACT. YIELD

CODE	MATERIAL	POUNDS	GALLONS	BATCH
GRIND IN STEEL BALL MILL TO 6-6 1/2 NS (16 HOURS):				
B-2063	Carbon Black	5.13	.35	14.16#
T-4372	Titanium Dioxide	102.32	3.00	282.40#
1-3372	Talc	57.21	3.75	157.90#
R-653	MM Alkyd Resin	94.20	12.00	259.99#
A-733	UO Amine Resin	60.37	8.00	166.62#
X-124	Xylol	79.99	11.11	220.77#
Y-573	Solvesso	27.44	3.20	75.73#
AFTER GRIND, ADD AND MIX:				
R-653	MM Alkyd Resin	61.84	9.00	170.68#
DUMP MILL AND WASH:				
X-124	Xylol	36.00	5.00	99.36#
ADD AND MIX:				
R-653	MM Alykd Resin	206.38	26.29	569.61#
V-427	V M & P	73.60	11.50	203.14#
M-943	Stabilizer Q	4.75	.50	13.11#
TINT WITH:				
HW - 259		4.49	.75	2.07gal
HW - 631		39.82	3.62	9.99gal
HW - 599		21.31	1.93	5.33gal
		874.85	100.00	

tration, assume the part is exactly the size illustrated. The space between them is what has been allowed by the designers. However, there could be no space allowance between the two parts, giving a zero allowance, or even a force-fit, which would mean a negative allowance.

It is unrealistic, because of variations in manufacturing, to expect the

Figure 4–8

Tolerance and Allowance

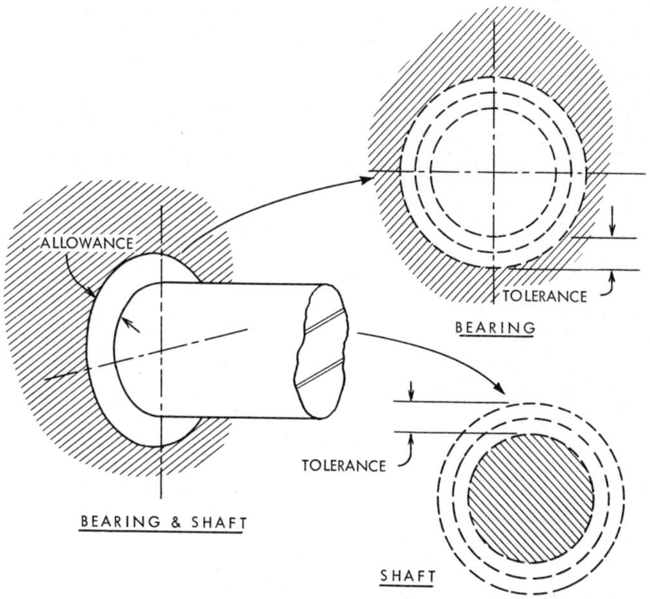

two parts to be exactly the sizes illustrated. Each part might vary, as is shown by the dotted lines in the second diagram. The difference between the two extreme dimensions is what can be tolerated. The variation in a part dimension is determined by the manufacturing process, while the designers specify within what limits the part will be acceptable. Hopefully, the designers' limits of acceptability will be greater than the tolerances dictated by the process. The tolerance is associated with one part, while the allowance refers to the mating of two parts. The system for maintaining quality is within the scope of this book, but the statistical applications for quality control are covered comprehensively by many excellent references and will not be included here.

Since so many products are made of iron, a few words about the characteristics and designation of this material will be included. Cast iron (*CI* on the product description) is an alloy of iron and carbon containing from 2 to 4 percent of carbon, 0.5 to about 3 percent of silicon, plus a small percentage of such elements as manganese, phosphorus, and sulphur. Its industrial importance comes from its capacity to be poured into molds of intricate shapes, thus reducing the machining time. It also has a high dampening capacity which makes it desirable for machine structures. And it has a high compressive strength, but it is not suitable for applications requiring high tensile strength.

Different types of cast iron result from different procedures of cooling the molten metal. Gray cast iron is the most common, but rapidly cooled cast iron—called white cast iron—is the basis for the very important material, wrought iron. The white cast iron castings are packed in an inert substance to prevent warping, then slowly heated and cooled for a period of several days. This changes the brittle white cast iron to highly malleable iron suitable for the agricultural, automotive, and other industries.

Mild or so-called plain carbon steels are basically alloys of iron with very little carbon and some small amounts of other elements. The low carbon steels have a carbon content between 0.05 and about 0.3 percent, while the medium carbon steels have a carbon content between 0.3 and 0.7 percent, and high carbon steels contain from 0.7 to about 1.3 percent. The low carbon steels are softer and therefore are used for such products as bolts, boiler plate, and similar products. Carbon can be added to the surface of this steel to give it a hard surface with a tough ductile interior. Medium carbon steels are used where requirements are more demanding, as for automobile crankshafts, axles, and similar parts. High carbon steel is used in tools, drills, reamers, springs, and other parts requiring a high quality.

If the steel is rolled while hot it is referred to as *hot rolled* (*HR*), and has a characteristic scaly, black surface. Cold rolled steel (*CRS*) has a smooth bright surface. Steels are designated on the product description by a code system. One common code, developed by the Society of Automobile Engineers (*SAE*), is referred to later in the chapter.

These are just a few aids to the reading of engineering prints. There are many other shorthand descriptions, such as *fao* for finish all over, with which one should become acquainted. The person working with engineering prints would do well if he obtained a copy of *American Standard Drawing and Drafting Room Practice*.

SIMPLIFICATION, DIVERSIFICATION, AND STANDARDIZATION

A thorough study of simplification, diversification, and standardization should precede any attempt to classify and code products, parts, etc.

Simplification. This is the process of eliminating all extraneous or marginal product lines. For example, a manufacturer of stoves may be producing 15 different models and decide to simplify the line by producing five.

Standardization. Often confused with simplification, standardization relates to a product or very closely related products. It is a criterion of size, shape, performance, and quality. A company producing automobile engines might standardize the size of gaskets, generator mountings, or other parts. Standardization may often lead to more and different products being available. This was the case when a pump manufacturer standardized the two end plates and bearings and produced a series of spacers and impellers of various thicknesses to give a broad range of pump capacities from which to choose.

Diversification. This process, the opposite of simplification, is a trend toward even broader lines of products.

There are certain forces within industry and society that, as a whole, bring about the processes of simplification and diversification. The force to diversify producers' goods is not nearly as strong as the force to diversify consumers' goods, and here is the secret of diversification. Many people, at least in the economy of the United States, are reluctant to buy products exactly like their neighbors'—or even very similar. While this is often referred to as "keeping up with the Joneses," it should be interpreted as "being different from the Joneses." This is a powerful force and one that is expressed through the sales departments of companies by an urge to create more diversified product lines. This process is accentuated when a number of companies strive to meet the competition created by other companies' diversifications.

The force to offset diversification often comes from the manufacturing function. Simplification means that the supervisor of manufacturing can reduce his inventories and take advantage of large-purchase quantities. By having long manufacturing runs, he can install special production equipment and reduce the set-up costs. Specialization, and all of the inherent savings, are natural outcomes of simplification.

One interesting case of successful simplification is the ultrasuccessful German Volkswagen. Apparently, customers who buy the Volkswagen are more interested in the economy and quality that comes from a one-product line than they are in the fact that all the cars look practically the same.

Anyone aware of the production history of the United States must know the importance of standardization. This important contribution to our outstanding success is said to have been originated by a New England inventor, Eli Whitney, who is probably better known for having invented the cotton gin. At one time he won a large government contract for firearms by showing that they could be produced with interchangeable parts.

The success of our electrical business depends upon the fact that the important characteristics of the power supply have been standardized, as have many of the sockets, connectors, and other accessories. This means that producers can make consumers' products in huge quantities at low cost. Wherever standardization has not existed, as in some of the early machine screw threads, phonograph records, cards for data-processing, and systems for color television, confusion has reigned, and at the expense of the consumer.

There are many agencies that work on the problem of standardization, and it is a wise management that sets up a "standards" function in its organization—not only to establish internal standards but to select additional standards from outside sources. Many trade and professional societies have standards committees which continually establish better standards. The American Standards Association is composed of representatives from trade and professional organizations, and is concerned with the unification of the effort to standardize.

The Army, Navy, and other government agencies have also striven to produce standards, and any manufacturer producing for them must be well acquainted with their requirements. The National Bureau of Standards has probably made the most profound contribution to the process of standardization in the United States. The story of its achievement is too extensive to relate here, but it makes fascinating reading for anyone who is seriously interested in the details of our manufacturing history.

CLASSIFICATION AND IDENTIFICATION

Many companies have found themselves in difficult times when their product line outstripped their code system and it became necessary to revise or start coding over again. This has led to confusion, not only among factory employees but also among customers, and has been reflected by a lower sales volume.

The advent of card-data processing has jolted many companies into overhauling their outdated coding methods, with painful repercussions upon both personnel and budgets. For instance, one large and well established machine tool builder decided to inaugurate a card-data-processing system in the payroll department, with the possibility of adding production control, inventory control, and other functions later. Because the coding system in use was not consistent with the card-data-processing requirements, it was essential to make some changes in the original code, which on the surface appeared to be fairly minor. Soon after the task was begun, the team processing the code changes had to be enlarged as numerous problems came up. It was discovered that the code changes had many ramifications which were not even dreamed of when the program was initiated.

Instead of some of the part numbers getting smaller under the new system, they became longer, requiring more space on the part. This meant an engineering change in the part, which in turn necessitated changes in the patterns and in the tools and fixtures. Some parts even had to be completely redesigned to give the part the proper balance. So what started out as a minor change in the system turned out to be an extensive overhauling of the entire product line. Nothing has been mentioned here about the difficulty experienced in making the changeover in the inventories, or the confusion experienced by the employees and the faithful customers.

This is just one experience of one large company. And it is true that it was a very old company, and that the founders had no way of knowing the extent of the company's growth or the impending birth of automatic data processing. However, no company devising a code system today should encounter these problems if proper consideration is given, but, surprisingly enough, this subject now receives less attention in literature than it did in the early days of scientific management.

THE MEANING OF CLASSIFICATION, IDENTIFICATION, SYMBOLS, AND CODES

Classification is the grouping of things by common attributes. The classes are identified by symbols. This system of symbols is called the code. Classifying is an economy-of-thought process which goes on whether we put tags on the classes or not. It goes on in the mind, although the individual is hardly aware that the activity exists, and a little introspection will verify this. One is continually classifying things and even people (a source of frequently dangerous generalization), and one in fact spends a great portion of his life making or memorizing classifications.

The process consists of establishing gross groupings of these things, and each large class is then subdivided into smaller classes. These subclasses, in turn, can be divided. The following classification of materials is typical of the process.

Class	*Subclass*	*Sub-subclass*
Raw Materials	Hot Rolled Metals	Rounds
		Hexagons
		Flats
		Squares
		Sheets
	Structural Shapes	Channels
		Angles
		Wide Flange
		Plates
		Car Channels
		Bar-size Angles

ECONOMIC CONSIDERATIONS

Within the classification process there may be subgroups with common characteristics which could profitably be put together. Since there are rarely two things which are identical, the classifying, subclassifying and sub-subclassifying could go on until each unit is a class by itself, but this would defeat the purpose of classifying. Our purpose is to get manageable groups which have some common meaning or purpose. If classification continues until it is no longer profitable for the purpose at hand, the returns on additional classification will start going up. The optimum point is very difficult to determine by quantitative means, but certainly an intuitive decision is close enough.

CONSIDERATIONS IN CLASSIFYING AND CODING

A symbol is one (or more) number, letter, or similar identification used to represent a class or subclass of things. It is the shorthand method used to refer to classes. So, while classification has to do with the grouping of things, symbols are used to identify the classes. Classification, by its very nature, must precede identification and symbolization.

The code is the arrangement of the symbols into some orderly structure. The symbols of the code are the "signals" which are the manifestation of the class information which is to be transmitted by the system. For example, a person wishing to convey information about a product from the sales department to the production department will write down the symbols of the code representing the product. These may in turn be translated into a set of hole symbols on a card, which will later be interpreted by machines back into a series of numbers or letters which are read by someone in the production department. By this means, a wealth of information is quickly and accurately conveyed.

Numerous ways of classifying and symbolizing have been used in manufacturing. Practically every aspect of the business of manufacturing is classified and coded, and it is not uncommon to find codes used for accounts, parts, blueprints, departments, materials, tools, and many other purposes. Some of these systems have outlived their usefulness, while some which have been discarded should probably be rediscovered. One will get a better insight into how a coding system should be developed by taking some of the considerations into account before he studies the various codes.

Symbols Should Have Multiple Functions

The symbol, as a whole, should of course have meaning, but the parts of the symbol should be put together according to a definite method so that each part conveys a message. This set of symbols is used in a code for grinding machines:

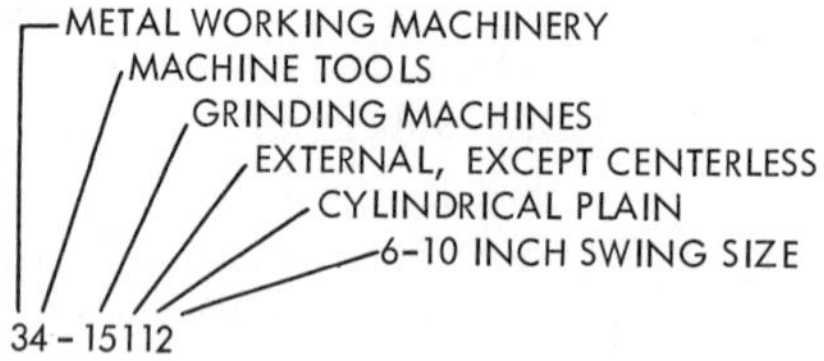

Figure 4-9
Code for Grinding Machines

Classifications and Codes Should Have an Open End

Classification and code systems should be constructed so that new classes can be added without making any changes in the basic system.

Subclasses Insertable

The system should be so designed that classes can be inserted within classes. Regardless of how a person tries to make a complete code, new divisions always develop or some are inadvertently left out. This difficulty can be overcome by leaving large "gaps" in the code.

Classification and Code Should Be Logical

This is an obvious observation yet one that is difficult to stress: The system should be thought through from one end to the other, and all possible exceptions should be taken into account. This process can frequently be pursued by means of a graphical layout of all the parts of an assembly.

Consider the Length of the Symbol

One cannot design a symbol system without considering the limitations of card-data-processing equipment. It is necessary to allocate a certain number of columns for a particular purpose, and this space cannot be enlarged at will. Since card space is usually severely limited, the number should be kept brief, but possible additions must be kept in mind. There are also certain limitations in the interpreting equipment which will be discussed under the section Card-data-processing Equipment.

Brevity in a symbol is desirable because it makes remembering and reproducing easier. Not only is the time required for transferring a symbol less, but so is the chance of making errors. Often, when symbols are typed on a form, the space is limited, and this should be considered reason enough for keeping the symbol brief.

Coordinate Classification and Symbol Systems

It is desirable to keep the number of code systems to a minimum in a factory and to interlock as many as possible with common terms. Occasionally one finds a separate code system for blueprints and parts which may lead to considerable confusion. By careful planning, these two systems can be merged so that the part number serves to identify both the print and the part. This system can be extended to the patterns, tools, dies, cost sheets, and throughout the factory; wherever it is necessary to identify the part.

Consider Subcontracting and Job-Lot Requirements

Frequently, companies that do subcontracting find they are producing the same product for a number of companies. Their manufacturing costs may be reduced by pooling the requirements of all the customers, but this makes the indexing system more complex. It is frequently necessary to use a cross-indexing technique. Study of the particular problem will often result in a suitable method.

Punctuation Should Be Used with Caution

Punctuation is useful in separating one class from another, to know where one class ends and another starts. It is also helpful as an aid to memorization of numbers. Punctuation is commonly used in library work (the Dewey Decimal System) and also in some office and accounting files. However, it has been found to be less desirable in factories because the periods, dashes, or whatever get lost when marked on rough materials. It should also be remembered that there is no way to identify the period on card-data-processing equipment, for seldom would you want to give up a space for that purpose.

Some numbering systems have letters inserted between numbers to give the effect of punctuation. The letter is commonly given some significance, and in engineering blueprints it frequently refers to the print size. *A* would indicate an $8\frac{1}{2}$ x 11 print, *B* would indicate an 11 x 17 print, etc., in multiples. The file drawers are designated by the letters and thus the prints are easy to locate. The strongest objection to using letters mixed in with numbers is the difficulty encountered when card-data-processing equipment is also used. Some operations become impossible, and even such basic operations as card punching become more difficult when letters are inserted.

Consider Aids to the Memory

This aspect of coding has been ignored in recent years. Taylor, along with others, was concerned with how easily a code system could be associated with the item it represents. The death blow was dealt this type of symbolization by the card-data-processing systems, but in many cases this reason for leaving letters out of a symbol is not enough. There certainly will be far fewer errors if the symbols aid the memory, and it is impossible to calculate the cost of errors caused by symbols that are difficult to remember—with all the accompanying frustrations to new employees and the irritations to customers. One important advantage of a memory-aiding code is reduction in learning time while a new employee tries to absorb all facets of a new job.

Consider the Product to Be Coded

Some products do not lend themselves to being coded by a number or letter system, and using colors is more satisfactory. This is true of some steel shapes, and we find that the bars in a warehouse are frequently marked with colors for quick identification. An excellent example of a color code, which is universally recognized, is the code used for electrical resistors (shown in Figure 4–10).

Figure 4–10

Resistor Color Code

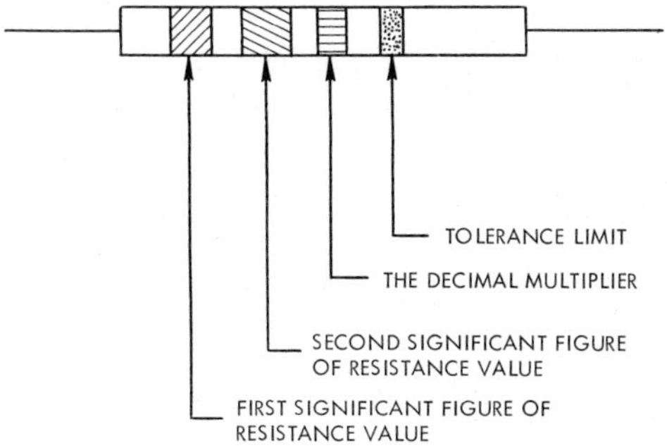

COLOR	SIGNIFICANT FIGURE	POWER OF 10	TOLERANCE
Black	0	10^0	
Brown	1	10^1	
Red	2	10^2	
Orange	3	10^3	
Yellow	4	10^4	
Green	5	10^5	
Blue	6	10^6	
Violet	7	10^7	
Gray	8	10^8	
White	9	10^9	
Gold		10^{-1}	∓ 5
Silver		10^{-2}	∓ 10
No color			∓ 20

EXAMPLES OF CLASSIFICATION AND CODING SYSTEMS

Many different classification and coding systems have been in favor at different times during the history of industry. Some have not been found suitable and therefore have been short-lived; others have been discarded without ample justification. It is not our intent to claim that only one classification and code system is suitable for all purposes, but rather to select and describe those which are representative and have been accepted. Coding systems can be cataloged as numeric, alphabetic, or a combination of the two.

Alphabetic Codes

Some straight alphabetic codes are not intended to aid the memory, and some are designed to help recall the object symbolized. Probably little can be said to justify the use of straight alphabetic codes, as compared to numbers, except that a letter position can represent one of 26 classes and a number only one of 10 classes. The straight alphabetic code, if very long, is difficult to remember; but if you have need for a short code, with more than ten numbers in each class, then perhaps you should consider it. You should be sure that it probably will never have to be used with machine punched cards.

It is better to use the Mnemonic Code, which is intended to aid the memory. This code, which was first devised by Taylor, borrows its name from Mnemosyne, the Greek goddess of memory, and makes use of a few letters to remind the user of what the code indicates. As an example, the departments of a shop may have the code letters, *TL*, *CH*, *ASM*, meaning, respectively, Turret Lathe, Cold Heading, and Automatic Screw Machines. Only three or four letters should be used together, or they start to lose their meaning (as anyone knows who has tried to interpret the letters designating various government agencies).

This technique of aiding the memory has been useful in designating small classification groups in industry and it should not be overlooked by the present designer of codes, despite some of the disadvantages attributed to it.

Numeric Codes

Numeric codes are favored today over alphabetical codes, and a number of widely accepted systems have been developed by government agencies, trade associations, and professional societies. One who is given the task of setting up a code would do well to explore all available codes and perhaps adapt one to his purpose. For example, a well-known and accepted coding system for steel was developed by the Society of Automobile Engineers, the SAE series. Every engineer should be acquainted with this system, which is given here in a brief form (Figure 4–11).

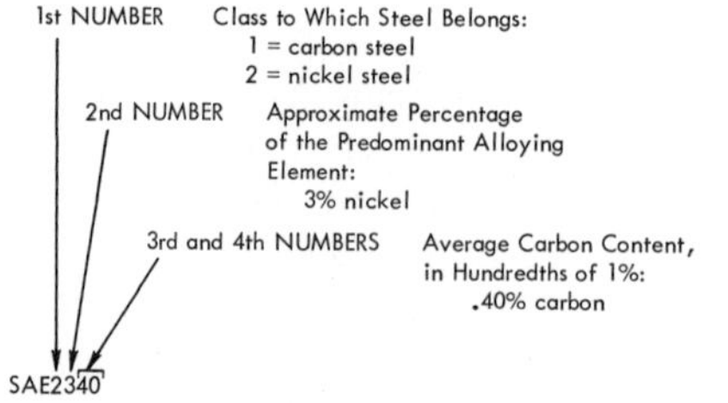

Figure 4–11
SAE Numbering System

EXAMPLES OF SPECIFIC CODES

Sequence Codes

The sequence method of coding consists of simply assigning numbers, starting with 1, to a list of items arranged in a particular order. There is no provision for classifying items with this method, and it should only be used if the list is not too long to be easily memorized. An example of a sequence code for listing employees on a payroll might look like this:

1. Ainsworth, Wilbur
2. Allen, Norman
3. Broome, Robert
4. Flack, Georgia
5. Flannigan, Roy

If new names are assigned to the list, they must take the next higher number, but this is awkward if the original list is in alphabetical order. This difficulty can be partially overcome by skipping numbers when originally setting up the table so that new names can be inserted later. This, of course, leaves much to be desired. Because of its simplicity, the sequence coding method has often been used, but often with drastic results. It should only be used when there is assurance that the list is static and not extensive.

Group Classification Code

This type of code uses succeeding digits of a number to indicate major, minor, and subminor classifications. An example of this is an abridgement of the full United States Standard Commodity Classification (Figure 4–12) to suit the purpose of metal manufacturers. This is given on next page, and its logic should be obvious. Raw materials are designated by the number 200. Thus all raw materials are prefixed with a 2. The second number, if a number *1*, refers to hot rolled material; if a number 2, to cold rolled material; 3 refers to structural shapes, etc. The meaning of the third number, which indicates a sub-subclassification, is evident.

Significant Digit Codes

Codes may include one or more digits which will indicate some qualification of the product, such as weight, dimension, capacity, or other factor. For example, the code described could be extended as shown. The symbol, *211–15*, would refer to a hot rolled bar fifteen-sixteenths of an inch in diameter.

Block Codes

Groups of blocks of numbers in sequence are used to represent classifications (without regard to the digit, tens, and hundreds grouping), as in the Group Classification Code. For example, a company producing television equipment might use the following numbering system:

1. Television antenna rotor—1 bearing
2. Television antenna rotor—2 bearing
3. Television antenna rotor—2 bearing and deluxe
4. Television antenna rotor—class left open for future product
5. Television antenna rotor—class left open for future product
6. Television antenna rotor—class left open for future product
7. Antenna array—1 stack
8. Antenna array—2 stack

Figure 4–12

Abridged Commodity Code

200 Raw materials
- 210 Metals hot-rolled
  - 211 Rounds
  - 212 Hexagons
  - 213 Flats
  - 214 Squares
  - 215 Sheets
- 220 Metals cold-rolled
  - 221 Etc.—same as above
- 230 Structural shapes
  - 231 Channels
  - 232 Angles
  - 233 Wide flange
  - 234 Plates
  - 235 Car channels
  - 236 Bar size angle
- 240 Metals, other forms
  - 241 Tubing
  - 242 Perforate sheet
  - 243 Key stock
  - 244 Shim stock
  - 245 Wire
  - 246 Miscellaneous castings
  - 247 Circles
  - 249 Miscellaneous
- 290 Miscellaneous
  - 291 Antimonial lead
  - 292 Sheet lead
  - 293 Pig lead

300 Fastenings
- 310 Bolts, machine, etc.
  - 311 Machine, sq hd
  - 312 Machine, hex hvy hd
  - 313 Machine, hex std hds
  - 314 Carriage bolts
- 320 Cap screws
  - 321 Round hd
  - 322 Flat hd
  - 323 Fillister hd
  - 324 Hex hd
- 330 Setscrews
  - 331 Headless, slotted cup pt
  - 332 Headless, slotted piv pt
  - 333 Headless, slotted oval
  - 334 Headless, slotted dog
  - 335 Sq hd, piv pt
  - 336 Sq hd, cup pt
  - 337 Recessed hd, cup pt
- 340 Machine screws
  - 341 Round hd
  - 342 Flat hd
  - 343 Fillister hd
- 350 Wood screws and nails
  - 351 Wood screw flat hd
  - 352 Wood screw rd hd
  - 353 Common nails
  - 354 Brads
  - 359 Miscellaneous
- 360 Nuts and washers
  - 361 Reg. C.P.S.F. nuts
  - 362 Slotted SAE nuts
  - 363 Check nuts
  - 364 Lock washers
  - 365 Flat washers
- 390 Miscellaneous
  - 391 Rivets, rd hd
  - 392 Rivets, flat hd
  - 393 Keys
  - 394 Cotter pins
  - 395 Drive screws
  - 396 Taper pins

400 Fabricated parts
- 410 Bearings
  - 411 Ball bearings
- 420 Cocks, all types
  - 421 Aircocks
- 430 Valves, all types
  - 431 Angle valves
- 440 Packing all types
  - 441 Garlock
- 450 Fabricated gaskets
  - 451 Geotze French type
- 460 Gages
  - 461 Pressure
- 470 Motive power
  - 471 Open motors
- 490 Other, n.o.i.b.n.
  - 491 Flexible couplings

500 Maintenance supplies
- 510 Electrical
- 520 Hardware
- 530 Heating
- 540 Plumbing
- 550 Transmission
- 560 Building supplies
- 570 Equipment supplies
- 580 Miscellaneous

600 Operating supplies
- 610 Files
- 620 Oils, acids, and chemicals
- 630 Paints and sundry
- 640 Pattern supplies
- 650 Abrasives
- 660 Welding and soldering
- 680 Miscellaneous

700 Pipe and fittings
- 710 Pipe and flanges
  - 711 Threaded pipe
  - 712 Flanged pipe
  - 713 Plain pipe
  - 714 Pipe nipples
  - 715 Companion flanges
  - 716 Blind flanges
  - 717 Floor flanges
  - 718 Common flanges
  - 719 Other
- 720 Union and union elbow
  - 721 Standard union
  - 722 Brass seated union
  - 723 Flanged unions
  - 724 Union elbows 90°
  - 725 Union elbows 45°
  - 729 Other
- 730 Elbows
  - 731 Elbows, 45°
  - 732 Elbows, 90°
  - 733 Elbow, street 45°
  - 734 Elbow, street 90°
  - 735 Elbow, reducing 45°
  - 736 Elbow, reducing 90°
  - 737 Elbow, street, reducing 45°
  - 738 Elbow, street, reducing 90°
- 740 Tees
  - 741 Tees, screwed
  - 742 Tees, reducing, screwed
- 750 Plugs
  - 751 Sq hd plug
  - 752 Solid plugs
  - 753 Countersunk plugs
  - 754 Slotted plugs
  - 755 Face bushings
  - 756 Hex bushings
- 760 Fittings, n.o.i.b.n.
  - 761 Caps
  - 762 Couplings
  - 763 Reducers
  - 764 Locknuts
  - 765 Return bends
  - 766 Y branches
  - 767 Crosses
  - 768 Cross reducing
- 790 Sundry
  - 791 Strainers
  - 792 Tube turns
  - 793 Thread protectors
  - 794 Pipe straps

By reserving vacant spaces in the numbering system, additional classifications can be added, but of course it is difficult to predict exactly what will be needed. The advantage of this type of code over the Group Classification is that it conserves space.

Dewey Decimal System

Material on classification and codes should include reference to the Dewey Decimal System, widely used in libraries, and which has found its way into industry, especially for referencing files. This system, which was published by Melvil Dewey in 1876, uses a class and subclass approach. To give some idea of how this system works, and how it can be expanded, consider the following example which was modified from the original:

6	Applied science
65	Business (which is an applied science)
658	Industrial management (subheading under business)
658.2	Industrial management of plants
658.21	Industrial management of plant locations

Characteristic of this system is the method of separating classes and subclasses by colons and periods. Such marks are considered too perishable to permit this code to be used universally in industry, however, because these important parts of the code are likely to be lost in the marking of steel and similar materials.

Consonant Codes

Where space is limited for coding purposes, there are means of abbreviation which might be useful. One widely used method is Consonant Coding, which consists of dropping all vowels beyond the first letter. The abbreviation as *MTRL* for material is a good example.

Coding and Decoding

To keep the process of coding and decoding from becoming a long and cumbersome operation in punched-card systems, prepunched master code cards are used. These are filed in the basic sequence of reference. Such a card may carry many items of data, all of which are not necessarily applicable to a single part of the operation. A common example is the master employee card used in payroll accounting. This card is usually filed by clock number and contains such items as employee name, location, occupation, rate of pay, social security number, dependents, and any other information needed to make out the employee's check, his tax deduction, etc. The use of the master prepunched card has the advantage of eliminating transcription error and the accompanying verification. Manual punching, which is time-consuming, is eliminated. The prepunched master code cards can be used to punch all or part of the information into detail cards. It is practical, at times, to fill in part of the information from the master card and to complete the card by hand punching.

A SYSTEM DESIGN FOR PRODUCT DESCRIPTION CHANGES

The system of revising the product description or process description is a design problem in itself. The changes must be made in a systematic and efficient manner or all sorts of problems will occur. For example, changes might be made on the print and not on the planning sheet, and if the operator forgets and works to the planning sheet he may be making scrap.

The flow chart for a typical system design that will take care of the necessary changes is shown in Figure 4–13. There are, of course, other systems which may be devised but it is helpful to have a checklist, as given below, when establishing a new system design.

Figure 4–13

A Product, or Process, Change System

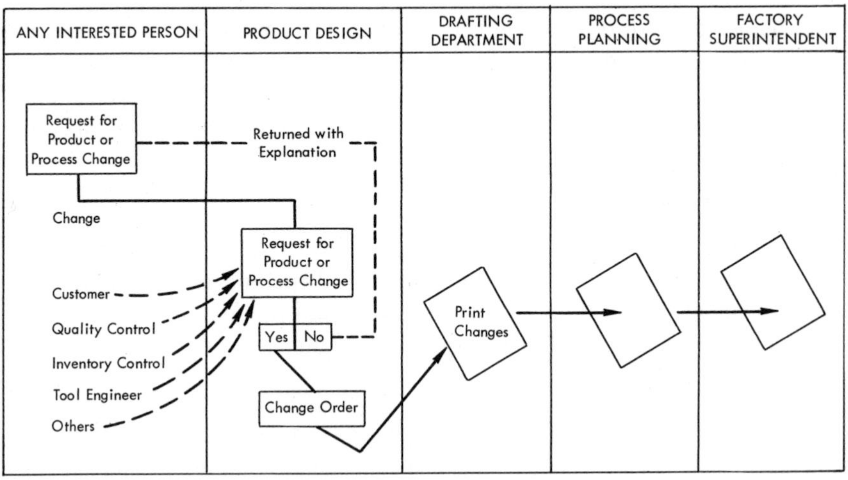

Checklist

1. Only those responsible for the functioning of the product should be permitted to authorize changes in the product description, and this is often true of the process description.
2. Changes should be cleared with the Quality Control Department to determine what effect the change will have on quality standards, replacement of gauges, etc.
3. Change suggestions should be originated by any interested person. A method for giving them proper recognition should be devised, for by no other means can full cooperation be expected. The authority for the change must, however, come from a central function, such as the design engineer.
4. Changes should be cleared with the customer—if it is a customer's order—to see if the product will still fit his requirements.

5. Changes should be checked with the inventory control. If old parts can be used before the change goes into effect, a method of phasing from the old to the new should be arranged.
6. If the product information is retained by the foreman or others, it is essential that the old information be destroyed and the new distributed.
7. Product changes should not be made by verbal order, but should be matters of record.

Drawings should have a block that is set aside for recording any changes which are made, and it is imperative that all changes be recorded to eliminate any misunderstanding at a later date. If the revision is minor and in no way affects the end use or the assembly of parts, it is customary simply to record the change on the print. If it is a major change, and the new and old parts are not interchangeable, the part print and number should be changed so there will be no confusion. This means the parts list and other records should also be changed to agree. A cross-indexing system may be needed between the new number and the old number in the inventory records. If the assembly bears a serial number, then it will be essential to record when the new part number went into effect. Only by this method can the customer who needs repair parts be assured of obtaining the ones he wants.

The management will be wise if it maintains a strong discipline regarding product changes. No changes of any sort should be permitted without proper written authority, which has gone through the established procedure.

DISTRIBUTION OF PRODUCT DESCRIPTIONS

Several systems are commonly used for distributing the product description to the production personnel when needed:

1. One method is to distribute a set of prints to each foreman. The foreman in turn issues them to the operators as needed. This, however, has proven inefficient, as the foreman, with his many duties, is not inclined to keep his files current. Consequently, the department product descriptions are out of date.
2. Another method is to maintain a file of prints in the production control department, which in turn issues them with the production orders and other forms in the route file. This system often requires an excessive number of prints.
3. Another common method is to have the production control department, or others needing prints, requisition them from the engineering blueprint department. This system is efficient and conserves material, but it also has the drawback of requiring a greater lead time.

DISTRIBUTION OF PROCESS INFORMATION

Once the processing is determined, it will probably remain without change. If, however, a change is needed, such as an additional operation, a request is sent to the planning department. If the requests are not sent to the planning department first, the costs are apt to increase, causing the usual repercussions from the cost department.

The process information is generally put on a master form which can be readily duplicated. This is necessary since a new set of forms will probably be needed every time an order is placed. The ozalid process is quite commonly used for this. The master is a clear piece of plastic upon which the standard information has been printed. The information for the particular plan can then be filled in by typewriter or pen. The spirit duplicating process is also frequently used for producing process information. With both of these processes, the master can be placed back in the file and used over and over again for different orders of the same product. Certain information which might change from time to time, such as quantities and order numbers, can be easily changed.

SECURITY OF PRODUCT INFORMATION

Many product and process descriptions reveal important and secret information which a company has spent a considerable fortune to obtain by research and development. Thus, it is obvious why a strict and rigid control over the security of the product and process design must be maintained. Companies doing military contracting must be especially cautious and, consequently, restrict the circulation of the product information, storing it in vaults when not in use. Companies which have "style" products, such as automobiles, also treat their product information with care.

The product or process description is the jelling of large investments of manpower. If the descriptions were destroyed, they could probably be replaced in time, but the loss in labor hours could be tremendous. Consequently, companies go to great effort to protect these assets. Companies which are one division of a multiple-division complex will undoubtedly store each other's production information, so if one set is destroyed another set is available. Other companies send their product information to vaults. Sometimes these are storage facilities in specially air-conditioned caves. Other companies follow the practice of microfilming all the product information and storing it in a vault. This method has been found so satisfactory by some companies that they microfilm all their drawings and the engineers and production people work with the films directly by means of special readers. One by-product of this process is greater ease of sending prints through the mail.

SUMMARY

The product information is an important input to the production control system. It is the instruction which tells the factory personnel what to produce. For some products a description of the end product, the *product description,* is all that is needed. For others, it is impossible or difficult to produce a meaningful product description, so a step-by-step *process description* is used. In many industries, the product and process descriptions are used together.

The change of the product description should follow a well designed system, for which there are certain well recognized criteria of design.

There is a logical procedure for the development of the process instruction, which includes determining all the suboperations, grouping these into operations, and, finally, placing the operations in a logical, efficient sequence.

Whatever the industry, there is a certain product and process information which is unique and which you will have to learn after you arrive on the job. This is something you should be aware of and look forward to with anticipation.

The production control systems are in reality communication networks of the most complicated type. If they are to be used efficiently, the messages transmitted must be received the same as sent. One of the most acceptable ways of doing this is to put the information into the form of a code. The very fact that this code is used repeatedly assures fewer errors in conveying messages. While it is difficult to say that there is one best method of classifying and coding information, there are certainly a number of distinct factors for efficient coding which should be taken into consideration.

Questions

1. Give an example of a company which produces a product which is not suitable for a pictorial product description.
2. How can a standard parts index save a company money?
3. Product descriptions for an assembly line are often verbal. What dangers do you see in this?
4. Make a sketch of a simple product, using the conventional views.
5. Frequently a statement is found on engineering drawings, "Don't scale the drawing." Why is this necessary?
6. Why does the metal working industry traditionally use both the product and process description?
7. Why is it undesirable to put dimensions on the operation sheet?
8. Consider some product with which you are familiar and for which you know the meaning of the suboperations. List the suboperations needed to produce the product. Group the suboperations into operations, and place the operations into some reasonable sequence.
9. Some companies identify the operation by the department number. Is there any objection to this?
10. Devise a code system suitable for some product with which you are acquainted.
11. Design a code system for your professional library.

12. What limitation does card-data processing impose on the design of the code system?
13. Discuss the affect mnemonic coding might have on training new employees and on their job satisfaction.
14. What justification is there for the straight alphabetic code system?
15. Design a method of distributing product and process information for a particular manufacturer. What procedure could be used for keeping this information up to date?

References

ADAMS, RICHARD F. "A Procedure for Determining the Work-Units of the Metalworking Machines." Unpublished thesis for MS., I.E., Purdue University, 1951.

AMERICAN SOCIETY FOR METALS. *Metals Handbook.* Cleveland: 1964.

AMERICAN SOCIETY OF TOOL AND MANUFACTURING ENGINEERS (FRANK W. WILSON, ed.). *Fundamentals of Tool Design.* Englewood Cliffs, N.J.: Prentice-Hall, Inc., 1962.

———. *Handbook of Fixture Design.* New York: McGraw-Hill Book Co., Inc., 1962.

———. *Tool Engineers Handbook.* 2d ed. New York: McGraw-Hill Book Co., Inc., 1959.

ARNELL, ALVIN. *Standard Graphical Symbols; A Comprehensive Guide for Use in Industry, Engineering and Science.* New York: McGraw-Hill Book Co., Inc., 1963.

BEGEMAN, MYRON LOUIS. *Manufacturing Processes.* 5th ed. New York: John Wiley & Sons, Inc., 1963.

DEGARMO, ERNEST P. *Materials and Processes in Manufacturing.* 2d ed. New York: Macmillan Co., 1962.

DOYLE, LAWRENCE E. *Manufacturing Processes and Materials for Engineers.* Englewood Cliffs, N.J.: Prentice-Hall, Inc., 1961.

EARY, DONALD F., and JOHNSON, GERALD E. *Process Engineering for Manufacturing.* Englewood Cliffs, N.J.: Prentice-Hall, Inc., 1962.

EVEN, ARTHUR D. *Engineering Data Processing System Design.* Princeton, N.J.: D. Van Nostrand Co., Inc., 1960.

GREENWOOD, DOUGLAS C. *Engineering Data for Product Design.* New York: McGraw-Hill Book Co., Inc., 1961.

GREENE, JAMES H. "Process Planning—Organized Methods Pay Dividends." *The Tool Engineer,* Vol. 4, No. 4. April 1958.

HEALY, WILLIAM L., and RAU, A. H. *Simplified Drafting Practice.* New York: John Wiley & Sons, Inc., 1957.

MACNIECE, E. H. *Industrial Specifications.* New York: John Wiley & Sons, Inc., 1953.

MELNITSKY, BENJAMIN. *Profiting from Industrial Standardization.* New York: Conover-Mast Publications, 1953.

STARR, MARTIN K. *Product Design and Decision Theory.* Englewood Cliffs, N.J.: Prentice-Hall, Inc., 1963.

CHAPTER **5**

Cost Information

The usual objective of production planning and control is to minimize costs, which in turn enhances the profit of a business. This is the primary mission, and although it may be interpreted as minimizing machine downtime, limiting scrap, increasing output, and other activities, all of these can be reduced to cost as a common denominator. It is therefore important that all production control personnel have a good grasp of cost terminology and be able to interpret their day-to-day decisions in these terms.

Cost, in itself, is not important to the manufacturer, but how costs influence profit is important. So important is the generation of profit that the word should be stamped on each page of this book as a reminder to you of your purpose in studying system designing and decision making for production planning and control.

It is true that there are other objectives of a business, such as the responsibility of furnishing an income to the employees, satisfying the ambitions of the managers, and perhaps even supplying a tax income to the government, but if a profit is not forthcoming, the capital investment will drift away to other investments where the rewards are greater. Even if you don't agree that profits are of primary importance, you will have to admit that profits are the basis for "scoring" the game. A manager, although he may have no investment in the business, is vitally interested in the profits because this is the way his success is measured, and, as we move down the industrial hierarchy, the contribution to profit will still be the basis for reward.

The relationship between profit and costs can be seen on the bar chart in Figure 5–1. As is obvious, the profit can be enhanced in two ways, by increasing the price or by reducing the costs.

The price of a product is established by the philosophy of the management and by the environment in which the product is being sold.

1. The price of a product may be established to meet the price of similar products on the market. This means management will have little control over the price.

Figure 5–1

Profit and Cost Relationships

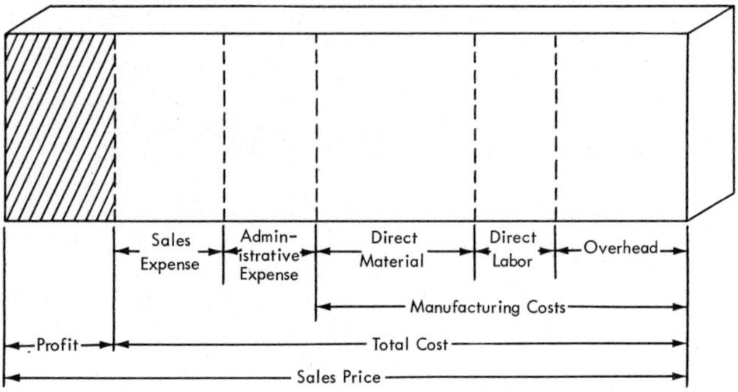

2. Some products are prestige items and the price is set high to accentuate that prestige. For example, fountain pens sold for the graduating senior must have a prestige price. It is difficult to imagine a loving aunt buying her favorite nephew a thirty-nine-cent pen for graduation, although it serves the same purpose (and becomes lost as quickly) as an expensive one.
3. Some companies have pursued a pricing policy of adding a fixed percentage to the cost of producing a product. These companies usually do not have a monopoly on the product, and are, in effect, pricing it to conform with other companies following a similar policy.
4. Products which are made by a secret process, or are patented, can be priced for what the market will stand. If there is no substitute and the product is essential—or the public thinks it is—the price can be far beyond any reasonable figure.
5. Companies have been known to price a product according to customers' buying habits. If the product is new to the prospective customers, the price might be lowered at first, but when the inertia of buying is established, prices will be gradually raised.

The price is reflected in the gross sales on the Profit and Loss Statement, A in Figure 5–2. From this is deducted the cost of goods sold, *B*, and the selling and administrative expenses, *C*, to arrive at the profit, *D*. It is evident that profit depends upon the difference between the price and the expenses. The selling and administrative expenses are outside the jurisdiction of the factory, and only the costs of manufacturing may be influenced. This explains why the emphasis here will be upon the *manufacturing costs*.

JOB ORDER COSTING AND PROCESS COSTING

In the discussion of many manufacturing techniques, a sharp line can be drawn between those used in the job shop factory and in the production line factory.

Figure 5–2

Profit and Loss Statement

TROY MANUFACTURING COMPANY
January 1 to December 31

A	Gross sales		$831,600
	Less: Sales returns and allowances		17,600
	Net Sales		814,000
B	Less: Cost of goods sold		
	Finished goods inventory, Jan. 1	$119,680	
	Cost of goods manufactured	579,040	
		698,720	
	Less: Finished goods inventory, Dec. 31	136,400	
			562,320
			251,680
C	Less: Selling and administrative expenses		
	General office expenses	23,200	
	Sales expenses	74,200	
	Bad debts	8,000	
			105,400
D	Net Profit		$146,280

Job Order Costing is used wherever it is convenient to accumulate the costs for each lot of material. For example, in the garment industry, where a limited number of each style is produced, the costs are accumulated for each *lot* or *order*. This is also the method used in the metal working industry, where the product goes through as a batch even though the batch may take considerable time to complete.

Process Costing is used where one or a few different products are produced and the costs can be accumulated for each *department* over a period of time. The unit costs are obtained by accumulating the departmental costs and dividing by the number of products produced.

The objective here is not to make an exhaustive study of accounting systems, but to outline a method of obtaining cost information from which day-to-day decisions can be made. The technique used for this purpose follows, in general, the job order costing method.

THE COST ESTIMATE FOR DECISION MAKING

Referring again to the bar chart (Figure 5–3), notice that the manufacturing cost is composed of three elements: *direct labor, direct material,* and *overhead.* This can be written as an important accounting equation, which should be committed to memory:

$$\text{Manufacturing costs} = \text{Direct labor costs} + \text{Direct material costs} + \text{Overhead costs}$$

Figure 5–3

Cost Estimating

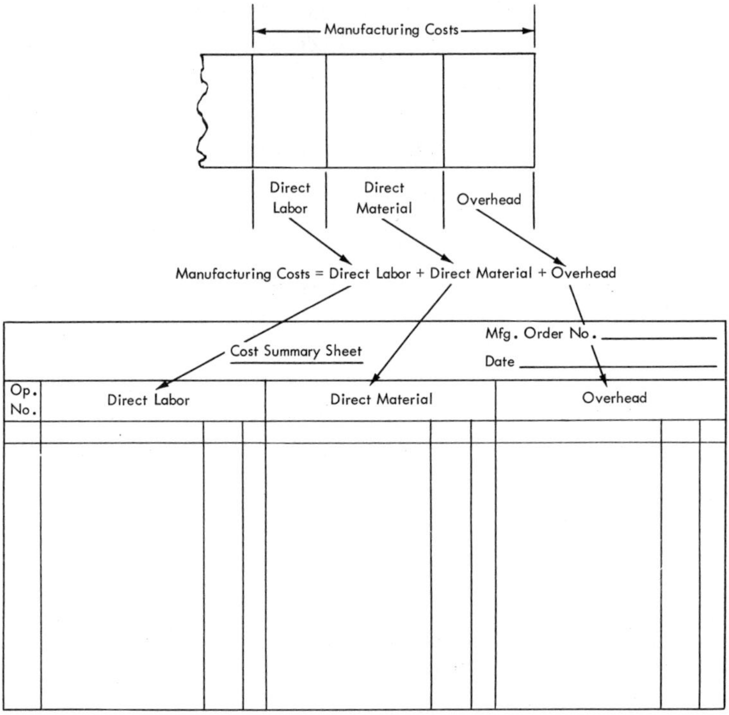

Remember, the objective is to arrive at the manufacturing cost as directly as possible, which makes it desirable to have a *Cost Summary Sheet* (similar to the one shown) which follows from the basic equation. Since it is necessary to obtain the data for these column entries, it is important that the three factors be defined precisely.

Direct material is all the material which can be readily charged to the product. Often this is more than the material seen in the end product, so it is of little use to use the definition of some accountants, "All of the material that can be seen in the end product." The material charged off to the product might consist of the usable material, plus stub ends of bars lost in a lathe process, the knotty pieces of wood in furniture making, the scrap from a punch press, or the broken bottles in a filling operation. As long as the costs belong to this production order, they should be charged to it. Otherwise they will be prorated throughout production.

Direct labor, like the direct material, is all the cost that can be justifiably charged to the product. Labor that cannot be charged directly to the product is caught up in the indirect labor account and, as we will see, prorated to all the jobs.

Overhead could be defined as the manufacturing costs less the direct material and direct labor costs. Since we are attempting to charge all the material and labor off to the order, we can say that the overhead is everything that is not included in these two categories. Included in the overhead expense are such items as water, electricity, coal for heating, taxes, insurance, and depreciation. How is it possible to charge these costs off to any particular product? It is done by adding them together and prorating them to the job by an elementary ratio method. Here is an example of how it might be calculated for a particular order, No. 598:

$$\frac{\text{Overhead dollars for No. 598}}{\text{Direct labor dollars for No. 598}} = \frac{\text{Overhead dollars spent last year}}{\text{Direct labor dollars for last year}}.$$

The unknown in this equation is, of course, *overhead dollars for order No. 598*. This would be an awkward equation for the cost clerk to use, so it is modified. The right-hand side of the equation, referred to as the *overhead rate*, is given to him as a percentage, such as 500%, which means that for every dollar of labor there are five dollars of overhead. Then, if both sides of the equation are multiplied by *Direct labor dollars for No. 598*, the equation will look like this:

$$\text{Overhead dollars for order No. 598} = \text{Direct labor dollars for No. 598} \times 500\%.$$

This is a good place to tell you that many words are synonymous with overhead, and *burden* is one of them. But you should not confuse the *overhead* with the *overhead rate*. Some of you are probably already questioning why direct labor dollars are used in the example. As you might suspect, there are other factors which could be used as long as they meet certain criteria. One obvious requirement is availability of information. As is apparent from the Cost Summary Sheet, the *direct labor cost* and *direct material cost* are available. In addition, there is *direct labor time* and the *quantity of material used*, such as pounds or square yards. Sometimes the direct material costs and labor costs are added to form the *prime cost*, which is also used to distribute the overhead.

The second requirement is that the overhead costs and the factor used in the denominator be correlated (as is shown in Figure 5–4). As the overhead increases on a job, so should the direct labor dollars, or whatever is being used to distribute the overhead. Some prefer to think of the overhead as having fixed, semivariable, and variable components, and to treat each separately. The overhead rate, at best, is just an estimate, so many companies are negligent in keeping it up to date.

Where data processing systems are in effect, some companies derive a new burden rate every month. The other extreme is the company which will go for years without updating its rates, and does so only when it finds it is out of competition or losing money. A company has been known to use a rate borrowed from another company, but with disastrous results. Overhead rates can be developed only by accumulating actual costs from company records. There is nothing sacred about certain overhead rates, and they can range from a couple of dollars per hour (or less) to more than a thousand dollars per hour.

Figure 5–4

Desired Relationship for Overhead Rates

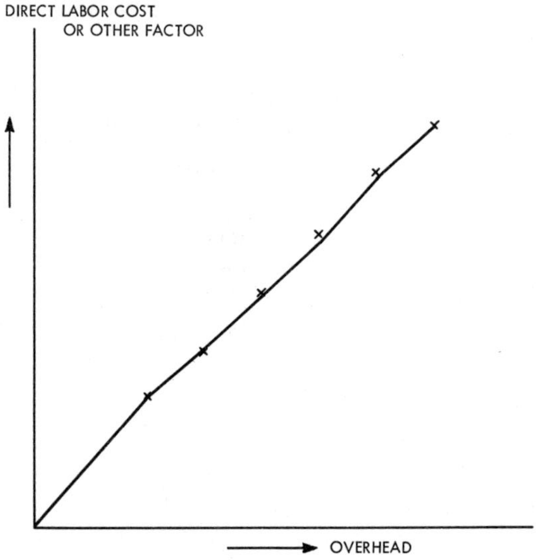

THE DANGER OF A COMMON OVERHEAD RATE

So far, it has been assumed that the factory processes are uniform and that all operate at full capacity. This can be a dangerous assumption if the company is using a plantwide overhead rate.

Figure 5–5

The Problem of a Plantwide Overhead Rate

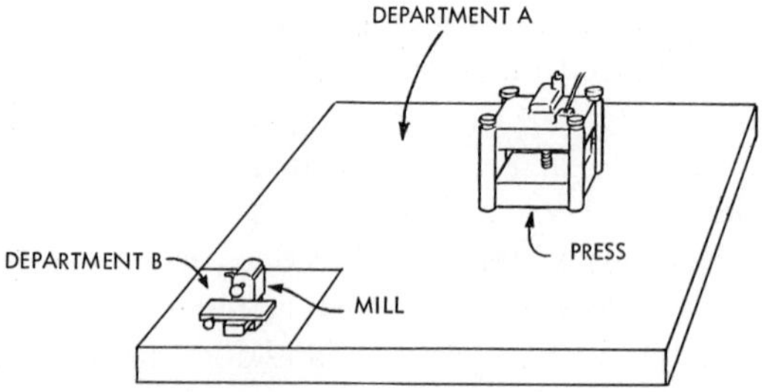

The danger can be pointed out in the hypothetical factory shown in Figure 5–5. Department A has a very expensive press while Department B has a considerably less expensive milling machine, used part of the time to process dies for the press but most of the time for subcontracting work. The overhead on these two machines accumulates at the rate of $100 per hour.

Since there are two machines, it might seem reasonable to divide the $100 between the two for a rate of $50 per hour per machine, and this in fact is just what happens when a plantwide overhead rate is used.

Now assume there is another company, that owns just a milling machine, and finds its overhead rate is $20 per hour; while still another company, owning just a press, has an overhead rate of $80 an hour. It is obvious that the company with both machines won't be able to compete with its milling machine since its overhead rate is $50 an hour compared with the $20 an hour charged by the competition. However, it will have cornered the market on the press work because its overhead rate is $50 an hour rather than $80 an hour. The only difficulty is that both machines must operate to cover the $100 per hour overhead which is accumulating. You undoubtedly will read in the financial section that bankruptcy has been declared.

The solution to this problem is to have an overhead rate calculated for each department. The overhead costs for each department, or work place, can be derived by the following equation:

$$\text{Overhead for department} = \text{Indirect labor for department} + \text{Indirect material for department} + \text{Indirect expenses for department}.$$

Each of the quantities on the right-hand side of this equation requires further explanation:

Indirect labor is that labor expense which can be charged directly to the production center. The fact that it is an *indirect* charge indicates that it cannot be charged directly to the product. Such expenses as labor for machine repairs can be charged to the department, and usually such labor is charged on a different-colored time card to distinguish it from the direct labor.

Indirect material is all material, such as repair parts, cutting oil, and similar items, which cannot be charged directly to the product, but can be charged directly to the production center.

Indirect expenses are all those overhead items which are not charged directly to the department. Since this information cannot be obtained directly, it is necessary to take each expense item and prorate it in some equitable way. This can be easily explained if we consider such an expense item as taxes for the factory building. The problem is to find the tax dollars to be charged to the department.

$$\frac{\text{Tax dollars for department}}{\text{Floor area for department}} = \frac{\text{Tax dollars for factory building}}{\text{Floor area for factory}};$$

$$\text{Tax dollars for department} = \text{Floor area for department} \times \frac{\text{Tax dollars for factory building}}{\text{Floor area for factory}}.$$

Each indirect expense item is considered and prorated on an appropriate basis to the departmental account. When all the costs—including indirect labor, indirect material, and indirect expenses—are accumulated for a department, they are divided by the direct-labor dollars, direct-labor hours, or other appropriate value which has been accumulated for the department to form a *departmental overhead rate*. The objective in establishing departmental overhead rates is to find true and equitable values. However, some companies adjust their cost figures arbitrarily to cover departments which are in the process of developing, or which the company wishes to justify for one reason or another. This defeats the purpose of a good cost accounting system and can have a discouraging effect on the departmental supervisors who are saddled with excessive overhead rates.

Do not lose sight of the objective in the estimating procedure. The *manufacturing cost* for a product is the desired goal, but the procedure starts way back where the indirect expenses are prorated to the departmental account. This account also accumulates the indirect material and indirect labor. If the direct-labor dollar method of applying overhead rates is used, the manufacturing expense for the department is divided by the dollars of direct labor used in that department. Remember that this, of necessity, is done with past information and will not necessarily reflect conditions as they exist now, but it is the best estimate that can be made.

The overhead is applied to the Cost Summary Sheet, along with the accumulation of direct labor and direct material costs, to complete the manufacturing cost for the product.

SOURCES OF COST INFORMATION

The various costs have been defined and the logic for developing the manufacturing cost has been shown. But what are the sources of these various cost data? This depends upon whether we are working before or after the fact. Working before the fact is the process of estimating, and the sources of the cost information are quite different from working after the fact. The flow of information into the cost summary sheet for *after-the-fact costing* is illustrated by Figure 5–6. The direct-labor costs are obtained

Figure 5–6

After-the-Fact Costing

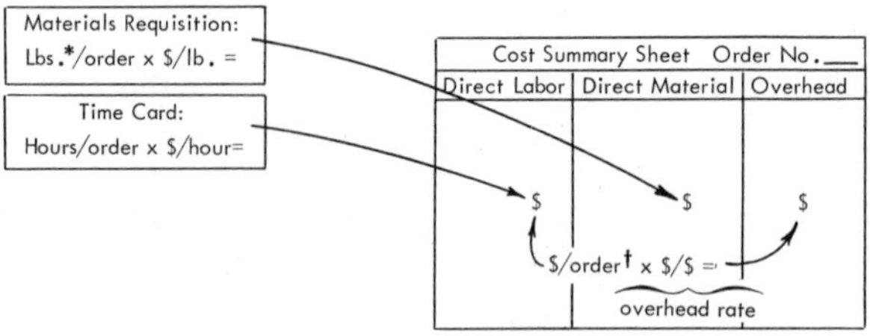

Source: Production Control Forms

* For the example, weight has been used as the unit of measure, but it could be any other, such as board feet, gallons, tons, etc.

† The overhead is applied on the basis of direct-labor dollars in the example, but it could just as well have been any of the other methods mentioned in the text.

from the time cards. The material costs are obtained from the materials requisitions which have gone through the stores record section to obtain both the cost and quantity. The overhead is applied using the overhead rate. The development of the overhead rate and the method of application are the responsibility of the accounting department.

The source of cost information for *before-the-fact costing* (or estimating [Figure 5–7]) is considerably different than that for after-the-fact costing. Since it is of greater importance to the subject of production planning and control, more time will be spent on it.

Figure 5–7

Before-the-Fact Costing (Estimating)

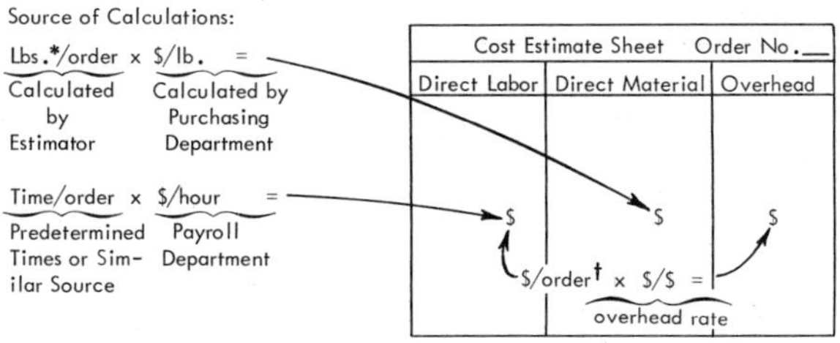

Source: Calculations

* For the example, weight has been used as the unit of measure, but it could be any other, such as board feet, gallons, tons, etc.

† The overhead is applied on the basis of direct-labor dollars in the example, but it could just as well have been any of the other methods mentioned in the text.

Direct Labor Costs

The time required to do a task can be derived by one of the methods described in Chapter 9. For estimating, usually the more precise methods are not necessary, and tables of gross times are suitable. Metal processing companies (and others) will frequently develop their own time data from actual experience. When the elapsed time is composed of machine-dictated time and man-dictated time, these two are calculated separately and then added:

$$(\text{Man time} + \text{Machine time}) \times \text{Labor rate} = \text{Direct labor costs.}$$

The labor rates are often tabulated for each production center, but the source of this information is the payroll department.

Direct Material Costs

Because the materials vary so greatly from product to product, it is difficult to generalize on the methods of calculation, but an example from the fastener industry will give you some idea of the process. Consider a small hexagonal head bolt made of brass. This could be made from a hexagon bar stock, which comes in lengths of about 15 feet. The problem is to determine the gross weight of the bolt.

Fortunately, a table in an engineering handbook will give the weight of the bar stock per inch. If the scrap is to be credited to the cost, the net weight of the bolt must also be found. This can be done quite rapidly by considering each part of the bolt as a geometric form: a cylinder, square, or hexagon. The weight per lineal inch for these forms can also be found in a table. The cost per pound of materials, including the shipping charges, can be obtained from the purchasing department. If the scrap is to be credited, it will be credited at the scrap price and not the price of the bar stock.

Overhead Costs

The overhead rate is furnished to the estimator by the cost accounting department. The way of applying, such as the direct-labor dollar method or direct-labor method, will not be decided by the estimator but will have been made by management at some earlier time.

EXAMPLE OF A COST ESTIMATE

How all the foregoing concepts fit together to produce an estimate is illustrated in Figure 5–8. The example is kept as simple as possible, yet it must still show the basic ideas. The cost estimating sheet, in this example, accompanies the operation sheet. This is logical since the process design must be decided before the costs can be estimated. Notice that this is just one process design, and there are probably others. For example, the number of cavities in the die might have been more or less than 16, and a different material might have been selected. All the alternatives should be considered by the process designer and should be checked by the costing methods shown. Often the costs have been previously worked out for various quantities, so decisions become automatic, and each process is not checked every time a product is made.

Our example is an actual cost estimate for a plastic company. You will notice that their cost breakdown is slightly different from the previous example. This is typical of the variation you can expect from industry to industry. In particular, you will find tooling and set-up costs handled in different ways. Some companies include these costs in the overhead while others add them to the total manufacturing costs.

DECISION MAKING

An understanding of the cost information developed in this chapter is essential for decision making throughout production planning and control.

Cost will be used for inventory control, scheduling, learning curve, and other decision-making models.

Cost is also used for the direct comparison between processes. The process planner may have to make a decision between mounting a part in a fixture for milling and mounting a part in a magnetic chuck to grind. The milling process will be much faster, but the fixture will cost more than would mount-

Figure 5–8

Example of a Cost Estimate

INDUSTRIAL PLASTICS, Inc.

Job Quotation Worksheet

Quote No. 2435
Date 12-16-64

Customer Keen Edge Knife Co.
Part Name Display Box Part No. —
Quote Promised 12-20-64 By TIM

MOLDS: Number of cavities 16 comb.
Machine Size
Cycle 30 sec.

COST: Hourly Production 864
Administration/hr. 4.80
Machine Overhead/hr. 3.25
Labor/hr. 4.80

MATERIAL: Type General purpose crystal
Lot Size —
Cost/lb. 1.45
Weight 50.7
Scrap 5.3
Weight-Gross 56.0

MISC. SUPPLIES:
Cartons 80
Tape 66

SUMMARY:

Raw Material	8	12		
Misc. Material	1	46		
Overhead	3	76		
Labor	5	56		
Manufacturing Costs			18	90
Administration			5	56
TOTAL PRODUCT COST				24.46
PROFIT			3	67
SELLING PRICE				28.13

DAILY PRODUCTION 20,736
WEEKLY PRODUCTION 103,680

Figure 5–8—Cont.

INDUSTRIAL PLASTICS, Inc.
Operation Sheet

Customer Keen Edge Knife Co. Date 1/23/65
Part Name Display Box Part No. —

Quantities 75,000 Date 4/1/65
75,000 5/1/65
75,000 6/1/65

Material G.P. Crystal Wt. 50.7

Operation No.	Operation Description	Die No.	Std. Times
10	Injection Mold	65-1392	30 sec/pc.

ing the part in the magnetic chuck for the slower process of grinding. A quick check of the costs for both processes will tell which is the best decision. Another example might be a choice between using some old cams for an automatic screw machine (which will take longer to do the job at hand) or some new, specially designed cams. The problem is whether the reduced production rate with the old cams will be more costly than making new cams. These and many other problems can be solved by making a direct comparison of cost between the two processes.

Although cost permeates all production planning and control, there are some special techniques for making decisions which should be discussed.

The Break-even Chart

The break-even chart is in reality two charts, one superimposed upon the other, and, for the sake of clarity, each will be discussed separately. The expense chart (Figure 5–9A) has expenses on the ordinate (vertical) axis and production on the abscissa (horizontal) axis. In the diagram the *fixed costs* are separated from the *variable costs*. Fixed costs remain fairly constant throughout a range of output: rent, insurance, and taxes, for example. The variable costs increase with production.

You are cautioned here to consider the cost with reference to the plant and not to the product. If you consider the product, you will become confused, as the fixed and variable cost concepts will be reversed. As production

Figure 5–9

Break-even Chart

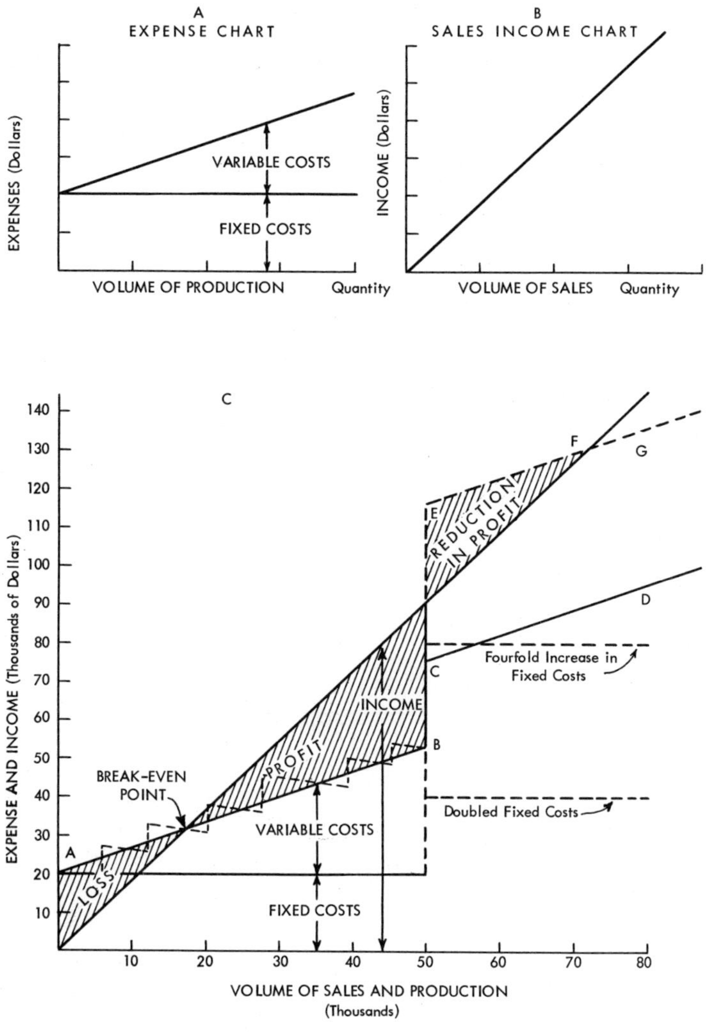

increases, the fixed costs per unit will become less and the variable costs will remain fixed. The concept of fixed and variable costs used in the diagram refers to the production center or factory.

The second chart is the sales income chart (Figure 5–9B). This chart also has production on the horizontal axis, as did the expense chart, but the sales income is on the vertical axis. It is assumed that when production is zero, the sales are zero. It is further assumed that sales income will increase linearly with production, which of course is not always true. When these two charts are superimposed upon each other, we have the typical break-even chart shown in Figure 5–9C.

The reason this is called a break-even chart is apparent upon inspection. The point at which the income exceeds the expenses is called the break-even point. This chart is an oversimplification of reality. The relationships, in most cases, won't be linear but will have steps—as represented by the dashed line.

The example given here is for a small company manufacturing a livestock spray which sells for $1.80 a gallon. The fixed expense for the factory is $20,000 a year with a maximum output of 50,000 gallons. The variable expense is $0.66 per gallon. It is apparent that the company must sell a little more than $30,000 worth to break even. The profits will be enhanced as more and more is sold because the fixed costs can be spread over more items. This chart, as we will see, can reveal interesting information for decision making.

Figure 5–10

Process Comparison Chart

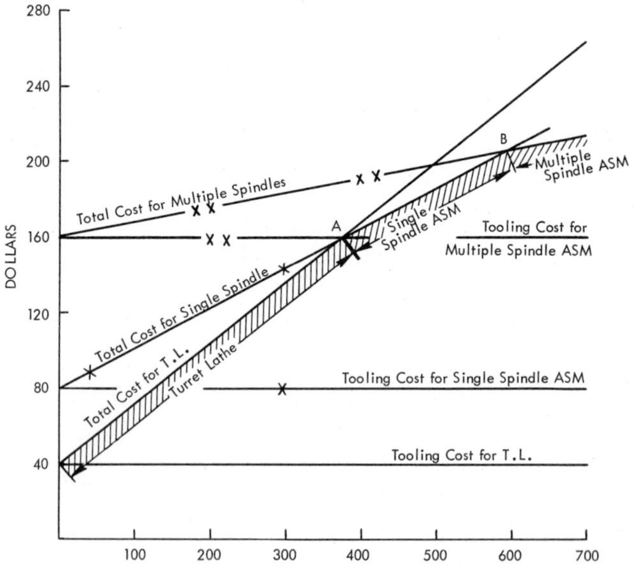

The capacity of the plant is 50,000 gallons a year, but what would happen if additional plant facilities were added to the picture? Suppose the plant were doubled in size and the fixed cost was also doubled (line *AB–CD*)? The profits will increase, but at a lower rate.

If the plant were increased fourfold, as shown by *A–B–E–F–G*, there would be a loss between *E–F* which must be offset against the profit. Not until this point is past will profit improve. This is a condition well worth remembering when one increases the size of a processing unit. The break-even chart can be used to simulate many conditions to obtain a better grasp of what changes will do to the profit.

Process Comparison Charts

Related to the break-even chart is the comparison chart (Figure 5–10). This chart is used for deciding whether to use one process or another. Typical of this decision is whether—for a particular product—a turret lathe, a single spindle screw machine, or a multiple spindle screw machine should be employed. The tooling costs will become progressively higher in each instance, but the labor costs per unit would be lower. The basic problem is to weigh the labor costs against the tooling costs. Below point A, it pays to use the turret lathe, and between A and *B* the single spindle automatic screw machine. The point where the lines cross, at A and *B*, is often called a break-even point, which is undoubtedly a carryover from the previous chart. This chart can also be used for simulation by varying the data. The numerous applications of this type of chart depend upon the imagination of the person seeking the answers for decisions.

Cost Reporting Charts

A form of cost report, which has been useful in some project work, is shown in Figure 5–11. This chart plots three kinds of information:

Actual costs: Those costs which have been incurred to date.
Budgeted costs: Those costs which have been anticipated.
Estimated costs for performance: Those costs which could be anticipated for the performance at this date.

Two examples are given in the chart. In the first example the actual costs are less than what had been budgeted for the elapsed time; however, the performance is less than had been anticipated. In the second example, the actual costs are more than the budgeted cost, but the work performed is greater than had been anticipated.

These are just a few of the charting techniques in which cost information can be applied for decision making. Other techniques are included throughout the book, so it is essential that you have a comprehension of how costs are derived.

COST ESTIMATING IN PRACTICE

A logic for estimating costs has been developed in this section, but not all companies follow the step-by-step procedure illustrated. Many companies are more likely to have someone estimating costs who has been in the business a long time. The process for estimating might go something like this:

This looks like a part we made three years ago for a certain company. We lost some money on that job so we will add 15 percent in order not to lose again. In

Figure 5–11

Cost Report Chart

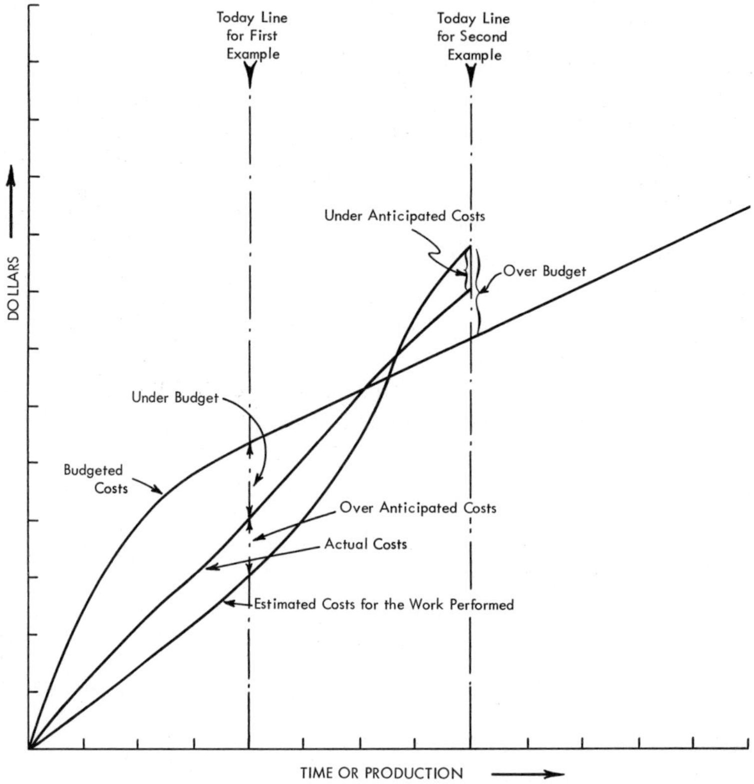

the meantime we have negotiated a new labor contract, so we will increase the price by 25 percent rather than by 15 percent. This part is a little thinner in some sections than was the other part, so we can reduce the cost by 10 percent, but there are two extra holes to drill and tap which increase the price by 20 percent. . . .

Amazingly, these estimates often prove correct to the penny, but one suspects that the factory workers *make* it come out that way. In some cases they may lose large sums of money—which are fortunately made up by some other estimate which has a compensating error. As in any process, it is well to understand the logic so as to realize the risks involved when a shortcut is taken.

SUMMARY

The price of a product is determined by many factors which are usually beyond the realm of the factory personnel. The factory contributes to the profit by reducing the manufacturing costs. The manufacturing costs for a product can be determined by four equations which should be first-hand knowledge to at least all supervisory personnel.

1) Manufacturing costs = Direct labor costs + Direct material costs + Overhead costs.

2) $$\frac{\text{Overhead costs for a job}}{\text{Direct labor costs for a job}} = \frac{\text{Overhead costs for last year}}{\text{Direct labor costs for last year}}.$$

(*The right-hand side of this last equation is known as the* overhead rate.)

If departmental overhead rates are needed instead of plantwide overhead rates:

3) Overhead for department = Indirect labor for department + Indirect material for department + Indirect expenses for department.

The indirect expenses may be calculated by an equation similar to No. 2 above:

4) $$\frac{\text{Indirect expense (taxes) for department in dollars}}{\text{Floor space for department in square feet}} = \frac{\text{Indirect expense (taxes) for factory in dollars}}{\text{Floor space for factory in square feet}}.$$

Of course, in this last equation, each indirect expense is prorated on an appropriate basis. The example has been for property tax, but it could have been for any other indirect expense, such as insurance, heating, etc.

The objective in the estimating procedure is to obtain the manufacturing costs, which means that the equations must be solved in the reverse of the order shown. Normally the accounting department will be responsible for Nos. 3 and 4, and will furnish the *overhead rate* for solving No. 2.

The costs can be obtained before the fact (estimating), or after the job is done, for cost comparison purposes. Costs are of vital importance to nearly all the activities of production planning and control, in fact this one word might be said to be the theme of this book.

Questions

1. Select several common products and suggest how the selling price is determined.
2. What are the three cost factors which make up the manufacturing cost? Where would you expect to obtain the information for each of these cost components?
3. Discuss how the production control department applies cost information to scheduling, expediting, and routing.
4. Estimate the cost of a product with which you are familiar, such as a spool of thread, a candy bar, or the like.
5. Why should burden rates be calculated from historical data?

6. Explain why burden rates are never right.
7. Give an example of a company which could use a uniform burden rate for an entire factory.
8. What could a company do about obtaining a true burden rate when it is just starting business?
9. Companies producing products on a production line may use job order costing systems. Explain why.
10. In choosing the denominator for the burden rate you should look for certain characteristics. What are they and why are they important?
11. Break-even charts are often drawn with straight lines. Is this realistic? Draw a chart for a particular company showing how you would expect the lines to appear.
12. Explain, by means of a break-even chart, why some companies find their profits reduced when they increase their production facilities.
13. It is not uncommon to find small industries operating out of the family garage and competing very well. When they expand to more luxurious facilities they often fail. Explain this by means of a break-even chart.
14. How many processes can be compared on one process comparison chart?

References

AMERICAN SOCIETY OF TOOL AND MANUFACTURING ENGINEERS (FRANK W. WILSON, ed.). *Manufacturing Planning and Estimating Handbook*. New York: McGraw-Hill Book Co., Inc., 1963.

BARISH, NORMAN N. *Economic Analysis for Engineering and Managerial Decision-Making*. New York: McGraw-Hill Book Co., Inc., 1962.

DICKEY, ROBERT IRVINE. *Accountants' Cost Handbook*. 2d ed. New York: Ronald Press Co., 1960.

FISKE, WYMAN, P., and BECKETT, JOHN A. *Industrial Accountant's Handbook*. New York: Prentice-Hall, Inc., 1957.

GRANT, EUGENE L. *Basic Accounting and Cost Accounting*. New York: McGraw-Hill Book Co., Inc., 1956.

GRANT, EUGENE L., and IRESON, W. GRANT. *Principles of Engineering Economy*, 4th ed. New York: Ronald Press Co., 1960.

HENRICI, STANLEY B. *Standard Costs for Manufacturing*. 3rd ed. New York: McGraw-Hill Book Co., Inc., 1960.

HOUGHTON, PHILIP S. *Estimating and Planning for Engineering Production*. London: Blackie & Son, Ltd., 1950.

KNOEPPEL, CHARLES E. *Profit Engineering*. New York and London: McGraw-Hill Book Co., Inc., 1933.

NORDHOFF, WILLIAM A. *Machine Shop Estimating*. 2d ed. New York: McGraw-Hill Book Co., Inc., 1960.

PARSONS, C. W. S. *Estimating Machining Costs*. New York: McGraw-Hill Book Co., Inc., 1957.

RAUTENSTRAUCH, WALTER, and VILLERS, RAYMOND. *Budgetary Control*. New York: Funk & Wagnalls in association with *Modern Industry*, 1957.

———. *The Economics of Industrial Management*. New York: Funk & Wagnalls Co. in association with *Modern Industry*, 1949.

STEDRY, ANDREW C. *Budget Control and Cost Behavior*. Englewood Cliffs, N.J.: Prentice-Hall, Inc., 1961.

TUCKER, SPENCER A. *Cost-Estimating and Pricing with Machine Hour Rates*. Englewood Cliffs, N.J.: Prentice-Hall, Inc., 1962.

VAN SICKLE, CLARENCE L. *Cost Accounting Fundamentals and Procedures*. 2d ed. New York: Harper & Bros., 1947.

VANCE, LAWRENCE LEE. *Theory and Technique of Cost Accounting*. Rev. ed. New York: Holt, Rinehart & Winston, Inc., 1958.

CHAPTER **6**

Forecasting the Quantity

Forecast Management

The prefix, or suffix, *fore* means *before* something, either in position or in time. In our usage, to be more specific, *fore*casting means the estimating of some quantity, stated either in numbers or value, to be produced and sold in the future.

We are all personally acquainted with forecasting and with some of its inherent dangers. For example, we are aware of the problems and results that accompany forecasting weather, baseball scores, presidential elections, or even how one's partner will bid his bridge hand. All of these forecasts, and many more, are plagued by numerous factors affecting their outcome.

Determining what will happen in the future is forecasting, and all profitable companies do this to at least some degree—although some don't put a name to it. We will first discuss the general problem of forecasting, its need and place in the organization, and then the statistical techniques which are either used extensively or hold promise of being useful.

THE PROBLEM

The problem, as stated in the definition, is to predict the sales at some future date. Designers make frequent predictions, but not always on a time scale. For example, the curve in Figure 6–1 is the stress-strain curve for a sample of steel which can be used to predict the performance of some part of a bridge structure. The problem is to determine, with some degree of certainty, how a part under consideration, such as the cables of the bridge, will perform under certain loads. This is a prediction that uses a scale other than time, but the engineer also forecasts on a time scale. The electronics designer is predicting on a time scale when he examines current or voltage variations.

Figure 6–1

Predicting with Stress-Strain Curve

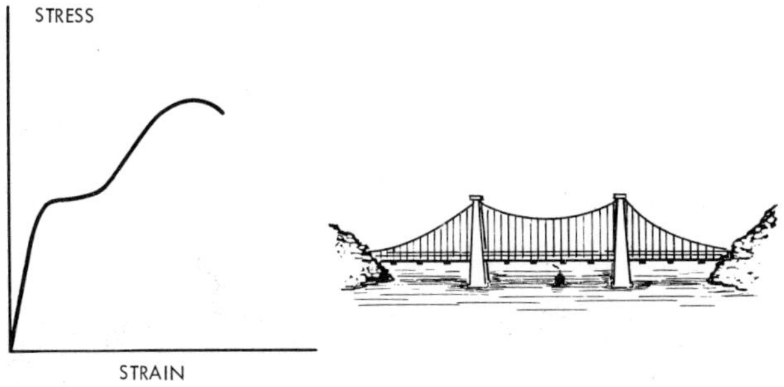

Forecasting sales is similar to the example but far more complex, because there are more factors influencing the problem—which in many cases are not definable or measurable. Scientists and engineers might scoff at industrial people for not being more quantitative, but it is not the lack of ability which makes them less quantitative, rather it is the more difficult problems they need to solve. Eventually, mathematical models will be developed for business changes as they have been for engineering phenomena, but they will be much more complex. Figure 6–2, showing variations in the economy, gives some idea of just how much more complicated the problem is.

NEED FOR FORECASTING

The sales forecast is the link between the external, uncontrollable movements of the economy and the internal, controllable affairs of the business. Therefore a sales forecast must be based on a careful analysis of external factors, as it is the foundation for planning all aspects of a company's operations. It dictates, among other things, production schedules, purchasing of inventory, capital expenditures, rental of warehouses, and budgets for labor. These activities, and many more, depend upon the sales forecast.

One might assume that forecasting is unnecessary if a company manufactures to order. To a degree this is true, but it is an oversimplification of the situation. It takes time to procure raw materials, personnel, and machines; to build parts, make them into subassemblies, and eventually into assemblies. Therefore it is essential that a company does some forecasting, especially if there is any variation at all in its output. Forecasting is no substitute for actual knowledge of a market, and subcontractors, in particular, would do well to create a close liaison with their customers and vendors.

Budgeting and forecasting go hand in hand, and the interest in budgeting during recent years has stimulated an interest in forecasting. There are a number of concrete advantages in having a good forecast:

Figure 6–2

American Business Activity

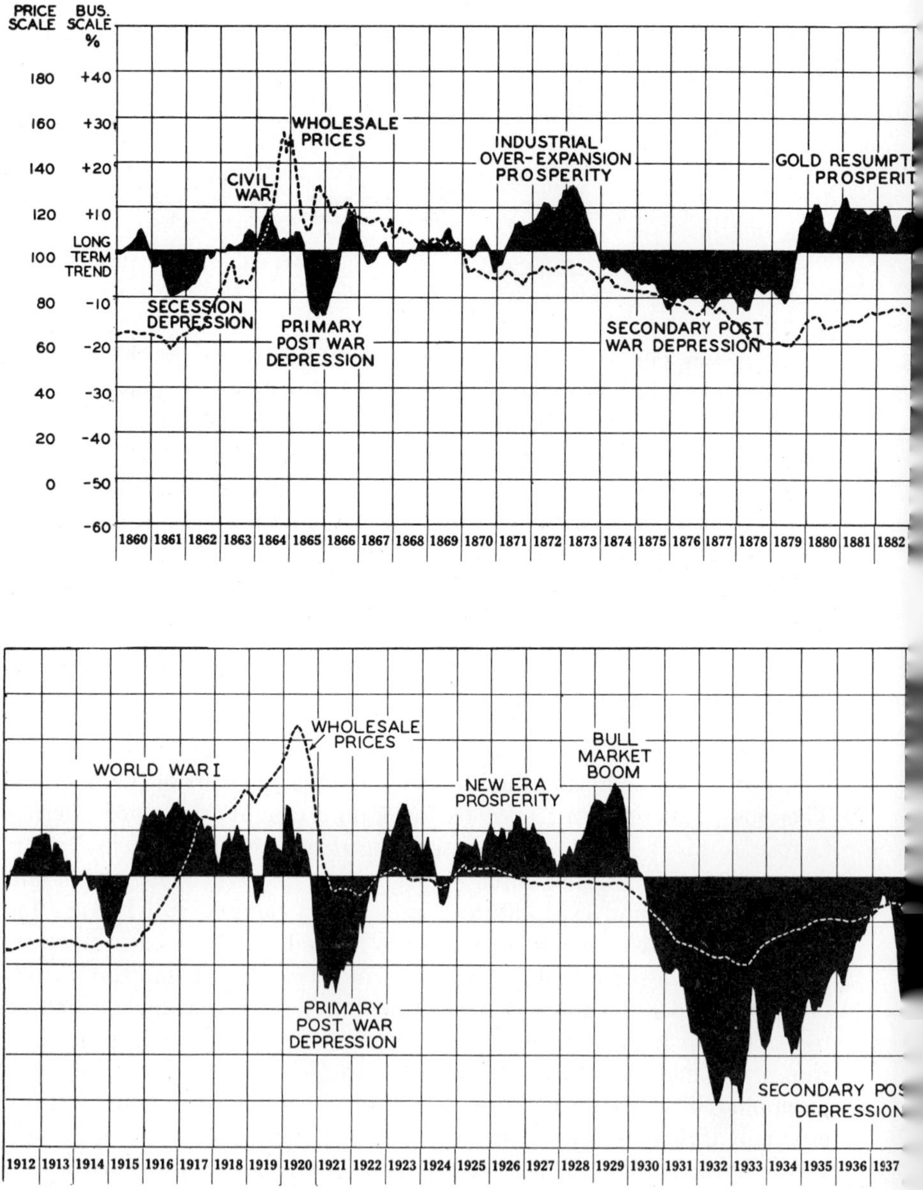

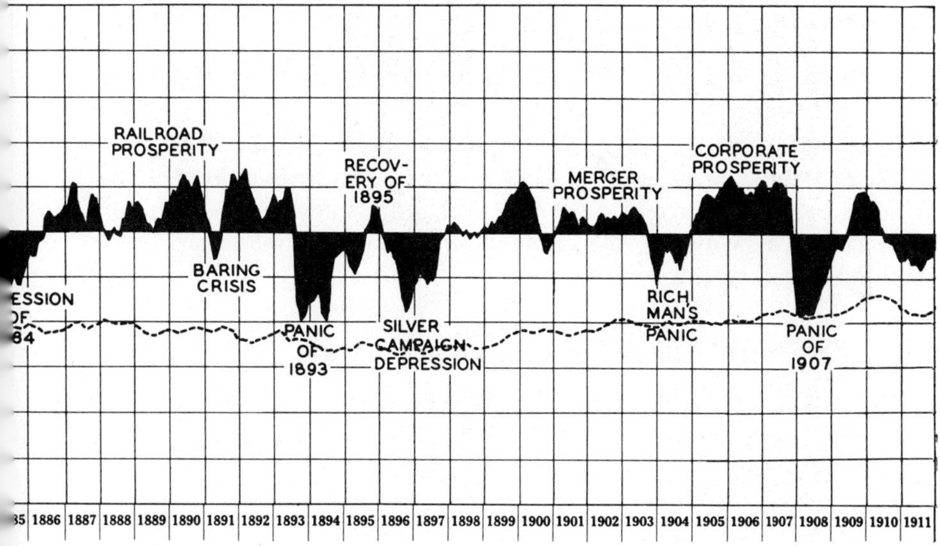
RAILROAD PROSPERITY
BARING CRISIS
RECOV-ERY OF 1895
PANIC OF 1893
SILVER CAMPAIGN DEPRESSION
MERGER PROSPERITY
RICH MAN'S PANIC
CORPORATE PROSPERITY
PANIC OF 1907
ESSION OF 84
1886 1887 1888 1889 1890 1891 1892 1893 1894 1895 1896 1897 1898 1899 1900 1901 1902 1903 1904 1905 1906 1907 1908 1909 1910 1911

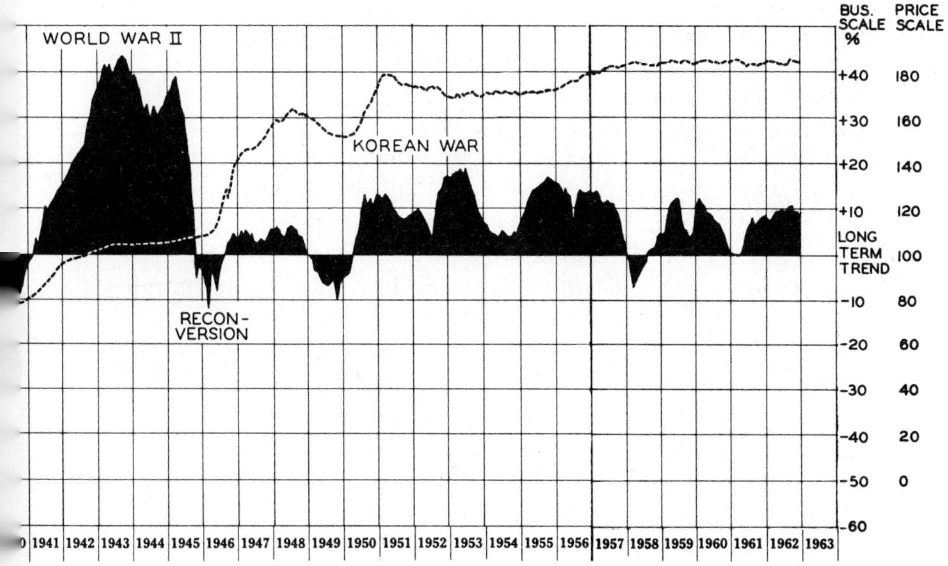
WORLD WAR II
RECON-VERSION
KOREAN WAR
BUS. SCALE %
PRICE SCALE
+40 180
+30 160
+20 140
+10 120
LONG TERM TREND 100
-10 80
-20 60
-30 40
-40 20
-50 0
-60
1941 1942 1943 1944 1945 1946 1947 1948 1949 1950 1951 1952 1953 1954 1955 1956 1957 1958 1959 1960 1961 1962 1963

1. Customers can be kept happy by being supplied the products they want as soon as they want them.
2. Cancelled orders, because of slow deliveries, can be eliminated.
3. A greater feeling of cooperation can be created in the factory.
4. Direct labor costs can be kept at a minimum by balancing work loads thus preventing overtime and reducing costly hiring and firing.
5. Inventories can be manipulated more efficiently.
6. Capital, in the form of both money and machines, can be used more effectively.

Forecasts are always wrong in the respect that the levels attained are hardly ever the same as anticipated. This must be understood by all those associated with the forecast. Seldom, if ever, will a guess about the future be exact—but how much better an *intelligent* estimate of the future, based on information, than a *wild* guess.

FORECASTING AND THE ORGANIZATION

The activities of a manufacturing business can be divided into three major functional groups: marketing, production, and finance. Marketing includes all the activities needed to move a product from the manufacturer to the consumer. Market research, part of marketing, is a critical and exhaustive investigation of the problems allied to getting a product to market.

Forecasting is just one activity in the market research picture, which includes studies of product acceptance, customer dissatisfaction, new uses of products, product simplification, and many other subjects which are fascinating but too extensive to dwell upon here.

Not many companies are large enough, or the sales forecasting critical enough, to warrant a market research organization. The function is usually served, in these situations, by the sales department, and the forecast may be nothing more exotic than a compilation of orders from which some idea of the trend can be gained. Even the companies with market research groups frequently delegate some of the forecasting function to the sales department.

Market research problems are often handled outside the organization, and there are a number of market research agencies available for manufacturers who do not wish to establish their own organizations. If the manufacturer passes the selling function on to other independent companies, he will probably pass on the sales forecasting. Advertising agencies have been taking on an increasingly important part of the market research function. Trade associations also serve a need in market research, for they can handle industry-wide problems which are beyond the scope of many companies.

The production control function is usually not responsible for forecasting, although occasionally it is driven to it by the default of others. Its task is usually limited to analyzing forecasts made by the sales department to develop master production schedules. Forecasts must be interpreted in terms of factory capacity. Thus the problems of matching forecasts to production conditions are, within narrow limits, those of production control. Wider variations will probably be the responsibility of upper management. If the forecast does not utilize all the plant capacity, a cut may have to be made in work hours, and, consequently, fewer goods will be produced; or management may decide finished goods should be stockpiled, or other markets found. If the forecasts are greater than capacity, the management must be satisfied with less than the total possible sales, or must increase production capacity by adding facilities or subcontracting to other manufacturers.

Forecasting often becomes a committee activity. Such a committee might include the production manager, sales manager, and treasurer. All these individuals will be able to contribute knowledge concerning their particular areas of responsibility, although there is the danger that one may unduly influence the others. The sales manager would have the factory make immediate delivery on anything and everything without regard to cost. The production manager wants an even flow of production, just slightly below full capacity, with large inventories available to balance out fluctuations in load. The treasurer wants to retain a high cash reserve to meet all contingencies, which means he would like to have small inventories. Thus the conflicting interests within the committee are obvious.

APPROACHES TO FORECASTING

Before going into any one technique of forecasting, let us take a look at all the methods so we can see them in perspective and dispose of those which promise to be of little value.

Forecasting for New Products

Forecasting demand for products which are established can often be a routine procedure, but forecasting demand for new products is considerably more difficult. In forecasting for old products, past information is available on which the future can be predicted. This is, of course, generally not true for new products. Some of the methods used for new product forecasting are:

Direct Survey Method. The prospective customers are asked what they intend to buy. As it is nearly impossible to ask *all* the customers, it is necessary to use sampling techniques and ask only a few. From the few it is possible to predict, with some degree of certainty, how the population will respond. Since the purchaser is likely to vacillate from day to day because of economic changes, political changes, style changes, and other reasons, surveys should be tempered by factors which account for these changes.

Indirect Survey Method. Another method of forecasting demand is by asking the people who know how the customer responds. Frequently the salesman knows, but his estimates are likely to be overly optimistic. Wholesalers, jobbers, and other middlemen are also solicited, for they have their fingers directly upon the pulse of the consumers' demand.

Comparing with Established Products. At times the product under consideration is comparable to an existing product, so sales figures can be compared. If it is an outright replacement for the present product, probably little difficulty will be encountered when the new product is properly introduced. If the new product is a substitute for a competitor's product, its acceptance will depend upon the advertising program and the customers' loyalty to the present product.

Limited Market Trial. Another method of forecasting the demand for a new product is to try selling it in a limited area to see how well it is accepted by potential customers.

Forecasting for Established Products

These are the methods which are common for forecasting sales of well established products:

Projection Method. This method is based upon the assumption that what has gone on before will continue. The relationship of sales with income, time, or other factors is projected ahead to determine what the sales will be in the future. This is illustrated in Figure 6–3. A line drawn through

Figure 6–3

Example of Projection Method

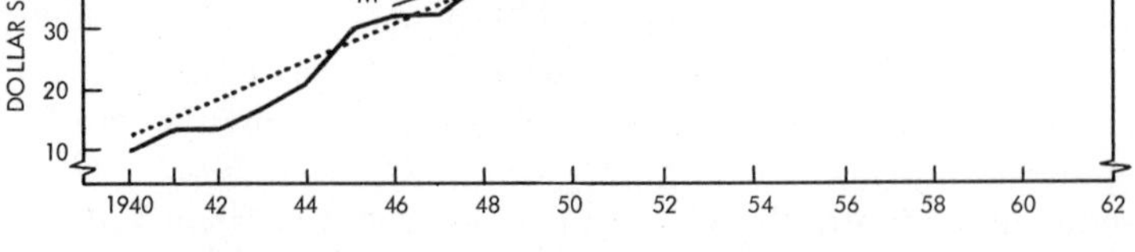

Source: "Finding and Evaluating Basic Data for Sales Forecasting," *Sales Forecasting Uses and Techniques*, by Alfred C. Scott (the Upjohn Co.) and published by the American Management Association, Special Report 16.

the known information is projected into the forecast area to predict what the sales volume will be for future periods.

Related Information Method. In this method (Figure 6–4), a predictor which varies directly with the sales volume is found. In this example the Federal Reserve Board Index is used. Of course the predictor must be available well in advance of the need. This means the predictor must either lead

Figure 6–4

Example of Related Information Method

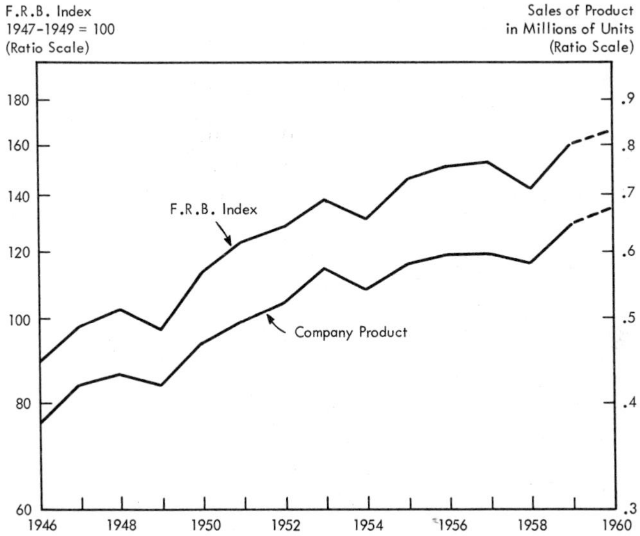

Source: John Neter and William Wasserman, *Fundamental Statistics for Business and Economics*, 2d ed., p. 809, copyright 1961 by Allyn and Bacon. Reprinted by permission of the publisher.

the sales or be a forecast itself for some time into the future. For example, the actual birth rates might be used to predict the sale of baby foods, or well established predictions of births might be used. These two techniques, the projection method and related information method, will be examined later by statistical techniques.

Statistics for Forecasting

The word statistics, as used in forecasting, has several quite distinctly different meanings. It may mean data or the collection of data, but to the more sophisticated it means the *principles of statistical inference.* Mathematical statistics can range from some very elementary ideas to extremely complicated theoretical concepts. Here we can touch only upon some of the more basic ideas, but you are urged to become acquainted with the excellent references in the bibliography.

Statistics, it should be understood, is a tool for the analysis of information and is not an end in itself. The subject will be developed with this in mind. To point the way for the discussion, the subjects will be covered in the following order:

1. Statistical Sampling
   a) Characteristics of normal distribution
   b) Characteristics of binomial and Poisson distributions

2. Statistics of Association
   a) Regression analysis
   b) Correlation analysis

LANGUAGE OF STATISTICS

A person involved with the statistical literature picks up the language quickly, even though there are often several symbols for one concept. The symbols used in this chapter are listed below in the Glossary of Terms, and will also be defined as used.

Glossary of Terms

(Greek letters will be used for *parameters* of a population; Latin letters will be used for *statistics* of a sample.)

a	Estimate of α, the Y intercept of a line.
b	Estimate of β, the slope of a line.
d	Deviation from a designated mean, X_d.
e	Deviation from a line.
f	Frequency.
i	Class interval.
n	The number in a sample.
N	The number in a population; in regression, the number of observations.
N*	The number of samples.
p	The probability that a success will occur.
$\bar{p}$	The sample proportion (read "p bar").
q	The probability that a failure will occur, $p + q = 1$.
r	Coefficient of correlation.
x	The deviation of a value from the mean.
x'	The deviation of a class mid-value from the mean.
X	A value in a series of values.
$\bar{X}$	Arithmetic mean of a series of values in a sample.
$\bar{\bar{X}}$	Arithmetic mean of sample means ("X double bar").
$\bar{X}_d$	A designated mean.
Y	An observed value of Y.
Y_c	A calculated value of Y.
$\bar{Y}$	Arithmetic mean of the Y values.
S	Standard deviation of a sample.
S_x	Estimated standard deviation of a population, computed from a sample.
$S_{\bar{x}}$	Standard deviation of the sample means.
S^2_x	Estimated variance of a population, computed from a sample.
S^2_y	Total variance to be explained.
$S^2_{y_c}$	Explained variance.
$S_{y \cdot x}$	Standard error of the estimate.
σ_x	Standard deviation of a population.
σ^2_x	Variance of a population.
$\sigma_{\bar{x}}$	Standard error of $\bar{X}$.
Σ	Add all the values in the interval ("capital sigma"). The interval may be designated by $\sum_1^n$ meaning sum the values from 1 to n.

STATISTICAL SAMPLING

Sampling, to determine the characteristics of a large body of information, is an everyday experience. The preview of next week's show at the local theater is a (biased) sample to urge you to return in the near future. Glancing through the magazines on a newsstand before buying is another sampling procedure used before making a decision.

Figure 6–5

Predicting the Size of Hats

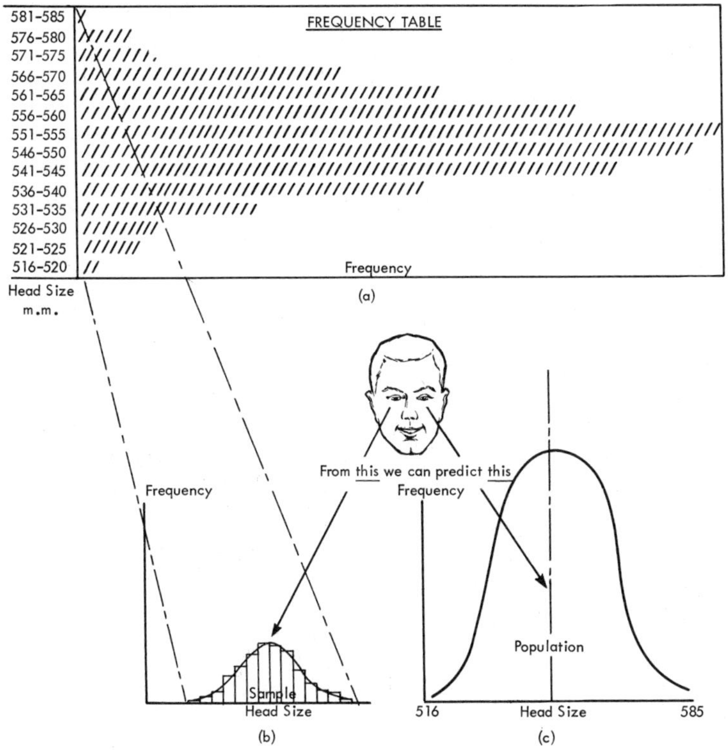

The manufacturer also uses sampling, consciously or not, to help him make decisions. For example, a manufacturer of hats is concerned about a new line for boys of a certain age group. How many should be made of each size? Mindful of a boys' school nearby, permission is obtained to measure the head size of each boy in the age group of interest. This is done quickly by recording the sizes on a frequency chart (as shown in Figure 6–5*a*).

Plotting the frequency of occurrences on the coordinate paper for each head size in the sample will give a distribution which looks something like the diagram in Figure 6–5*b*. This stair-step diagram is called a *histogram*. The group of boys under observation is called the *sample* and the potential market for boys buying the manufacturer's hats is called the *population*. We might predict the distribution of the population from the histogram (Figure 6–5*c*).

As the sample size gets larger and larger, one would expect the sample distribution to look more and more like the population. The problem is to predict the characteristics of the population from what we can learn about the sample. It is apparent that the statistical inference can be made from the sample. But what about this sample? Will any sample do? The sample must be a *probability sample* if it is to be used for statistical inferences. Although the simple random sample is only one form of probability sampling, our interest will be focused on this method. "Selected at random" indicates that each possible sample has the same probability of being drawn.

First we will discuss characteristics of the sample and later show how the sample can predict the characteristics of the population. This is the problem, but what are these characteristics with which we are concerned?

The symmetrical distribution, shown by the smooth line through the histogram in Figure 6–5*b*, is the most important distribution in statistics and is referred to as the *normal distribution* or, for obvious reasons, the *bell curve*. It is the result of a large number of additive effects and is often representative of information found in the sciences as well as in industry. It is basic to many sampling plans.

What would you want to know about the distribution of head sizes if you were the hat manufacturer? Certainly the average size, the largest, and the smallest sizes, and, if you could have more information (which you could), you would ask for the percentage of each size you expect to sell. The arithmetic mean, often referred to as the average, is, as you know, the total of all the values of a group divided by the number in the group. This is stated by the equation:

$$\overline{X} = \frac{\sum_{i=1}^{n} X_i}{n}$$

$\overline{X}$ = arithmetic mean of a sample
X_i = value of the *i*th observation in the sample
n = number in the sample

The capital sigma, Σ, means "add all the X values from 1 to *n*" and gives a simple way of showing the total of the values of X. No longer will the interval 1 to *n*, over which we are adding, be expressed; and we will always assume that we are totaling all the values in the interval.

The arithmetic mean, $\overline{X}$, (called "X bar") is only one of the measures of *central tendency*. There are others, such as the *median* (the middle number in a series of consecutive numbers) and the *mode* (the number which occurs most frequently). As you might guess, on a normal curve all these measures—mean, median, and mode—fall at the same place.

Several curves could have the same average, and be normal distributions,

Figure 6–6

Distributions with Same Mean but Different Dispersion

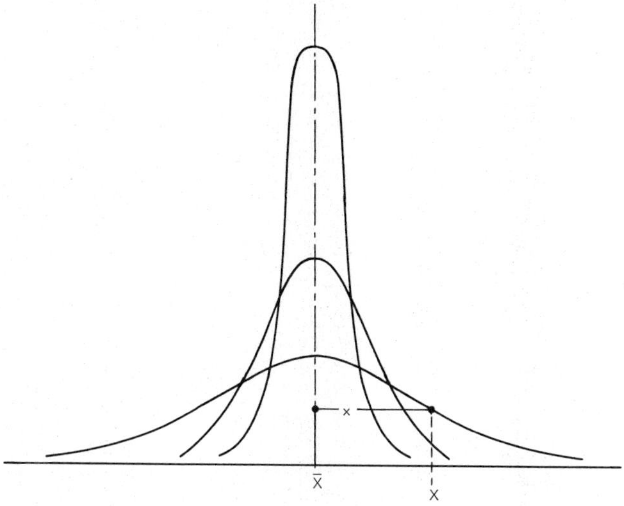

but look like any of the three curves in Figure 6–6. The difference is in the dispersion. The manufacturer might be satisfied by knowing the two extreme head dimensions, but there is a better measure of dispersion called the *variance*, and its next of kin, the *standard deviation*. Let us look at these together and compare them briefly before proceeding.

Variance of a Sample Size n:

$$S^2 = \frac{\Sigma(X - \overline{X})^2}{n} = \frac{\Sigma(x)^2}{n}$$

The variance, S^2, is also called the *mean square error.*

Standard Deviation of a Sample Size n:

$$S = \sqrt{\frac{\Sigma(X - \overline{X})^2}{n}} = \sqrt{\frac{\Sigma(x)^2}{n}}$$

The standard deviation, S, is also called the *root mean square error.*

The variance and the standard deviation look alike with one exception. The standard deviation is the square root of the variance, or the variance is the standard deviation squared, whichever way you care to look at it. But one should not pull equations out of the air like this without explanation of what they measure.

As we know, $\overline{X}$ is the average value, so if we subtract it from the individual X's, as shown in the previous figure, we have the differences or variability around the mean, which will be designated by small x's. Some of these will be negative, which will balance out the positive values, giving a total of zero.

If negative numbers are squared, they result in positive numbers. So if we do this, $(X - \overline{X})^2$, we get positive values which are then totaled over the entire interval, as indicated by the capital sigma (Σ). This total is then divided by n. The engineer will recognize an analogy between the mean as the first moment about the origin, and the variance as the second moment about the mean.

Up to this point we have singled out the sample for discussion because we cannot conveniently obtain information about the population and must project our knowledge from a sample. Here we shall pause and compare the sample *statistic* with the population *parameter*. To minimize the confusion we shall want to use a different set of symbols for each. Here are symbols which are fairly common in the literature:

Symbols Used for Samples (Statistic)		*Symbols for Samples When Used to Estimate the Population*		*Symbols for Populations (Parameters)*	
S	Sample standard deviation	S_x	Estimated standard deviation of a population predicted from a sample	σ_x	Standard deviation for the population (lower case *sigma*)
n	Number of items in the sample	n	Number of items in the sample	N	Number of items in the population
$\overline{X}$	Sample mean	$\overline{X}$	Sample mean	μ	Population mean (*mu*)

Notice this confusing point. The capital sigma was used for summing a series of numbers, but here the lower case sigma, σ, indicates the population standard deviation. There is no relationship between the meanings of these two symbols. Also notice that S is used to indicate the sample standard deviation and S_x is used for the estimated standard deviation of a population predicted from a sample.

The population mean can be estimated by the sample mean, so this is true:

The *sample mean* is an estimate of the *population mean*:

$$\overline{X} = \Sigma X/n \qquad \mu = \Sigma X/N$$

The greatest difficulty lies in estimating the standard deviation. To introduce sampling it was implied that the sample deviation is a good predictor of the population standard deviation. This is not a bad assumption for large sample sizes, but it introduces some error when the sample is small. The *estimated standard deviation of a population* will be designated by S_x, and the relationship between it and the population standard deviation, σ_x, is as follows:

Sample standard deviation is an estimate of the *population standard deviation*:

$$S_x = \sqrt{\frac{\Sigma(X - \overline{X})^2}{n - 1}} \qquad \sigma_x = \sqrt{\frac{\Sigma(X - \mu)^2}{N}}$$

The $n - 1$ accounts for the degrees of freedom[1] and is used instead of n so that we will obtain an unbiased estimator. That is, the estimators will not favor an incorrect answer which, in the case of using n, would on the average cause the estimate of σ_x to be small. It is obvious that the larger the sample the smaller the difference between n and $n - 1$, so it is common to use n for large samples.

The standard deviation has an interesting characteristic. The more the X's are dispersed the greater will be the standard deviation. However, for a normal curve, the distribution of the X's will follow the pattern shown in the diagram in Figure 6–7.

Figure 6–7

Relationship between Standard Deviation and Frequency

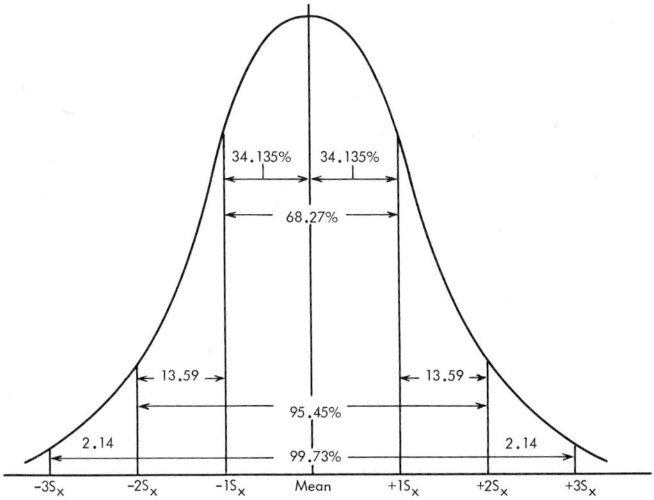

What this says is that 68.27 percent of the cases will fall within one standard deviation, either side of the mean; 95.45 percent of the cases within (plus and minus) two standard deviations; and 99.73 percent within (plus and minus) three standard deviations of the mean.

Tables are available (Figure 6–8) which give the area under the normal curve for any practical multiple of standard deviations. To enter the table, the X value is expressed in standard deviations called Z values.

[1] Degrees of freedom, the maximum number of mutually independent variables in a system. For example, if three items total 9 and two of them are 3 and 4, the third must be 2. For a sample size n, there are $n - 1$ degrees of freedom.

$$Z = \frac{(X - \mu)}{\sigma}$$

Since population values are not known, it is necessary to estimate Z from a sample (using the following equation). This is applicable only when large samples are available and when it is known that the sample is representative of the inference population which is known to be normal.

$$Z = \frac{(X - \overline{X})}{S_x}$$

For example, if $X = 8$, $\overline{X} = 4$, and the estimated standard deviation S_x is 2, the Z value would be $\frac{8 - 4}{2} = 2$. Entering the table, we find that 47.72 percent of the area is between X and $\overline{X}$. This is illustrated in Figure 6–8. If we were interested in the area between plus and minus X, as we might be, the area would simply be 95.45 percent. From this table it is obvious that we can obtain information for any multiple of standard deviations.

Following the procedure just given, the hat manufacturer can determine the quantity of each size hat he should manufacture. But can you imagine the trouble it would cause to take the sample items, subtract them from the mean, square them, add them, and extract the square root? Even the thought is fatiguing, so let us strive to find a simpler method. The evolution of reaching a practical model will be given briefly. In the following equations n will be used instead of $n - 1$ because it is assumed the samples are large, and we will start with the sample standard deviation in the form just given.

First Improvement: Rather than subtract the individual X's from the mean, $\overline{X}$, as shown in the previous equation, the following equation in terms of X's can be used:

$$S_x = \sqrt{\frac{\Sigma X^2}{n} - \left(\frac{\Sigma X}{n}\right)^2}$$

Second Improvement: By grouping data for convenience, the information can be tabulated in a frequency distribution as shown earlier. The equation can then be changed to account for the form of the data.

$$S_x = \sqrt{\frac{\Sigma f x'^2}{n}}$$

(x' is the deviation of a class midvalue from the mean; f is the frequency.)

Third Improvement: Determining x' is obviously difficult so, rather than use the average, the midvalue of any class can be used as the assumed mean. Calculations are made with the deviations around this value and then corrected:

$$S_x = \sqrt{\frac{\Sigma f d^2}{n} - \left(\frac{\Sigma f d}{n}\right)^2}$$

(d is the deviation of an X from any designated mean $\overline{X}_d$.)

Figure 6–8

Areas of a Standard Normal Distribution for *Z* Values

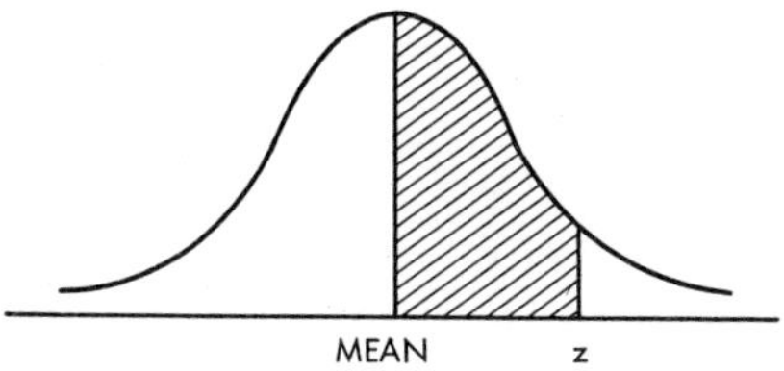

Table of Areas from Mean to Distances *Z**

Z	.00	.01	.02	.03	.04	.05	.06	.07	.08	.09
0.0	.0000	.0040	.0080	.0120	.0160	.0199	.0239	.0279	.0319	.0359
0.1	.0398	.0438	.0478	.0517	.0557	.0596	.0636	.0675	.0714	.0753
0.2	.0793	.0832	.0871	.0910	.0948	.0987	.1026	.1064	.1103	.1141
0.3	.1179	.1217	.1255	.1293	.1331	.1368	.1406	.1443	.1480	.1517
0.4	.1554	.1591	.1628	.1664	.1700	.1736	.1772	.1808	.1844	.1879
0.5	.1915	.1950	.1985	.2019	.2054	.2088	.2123	.2157	.2190	.2224
0.6	.2257	.2291	.2324	.2357	.2389	.2422	.2454	.2486	.2518	.2549
0.7	.2580	.2612	.2642	.2673	.2704	.2734	.2764	.2794	.2823	.2852
0.8	.2881	.2910	.2939	.2967	.2995	.3023	.3051	.3078	.3106	.3133
0.9	.3159	.3186	.3212	.3238	.3264	.3289	.3315	.3340	.3365	.3389
1.0	.3413	.3438	.3461	.3485	.3508	.3531	.3554	.3577	.3599	.3621
1.1	.3643	.3665	.3686	.3708	.3729	.3749	.3770	.3790	.3810	.3830
1.2	.3849	.3869	.3888	.3907	.3925	.3944	.3962	.3980	.3997	.4015
1.3	.4032	.4049	.4066	.4082	.4099	.4115	.4131	.4147	.4162	.4177
1.4	.4192	.4207	.4222	.4236	.4251	.4265	.4279	.4292	.4306	.4319
1.5	.4332	.4345	.4357	.4370	.4382	.4394	.4406	.4418	.4429	.4441
1.6	.4452	.4463	.4474	.4484	.4495	.4505	.4515	.4525	.4535	.4545
1.7	.4554	.4564	.4573	.4582	.4591	.4599	.4608	.4616	.4625	.4633
1.8	.4641	.4649	.4656	.4664	.4671	.4678	.4686	.4693	.4699	.4706
1.9	.4713	.4719	.4726	.4732	.4738	.4744	.4750	.4756	.4761	.4767
2.0	.4772	.4778	.4783	.4788	.4793	.4798	.4803	.4808	.4812	.4817
2.1	.4821	.4826	.4830	.4834	.4838	.4842	.4846	.4850	.4854	.4857
2.2	.4861	.4864	.4868	.4871	.4875	.4878	.4881	.4884	.4887	.4890
2.3	.4893	.4896	.4898	.4901	.4904	.4906	.4909	.4911	.4913	.4916
2.4	.4918	.4920	.4922	.4925	.4927	.4929	.4931	.4932	.4934	.4936
2.5	.4938	.4940	.4941	.4943	.4945	.4946	.4948	.4949	.4951	.4952
2.6	.4953	.4955	.4956	.4957	.4959	.4960	.4961	.4962	.4963	.4964
2.7	.4965	.4966	.4967	.4968	.4969	.4970	.4971	.4972	.4973	.4974
2.8	.4974	.4975	.4976	.4977	.4977	.4978	.4979	.4979	.4980	.4981
2.9	.4981	.4982	.4982	.4983	.4984	.4984	.4985	.4985	.4986	.4986
3.0	.49865	.4987	.4987	.4988	.4988	.4989	.4989	.4989	.4990	.4990
4.0	.4999683									

* For Z = 1.93 (illustration), shaded area is .4732 out of total area of 1.

Source: John Neter and William Wasserman, *Fundamental Statistics for Business and Economics*, 2d ed. (Boston: Allyn and Bacon, Inc., 1961), p. 809. Reprinted by permission of the publisher.

The mean can be calculated:

$$\overline{X} = \overline{X}_d + \frac{\Sigma fd}{n}$$

Fourth Improvement: To shorten the process even more, the deviations can be taken in terms of classes:

$$S_x = i\sqrt{\frac{\Sigma f(d')^2}{n} - \left(\frac{\Sigma fd'}{n}\right)^2}$$

(d' is the deviation of a class midvalue from the assumed mean in terms of classes; i is the class interval.)

And the mean is:

$$\overline{X} = \overline{X}_d + i\left(\frac{\Sigma fd'}{n}\right)$$

Since this fourth improvement is the most efficient, it will be used to solve the hat size problem. The information for the hat size problem is

Figure 6–9

Determination of Hat Sizes

Head Size m.m.	Frequency	Midvalue of Class	d'	fd'	$f(d')^2$
516–520	2	518	−6	−12	72
521–525	7	523	−5	−35	175
526–530	9	528	−4	−36	144
531–535	20	533	−3	−60	180
536–540	38	538	−2	−76	152
541–545	58	543	−1	−58	58
546–550	65	548	0	0	0
551–555	68	553	1	68	68
556–560	54	558	2	108	216
561–565	39	563	3	117	351
566–570	24	568	4	96	384
571–575	9	573	5	45	225
576–580	6	578	6	36	216
581–585	1	583	7	7	49
	$n = \Sigma f = 400$			200	2290

$$\overline{X} = \overline{X}_d + i\left(\frac{\Sigma fd'}{n}\right) = 548 + \frac{5 \times 200}{400} = 550.5$$

$$S_x = i\sqrt{\frac{\Sigma f(d')^2}{n} - \left(\frac{\Sigma fd'}{n}\right)^2} = 5\sqrt{\frac{2290}{400} - \left(\frac{200}{400}\right)^2}$$

$$= 5\sqrt{5.725 - .25}$$

$$S_x = 11.70$$

$$\overline{X} + 3\,S_x = 585.6$$

$$\overline{X} - 3\,S_x = 515.4$$

given in a form that can be readily solved by the last set of equations. As can be seen from the information, we would expect that the average hat size would be 550.5 m.m., and the two extremes would most likely be three sigma either side of the mean, which is 515.4 m.m. and 585.6 m.m. The number of hats that one could expect to sell between 566 m.m. and 576 m.m. could be calculated in this way:

$Z \cong \dfrac{X - \bar{X}}{S_x}$ = (?) which includes (?)% of the area

$Z_1 \cong \dfrac{576.0 - 550.5}{11.70} =$ 2.18 which includes 48.54%

$Z_2 \cong \dfrac{566.0 - 550.5}{11.70} =$ 1.32 which includes 40.66%

7.88%

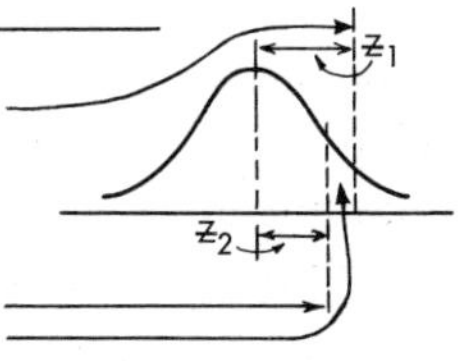

This, of course, has been predicted on only one sample, and we would guess that there could be some differences among samples. So now we will turn to the problem of establishing confidence limits.

CONFIDENCE INTERVALS FOR ESTIMATES

In the hat size problem the assumption of a normal population was made, which was probably not too far from the truth. Now we will turn our attention to problems where the population distribution might take practically any form, and we will be concerned with determining the average value within certain confidence limits. Before discussing how this type of problem is approached, some of the basic theory should be discussed, although we cannot digress long enough to develop proofs.

The Central Limit Theorem is regarded as the most important in statistics: *If simple random samples of sufficiently large size are drawn from almost any population, the sampling distribution of the sample means, $\bar{X}$'s, is approximately normal.*

Individual sample values tend to be distributed as the population is distributed, but the distribution of sample means $\bar{X}$ takes on the form of the normal distribution.

The arithmetic mean of the sample means, $\bar{\bar{X}}$ (*X double bar*), tends to be the same as the arithmetic mean of the population, μ.

$$\mu \cong \bar{\bar{X}} \cong \frac{\Sigma \bar{X}}{N^*}$$

(N^* is the number of samples, not the number of items.)

In other words, we do not need to total all the individual values, but can total the mean of the samples.

The standard deviation of the sampling distribution $S_{\bar{x}}$ is:

$$S_{\bar{x}} = \sqrt{\frac{\Sigma(\bar{X} - \bar{\bar{X}})^2}{N^*}}$$

The standard deviation, $S_{\bar{x}}$, of the sampling distribution is an estimate of $\sigma_{\bar{x}}$. The relationship between the *standard error of the mean,* $\sigma_{\bar{x}}$, and the population standard deviation is given by the following for a finite population:

$$\sigma_{\bar{x}} = \frac{\sigma_x}{\sqrt{n}} \cdot \sqrt{\frac{N-n}{N-1}}$$

(N is the population size; n the sample size.)

As the population grows larger and larger, the value under the second radical, called the *finite correction factor,* approaches 1. If the portion sampled does not exceed 5 percent of the population, the equation can be simplified by dropping out the correction factor, resulting in the equation:

$$\sigma_{\bar{x}} = \frac{\sigma_x}{\sqrt{n}}$$

The tendency of the means of samples to form a normal distribution is a most convenient characteristic because we can turn to the normal distribution tables, as illustrated, and bring forth all sorts of information from which to make decisions. And this is what we will do now.

A washing-machine company, planning its future sales of replacement

Figure 6–10

Time before First Service

Service Time (X = Years to nearest one-half year)

X	X^2	X	X^2	X	X^2
3.5	12.25	5.5	30.25	7.0	49.00
0.0	0.0	7.0	49.00	2.0	4.00
1.5	2.25	2.5	6.25	.5	.25
5.5	30.25	1.5	2.25	1.0	1.00
4.0	16.00	8.5	72.25	6.0	36.00
7.5	56.25	0.0	0.00	.5	.25
2.0	4.0	3.0	9.00	3.0	9.00
4.5	20.25	8.5	72.25	4.0	16.00
6.0	36.00	0.0	0.00	5.5	30.25
8.0	64.00	6.0	36.00	6.5	42.25
9.0	81.00	4.5	20.25	5.0	25.00
7.5	56.25	4.5	20.25	9.0	81.00
5.5	30.25	6.5	42.25	5.0	25.00
2.5	6.25	5.0	25.00	4.5	20.25
3.0	9.00	2.5	6.25	6.0	36.00

$\bar{X} = \Sigma X/n = 201.0/45 = 4.47$ years

$S_x = \sqrt{\Sigma X^2/n - (\Sigma X/n)^2} = \sqrt{\frac{1190.5}{45} - \left(\frac{201.0}{45}\right)^2} = \sqrt{6.46} = 2.54$ years

$S_{\bar{x}} = S_x/\sqrt{n} = 2.54/\sqrt{45} = 2.54/6.72 = .38$

And since $\bar{X}$ is a good estimate of $\bar{\bar{X}}$, which is a good estimate of μ, the limits are:

Upper limit $= 4.47 + 3 \times .38 = 5.61$ years
Lower limit $= 4.47 - 3 \times .38 = 3.33$ years

parts, wishes to know the average number of years that a particular machine has been used before being serviced for the first time. It is obviously impossible for the company to obtain this information from the ten thousand customers who have bought the machines, so it must resort to a sampling technique.

The company is able to obtain information from a sample of 45 (as shown in Figure 6–10). If it were possible to get numerous samples, the average of the averages, $\bar{\bar{X}}$, of the samples would tend to be the same as the average for the population mean, μ. The problem is how far away from the sample mean is the population mean if we wish to be right in estimating μ 95 percent of the time?

The reasoning behind the solution to this problem can be shown better graphically (Figure 6–11). The diagram, Figure 6–11*a*, represents the distribution of $\bar{X}$ values, the $\bar{\bar{X}}$ being an estimate of the true mean, μ. If our particular sample has an $\bar{X}$ value (shown in Figure 6–11*b*), it is possible to add confidence limits of any size to either side as shown. For a confidence interval of 95 percent, the confidence limits would be $2\sigma_{\bar{x}}$ either side of $\bar{\bar{X}}$. This means that, by chance alone, we can be sure the interval $\bar{\bar{X}} \pm 2\sigma_{\bar{x}}$ includes μ 95 percent of the time and 5 percent of the time it will not. This latter situation of being outside is illustrated in Figure 6–11c.

Figure 6–11

Establishing Confidence Limits

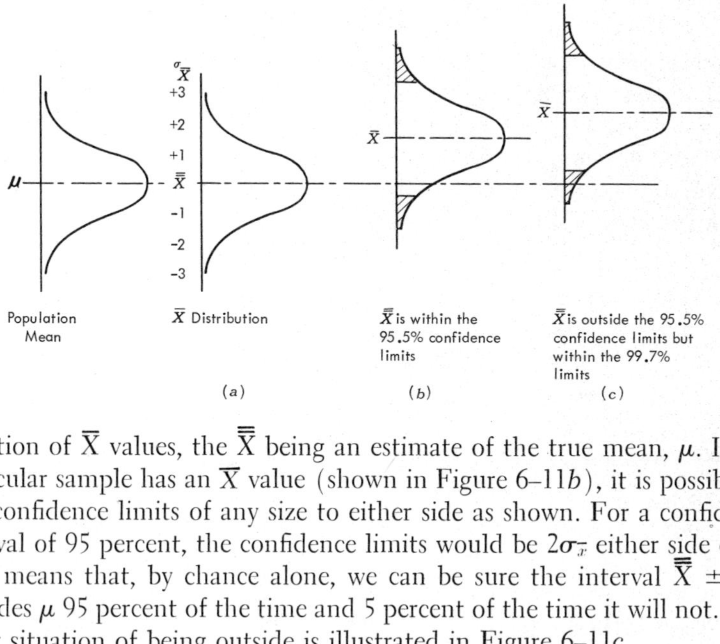

Any confidence limits may be chosen. As you will recall, $\pm 3\sigma_{\bar{x}}$ will give a 99.73 percent confidence, and any other values can be chosen from the table of Z values.

Continuing with the data for the washing-machine example, you will find the calculations for the sample mean, $\bar{X}$, and the standard deviation of the sample, S_x, in the previous table. The sample standard deviation, S_x, is an estimate of the population standard deviation, σ_x.

We are 99.73 percent sure that the interval 3.33–5.61 includes μ. Notice that the spread depends upon the assurance desired, as expressed by 3 for the Z value, and also the size of the sample. The confidence limits decrease as the sample size becomes larger.

THE BINOMIAL DISTRIBUTION

The probability distribution discussed applies to information which can be classified quantitatively. But there are also methods of handling qualitative information, such as defective or nondefective parts, yes or no answers on a questionnaire, and other similar evaluations. The binomial distribution, first recognized by Bernoulli, applies to phenomena which can be classified qualitatively into two classes, and it is closely related to the binomial theorem you studied in high school.

One seldom finds coin-tossing as an industrial process, at least during working hours, but it does serve a useful means of explaining industrial processes. Therefore assume a perfect coin, that will fall, when tossed, heads up (H) half the time, and tails up (T) the other half. The probability (p) of throwing a head is one chance in two, expressed as $\frac{1}{2}$ or .50.

If two coins are thrown, the possible outcomes are: HH, HT, TH, and TT. Even though the probability of a head or tail for each toss is equal, the probability of the combinations are obviously not. The probability is the ratio of the occurrence of a particular outcome to the sum of all possible outcomes. This is more readily seen by a tabulation (Figure 6–12). Since order is not important, HT is the same as TH.

Figure 6–12

Probabilities for Binomial

Tossing Two Coins

Possible Outcomes	*HH*		*HT*		*TT*		
Number of heads, *X*	2		1		0		
Probabilities, *p*	1/4	+	2/4	+	1/4	=	1
	25%	+	50%	+	25%	=	100%

Tossing Three Coins

Possible Outcomes	*HHH*		*HHT*		*HTT*		*TTT*		
			HTH		*THT*				
			THH		*TTH*				
Number of heads, *X*	3		2		1		0		
Probabilities, *p*	1/8	+	3/8	+	3/8	+	1/8	=	1
	12.5%	+	37.5%	+	37.5%	+	12.5%	=	100%

The word *success* is used as a convenient way of indicating the occurrence of an event, which in this example will be a head, while *failure* is used to indicate that an event did not occur. Let p denote the probability that a success will occur and q the probability that a failure will occur. Since either a success or a failure must occur, $p + q = 1$. From this it is apparent that the sum of all outcomes must equal one. The values in the table could have been obtained by expanding the binomial $(p + q)^n$. The n is the number of trials.

Since in this case $p = \frac{1}{2}$ and $q = \frac{1}{2}$, we can expand the binomial:

For 2 coins:

$$(p + q)^n = p^2 + 2pq + q^2 = 1/4 + 2/4 + 1/4 = 1$$

For 3 coins:

$$(p + q)^n = p^3 + 3p^2q + 3pq^2 + q^3 = 1/8 + 3/8 + 3/8 + 1/8 = 1$$

These distributions are shown graphically in Figure 6–13.

Figure 6–13

Binomial Distribution

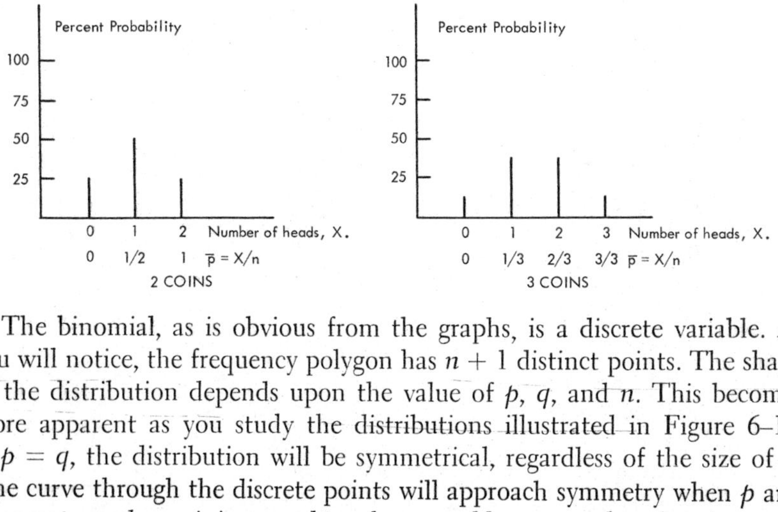

The binomial, as is obvious from the graphs, is a discrete variable. As you will notice, the frequency polygon has $n + 1$ distinct points. The shape of the distribution depends upon the value of p, q, and n. This becomes more apparent as you study the distributions illustrated in Figure 6–14. If $p = q$, the distribution will be symmetrical, regardless of the size of n. The curve through the discrete points will approach symmetry when p and q are *not equal*, as n is increased to a larger and larger number. As n increases without limit, the binomial approaches the normal curve which we have discussed. In fact, if $p = q$, and n is greater than 20, a normal curve is considered a good approximation and the same tables can be used as were used for the normal distribution. Special tables are available for samples smaller than 20.

The binomial distribution, like other distributions, has a mean and a standard deviation. While the mean can be calculated in the usual method, a more direct way is available.[2]

$$\mu = np$$

[2] John Neter and W. Wasserman, *Fundamental Statistics for Business and Economics* (Boston: Allyn and Bacon, Inc., 1961), p. 306.

Figure 6–14

Binomial Probability Distribution for Different Sizes of *p* and *n*

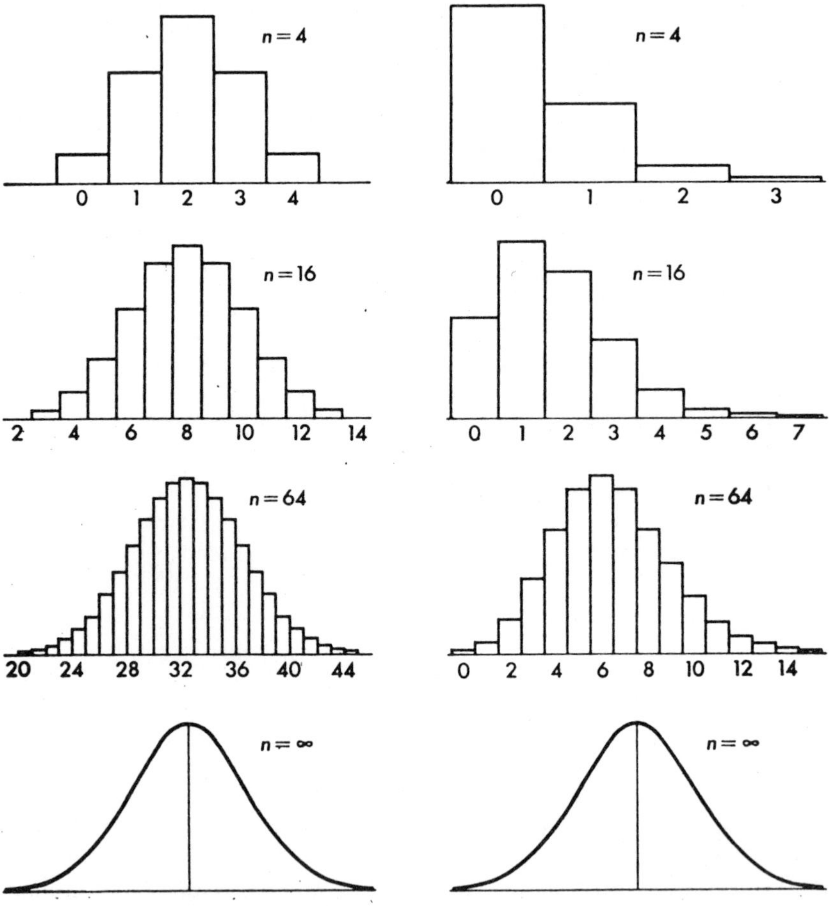

Binomial probability distribution, $p = 0.5$.

Binomial probability distribution, $p = 0.1$.

Applied Business and Economic Statistics, Ya-Lun Chou; Holt Rinehart & Winston

And the standard deviation of the X's is:

$$\sigma_x = \sqrt{npq}$$

By following the logic of establishing confidence limits for normally distributed data, a set of confidence limits can also be established for the yes–no type of information.

DISTRIBUTION OF SAMPLE PROPORTIONS

The X and the σ_x in the previous discussion indicated that our interest was in the *number* of X's, but more often, as in work measurement, our interest is in the *proportion* of X's.

Figure 6–13 will give us an insight to a useful relationship between X and the sample proportion X/n, referred to as $\bar{p}$ (read *p bar*). Notice in the coin flipping, using two coins, that the proportion X/n has values of 0, ½, and 2/2, which coincide with the occurrence of X equal to 0, 1, and 2. The same coincidence occurs for the illustration using three coins, and, for that matter, any other number of coins. This means, fortunately, that we can resort to the normal curve when making predictions under certain conditions, as described when discussing the distribution of X's.

Our interest is in predicting the population proportion and appropriate confidence limits. The sample proportion, $\bar{p}$, is a good point estimate of the population proportion. Since the sampling distribution of $\bar{p}$ is approximately normal for large samples, we can determine the confidence interval by a method similar to the one described before:

$$\text{Confidence interval} = \bar{p} \pm Z\sigma_{\bar{p}}$$

The standard deviation, $\sigma_{\bar{p}}$, for the sampling distribution of $\bar{p}$, can be expressed:

$$\sigma_{\bar{p}} = \sqrt{\frac{\bar{p}(1-\bar{p})}{n}}$$

The reader can envision how this logic can be applied to a problem of polling customers where the only available answers are yes's and no's. An application of the foregoing equations will be found in Chapter 9 which takes up determining time values where they are applied to *work sampling*.

A knowledge of the binomial is essential in order to understand the other distributions more fully. Its application is in the area where qualitative answers, yes–no, accept–reject, working–nonworking, are available.

The normal and binomial distributions, along with the Poisson, are considered classical distributions. The Poisson distribution is the limit of the binomial distribution when p is very small and n is very large. The distribution has been called the *law of improbable events* because it may be used to describe the behavior when the occurrence of an event is rare. The Poisson distribution has applications in the analysis of queues—that is, queueing theory—and in inventory problems.

The subject of sampling has been introduced because of its importance in forecasting in its own right. It is also basic to the more sophisticated techniques to come.

STATISTICS OF ASSOCIATION

Up to this point we have discussed data with only one variable, commonly called *univariate* data. Next we are concerned with determining associations among things. This should not alarm you, for you probably make a number of decisions each day by association. For example, you know there is some relationship between the number of fish in a lake and the number of fish you catch, and consequently you usually try to fish in lakes where there is a large number of fish.

There are two common statistical techniques used in the analysis of bivariate data:

Regression Analysis: The derivation of a numerical relationship between two or more groups of data. The objective is to predict the value of one variable from the value of another variable.

Correlation Analysis: This is the measurement of the *degree* of relationship among the variables under consideration.

Frequently, these two subjects, regression analysis and correlation analysis, are grouped under one title, *correlation*. If the relationship is between just two sets of data, it is referred to as a *simple correlation* or *simple regression analysis*; but when more sets of variables are under consideration it is referred to as a *multiple correlation* or *multiple regression analysis*. Both regression and correlation analysis techniques will be developed in the coming sections.

REGRESSION ANALYSIS

In the simple regression analysis we attempt to derive a numerical relationship between two groups of matched observations, so by having information about one we can predict the value of the other. The variable to be predicted is referred to as the *dependent variable*, while the value used in predicting is called the *independent variable*.

Regression analysis is a sophisticated but meaningless name for this technique because *regress* means the act of going or coming back, which is the way a characteristic between fathers and sons behaved in an early statistical study. Since that time this word has been applied to all relationships like the one just mentioned. Meaningful or not, we are stuck with this name.

We will progress from the simplest form of regression study to relatively complicated methods. Before deriving a numerical relationship, it should be mentioned that a great deal of forecasting can be done without any knowledge of mathematical regression techniques by merely extending an appropriate line through the data by inspection (as shown in Figure 6–15).

Figure 6–15

Regression by Inspection

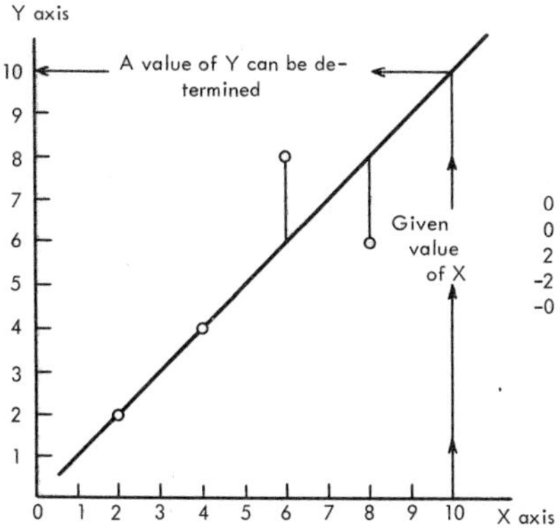

	Points	X	Y
0	1	2	2
0	2	4	4
2	3	6	8
-2	4	8	6
-0	5	10	10
		30	30

The points representing the data form a scatter diagram or *scattergram*. If the line is properly drawn, the sum of the negative vertical deviations will just equal the sum of the positive vertical deviations. Now it is apparent that we can predict the value of Y for any value of X, and we can even extend our prediction beyond the array of points, if we are willing to assume certain risks.

The Regression Equation by Inspection

An equation for a trend line gives a concise statement of the trend, making it possible to predict values of the dependent variable without tedious plotting. This is highly desirable when you are asking a computer to do the dirty work. An equation also makes it possible to isolate and study different causes and effects.

As we determine the location of a geographical point by describing how far north and how far east it is from some known point, so can we tell the location of a point on a straight line (Figure 6–16) by describing how many X units and how many Y units it is from the origin. For example, P_1 is X_1 and Y_1 distances from the origin.

The equation for the line tells us the relationship between these distances as the point moves along the line. Given one value, we can solve the equation for the other. One method of developing the equation for the line is by considering the similar triangles, *A* and *B*. The short side of one triangle is to its long side as the short side of the other triangle is to its long side, which can be said more conveniently in this form:

$$\frac{Y_1 - a}{X_1} = \frac{2}{3}$$

$$Y_1 = a + 2/3\, X_1$$

Figure 6–16

Regression Equation by Inspection

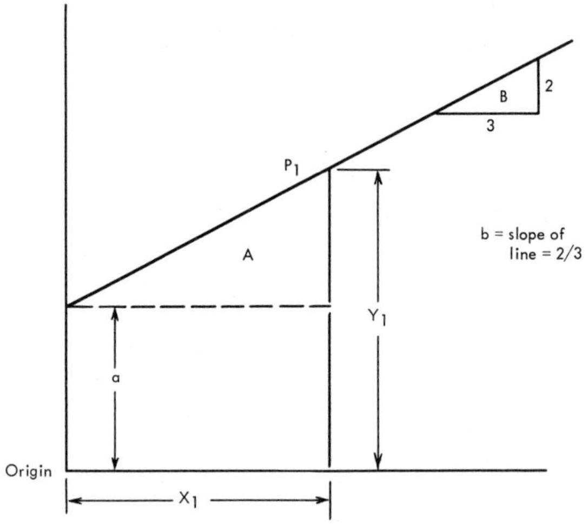

It is apparent that a is the intercept of the line with the Y axis when X is zero and b is the slope of the line. So the generalized equation can be written:

$$Y = a + bX$$

The a and b are called the *regression coefficients.*

This equation is no better than the line which we drew. We have a still better, if more tedious, way to develop the equation, which will assure the best fit, in the *least squares* sense.

Regression Equation by Least Squares

In fitting the line by eye, remember that we tried to put the line through the scattergram so the sum of the positive deviations from the line would just equal the sum of the negative deviations.

When either positive or negative numbers are multiplied by themselves (squared), they produce positive numbers. So, if all the deviations from the line are squared, they become positive, and the problem is no longer to offset negative against positive but to minimize the total. The *least squares method,* as the name indicates, attempts to make the total of all the deviations squared, the minimum or least value. This is easy to envision, in Figure 6–17, when we observe that the objective is to minimize the areas of the squares.

The heart of this method is to determine the regression coefficients a and b under the following conditions:

Figure 6–17

Regression Equation by Least Squares

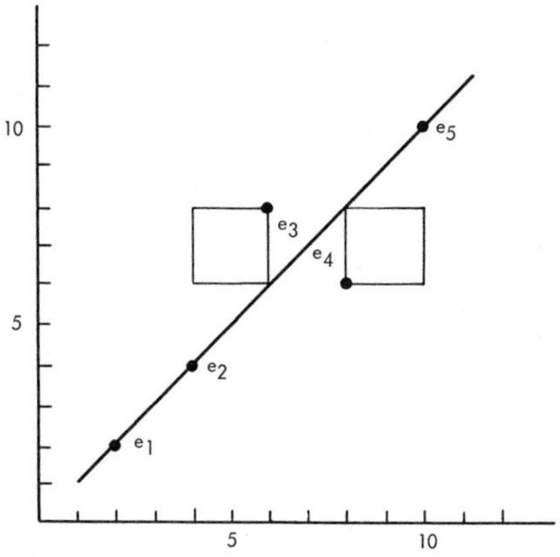

Point	e values
1	0
2	0
3	+2
4	-2
5	0

1. The sum of the vertical deviations from the regression line equal zero. That is, all the plus deviations above the line should just equal all the negative deviations.
2. The deviations, e, from the regression line, when squared, e^2, and summed, $\sum_1^N e^2$, must be less than for any other straight line that might be drawn through the points. The conditions for *1*, above, are met when the condition for this part is satisfied.

As you can see on the last figure, e is the difference between the plotted value, Y, and the calculated value on the line, Y_c. Our objective, of course, is to minimize the sum of all the squares of these differences. Starting with the equation for the line, we can put it into terms of the error, e, by this method:

$$Y_c = a + bX$$

Y_c is the calculated value. Multiply both sides of the equation by -1.

$$-Y_c = -a - bX$$

Add Y to both sides:

$$(Y - Y_c) = -a - bX + Y$$

since $e = (Y - Y_c)$, and we wish to sum all of the squares of the e's.

$$\sum_1^N (e^2) = \sum_1^N (Y - Y_c)^2 = \sum_1^N (Y - a - bX)^2$$

We can minimize the value of the error term by taking the first derivative and setting it to zero,[3] first taking the derivative with respect to a:

---

[3] This method is used again in Chapter 8 for optimizing lot sizes.

$$\frac{\partial\left(\sum_{1}^{N} e^2\right)}{\partial a} = -2\sum_{1}^{N}(Y - a - bX)$$

$$0 = -2\sum_{1}^{N}(Y - a - bX)$$

The −2 can be disposed of by dividing both sides by −2. It is understood that all deviations, $e_1, e_2 \ldots e_n$, will be considered, so we can omit the interval of the summation sign, Σ. Also, when a constant is summed over N observations, it is just the same as multiplying the constant by N. We can just say Na instead of Σa. This leads to a much cleaner way of writing the equation just given:

$$0 = \Sigma Y - Na - b\Sigma X$$
$$\Sigma Y = Na + b\Sigma X$$

The equation in this last form is called the *first normal equation*. Going through the same procedure for the regression coefficient b:

$$\sum_{1}^{N} e^2 = \sum_{1}^{N}(Y - a - bX)^2$$

$$\frac{\partial \sum_{1}^{N} e^2}{\partial b} = -2\sum_{1}^{N}(Y - a - bX)(X)$$

$$\sum_{1}^{N} YX = a\sum_{1}^{N} X + b\sum_{1}^{N} X^2$$

$$\Sigma YX = a\Sigma X + b\Sigma X^2$$

This is the *second normal equation*.

We could determine the regression coefficients, and consequently the estimating equation from the normal equation above, but it would be tedious. So it is better if we have a short cut. This will be discussed by means of an example.

An Application of Regression Analysis

Before continuing with the development of statistics, an application of regression analysis will be useful to create a better understanding.

The problem is to obtain an equation for a best fit line, in the least squares sense, from which we can extrapolate information. This means finding the values for a and b for the normal equations, using the simultaneous equation solution. This is not a very enjoyable prospect when there are many large values, so let us explore a short cut and shift the axis to the mean value of X and Y.

1. Express X and Y as deviations, x and y, from their respective means:

$$\Sigma y = Na + b\Sigma x$$
$$\Sigma xy = a\Sigma x + b\Sigma x^2$$

2. The sums of the deviations from their means are zero, so:

$$\Sigma y = 0 \text{ and } \Sigma x = 0,$$

which means that these terms will drop out of the equation, and therefore the second equation becomes:

$$\Sigma xy = b\Sigma x^2$$

$$b = \frac{\Sigma xy}{\Sigma x^2},$$

which gives the slope of the line which is one of the regression coefficients.

3. For the value of *a*, the other regression coefficient, insert the value *b* in the first equation, $\Sigma Y = Na + b\Sigma X$. This can be written in a more convenient form:

$$a = \overline{Y} - b\overline{X}$$

4. Σxy and Σx^2 for determining *b* can be derived directly from the values of X and Y.[4]

$$\Sigma xy = \Sigma XY - \frac{(\Sigma X)(\Sigma Y)}{N}$$

$$\Sigma x^2 = \Sigma X^2 - \frac{(\Sigma X)^2}{N}$$

This short cut method can now be used to solve a forecasting problem.

The information shown in Figure 6–18 is for a particular industry's domestic sales versus the disposable income.[5] With an available prediction of disposable income, it is possible to predict the domestic sales. This company, knowing its share of the domestic sales, can predict its sales for any given forecast of disposable income. The information given is tabulated in the first two columns of Figure 6–19.

The method of calculating the company's sales by the short-cut method is shown at the bottom of the table in Figure 6–19.

Dispersion about Regression Line

It is extremely doubtful that the forecasted figure will agree exactly with what actually transpires, and if it doesn't agree it would be desirable to know whether the disagreement could have come about by chance or whether it is the result of some assignable cause. This brings us to the development of a confidence interval, sometimes called a confidence band, for the calculated regression line.

The vertical distance between the actual Y value and the calculated Y value, Y_c, is $(Y - Y_c)$. These differences form a distribution about the

[4] Robert Ferber, *Statistical Techniques in Market Research* (New York: McGraw-Hill Book Co., Inc., 1949).

[5] Example taken from "What Management Expects of Forecasting," B. E. Estes, Director of Commercial Research, U.S. Steel Corp., *Sales Forecasting, Special Report 16,* American Management Association, 1515 Broadway, New York 36, N.Y.

Figure 6–18

Domestic Sales versus Disposable Income

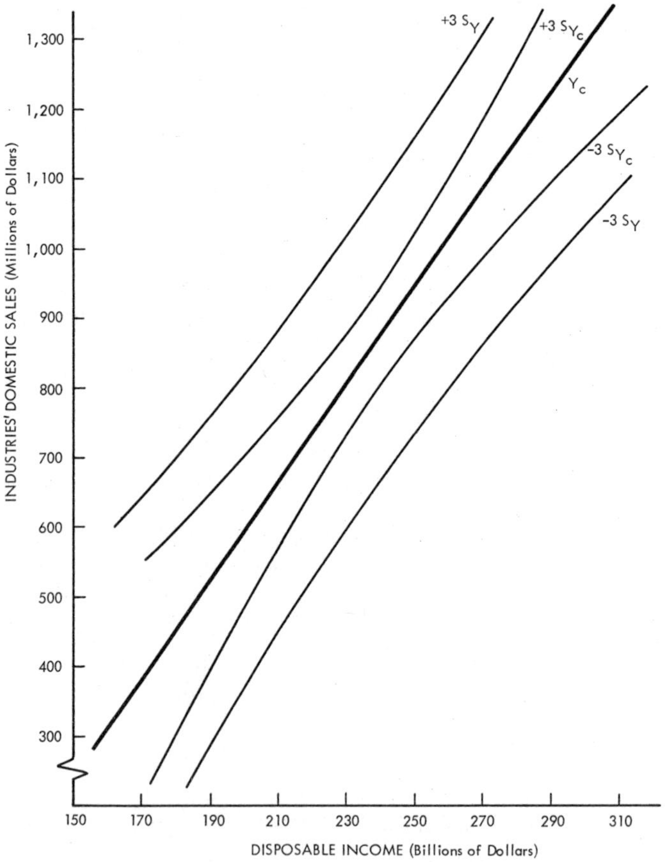

regression line analogous to the standard deviation about the mean, but it bears the name, *standard error of the estimate,* $S_{y \cdot x}$.

$$S_{y \cdot x} = \sqrt{\frac{\Sigma(Y - Y_c)^2}{N - 2}}$$

The standard error of the estimate is often mistakenly used to develop confidence bands, represented by the parallel lines $Y_c \pm tS_{y \cdot x}$. The multiplier, *t*, is used rather than Z because we are concerned with a small sample. This would be correct only if there was assurance that the calculated line was the true regression line. Remember, the line itself is calculated from a sample and is subject to sampling errors.

The error in the line is expressed in the variances of the two regression coefficients in the linear equation. In fact, the variance of Y_c for a given

Figure 6–19

Industry Domestic Sales versus Disposable Income

Y Sales (Billion Dollars)	X Disposable Income (Billion Dollars)	XY	Y^2	X^2
.435	181.6	78.996	.189225	32,978.6
.621	206.1	127.988	.385641	42,477.2
.819	226.1	185.176	.670761	51,121.2
.879	236.7	208.059	.772641	56,026.9
.933	250.4	233.623	.870489	62,700.2
.970	254.8	247.156	.940900	64,923.0
1.070	274.0	293.180	1.144900	75,076.0
1.180	284.0	335.120	1.392400	80,656.0
$\Sigma Y = 6.907$	$\Sigma X = 1913.7$	$\Sigma XY = 1709.299$	$\Sigma Y^2 = 6.366957$	$\Sigma X^2 = 465{,}959.1$
$N = 8$				

$$b = \frac{\Sigma xy}{\Sigma x^2} = \frac{\Sigma XY - \dfrac{(\Sigma X)(\Sigma Y)}{N}}{\Sigma X^2 - \dfrac{(\Sigma X)^2}{N}}$$

$$\Sigma XY = 1709.299$$

$$\frac{(\Sigma X)(\Sigma Y)}{N} = \frac{1913.7 \times 6.907}{8} = 1652.223$$

$$\Sigma xy = 57.076$$

$$\Sigma X^2 = 465959.1$$

$$\frac{(\Sigma X)^2}{N} = \frac{(1913.7)^2}{8} = 457780.9$$

$$\Sigma x^2 = 8178.2$$

$$b = \frac{57.076}{8178.2} = .0069$$

$$a = \overline{Y} - b\overline{X} = \frac{6.907}{8} - .0069 \times \frac{1913.7}{8}$$

$$= .863 - 1.670 = -.807 \text{ billion or } -807 \text{ million}$$

value of X, X_p, is the sum of the variances due to the coefficients in the regression model $(Y_c - \overline{Y}_c) = a + b(X - \overline{X})$.

$$S^2_{Y_c} = \frac{S^2_{y \cdot x}}{N} + \frac{S^2_{y \cdot x}(X_p - \overline{X})^2}{\Sigma(X - \overline{X})^2}$$

$$= \frac{S^2_{y \cdot x}}{N} + \frac{S^2_{y \cdot x}\, x^2_p}{\Sigma x^2}$$

$$S_{Y_c} = S_{y \cdot x}\sqrt{\frac{1}{N} + \frac{(X_p - \overline{X})^2}{\Sigma(X - \overline{X})^2}} = S_{y \cdot x}\sqrt{\frac{1}{N} + \frac{x^2_p}{\Sigma x^2}}$$

where:

$$\frac{S^2_{y \cdot x}}{N} = \text{variance for the regression coefficient } a$$

$$\frac{S^2_{y \cdot x}}{\Sigma x^2} = \text{variance for the regression coefficient } b$$

For large samples of 30 or more, any desired confidence level for Y_c can be established by multiplying S_{y_c} by an appropriate Z value (as was illustrated in Figure 6–10). Plus or minus $3S_{y_c}$ would give a confidence band of 99.7 percent, while $2S_{y_c}$ would give a confidence band of 95.45 percent. For example, the 99.7 percent confidence band for Y_c is:

$$Y_c \pm 3\,S_{y\cdot x}\sqrt{\frac{1}{N}+\frac{(X_p-\overline{X})^2}{\Sigma(X-\overline{X})^2}},\ \text{or,}\ Y_c \pm 3\,S_{y\cdot x}\sqrt{\frac{1}{N}+\frac{x^2_p}{\Sigma x^2}}$$

The x^2_p is the square of the X_p value being estimated in deviation units. The Σx^2 and N are for the whole sample and remain the same for all calculations of S_{y_c}.

The confidence band for the individual Y's is even wider, as it includes the variance $S^2_{y\cdot x}$ around the regression line. So the variance for the Y's is:

$$S^2_y = S^2_{y\cdot x} + \frac{S^2_{y\cdot x}}{N} + \frac{S^2_{y\cdot x}(X_p-\overline{X})^2}{\Sigma(X-\overline{X})^2},\ \text{or,}\ S^2_{y\cdot x} + \frac{S^2_{y\cdot x}}{N} + \frac{S^2_{y\cdot x}\,x^2_p}{\Sigma x^2}$$

And it follows that the 99.7 percent confidence band for Y is:

$$Y_c \pm 3\,S_{y\cdot x}\sqrt{1+\frac{1}{N}+\frac{(X_p-\overline{X})^2}{\Sigma(X-\overline{X})^2}},\ \text{or,}\ Y_c \pm 3\,S_{y\cdot x}\sqrt{1+\frac{1}{N}+\frac{x_p{}^2}{\Sigma x^2}}$$

The development of the confidence bands, so far, has been based on a large sample, and it was appropriate to use Z values. In the example illustrated, Domestic Sales versus Disposable Income, the sample cannot be considered large, so we must modify the confidence bands to account for the small sample. This may be done by using the *t* distribution, which is applicable where only small samples are available. The *t* tables are used in a way which is similar to the table of Z values except to enter the table it is necessary to know the acceptable confidence level and the degrees of freedom in the equations. The degrees of freedom are $N - 2$ because there are two regression coefficients.

The method of calculating $S_{y\cdot x}$ has been passed over lightly but you can see that finding $(Y - Y_c)$ for all the points would be a most tedious task. Fortunately, $S_{y\cdot x}$ can be found directly from the values of Y and X:

$$S_{y\cdot x} = \sqrt{\frac{\Sigma Y^2 - a\Sigma Y - b\Sigma XY}{N-2}}$$

For a small sample, a better answer is obtained if $N - 2$ is used in the denominator to account for the degrees of freedom lost in the regression coefficients.

The illustration of the data, Domestic Sales versus Disposable Income, with the bands for S_{y_c} and S_y, makes the difficulty of prediction appear obvious. Certainly parallel bands, $Y_c \pm 3S_{y\cdot x}$ would be of little help in a prediction. As is apparent, the farther one goes to the right of center the more questionable becomes the prediction.

Interpreting the information leads to some interesting observations. For example, the predicted value of sales when the disposable income reaches \$240 billion is \$868 million, with a range of plus or minus \$213 million for 99.7 percent confidence. The same values for \$300 billion is \$1,287 million, with a range of plus or minus \$251 million. It is apparent what the effect of the widening band has upon the prediction. When the band is too wide to be practical, one must work on reducing either $S_{y \cdot x}$ or the total variance of Y.

CORRELATION ANALYSIS

Correlation analysis is the other commonly used technique for evaluating the relationship between two groups of data. Recall, in the regression analysis just discussed, we were striving for a graphical or numerical relationship between the variables under consideration. However, at times, we are interested only in the degree of the relationship, without regard to the quantitative aspects.

In the last of the preceding section we developed the *standard error of estimate* as a measure of the closeness of the relationship. Shortcomings of that system are:

1. The standard error of estimate is an absolute measure of the relationship and has little meaning unless one is well acquainted with the data.
2. The standard error of estimate is in the same units as the data, so relationships based on units of different size or even units of different types cannot be compared.

The faults are overcome by the *coefficient of correlation*, r, or the closely related *coefficient of determination*, r^2, to be discussed in this section. These coefficients do not attempt to distinguish between dependent or independent variables, but present an abstract number.

These numbers are readily explained by Figure 6–20, which illustrates that the total sum of the squares of the deviations is equal to the explained sum of the squares of the deviations plus the unexplained sum of the squares of the deviations.

The coefficient of determination, r^2, is defined as:

$$r^2 = 1 - \frac{\text{Unexplained sum of squares}}{\text{Total sum of squares}}$$

$$r^2 = 1 - \frac{\Sigma(Y - Y_c)^2}{\Sigma(Y - \bar{Y})^2}$$

When the difference between the calculated value Y_c and the actual value Y, for all observations, becomes zero, the ratio between the unexplained and the total sum of squares becomes zero, yielding an r^2 value of 1. When X contributes no information about Y, the numerator and denomi-

Figure 6–20

Correlation Analysis

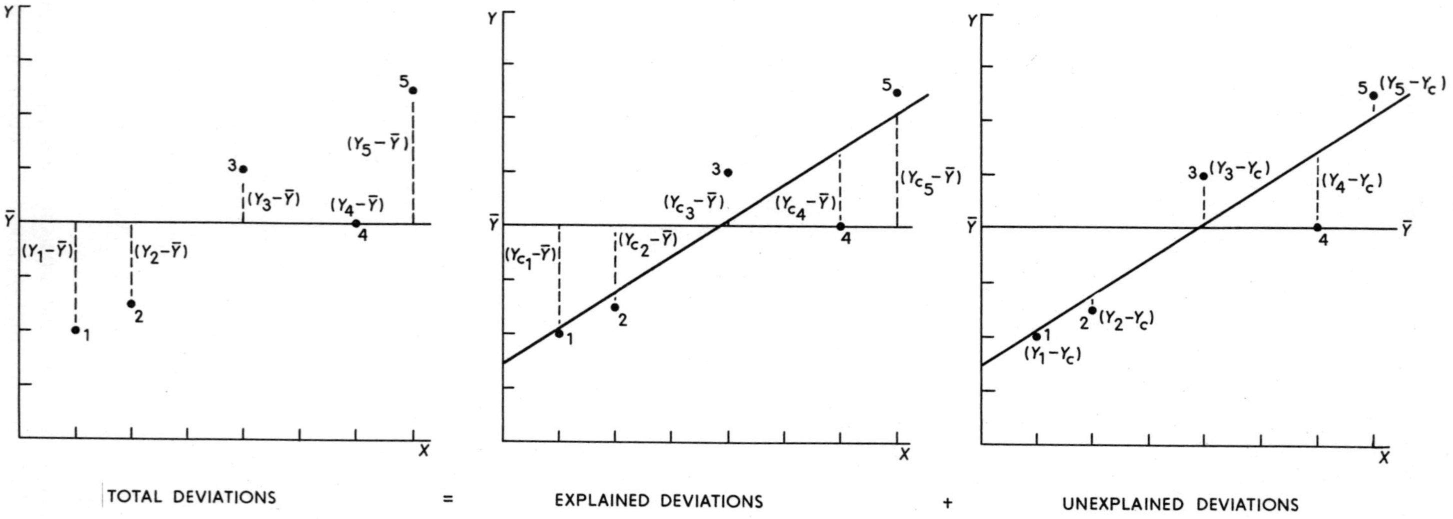

nator are equal, making the ratio between the unexplained and the total sum of squares equal to 1, which results in an r^2 value of 0.

This illustration should give you some comprehension of why r^2 can range between 0, indicating no relationship, to 1, indicating a perfect relationship. Its square root, r, the coefficient of correlation, can range between +1 to 0, to a −1, this latter indicating a perfect inverse relationship. This explanation has been limited to the situation of predicting Y from X. As you would expect, X could have been predicted from Y, which would complicate the explanation. Probably the best-known equations for obtaining the coefficient of correlation are these:

$$r = \frac{\Sigma xy}{\sqrt{\Sigma x^2 \Sigma y^2}}$$

This can be expressed in terms of the measured values:

$$r = \frac{\Sigma(X - \overline{X})(Y - \overline{Y})}{\sqrt{\Sigma(X - \overline{X})^2 \Sigma(Y - \overline{Y})^2}}$$

For ease in computing the coefficient of correlation, the following equation might be used:

$$r = \frac{N\Sigma XY - (\Sigma X)(\Sigma Y)}{\sqrt{[N\Sigma X^2 - (\Sigma X)^2][N\Sigma Y^2 - (\Sigma Y)^2]}}$$

This correlation measure can be used when we wish to determine the degree of relationship without any concern for the functional relationship. For example, if we had wished to determine the degree of relationship for the sales to disposable income, we could have used the correlation coefficient.

Examples of Correlation in Forecasting

Correlation has an interesting application where there are two series of events running side by side (as shown in Figure 6–21, top). The first might be called a synchronous series, while the second might be called a leading series.

These two relationships, where correlation can be found to be useful, are described more fully:

Synchronous Series: In this situation two series of events move together step by step. One series of events, perhaps a government index, is in itself a prediction which is available in advance of the time that the product forecast is needed. Relating these two values make it possible to predict sales from the index.

Leading Predictors: Frequently, a series of events leads the series being predicted (as in Figure 6–21, bottom). Croxton and Cowden[6] propose an ingenious way of solving such correlation problems:

1. Plot each of the series on separate transparent papers, making sure that the horizontal scale is the same for each.

[6] P. E. Croxton and D. J. Cowden, *Applied General Statistics* (2nd ed.; Englewood Cliffs, N.J.: Prentice-Hall, Inc., 1955).

Figure 6–21

Application of Correlation to Forecasting

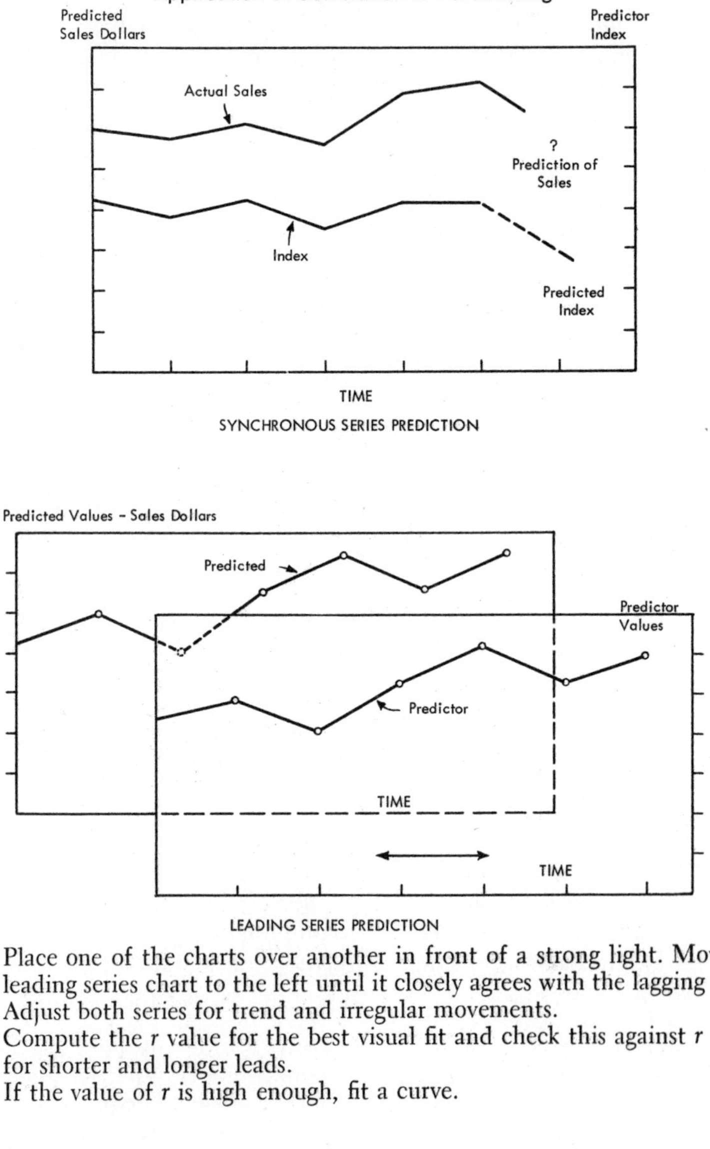

2. Place one of the charts over another in front of a strong light. Move the leading series chart to the left until it closely agrees with the lagging series.
3. Adjust both series for trend and irregular movements.
4. Compute the *r* value for the best visual fit and check this against *r* values for shorter and longer leads.
5. If the value of *r* is high enough, fit a curve.

TIME SERIES

There is one large area of statistical analysis in which the independent variable, on the horizontal axis, is time. A *time series* is chronological data which has some quantity, such as sales dollars, sales volume, or other information, as the dependent variable and units of time as the independent variable.

The movements or variations of the dependent variable can be divided into four distinct components which can be studied independently. These are called *trend, cyclical, seasonal,* and *irregular* variations. A more extensive description of the movements of the time series will be of value. Starting with the longest periods of movement:

Trend Variations: Changes which occur over a long period of years. When all the intermediate variations are not considered, a time series frequently shows a tendency to increase or decrease.

Cyclical Variations: These changes occur over a shorter period of years and show some evidence of periodicity. They can be compared with a pendulum or spring-mass system in the field of mechanics. As we all know, when a pendulum is set in motion it attempts to reach its point of equilibrium, but overshoots this position. In attempting to return to equilibrium, it again overshoots, and so goes through a series of vibrations until it finally attains the rest position. If there is an outside disturbance, this gyration can continue indefinitely. There may be several cycles with different time periods in effect at the same time, one superimposed upon the other. Industries would like to predict the cycles, and many attempts have been made to correlate them with phenomena such as weather and sun spots, but with little success.

Seasonal Variations: The most common periodic movement is the seasonal variation which occurs, with some degree of regularity, in the span of a year. These variations are caused by climate conditions, such as the effect of the sun and good weather on lawns, which in turn affects the sale of lawn mowers, fertilizers, lawn furniture, and similar commodities. Social customs have a strong influence, such as the effect of spring housecleaning on the sale of home furnishings, Christmas on the sale of toys, and Easter on the sale of hats. Attempts are made to iron out seasonal variations by building up demand for off-season use of the product or by manufacturing another product for off-season use.

Irregular Variations: These are movements which occur without any particular rhythm. They may be important enough to make a noticeable shift in the time series or they may be only temporary surges of no lasting importance. They can be correlated with some event, such as the start or end of a war, epidemic, or other crisis. They can also be caused by something as trivial as a scene in a movie, as when Clark Gable appeared in a movie sans underwear shirt, causing the sale of underwear shirts to go into a tailspin.

The four classifications of time series movements are of importance because we may wish to isolate one effect and study it alone; or we may also wish to remove one effect, such as a trend, to study the others.

The decomposition of the time series is accomplished by the model:

$$O = T \times C \times S \times I$$

where O equals the Observed value, T equals the Trend, C equals the Cycle, S equals the Seasonal, and I equals the Irregular.

An additive model is used at times, but the multiplicative model is preferred because it can be used with percentage changes rather than absolute changes.

Since this is a multiplicative model, it is only necessary to divide by the appropriate factor to remove its effect. For example, to de-trend the series, we can divide by T, so $O/T = T \times C \times S \times I/T$, or, to remove the effect of the cycle, $O/C = T \times C \times S \times I/C$.

The percentages used in these models are good examples of index numbers and are worthy of a separate discussion.

INDEX NUMBERS

Index numbers are a series of percentages showing change in price, quantity, or value, with reference to a base. The choice of the base is arbitrary but should usually be selected to give an unbiased picture. Often, but not necessarily, the base is for the first period or for the average of several of the initial periods. The numbers given here illustrate the development of index numbers.

Year	*1st*	*2nd*	*3rd*	*4th*
Sales	37	39	43	47 thousand
Base		39 (an arbitrary choice)		
	37/39	39/39	43/39	47/39
Index	95%	100%	110%	120%

Indexes are classified by the way they are formed:

Simple index: The example given is a typical simple index, one value divided by the base.

Simple aggregate index: Several values, such as the price of corn and wheat, are added and divided by the base period total. The result is multiplied by 100 to form a percentage.

Average of relatives index: Two or more indexes are added together and averaged.

Weighted aggregative index: In the average relative index, each component has an equal influence. In the weighted aggregative index, the statistician applies weighting factors to the components as he thinks necessary. Determining the weighting factors can be a study in itself.

The index plays an important part in forecasting as well as in the analysis of the economy. We are all aware of cost-of-living indexes, market indexes, and others. It is now time to put these concepts in their proper perspective by illustrating them with an example. The reader should not confuse this example, which has time as the independent variable, with the earlier example, which has disposable income as the independent variable.

EXAMPLE OF A FORECASTING PROBLEM

The example will proceed in steps:

1. The long-term forecast, Y_c = Trend.
2. Forecast modified by the influence of the cycle, Y_c = Trend × Cycle.
3. Short-term forecast to account for the seasonal Y_c = Trend × Cycle × Seasonal.

Step 1. Yearly Demand Forecast, Y_c = Trend

The yearly sales for a particular pharmaceutical product are shown graphically in Figure 6–22. The problem is to extend the information into the future and predict what the sales might be for any year. We can do this best by finding the regression equations for the best-fit line. From this can be predicted the value of Y, sales, for any value of X, years.

Figure 6–22

Yearly Sales of a Pharmaceutical Product

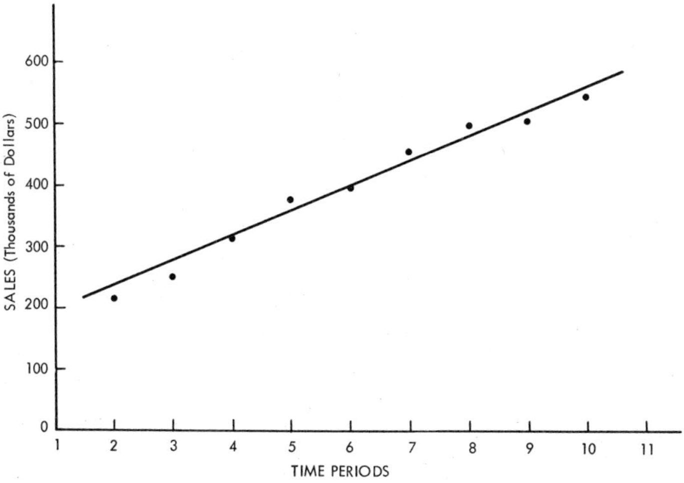

The solution of the problem is shown in Figure 6–23. The calculations are somewhat simplified over the previous example because any year we wish may be chosen for the origin. By taking the origin as the middle year, the sum of X values becomes zero. The normal equations become:

$$\Sigma Y = Na$$
$$\Sigma XY = b\Sigma X^2$$

The yearly sales, plotted on the graph, are shown in column 3 of the table. At the bottom of the table you will see the equations needed for determining the regression coefficients, *a* and *b*. As can be seen, the value of *a* is 394,300. Knowing this and the value of *b*, it is relatively easy to predict the value of Y_c for any year in the future. For example, the forecast for the twelfth year is:

$$Y_c = a + bx$$
$$Y_c = 394{,}300 + 39{,}879 \times 6$$
$$Y_c = 633{,}574 \text{ dollars}$$

Figure 6–23

Data for the Yearly Sales for a Pharmaceutical Product

(1) Year	(2) x Deviations (One-Year Units)	(3) Y Sales-TCI-\$	(4) xY	(5) x^2
1	−5	204,875	−1,024,375	25
2	−4	219,190	−876,760	16
3	−3	252,324	−756,972	9
4	−2	317,258	−634,516	4
5	−1	372,356	−372,356	1
6	0	402,140	0	0
7	+1	451,020	+451,020	1
8	+2	480,010	+960,020	4
9	+3	503,060	+1,509,180	9
10	+4	543,870	+2,175,480	16
11	+5	591,200	+2,956,000	25
$N = 11$	$\Sigma x = 0$	$\Sigma Y = 4{,}337{,}303$	$\Sigma xY = +4{,}386{,}721$	$\Sigma x^2 = 110$

Calculations for a	Calculations for b	Calculations for Y_c
$a = \Sigma Y/N$	$b = \Sigma xY/\Sigma x^2$	$Y_c = a + bx$
$a = \dfrac{4{,}337{,}303}{11}$	$b = \dfrac{4{,}386{,}721}{110}$	$Y_c = 394{,}300 + 39{,}879x$
		x = years
$a = 394{,}300$	$b = 39{,}879$	Y = dollars
		Origin: July 1, 6th year.

Step 2. Yearly Demand Modified for Cycle Variation: Y_c = Trend x Cycle

As we have noted, there is a cyclic variation imposed upon the long-term trend, so it would seem obvious that the value obtained for the example so far should be modified for the effect of the cycle.

If a general business forecast predicts an increase or decrease of activity, we can modify the trend by:

$$\text{Trend} \times \text{Cycle} = \text{Forecast}$$

Obtaining the value for the cycle variation is a statistical task in itself, but for the example assume the value for next year will be +4 percent:

$$633{,}574 \times 104\% = 658{,}917 \text{ dollars}$$

Step 3. Short-Term Forecast to Account for Seasonal: Y_c = Trend x Seasonal x Cycle

Those responsible for the day-to-day operations of a factory will be interested in short-term forecasts for determining inventories, labor, and other needs. The monthly forecasts can be made by fitting a trend line to the monthly data, but this would be tedious and unnecessary as it is possible to adjust the yearly trend line. Starting with the trend line, $Y_c = a + bx$, developed for the yearly forecast, it can be modified for monthly forecasts:

The a value, the arithmetic mean of the annual total, is divided by 12 to obtain the mean of the monthly total.

The value of b must be divided by 12 × 12. This can be explained in this way. Dividing b by 12 reflects the annual increase in the monthly data. Dividing by 12 again, we have the monthly increase per month.

The revised equation is:

$$Y_c = a/12 + bx/12 \times 12$$

It is simple enough to calculate the monthly forecast, but there is the problem of determining the correct x value for any given month. First, examine the position of the origin.

For a trend line fitted to an *odd* number of years, the origin is *centered* on July 1st of the middle year.

For a trend line fitted to an *even* number of years, the origin is centered on January 1st, dividing the years.

An example will show how the value of x is determined. Let us assume that we wish to know the value for the month of October of the twelfth year.

From July 1st to January 1st	6	months
From January 1st of the 7th year to January 1st of the 12th year	60	"
From January 1st of the 12th year to October 1st of the 12th year	9	"
From October 1st to middle of October	.5	"
$x =$	75.5	months

Inserting this value of x into the equation for trend, the value for October can be estimated:

$$Y_c = a/12 + bx/144$$
$$Y_c = 394{,}300/12 + 39{,}879 \times 75.5/144$$
$$Y_c = 52.244 \text{ dollars}$$

This value for the month of October has not been adjusted for cyclical changes. Applying the cycle variation:

$$Y_c = 52{,}244 \times 104\%$$
$$Y_{c\,\text{Oct.}} = 54{,}334 \text{ dollars}$$

Since the irregular variations cannot be forecast, it is only possible to add the seasonal variation. Obtaining a seasonal index can be done by following the steps shown in Figure 6–24. The sales for each month of the previous year are given in column 2. These are totaled and then averaged. The average forms the base for this index. It would be better if several years had been used in developing the index, but this will illustrate the idea. The next step is to adjust the forecast in the last example for the seasonal variation:

$$\text{Forecast} = \text{Trend} \times \text{Seasonal} \times \text{Cycle}$$
$$\text{Forecast} = 54{,}334 \times 119.6\%$$
$$\text{Forecast} = 64{,}983 \text{ dollars}$$

Figure 6–24

Monthly Sales Index

Month *Column 1*		*Sales/Month (Nearest $100)* *Column 2*	*Index* *Column 3*
1	Jan.	39,300	79.8%
2	Feb.	44,700	90.7
3	March	46,300	94.0
4	April	49,200	99.9
5	May	49,800	101.1
6	June	49,100	99.7
7	July	58,200	118.1
8	Aug.	68,100	138.2
9	Sept.	57,100	115.9
10	Oct.	58,900	119.6
11	Nov.	40,600	82.4
12	Dec.	29,900	60.7
		591,200	

Example: $\dfrac{\$591{,}200}{12 \text{ mo.}} = \$49{,}267/\text{mo.}$

$\$29{,}900/\$49{,}267 = 60.7\%$

The example presented indicates the logic of developing a forecast by means of regression techniques and should establish in your mind a structure for approaching such problems. But do not be misled by the mathematical preciseness. There are any number of changes that could come about, such as technological advancements, consumer desires, political and economic developments, and many others which could have a profound effect upon the forecast. The unwary could make dangerously misleading forecasts with these techniques but the astute industrialist can find them an important tool in obtaining a sales forecast with logic.

NON-LINEAR TRENDS

For short periods of time the straight line may be adequate as a predictor, but for periods of longer duration a curved line may be needed.

The straight line equation, $Y_c = a + bX$, can be expanded into a family of curves. The first, second, and third degree curves are the most useful.

First degree	$Y_c = a + bX$	Straight line (no curve)
Second degree	$Y_c = a + bX + cX^2$	One bend in curve
Third degree	$Y_c = a + bX + cX^2 + dX^3$	Two bends in curve

In fitting a first degree curve, two normal equations were used, but for a second degree curve three normal equations are needed, and for a third degree curve, four normal equations are needed, etc.

The form of such a set of equations for a second degree curve is illustrated here:

$$\Sigma Y = Na + b\Sigma X + c\Sigma X^2$$
$$\Sigma XY = a\Sigma X + b\Sigma X^2 + c\Sigma X^3$$
$$\Sigma X^2Y = a\Sigma X^2 + b\Sigma X^3 + c\Sigma X^4$$

The third degree set of equations includes one more equation of similar form.

In addition to these there are other non-linear trends which have found wide application in forecasting.

GROWTH CURVES

The long-term trend pattern for many industries and products has indicated a growth pattern not unlike that to be found in the biological sciences. The growth is slow at first, with a gradual acceleration. Eventually, the growth starts to decelerate, and in time stops. This phenomena (shown in Figure 6–25) is prevalent throughout the world where growth is involved, and is a valuable predictor for those responsible for forecasting.

Figure 6–25

Example of Gompertz Curve

Domestic Consumption of Rayon Filament Yarn (1920–52) and Trend

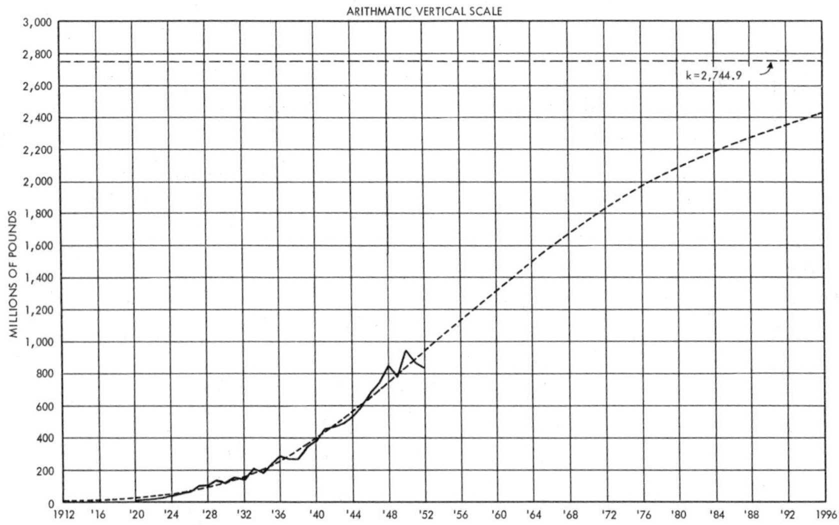

Frederick E. Croxton and Dudley J. Cowden, *Applied General Statistics*, 2nd ed., © 1955, by permission of Prentice-Hall, Inc., Englewood Cliffs, N.J.

Of the various growth curves, the two of greatest importance are the *Gompertz Curve*, and the *Logistic*, frequently referred to as the *Pearl-Reed Curve* (shown in Figure 6–26). Both of these are *S* curves of similar shape (as illustrated). Other examples of these curves as prediction devices can

Figure 6–26

Example of Logistic or Pearl-Reed Curve

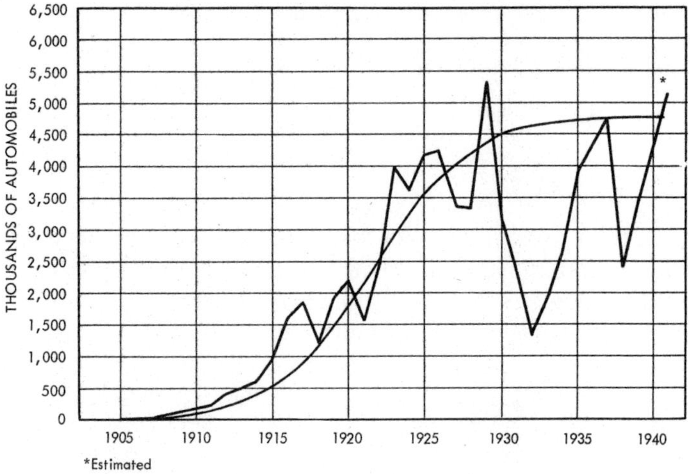

Source: W. A. Neiswanger, *Elementary Statistical Methods* (New York: Macmillan Co., 1943), p. 536.

be found in most of the statistical economic texts. These curves, like the straight line, can be fittted to data and used in forecasting in a similar if more complicated fashion.

MOVING AVERAGE

The moving average is essentially a descriptive method of forecasting and does not produce a mathematical trend equation. This technique has found favor by some forecasters because of its simplicity.

The moving average substitutes the mean of a series of items for the given series of items. The mechanics are more readily understood by considering Figure 6–27. For example, consider a series of three items. These three items are added and averaged and inserted in column 2. For the next average, the first item is dropped and the fourth one picked up. If just three values are used in the moving average, one point is missing on either side of the center, and if five values are used, two points on either side of the center are lost. This indicates one of the difficulties of this method; it is always behind.

The length of the series of items averaged should be equal to the *period* of the data. For seasonal data, a twelve-month period is often suitable, although, because it is an even number of items, it increases the difficulty of calculating.

Figure 6–27

Moving Average

MONTH	SALES	3-MONTH MOVING AVERAGE	5-MONTH MOVING AVERAGE
1	$39,300		
2	44,700	$43,433	$45,860
3	46,300	46,733	
4	49,200	48,433	
5	49,800	49,366	
6	49,100	52,366	
7	58,200	58,466	
8	68,100	61,133	
9	57,100	61,366	
10	58,900	52,200	
11	40,600	43,133	
12	29,900		

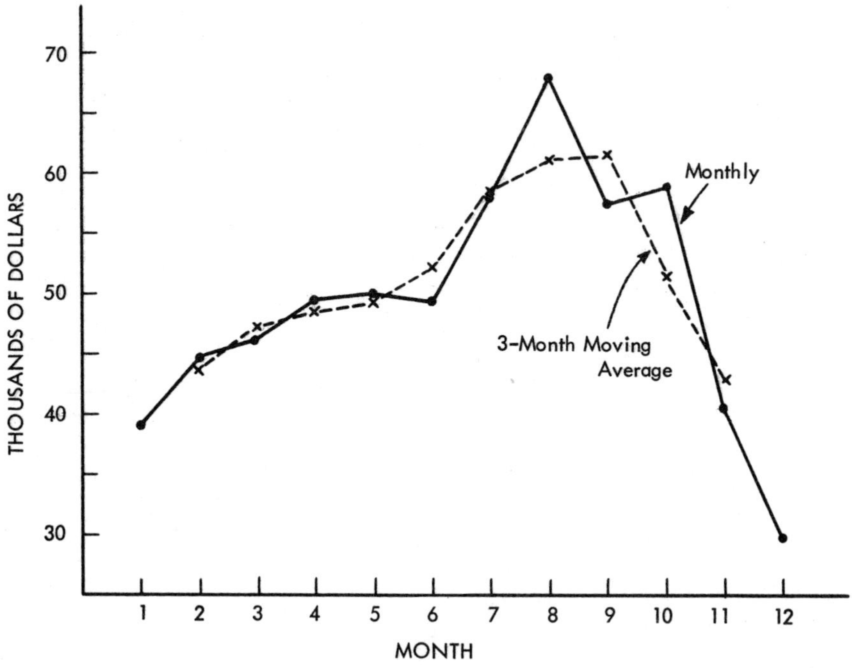

A forecast is made by extrapolating the trend of the moving average into the area of prediction. This can be done by means of the chart and subjective judgment.

EXPONENTIAL SMOOTHING

Robert G. Brown of Arthur D. Little, Incorporated, has developed the technique of exponential smoothing for forecasting.[7] Exponential smoothing is a special kind of weighted moving average which is especially suitable for data-processing applications. A new estimate is a weighted sum of the old estimate and the demand occurring in the most recent period since the last review. This estimate does not include any specific considerations for trend, but the technique can be extended to include the calculation of the trend.

The logic is easier to follow by a series of diagrams:

1.

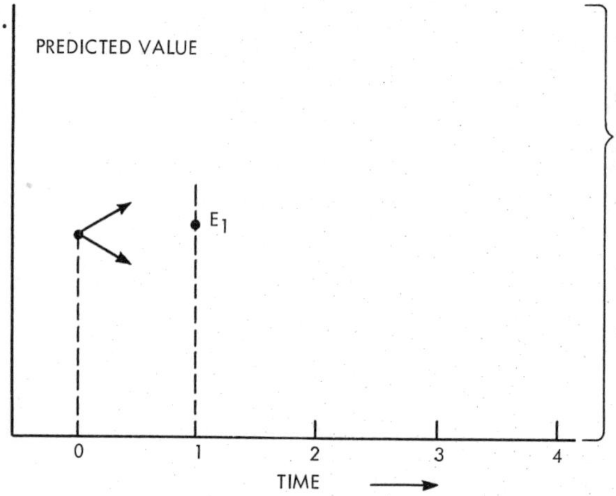

The forecast must be started with some judgment value, at some instant of time, 0, as shown. Now predict the sales, E_1, that will be made through the first period. Starting with no information in the past, we can do nothing more until the end of the first period, when we will predict again.

2.

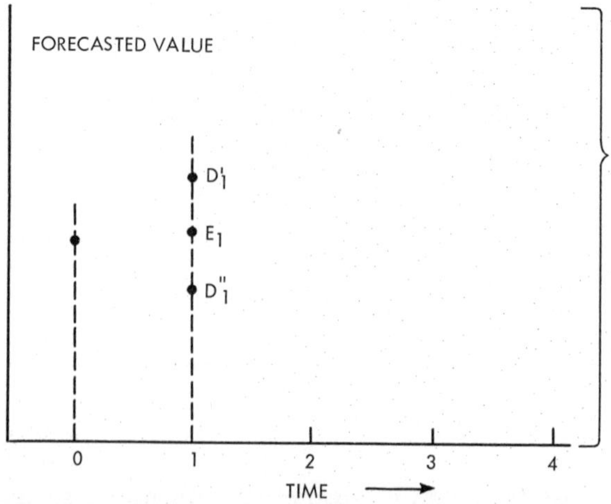

We would be lucky if the demand, D_1, during the period agreed with the estimate, E_1. It is more than likely that it will be above or below the estimate, as shown in D'_1 or D''_1.

[7] Robert G. Brown, *Statistical Forecasting for Inventory Control* (New York: McGraw-Hill Book Co., Inc., 1959), used by permission.

3.

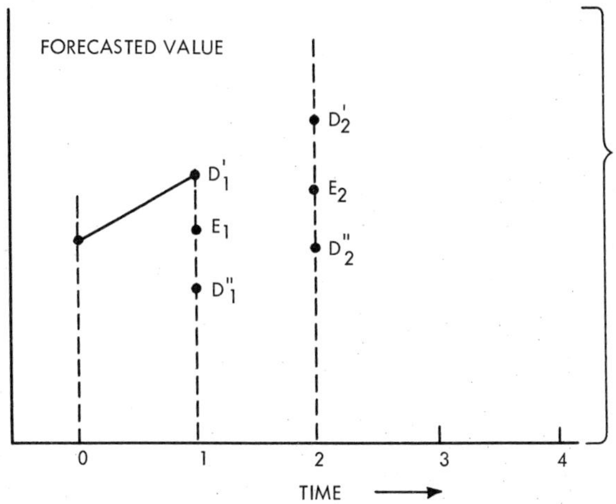

To make the new estimate, E_2, start with the value of E_1 and modify it by some fraction of the amount that the demand, D_1, missed in the previous estimate. So we have:

New estimate = Last estimate + α (Current demand − Last estimate).

$$E_2 = E_1 + \alpha (D_1 - E_1)$$

Alpha, α, is called a smoothing constant and has a value between zero and one. If the value is small, in the order of .001, the response will be slow and gradual. A value such as 0.5 will cause a quick response. In actual practice, companies have found 0.1 is a satisfactory smoothing constant.

The greater the difference between the estimate made for the last period and the actual demand this period ($D_1 - E_1$), the greater will be the adjustment for the next period. If the difference is negative, rather than positive, this change is also taken care of automatically by the equation.

We are justified in calling this estimate an average in the same sense that we use the term *moving average*. This is seen more readily by changing the previous equation:

$$E_2 = E_1 + \alpha(D_1 - E_1)$$

to:

$$E_2 = \alpha D_1 + (1 - \alpha)E_1$$

New estimate = α(Current demand) + $(1 - \alpha)$ (Last estimate)

As we accumulate the new estimates over a number of estimating periods, we are doing the following: The last estimate of the above equation could be replaced by the new estimate of the period before. This, of course, will include a last estimate again, which can be replaced by the appropriate new estimate, and this procedure can be carried on indefinitely:

New estimate = α(Last demand) + $(1 - \alpha)$ [α(Last demand) + $(1 - \alpha)$ Previous last estimate]

This, continued, would become cumbersome, so we resort to the symbols; only notice now that we are extending the subscripts back in time rather than forward.

$$\text{New estimate} = \alpha D_0 + \alpha(1-\alpha)D_1 + \alpha(1-\alpha)^2 D_2 + \ldots + \alpha(1-\alpha)^{k-1}D_{k-1} + (1-\alpha)^k \text{[estimate made } k \text{ months ago]}$$

where:

$$D_0 = \text{demand last month}$$
$$D_1, D_2 = \text{demand one and two months ago}$$
$$D_k = \text{demand } k \text{ months ago}$$

Continue this process long enough and the factors $(1 - \alpha)^k$ become smaller, and the early information has no appreciable effect on the present estimate. If the sum of the weights is equal to 1, the estimate can be called an average, and the sum of the weights $\alpha + \alpha(1 - \alpha) + \alpha(1 - \alpha)^2 + \ldots + \alpha(1 - \alpha)^k + \ldots$ does equal 1.0.

$$\text{New average} = \alpha(\text{Last demand}) + (1 - \alpha)(\text{Old average})$$

This equation will respond to random changes, but if there is a consistent trend the estimates will be biased and will fall below the demand. Now let us see how we can account for the trend. The trend can be estimated by the following equation:

$$\text{Current trend} = \text{New average} - \text{Old average}$$

This trend is the amount by which the average increases in one month. The random fluctuations in demand will cause variation in the estimated average demand, and therefore the current trend. The average trend can be computed:

$$\text{New trend} = \alpha(\text{Current trend}) + (1 - \alpha)(\text{Old trend})$$

Brown has shown that this method of computing the trend is the equivalent of the least squares method, if the weights given to the demand in each previous month are the same as those used in computing the average.

The correction for the lag caused by the trend is:

$$\text{Expected demand} = \text{New average} + \frac{(1 - \alpha)}{\alpha}(\text{New trend})$$

The practical aspects of this method of forecasting are fairly obvious since it is only necessary to store the previously calculated values for the average and the trend.

NONSTATISTICAL FORECASTING DECISIONS

This chapter has been primarily devoted to statistical techniques used in forecasting. Needless to say, not all forecasting questions can be answered by quantitative methods as described, so one must make decisions by other means. Such factors as the domestic and foreign political climates must often enter into forecasting decisions. Frequently, styles and fads must be considered, along with such imponderables as the weather. These subjects cannot be covered in depth, but some are worthy of mention.

The purchasing pattern of producer goods (goods used to produce other goods) often varies more drastically than consumer goods (goods used by the consumer). Anyone responsible for forecasting will naturally take this into account.

The decision process for buying producer goods is frequently considered to be more objective than the decision process for buying consumer goods. The motives for purchasing producer goods is frequently based upon economic considerations alone, and the buyers, being professionals, have greater experience and buy with less emotion.

The elasticity of demand concept isn't usually considered as a forecasting technique, but a knowledge of how price affects demand is useful in forecasting.

We all know that, generally, as the price of a product is increased, the demand will decrease, and, as the price of the product is decreased, the demand will increase. This relationship can be plotted as a demand curve, as shown in Figure 6–28. Those products shown by curve (*a*) are little affected

Figure 6–28

Price and Quantity Relationships

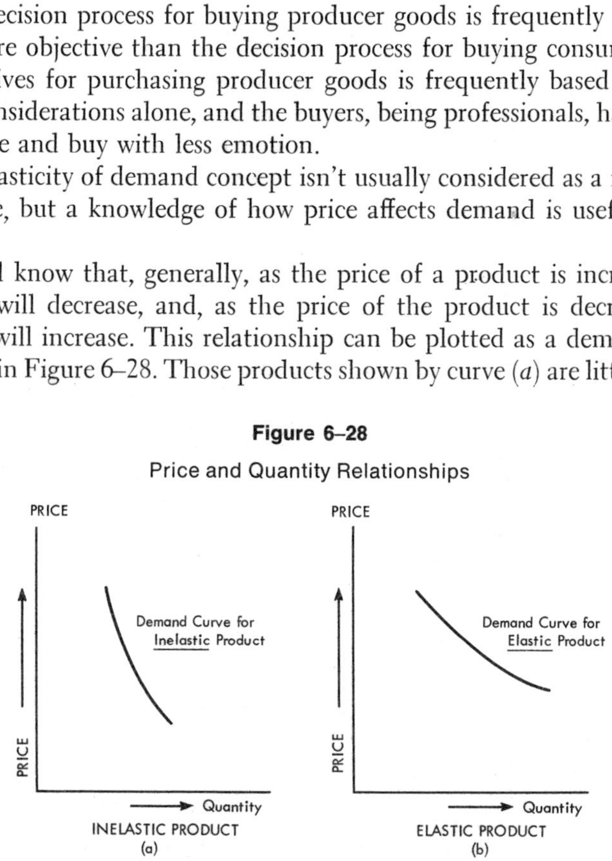

by any change in price and are said to be inelastic. Those for which the quantity varies considerably with the price change, as in (*b*), are said to be elastic. In other words, the demand is stretchable or not, depending upon how important the product is to the well-being of the customer.

The reason for this phenomenon is fairly obvious. As the prices are lowered for a product such as butter, people will start using it rather than a cheaper spread. If the price goes low enough, it may become the raw material from which other products are manufactured.

It is possible for a company to test the elasticity of a product by a controlled experiment. Field testing of the elasticity of consumer products is often done in cooperation with dealers. Typical of such studies would be to place a product in a store and change the price level from time to time to see how this affects the sales.

The addition of a tax to a product with an elastic demand curve could affect the demand to the extent of making it unprofitable to produce. Such changes in demand are of vital importance to the manufacturer. This is why elasticity of demand and external forces can have a profound effect upon the forecast.

These are just a few examples of the many factors to be considered when making a forecast. As illustrated, some information for forecasting can be handled analytically but other information cannot. Regardless of the source of information, the forecast serves as a link between the external environment and the internal operations of the business. It is, therefore, an important input to the system design of production control.

SUMMARY

The sales forecast is the link between external, uncontrollable movements of the economy and the internal, controllable affairs of the business. Although sales forecasting is an important function, its place in the organization will depend upon personnel available, type of product being sold, and many other factors.

Regardless of how forecasting is organized, the forecasting decision deserves the best information available. Statistics is an important tool for making these decisions. Of these tools, sampling, regression, and correlation present the most useful applications.

Questions

1. Give several examples of predictions which you make every day in which there is some uncertainty.
2. Who in the manufacturing organization should be responsible for sales forecasting? Justify your choice.
3. Select a company and outline a procedure for making a sales forecast.
4. Discuss the relationship between sales forecasting and the success of some particular manufacturing company.
5. What effect would good sales forecasting techniques have on the various departments of a manufacturing business?
6. Have you ever participated in a market survey? Explain.
7. What is meant by a random sample?
8. What are the characteristics needed to describe a population?
9. Why is the subject of sampling statistics of importance to forecasting?
10. What is the difference between regression analysis and correlation analysis? When would you use each one of these techniques?
11. Why is the central limit theorem important in the application of statistical procedures?
12. What are the four components of variation in a time series?

13. Discuss the growth curve for one of the following products: colored television, Salk vaccine, hoola hoops, bottle caps, plastic wading pools.
14. What are the advantages of the exponential smoothing technique used in forecasting?
15. Suggest some information which would be highly correlated with the sales of one of the following: household appliances, school furniture, animal vaccines, car accessories.

References

ABRAMSON, ADOLPH G., and MACK, RUSSELL H. *Business Forecasting in Practice: Principles and Cases.* New York: John Wiley & Sons, Inc., 1956.

BASS, F. M.; BUZZELL, R. D.; GREENE, M. R.; LAZER, W.; PESSEMIER, E. A.; SHAWVER, D. L.; SCHUCHMAN, A.; THEODORE, C. A.; and WILSON, G. W (eds.), *Mathematical Models and Methods in Marketing.* Homewood, Ill.: Richard D. Irwin, Inc., 1961.

BASSIE, V. LEWIS. *Economic Forecasting.* New York: McGraw-Hill Book Co., Inc., 1958.

BRATT, ELMER CLARK. *Business Cycles and Forecasting.* 5th ed. Homewood, Ill.: Richard D. Irwin, Inc., 1961.

BROWN, ROBERT GOODELL. *Smoothing, Forecasting, and Prediction of Discrete Time Series.* Englewood Cliffs, N.J.: Prentice-Hall, Inc., 1963.

———. *Statistical Forecasting for Inventory Control.* New York: McGraw-Hill Book Co., Inc., 1959.

CHOU, YA-LUN. *Applied Business and Economic Statistics.* New York: Holt, Rinehart & Winston, Inc., 1963.

CRISP, RICHARD D. *Market Research.* New York: McGraw-Hill Book Co., Inc., 1957.

CROXTON, F. E., and COWDEN, D. J. *Applied General Statistics.* 2d ed. Englewood Cliffs, N.J.: Prentice-Hall, Inc., 1955.

ESTES, B. E. "What Management Expects of Forecasting," *Sales Forecasting,* Special Report 16. New York: American Management Association, 1956.

EZEKIEL, MORDECAI, and FOX, KARL A. *Methods of Correlation and Regression Analysis, Linear and Curvilinear.* 3rd ed. New York: John Wiley & Sons, Inc., 1959.

FERBER, ROBERT. *Statistical Techniques in Market Research.* New York: McGraw-Hill Book Co., Inc., 1949.

FRANK, RONALD E.; KUEHN, ALFRED A.; and MASSEY, WILLIAM F. *Quantitative Techniques in Marketing Analysis.* Homewood, Ill.: Richard D. Irwin, Inc., 1962.

GRIFFEN, JOHN I. *Statistics Methods and Applications.* New York: Holt, Rinehart & Winston, Inc., 1962.

KAUFMANN, ARNOLD. *Methods and Models of Operations Research.* Englewood Cliffs, N.J.: Prentice-Hall, Inc., 1963.

KURNOW, ERNEST; GLASSER, GERALD J.; and OTTMAN, FREDERICK R. *Statistics for Business Decisions.* Homewood, Ill.: Richard D. Irwin, Inc., 1959.

LYLE, PHILIP. *Regression Analysis of Production Costs and Factory Operations.* 3rd ed. Edinburgh-Tweeddale Court, London: Oliver & Boyd, Ltd., 1957.

MARKET RESEARCH SOCIETY, INC. *Business Forecasting*. London: Oakwood Press, 1958.

MOSTELLER, FREDERICK; ROURKE, ROBERT; and THOMAS, GEORGE B., JR. *Probability and Statistics*. Reading, Mass.: Addison-Wesley Publishing Co., 1961.

NEISWANGER, WILLIAM A. *Elementary Statistical Methods as Applied to Business and Economic Data*. Rev. ed. New York: The Macmillan Co., 1956.

NETER, JOHN, and WASSERMAN, WILLIAM. *Fundamental Statistics for Business and Economics*. Boston: Allyn and Bacon, Inc., 1961.

SMITH, C. FRANK, and LEABO, D. A. *Basic Statistics for Business Economics*. Homewood, Ill.: Richard D. Irwin, Inc, 1960.

SPENCER, MILTON H.; CLARK, COLIN G.; and HOGUET, PETER W. *Business and Economic Forecasting*. Homewood, Ill.: Richard D. Irwin, Inc., 1961.

WALKER, HELEN MARY, and LEV, JOSEPH. *Elementary Statistical Methods*. Rev. ed. New York: Holt, Rinehart & Winston, Inc., 1958.

WRIGHT, WILSON EDWARD. *Forecasting for Profit*. New York: John Wiley & Sons, Inc., 1947.

CHAPTER 7

Inventory Systems

The Inventory Control Function

The inventory control function should be discussed not only as an input to the production control system but also as a system in itself, for the information from the inventory system is an input to the purchasing system and the cost system, as well as to the production system. The inventory function is also a system with inputs from the production function, purchasing function, and others. Thus it might be difficult to decide where in the development of a system design this subject should appear, but, since we are talking of inputs in general, the discussion of inventories and how they are controlled should come early.

THE MEANING OF INVENTORY

The word inventory has so many meanings that it often leaves the new student of the subject a bit bewildered. An inventory refers to the movable articles of a business which are eventually expected to go into the flow of trade. Inventory is also used to indicate the value of these goods. Frequently it is used to designate a detailed list of the articles, with perhaps the description, identification number, quantity, and value. Inventory can also be used as a transitive verb to indicate the counting and listing of goods. We frequently hear such statements as "Companies usually *inventory* their goods on the first of January." The meaning of these different usages soon becomes apparent.

CLASSES OF INVENTORY

Industries find that it is far more convenient to establish classes of inventory rather than to throw everything together into one class. They separate those goods which have had no work done on them from those which have had some work done, and both from those which are finished. The advantages of making these classifications will be obvious as you become more aware of the problems involved.

The common inventory classifications found in industry are:

Raw Materials
Materials in Process
Finished Products
Component Parts
Supplies

The term raw materials can have two quite distinct meanings to the economist. First, it can mean that the material has just been extracted from nature. For example, iron ore, crude oil, and coal would all be raw materials in this sense. The other meaning, understandable to both economist and the accountant, is that raw materials are those goods which have had no work added to them *in the plant in which they are situated.* This is the definition which will be used here.

Raw materials, then, can sometimes be considered as finished materials. For example, iron pigs are finished products for the blast furnaces, but raw materials for the foundry. Rough castings are the finished goods for the foundry, but raw materials for the machine shops. And, in turn, the finished castings may be the raw materials for a manufacturer of generators.

The relationship among the classes—raw materials, materials in process, and finished goods—can be shown more vividly by a chart of costs versus operations (Figure 7–1).

Figure 7–1

Relationship of Material Costs

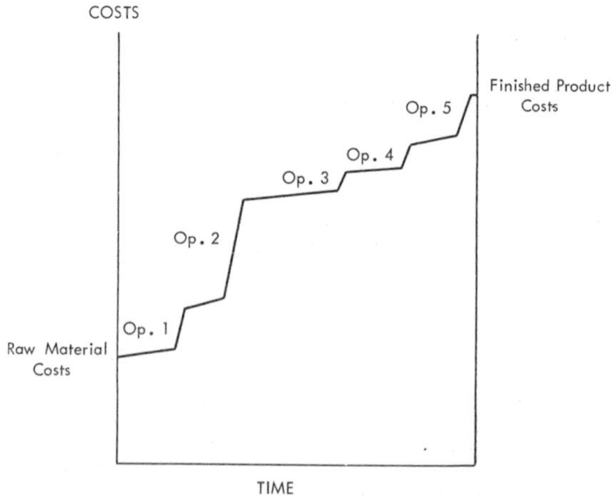

The raw material comes into the plant with an inital cost, shown on the left of the chart. As it remains in storage, it "gains" some cost, but the major cost contributions come at the various operations shown on the chart. After the material starts through the steps of the process, it is considered as material in process. Of course it eventually reaches the end of the processing and becomes a finished product.

At the end of the fiscal period the cost of the raw materials is easily obtained (for inventory purposes) from the invoices or lists of merchandise sent from the vendors. The finished-goods cost is fairly easy to obtain by accumulating the labor costs, materials costs, and overhead. The real difficulty is finding the cost of materials in process at some particular stage. So, when the inventories have to be evaluated, it is more easily done in either the raw materials form or in the finished product form. This is often impossible to arrange without considerable loss in production.

Component parts are either manufactured or purchased units which are carried in stock. A distinction may be needed between simple parts, such as washers and bolts, and complex items, such as motors, generators, and other subassemblies which will eventually go into the assemblies. The situation becomes more complicated because these subassembly units might be sold as replacement parts or used in the production of final assemblies. The complex subassemblies are, at times, kept in a separate inventory grouping under such as title as Assemblies.

Supplies are items which are not included in the final product, except in a very minor way: such things as lubricating oil, repair parts for machines, cleaning and polishing materials, and similar indirect cost items.

These are the classifications, although they may have different names, which most companies find will cover their needs. A company should, however, as it thinks necessary, break its inventory down into classes.

THE IMPORTANCE OF INVENTORIES AND THEIR MANAGEMENT

It is difficult to pick up the financial section of a newspaper without finding some reference to the status of inventories. Such a comment as the following is commonplace and typical: "Economists say that an efficient clean-up of the heavy carryover of this year's inventory of cars, and brisk early sale of next year's models, would lead to a high automobile production and would stimulate a comfortable rise in the output of steel, copper, glass, tires, textiles, and other material."

The values of inventories in an industry are watched carefully by investors and regarded as bellwethers of industry. When raw material inventories build up, it shows some optimism in the future sales of a product. Permitting inventories to become depleted is apt to indicate a pessimistic attitude by the industry.

The inventory is of such great consequence to the manufacturer that it shows up in the most important financial statements, the Balance Sheet (Figure 7–2) and the Profit and Loss Statement (Figure 7–3).

Figure 7–2

Balance Sheet (Statement of Financial Position)

	May 31, 196	May 31, 196
CURRENT ASSETS:		
Cash	$ 6,769,180	$ 10,436,420
Temporary cash investments, at cost	14,091,774	44,494
Receivables, less allowance for doubtful accounts o[illegible] $927,000, respectively	44,179,473	40,856,243
Inventories [illegible]	50,881,396	53,644,821
Advances on purchases	2,802,895	5,501,391
Prepaid expenses	1,625,947	1,969,672
Total current assets	$120,350,665	$112,453,041
CURRENT LIABILITIES:		
Notes payable	$ 11,363,198	$ 19,152,955
Trade accounts payable	22,261,720	20,141,457
Accrued liabilities and miscellaneous accounts payable	10,645,696	10,151,255
Dividends payable	930,173	899,299
Current portion of long-term debt (Note 4)	472,082	1,106,799
Taxes on income	3,907,760	3,513,450
Total current liabilities	$ 49,580,629	$ 54,965,215
WORKING CAPITAL	$ 70,770,036	$ 57,487,826
PROPERTY, PLANT, AND EQUIPMENT (Note 3)	64,211,251	65,975,109
GOODWILL ARISING UPON CONSOLIDATION (Note 1)	3,154,704	2,880,332
INVESTMENTS AND OTHER ASSETS	2,607,209	1,887,981
	$140,743,200	$128,231,248
DEDUCT:		
Deferred taxes on income (Note 5)	$ 334,944	$ 564,210
Long-term debt, non-current portion (Note 4)	38,736,752	27,512,828
Minority stockholders' interest	1,499,401	1,423,913
	$ 40,571,097	$ 29,500,951
NET ASSETS	$100,172,103	$ 98,730,297
STOCKHOLDERS' EQUITY:		
$4 cumulative preferred stock (redeemed during the year)	$ —	$ 2,539,800
Common stock (Note 6)	36,821,420	36,710,117
Accumulated earnings, retained and used in the business (Note 4)	63,350,683	59,480,380
	$100,172,103	$ 98,730,297

Source: The Pillsbury Company

As shown in the simplified version of the balance sheet, the inventory value appears on the assets side. It is part of the property owned by the company, and the managers—as well as the stockholders—are interested in knowing just how well this property is used. The most recent inventory value and the previous value are both shown on the profit and loss statements as a means of calculating that most important figure: the profit or the loss. There are also a number of relationships among the inventory value and other values, shown on both the balance sheet and the profit and loss statement, which indicate the efficiency of an industrial organization.

Figure 7–3

Profit and Loss (Statement of Earnings)

	Years ended May 31, 196	196
INCOME:		
Net sales of products and services	$446,361,776	$419,798,321
Interest and miscellaneous income	1,728,523	1,168,545
	$448,090,299	$420,966,866
COSTS AND EXPENSES:		
Cost of products and services sold	$344,415,269	$326,661,702
Selling, general, and administrative expenses	81,403,139	74,972,909
Interest and debt expense	2,990,232	3,127,637
Miscellaneous deductions	1,278,632	1,268,904
	$430,087,272	$406,031,152
EARNINGS BEFORE TAXES ON INCOME	$ 18,003,027	$ 14,935,714
TAXES ON INCOME (Note 5)	9,000,000	7,113,453
NET EARNINGS	$ 9,003,027	$ 7,822,261

Cost of Products includes starting inventory plus purchases less ending inventory.

IMPORTANCE OF A GOOD INVENTORY CONTROL SYSTEM

Before we expand the subject of inventories it will be well to emphasize the importance of good control over the inventory.

1. A good inventory control system minimizes the possibility of delays in production. Depletion of an item's inventory quantity may indicate a sad and dangerous condition for a factory.

   Consider what would happen if an automobile company ran out of sheet steel. The plant would have to close down, discharge its employees, stop processes (which cannot be started again overnight), advise its carriers that there would be no cars to deliver, and inform unhappy customers that they would have to wait. Probably the dividends would be lower, which would make the stockholders unhappy, and they would proceed to replace the management that let this happen in the first place. This is a black picture, but it is the sort of thing that happens to companies with poor inventory control.
2. A good inventory control system permits a company to exercise economies in many ways. It eliminates duplication in ordering and encourages a better utilization of available materials by interdepartment or intercompany transfers. Purchasing economies can be exercised by obtaining quantity and shipping discounts.
3. A good inventory control system is essential for an efficient accounting system. This is especially true for the materials aspect of cost accounting.
4. A good inventory control is a deterrent to dishonest people who might steal materials from the factory. Also, a good inventory control stimulates respect for the material, minimizing losses caused by damage in careless handling. And, of course, a good inventory control system is desirable to expedite the production of the financial statements.

Inventory Control and the Organization

The inventory control function can be in one of several places on the organizational chart. Its exact location depends upon the financial condition of the company, the product which is being produced, and, not of least importance, the people who are involved. From the manufacturing viewpoint, the best place to have the inventory function is directly under the manufacturing supervisor. It is often, however, under the supervision of accounting, and occasionally one finds it under the supervision of the purchasing agent. The purchasing agent, closely connected with the vendor, is sensitive to new products coming out and can often buy to advantage if he knows the inventory. In case a company is short of working capital, or is buying in a speculative market, the treasurer should keep a close watch on the inventory.

One possibility in organizing the inventory control function is to split it between finished goods and raw materials. The factory might have supervision of the raw materials and the sales department might take over the supervision of the finished inventory. The sales department's control should not extend back into the production function, for its objectives are frequently different and this can cause confusion.

INVENTORY CONTROL AND THE ACCOUNTING FUNCTION

The production personnel are interested in the physical flow of inventories as it affects production, and consequently have become more and more involved in the accountant's realm of recording the value of inventories. The two areas, production and accounting, are so closely interrelated that it is well for both to be cognizant of the interests and objectives of the other.

Van Sickle states that the cost accounting department performs five principal functions in handling the details of the stores inventory:

1. It supervises the stores inventory auxiliary ledger records pertaining to the receipts, issues, and balance of all store items.
2. It maintains an up-to-date price record of all items kept in the storeroom by revising the unit prices of any items when the purchase invoice indicates the necessity for their revision.
3. It prices the stores requisition and makes the extensions and totals thereon for all items issued.
4. It prepares cost summaries showing the cost of materials and supplies consumed.
5. It prepares the factory journal or journal voucher entries for all store items issued, spilled, salvaged, and scrapped, and for the estimated shrinkage of the stores inventory.[1]

---

[1] Clarence L. Van Sickle, *Cost Accounting Fundamentals and Procedures* (2d ed.: New York: Harper & Brothers, 1947).

The accountant has found it necessary to improve his recording systems as industry has become more complex and demanding. He has found it necessary to divide and subdivide accounts to paint a more realistic financial picture and to cash in on the specialized abilities of various individuals.

In the most elementary form of cost accounting, all the costs of manufacturing are subtracted from the income for any period of time. Among the costs of manufacturing is the cost of material, which is obtained by adding the cost of the initial inventory to the material purchases and deducting the cost of the remaining inventory. In today's more complex accounting systems, there are numerous records in which the daily transactions are recorded. These accounts, pertaining to the control of inventories, are shown in the flow diagram of Figure 7–4.

Figure 7–4

Accounting for Inventories (Dollars)

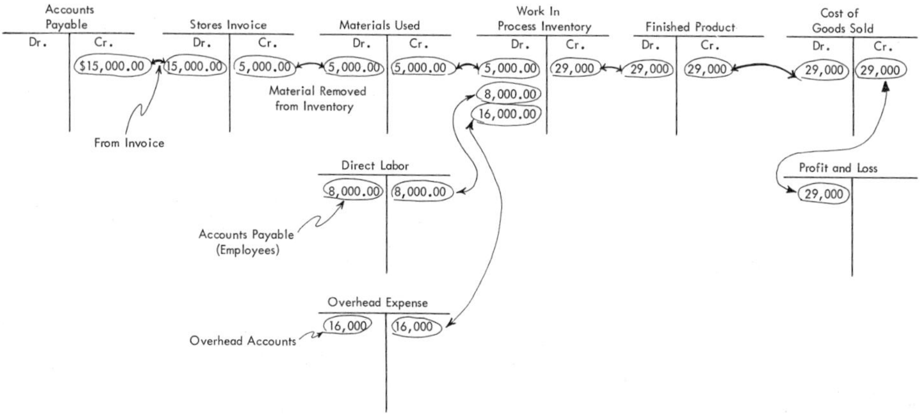

A word about the flow of the entries shown in the diagram might be useful for those unfamiliar with accounting procedures. Most all accounting today is *double entry*, which means that two entries will be made for each transaction. The two entries which are associated on the diagram are connected by an arrow, but there are numerous alternatives to the accounting procedure shown.

The cost accounting records are affected not only by the inventory transactions but also by the general accounts, which include accounts payable and the cash account. The flow of materials into the inventory and the payment procedure are shown in Figure 7–5.

This has been a sketchy overview of the accountant's part in the inventory procedure, but if you are a serious student of manufacturing you will become thoroughly familiar with accounting, and, in particular, cost accounting. Probably no other subject can give you such an important insight into manufacturing.

Figure 7–5

General Accounting Procedure for Receiving

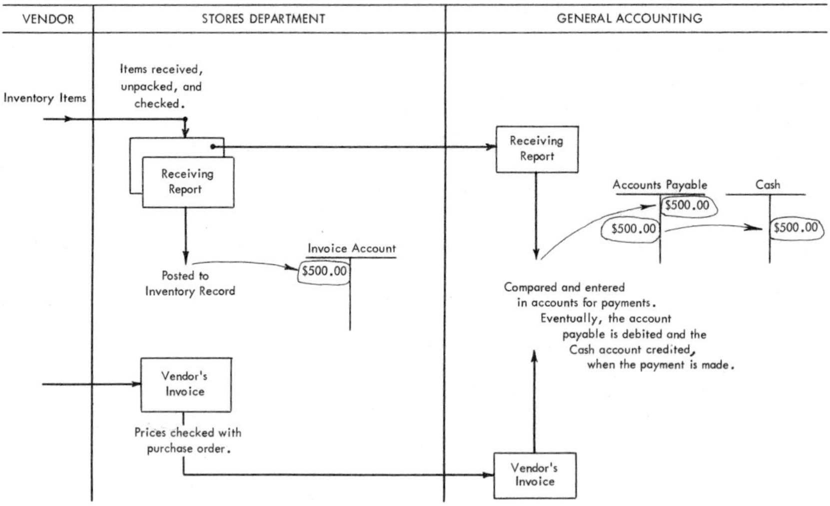

INVENTORY CONTROL AND THE PURCHASING FUNCTION

Nearly everyone seems to get involved in the inventory control procedure, but the purchasing department is particularly involved. A common practice followed for the purchasing cycle is shown in Figure 7–6. The purchase requisition is initiated by a person with authority, and, most frequently, by someone involved in the inventory records.

If the order is one of high value, it is not too uncommon to request price quotations from several vendors. This, however, is a slow process, and usually the purchase order is placed directly with a vendor on the basis of known quality, service, transportation cost, or other criteria.

This is not the place to study the purchasing function intensively, but probably no other function can contribute more to an efficient manufacturing operation.

INVENTORY CONTROL AND THE SALES FUNCTION

The finished inventory is withdrawn by the authority of the *sales order*. A typical chain of events for the sales order is shown in Figure 7–7. This is a typical procedure, but there are simpler and more complex methods for consummating the sale of the product.

Figure 7–6

Purchasing Procedure

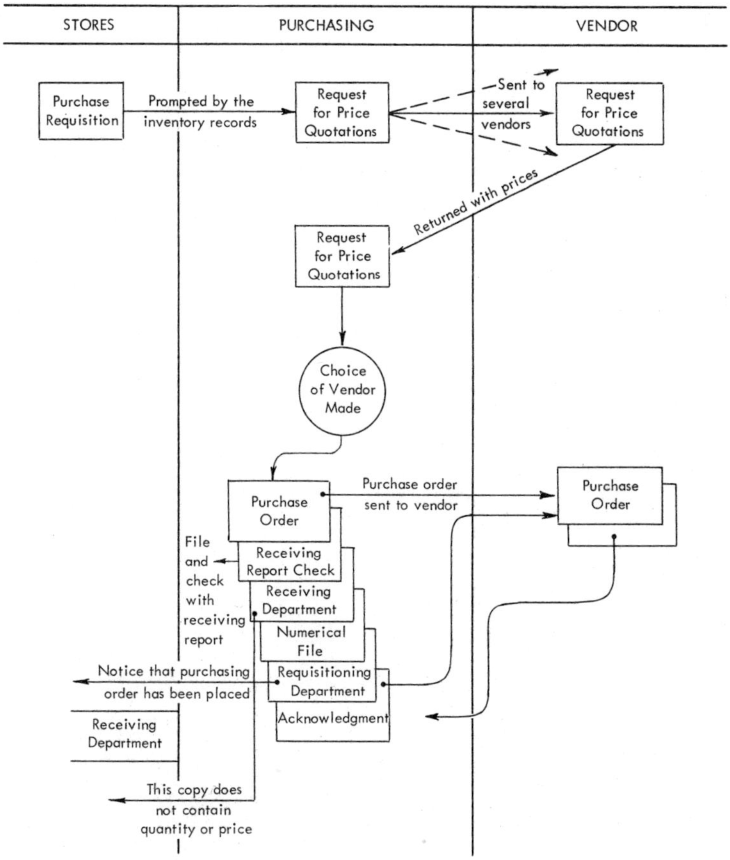

Figure 7–7

Sales Procedure

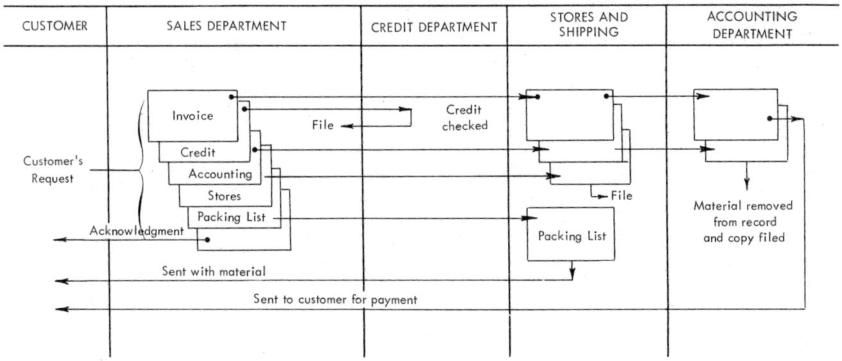

INTERNAL ORGANIZATIONAL CONTROL FOR THE INVENTORY FUNCTION

The physical inventory count, which must be taken once a year, is a check against errors and theft, but once a year is sometimes not often enough for keeping the best control. If there is an error in the records, it should be detected as soon as possible, before the stores run out of materials which are essential for production. On the other hand, dishonest employees in the factory should be found out as soon as possible. The very fact that inventory is checked periodically will often keep employees honest.

One way of patrolling the inventory is to set up a three-way check among the stores keeper, the inventory record clerk, and some other responsible person (such as the assistant to the works manager). At intervals, perhaps once a week, the assistant chooses some product numbers at random. He makes a simultaneous request for counts, from both the inventory record clerk and the stores keeper. If the counts do not agree, the discrepancies can be investigated and corrected at once. This three-way check minimizes any cover-up of records, which otherwise could go on year after year.

ORGANIZATIONAL DIVISION OF THE INVENTORY CONTROL FUNCTION

There are three distinct functions in inventory control: the actual receiving and shipping (with the required checking of goods), the storekeeping, and the recordkeeping. All three activities can be located in one place, or they can be distributed around the plant in separate localities. If separated, more communication among the groups is necessary and the system becomes more complex. In addition to the above functions, the inventory control group frequently serves other purposes. They sometimes salvage and rework material, and often prepare material for production. This is especially common in the metal working industry, where it is necessary to cut materials to length.

Inventory Records

Many small companies operate efficiently without any written records of their inventories. The number of items is so few and the quantities so small that one man can keep track of them. This method depends upon an occasional physical count of the items, known as a *physical inventory*. For many small companies this method is the cheapest and most efficient, and a complex and expensive system should never be imposed upon them.

MATERIALS BUDGETS FOR CONTINUOUS MANUFACTURING

In continuous manufacturing, the materials needs should be budgeted on the basis of the sales forecast (which was discussed in Chapter 6). By anticipating the materials needed on a weekly or monthly basis, the shipments of materials can be kept flowing with a minimum of delay. The materials for production can be received, processed through the inventory control, and go directly to work in process without any excessive handling within the plant. The materials budget can be made a year in advance; and minor adjustments can be made throughout the year, as necessary, to meet changing demand and production.

THE USE OF BIN TAGS FOR INVENTORY CONTROL

The bin tag, used in two quite distinctly different systems, is found in many companies today. In the first situation, the bin tag is the only form of written record kept on the storeroom items. The tag, which is fastened to the front of each bin, has all the identification information, such as part number and part name. In the body of the tag is space to record the withdrawals and additions. This is done at the time by the storeroom clerk. This system, however, leaves much to be desired. The clerk frequently fails to fill in the necessary information because he doesn't have a pencil, his hands are full, or he "just forgets."

In the second situation, the bin tag is used as a supplemental record to that which is kept by the inventory clerk. The record on the bin tag and the inventory record should agree. This method of using the bin tag doubles the work that has to be done and is probably not worth the effort.

PERPETUAL INVENTORY

The perpetual inventory record is a running account of the incoming materials, outgoing materials, and the balance on hand. At practically any instant one should be able to check the perpetual inventory and determine the quantity on hand and the activity of the particular item. The perpetual inventory record can take many forms which assist in the rapid transfer of information, but for simplicity's sake consider here that the inventory information is placed on a card. This card has two distinct sections: the heading, where all of the unchanging information is placed, and the body, where the changing information is to be found. A short discussion of these two sections will point out the type of information that might be needed. It cannot be stressed too strongly that information not put to useful purposes should be left off the record.

Figure 7–8

Heading for Perpetual Inventory Record

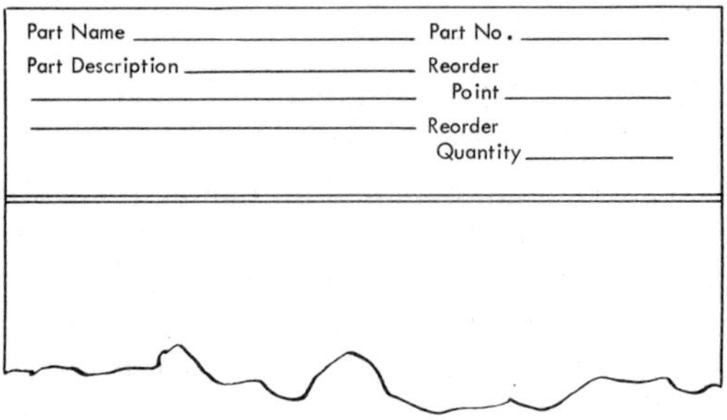

In the heading, shown in Figure 7–8, the following might be found:

Material Designation: The part name and number should be shown clearly at a position on the form that makes it convenient to leaf through the forms and find the desired card.

Part Description and Size: A brief description of the part, with the size and any other important information, should be contained on the card.

Reorder Point: This should contain the information that will indicate the reorder time to the recordkeeper. He will be able to check the quantity on hand with the order point.

Reorder Quantity: When the clerk makes out the requisition for materials, the order quantity should be readily available; and this is a convenient place to keep the information.

Many companies have additional information on their inventory cards. For example, it might be desirable to include the reserve quantity on the card to show when the inventory goes below the danger point. When the reserve quantity is omitted, the clerk must be aware of items which should be watched carefully. The product specification, or a description of the material from which the product is made, might be carried on the inventory card. If the item is purchased from the outside, the list of vendors can be kept on the card, along with the ordering priority. The location of the material in the storeroom can be indicated as well. The record is a useful place to keep information about the product, but care should be exercised to keep the record from becoming cluttered with a lot of useless information which will lead to the introduction of errors and delays.

The essential information included in the body of an inventory record card (Figure 7–9) tells us about the incoming and outgoing material, and what is on hand. There are other items which we will discuss, but this is the minimum that one could expect. In each incoming and outgoing column should be sufficient information to determine the person responsible for making the entry, the date the entry was made, and the source document—such as the materials requisition, stores record, etc. Other columns of information find their useful purpose in the inventory record, but first the flow of information into this simple record should be shown.

Figure 7–9

Body of Perpetual Inventory Record

RECEIVED			ISSUED			BALANCE
Date	Order No.	Quantity	Date	Order No.	Quantity	Quantity

FLOW OF INFORMATION IN AND OUT OF INVENTORY CARDS

Since there is a difference in the flow of information for raw materials records and finished goods, each will be discussed separately. Figure 7–10

Figure 7–10

Flow of Information for Raw Materials Inventory

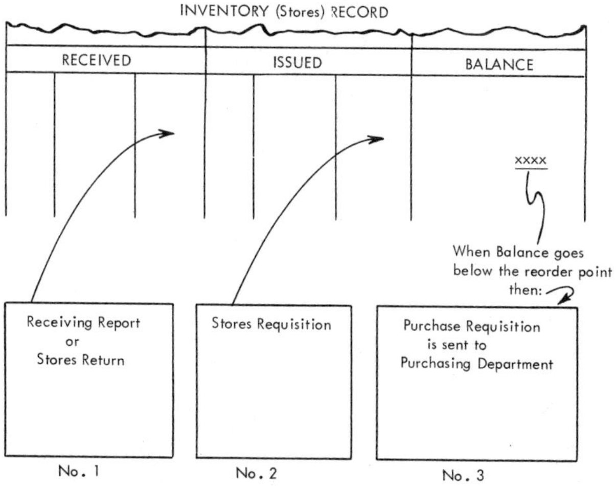

shows the elementary raw materials record, with the accompanying input and output information. Each of these will be discussed briefly.

Number 1 (in the illustration) is the receiving report. The receiving department maintains a file of unfilled purchase orders against which it checks incoming shipments. The receiving report is the form which is used by the receiving clerk to notify the inventory clerk that material has been received.

This should give all the pertinent information, such as the quantity, date, rejections if any, etc. One might ask why a copy of the purchase order should not be used for this purpose. It could, if the entire order is filled at one time. Since this does not occur frequently, separate receiving reports for each shipment must be made out. As we will see later (in the design of systems), several copies of the receiving report are made out at one time and sent to different departments for various purposes.

Figure 7–11

Typical Forms

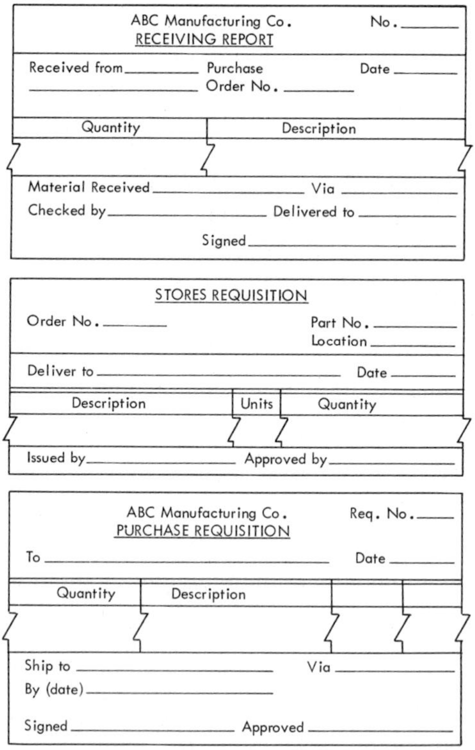
ABC Manufacturing Co. No. ______
RECEIVING REPORT

Received from ______ Purchase Order No. ______ Date ______

Quantity	Description

Material Received ______ Via ______
Checked by ______ Delivered to ______
Signed ______

STORES REQUISITION

Order No. ______ Part No. ______
Location ______

Deliver to ______ Date ______

Description	Units	Quantity

Issued by ______ Approved by ______

ABC Manufacturing Co. Req. No. ______
PURCHASE REQUISITION

To ______ Date ______

Quantity	Description		

Ship to ______ Via ______
By (date) ______
Signed ______ Approved ______

Number 2, the stores requisition, is an authorization to remove material from stores. One might consider that the stores clerk is responsible for all stock, and, if he doesn't have the material on hand, he must have a record to show why—and where—it has gone. The stores requisition serves much as a personal check does on a bank account. This form will usually originate in the production control department. After the material is issued by the stores clerk, the quantity will be deducted from the stores record and the stores requisition will be forwarded to cost accounting for calculating the cost of the product.

Number 3, the purchase requisition, is a signal or authorization to the purchasing agent of a company to procure the goods described. This, of course, cannot be issued by just anyone but must come from an authorized person, such as the inventory clerk.

Figure 7–11 shows a set of typical forms which might be used for the receiving report, stores requisition, and purchase requisition.

The stores requisition will seldom be made out for exactly the quantity used in production; it will also take into account the quantity of material that might be spoiled during manufacturing. If this excess material is not used, or if material is returned for some other reason, there must be some provision for doing this. The "storage return" or "credit" requisition is the form that is made out for this purpose and might be considered as a stores requisition in reverse. It should contain the same information.

Before going to more complicated stores records, let us see how the stores record for finished goods would be different from the one just illustrated. In Figure 7–12 we have a flow chart that depicts the inputs and outputs for the finished goods inventory.

Figure 7–12

Finished Goods Inventory

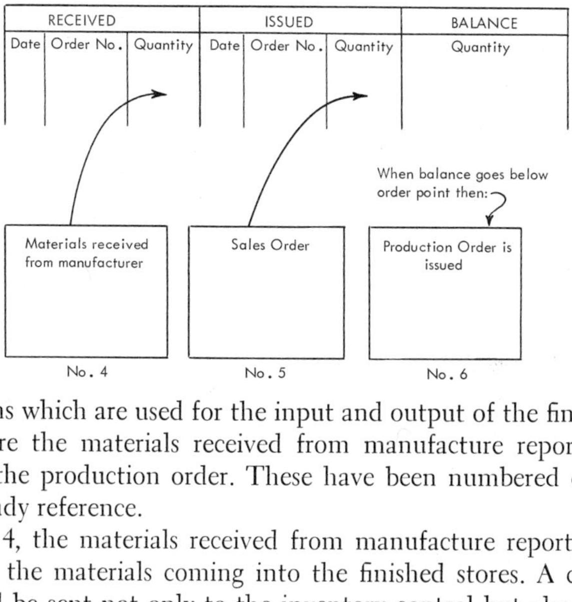

The forms which are used for the input and output of the finished goods inventory are the materials received from manufacture report, the sales order, and the production order. These have been numbered on the flow chart for ready reference.

Number 4, the materials received from manufacture report, is used to account for the materials coming into the finished stores. A copy of this form should be sent not only to the inventory control but also to the production and accounting departments. At times, the manufacturing order might serve the purpose of materials received from manufacture report. This report serves the same purpose for the finished stores record as does the receiving report for raw materials.

Number 5 is the sales order, which is the authorization to remove the finished goods from the inventory.

Number 6 is a production order, or production requisition, which serves as a signal and authorization for manufacturing to produce goods to fill up the inventory which has become depleted (as shown) when the balance on hand is compared with the order point.

The component part inventory record will be slightly different from the raw materials record and the finished goods record. If the component is a purchased component, it will have the same inputs and outputs as the raw materials record. However, if it is a manufactured component, it will differ from the finished goods inventory record in that the sales order will be replaced by the stores requisition.

RECORDS FOR ADDITIONAL INFORMATION

The perpetual inventory record—with its three columns, received, issued, and balance—is sufficient for many inventory systems, but occasionally more information may be desirable (as is shown in Figure 7–13).

An *ordered* column should be added to the inventory record form if the ordering cycle is so long that one or more orders might be out at one time. The purpose of this column is to prevent making repeated orders for materials when they are not needed. The input of information for this column would, of course, be the purchase order for raw materials and components and the manufacturing order for finished goods and manufactured components. The ordered column should only be added to the record when multiple orders are being made and when it is costly to have duplicate orders delivered. Adding the column may cause errors which would not occur on the illustrated, simpler form.

Similar reasoning could be used for an *apportioned* column. If the materials go directly into production after the requisition has been made, there is no need for the apportioned entry. If, however, there is a delay which would cause a serious overdraw on the materials on hand, then this column should be added. The input of the apportioned column would come from the manufacture order.

PHYSICAL INVENTORIES

The physical inventory is an actual count of the materials on hand. This often entails considerable expense and trouble, and one might ask what is the point of keeping the elaborate perpetual inventory if periodic checks are still made by counting the goods. There are a number of good reasons why this must be done.

Operating the plant without delays is imperative to the management, which wishes to make a profit, as well as to the employee, who is concerned with his income. More than once, a plant or department has had to close down temporarily because of a lack of parts, parts which appeared on the record but could not be found in the storeroom. They had disappeared because of an error in the record, carelessness, or theft. This would be reason enough for a periodic check, but there are also many others.

Figure 7–13

Records for Additional Information

Part Name *Bracket Motor Mount*

Part Description *C.I. Bracket, 3″ center, ½″ holes.*

Order Point 1000

Order Quantity 8000

Part No. 8A-1036

1. Ordered			2. Received		3. Balance on Hand		4. Issued			5. Apportioned but Not Issued			6. Available for New Orders	
Date	Order No.	Quantity	Date	Quantity	Date	Quantity	Date	Order No.	Quantity	Date	Order No.	Quantity	Date	Quantity
					6/16	3000							6/16	3000
						1800	6/20	MO-98	1200				6/20	1800
						800	7/12	MO-127	1000				7/12	800
7/15	P.O.-950	8000											7/15	8800
										7/22	MO-316	2400	7/22	6400
						200	7/28	MO-316	600			—600		
		0000	8/1	8000	8/1	8200								

One of the most important reasons for taking a physical inventory is because banks and the government will not accept a count that is taken from the record and not substantiated by a physical count. The reason for this is apparent when one realizes that the value of the inventory at the start of the accounting period and at the end of the accounting period enters into the calculation of the profit. It is quite natural that the Bureau of Internal Revenue, which taxes profit, is concerned with how these values are obtained.

Several methods are commonly followed in taking the physical inventory.

1. Whenever a requisition is placed, the material in the stores, which should be at a minimum, is checked against the record.
2. Each day the storeroom clerk checks the balance of a few items against the record. This is scheduled so that by the end of the year all of the items have been checked.
3. A physical count at the end of the accounting period, of six months or a year, is the most common method. Under this plan the activities in the storeroom are suspended for a day or so while the material is counted. This means an unusual demand upon the stores and factory personnel, and frequently the manufacturing activities will have to be closed down, adding another cost to this operation.

In effect, the physical inventory should be taken instantaneously—as if a photograph of all the quantities were taken at one time. This, of course, is impossible, so activities have to be suspended while a "time exposure" is taken. There are, however, various ways that the time can be shortened. Tape recorders and photographs are methods that have been used. The inventory clerks read off the quantities stored into a tape recorder and later a secretary types off a list. The photographic technique can be used where the material can be arranged to be counted in the photograph and where nothing is hidden from view.

Figure 7–14

Inventory Tags for Physical Inventory

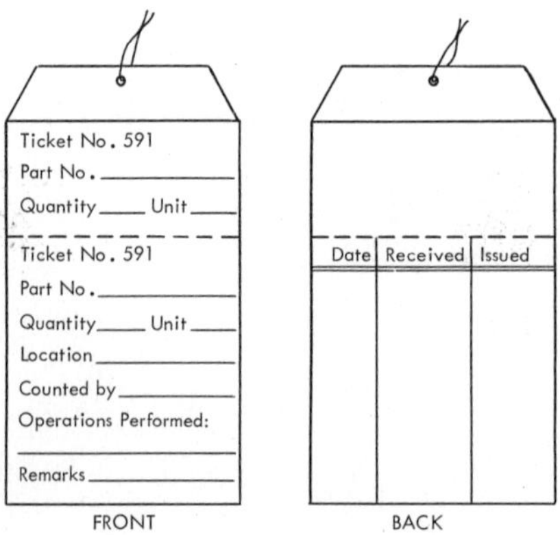

In any method of taking the physical inventory, the first step should be to have the stock in good condition, piled in an orderly fashion, and consolidated so it can be counted rapidly.

Probably the most common method of taking inventory rapidly is to use a serrated tag (Figure 7–14), which is fastened to each inventory item or group of items. This can be done well in advance of the time that the inventory is to be taken. The least active items can be tagged and counted first. Entries can be made on the card later if there are any additions or subtractions. At the instant the inventory is to be taken, the clerks can rapidly go through the stock room and tear off the bottom half of the card, leaving the top of the tag with the item. The tags can then be checked with the inventory record and, where there are discrepancies, a recheck can be made. With the tag serial number, and the location of the material, it is quite simple to find any errors.

DIFFICULTIES ENCOUNTERED IN INVENTORY CONTROL

A difficulty is encountered in the inventory control procedures when material in process cannot be completed because of some delay in the processing. Perhaps a tool has broken down and it will be some time before it is repaired, or perhaps a rush order has come in that will delay the production of parts in process. Leaving the parts on the production floor often is not desirable because of the space they take up or because they might become damaged.

Part numbers refer to either a raw material or finished goods, so materials in process have no unique number. If the material in process is placed in storage under the finished product number, the records will be incorrect, and if it is not numbered, will become lost or forgotten. These "orphaned" materials in process should be given every consideration and adequate cross-references and codes should be set up to prevent any loss.

One knotty problem encountered in inventory control is that subassemblies carried in stock can be drained off in two directions. They can be sent into production to produce a final assembly; or they might be shipped out for replacement parts. Consequently, production of assemblies can be delayed because of a lack of subassemblies which were in the inventory when production started.

The Flow and Pricing of Inventories

If inventories did not change with time, did not deteriorate, change styles, or otherwise become less desirable, there would be no problem of inventory flow. But because they do change, there is an inventory flow problem which management must face. The problem can best be described, as before, by an analogy.

In the first-in–first-out (FIFO) process, the material which flows in first is the first to flow out. It is as if a viscous fluid, which never mixes, is flowing through the tank. This is the ideal flow of inventories when such changes as the age hardening of steel or the spoilage of dairy products might occur. But, as everyone knows, excessive time delays in such inventories as dairy products can cause customer dissatisfaction. This method can cause considerable difficulty in materials handling because it is necessary to have old stock continuously accessible.

The last-in–first-out (LIFO) method is suitable for items which do not deteriorate. Pipe fittings are typical of such products which, in fact, appear to gain in value with their griminess. With such material, the new stock can be placed in front or on top of the old material, and we can expect seldom if ever to see the first material received.

The gas in the storage tanks of a filling station would characterize a mixed inventory. When the tank is refilled, the contents take on the *average* characteristics of all the gas.

While the physical flow of the inventory is obviously important, there is a closely related problem of pricing the inventory, which is also important.

PRICING THE INVENTORY

If the material was purchased and sold instantaneously, or if the prices never fluctuated, we would not need to be concerned with the pricing of the inventory. But since it doesn't always move quickly, and prices do change, management must be concerned with the pricing of the inventory as it goes into the cost sheet for the finished product. As we will see, the profits can be understated or overstated, depending upon how the inventory is priced. And when we are tampering with profits we are awakening a whole host of interested parties, ranging from the employee working on a profit-sharing plan to the Bureau of Internal Revenue standing by to tap its share, based on the profits of the company.

There are two acceptable methods of inventory evaluation, *cost* and *cost or market*, whichever is the lower. This would appear to be a relatively easy problem. Choose the method, stick with it, and never give it another thought. But it is not that simple, for which cost shall we use? Shall we use that of the first material purchased, or that of the latest material purchased? The common methods used can be summarized:

1. Cost
   a) First-in–first-out (FIFO)
   b) Last-in–first-out (LIFO)
   c) Average
2. Cost or market, whichever is lower.

FIFO, LIFO, and Average sound like the same words we used when discussing the flow of inventories. The analogy is the same, but we should recognize that the material could flow in the FIFO fashion and be priced in the LIFO fashion, and vice versa.

Since the choice of the above methods can have a profound effect upon the balance sheet and the profit and loss statement, let us take a look at the simple one-item inventory and price it under the three methods illustrated. We will first consider a case of prices increasing, and you may wish to try a similar example with prices decreasing.

FIFO Method:

In	*Out*	*Balance*	*Price*	*Transaction*
		00		
50 gal.		50 gal.	50¢	+$25.00
100 "		150 "	75	+ 75.00
	60 gal.	90 "	{50 at 50¢ 10 at 75¢	− 32.50

LIFO Method:

In	*Out*	*Balance*	*Price*	*Transaction*
		00		
50 gal.		50 gal.	50¢	+$25.00
100 "		150 "	75	+ 75.00
	60 gal.	90 "	60 at 75¢	− 45.00

Average Method:

In	*Out*	*Balance*	*Price*	*Transaction*
		00		
50 gal.		50 gal.	50¢	+$25.00
100 "		150 "	75	+ 75.00
	60 gal.		50 at 50¢ 100 at 75¢	− 40.00

Summary of Results:

	FIFO	*LIFO*	*Average*
Cost of material sold	$32.50	$45.00	$40.00
Remaining inventory cost	67.50	55.00	60.00

It will be worthwhile to make an analysis of this simple example, so let us look at the FIFO method first. Since the prices are going up, we can expect to pay at least the most recent price of 75¢ a gallon for the next purchase, or $45 to replace the 60 gallons sold. This same amount of material was priced out at $32.50, so we have wiped out $45 minus $32.50, or $12.50, of any profit we might have anticipated just by the act of replacing the inventory. Not a very profitable transaction, is it? So, in an increasing market, it would be wise to price the inventory on the LIFO basis rather than on the FIFO basis. What does this do to the value of the remaining inventory? It is out of date, so the inventory shown on the balance sheet will appear out of date, and the true value of the company's assets will not be revealed. One can't have his cake and eat it, apparently. Either the profit and loss statement will be accurate and the balance sheet will be out of date, or the reverse will be true.

The Average method is a tedious, time-consuming technique which will require excessive clerical time. Perhaps the most common way of evaluating the inventory is by the *cost or market*, whichever is lower, method. This presents a very conservative evaluation for both the balance sheet and the profit and loss statement. By this plan, if the replacement cost of an item is lower than the invoice cost, then replacement cost is used as the value of the item.

On the other hand, if the invoice cost is less than the replacement cost, then the invoice cost is used as the basis of evaluation.

The profit, the value of the inventory, and thus the business, are strongly influenced by the method chosen for pricing the inventory. It is therefore of vital concern to the stockholders and management, but it is the Bureau of Internal Revenue of the United States Treasury Department which exercises the greatest regulatory force. They are interested because it is the profit which is taxed, and if the profit can be changed so can the taxes.

The Treasury Department has issued numerous rulings on inventory evaluation. A businessman is permitted to use any recognized method of inventory evaluation as long as he uses the same method consistently. Ordinarily the business must obtain permission to change method, and probably this permission would be difficult to obtain from year to year.

Inventory Storage

The actual storing and moving of the materials in an inventory might be considered as analogous to the operation of a filing system. As in a filing system, we wish to place and withdraw materials as rapidly and economically as possible. More than one efficient factory has been hampered by an inefficient inventory storage system. While space does not permit an adequate discussion of the materials-handling equipment used to manipulate the materials, we can discuss some of the more efficient ways of locating materials in storage spaces. First we will discuss some of the systematic storage procedures, and then discuss the complicating apects of inventory storage.

SYSTEMATIC STORAGE PROCEDURES

Storage by Part Number

In this procedure, the parts are stored in the sequence of their part numbers. This is satisfactory if all the parts are small and have similar characteristics. What do you do, however, when one part is a five-foot pulley and the next a small key that holds the pulley on the shaft? Or one part is a transformer housing, and the next part in the sequence a can of highly inflammable and messy cooling oil used in the transformer?

In general, this system of storing by part numbers is suitable for small parts where the quantity on hand remains fairly uniform. Bolts, rivets, nails, and similar items which are used in small quantities can be stored very conveniently by this method, but if we are talking about carloads of such items, then there are better storing systems.

Storage by Coordinate Index Number

In this procedure the storage area is laid out in a coordinate index system, and a cross-reference is established between the part number and the index.

Figure 7–15

Storage by Coordinate Index

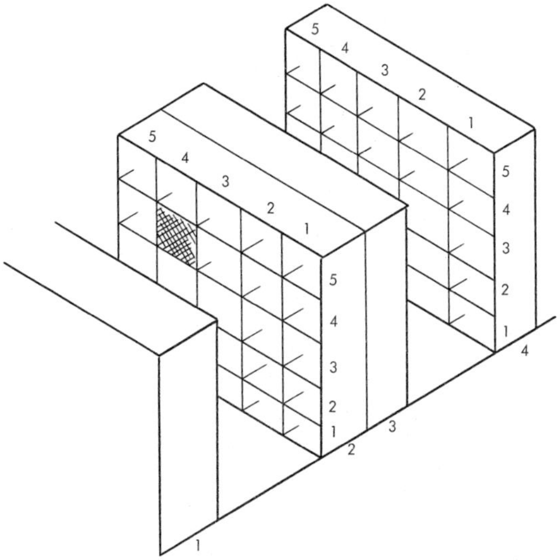

One way of setting up the index is to number the storage spaces, as in Figure 7–15. The aisles are numbered in sequence, as are the rows and levels of bins. A number, such as 2–4–4, would indicate the bin in the second aisle, fourth column, at the fourth level. To this could have been added a number to designate the particular storage area.

Instead of locating material by part number, the location of the material is shown on the inventory record or on a special index sheet. This requires a little more time in the recordkeeping, but it permits greater flexibility and more efficient utilization of space. If there are excess parts for a certain area, they can overflow into another space, just as long as the cross-reference is made. When the inventory is reduced, the space can be utilized for other purposes.

Storage by Serial Index Number

Rather than establish index number by coordinates, some companies prefer numbering the storage spaces in sequence. This has some advantage for areas which are not perfectly rectangular, but, until personnel is familiar with the locations, it might take a longer time to find any particular part. There is also some advantage in this system since the numbers need not be in blocks, as in the coordinate system.

Storage by Frequency of Use

Some organizations have made extensive studies to determine their most frequently used material. Those products which are withdrawn most often are located near storage area exits. Other companies place some of these materials near the point of use and maintain additional material in remote storage areas. This latter method is likely to make the recordkeeping somewhat more complicated. The index number method is still quite suitable for frequency-of-use storage procedures.

COMPLICATING ASPECTS OF INVENTORY STORAGE

There are many reasons why storage of materials becomes more complicated than would appear necessary. In attempts to conserve space, inconvenient and undesirable space is often used. Frequently the space is not symmetrical, so it becomes difficult to install standard racks, and it is nearly impossible to lay out the space to take advantage of a uniform indexing system. These spaces are in out-of-the-way places, with inadequate access for the materials-handling equipment available.

Often city ordinances and fire insurance policies require that inflammable materials be placed in remote locations. Some materials have disagreeable or corrosive characteristics that make it desirable to locate them away from the usual storage area.

Heavy parts and materials that have to be handled by large materials-handling equipment should be placed in bays where the necessary moving equipment is available. Large tools and dies can often be covered with a preservative and stored in open yards. This means that equipment must be available to move the tools and dies to the cleaning area as well as to and from the production areas.

Often material can be stored at the point of use. This can save many dollars by reducing the warehouse supervision costs, but it can be done only if the value of the material is so small as to be unimportant, or its size and shape such that it cannot be carried out without being detected. Some companies, making good use of this technique, store metal bars near the work place, using a color code painted on the floor area to indicate when it is time to reorder and when the stock is dangerously low. This assumes that the material is always removed and replaced in a particular order.

Field warehousing seems to be increasingly popular with companies fabricating products out of steel. The raw materials are set aside in a restricted area under the supervision of a bonded warehouse man who represents the vendor. The material in the restricted area is the property of the vendor and does not belong to the customer until it is properly checked out by the warehouse man. For companies operating on a limited amount of capital, field warehousing offers many advantages.

Many of the storage problems encountered by factories are unique and it is impossible to delineate all of the possibilities and possible solutions. A logical, analytical approach should result in a solution satisfactory to the particular problem.

SUMMARY

The importance of the inventory control function has been reviewed in this chapter, along with the organization and procedures required for efficient operations. The impact of pricing methods upon the financial statements was discussed and special attention was given to efficient ways of organizing storage space.

In recent years the emphasis has been on inventory theory, the selection of the order point, and order quantity. This emphasis has come about because of the advent of the computer and the techniques of Operations Research.

There are savings to be made for a company in the inventory theory, but there are also savings to be made in the subjects discussed in this chapter. Do not stumble over these methods in an effort to get to the more sophisticated, but not easily applied, inventory theory.

Questions

1. What are the classes of inventories that you might expect to find in a particular industry? Give an example of an item which might be found in each class.
2. Where on the organizational chart might one find an inventory control department? Discuss the reasons for this and the advantages.
3. Is it necessary for the individual responsible for the inventory control to know about the procedures and operations of the other departments? Explain your answer in full.
4. What purpose does each of the following serve?
   a) Receiving report.
   b) Invoice.
   c) Purchase requisition.
   d) Request for price quotation.
   e) Purchase order.
   f) Packing list.
   g) Stores requisition.
   h) Sales order.
   i) Returned-to-stores record.
5. Is a written perpetual record of the inventory always imperative? Explain your answer.
6. Under what conditions would it be desirable to have an "on order" column on the inventory record? What conditions would dictate an "apportioned" column?
7. Outline the characteristics you would look for when hiring an inventory record clerk.
8. Why is a physical inventory essential?
9. Outline the procedure for taking a physical inventory. Design the forms and explain how they will be used.
10. Explain why the method of pricing an inventory is important.
11. Describe a situation where storing material by part number would be suitable. What problems must you consider?

12. Give an example of a situation where the first-in method of handling material is suitable.
13. Discuss the effect of an efficient inventory control system upon the rest of the factory.

References

(See end of Chapter 8)

CHAPTER 8

Inventory Decisions

A useful analogy can be made between a simple fluids system and the inventory system. This analogy is not too far from reality and might have an application in the storage and control of oil, chemicals, or similar fluids.

Figure 8–1*a* illustrates a tank being filled with fluid at the top which can

Figure 8–1

Inventory Concepts

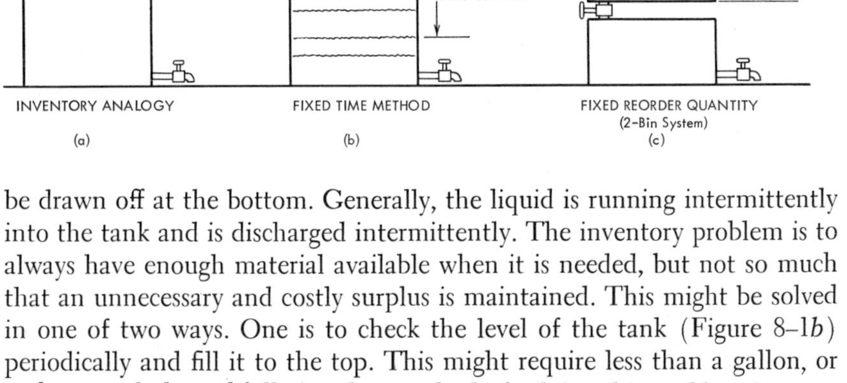

be drawn off at the bottom. Generally, the liquid is running intermittently into the tank and is discharged intermittently. The inventory problem is to always have enough material available when it is needed, but not so much that an unnecessary and costly surplus is maintained. This might be solved in one of two ways. One is to check the level of the tank (Figure 8–1*b*) periodically and fill it to the top. This might require less than a gallon, or perhaps a whole tankfull. Another method of solving this problem is to reorder every time the fluid gets to a certain level (as illustrated in Figure 8–1*c*). This might be done by setting up a reserve tank, which is drawn upon when the first tank is empty.

Checking the tank periodically is a fixed review time method of ordering, which is frequently referred to as the ordering cycle method. Ordering at the time the tank reaches a certain level is a fixed reorder point method, and this is frequently referred to as the two-bin method. The reason for it being called the two-bin method is obvious from our analogy since we have one tank or bin which holds the regular supply and another tank or bin which is drawn on after the first is depleted.

The above analogy is made clearer by a graphical description (Figure 8–2*a*). This is the typical saw-tooth chart used to illustrate inventory control

Figure 8–2

Graphical Inventory Concepts

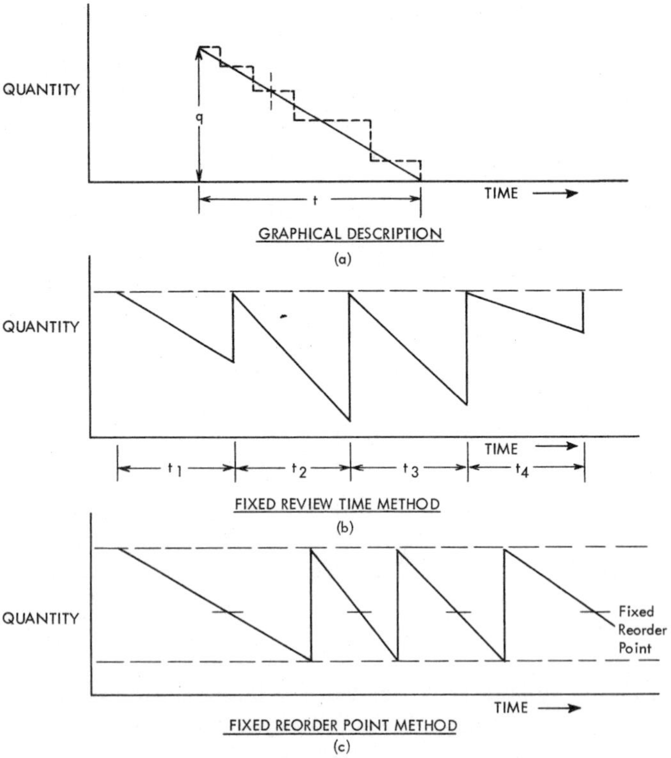

problems. On the horizontal axis is plotted time, while on the vertical axis quantity is plotted. The withdrawal of different size lots with different time intervals is illustrated by a stepped line. If the quantity and time increments are nearly uniform from period to period, we can, with some justification, smooth out the stair steps and represent them with a straight line.

The inventory starts with some quantity, q, which is gradually removed until it approaches zero in time, t. The slope of the line, q/t, shows the average quantity of inventory used per unit of time.

In the fixed review time or cyclic ordering method (Figure 8–2*b*) the time, *t*, remains fixed and the order quantity varies. The inventory items are kept under a periodic surveillance so that once a month, once a week, once a day, or some other such period, an order is placed which will bring the inventory up to the established level.

In the fixed reorder point method (Figure 8–2*c*) the quantity on hand is checked every time material is removed from the inventory. When it reaches a certain point, a quantity of a fixed size is ordered.

The inventory theory problem can now be summarized:

For the fixed review time method:

1. The quantity is reviewed periodically. The frequency of the review is still to be answered.
2. The order is placed for a quantity sufficient to replenish the inventory.

For the fixed quantity method:

1. The inventory is withdrawn to a point where there is just sufficient material to cover the replenishment time.
2. The order is placed for a quantity which optimizes the cost factors.

This amounts to determining *when* and *how much* to order, and we shall now proceed to study these questions in a logical order.

FIXED REVIEW TIME METHOD

Computers have stimulated an increasing interest in the fixed review time method because it is relatively easy to check a large number of inventory items periodically. Fixed review time can also be used in a manually operated system if the inventory consists of just a few items, or if the records can be displayed as bar charts which can be quickly reviewed.

Reviewing the inventory status by a computer, rather than manually, is still a time-consuming and costly operation. Frequently, the inventory quantities are recorded on a magnetic tape which must run from end to end checking item by item. A more efficient system would have the items grouped by optimum review times: those to be reviewed daily could be on one tape, those to be reviewed weekly on another tape, etc.

An intuitive decision can be made concerning the length of the review period by considering the cost of short versus long review periods. As the length of the review period is increased, the clerical cost of reviewing and updating the records is decreased, because there is less labor involved (Figure 8–3). As the review period increases, the period of ignorance is increased because of the variability of demand and lead time. This means that larger reserves will be needed, which will increase the carrying costs as shown on the diagram. The total of the carrying and reviewing cost is shown as one curve on the diagram. We are, of course, interested in finding the minimum total cost, which is obviously the lowest point on the curve. Equa-

Figure 8–3

Cost of Review

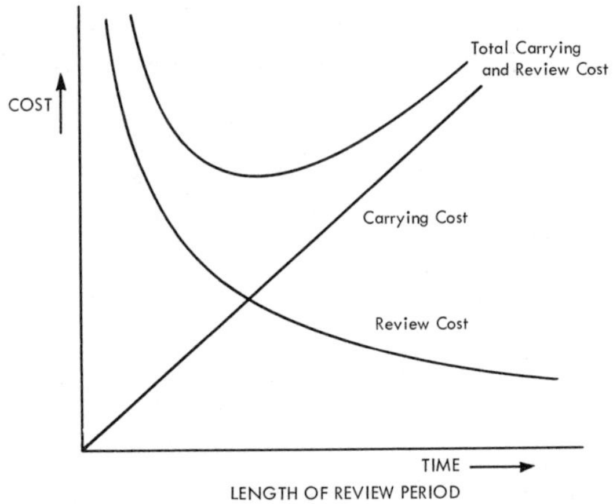

tions have been developed along the lines described here, but probably many refinements and simplifications will have to be made before they become generally acceptable.[1]

In actual practice there are problems which occur when the fixed review time method is used. As is apparent on the saw-tooth chart, when the time is fixed, the reorder quantity will vary, which means that it will be difficult to take advantage of economic order quantities. It is true that the person in charge of the inventory may take the option of ordering or not ordering at the review period. When only a small quantity is needed, the decision may be not to reorder, but this brings up the chance of a human error and the next review period might find the stock dangerously low.

FIXED ORDER QUANTITY METHOD— UNDER CERTAINTY

Let us expand on the fixed order quantity method, shown in Figure 8–4, in which again the slope of the line represents the average use of material.

It would be desirable if the ordered quantity could be received at the very instant the stock was depleted, but to set up a system on this basis would be far too risky. Even if we took into account the probabilistic nature of demand, as we will do later on, we would be taking the risk of running out by failing to recognize the human element in the system.

Many inventory control models fail to take into account that even the most mechanized and computerized inventory control systems include people whose mental functions are often of a two-state nature: they either

---

[1] John J. Fox, *Inventory Management: Statistical Techniques for Inventory Management with UNIVAC Systems,* Sperry Rand Corporation, 1962.

Figure 8–4

Fixed Order Quantity Method under Certainty

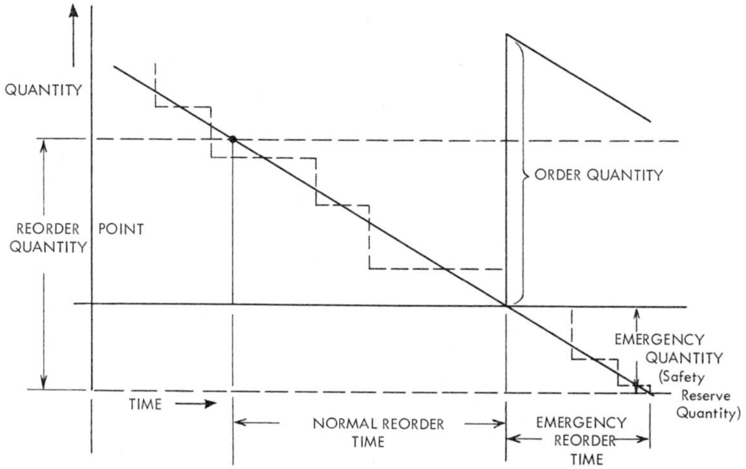

remember to do something or they forget to do something. And if they forget, they often forget forever—until reminded. These people form the numerous links between the inventory records and the production and delivery of the material. They may be the people in the inventory department, in the purchasing department, or even in some isolated railroad express office. Because of this, it is essential that some safety device be built into the system. This is the *safety reserve* shown in the diagram.

Safety Reserve Quantity

The safety reserve quantity is based on the time that it takes to obtain material in an emergency. Usually a factory knows what delay can be expected in obtaining material in the usual course of events, and it is also known that this time can be shaved considerably in an emergency by giving orders special rush priority, which may mean revising schedules, "robbing" orders, shipping by air express, and other expedients. Of course, this is very expensive and should not be permitted to occur too frequently. The emergency quantity signal may or may not be present on the inventory records, but often inventory clerks are aware of these danger points and will act "automatically."

Reorder Point

The reorder point quantity appears on the inventory record and is the "flag" for the inventory clerk, indicating when an order should be placed. If the demand is constant, as we are assuming throughout this section, the reorder point should be the safety reserve quantity plus what will be used during the time the order is being placed and delivered. In other words, it is the sum of the normal and emergency reorder time multiplied by the quantity used per day.

One obvious question: What is the normal reorder time? This, of course, will vary from vendor to vendor, and many companies prefer to use several vendors in order not to be dependent upon one. This has the advantage of making vendors more competitive. The names of the vendors can be listed on the inventory record along with typical delivery times. As you can imagine, delivery time variations among vendors can be considerable.

The best policy might be to establish the reorder point to account for the maximum reorder time, or to let the inventory clerk choose the vendor by considering the rate of withdrawal and any impending emergency. If the demand is great, the order can be placed with the vendor who can deliver the goods the fastest.

THE APPLICATION OF THE TWO-BIN SYSTEM

This type of inventory control, just discussed, has been described as a two-bin system, which refers to two separate groups of inventory items. That quantity above the reorder point is the first bin and that quantity below the reorder point is the second bin. The reference to two bins might mislead the reader into thinking that there must be two distinct storage areas. This is not true, for all the material may be stored together and the only distinction between the two groups would be made on the inventory card.

On the other hand, it may actually be that the two groups are separated. For example, and especially when a perpetual inventory is not kept, it is quite common to box up a reserve quantity and set it to one side in the inventory area. When the first bin runs out and the reserve is opened, an order is placed. This same arrangement can be worked out with a bin replacing the boxed material; and from this the name of the two-bin system was derived.

PROBABILISTIC INVENTORY MODELS

Let us briefly review the model of inventory under the conditions of certainty before exploring the application of uncertainty. In Figure 8–5 we have the typical saw-tooth chart, representing the withdrawal and replenishment of inventory, with quantity on the vertical axis and time on the horizontal axis. This is the fixed reorder quantity system which has been discussed, but it does not include an emergency quantity—which we intend to develop by a method slightly different than before.

The problem is to determine the quantity to which the inventory can be reduced before an order must be placed if it is to be received before the stock is depleted. Why quantity? Because this is the form of the information available in the records. This quantity must be translated eventually

Figure 8–5

Typical Saw-Tooth Chart

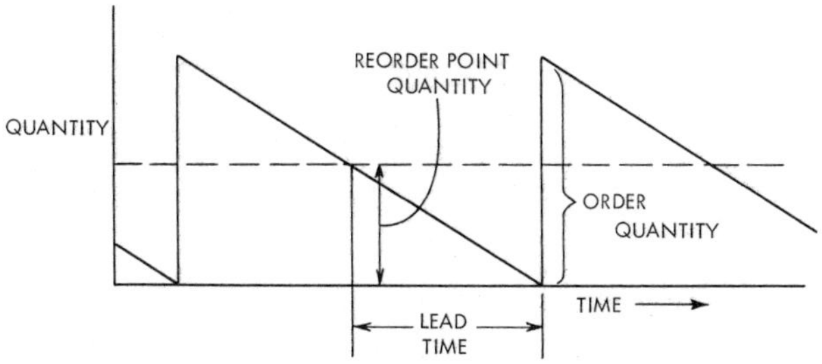

into time because this is the form of the replenishment information.

If the stock could be replenished instantaneously, this order point could be near the point of depletion. Since the stock cannot be obtained immediately, a *lead time* must be provided for the replenishment of stock. This conventional way of illustrating the problem can lead to some confusion and error, so a more elaborate illustration, Figure 8–6, will be developed.

Figure 8–6

Withdrawal and Replenishment Cycle

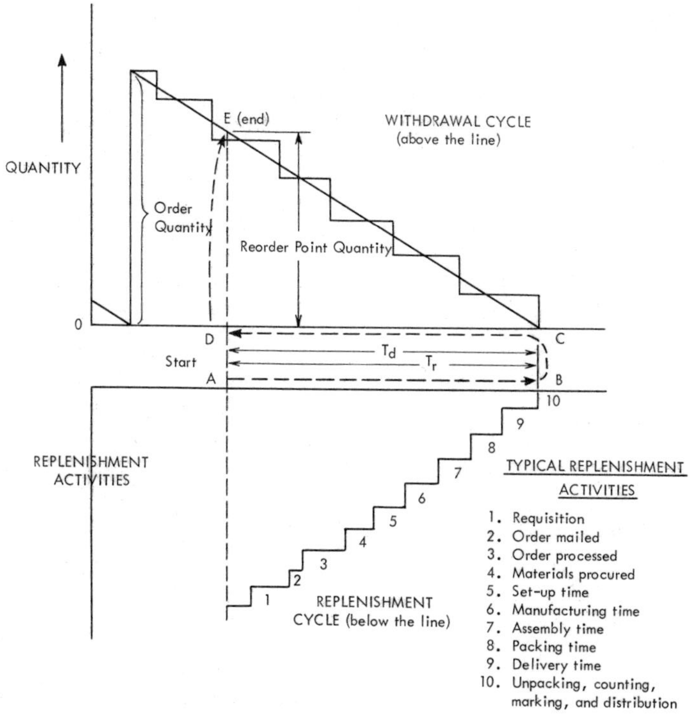

The part of the diagram above the horizontal time axis illustrates the withdrawal cycle, as shown before, but the part below the axis illustrates the replenishment cycle.

The various replenishment activities are extended along the vertical axis, and the horizontal axis, of course, represents time. The completion of each of the various activities in the replenishment cycle is represented by a step in the line. The time to replenish the stock, either by placing an order with a vendor or with the company's facilities, is shown by T_r. The time for depleting the stock is shown by T_d.

In the first illustration we will consider the times for depletion and replenishment as being fixed or certain. In the ideal situation the time for replenishment should be exactly equal to the time of depletion, $T_r = T_d$. It should be apparent that if the material is used sooner than it is replaced—that is, T_d is less than T_r—there won't be any on hand to fill the need; but if T_r is less than T_d, we will have stock on hand before it is needed. We are assuming for the moment that the inventory can go down to zero since the problem is to eventually find the emergency stock needed under uncertain conditions.

The ideas developed here are not exotic, for this problem is no different than the one faced by a housewife. She must predict how fast the family is going to drink milk, as well as the milkman's delivery time, so that the depletion and the delivery time nearly coincide—she hopes.

We can now see that there is a sequence of steps in obtaining the reorder point quantity. First the replenishment time, T_r, is determined, which in turn determines the depletion time, T_d, from which the reorder point quantity can be calculated. To see this, follow the letters, A, B, C, D, and E on Figure 8–6.

$$\text{Reorder point quantity} = \text{Replenishment time} \times \frac{\text{Quantity withdrawn}}{\text{Time}}$$

Our model doesn't represent the real world because, as you know, the rate of withdrawal will vary, causing the withdrawal time to vary, and the replenishment time will also be subject to variations. This is why we are interested in inventory policies under conditions of uncertainty.

We will now turn to the discussion of probabilistic models. First, we will discuss the effect of the variability in general, making some initial assumptions about the variability, and later we can discuss the variability in detail. From now on, all the stepped withdrawal and replenishment lines will be represented by straight lines to keep the illustration uncluttered. We will use our previous illustration and add the variability concept, as shown in Figure 8–7.

Not only is the average time illustrated for the depletion and withdrawal cycles, but also the minimum and maximum time for each. The frequency of the time values between the extremes can be represented by distributions

Figure 8–7

Probabilistic Model

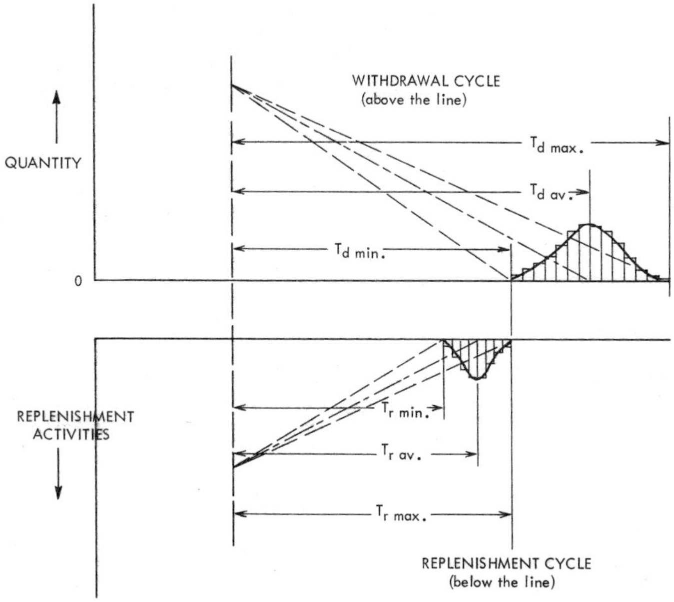

which at first will be assumed to be normal. Using this assumption, three standard deviations either side of the mean will include nearly all of the possibilities. At this point there is no reason to believe that these distributions will be normal, but it is more convenient to discuss them as if they were.

Pause for a moment and review what we are doing. It takes time to replace the stock in an inventory and we must have a signal that says, "Now is the time to start the replacement cycle, if we wish to have the material arrive on time." This signal is the reorder point quantity.

Before going farther with this model, to explore the relationship between the withdrawal and replenishment distributions, it will be worthwhile scrutinizing each distribution more carefully.

The Replenishment Distribution

This distribution is made up of a series of events which it is sometimes assumed will add together to form a normal distribution. The Poisson distribution has also been assumed to be a good model. Some samples of data, however, have exhibited distinct bimodal distributions for the total replenishment times. This might be expected because of the impact of weekends upon the series of events. But, beyond this, there are causes which could contribute to weird-looking empirical distributions, such as the effect of the heavy holiday traffic on the railroads, which in turn influences the schedules of freight and express. The coincidence of large orders arriving on the same day would have an important impact on delivery dates. These are just a couple of the causes that can affect the processing of an order—in addition to general economic conditions.

Some attempts have been made to fit the curve developed by empirical data obtained from the records, but this might lead to hazardous conclusions if the economy were to suddenly change. When business is booming, vendors will probably be slow in filling orders; during depressed periods they will not only hasten to fill orders to keep valuable customers but will also have facilities available to fill the orders. Perhaps no distribution is suitable for these changes, and we may need an elastic distribution which changes from season to season and year to year.

Including the variability of the replenishment cycle in the inventory reorder model complicates it to such an extent that many models ignore it completely. Although the replenishment time may be extremely long, the variability for replenishment in most industrial situations is probably relatively small when compared with others.

The Withdrawal Distribution

This distribution is also suspect, as illustrated in Figure 8–8. Let us discuss withdrawals as a series of events occurring during time periods, such as

Figure 8–8

Withdrawal Distribution

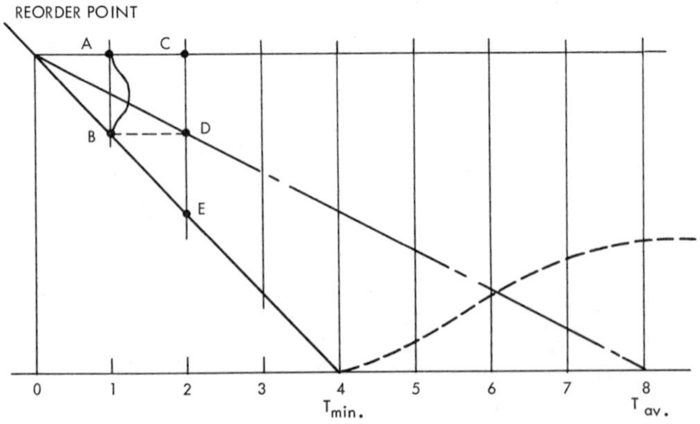

days, as shown on the diagram. The probability of the various possible withdrawal quantities can be illustrated, for the moment, by a distribution as shown at the end of the first day. The series of events will be easier to follow if they are considered period by period:

End of the first period: It is conceivable that at the end of the first period no material will have been withdrawn, as shown at A, or the maximum quantity might have been withdrawn, as shown at *B*. These are, of course, the extreme conditions, and any quantity between the two could have been withdrawn, as described by the probability distribution.

End of the second period: If the first withdrawal period left the inventory at A, we can see that the second period might have left the inventory at *C* or *D*, or some place in between. If the first period had the maximum withdrawal, as shown by *B*, then we might have had for the second period no withdrawals, as shown at *D*, or some maximum value, as shown at *E*, or again some value in between.

Continuing this line of logic, we obtain a line with the T_d minimum intersecting the *zero* quantity line, as shown on the diagram. If the average withdrawal should occur during every time period, we can project that line to intersect with the time axis too, but what about the other extreme? The line extending horizontally is accounted for in some economic lot-size models by obsolescence, and this is just what we have if the line extends as shown.

Even the distributions for each day, as shown in the illustrations, are questionable. If we were considering steel inventories, we would find the distributions skewed to the left if a steel strike were in the offing and skewed to the right if hard times were upon us. These distributions might be independent, or they might be dependent.

This situation is not unlike that faced by the owner of the local candy store. When a child, clutching a coin in his grimy little hand, gives a glance at the candy display but wanders on down the street to emerge from the ice cream store with a cone, the candy store owner knows he has lost a sale. The opportunity to fill this exact need for the child is lost forever. The child may pass this way again tomorrow, but it won't be to fill the same need—only another one. This decision depends upon the satisfactions gained for the amount of money spent. If the cost is too high, there will be substitution.

This same thing occurs in commercial buying. Steel is compared with aluminum and wood with plastic. If the price of the product is too high, and satisfaction can be gained in some cheaper way, the shelves will remain full and the withdrawal line will be horizontal. This can be a sudden change —occurring overnight—if the price of the substitute is lowered.

The decisions, on the other hand, might be dependent. It is not unusual for a customer to defer the purchase of some article because of a shortage of capital, inclement weather, or other reason, and, as a result, double his purchases the following period. In other words, he lets the pipeline run low and fills it by placing one large order.

The foregoing indicates some of the difficulties encountered in describing the withdrawal cycle.

COSTS OF OVERSTOCKING AND UNDERSTOCKING

Let us now take a better look at the withdrawal cycle, assuming a near normal distribution, as shown in Figure 8–9*a*. This first diagram shows a situation in which there is virtually no chance of running out, if there is no variability in the replenishment cycle.

Figure 8–9

Cost of Stockpiling Material

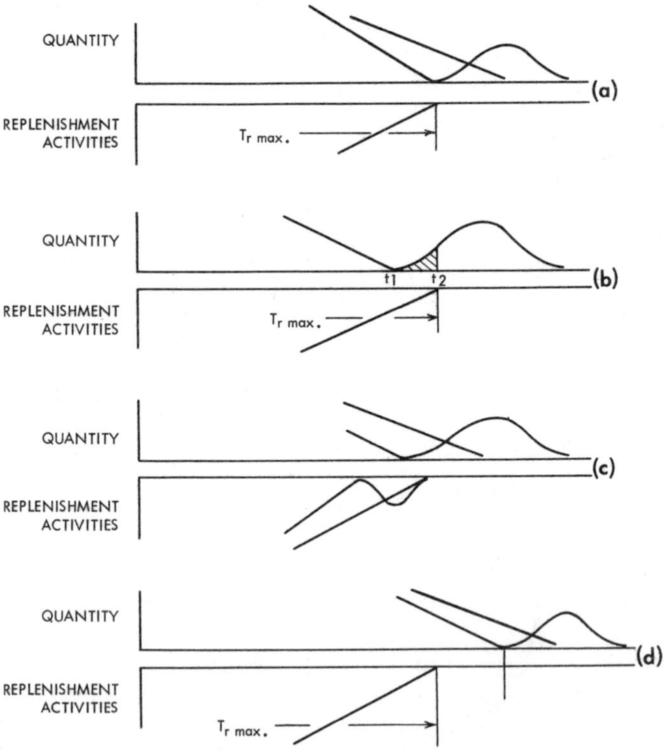

In the second example, *b*, with the replenishment time still fixed, there is an opportunity of depleting the stock before it is replaced. The costs of running out, which may entail shutting down production lines, air-expressing parts, and other expenses, must be weighed against the costs of maintaining an inventory for the period of time $t_2 - t_1$. This stockpiling has been the cause for some alarm, and perhaps rightly so, but it should be compared with the costs that might occur in case of a shortage.

The risk-taking problem becomes more complicated in the third illustration, *c*, when one tries to consider the variability both in the withdrawal and the replenishment distributions. This is especially difficult when little is actually known about each.

The fourth illustration, *d*, shows what can happen if the lead time is set too long or the inventory clerk has been extremely careless in placing the order before it is signaled. The distance between the distributions would be extended, as shown, but the effect would be to increase the safety only very slightly, and at excessive costs.

FACTORS TO CONSIDER IN THE PROBABILISTIC MODEL

It should be evident by now that the development of a probabilistic model is not exactly straightforward. In addition to the problems discussed, there are other factors which influence the effectiveness of any model.

The Effect of Business Trends

We have not taken into account the effect of business changes. What might be a good reorder point in one economic condition might be a poor one at another time. The Good Humor Man would be foolish to lay in a huge supply of ice cream just because he had unusually high sales on a freakishly hot day in October. Probably a good indicator would be the steepness of the withdrawal line as it passes through the reorder point. In a system using clerks, these rates are detected and taken into consideration—a computer is not programmed to judge this change and something is bound to be lost as a consequence.

Factory Scheduling and Withdrawals

The operation of the factory and the inventory are not as unrelated as might have been implied in the previous discussion. The withdrawal of raw material inventories in a job shop is at the mercy of the way the jobs are scheduled to the shop. Consequently, the withdrawal of material can be controlled by what is happening in the factory and the withdrawal distribution is not the result of chance causes alone.

Multiple Use of Inventory Items

The inventory problem is often compounded because a certain item is used in different products. While this makes it more difficult to predict withdrawals, it does permit some trade-offs to compensate for excessive withdrawals.

Cost of Not Filling an Order

There have been attempts to evaluate the cost of not satisfying a need, but we cannot forget that the customer, especially in a retail situation such as a bakery, has some opportunity to make a trade-off. Perhaps he might not get the exact item he wants from the vendor, but he will probably find an acceptable substitute. The customer's buying habits are probably not established on one item alone but upon all the items he carries out in his market basket. There is considerable inertia in a customer's buying habits, but we should remember that if we turn a customer away too often we will lose his loyalty and he will look to other vendors to satisfy his needs.

The manufacturer and the wholesaler have several means of satisfying a customer's needs. Part of an order might be back-ordered, which could be quite satisfactory to the customer since he will not have to store the material and can defer payment. He would probably just as soon fit his withdrawal cycle to the vendor's deliveries if he didn't lose by doing so.

There are other trade-offs which can be made by the vendor that might be satisfactory. He might be able to "rob" other orders, which are not needed immediately, or he might borrow from another manufacturing unit, district warehouse, or friendly customer, and it is not uncommon to borrow from a friendly competitor. While these methods might not be the most satisfactory, they remove some of the hazards in establishing a reorder point. At any rate, the cost of not satisfying a need is probably far too complex to be answered by a single factor in an equation.

Reorder Points and People

One cannot overlook the fact that the withdrawal and replenishment cycles are under the supervision of people. In the replenishment cycle the people are naturally going to work toward the scheduled time (which they seldom will beat, but frequently go beyond). So, because of people alone, the replenishment distribution will probably tend to be skewed to the left.

There will be tendencies throughout for individuals to "pad" data for their own protection. This always makes it difficult to obtain any true picture of a time or quantity estimate.

WHAT IS THE SOLUTION?

No case has been made for a unique method of solving the reorder point problem under uncertainty. Rather, the complexity of the problem has been highlighted with the hope that the reader will not place false hope in a particular technique.

With what little we know about the types of distributions it would seem like a waste of time to go all-out for the curve-fitting methods. The problem becomes particularly complex when we consider inventories containing thousands of different items, although some efficiency can take place by grouping items into families.

The quickest and easiest way of obtaining a reorder point quantity would appear to be the product of the maximum replenishment time and the maximum usage rate. Should this give excessive inventories, it will then be necessary to reduce the quantities, realizing that a certain amount of risk is being taken.

When the savings are being considered for a certain risk, be sure to evaluate it not in abstract terms but in relationship to the cost of closing down the plant, the total plant investment, and other important cost factors.

THE ORDER QUANTITY

Up to this point we have given our attention to the problem of *when* to reorder. Now it is time to turn our attention to *how much* to order. The fixed-order-quantity method, just described, has only one value lacking to make the picture complete. This is the *economic order quantity*, which will also be posted on the heading of the inventory record, with the reorder point quantity, for the convenience of the clerk when reordering.

The quantity that is to be ordered during a certain time can be considered as one or more *lots*. The lot is that group or batch of material that has the same identity for convenience in ordering or manufacturing. Lots are designated because of economic reasons, or for the convenience of the customer, process control department, quality control department, shipping department, or other. The *economic lot size* is that quantity which can be purchased or produced at a minimum cost.

While the method of solving the economic lot-size problem is practically the same for purchased lots and manufactured lots, it should be obvious that the factors entering into the decision will be different. In purchasing from a vendor, quantity discounts should be taken into consideration as well as discounts given by transportation companies for moving large quantities.

The relationship between the lot size and the number of lots produced should be emphasized. The more often lots are produced, the smaller they need to be to satisfy the inventory requirements. Of course, the reverse is also true: large lots need be produced more infrequently. This can be easily visualized on the "saw-tooth" chart of Figure 8–10. On the left, only one large lot is made during the inventory period to last for the whole period. On the right, a number of lots are made and each one has to last but a

Figure 8–10

Order Frequency

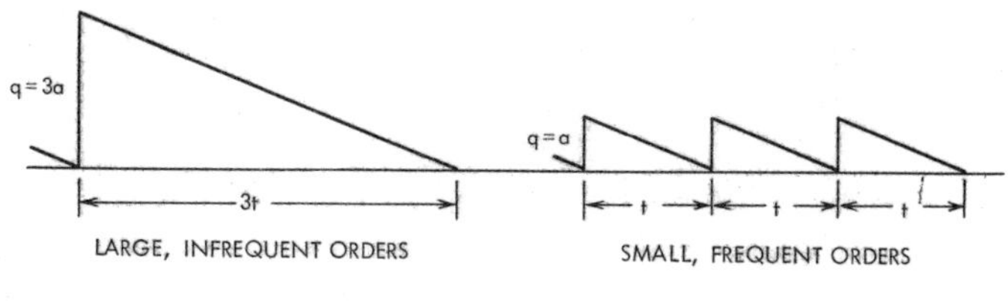

fraction of the total time. In either case, the product of the number of lots and the lot size must be equal to the total demand for the inventory period. Be sure, when you are considering economic lot size problems, that you remember the inverse relationship between lot sizes and number of lots.

It is imperative that the manufacturing engineer fully understands the logic of the economic lot-size problem and knows how it is solved. While few companies use elaborate methods of determining the economic lot size, the individuals responsible for the decision should recognize those factors that go into the elaborate formulas and how they influence the decision. The factors and logic of solving the economic lot size should be understood even though a crude rule-of-thumb method might be used.

The solution of the economic lot-size problem is to minimize the inventory cost. This quickly becomes evident if one studies the two curves in Figure 8–11. No. 1 represents preparation costs plotted against lot sizes; and a curve, No. 2, represents carrying costs plotted against lot sizes.

Figure 8–11

Preparation versus Carrying Costs

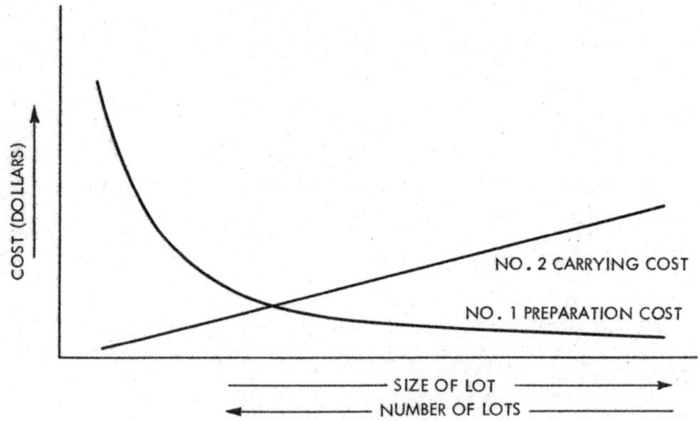

The preparation costs will include such items as preparing the paper work for the order, setting up the machine, and any other costs which are repeated every time an order is placed. The carrying costs are those costs, such as insurance, taxes, etc., having to do with maintaining the inventory for a period of time. As you can see, on the left side of Figure 8–11, the preparation costs for many lots would be large but the carrying costs would be small. On the right, the reverse is true. So our objective in determining an economic lot size is to bring the total of these two groups of costs to a minimum and thus find the lowest possible cost per part in inventory.

The costs for economic lot-size decisions can be brought into sharper focus by listing those costs which tend to make a lot size larger, and by listing separately those costs which tend to make a lot size smaller.

Those factors which tend to make a lot size large are:

1. *Preparation cost:* This includes the costs of preparing the paper work, blueprints, etc., for the order and also the set-up cost for the machines. Set-up cost is the expense of getting the machine ready for production. One question which comes up is whether or not this should include the cost of the machine's being *out* of production. This is typical of the type of question we will run into as we develop the models needed.

Those factors which would tend to make a lot size small are:

1. *Storage or warehousing charge:* This charge, which is self-explanatory, should be for the maximum space used for the items unless it is possible to utilize the space as the inventory is contracted.
2. *Interest charge:* This is the interest on the capital invested, and again we are faced with one of those inscrutable questions. Should this interest rate be what one can expect to earn in the business, or should it be the rate of loaning money or perhaps borrowing money?
3. *Insurance and tax charge:* This would include the insurance on property for both fire and theft as well as property taxes.

DEVELOPING THE ECONOMIC LOT SIZE MODEL

At first we will discuss a very simple model for economic lot sizes, then progress to more sophisticated ones. The simplest model is most frequently used by industry and is the one proposed by one of the largest manufacturers of card-data processing equipment. Although the logic of the simple formula is paved with errors and weak assumptions, it is the one which is used as a starting point for more elaborate models.

For the first model, here are some simplifying assumptions (which can be removed at a later date):

1. The order is placed so that it is received at the time the stock is depleted. In other words, we are not taking into consideration any emergency reserve.
2. The inventory carrying cost is applied to the average inventory value. This means we are not taking into account all the storage costs and the other costs which do not collapse with the decrease in the size of inventory.
3. The unit cost will remain constant throughout the range of production under consideration.

Since our objective in the determination of the economic lot size is to find the lowest yearly inventory cost, it is necessary to express the yearly cost which we intend to optimize.

The total yearly inventory cost is the total of the three costs, as illustrated on the diagram in Figure 8–12.

1. Cost of preparation for production
2. Cost of carrying the inventory
3. Cost of the products in inventory

Equations: 1 + 2 + 3 = 4. Total Yearly Inventory Costs.

Figure 8–12

Economic Lot Sizes

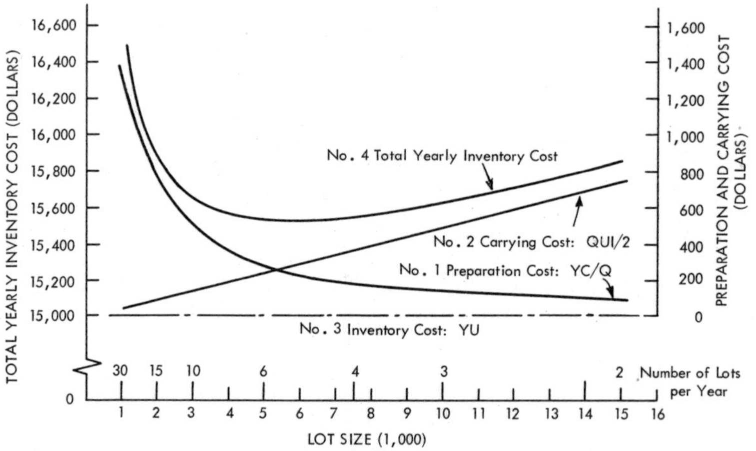

Each of these three costs, 1, 2, and 3, can be defined further:

1. Cost of preparation for production ($/year) equals:

$$\frac{\text{Yearly demand (units/year)}}{\text{Quantity (units/lot)}} \times \text{Cost of order preparation (\$/lot)}$$

$Y =$ Yearly demand in units/year
$Q =$ Economic lot size in units/lot
$C =$ Preparation costs in dollars/lot

Cost of preparation for production $= YC/Q$

2. Cost of carrying inventory for year ($/year) equals:

Average inventory on hand during year × Cost per part × Carrying charge in percentage of part cost

$Q/2 =$ Average inventory carried during the inventory period
$U =$ Unit cost, which is the sum of the direct labor, direct material and overhead, in $/unit
$I =$ Total of all carrying charges expressed as a percentage of the cost of the parts carried in stock for the year

Cost of carrying the inventory $= QUI/2$

3. Cost of inventory ($/year) equals:

Yearly demand in units/year × Cost/unit, or, (as has been defined):

Cost of the inventory $= YU$

Expressing the total yearly inventory cost, *TYIC*, with symbols, we have:

$$TYIC = YC/Q + QUI/2 + YU$$

This gives the total yearly inventory cost; and all the items on the right side of the equation can be determined from the records (except Q). The estimate of the yearly demand, Y, is obtainable from the inventory records; the rest of the information should be found in the cost records.

The problem is still not solved, and the task of obtaining the lowest economic quantity still lies ahead. To do this we have a choice of several methods. Because it is the most revealing, let us examine the graphical solution first, using data for a typical problem.

GRAPHICAL SOLUTION FOR INVENTORY DECISIONS

An electrical appliance manufacturer wishes to know what the economic quantity should be for a plastic impeller when the following information is available.

The average daily requirement is 120 units and the company has 250 working days a year, so the total yearly requirement, Y, is approximately 30,000 units a year. The manufacturing cost, U, which includes the direct labor, direct material, and overhead, is 50 cents each. The sum of the annual rates for interest, insurance, taxes, etc., is 20 percent of the unit cost, and the cost of preparation is \$50 per lot.

$$
\begin{aligned}
Y &= 30{,}000 \text{ units} \\
C &= \$50/\text{preparation} \\
U &= 50¢/\text{part} \\
I &= 20\%
\end{aligned}
$$

These costs, inserted in the equation, would give the following:

$$
TYIC = \frac{30{,}000 \text{ units/year} \times \$50/\text{lot}}{Q \text{ units/lot}} + \frac{Q \text{ units/lot} \times 50¢/\text{part} \times 20\%}{2} + 30{,}000 \text{ units/year} \times 50¢/\text{part}
$$

Figure 8–12 shows the quantity plotted on the horizontal axis, and costs, *TYIC*, on the vertical axis.

It is quite apparent that if only one lot is produced the cost for the year is very high, and that it drops rapidly as more lots are produced—until a lot-size value between 5,000 and 6,000 is reached. As each additional lot is added, and the lot sizes are made smaller, the costs start to go up again. The economic lot size is, of course, where the curve dips at its lowest point, between 5,000 and 6,000.

The third factor, YU, in the equation remains constant and it is easy to see that it in no way affects the solution. All it does is to raise the base from which we start. The same solution would have been obtained if we had left out that part of the equation entirely. We could have done just as well if we had ignored part 3 of the equation and plotted only parts 1 and 2. However, it is better that you see the complete development of the equations.

The graphical solution is tedious, compared with the mathematical models which follow, but it has an advantage (which no other method presents) in that it shows the sensitivity of the costs to slight changes in lot size.

TABULAR SOLUTION

The lowest total yearly cost can be seen by reference to the table of costs, Figure 8–13, which was assembled for plotting the information. By observ-

Figure 8–13

Tabular Method

Lots/Year	*Q* Lot Size	*YC/Q* Prep. Cost No. 1	*QUI/2* Carrying Cost No. 2	*YU* Inv. Cost No. 3	Total Cost No. 4
1...........	30,000	$ 50.00	$1500.00	$15,000.00	$16,550.00
2...........	15,000	100.00	750.00	15,000.00	15,850.00
3...........	10,000	150.00	500.00	15,000.00	15,650.00
4...........	7,500	200.00	375.00	15,000.00	15,575.00
5...........	6,000	250.00	300.00	15,000.00	15,550.00
6...........	5,000	300.00	250.00	15,000.00	15,550.00
7...........	4,286	350.00	214.00	15,000.00	15,564.00

ing the row showing the *TYIC*, one can see that the cost starts high ($16,550 for one lot), decreases to less than $15,550, and starts going back up again. The lowest cost is somewhere between lot sizes of 5,000 to 6,000, just as was shown on the curve.

NOMOGRAPH SOLUTION

Companies have found that solving the economic lot size by graphical means, tabular solutions, or by equations has been far too cumbersome and expensive, so they have resorted to the use of nomographs. Figure 8–14 is typical of this method of solving the economic lot-size problem.

THE CALCULUS METHOD OF SOLVING THE ECONOMIC LOT SIZE PROBLEM

The slope of a line is described by the value of a small segment of y (called *delta* y) over the small segment of x (*delta* x), as shown in Figure 8–15. Thus the value of $\Delta y/\Delta x$ is said to be the slope of the line. The slope at any point on the line can be determined as $\Delta y/\Delta x$ becomes infinitesimal. This is done by the methods of differential calculus.

We can observe that the value of the slope changes from negative to

Figure 8–14

Nomograph Solution

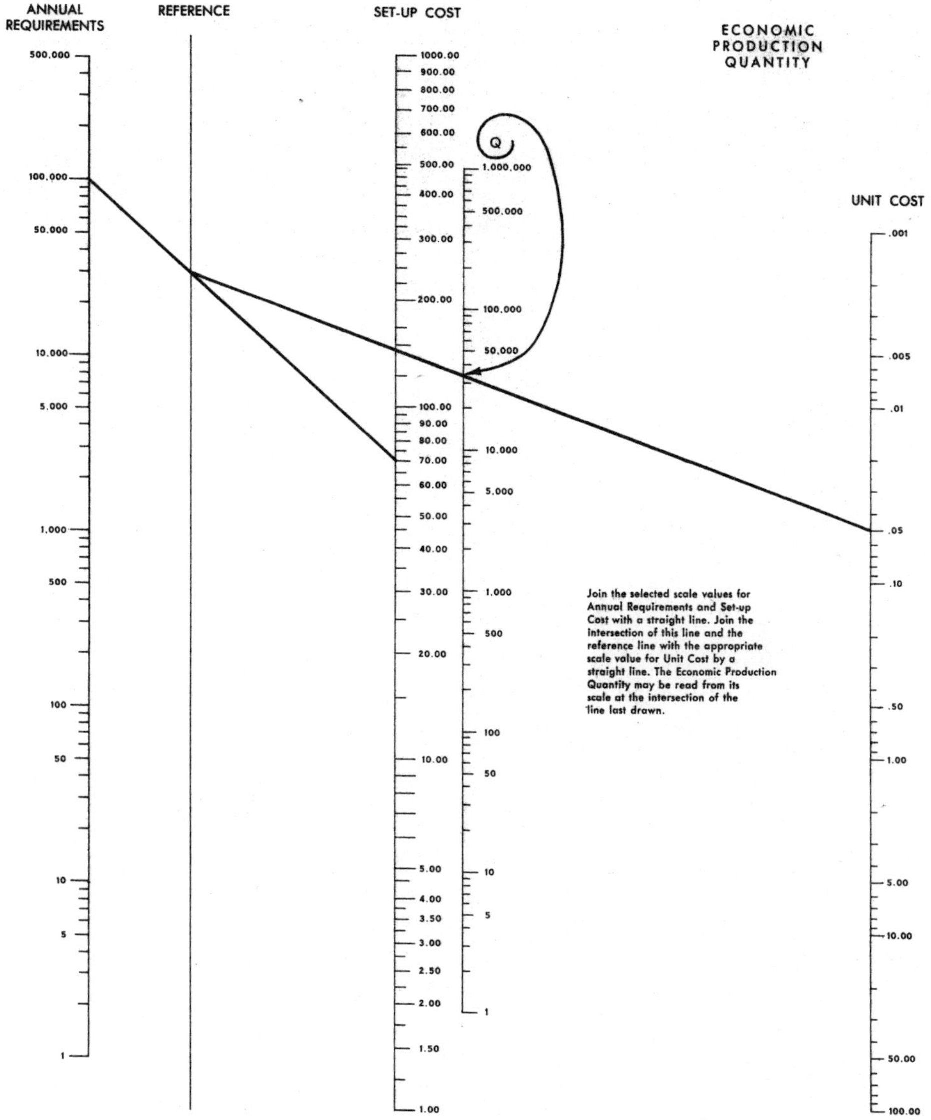

Source: International Business Machines Corp.

positive as we move along the curve. It becomes apparent that the lowest point on the curve—and the one we are searching for—has a slope of zero. This is found by taking the first derivative of the function *TYIC*, setting it to zero, and solving for the value of *Q*:

Figure 8–15
Calculus Solution

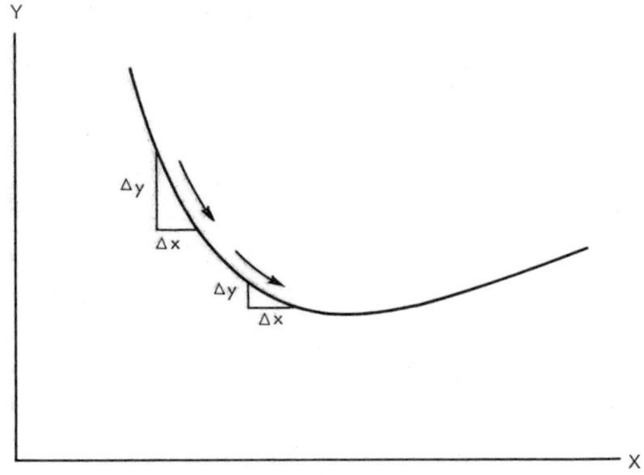

$$TYIC = YC/Q + QUI/2 + YU$$
$$d(TYIC)/dQ = -YC/Q^2 + UI/2 + 0$$
$$d(TYIC)/dQ = 0$$
$$Q = \sqrt{2YC/UI}$$

We can now solve our example by this method:

$$Q = \sqrt{\frac{2 \times 30{,}000 \times 50.00}{.50 \times .20}}$$
$$Q = 5{,}477 \text{ parts}$$

Notice that the value of YU dropped out of the solution, and remember that in our graphical solution we discovered the same to be true.

The equation, $Q = \sqrt{2YC/UI}$, states that the economic lot size varies directly with the square root of the yearly demand and preparation costs, and indirectly with the square root of the carrying costs. This leads to some interesting observations. If the yearly demand for a product went from 100 to 10,000, which would be an increase of 100 times, the economic lot size would be only 10 times larger if all the other factors in the equation remained the same. It is important to management to realize that stock need not be increased in the same ratio as sales or production. Also, as the value of I is increased from, for example, 9 to 16 percent, the economic quantity will be reduced by about 30 percent.

Another important consideration is the shape of the curve at its minimum value. Since it is quite flat near the economic lot-size value, it is not critical for a considerable range of values. This indicates that the decision is not as important as one might imagine. This is a point management should keep in mind as the cost of economic lot-size decisions is considered.

This equation, $Q = \sqrt{2YC/UI}$, with perhaps some slight modifications, is used by the majority of firms which use equations. One of the largest manufacturers of card-data processing equipment suggests this model to its customers. This model is also the one which pops up in the area of mathematical programming upon which more elegant models are developed. However, anyone who has had experience in factory operations must question the assumptions and factors that are used in the equation.

CONSIDERATIONS AND MODIFICATIONS OF THE CARRYING CHARGE

The cost of the inventory carrying charge was calculated on half of the average economic lot size. This would be justifiable if the costs of carrying the inventory were to go up and down with the quantity of inventory on hand. A little consideration of the components of this cost will disclose the unreasonableness of dividing all carrying costs by two. Here are the elements of the inventory carrying costs for your consideration:

Obsolescence of the inventory items
Depreciation of the inventory items
Transportation and handling of the items in inventory
Property taxes on the items in inventory
Storage facility charges
Insurance on the inventory
Interest on the value of the inventory

Each of these items must be evaluated by the company concerned; and it is probable that this is one of the most difficult aspects of the inventory control problem, and one that seems to be often totally ignored.

The obsolescence and depreciation of the inventory is peculiar to the particular industry being studied. For a company producing a high-style product, this would be appreciable, but for a company producing such items as pipe fittings it is relatively low. These costs, as well as the transportation and handling charges, could better be associated with the total economic lot size rather than one-half of it, as shown in many economic lot-size formulas.

Property tax and insurance charges can be best accumulated by the accountant. These depend upon the management policies of the company as well as external forces beyond its control.

The storage charge could seldom be added for one-half the total inventory for the space, in most cases, is not collapsed or used for something else. The bins will exist for an item whether there is one part or fifty thousand. The storage charges for a tank of chemicals cannot be reduced as the quantity is reduced. It becomes quite evident that some charges remain fixed regardless of the size of the inventory, and, in reality, the value of I should be divided into two factors, I_f and I_v, to represent those charges which remain fixed and those which vary with the value of the inventory. Each item will have to be studied by both the production management and the accountant before a decision can be reached as to the appropriate value.

Making this modification in the formula we have the following:

$$\text{Cost of carrying inventory for year} = QUI_v/2 + QUI_f$$

Thus the equation is:

$$TYIC = YC/Q + QUI_v/2 + QUI_f + YU$$
$$TYIC = YC/Q + QU(I_v/2 + I_f) + YU$$
$$d(TYIC)/dQ = -YC/Q^2 + U(I_v/2 + I_f)$$
$$Q = \sqrt{YC/U(I_v/2 + I_f)}$$

It is not easy to select the correct value for interest. One can get numerous answers to this question. The interest rate on borrowed money might be suggested or the interest rate on loaned money might be proposed. Norton has made extensive economic studies and suggests that it should be the minimum attractive rate of return instead of interest rate on borrowed money.[2] In other words, it should be the rate of return that the company earns in its operations, otherwise it will not account for the risks involved. A low interest rate will affect the lot-size formula in such a way as to make the lot size larger than it should be.

CONSIDERATION OF THE SAFETY RESERVE QUANTITY

On first thought it might appear that the safety reserve quantity should have been taken into consideration. We expect to replace the inventory when the level reaches the safety reserve quantity so that the economic lot-size equation would pertain only to carrying the safety reserve during the inventory period. This can be written as an equation:

$$\text{Carrying charge for safety reserve} = \text{Safety reserve quantity} \times \text{Unit cost} \times \text{Annual rate}$$

If this additional carrying charge is added to the economic lot-size equation it will have no influence on the final answer. This is apparent when one recognizes that the above equation does not contain Q. This is similar to the costs of the products in inventory, represented by factor 3 in the development of the economic lot-size equations.

CONSIDERATION OF NONINSTANTANEOUS INPUTS

Up to this point we have considered the inventory input as being instantaneous—as exhibited by the vertical line *O–A* on the saw-tooth chart of Figure 8–16. Frequently, the production would extend over a period of time, as shown by *O–B*. The slope of this line, r/t, is obviously the replenishment rate in quantity per day, week, or other unit of time. The quantity produced,

[2] W. Grant Ireson and Eugene L. Grant, *Handbook of Industrial Engineering and Management* (Englewood Cliffs, N.J.: Prentice-Hall, Inc., 1955), p. 143.

Figure 8–16

Noninstantaneous Inputs

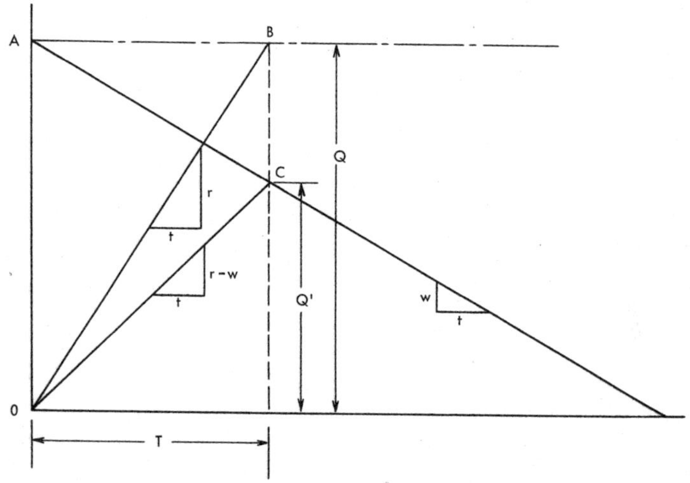

Q, which should be an economic order quantity, is the product of the rate, r/t, and the time period, T, $Q = Tr/t$.

If the material is withdrawn from the inventory at a rate, w/t, while it is being replenished at a rate, r/t, we will develop a line, O–C, with a slope of $(r - w)/t$. It should be noted here that the replenishment rate, r/t, will have to be equal or greater than the withdrawal rate, w/t, or we will run out of stock.

Since the material is running into the inventory while it is also trickling out, we won't need as large a storage space as we did when the inventory replacement was instantaneous. This results in a reduction of the inventory carrying charges, but by how much?

The maximum inventory on hand is as shown on the diagram by Q'. As is customary, the carrying charge is applied to only the average quantity on hand, $Q'/2$. Q' is the product of time period, T, and the rate, $(r - w)/t$.

Starting with $Q' = T(r - w)/t$ and $Q = Tr/t$, we can express Q' in terms of Q:

$$Q' = \frac{Q}{r}(r - w) = Q(1 - w/r)$$

Entering this quantity in the original equation for the storage carrying cost, we have:

Original Equation:

$$\text{Total yearly inventory cost} = \text{Cost of preparation} + \text{Cost of carrying} + \text{Cost of inventory}$$

$$TYIC = YC/Q + Q'UI/2 + YU$$

Revised Equation:

$$TYIC = YC/Q + Q(1 - w/r)\,UI/2 + YU$$

$$\frac{d(TYIC)}{dQ} = -YC/Q^2 + \frac{UI(1 - w/r)}{2}$$

$$Q = \sqrt{\frac{2YC}{UI(1 - w/r)}}$$

It is apparent that the noninstantaneous input equation is slightly more complex than the instantaneous input equation, but probably not so much as to rule out its use. However, before making a general application of this equation, studies regarding the sensitivity should be made.

CONSIDERATION OF LONG ORDER TIMES

So far in our examples the order time has been less than the time it would take to use the material. This doesn't always occur, and frequently we find that it is necessary to have several orders in progress. This situation is more easily seen by Figure 8–17. In *a* we have the situation which has been used in the previous models, in *b* the lead time approaches the usage time, and in *c* the lead time exceeds the usage time by *t*. Several order cycles are shown in Figure 8–18.

It is evident that the quantity ordered at 1 will not be delivered before the inventory is depleted, so there must be an order on its way that will build up the inventory, Q. The material ordered at 1 will be delivered to rebuild the inventory, Q_1. The material ordered at 2 will rebuild the inventory at Q_2, etc. The reorder-point quantity is then determined by extending *t* to the line representing the rate of usage.

In practice, the inventory clerk must be alerted to expect more than one order out at a time. This method of development could expand through as many cycles as necessary.

CONSIDERATION FOR PRICE BREAKS AND SHIPPING DISCOUNTS

The costs that go into the price of a product can vary extensively throughout the range of possible purchased quantities. These different price levels are called "price breaks" and come about for various reasons. Price breaks occur in purchased items because the vendors frequently give quantity discounts at different quantity levels. In addition, price breaks are offered by transportation companies with carload—as opposed to less-than-carload (LCL)—prices. In manufactured products there are price breaks which are caused by differences in processing, such as the difference in costs for producing parts on an engine lathe rather than on an automatic screw machine.

Sometimes these price breaks are such that it is not easy to determine

Figure 8–17

Long Order Times

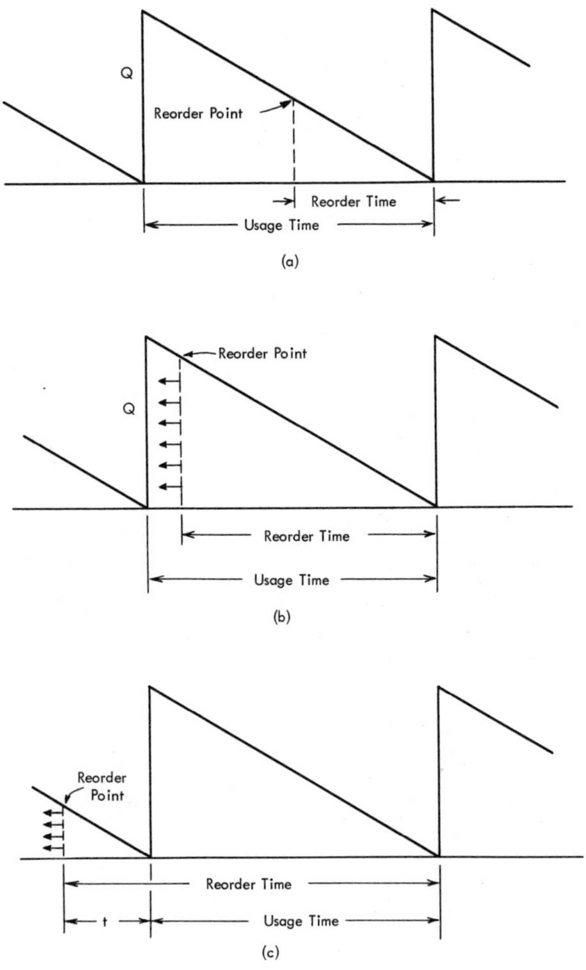

Figure 8–18

Several Order Cycles

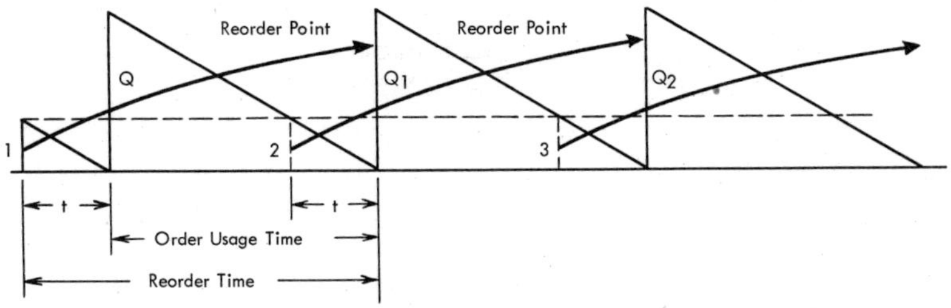

the economic lot size for any particular condition. When this is true, the best procedure is to figure the costs for several alternatives and simply choose the best.

OTHER CONSIDERATIONS

There are various combinations of the quantity-constant and time-constant systems. The time-constant system has the inherent danger that a sudden draw on the inventory will go unnoticed and it will be too late to wait for the usual reorder time. To overcome this, a reorder point is used in conjunction with the time constant system.

In other cases a company may check its inventory items periodically but only place orders for those items which are close to the reorder point. As can be seen, many variations can be played upon these two themes.

SOME COMMENTS ON ECONOMIC LOT-SIZE FORMULAS

This statement will be open to criticism from those who like "elegance" of inventory models regardless of the cost. But probably economic lot decision making should itself come under the scrutiny of an economic study.

Economic lot-size formulas, similar to the ones discussed, have been around since the turn of the century. After having nearly been dropped, they have recently been rejuvenated by the application of statistics and high-speed computers which make the complicated and tedious formulas more suitable for "ambitious" electronic slaves.

The curve of the example problem shows that it would be much better to err on the side of small lots rather than that of large lots. This is characteristic of these curves and should be taken into consideration when making the decision, with or without the aid of the economic lot-size formulas. However, if the risk is high, then the decision should be made as far to the left as possible, which will also increase capital turnover. Many companies operate with so little working capital that they should not consider economic lot sizes. Also, notice how flat the curve is near the bottom. Thus, moving either way from the economic lot size has no drastic effect upon the resulting costs. Again, this should be kept in mind when making the decision.

What sense do elaborate equations make if they do not conform to the facts of life in a factory? The lot size may call for 1,000 parts as an economic lot size, but we discover that the tumbler used for polishing the parts holds just 750 parts, and to run 1,000 we would have to run a tumbler only part full. This doesn't make good sense, so the number should be increased or decreased to come out with even lots in the tumbler operation. Or perhaps we find this lot size would take a half hour longer than the time required for each shift. If we can reduce the time by half an hour, one of the night set-up men can make the change and the machine will not be out any productive time. This makes sense; so whenever economic lot-size formulas are used they should be tempered with good judgment.

Often the type of people who will be responsible for economic lot-size decisions is forgotten. Certainly we can't expect to use a high-level staff man for setting the numerous lot sizes; it will more likely be a clerk with perhaps less than a high school education. It would be foolish to ask him to work a complicated equation.

Also we know that no solution to a problem can be any better than the information that goes into the problem. It was evident earlier that there were some questions about some of the factors that are fed into the equations.

A good way of establishing economic lot sizes is to have a committee formed of the inventory clerk, the plant manager, foremen involved, materials handling supervisor, and other interested parties. After a full understanding of the philosophy of economic lot sizes they can progress to the establishment of economic lot sizes, taking into account the size of tote pans, set-up times, receiving methods, and other factors which bear upon the decision and to which the computers cannot possibly give attention.

INVENTORY POLICIES VERSUS THEORY

Modern inventory theorists often do not take into account the management policies which override some of the most elaborate models. As an example, one small manufacturer of electric measuring instruments knows that he has little to offer the customer in the way of advanced research and production facilities. He does know that one of his biggest selling points is his immediate delivery service. He therefore keeps on hand a carload of instruments so he can make shipments at once. By being able to do this he has been able to stay in business among some of the sharpest competition.

Another example of theory being overridden by practical policy is when a company is operating on little working capital. The economic lot-size formulas may suggest quantities which will cause such drastic problems as making it impossible for a company to take advantage of discounts on accounts payable, or perhaps delaying the payroll. One could think of a number of examples when it is advisable to override the economic lot-size decisions. One should, of course, realize that the theory is helpful in making decisions, but the cost of the inventory alone may not be the only thing to consider.

THE ABC ANALYSIS OF INVENTORY

H. Ford Dickie of the General Electric Company devised a method of analyzing inventories (Figure 8–19) which has been effective not only for his

Figure 8–19

The ABC Analysis

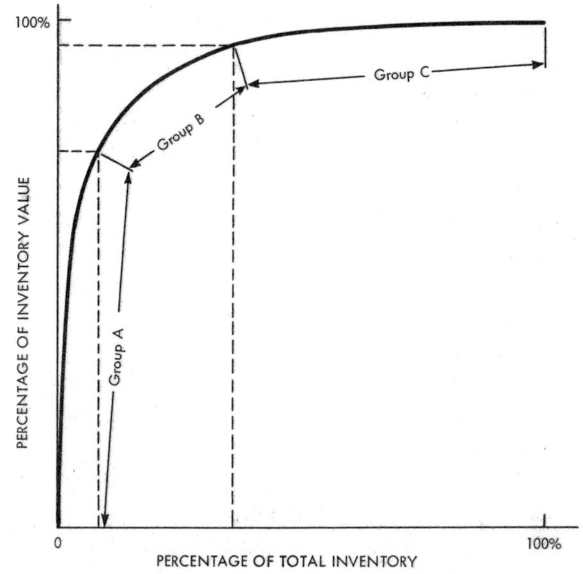

company but for others. The "ABC" method is simply being concerned about products in accordance with their value. In many inventories it can be observed that a *few* of the products, group A, account for the *greatest* cost; some of the items, group B, accounts for a *small amount* of the cost; and group C accounts for a *very* small amount of the cost.

The items in group A should be watched very carefully. For example, the diesel motor is the most costly item in the manufacture of diesel locomotives. Thus, during the assembly, templets are substituted for the engine, which is delivered at the last moment, saving handling and investment costs. Items in group B are watched with some care and kept under surveillance with normal inventory control procedures.

The items in group C are not subjected to the usual paper work. Stock is ordered in this category for a number of months, and when the parts are received enough is set aside, packaged, or otherwise separated to take care of the needs for a reordering cycle. So no records are kept for C items, which would normally constitute the bulk of entries in a perpetual inventory system. When the material is depleted to the point that the material set aside is required, an order is placed. This is, of course, the two-bin system described before. (This does not mean that these products are treated carelessly; they are not. Checks should be made periodically to prevent quantities of materials from disappearing.)

Some companies have found it desirable to divide their inventory clerical force along the lines of the ABC grouping. This is probably desirable because of the difference in philosophy needed by people handling these various types of goods.

One plant in the General Electric complex reported that the stock posting on one line was reduced from 17,000 to 1,500 per year. This saving would compensate for occasionally being out of stock, some emergency orders, and possible thefts.

One weakness of the ABC analysis should be pointed out. Although the items in the C category might have very little cost they may be extremely important in the production of a product. It is conceivable that a small special washer might be just as important in the production of a product as an expensive diesel engine—at least production could be stalled just as quickly for want of one as for the other. This does not prevent us from using the ABC technique, but it points out the necessity of watching all items—and especially those which are vital to production.[3]

QUANTITY REQUIREMENTS BY LEVEL-BY-LEVEL PRODUCT "EXPLOSION"

It is extremely difficult to determine the exact number of parts which are used when there are several levels of assembly. The level-by-level product explosion technique is a logical, orderly method which is readily applied in card-data processing as well as in computer systems. The alternative is to make a detailed breakdown of the product.

The level-by-level requirements explosion is illustrated by Figure 8–20. In this example we are interested only in collecting information about part P–1 (and therefore the illustration is simplified by the omission of all information which does not lead to P–1). As indicated by the code at the head of the first column, the first number indicates the part number; the second number the level; and the third the quantity. This method of numbering is used primarily for illustrating the product explosion system and is not necessarily a suggested method for product numbering. The level and the quantity used for each level may be placed on the record, but not necessarily as part of the product number.

The way of accumulating the quantity of parts needed for the final assembly is illustrated in the table at the bottom of the illustration. This procedure can be used for every part and subassembly used in the completed machine.

MEASURE OF EFFICIENCY FOR INVENTORY

The turnover ratio is frequently used as a measure of the efficiency of an inventory control system. This ratio is expressed as:

[3] H. Ford Dickie, *Key Consideration to Inventory Management* (Manufacturing Series, No. 207) (New York: American Management Association, 1953).

$$\text{Turnover} = \frac{\text{Quantity used during a period of time}}{\text{Average inventory on hand}}$$

Figure 8–20

Product Explosion

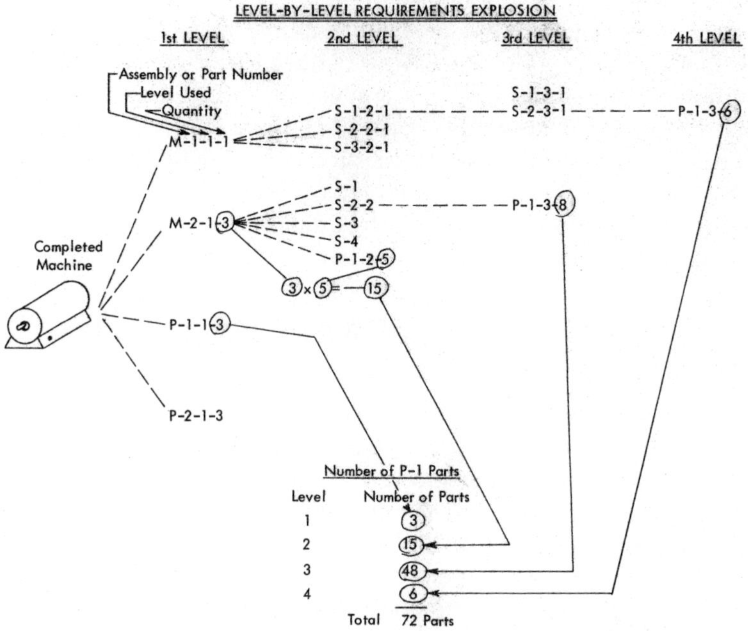

The higher the inventory turnover the more efficiently the inventory is being handled, and the more effective the use of capital. This ratio varies considerably from company to company and industry to industry. A good management will know what is acceptable in its industry and strive to better it.

FUTURE OF INVENTORY CONTROL THEORY

In recent years management has learned some of the many advantages of good inventory control procedures. Efficient inventory management has been credited with playing an important role in the unprecedented and sustained prosperity of our time.

Executives will undoubtedly be exploring the possibility of applying some of the more sophisticated inventory models. Those who are developing inventory models will probably start looking more closely at the real-world conditions in which their techniques are to operate. Designing the models within the restrictions of the industrial conditions will become more important, but of greater importance will be a thorough testing to determine the efficiency of the models.

Rhocrematics is a concept of integrated material flow. This science of material flow consists of developing a framework within which the whole distribution function can be examined. This "horizon-to-horizon" thinking about the material problems will certainly produce some new and better solutions.

Communications, in its improved forms, is bound to have an important impact upon inventory problems. Data-Phones will convey information between data-processing centers to allow executives new dimensions in decision making.

More and more information is becoming available at a faster and faster rate, but—what is probably more important—we are training people to be competent enough to use it efficiently.

SUMMARY

Inventory decision-making problems are of two kinds: when to order and how much to order. The decision of when to order may be based on either a constant review time or on a constant reorder quantity, the latter being favored by most companies.

The order-quantity decision is a problem of minimizing both the total costs of maintaining an inventory and the costs of placing an order.

There has been a tendency to make inventory decisions more complex than they deserve, but it is useless to be concerned about factors in equations which have little influence on the decision. It should also be kept in mind that the answer can be no more accurate than the information which is used in the model. However, the reasoning behind inventory models can be useful as a guide for day-to-day decisions of when and how much to order.

Questions

1. How well does the saw-tooth chart illustrate the inventory control situation?
2. Which is the more common system: fixed-order quantity or fixed-order time?
3. Which inventory system—fixed-order time or fixed-order quantity—does each of the following use: housewife, filling station owner buying gas, homeowner buying fuel oil, automobile owner buying gas?
4. The frequency of reviewing the inventory on a fixed-time basis should minimize the total of two costs. What are these costs? How easy would it be to determine these costs? Are these costs linear wih respect to the length of the review period?
5. Define the following: order quantity, reorder point quantity, safety reserve quantity.
6. What is the purpose of the ABC inventory control method? Describe how it might be used in the manufacture of electrical appliances. Is it possible that a C product is more important than an A product? Explain.
7. Discuss the dangers of both overstocking and understocking material in a manufacturing company.

8. Relate economic conditions to the economic order quantity.
9. The economic lot size attempts to minimize the total of two costs. What are they? How easy are they to obtain?
10. Why is it that the cost of the products in the inventory does not affect the economic lot size?
11. Discuss the strengths and weaknesses of the economic lot-size equations from an applied viewpoint.
12. A hardware company produces over 10,000 different items. Suggest how they can use economic lot-size formulas without excessive cost.

References

ALFANDARY-ALEXANDER, MARK. *An Inquiry Into Some Models of Inventory Systems*. Pittsburgh: University of Pittsburgh Press, 1962.

AMERICAN MANAGEMENT ASSOCIATION. *Company Approaches to Production Problems: Inventory, Warehousing, Traffic*. Manufacturing Series 220. New York, 1955.

———. (H. FORD DICKIE, ed.). *Key Consideration to Inventory Management*. Manufacturing Series No. 207. New York, 1953.

AMERICAN PRODUCTION AND INVENTORY CONTROL SOCIETY (CLIFFORD M. BAUMBACK, ed.). *Management of Lot Size Inventories*. Chicago, 1963.

AMMER, DEAN S. *Materials Management*. Homewood, Ill.: Richard D. Irwin, Inc., 1962.

ARROW, KENNETH JOSEPH; KARLIN, SAMUEL; and SCARF, HERBERT. *Studies in the Mathematical Theory of Inventory and Production*. Stanford, Calif.: Stanford University Press, 1958.

BOWMAN, EDWARD H., and FETTER, ROBERT B. *Analysis for Production Management*. Homewood, Ill.: Richard D. Irwin, Inc., 1957.

BREWER, STANLEY H. *RHOCHREMATICS, A Scientific Approach to the Management of Material Flows*. Seattle, Wash.: Bureau of Business Research, College of Business Administration, University of Washington, 1960.

———, and PARKER, DONALD D. *Rhochrematics in the Flow of Parts and Accessories*. Seattle, Wash.: Faculty Research and Publications, College of Business Administration, University of Washington, 1962.

BRIGGS, ANDREW J. *Warehouse Operations Planning and Management*. New York: John Wiley & Sons, Inc., 1960.

BUCHAN, JOSEPH, and KOENIGSBERG, ERNEST. *Scientific Inventory Management*. Englewood Cliffs, N.J.: Prentice-Hall, Inc., 1963.

FETTER, ROBERT B., and DALLECK, WINSTON C. *Decision Models for Inventory Management*. Homewood, Ill.: Richard D. Irwin, Inc., 1961.

FOX, JOHN J. *Inventory Management, Statistical Techniques for Inventory Management with UNIVAC Systems*. New York: Sperry Rand Corporation, 1962.

GREENE, JAMES H., and COLLIER, JAMES A. "The Dynamics of Packaging," *Material Handling Engineering*, Vol. 14, No. 8 (May, 1959), p. 96.

———, and RAYMOND, MURRAY. "Here's How Photography Can Eliminate Inventory Handling," *Flow*, Vol. 13, No. 11 (August, 1958), p. 51.

HADLEY, GEORGE, and WHITIN, T. M. *Analysis of Inventory Systems*. Englewood Cliffs, N.J.: Prentice-Hall, Inc., 1963.

HANSSMANN, FRED. *Operations Research in Production and Inventory Control*. New York: John Wiley & Sons, Inc., 1962.

HOLT, CHARLES C. *Planning Production, Inventories, and Work Force*. Englewood Cliffs, N.J.: Prentice-Hall, Inc., 1960.

MELNITSKY, BENJAMIN. *Industrial Storeskeeping Manual*. Philadelphia: Chilton Co., 1956.

———. *Management of Industrial Inventory*. New York: Conover-Mast Publications, 1951.

NEUSCHEL, RICHARD F., and JOHNSON, H. TALLMAN. *How to Take Physical Inventory*. New York and London: McGraw-Hill Book Co., Inc., 1946.

RAYMOND, MURRAY R. "The Use of Photographic Techniques in Making the Physical Inventory." Unpublished thesis for M.S., I.E. Lafayette, Ind.: Purdue University, 1955.

SCARF, HERBERT E.; GILFORD, DOROTHY M.; and SHELLEY, MAYNARD W. *Multistage Inventory Models and Techniques*. Stanford, Calif.: Stanford University Press, 1963.

SESPANIACK, LAWRENCE J. "An Application of Combinatorial Statistics to the Determination of the Order Point." Unpublished thesis for M.S., I.E. Lafayette, Ind.: Purdue University, 1957.

STARR, MARTIN KENNETH, and MILLER, DAVID W. *Inventory Control: Theory and Practice*. Englewood Cliffs, N.J.: Prentice-Hall, Inc., 1962.

WAGNER, HARVEY M. *Statistical Management of Inventory Systems*. New York: John Wiley & Sons, Inc., 1962.

WELCH, W. EVERT. *Tested Scientific Inventory Control*. Greenwich, Conn.: Management Publishing Corp., 1959.

WHITIN, THOMSON M. *The Theory of Inventory Management*. 2d ed. Princeton, N.J.: Princeton University Press, 1957.

CHAPTER 9

Scheduling Information

Regardless of the activity, it is essential to have time estimates if we expect to develop an efficient schedule. A good student, with his numerous activities to perform, has an idea of how long it takes to do each one. He knows how long he takes to do an experiment, do a report, attend a class—and all the other things that fill his time—for only with this scheduling knowledge can he possibly be an efficient student. This analogy can be carried into the industrial world by saying that only factories with accurate time information can expect to operate with any degree of efficiency.

Since we are interested in the efficient planning and control of a factory, it is essential to know the best ways to develop the necessary time information. This subject makes up part of this chapter, but we must also know the strengths and weaknesses of these time data. In addition, you will observe the effect of learning upon time estimates. You will also become acquainted with the various *industrial calendars* found in today's factories.

USE OF TIME ESTIMATES

Our major interest in time values for tasks is in their application to scheduling, but this is not their only use. For example, time estimates are tied directly to the wage incentive plan. They are also used in the scientific cost estimate, as we have seen. Where the activities are composed of several men or machines, the time estimates can be used to balance the loads. Motion study, which is the analysis and improvement of methods of doing work, goes hand in hand with the determination of time values, for how else could the improvement be measured?

With all the various uses for time estimates it is little wonder they do not meet all the objectives. Also, it is reasonable to expect different degrees of accuracy to be required for the various uses. This is true, and we should be able to select the proper measuring tool for the work to be done.

Methods for Estimating Time Values

A number of techniques are used in determining the time required for factory and office activities. Some of these methods can only give crude approximations of the actual time while others can give quite accurate information. The common methods will be briefly discussed in this order:

1. Time estimates based on past experience
2. Stop-watch time study
3. Elemental standard data
4. Predetermined motion-time data
5. Work sampling

PAST EXPERIENCE ESTIMATES

Probably no self-respecting devotee of scientific management would ever recognize this method of obtaining time information. Nevertheless, the technique does exist to a considerable extent when the information is used for scheduling. This method is practiced by recording the past performance of an operation, often directly on the operation sheet. When this job, or a similar one, is to be run again, the information is pulled from the file and used with perhaps some modifications for changes in machines, operators, materials, and the other variables. Lacking this past performance record, a *guesstimate* is made using the past experience of similar projects familiar to several production people. Such estimates should not be used as a basis for wage payments, of course, but in scheduling they can be used satisfactorily if the personnel are experienced and no better information is available.

STOP-WATCH TIME STUDY

Stop-watch time study is the most common method of measuring the time that it takes to accomplish a task. Dr. Ralph M. Barnes, a pioneer developer of this tool of scientific management, defines time study thus:

> Time study is used to determine the time required by a qualified and well-trained person working at a normal pace to do a specified task.[1]

The objective of the time study is to determine the *standard time*. This is defined as the time it takes to do a task, usually expressed in minutes per part. At a glance, it would appear that this can be obtained by going out on the factory floor with a watch and timing the task, but it isn't quite that simple.

First, when you time the task you have no assurance that the worker is doing the task at a *normal pace*, for he may be working faster or slower than the average. Therefore it is necessary to modify or *normalize* the task time

[1] Ralph M. Barnes, *Motion and Time Study: Design and Measurement of Work* (5th ed.; New York: John Wiley & Sons, Inc., 1963), p. 348.

as measured by the watch. Second, we usually cannot time the task all day, and therefore cannot include all the additional time needed for personal needs and other delays which are inherent in the work. It is obvious that the time values we obtain during our short stay on the factory floor will have to be modified in two ways: one, to make them represent the normal pace; second, to allow for the unavoidable delays that occur during the task.

There are some variations in the way stop-watch time studies are made, but the following discussion will give a brief summary of a common method. The equipment used by the time study analyst consists of time study data sheets, conveniently secured to a clipboard to which a decimal stop watch is attached (Figure 9–1). The analyst takes up a position from which he can

Figure 9–1

Time Study Recording Equipment

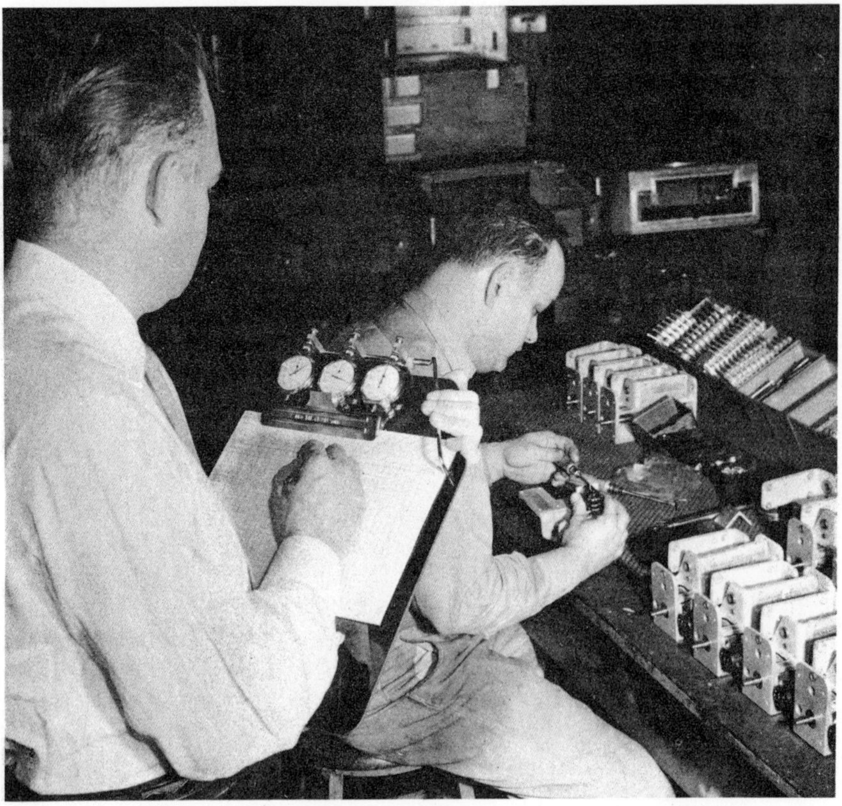

Courtesy of Meylan Stopwatch Corporation

conveniently observe both the task being performed and the watch and board. It should be pointed out that there are other timing methods used, such as strip recorders, but the common method is the decimal stop watch.

The entire stop-watch procedure can be best understood by following it step by step. The recorded results of these steps are indicated directly on the time sheet (Figure 9–2).

Step 1. Observe and Record Job Conditions. First, the analyst should observe the job for a period of time and discuss it fully with the foreman in charge, as well as with the operator doing the work. It is essential that the task conditions be recorded so that they can be reconstructed at some time in the future if need be. Therefore, every detail of the task must be recorded.

Step 2. Establish the Cycle Elements. The operation cycle is divided into elements. This is important to assure that the entire operation is recorded and to separate machine elements, which tend to remain the same, from man-controlled elements, which may vary. As we will see later, these elements might be used to synthesize standard times for other tasks as well. Also, in some time study techniques the normalizing is done element by element rather than for the whole cycle.

Step 3. Time the Elements. The next step is to observe the operator doing the task a number of times, recording the time taken for each element. There has been some controversy as to whether the watch should run continuously, with the analyst taking the time at the end of each element, or whether the watch hands should be "snapped back" to zero at the end of each element. Both methods appear to give good results.

This phase of the stop-watch time study is a sampling procedure, and we must take a large enough sample to represent the population. This is an extensive subject, but the recognized texts in the field not only develop the statistics behind the sampling procedure, they also have tables and charts which can be used in determining the correct number of readings.

Step 4. Normalizing the Recorded Time. According to our definition, we wish to determine the normal pace needed to do a specified task. We have used the word normalize as being more descriptive, but the process is more commonly called *rating*. In the rating process the time study analyst compares the actual performance of the operator with a concept of *normal performance*. This concept of normal performance is frequently reinforced by observing rating films in which a number of levels of performance are known. The results of Step 4 is the *normal time*. There are various other ways of rating, one being *objective rating*, in which each element is rated.

Step 5. The Addition of Allowances. The normal time developed in Step 4 is usually obtained over a relatively short period, so it does not account for any rest, personal time, or other delays. Since these are to be expected, we must increase the normal time. This information is usually in a table prepared from all-day time studies.

Briefly, these have been the steps in making a stop-watch time study, but the method might be more obvious if we simply state the equations used in obtaining the *standard time*.

Selected time × Rating = Normal time (also called *base time, leveled,* or *rated time*)

Figure 9–2

Time Study Data Sheet

Form 762

GEAR AND TOOL COMPANY

TIME STUDY DEPT.

SHEET 1 OF 2

DATE	6-13
TIME STUDY NO.	26568
PART NAME	Contact & Brush & Cable Assy.
ROUGH PART NO.	26 - 3 - 87
FIN. PART NO.	402235-A-1
APPLIED TO:	
OPERATION	Assemble terminal & washer one end of cable washer insulator over terminal stud- Assemble to cover & rubber shell, assemble washer & nut, fold- Cable inside cover.
MACHINE TYPE, NAME AND NO.	
OPERATION NO.	1
DEPT. CODE	GA
NO.	70
NO. MACH'S	
POINTS 60 GROUP	60
OPER'D	1

QUAN.	TOOLING: (Include all data necessary to duplicate set-up)	NO. OF CUTS	DEPTH OF CUT	LGTH. OF CUT	SPEED	SPDLE GEARS	FEED	FEED GEARS	TIME (SEC.)
	Special screwdriver with socket welded on aluminum hammer.								

JIGS & FIXTURES: Stud type fixture to assemble terminal, wire & washer. D-933976, fixture for assembly

INSPECTION: 100 % visual check for alignment, etx.

SIZE: ROUGH	
FINISH	
WORK: FROM:	Box
TO:	Box
MATL:	
RGH. WT.	
NO. PCS./CYCLE	
REMARKS:	

ALLOWANCES:	HANDLING	MACHINE
MINIMUM DELAY	2	
PERSONAL	4	
FATIGUE	5	
Clean up	1	
TOTAL	12	

SUMMARY:	NRML. TIME	12-1/2%	ALL'A. %	ALL'A. TIME
PC. HANDLING	1.			
MACH. HANDLING				
MACHINE TIME				
HANDLING, INTERNAL TO MACH. TIME				
TIME ALLOWANCES				
TTL. NRML. TIME		xxx	xxx	xxx
TTL. ALL'D. TIME	x.......%	xxx	xxx	
NORMAL EXPECTED PCS. PER HR. NET			xxx	xxx
ALLOWED EXPECTED PCS. PER HR. NET		xxx	xxx	(a)

OCCU. CODE NO. LABOR GRADE

INCENTIVE RATE COMPUTATION BASE (Expected Earnings minus Payroll Additions) (b)

RATE PER 100 PCS. (b) $........ x 100 .... = $ (a) MACH

PREVIOUS RATE:

SET UP:

JOB ALLOWANCES: None

Free effort

REASON:

SKETCH WORK AREA AND PARTS:

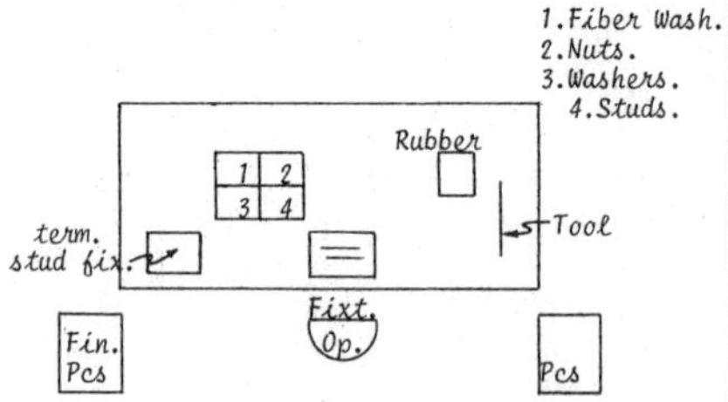

OPERATOR:	T.I.M.	FOREMAN:	R.O.B.	O. M. CARD:	7-1-68	APPROVED BY:	RATE ISSUED:
CLOCK NO.:	6927	TIME STUDY BY:	B.M.				

To the *normal time* must then be added the allowance to obtain the *standard time*

Normal time + (Normal time × Allowance) = Standard time

To start with, we obtain the *selected time* for the task. We have divided the task cycle into distinctive, easily measured elements, and have determined the time for a number of cycles of these elements which will give a representative sample. The number of cycles must be large enough to assure

Figure 9–2 (continued)

DATE: SHEET 2 OF 2

TIME STUDY SHEET

START	STOP	ELAPSED	PART AND OPERATION:
2:30	4:30	--	Contact & Brush & Cable Assy--

DESCRIPTION OF ELEMENT (PERFORMANCE RTG. CYCLE)	1	2	3	4	5	6	7	8	9	10	TTL	AV.	SLCT	PERF. RTG.	Norm TIME
1. Position washer fix. stud	8	9	9	8	9	7	10	7	6	7	2.32				
pos. cable & stud - hit stud-	08	94	84	36	18	99	04	83	59	38	28	0829			
2. Pick up cable assembly, pos	13	12	16	8	9	10	13	13	10	10	3.16				
stud & bend wire down.	21	06	00	44	27	09	17	96	69	48	28	1129			
3. Pos. fiber washer over	16	12	16	8	11	19	12	13	18	17	4.03				
term. stud & pos. cover over stud-	37	24	16	52	38	28	29	09	82	65	28	1439			
4. Pick up rubber shell &	8	10	10	12	10	11	10	8	12	14	3.20				
fit washer into shell & shake to seat.	45	34	26	64	48	39	39	17	94	79	28	1143			
5. Pick up special socket	12	11	8	16	10	8	10	9	9	10	2.77				
wrench, position nut into socket & then to shell-	57	45	34	80	58	60	49	26	03	89	28	0989			
6. Position to terminal stud	15	16	16	18	19	14	15	14	15	16	4.17				
start nut - secure nut-	72	61	50	98	77	74	64	40	18	05	28	1489			
7. Pick up assembly, remove	13	14	15	11	15	20	12	13	13	14	4.95				
wrench. Alignment, bend wire per print.	85	75	65	09	92	94	76	53	31	19	28	1411			
												8429			
					.8429 X 1.10 = .9272										
					.9272 + (.9272 X 12%) =										1.0384

CODES:

that the times are representative. A common way of obtaining a representative time for the cycle is to add and average all the readings. This cycle time is referred to as the selected time.

The selected time, as we know, may not be representative of a normal pace, so the time study analyst must modify it by multiplying by a rating factor. As we will see later, it is the rating factor which might cause us difficulty in applying the standard times to scheduling. This subject is worthy of a lengthy discussion but we should first see how it is part of the other methods of estimating time values. To the normal time must be added time for rest and personal needs. This is done by the allowance, which varies from task to task, depending upon the specific requirements of that task.

ELEMENTAL TIMES

In certain kinds of work, such as in the metal working industry, standard times can be synthesized from the elements of previous time studies. For example, in simple drilling operations the time for loading the jig is nearly the same for a family of tasks. The machine time, on the other hand, will vary from task to task because of the size and depth of the hole to be drilled. The same is true for milling operations, lathe operations, and many other tasks. Consequently, we can separate the man-time from the machine-time, calculate each separately, and then combine them into a standard time.

Man Time

Standards departments take advantage of the similarity among jobs and accumulate the times for common elements, which they then compile into a table. Lacking time study data of their own, they might resort to one of the compilations of data (Figure 9–3) available in one of the commercially available handbooks. This is for one simple operation, but these books cover

Figure 9–3

Elemental Times for Drilling*

8. Unit time to sharpen drill	See Table 68	
9. Personal allowance		5%
10. Fatigue allowance	See Chap. IV	

Method 2.—To be used for the drilling of one hole in bolts, small tubes or shafts, cotter-pin holes, etc. A small jig is used, and the part is held in place by one setscrew.

		Minutes
1. Pick up part from tote pan, and install in jig.............		.120
2. Position jig and work on table under spindle..............		.060
3. Advance drill to work..................................		.030
4. Drill, ream, tap, etc.	See Tables 69–78	
5. Clear drill		.020
6. Release part from jig..................................		.080
7. Aside with part to tote pan............................		.050
8. Blow jig and table clean to receive next load..............		.100
9. Unit time to check part	See Chap. IV	
10. Unit time to sharpen drill	See Table 68	
11. Personal allowance		5%
12. Fatigue allowance	See Chap. IV	

* W. A. Nordhoff, *Machine Shop Estimating* (New York: McGraw-Hill Book Co., Inc., 1947).

most of the common machine tools. Other information is available for other industries as well.

Machine Time

Often the times for machine operations are compiled in a table. The time it takes for threading one inch of rod in various diameters and materials is an example. Sometimes this information is not attainable and one must work from the basic information of feeds, speeds, and depth of cut. This is a subject with which you should be familiar and one which will be discussed later in this chapter.

Predetermined Motion-Time Standards

Predetermined motion-time standards are more refined than the elemental time methods just described. In the elemental time method the units measured were gross compared with the units used in predetermined motion times. The characteristic of the predetermined motion-time standard is to consider the basic motions for which extensive time data have been obtained by such techniques as time study, frame-by-frame analysis of motion pictures, and, more recently, by electronic instrumentation.

There are a number of predetermined motion-time standard systems available which go under such names as Methods Time Measurement (MTM), Work Factor Plan (WF), Basic Motion-Time Study (BMT), and others. The basic motions, with their associated time values for the MTM system, are shown in the following tables (Figure 9–4). These values are all normalized but do not include any allowances. To show how quickly this system can be put to the task of calculating a standard time, observe the calculations for the illustration in Figure 9–5.

These motion times can be used to engineer the methods and times for tasks even before the task is actually performed by an operator. In actual practice, on highly repetitive work the time for an operation is synthesized directly from the tables shown in Figure 9–4. On less highly repetitive work, standard data elements, such as the one shown in Figure 9–5, are first built up. Then these elements are used for the establishing of methods and standards. By means of the process of building up standard elements from the basic motion data, nonrepetitive work—such as the building of an entire ship and various kinds of maintenance work—has been successfully placed on standard, even to the setting of incentive rates.

WORK SAMPLING

Work sampling is a method of analyzing and evaluating the time used for work by a series of random observations which are extended over a period of time. This technique also goes under the name of *ratio delay* because one

Figure 9–4

MTM Tables

TABLE I—REACH—R

Distance Moved Inches	Time TMU A	Time TMU B	Time TMU C or D	Time TMU E	Hand in Motion A	Hand in Motion B
¾ or less	2.0	2.0	2.0	2.0	1.6	1.6
1	2.5	2.5	3.6	2.4	2.3	2.3
2	4.0	4.0	5.9	3.8	3.5	2.7
3	5.3	5.3	7.3	5.3	4.5	3.6
4	6.1	6.4	8.4	6.8	4.9	4.3
5	6.5	7.8	9.4	7.4	5.3	5.0
6	7.0	8.6	10.1	8.0	5.7	5.7
7	7.4	9.3	10.8	8.7	6.1	6.5
8	7.9	10.1	11.5	9.3	6.5	7.2
9	8.3	10.8	12.2	9.9	6.9	7.9
10	8.7	11.5	12.9	10.5	7.3	8.6
12	9.6	12.9	14.2	11.8	8.1	10.1
14	10.5	14.4	15.6	13.0	8.9	11.5
16	11.4	15.8	17.0	14.2	9.7	12.9
18	12.3	17.2	18.4	15.5	10.5	14.4
20	13.1	18.6	19.8	16.7	11.3	15.8
22	14.0	20.1	21.2	18.0	12.1	17.3
24	14.9	21.5	22.5	19.2	12.9	18.8
26	15.8	22.9	23.9	20.4	13.7	20.2
28	16.7	24.4	25.3	21.7	14.5	21.7
30	17.5	25.8	26.7	22.9	15.3	23.2

CASE AND DESCRIPTION
A Reach to object in fixed location, or to object in other hand or on which other hand rests.
B Reach to single object in location which may vary slightly from cycle to cycle.
C Reach to object jumbled with other objects in a group so that search and select occur.
D Reach to a very small object or where accurate grasp is required.
E Reach to indefinite location to get hand in position for body balance or next motion or out of way.

TABLE II—MOVE—M

Distance Moved Inches	Time TMU A	Time TMU B	Time TMU C	Hand in Motion B
¾ or less	2.0	2.0	2.0	1.7
1	2.5	2.9	3.4	2.3
2	3.6	4.6	5.2	2.9
3	4.9	5.7	6.7	3.6
4	6.1	6.9	8.0	4.3
5	7.3	8.0	9.2	5.0
6	8.1	8.9	10.3	5.7
7	8.9	9.7	11.1	6.5
8	9.7	10.6	11.8	7.2
9	10.5	11.5	12.7	7.9
10	11.3	12.2	13.5	8.6
12	12.9	13.4	15.2	10.0
14	14.4	14.6	16.9	11.4
16	16.0	15.8	18.7	12.8
18	17.6	17.0	20.4	14.2
20	19.2	18.2	22.1	15.6
22	20.8	19.4	23.8	17.0
24	22.4	20.6	25.5	18.4
26	24.0	21.8	27.3	19.8
28	25.5	23.1	29.0	21.2
30	27.1	24.3	30.7	22.7

Wt. Allowance: Wt. (lb.) Up to	Factor	Constant TMU
2.5	1.00	0
7.5	1.06	2.2
12.5	1.11	3.9
17.5	1.17	5.6
22.5	1.22	7.4
27.5	1.28	9.1
32.5	1.33	10.8
37.5	1.39	12.5
42.5	1.44	14.3
47.5	1.50	16.0

CASE AND DESCRIPTION
A Move object to other hand or against stop.
B Move object to approximate or indefinite location.
C Move object to exact location.

TABLE III—TURN AND APPLY PRESSURE—T AND AP

Weight	30°	45°	60°	75°	90°	105°	120°	135°	150°	165°	180°
	Time TMU for Degrees Turned										
Small— 0 to 2 Pounds	2.8	3.5	4.1	4.8	5.4	6.1	6.8	7.4	8.1	8.7	9.4
Medium—2.1 to 10 Pounds	4.4	5.5	6.5	7.5	8.5	9.6	10.6	11.6	12.7	13.7	14.8
Large— 10.1 to 35 Pounds	8.4	10.5	12.3	14.4	16.2	18.3	20.4	22.2	24.3	26.1	28.2

APPLY PRESSURE CASE 1—16.2 TMU. APPLY PRESSURE CASE 2—10.6 TMU

Figure 9–4 (continued)

TABLE IV—GRASP—G

Case	Time TMU	DESCRIPTION
1A	2.0	**Pick Up Grasp**—Small, medium or large object by itself, easily grasped.
1B	3.5	Very small object or object lying close against a flat surface.
1C1	7.3	Interference with grasp on bottom and one side of nearly cylindrical object. Diameter larger than ½″.
1C2	8.7	Interference with grasp on bottom and one side of nearly cylindrical object. Diameter ¼″ to ½″.
1C3	10.8	Interference with grasp on bottom and one side of nearly cylindrical object. Diameter less than ¼″.
2	5.6	**Regrasp.**
3	5.6	**Transfer Grasp.**
4A	7.3	Object jumbled with other objects so search and select occur. Larger than 1″ x 1″ x 1″.
4B	9.1	Object jumbled with other objects so search and select occur. ¼″ x ¼″ x ⅛″ to 1″ x 1″ x 1″.
4C	12.9	Object jumbled with other objects so search and select occur. Smaller than ¼″ x ¼″ x ⅛″.
5	0	Contact, sliding or hook grasp.

TABLE V—POSITION*—P

CLASS OF FIT		Symmetry	Easy To Handle	Difficult To Handle
1—Loose	No pressure required	S	5.6	11.2
		SS	9.1	14.7
		NS	10.4	16.0
2—Close	Light pressure required	S	16.2	21.8
		SS	19.7	25.3
		NS	21.0	26.6
3—Exact	Heavy pressure required.	S	43.0	48.6
		SS	46.5	52.1
		NS	47.8	53.4

*Distance moved to engage—1″ or less.

TABLE VI—RELEASE—RL

Case	Time TMU	DESCRIPTION
1	2.0	Normal release performed by opening fingers as independent motion.
2	0	Contact Release.

TABLE VII—DISENGAGE—D

CLASS OF FIT	Easy to Handle	Difficult to Handle
1—**Loose**—Very slight effort, blends with subsequent move.	4.0	5.7
2—**Close** — Normal effort, slight recoil.	7.5	11.8
3—**Tight** — Considerable effort, hand recoils markedly.	22.9	34.7

TABLE VIII—EYE TRAVEL TIME AND EYE FOCUS—ET AND EF

Eye Travel Time $= 15.2 \times \frac{T}{D}$ TMU, with a maximum value of 20 TMU.

where T = the distance between points from and to which the eye travels.
D = the perpendicular distance from the eye to the line of travel T.

Eye Focus Time = 7.3 TMU.

Figure 9–5

MTM Example Problem

METHODS ANALYSIS CHART REFERENCE No. ______

PART "C" Clamp DATE ______ STUDY No. ______

OPERATION Remove small "C" Clamp ANALYST ______ SHEET No. ______ OF ______ SHEETS

DESCRIPTION — LEFT HAND	No.	L H	TMU	R H	No.	DESCRIPTION — RIGHT HAND
Reach for clamp		R24B	21.5	R24B		Reach to clamp handle
Grasp clamp		G1A	2.0	G1A		Grasp handle
			16.2	AP1		Loosen (apply pressure)
			9.4	T180S		Turn handle
			4.0	RL1	2	Release
			18.8	T180	2	Turn hand back
			4.0	G1A	2	Grasp handle
			18.8	T180S	2	Turn handle
Regrasp clamp		G2	5.6	RL1		Release
Remove clamp		M16B	15.8			
Lay aside clamp		M24B	20.6			
Release		RL1	2.0			
			138.7			

No.	ELEMENT DESCRIPTION	ELEMENT TIME TMU	CONVERSION FACTOR / LEVELED TIME	% ALLOWANCE	ELEMENT TIME ALLOWED	OCCURRENCES PER PIECE OR CYCLE	TOTAL TIME ALLOWED
						TOTAL	

of the first applications was to determine the ratio between the delay and the actual work being performed.

While our main interest here is in developing standard times for scheduling, it should not be concluded that this is the only application for this technique. It is useful in determining the allowances as used in stop-watch time study, balancing work loads in multiple man-machine operations, and other instances when work is to be measured.

Work sampling has the advantage over conventional stop-watch studies in that special skill is not required for observations and a high degree of accuracy is obtained without constant observation. In fact, the answer given by work sampling might be more accurate than all-day studies.

First observe how a standard time is calculated by means of work sampling; then we shall develop more fully the logic behind this valuable measuring tool. The standard time for a task by work sampling can be calculated in the following manner:

$$\underset{\text{(min./part)}}{\text{Standard time}} = \frac{\underset{\text{(in min.)}}{\text{Total time}} \times \underset{\text{(in percent)}}{\text{Working time}} \times \underset{\text{(in percent)}}{\text{Performance index}}}{\text{Total number of pieces produced}} + \underset{\text{min./part}}{\text{Allowance}}$$

Information for the above equation is to be found in several places:

Total time, in minutes, can be found in the past experience of the time cards.

Working time, in percent, is to be found in the sampling technique to be discussed.

Performance index, in percent, is the same objective method as used in the stop-watch time study, for rating.

Allowances are determined in the same way as those used in the stop-watch time study. Both the rating factor and the allowances might have been the result of a work sampling study.

Total number of parts is available from the company's records.

We shall now proceed to discuss how the percentage of working time is obtained, since it is the only factor not readily available for the equation.

Work Sampling is based on the laws of probability, discussed in Chapter 6. By determining the characteristics of a sample it is possible to predict the characteristics of a population. The standard time for a task extending over a long period can be obtained by merely taking a sample of data. This can be seen by means of an illustration. Assume there is some task which runs for a period of eight hours, represented by the lines in Figure 9–6. This, incidentally, could be a man and machine activity, running simultaneously, in which case we could have used one bar to represent each activity. To keep the example straightforward, consider one man working eight hours, or 480 minutes, so the bars represent 480 discrete time units.

If the man's activity was observed and recorded all day, it would be seen that he works most of the time. In fact, the example shows the man working 80 percent of the time and not working 20 percent of the time (as represented by the dark bar).

This all-day observation is too expensive and might even be impossible if we were observing a number of activities. Sampling is a better method and, strange as it may seem, can be more accurate.

The sample taken must be random; that is, every minute of the working period must have an equal chance of being the one observed. One way of doing this is to number the time increments on the chart from 1 to 480, then

Figure 9–6

Work Sampling Example

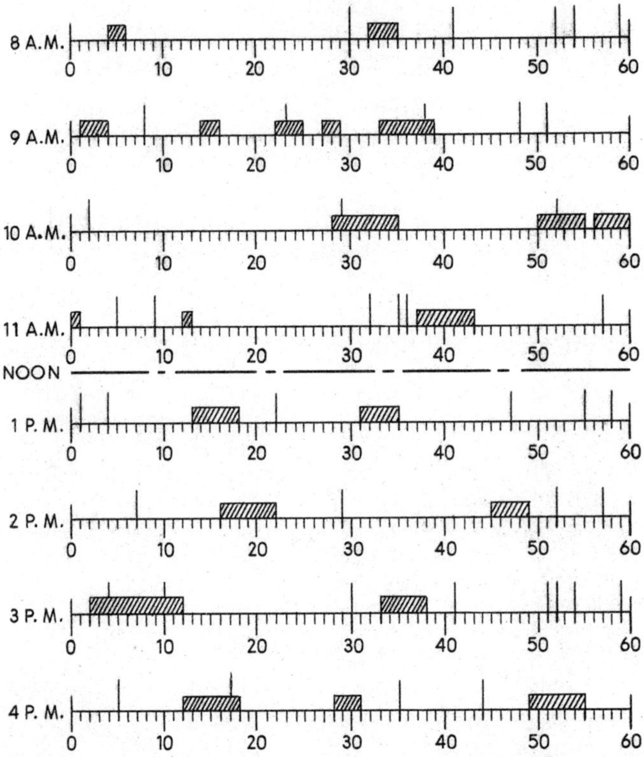

to take a similar amount of numbered chips, shake them in a container, and draw them at random. For example, if a sample of 40 was taken, the times indicated on the bar chart by short vertical lines might have been drawn. A more sophisticated and less tedious method would have been to select numbers from a random number table (to be found in many statistical texts). The results might have been:

Number of times observed *not* working .... = 7
Number of times observed .... = 40

$7/40 = p$

The ratio between the number of times observed not working and the number of times observed is a sample proportion, p, which is used to predict the true proportion, p'. The symbols in this discussion will conform to the literature of work sampling rather than to the statistics of forecasting to be found in Chapter 6. The concepts are the same, so you should encounter little difficulty in transferring your knowledge or in reading the work sampling literature.

The observations, being either "yes" or "no," form a binomial distribution which fortunately can be approximated, in this case, by a normal distribution.[2] Consequently, we can use the normal-curve tables referred to earlier to determine the probability of obtaining any proportion, p, of a sample.

The standard deviation for a binomial distribution is:

$$\sigma_p = \sqrt{\frac{p(1-p)}{n}}$$

p = Sample proportion of occurrences expressed as a decimal or percent
n = Number of items in a sample

Pursuing the same logic used in the previous discussion of statistics, two standard deviations either side of the mean will include 95.4 percent of the occurrences. Thus we say the confidence limits are 95 percent (rounded), which means that events could occur outside these limits 5 percent of the time just by chance. The value of the standard deviation, as can be seen from the equation, is dependent upon the value of p and n, but the acceptable dispersion in terms of σ_p is established as a policy. These two viewpoints can be grasped easier by a diagram, Figure 9–7. First, you should be cautioned

Figure 9–7

Logic of Sampling for Work Sampling

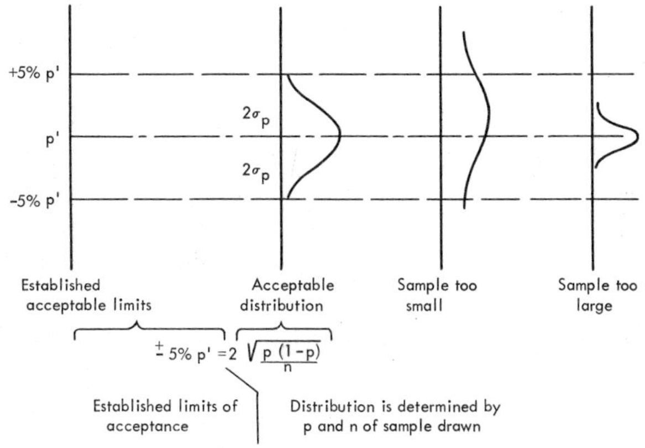

that p is varying from sample to sample and, while it is illustrated on the diagram as being in one position, it is in reality constantly shifting until we zero in on the true value, p', as the sample size becomes larger.

The established acceptable limits, or accuracy, a, is often set at ± 5 percent p'. This seems to be a workable value, and, for the example—where we believe the true p' is 20 percent—the limits would be established at 19 percent and 21 percent.

[2] Refer to Chapter 6. The normal-curve approximation is fairly good under the conditions of work sampling.

It is apparent that the standard deviation decreases directly with the square root of the sample size. It would not be economical to take an extensive sample if it were not needed. The problem is to solve the equation for n, but there is another unknown in the equation, and that is p. The solution to this dilemma is to first take a sample to get a rough approximation of p, insert that in the equation, and solve for n. When a sample of n has been collected, recalculate p, and from this calculate a new value of n until the $2\sigma_p$ is within the accuracy established. To get some idea of how p and n are interrelated, study Figure 9–8.

Figure 9–8

Observations Required for Work Sampling*

Number of Observations Required
95 Percent Confidence

	Relative Error			Absolute Error	
p \ a	1%	5%	10%	1%	3.5%
10	360,000	14,400	3,600	3,600	294
20	160,000	6,400	1,600	6,400	522
30	93,300	3,730	935	8,400	686

* Ralph M. Barnes, *Work Sampling* (2d ed.; New York: John Wiley & Sons, Inc., 1957), pp. 30, 36.

From the table it becomes obvious that the number of readings required becomes extensive if p and the limits of accuracy, a, are small. This has brought some to consider the use of an *absolute* measure of accuracy, a percent, rather than a *relative* measure, $p \pm a$ percent. Further information regarding this can be found in the work sampling references listed in the Bibliography.

The following is a step-by-step procedure for determining the standard time by work sampling:

Step 1. Policy has been established in the standards department that p will be within ± 5 percent, with a 95 percent confidence.

Step 2. An initial study shows the operator was idle 16 times out of 100, or 16 percent of the time; $p = 16$ percent.

Step 3. Determine the number of readings needed. The accuracy ± 5 percent must be included in 95 percent, or roughly $2\sigma_p$, either side of the mean.

$$.05p = 2\sqrt{\frac{p(1-p)}{n}}$$

$$n = \frac{4p(1-p)}{0.0025p^2}$$

$$n = \frac{4 \times .16(1-.16)}{0.0025 \times .16^2} = 8400 \text{ readings}$$

Step 4. Part way through the study it appeared that the p value was nearly 20 percent rather than 16 percent, as thought at first. This is of interest because the size of the sample can be reduced.

$$n = \frac{4p(1-p)}{0.0025p^2} = 6400 \text{ readings}$$

Step 5. The p value is checked periodically to see if it is within the limits desired. It is finally determined that $p = 19$ percent. This can now be included in the standard time equation. (Note: Only the delay time, as a percentage of the entire time, has been developed here. All other information for the standard time will be found elsewhere in the standards department.)

Step 6. Calculate the standard time:

$$\underset{\text{(min./part)}}{\text{Standard time}} = \frac{\underset{\text{(in min.)}}{\text{Total time}} \times \underset{\text{(in percent)}}{\text{Working time}} \times \underset{\text{(in percent)}}{\text{Performance index}}}{\text{Total number of pieces produced}} + \text{Allowance}$$

$$\underset{\text{(min./part)}}{\text{Standard time}} = \frac{15{,}000 \text{ min.} \times (1.00 - .19) \times .95}{4300 \text{ parts}} + 15 \text{ percent allowance}$$

$$\text{Standard time} = 3.09 \text{ Minutes/part}$$

The five ways of determining the time needed to perform a task have been developed. It is not supposed that from this you will become a proficient technician, but you should have some insight into the source of time information before discussing how it is applied to systems design.

ERRORS CAUSED BY RATING

A basic difficulty in using the standard times developed by the methods described is that they are used primarily with wage incentive systems, and the objectives are somewhat different than they are for scheduling. This problem can be pointed out by means of a diagram (Figure 9–9).

An incentive is no incentive at all unless it affects most of the people. This means that both the good and the poor operators must come under the incentive system. However, there is considerable difference between the good operator and the poor operator. In fact, it has been shown that this relationship is in the order of two to one. The best worker produces two times as much as the poorest, and the workers in between these two extremes would form a frequency distribution as shown. Because most workers should make incentive pay, the standard of performance is set to the left of the average performance.

How far to the left the standard performance should be depends upon the policy of the company. The average worker is usually expected to earn 25 to 30 percent incentive, which would place the standard of performance to the left on the curve, as shown.

This means that if standard times are to be used for scheduling, they must be adjusted. This can be done on a gross basis by multiplying the times by a factor which takes account of all discrepancies between the calculated

Figure 9–9

Time Study Rating

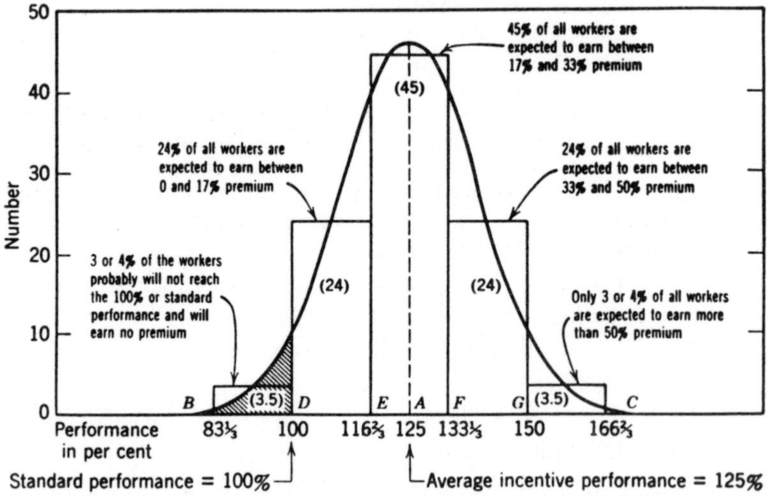

Source: Ralph M. Barnes, *Motion and Time Study: Design and Measurement of Work* (5th ed.; New York: John Wiley & Sons, Inc., 1963), p. 394.

times and the actual times. Some companies ignore this discrepancy, feeling their scheduling plan is so loose that the error makes little difference.

DETERMINING MACHINE CONTROLLED TIMES

Not all tasks are controlled by the movements of an operator. Consequently, it is necessary to calculate by different means the time needed for the machine time. Only metal working is discussed here, but task times can be determined for other processes, too.

The rate at which metal is removed in a cutting operation is determined by three factors:

Speed: The rate at which the tool passes the work or the work passes the tool; given as feet per minute.

Feed: The distance the tool moves in a cycle of operation; given in inches per revolution.

Depth of cut: The right angle distance between the old surface and the newly cut surface; given as inches per pass.

These three concepts become more obvious when we see them on the simple diagram, Figure 9–10. It is of interest to note that we are talking about three different movements, and this corresponds to the three dimensions of the object we wish to alter.

The optimum relationships for speeds, feeds, and depths of cuts have been determined for the common materials, common cutting materials, and

Figure 9–10

Determining Machine Controlled Time

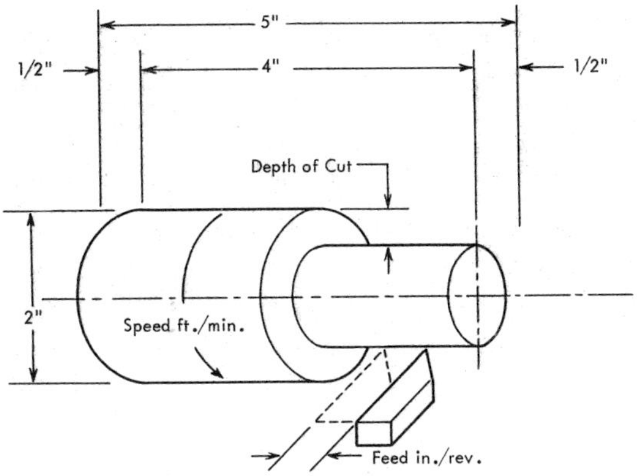

the finish desired on the part. This information is available in many engineering handbooks. For example, to determine the time for removing the material on the simple cylinder, as shown, we could find in a handbook that the speed, feed, and depth of cut for mild steel, cut by high-speed steel, should be:

Speed: 200 ft./min. Feed: .020 in./rev. Depth of cut: .125 in.

From the speed and the diameter of the part, we can determine the correct rotational speed:

$$\frac{\text{Speed (ft./min.} \times \text{12 in./ft.)}}{\text{Circumference } (\pi \times \text{D in.})} = \frac{\text{200 ft./min.} \times \text{12 in./ft.}}{\text{2 in.} \times \text{3.14/rev.}}$$

$$\text{since } 12/\pi = \text{approximately 4, then:}$$

$$\frac{\text{200 ft./min.} \times \text{4 in./ft.}}{\text{2 in./rev.}} = \text{400 rpm.}$$

This is a theoretical speed, and, if such a speed isn't available on the machine, it is necessary to adjust the theoretical speed accordingly. Whether one adjusts the speed up or down depends upon the finish desired, the capabilities of the machine, how decrepit it is, and other factors. For the example, assume 425 rpm is the nearest actual speed.

Next we need to know how many revolutions are required. Since it would be unlikely that the tool would start and end on the piece, we must add a little tool travel on each end. This is called "cutting air." Our calculations continue in this way:

$$\frac{\text{Length of part (inches) + Additional length (inches)}}{\text{Feed (in./rev.)}} = \text{Rev. /part}$$

$$\frac{(4 + \tfrac{1}{2} + \tfrac{1}{2}) \text{ in./part}}{\text{.020 in./rev.}} = \text{250 rev./part}$$

From the above information we can determine the time per cut or pass:

$$\frac{\text{Revolutions/part}}{\text{Revolutions/min.}} = \frac{250 \text{ rev./part}}{425 \text{ rev./min.}} = .59 \text{ min./part}$$

But this is for only one pass, and for the surface desired it may be necessary to take several passes. Assume in this case we need three:

$$\text{Minutes/part/pass} \times 3 \text{ passes} = .59 \times 3 = 1.77 \text{ min./part}$$

These same basic ideas can be extended to drilling, boring, milling, planing, and similar operations. For other processes there are other ways of determining the time that it will take to do a task. For example, press times can be determined by finding the cycles per minute.

Machine controlled times are often necessary in calculating time data for scheduling as well as for estimating costs.

The Effect of Learning on the Data

Most industries have established standards of performance, with little or no consideration for the improvement that comes about by the repeated performance of a manual task. This improvement phenomenon is such a commonly observed experience that it seems peculiar no practical use was made of it until recently. Even now it has not been universally accepted. Although a company may not wish to apply the learning curve phenomenon by using the simple logarithmic charts described here, it should be aware of the learning phenomenon in general, and take advantage of it to predict costs, estimate capital requirements, enter into contracts, and perform all the other activities which require accurate predictions of production times.

The learning curve is the graphical representation of the very well known fact that a worker learns as he works. The more often he repeats a task, the more proficient he becomes. As he becomes more proficient, his production rate increases, which of course means that the production time decreases.

While in the past many people in industry must have been aware of this phenomenon, and perhaps occasionally took some recognition of it in their predictions, it was not until the Second World War that it became generally known and used to any extent.

Airframe manufacturers were one of the first to use the learning curve in predictions, probably because the large number of labor hours and consequent high costs required in constructing each frame helped to make the phenomenon so obvious. Soon the usefulness of the learning curve came to the attention of the Armed Forces and they put the Stanford Research Institute to work making a statistical study of the direct labor costs going into airplane frames. It became apparent that each type of frame—bombers, fighters, and so forth—had its own initial production time (as might be expected), but the rates of improvement for all frames were remarkably similar. In fact, they were all so similar that the industry's improvement characteristic of 20 percent has been carried over to other industries without ample proof of the similarity—and probably without adequate justification.

CONSTRUCTION OF THE LEARNING CURVE

The first relationship which will be discussed is the cumulative average man-hours/unit as they are related to the cumulative number of units produced. The cumulative average man-hours/unit is the total number of production hours accumulated since production began, divided by the number of units produced. As the time for each succeeding unit becomes less, the cumulative average becomes smaller and smaller. It should be recognized that this average time will never become as small as the total man hours for a specific unit because it is influenced by the early, less efficient production.

As an example, consider wiring an electrical control panel, which takes 100 hours to produce the first product. Each time the production is doubled there is a 20 percent improvement. Another way of saying this is that each time production doubles, the cumulative average man hours is 80 percent of the previous production level. This can be seen in the following form:

			Cumulative Average Man-hours/unit
First unit takes:			100
First 2 units take:	$\frac{2 \text{ parts} \times 100 \text{ hours} \times 80\%}{2 \text{ parts}}$	=	80
First 4 units take:	$\frac{4 \text{ parts} \times 80 \text{ hours} \times 80\%}{4 \text{ parts}}$	=	64
First 8 units take:	$\frac{8 \text{ parts} \times 64 \text{ hours} \times 80\%}{8 \text{ parts}}$	=	51.2

Before plotting this information, look at the right-hand column of the table above and predict what is going to happen as cumulative times are plotted against cumulative units. The differences between succeeding units are 20, 16, and 12.8 hours. As is to be expected, the greatest reduction of time occurs in the early stages of production and tapers off gradually as production continues. If this information shown above is placed on a chart (Figure 9–11) the change in production rate is dramatic.

The curve shown illustrates the change vividly, but it makes the construction and subsequent reading a little more difficult than if the equation were converted to logarithms and plotted on logarithmic paper (Figure 9–12).

Figure 9–11

Learning Curve

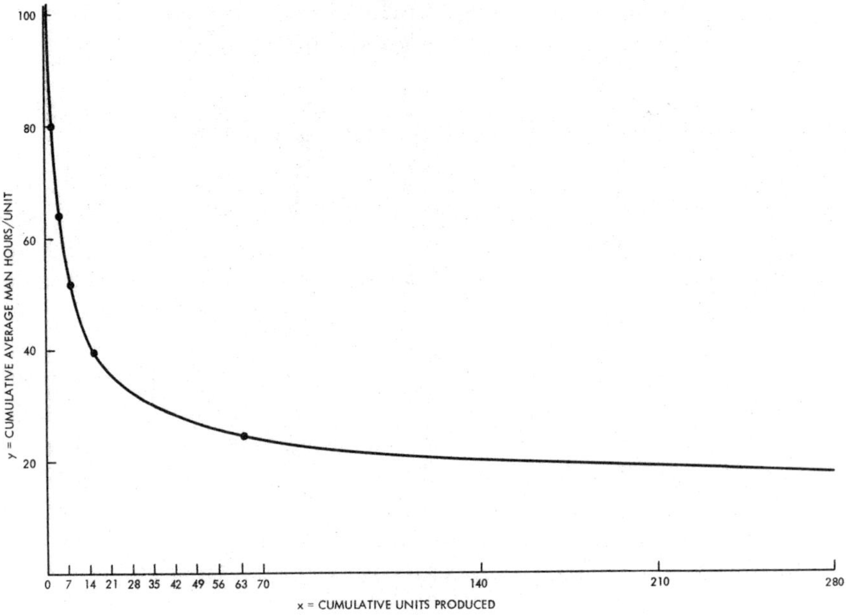

Figure 9–12

Learning Curve, Log-log

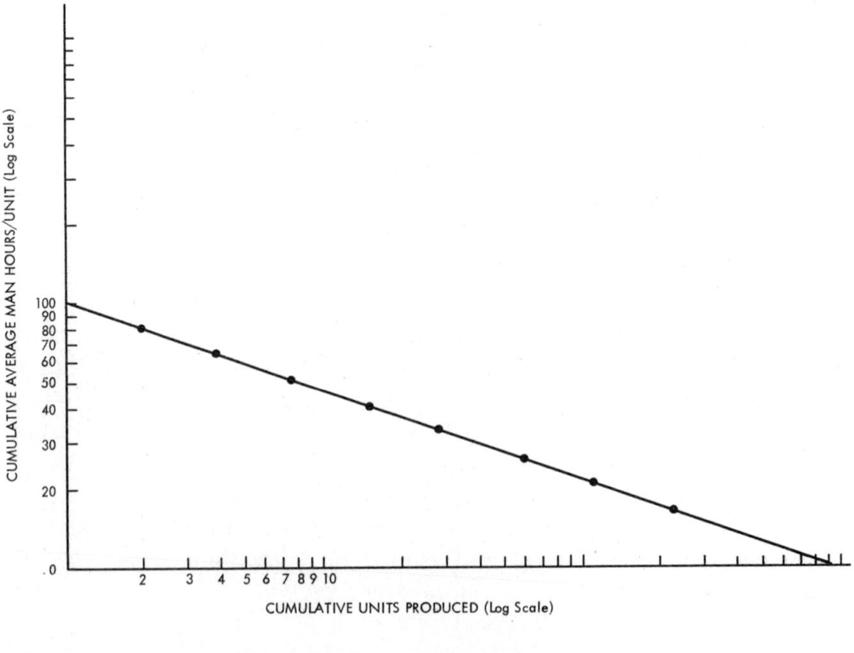

The equation of the curve just illustrated is given by:

$$Y = KX^{-n}$$

Y = Cumulative average man-hours/unit for any number of units, plotted on Y axis
K = Number of man-hours to build the first unit
X = Cumulative number of units produced
n = The exponent of the curve which will, in the example, be negative

This equation, $Y = KX^{-n}$, can be restated in terms of logarithms thus:

$$\log Y = \log K + (-n)\log X$$

For those who have forgotten, the product of two numbers, K and X, is found by adding their logarithms. The logarithm of a number raised to a power, X^{-n}, is the product of $-n$ and the logarithm of the number, or $-n \log X$.

By this familiar technique of changing to logarithms we have simplified the graphic representation of the problem by putting the information in a linear form. For just a moment let us pause and interpret the above equation in terms of its graphical presentation. The first term, log Y, is equal to log K when X is one. This value, log K, therefore, is the intersection of the curve with the Y axis. The letter n in the expression is the slope of the line, and will be negative because the line slopes from left to right. In addition to having a straight line, which is easier to interpret, another bonus is obtained because, as you will see, log-log paper keeps the chart within reasonable bounds.

The slope of the line, n, can be derived:

$$Y = KX^{-n}$$
$$Y = K/X^n$$
$$X^n = K/Y$$
$$n \log X = \log K - \log Y$$
$$n = \frac{\log K - \log Y}{\log X}$$

It turns out that n is the log (percent of learning curve) divided by log 2. This might be seen more clearly if we consider the equation when the production is doubled, using the previous data of 100 hours for the first unit and an 80 percent learning curve.

First doubling: $$n = \frac{\log 100 - \log (100 \times .80)}{\log 2}$$

Double production again: $$n = \frac{\log 100 - \log (100 \times .80 \times .80)}{\log 4}$$

$$n = \frac{\log 100 - \log 100 - \log .80 - \log .80}{\log 2 + \log 2}$$

$$n = \frac{-2 \log .80}{2 \log 2} = \frac{-\log .80}{\log 2}$$

This step was taken to make it apparent that doubling factors cancel out and the slope remains, log (percent of learning curve) /log 2. From this basic equation, $Y = KX^{-n}$, several other significant and useful equations can be derived.

Total Man Hours

Many times it would be convenient to know what the total man hours are for any level of production. This can be determined by obtaining the product of the cumulative average man hours per unit and the number of units produced.

$$T = YX$$

T = Total man hours required to build a (predetermined) number of units

or we can say:

$$T = KX^{-n} \times X$$

So, in effect, we are saying only that the product of the cumulative average time for each unit, KX^{-n}, and the number of units, X, is equal to the total time it takes to produce a quantity. From this equation it is possible to go on and develop an equation for determining the time it takes to produce any one unit.

Unit Time

The unit time for any unit is derived with a little more difficulty, starting with the total time just derived. Remember that, so far, the average time, Y, for all units up to a certain point has been derived. The unit time, U, will give the time required for any one unit without including all the production which has gone before.

$$T = KX^{-n} \times X$$
$$T = KX^{-n+1}$$
$$T = KX^{(1-n)}$$

If the first derivative of the total man hours is taken with respect to units:

$$\frac{dT}{dX} = (1 - n)KX^{-n}$$
$$U = \text{man hours/unit} = (1 - n)KX^{-n}$$

Since $KX^{-n} = Y$, the cumulative average man hours per unit, we can see that the time to produce any one unit is merely the product of Y and $(1 - n)$. The values of n and $(1 - n)$ can be obtained from logarithm tables, but some common ones will be given here for convenience (Figure 9–13).

The three important relationships of the learning curve have been given. It might be well to turn our attention back to the example problem men-

Figure 9–13

Learning Curve Values

Efficiency	*Learning Curve Value*	*n*	1 − *n*
35%	65%	.624	.375
30	70	.515	.485
25	75	.415	.585
20	80	.322	.678
15	85	.234	.766
10	90	.152	.848
5	95	.074	.926

tioned previously for wiring the electrical control panel and see how these relationships are used.

The Production Control department would like to know how long it will take to produce the first 70 control panels and also the maximum time for each of the succeeding 10 panels. In brief, how long will it take to produce 70, T, and how long will it take to produce the 71st panel?

The cumulative average hours, Y, is:

$$Y = KX^{-n}$$
$$\log Y = \log K - n \log X$$

Example

$$\log 100 = 2.00000$$
$$-.322 \log 70 = -.59412$$
$$1.40588$$

and the number for this logarithm is 25.46 hours.

Since T equals YX,

Total hours = 25.46 hours/panel × 70 panels = 1782 hours

The unit time for the 71st panel is:

$$U = (1 - n)KX^{-n}$$
$$\text{Unit time} = .678 \times 25.46 = 17.26 \text{ hours}$$

While we have shown the calculations here, it is much simpler, of course, to select the information from the curves. Check the calculations with the curve and see if they compare. The "unit times" can also be plotted on a curve for ready reference.

This is the kind of information that is needed by every production control department, as well as by other branches of management, if both are going to operate with any reasonable accuracy.

This technique has some "opportunities" for error and certain precautions should be taken. The relationship that has just been considered between the number of products produced and the cumulative average hours is probably not caused entirely by the worker's learning experience because there are *many* factors which could influence the curve. These factors might include improvements in production design, new tooling, innovations by the industrial engineering group, improved management, etc. This means that the learning curve is probably not an absolutely scientific tool but has overtones of empiricism. This does not particularly matter as long as we don't accept it as being infallible. The important thing is that the curves seem to show a consistent pattern of behavior which is reliable enough to use in the production situation.

Learning curves are applicable primarily to hand and assembly operations where the learning factor is significant. Machines, by themselves, do not learn to run any faster, and, as could be expected, the learning curve will be steep for manual operations and flat for machine operations. While the aircraft industry has found the 80 percent curve universally acceptable, there are other industries which would have a 90 or 95 percent curve, or an even flatter curve. Others may experience steep, 65 or 60 percent learning.

Shifts in the use of direct labor, such as the purchase of parts on the outside, can cause errors in the curves by showing abrupt declines in the labor used. A shift in the proportion of direct labor to indirect labor may also be misleading. For example, a reduction in low-cost direct labor might be made at the expense of high-cost indirect labor. Any changes in the direct labor costs at the expense, or benefit, of other costs should be handled with caution.

New innovations in the process should also be handled with caution for it is possible that they would cause a large jump in the curve, either plus or minus, with the start of a new learning curve. Of course the direct labor costs are frequently influenced by the level of production. As a productive unit operates near its maximum, the direct labor may be reduced. At least, there is some level of production which is optimum, and any variations in labor efficiency from this cause should not be interpreted as learning. If the production is intermittent, the curve cannot be expected to be smooth since there will be a certain amount of relearning every time the production is restarted.

It has already been shown how the learning curve might be used for scheduling information and advising customers of delivery dates, but this is not the limit of its usefulness—even though it is important enough to make it universally acceptable.

Instead of using units for the X axis it is possible to use *pounds* of material. This makes it possible to predict and compare the cumulative hours on the basis of weight of material and not on units, thus giving a broader application from product to product.

The learning curve can be used in the decision to buy or to make component parts. A contractor should consider whether or not his subcontractor has a flatter learning curve than his own. If it is flatter, even though it may start at a lower level, the alternative to make the component obviously should be considered.

In the planning of capital expenditure (Figure 9–14) the learning curve

Figure 9–14

Capital Planning with Learning Curve

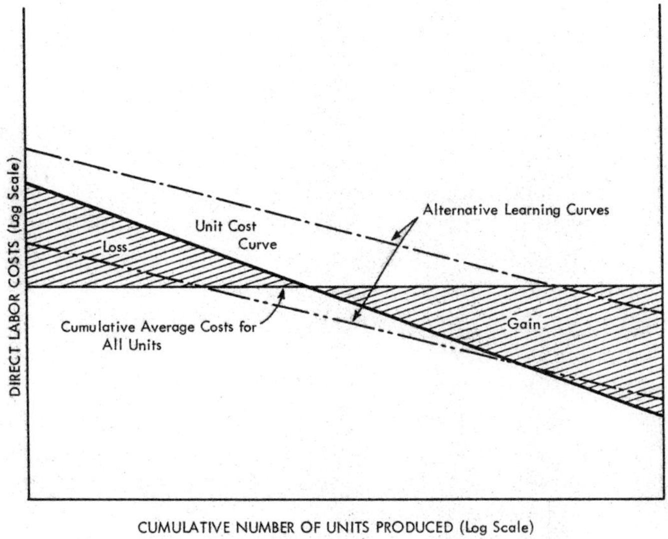

has some obvious applications. For example, the unit-cost curve will cross the cumulative average-cost curve (as shown). To the left of this intersection there is a financial drain on the business while at the right there is a financial return. Knowing this, the people responsible for the budget can do a better job of planning. The purchasing agent can also use this in his dealings with the subcontractors to advise them on costs. By using the learning curve it is possible to predict budgets and come up with reasonable data at each step; it is not necessary to wait until the end for cumulative data.

For large assemblies, where considerable area is necessary for large jigs and fixtures, the learning curve finds an application in space utilization. The space can be determined for each production level for different products and, consequently, building space can be used to the utmost.

As is obvious, the time—at least at the beginning of production—will have some wide variations. This makes scheduling of subsequent quantities very difficult. Therefore the learning curve is an obvious tool for smoothing out the production schedule of jobs with high percentages of learning. If the total number of employees and the hours available are known, it is possible to work backwards and determine the delivery schedule. By taking the cumulative average learning curve and projecting on it the total number of man hours, the production schedule can be determined.

Practically any industry could use the learning curve if there are tasks which require a large percentage of man-controlled operations rather than machine-controlled operations, and where the product or parts of the product are being made repeatedly.

Industrial Calendars

It is in keeping with industries' standardization efforts that they have frequently put into practice standardized calendars. It is nearly impossible to compare sales, costs, and other production figures without standardizing the time period for which they are being compared. It is not uncommon to hear such statements as "the sales for last month were 5,000 units," but unless we know something about the number of days in last month, the number of weekends included in the month, and the number of vacations we know very little about the sales figure. The working time might vary as much as 10 percent from month to month.

Attempts to make the industrial calendar uniform have been tried, with unusual success, for many years. There are various ways of making the calendar periods uniform, but probably the 13-period calendar has been the most successful. Companies using the "13-month" system divide their year into 13 equal periods—of 4 weeks, or 28 days, each. The year is divided into quarters of 3 "months" each, for accounting purposes, with the vacation period falling into the extra "month."

Some companies have used the so-called 4–4–5 quarter plan in which the first and second month of a quarter contain 4 weeks each and the third month contains 5. Still other companies, also wishing a uniform calendar, have employed other plans.

In all these plans there is the problem of the extra days "left over" after the periods are made as uniform as possible. Also there is the question of the extra day occurring because of leap year. Quite commonly days are carried forward until they accumulate to a full-week period. The pros and cons of uniform industrial calendars can more readily be summarized in a list of advantages and disadvantages.

ADVANTAGES OF UNIFORM CALENDAR

1. Each month is made up of exactly the same number of days, which makes it possible to compare successive months, as well as the months, themselves, from year to year.

2. It is not necessary to keep in mind the number of days in each month and then try to make necessary adjustments. Comparisons can be made on the basis of costs, output, and other variables without considering the number of days in the denominator.

3. Payrolls can be closed at the end of a week, which eliminates the usual letdown in production when a pay period ends in the middle of a week. This has been an advantage to the community as well because there is a tendency for bills to be paid regularly and promptly.

4. It is easier for employees to determine what is required of them; it

gives them a means of measuring progress; and they appreciate more uniform pay periods.

5. Physical inventories can be taken over the weekends without any interruptions. Since the plant will probably be closed down, it is easier to determine what material is in process and what isn't.

DISADVANTAGES OF UNIFORM CALENDAR

1. It becomes difficult to compare cost figures with companies not operating on the same plan.

2. External accounting, such as accounts receivable, will have to be carried out on a 12-month basis or other arrangements made.

3. Thirteen closing periods for the accounts will add to the clerical costs.

4. Banks and exchanges require reports on the monthly and quarterly basis.

5. The names of the months will have to be disregarded and numbers used for identification.

NUMBERING PRODUCTION DAYS

Whether or not a company uses a standardized calendar, it can obtain considerable advantage from numbering its production days consecutively so that certain *production days* can be referred to instead of a certain month and day in the month. A calendar printed to show the number of the production days is shown in Figure 9–15. This system eliminates many misunderstandings and—best of all—gives a common time-language for the entire factory by which production goals can be set.

SUMMARY

Time is the "keystone" for all factory operations. Investments must have a pay-off within a certain time. Inventories must be turned over within a certain time. Labor is paid for its work on the basis of time, and customers expect their orders filled by a certain time.

The system designer measures the input to the factory in units of time. The feedback is also recorded in units of time. Ultimately, the efficiency of the system is determined by how well time is utilized.

Since time is the common denominator of many aspects of planning and controlling factory operations it is important that you know how time information is obtained. There are a number of common ways of developing time information; these include past estimates, stop-watch time study, elemental standard data, predetermined motion-time data, and work sampling. These methods are usually not designed for scheduling and cost estimating, and, therefore, must be adjusted for these purposes.

Figure 9–15

Production Calendar

JANUARY

BLK.	MON.	TUES.	WED.	THURS.	FRI.
1	NEW YEAR HOLIDAY	[1] 3	[2] 4	[3] 5	[4] 6
2	[5] 9	[6] 10	[7] 11	[8] 12	[9] 13
3	[10] 16	[11] 17	[12] 18	[13] 19	[14] 20
4	[15] 23	[16] 24	[17] 25	[18] 26	[19] 27
5	[20] 30	[21] 31			

FEBRUARY

BLK	MON.	TUES.	WED.	THURS.	FRI.
5			[22] 1	[23] 2	[24] 3
6	[25] 6	[26] 7	[27] 8	[28] 9	[29] 10
7	[30] 13	[31] 14	[32] 15	[33] 16	[34] 17
8	[35] 20	[36] 21	[37] 22	[38] 23	[39] 24
9	[40] 27	[41] 28			

MARCH

BLK.	MON	TUES.	WED.	THURS	FRI.
9			[42] 1	[43] 2	[44] 3
10	[45] 6	[46] 7	[47] 8	9	[49] 10
11	[50] 13	[51] 14	[52] 15	[53] 16	[54] 17
12	[55] 20	[56] 21	[57] 22	[58] 23	[59] 24
13	[60] 27	[61] 28	[62] 29	[63] 30	[64] 31

When people repeat tasks time after time they become more proficient, which in turn reduces the time. This, in many cases, will influence the schedule and should be accounted for when establishing the time relationships among jobs.

Conventional calendars are not always the most useful media for regulating factory activities, and many companies have found that uniform calendars offer many advantages.

If you have never given consideration to the importance of time as it affects our lives, perhaps now is the time to start—using some of the many time-regulating techniques discussed in this book.

Questions

1. What are the applications of time estimates in a factory?
2. What are the strengths and weaknesses of the various methods of estimating the time to do a task?
3. Give an example of a job which could be estimated from:
   a) Past experience.
   b) Predetermined motion-time data.
   c) Work sampling.
4. In what two ways is the actual measured time adjusted in a stop-watch time study? To what degree does this affect the objectivity of the techniques?
5. What advantages does the work sampling method have over the other methods?
6. What information would you need to determine how long it takes to turn a metal cylinder on a lathe? What is the source of this information? How does the theoretical information compare with the actual information?
7. In what situations would the effect of learning be important?
8. How does the time study analyst cope with the problem of learning?
9. Why is the log-log graph of the learning curve used?
10. Compare the advantages and disadvantages of the uniform calendar.

References

ABRUZZI, ADAM. *The Theory and Practice of Standard Data.* New York: American Society of Mechanical Engineers, 1953.

———. *Work Measurement, New Principles and Procedures.* New York: Columbia University Press, 1952.

———. *Work, Workers, and Work Measurement.* New York: Columbia University Press, 1956.

ANDRESS, FRANK J. "The Learning Curve as a Production Tool." Cambridge, Mass.: *Harvard Business Review*, Vol. 32, No. 1, p. 87.

BARNES, RALPH M. *Motion and Time Study: Design and Measurement of Work.* 5th ed. New York: John Wiley & Sons, Inc., 1958.

———. *Work Sampling.* 2d ed. New York: John Wiley & Sons, Inc., 1957.

CURRIE, RUSSEL MACKENZIE. *Work Study.* London: Pitman, 1961.

HADDEN, ARTHUR A., and GENGER, VICTOR K. *Handbook of Standard Time Data for Machine Shops.* New York: Ronald Press Co., 1954.

HANSEN, BERTRAND L. *Work Sampling for Modern Management.* Englewood Cliffs, N.J.: Prentice-Hall, Inc., 1960.

HEILAND, ROBERT E., and RICHARDSON, WALLACE J. *Work Sampling.* New York: McGraw-Hill Book Co., Inc., 1957.

HUGHES, R. C., and GOLEM, H. G. *Production Efficiency Curve and Its Application.* San Diego, Calif.: Arts and Crafts Press, 1944.

KRICK, EDWARD V. *Methods Engineering: Design and Measurement of Work Methods*. New York: John Wiley & Sons, Inc., 1962.

MUNDEL, MARVIN E. *Motion and Time Study, Principles and Practice*. Englewood Cliffs, N.J.: Prentice-Hall, Inc., 1960.

NADLER, GERALD. *Work Design*. Homewood, Ill.: Richard D. Irwin, Inc., 1963.

NIEBEL, BENJAMIN W. *Motion and Time Study*. 3rd ed. Homewood, Ill.: Richard D. Irwin, Inc., 1962.

NORDHOFF, W. A. *Machine Shop Estimating*. New York: McGraw-Hill Book Co., Inc., 1947.

PAPPAS, FRANK F., and DIMBERG, ROBERT A. *Practical Work Standards*. New York: McGraw-Hill Book Co., Inc., 1962.

PARSONS, G. W. S. "The 80% Learning Curve." *Modern Machine Shop*, March, 1960.

SECTION THREE

System Designing

CHAPTER 10

Organization and Physical Facilities

It would be difficult to consider the design of a system without taking into consideration the organization and physical facilities of the factory, for frequently the system design is limited by the characteristics of these two factors. The system may not need improvement at all, but the organization or physical facilities might need drastic overhauling. At any rate, the system designer will be wise to become well acquainted with the standards of acceptable organizations and facilities.

The Organization

Organizations are living dynamic organisms. Parts of the organism are growing and expanding while other parts are dormant, or even dying. As the organization grows, there are separations not unlike those that occur in the reproducing process of the cell. There is a time aspect of the organization's growth as different parts play important roles at different times during the life span. It is this dynamic aspect of an organization which makes it as difficult to deal with as to describe. One way of getting a grasp of the entire operation is by means of the organizational chart.

THE ORGANIZATIONAL CHART

The organizational chart is a symbolic method of representing the organization. Usually a box, or rectangle, is used to represent a function performed by the plant manager, secretary, foreman, production control supervisor, and others. These boxes are interconnected to designate their relationship, as shown in Figure 10–1. The lines of authority and responsibility are inferred by the level of the boxes, as indicated on the diagram.

Figure 10–1

Typical Organizational Chart

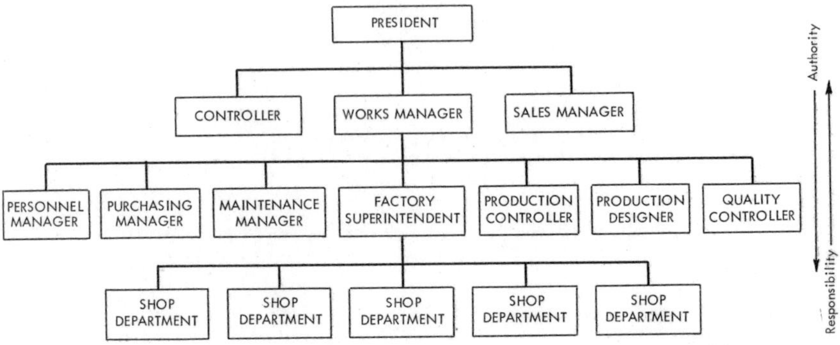

Other sets of symbols have been used, such as circles instead of boxes, and occasionally we find a chart inverted so that those functions with the least authority are shown at the top, giving the effect of an inverted pyramid.

Organizational charts are desirable for any organization, but they do not tell all the story. There is no way of showing the channels of communications which exist as a result of empathy, union leadership, sports activities, and family ties, but the charts do serve as a basic structure and enforce a certain degree of discipline—which would not otherwise exist—upon an organization.

ORGANIZATIONAL DYNAMICS

Before launching into a discussion of the principles involved in designing an organization, it is well to become aware of the growth of an organization. Very frequently an organization starts with just one man (Figure 10–2) who wants to go into business. More often than not, he has a limited amount of capital, and so is an inventor, engineer, capitalist, manufacturer, and salesman all at one time. This puts a strain on his abilities, and, as he is able to afford the luxury of more help, he adds people to his organization. Perhaps he hires a salesman, a bookkeeper, and a production worker or two. So he has the first organization representing the factory's major functions. As growth continues, additional workers are added, which increase the owner's headache as he attempts to communicate with more and more people.

It won't be long before he sheds all these individual communications and delegates one person to take all the communications in finance, another person all the communications in sales, and another person for manufacturing. These groups will not all grow at the same rate, so eventually some individuals will have more employees reporting to them than others. Such would be the case in production, and it may be desirable to establish another layer of centralization.

Figure 10–2

The Development of an Organization

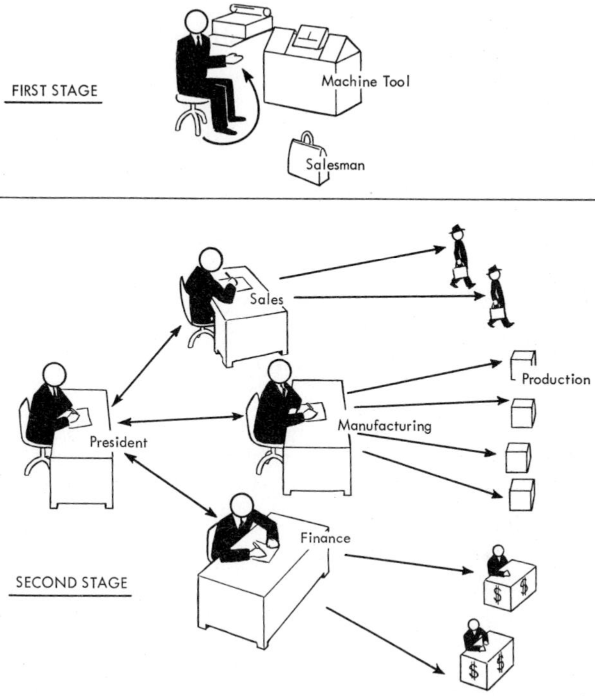

This organization, responsible for production, is called the *line organization*; it is typified by authority extending down through the organization from the president, and responsibility reaching back up through the organization from the lowest level to the president. This, however, is a rather limited usage of the term line organization, and it is frequently used to refer to any organization within which authority and responsibility exist.

As an organization grows, it is apt to come under the influence of another growth formation. For example, in our earlier illustration the president-owner might have hired someone to help him, perhaps a typist-secretary, who would have no authority except as it was relayed through the president. The position of the typist-secretary, who is only advising, is that of *staff*. A better example might be the factory manager, who, finding that he was overloaded with detail, hired a person to take over the paper work necessary for controlling production. The factory manager still maintains complete control and the staff worker merely advises him in which order the work should be performed.

Within the structure of an organization, as in many other things, it is difficult to find situations which are either black or white. And one seldom finds a staff position, for example, which is purely advisory. The line function, associated with the staff position, is often quite willing to give up or delegate some of its authority to the staff, at least as far as routine problems are concerned. This is what happens with the production control function. The production control function belongs with the factory manager, but the detail work would load him down to the extent that he would be unable to accomplish anything else. So he sets up a special group to take care of this area of activity. The factory manager will have to act only when something unusual comes up and the production control manager's authority is challenged. In time the area of authority will become well defined, so that the factory employees will know the realm within which the production control manager operates.

When a staff position has some area of authority, it is described as a *functional staff position*. Most staff positions come under this description because they exert some authority—if for no other reason than being at a higher level than some other positions.

Before going further, you should have some idea of what a full-fledged organization looks like, but how can one observe anything as nebulous as an organization? Our only method is through the organizational charts shown in Figure 10–3. Here is a chart showing most of the major functions to be found in a manufacturing concern, but to say this is the way the organization actually functions would be extremely naïve.

DESIGN CONSIDERATIONS FOR CONTROL: PRINCIPLES

This being a book on the design of systems, it would be highly desirable if material of a quantitative nature could be furnished for designing an organization. Regrettably, this type of information is not available, but there are some acceptable principles of design which one should use. Some of these principles are obvious while others are intuitive, but they seem to have produced exceptional results. These principles and a brief statement about each will be given in this section.

Apply Analytical Techniques

The organization is a system, and therefore the method of logic discussed in Chapter 2 is a very useful tool in designing the organization. This, of course, includes obtaining all the facts about the problem and pursuing the same step-by-step procedure of logic as used in any other type of system.

Too frequently, organizational changes are made hastily, without due consideration for all the side effects. Remember, the organizational changes under consideration might have an impact upon other parts than the ones you wish to change. This might be checked by simulating the changes.

Figure 10–3

Factory Organizational Chart

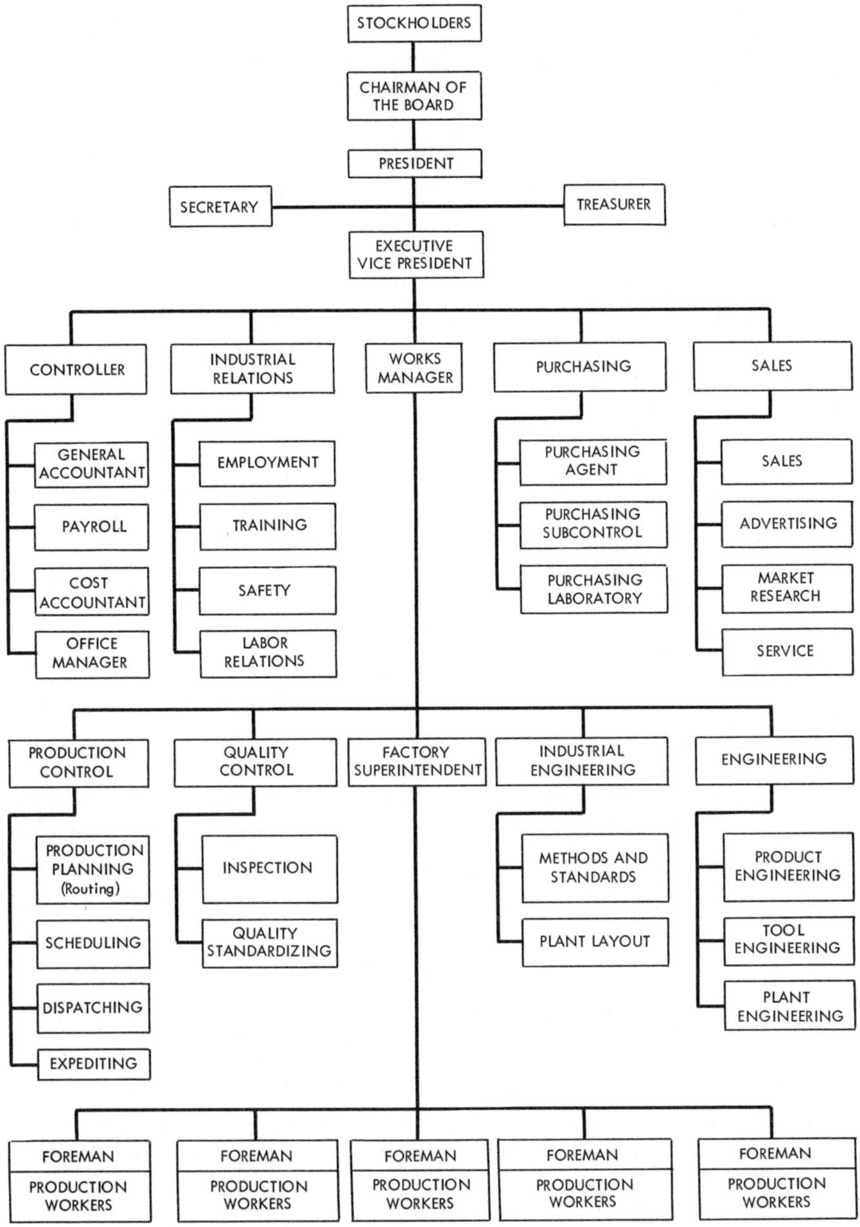

Define Objectives

The objectives of an organization, be it an entire factory or just a small department, should be stated and well known to all the employees. The top management should state the objectives in writing, in broad terms; while at each level below, the objectives should be restated in greater detail, as they affect the group.

If the officials of a company have decided they will produce only a high quality product without regard to cost, this should be known up and down the organization. It would be most inefficient, if, by not stating the objectives, some employees thought that the emphasis should be placed on quality while others thought the emphasis should be placed on price. It is obvious there would be no end to the conflicts that would arise.

Design around Functions, Not People

Organizations should be designed around the essential functions and not around the available people. Ideally, the organizational structure should be designed without regard to individuals so the system remains stable, regardless of how people are moved from position to position. On the organizational chart it is best if the names of individuals do not appear at all.

We are, of course, speaking of the ideal organizational design, and seldom will it be possible to design the organization without giving some consideration to the individuals available. In the long run, however, designing around people is dangerous and leads to empire-building and too great a dependence upon certain key individuals.

Define Lines of Authority and Responsibility

Basic to the design of an organization is the fact that authority extends downward through the organization while responsibility extends upward, as has been illustrated on the charts. Each echelon is responsible for the activities of the echelons below and has authority over those echelons, for it is basic to the design of an organization that an echelon should not be responsible for the actions of a group if it does not have authority over it also. Responsibility and authority must be well-defined, and one must not have responsibility over something for which he does not have authority.

Strive for a Balanced Organization

An old truism in engineering design is: *If it looks right, it is probably designed right,* and the same follows for an organizational structure. It should be well balanced, and one should look for inefficiencies where the organization appears to be overbalanced. A company which uses a large number of expediters for the size of the production force is suspect, and a close scrutiny will undoubtedly show an inefficiency in the production control department.

Policies Should Be Established

One would not consider designing a structure without dictating the specifications of the components making up the whole. In the same way, the functional components of an organization must have specifications laid down. The policies indicate the limits of response for a part of the system. As in any design, these should be written down clearly and specifically so they can never be misinterpreted. In a well designed organization this is done by a policy manual. The company, as well as each department, should maintain a policy manual, to be referred to at any time.

Include Exception Principle

No competent designer would design a system without taking into consideration the possibility of an overload, and the same should be true in an organizational design. There are times when the problems just don't fit the routines covered by the policy manual, so provisions must be made for these conditions. This is commonly called the "exception principle."

This might be illustrated by functions 1, 2, 3, and 4, coming under A's authority and responsibility. These four functions normally operate within the limits of the policy established for them. If something unusual comes up, an *exception,* it is referred to A. This chain extends on up through the organization and can account for the highly efficient way some organizations operate. In contrast to this system, we have situations where a large share of the questions filter up through the organization for decisions, with resulting inefficiencies.

Allow for Growth

As stressed in the Introduction, all organizations are dynamic and are usually expanding if they are healthy. This means that an organization cannot just be designed for today; every possible direction for expansion must be taken into consideration. Bridge designers take into consideration the advent of heavier vehicles and increased volume to the extent of providing for the addition of roadbeds and even double decks. The same philosophy must follow in the design of an organization. Today, a manufacturing organization must consider that production control might grow through the card-data-processing stage into extensive computer processing. This can result in radical changes in the organizational structure as the functions become more centralized.

Span of Control

This idea, probably first defined by Henri Fayol, pioneer organizational theorist, has a close analogy in engineering systems. It is essential that any one component of a system be able to withstand all the inputs leading to it. One circuit feeding several circuits must be able to handle the flow of current of all the individual circuits. A beam supporting others must be able to support the sum of the loads.

In an organization, the individual in a function must be able to exercise authority and accept responsibility for the aggregate of functions below him on the organizational chart. Standards have been established for the *span of control* for an individual, but it is doubtful that they are meaningful, the reason being that we actually do not have any specifications for the individual. What might be a light load for one could be a heavy load for another. In any case, the span of control should be kept at a workable and efficient level.

Strive for Simplicity

The organization should be designed as simply as possible to perform the function it is to serve. Any frills will undoubtedly affect the function in an adverse manner and will add to the overhead.

Minimize Costs

As in every design, cost should be taken into consideration. The cost of a design improvement must be compared with the value of the improvement. Not only must the increase in cost and value be considered, but the cost of increasing the reliability of the system must also be taken into consideration.

Standardization

In all designs we try to get the highest efficiency by standardizing the components. This concept can be carried over into the organizational design by having the functions standardized. People filling these functions can then be readily shifted as desired. This tends to develop experts in these activities with extensive knowledge and skill. This may be seen on a production line, where one job is the tightening of a bolt, and may also be found in the controller's office, where one job is taking care of a certain part of the accounts payable. One danger of this policy, if carried to the extreme, is that no individuals are trained in breadth to fill the higher echelons.

Departmentalization

The design of the organization should include well defined departments with established and recognized boundaries. This is helpful in developing team spirit, an essential ingredient in any organization. Where departmental boundaries are not well defined there is apt to be a shifting of responsibility and unbalanced workloads. Energetic workers will constantly increase their workloads while departments with lazy people will constantly do less.

We know it is efficient to group similar things into classes, and this follows in the organizational design. Similar activities should be grouped under one function.

Keep Lines of Communication Short

The lines of communication should be just as short and direct as possible. The more times a commnunication has to be repeated, the more possibilities there are for errors to occur. Long lines of communication also account for unnecessary delays.

No set of principles will account for all the design problems you will encounter in industry. Often an organization grows up not knowing exactly what its final objective is. People are hired at levels beyond their abilities, or they do not continue to produce; but rather than replace the people in the function, the function is isolated by establishing a duplicate or similar function. This is especially typical of a family-owned business where a home must be found for some of the more ineffective members of the clan. Often members of an organization collect a political power which would cause a disturbance if they were replaced. Instead of being replaced, these individuals are merely sealed off and left to wither. This is not unlike the growth of any other organism which becomes infected: the diseased portion is isolated.

THE ORGANIZATION AND SYSTEM DESIGNING

There is little doubt that the factory organization is a system; and the production control function within the organization is just a subset of the larger system. Since it is a system, the method of logic for designing a system is a suitable approach for designing and redesigning the organization.

You are studying system designing so that eventually you will be able to put your knowledge into practice by developing improved control systems. Often the efficiency of the control system depends upon how well the organization is designed. It is, therefore, imperative for you to learn how to analyze and improve the organization. At least you should be aware of structural weaknesses if redesigning the organization is not permissible.

The organization is a complex system about which little is actually known. Contrary to the knowledge available in many physical systems, we are never quite sure what effect the changes made on one part of the system will have on others. Eventually, we can hope to have such useful design information, but not in the present state of the art. Now, we must depend upon *design considerations*, which are hardly more than rules-of-thumb for designing the organization.

The Physical Facilities

Routing the product through the processes of an existing plant is part of the *process designing* activity. However, modifying the plant facilities to conform to the process is the *plant layout* activity. These two approaches are merely different ways of attacking the same problem.

If the production set-up times are short, it will generally pay to route the product from one machine to another. However, if the production set-up times are long, and if it is otherwise feasible, the equipment should be arranged so the materials flow directly from one operation to the next.

Because of these two facets of the same problem, we find factory facilities organized in two distinctive patterns.

Job Shop: Machines are grouped primarily by the kind of work they perform.

Production Line: Machines are grouped by the sequence of operations required on the product.

The two terms used here are the ones that are recognized in industry, but others are used in the literature. For example, the job shop is often referred to as a *process* or *functional layout,* while the production line is referred to as the *product* or *line layout*. But what causes a management to decide whether or not the job shop or the production line is the most suitable for its purpose?

There are several reasons for making the decision, one way or the other, but the important one is the length of the set-up time—or how long the machines will be doing a particular job. If the machines are to be used for just a short time for a particular job, and the flow pattern will change drastically from job to job, then it is probably desirable to group the machines by the kind of work they perform.

The type of layout should not be associated with the quantity of product alone. For instance, nails are produced in large quantities in plants laid out as job shops. Why? Because the headers, which produce the nail heads, are noisy, and the plating processes have disagreeable fumes.

There are other reasons, besides the length of set-up time, which dictate a job shop layout. In some cases the process may require air-conditioning, or the process may be screened from public view because it is secret, or perhaps the layout is dictated by the weight of the product or by machines which might overstress the floor in some areas.

It is not intended to imply that a factory must be either a job shop or a production line, for it is frequently a combination of both. It is common to find a factory producing parts in a job shop but assembling on a production line. In this case, the parts are produced at such a high rate it does not pay to maintain production lines for them. Occasionally, a job shop finds that a certain sequence of operations occurs so frequently it is desirable to put several machines together in a line, such as placing a drilling machine in the lathe department for the frequent drilling jobs that need to be made on turned spindles.

THE TOOLS OF PLANT LAYOUT

The many excellent references to plant layout furnish adequate descriptions of the various tools for improving the plant layout design. Space will permit only a brief coverage of the subject here.

Process Chart

As shown in Figure 10–4, the process chart is a quick way of analyzing the process. Starting with the operation sheet, or with the actual flow

Figure 10–4

Process Chart (Original)

INDUSTRIAL ENGINEERING DIVISION

PROCESS CHART

SUMMARY	
OPERATIONS	7
TRANSPORTS	0
TEM. STORAGE	8
PER: STORAGE	1
INSPECTION	1
VERT. DISTANCE	–
HORIZ. DISTANCE	44
TIME	1.01

OPERATION ASSEMBLE DEMONSTRATION PACKAGE
PRODUCT CONSUMER PACKAGE
DEPARTMENT ASSEMBLY
PRESENT X PROPOSED

BINDER	37X-4
CHART	1
SHEET	1 OF 1
CHARTED	James Jones
DATE	3/22/64
CHECKED	GCH
APPROVED	GCH

NO.	DIST. IN FEET	TIME IN HOURS	OPER'N	TRANSP.	PERM.ST	INSP'N	DESCRIPTION
1.	2	.12	1				Pick up bindings – dispose to tote box.
2.	2				T		Storage prior to next operation.
3.	2	.14	2				Assemble bindings, holders, and tapped bearing insert into outer container using special pliers – dispose to tote box.
4.	2				T		Storage prior to next operation.
5.	4	.15	3				Fasten container to body with screw.
6.	4				T		Storage prior to next operation.
7.	4	.27	4				Insert holding screws, attach advertising and place outer cover on container at work place 1 or 2 – dispose to tote box.
8.	4				T		Storage prior to next operation.
9.	3	.10	5				Seal rip string to cover – dispose to tote box.
10.	3				T		Storage prior to next operation.
11.	2	.09	6				Notch container – dispose to tote box.
12.	2				T		Storage prior to next operation.
13.	2	.07				1	Inspect container – dispose to tote box.
14.	2				T		Storage to next operation.
15.	2	.07	7				Label container – dispose to tote box.
16.	4				T		Accumulate packages.
17.							Storage prior to packing.

TEMPORARY STORAGE CAN BE DENOTED BY △T

KPφ 34081B

of the product on the floor, a chart is made which shows every step of the process. A well accepted set of symbols for charting has been established which represents operation, move, storage, and inspection. Others might be

Figure 10–5

Process Chart (Revised)

INDUSTRIAL ENGINEERING DIVISION

PROCESS CHART

SUMMARY	
OPERATIONS	5
TRANSPORTS	0
TEM. STORAGE	4
PER: STORAGE	1
INSPECTION	1
VERT. DISTANCE	–
HORIZ. DISTANCE	24
TIME	.60

OPERATION ASSEMBLE DEMONSTRATION PACKAGE

PRODUCT CONSUMER PACKAGE

DEPARTMENT ASSEMBLY

PRESENT ______ PROPOSED X

BINDER	37X-4
CHART	1
SHEET	1 OF 1
CHARTED	James Jones
DATE	3-27-64
CHECKED	GCH
APPROVED	GCH

NO.	DIST. IN FEET	TIME IN HOURS	OPER'N	TRANSP.	PERM.ST.	INSP'N	DESCRIPTION
1.	1	.12	1				Pick up bindings – dispose to special holder.
2.	2	.11	2				Assemble bindings, holders and key slot bearing and insert into container using special pliers – dispose to tote box.
3.	2				T		Storage prior to operation.
4.	2	.13	3				Insert holding screws, attach advertising and place outer cover on container – dispose to tote box.
5.	2				T		Storage prior to next operation.
6.	7	.13	4				Seal rip string to cover and notch container – dispose to tote box.
7.	2				T		Storage prior to next operation.
8.	2	.11	5				Inspect and label container – dispose to tote box.
9.	4				T		Accumulate packages.
10.					△		Storage prior to packages.
11.							
12.							
13.							
14.							
15.							
16.							
17.							

TEMPORARY STORAGE CAN BE DENOTED BY △(T)

KPφ 34081B

added as needed. (And this chart is, of course, not the final objective of this technique.)

The next step is to analyze the flow for any unnecessary delays, operations out of sequence, or other signs of inefficient operation. From this analysis a new and improved chart is drawn, as shown in Figure 10–5. This now becomes the model for the improved plant layout. It should be apparent that this is a far more efficient way of analyzing and improving the factory layout, as compared with actually moving the machines about on the factory floor.

Flow Process Diagram

As illustrated in Figure 10–6, the flow process diagram is related to the charting technique just discussed, but it has the advantage of showing the

Figure 10–6

Flow Process Diagram

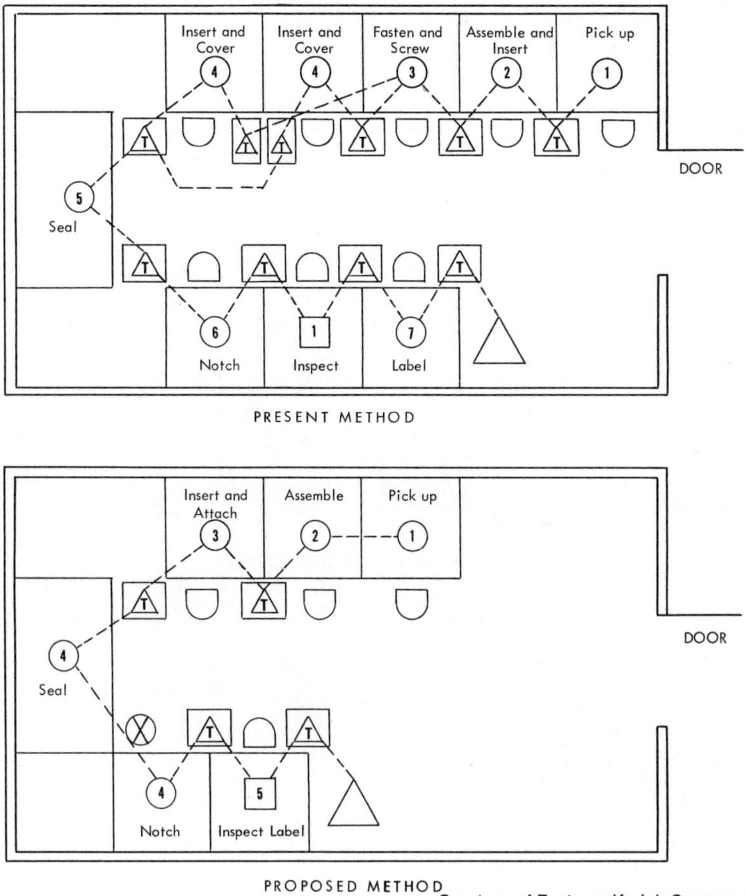

Courtesy of Eastman Kodak Company

flow of the product on the floor diagram. Long hauls of materials and points of traffic congestion will show up more quickly on the diagram than on the chart. A disadvantage is that the floor diagram has to be made, but frequently this can be just a rough sketch.

Two-Dimensional Layouts

This tool of plant layout consists of the floor plan with templates of the production equipment placed in the proper positions. The templates can be homemade or purchased, of heavy paper or plastic. They can be shifted to represent various layouts. Obviously, it is easier to envision the plant and flow of materials with this type of layout than it is with the flow process diagram.

Three-Dimensional Layouts

These layouts are made with models which are easily produced in a model shop, or purchased. They are usually made to the scale of one-quarter inch equals one foot. The advantage of this layout (Figure 10–7) over the previous method is the ease of envisioning all the details, including the inter-

Figure 10–7

Three-Dimensional Layout

Courtesy of General Motors Engineering Journal

ferences that might be caused by machines and materials. These model layouts are also used for such a purpose as introducing new employees and visitors to the complexity of the factory.

Mentioned here are the most important tools of plant layout, and with them remarkable savings can be made in the plant operation. There are other techniques, and refinements of the methods discussed here, with which everyone interested in the efficient operation of a factory should become familiar.

PLANT LAYOUT DESIGN CONSIDERATIONS

As in organizational design, it is difficult to state any quantitative design criteria for plant layout, but there are a number of well accepted design considerations. Some of the most important ones are:

Material Flow Should Comply with the Steps of the Process

The most efficient way to manufacture a product is to organize the machines so that the material flows the shortest possible distance, directly from one machine to the other, with little or no delay.

Move Material at a Minimum Cost

It is an old cliché that the best solution to a materials-handling problem is not to move the material. If this is impossible, then move it by gravity. And if this is not possible, usually the next best way is to move it by power. If people must move the material, it should be moved by the cheapest labor possible.

Minimize All Production Delays

Production delays should be minimized for several reasons. They are the source of customer dissatisfaction. Inventories will increase with the consequent costs of warehousing and large investments. The smooth flow of material at a constant rate will have a favorable effect upon the morale of the factory personnel.

Utilize Space for Production

The primary purpose of the factory is to produce goods. Any space that is not used for this purpose should be suspect. Of course there must be space for storage, aisles, and service areas; and the plant personnel should not feel crowded, but steps should be taken to make as much of the space as productive as possible.

Provide for Adequate Storage

Often unexpected production delays occur. When possible, these should be predicted and provision made for storing the material. The stored material should be protected and out of the way of normal production.

Maintain Material Identification

In many situations it is essential that the material be moved through the factory without losing its identity. This is especially true when material is not easily recognized as belonging to a particular product or order. It is also true when the quality record must be maintained for some time in the future, as for aircraft components. But identification is also important for production control in a job shop, where parts are moved through the factory in lots. Periodic scrap drives are the costly result of not placing enough emphasis upon this design consideration.

Keep Direct Labor Productive

It is not uncommon to find direct laborers moving material, running errands, and other nonproductive activities. Direct labor should be kept productive, and actively producing the product.

Keep Machine Loads Balanced

On the production line, it is desirable to keep the workloads balanced from machine to machine so that each is operating near its full capacity. When several machines are being operated by one person, an effort should be made to arrange the work so that the machines and the individuals are as productive as possible.

Minimize Capital Investment

This design consideration appears at many points in the plant design, as when machines have been overdesigned and when idle machines and idle inventory are permitted—all indications of poor utilization of capital investment.

Design for Flexibility

Seldom would a plant be designed and built without the consideration of future alterations. Changes in volume, changes in product design, the addition of new and better processes, all these indicate the necessity for a flexible design.

Maintain Quality Standards

A product can lose its value as it travels through the plant because it becomes contaminated, deteriorates, or is just shopworn. Every effort should be made in the layout of the plant to maintain the quality of the product and not decrease its value.

Apply Methods Improvement to Work Center

The plant layout design is not completed until each work center is carefully scrutinized and improved, for here is a point that will yield a big payoff.

Consider the Employees' Safety and Comfort

Safety measures can be directly reflected by the reduction of insurance premiums, but there are also indirect rewards that can be gained by a company practicing good safety rules. Delays in production can be kept at a minimum, and morale can be markedly improved if personnel realize that their safety is of importance to the management.

Provide for Efficient Supervision and Control

Departments should be of a size that can be efficiently supervised, and the processes should be grouped to offer the best supervision possible. Control offices and dispatch boards should be conveniently located to eliminate any undue delays and reduction in production time. *Feedback links* to the production control system should be immediate and accurate.

PHYSICAL FACILITIES AND SYSTEM DESIGNING

Recalling the definition of a system, there is little doubt that the factory facilities form a system. A very complex system it is, of machines and other physical facilities which function together for a common purpose. Therefore the steps of logic used in system designing are applicable to the design of the physical facilities:

1. Become aware of the problem.
2. Define the problem.
3. Locate, evaluate, and organize information.
4. Discover relationships and formulate hypotheses.
5. Evaluate the hypotheses.
6. Apply the solution.

The objective in *system designing for production control* is usually the imposition of control on the present layout of the physical facilities, however it does not rule out the design or redesign of the physical facilities to meet the control requirements. Usually, books and college courses which emphasize the physical facilities come under the subject of *plant layout.* Production control and plant layout are highly correlated and are two different ways of looking at similar problems.

SUMMARY

The design of a system cannot be considered without taking into account the environment within which it is to operate. In the factory the environment consists of the organization and the manufacturing facilities. Often any system imposed upon this environment will fail because of these two factors.

Organizations are depicted by charts, but these often tell only part of the story. The sciences of organization and facilities design have not matured to the point where all the numerous relationships can be described by equations, but, as in other disciplines, this has not prevented us from designing. The designing is facilitated by a number of well-known and accepted design considerations which are practiced by competent designers.

Questions

1. Is the organizational structure for a factory likely to change as it matures? Explain your answer. If the organization does change, where would you expect the greatest change?
2. How efficiently does an organizational chart explain an organizational structure?
3. As related to the organization, define:
   a) Line.
   b) Staff.
   c) Functional staff.
4. Which organizational design consideration do you consider the most important? Explain why.
5. In what type and size plant will the plant layout function play an important part? Explain your answer.
6. What advantage does a three-dimensional layout have over a two-dimensional layout?
7. Does a manufacturing plant ever include both job shop and production line layouts?
8. Job shop layouts are associated with what type of product? Production line layouts are associated with what type of product?
9. Which plant layout design consideration do you consider the most important? The least important? Explain why.
10. Draw an organizational chart for a company with which you are acquainted. Redesign the organization and explain how you have used the *design considerations*.
11. Choose one of the plant layout techniques and illustrate an original, and a revised, factory system. Explain how you have used the plant layout *design considerations* in making the revised layout.

References

APPLE, JAMES MACGREGOR. *Plant Layout and Materials Handling*. 2d ed. New York: Ronald Press Co., 1963.

BROOM, HALSEY N. *Production Management*. Homewood, Ill.: Richard D. Irwin, Inc., 1962.

DEMIANIUK, F. S. *The Technological Principles of Flow Line and Automated Production*. Translated from the Russian by O. M. Blumn. Edited by E. Bishop. Oxford, England: Pergamon Press, 1963.

GREENE, JAMES H. "Is Current Layout Thinking Obsolete?" *Modern Materials Handling*, Vol. XIII, No. 12 (December, 1958), p. 70.

IMMER, JOHN R. *Layout Planning Techniques*. New York: McGraw-Hill Book Co., Inc., 1950.

MOORE, JAMES M. *Plant Layout and Design*. New York: Macmillan Co., 1962.

MOORE, FRANKLIN G. *Manufacturing Management*. 4th ed. Homewood, Ill.: Richard D. Irwin, Inc., 1965.

MUTHER, RICHARD. *Production-Line Technique*. New York and London: McGraw-Hill Book Co., Inc., 1944.

———. *Systematic Layout Planning*. Boston: Industrial Education Institute, 1961.

ROSCOE, EDWIN SCOTT. *Organization for Production*. Rev. ed. Homewood, Ill.: Richard D. Irwin, Inc., 1959.

REED, RUDDELL. *Plant Layout*. Homewood, Ill.: Richard D. Irwin, Inc., 1961.

CHAPTER 11

Manual Control Systems

In many respects, all that has gone before is culminated in this chapter. You will remember that system designing was defined as: conceiving and planning in the mind a complex unity of many diverse parts to exercise restraining influence over the making of goods.

The emphasis now will be upon how the systems are analyzed and synthesized to fit the various components together in an efficient system. Again it should be stressed that the signal and the system are two separate things: the system is being discussed and not the decisions that are imposed upon the system. The system might carry the signals perfectly, but if the signals are imperfect the message will be imperfect.

This section will include chapters covering the entire gamut of manufacturing control system designing, from the simplest flow of paper work for manual systems to the more complicated computer programming. Discussion of computer programming in these surroundings should not be startling if one considers the basic problem of assembling a group of components for conveying information and carrying out instructions. In a noncomputerized system, people are asked to follow the system that has been established. In a card-data-processing system, the instructions are given to the personnel in the data-processing center, who in turn give them to the machines by instructions wired on the panel. In electronic data processing the instructions are also carried out by the personnel as well as by the computer which is instructed by its program.

In an era of electronic gadgetry, the computers have gained an aura of exotic mystery, but in reality they are not as complex as the human being. The computer is more predictable since it interprets instructions only as written. It can only make the logical decisions which are given to it in the computer program. This is not true for the human being, who, fortunately, or unfortunately, makes decisions on his own.

This section is divided into three distinct techniques:

Chapter 11: System designing for manual methods;

Chapters 12 and 13: System designing for card-data processing.

Chapters 14 and 15: System designing for computers.

Each of these system-designing techniques is considerably different from the other. This is regrettable, because there is little carryover of knowledge from one to another. This difference in techniques is caused by the differences in history as well as by some differences in organizational structure. Generally, all card-data-processing equipment and computer equipment is placed in one central location, under the supervision of one person whose knowledge is machine-orientated. He, however, becomes deeply involved in payroll, inventory control, accounts payable, and many other functions of the company. This development undoubtedly has a profound effect upon the organizational structures, and it is worthy of extensive research.

System Designing for Manual Methods

Factory managers are accustomed to thinking of the step-by-step process needed to produce their products and constantly look for means of improvement in order to reduce direct costs and thereby increase profits. A parallel can be drawn between the product process and the paper work procedure; the procedure being a *series of related clerical steps used to process a business form.* Improvements here are revealed in the reduction of both direct and indirect costs, which also increase profits; and profits produced in this way are just as good as those produced by process improvement. Since more companies have given less attention to their procedures than they have to their processes, the opportunities for profit-hunting by procedure analysis usually are excellent.

Some of the numerous opportunities for improvements and savings are: savings in costs by a reduction in the number of business forms and by elimination of unnecessary steps in their processing; improved customer relations by a reduction in the order processing time and by more efficient handling of the customers' inquiries; and improved employee relations by well outlined methods and by fixed responsibility while training time is reduced.

STEPS OF THE SYSTEMS ANALYSIS

Systems analysis consists of three steps:

1. *Paper-flow Charting.* This step consists of showing the flow of the paper work by some schematic arrangement. After a suitable chart is drawn, the flow is analyzed for possible improvements and a new improved procedure is developed.

2. *Design of Forms.* All the forms are designed, or redesigned, so that they can be used efficiently. This means forms must be designed to satisfy a well-thought-out set of criteria for efficiency.

3. *Procedures Manual.* Step-by-step instructions must be written to show how the improved procedure is to be operated. This could be considered as the rulebook by which the procedures are played. Changes can and should be made, but only after adequate consideration.

Preceding any attempt at paper-flow charting, the procedures analyst should become acquainted with the organization. If a chart of the organization is unavailable, one must be produced which will assist the analyst in getting orientated. The analyst should accept some responsibility in suggesting changes which will make a more efficient organizational structure.

The Paper-flow Charting

After an overall view of the organization is obtained it is essential to produce a detailed picture of the present system. To do this it is necessary to interview each employee involved and to record his part in the procedure. This is not always easily done, for employees frequently find it difficult to relate everything they do. The analyst must be patient in his endeavors to draw out the necessary facts and must be skilled in separating fact from fiction. He must also take care not to become involved in the personal problems of the employee. Several interviews are sometimes necessary before the information chinks are filled.

A verbal description alone is confusing to analyze, so the acceptable method is the graphic paper-flow chart, an example of which is shown in Figure 11–1.

To explain the chart one must know the language. There are many languages, or sets of symbols, to be found in the literature, but a useful code is the one shown in Figure 11–2. Since this code is just a tool, you should feel free to alter or add to it to serve your purpose.

As with any language there must be rules, such as: Charting should start in the upper left-hand corner and progress downward and to the right. The vertical axis shows the sequence of chronological events, with the first events at the top. Columns on the chart may be used to represent different forms, or, as in the example, different departments through which the paper forms flow. Charting only the paper flow would serve little purpose; it is necessary to analyze the flow for possible improvement. This can best be done by asking questions such as:

System Design Checklist

_____ Can any forms be eliminated?
_____ Can any step be eliminated?
_____ Can any other person do the operation better?
_____ Can any steps be combined to advantage?

Figure 11-1

Paper-Flow Chart

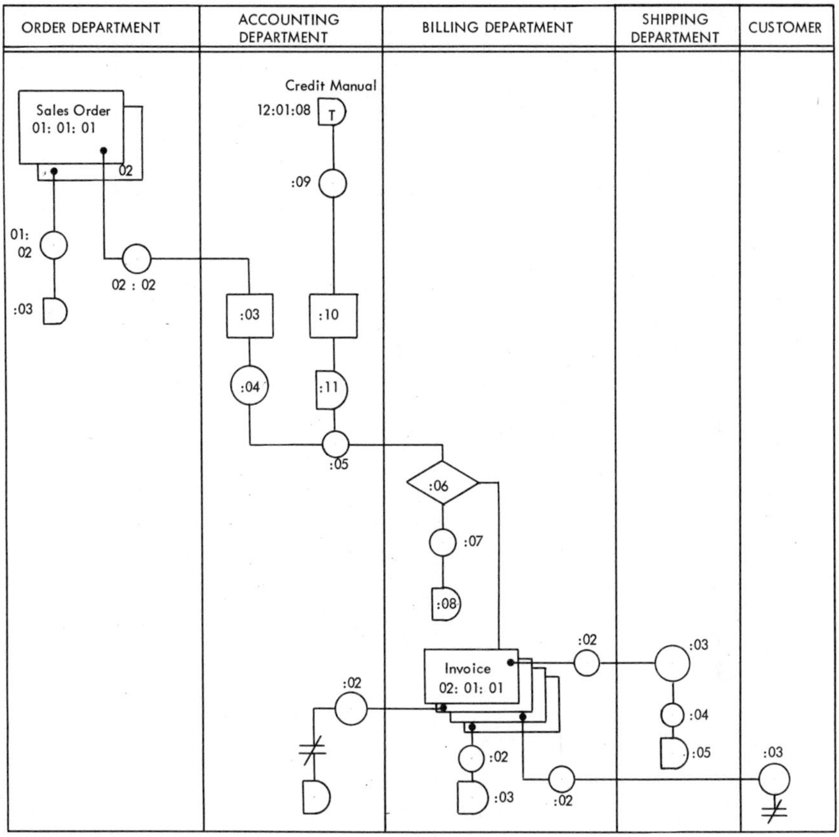

______ Can any steps be subdivided to advantage?
______ Can the sequence of steps be improved?
______ Can spot checks be substituted for 100 percent inspection?
______ Can the originator of a form furnish more information, and on a better form?
______ Are workloads balanced?
______ Could a lower-paid employee do the operation?
______ Can delays be eliminated or utilized for other operations?
______ Can the travel distance be reduced?
______ Can bottleneck operations be scheduled better?
______ Can forms be presorted while completing an operation?
______ Can any filing operation be eliminated? Why save this form?
______ Is a record being kept in more than one place?
______ Can any employee offer suggestions to improve the procedure?

There are other questions the inquisitive mind must ask (make a practice of it) for no checklist will ever supplant the curiosity of the good analyst.

Figure 11–2

Paper-Flow Charting Symbols

SYMBOL	NAME	DESCRIPTION
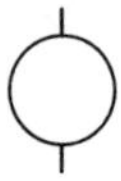	Operation	Work being done on a form: information being added, balance being extended, etc.
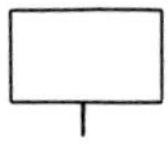	Origin Operation	Operation when it is the origination of a form.
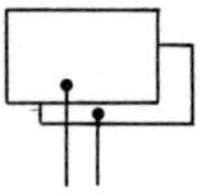	Origin Operation	Operation when it is the origination of more than one form.
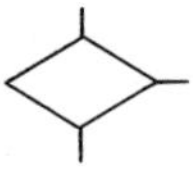	Operation Take-off	Operation when information is transcribed to another form. Horizontal line connects the two forms.
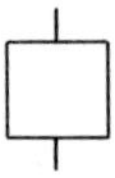	Inspection	Determination of the correctness of information.
	Move	Form is moved from one location to another.
	File	Form is placed in an organized filing system.
	Temporary File	Form awaiting to be moved for further work.
	Disposal	Form is destroyed.
	Break	A break in the procedure analysis indicating something that is not pertinent to the study.

Of course, asking the questions is not enough; a new chart must be developed showing the improved method, and getting the improved method into use is the ultimate goal.

During the analysis one should see many opportunities to improve the design of the form used. Frequently the type of form will be abandoned in favor of a form which can be handled easier or which will present information in a more vivid fashion.

Design of Forms

The design of business procedure forms is merely applied-common-sense. In general, the thing to keep in mind is how easy it is to add or remove information, whether this be by hand or by machine. But since it is difficult to keep all the numerous considerations in mind, a checklist is the best approach.

Form Design Checklist

_____ Is this form necessary, or is its purpose served by another form?
_____ Does this form have a title which really describes its purpose?
_____ Are there adequate instructions on the form for its general use?
_____ Are sorting symbols in the most convenient place?
_____ If the form is a traveler, does it need a space for addressor and addressee?
_____ Is the form of a suitable size for filing?
_____ Are there adequate margins for binding?
_____ Can both sides of the form be used?
_____ Will the forms get dirty? If so, how should they be protected?
_____ Is common information grouped in blocks? Is all the information used by one person or department placed in one location?
_____ Are data which could cause serious transcription errors separated on the form?
_____ Is the information in convenient sequence for transcription?
_____ Can more common information be printed on the form, rather than filled in?
_____ Are spaces adequate for the information to be filled in?
_____ Do the printed lines conform to typewriter spacing?
_____ Is print arranged for a minimum number of typewriter stop settings? (Stop settings should conform to other business forms in use.)
_____ Would horizontal or vertical lines help reduce errors?
_____ Can check boxes be used as a substitute for written-in information?
_____ Can any wording be misinterpreted?
_____ Can a common sketch, with fill-in spaces for specifications, be substituted for blueprints or other descriptive material?
_____ Is all the information necessary?
_____ Does the form create a good appearance? Would it create a good mental attitude in the user?
_____ Will colored paper help in identification or filing?
_____ Can the employee who uses the form suggest improvements?

Written Standard Procedure

Improved procedures and new forms will be worthless unless the employees accept them as their own and follow them to the letter. The only thing to do is to freeze the system in a *Written Standard Procedure*. The Written Standard Procedure includes simple direct instructions in how the forms are to be used. It offers many advantages by serving as an instruction to new employees: they can see the whole picture as well as their own small part. It also prevents conflicting procedures from being inaugurated, and it presents a basis for job descriptions and disciplines.

The method of writing a Written Standard Procedure is simple. For each symbol on the chart there should be a short imperative statement. The instructions should be direct, care being taken not to insult the reader but leaving no question in his mind regarding his duty. The steps in the procedure should be indexed in some organized fashion. A simple, convenient way of doing this is to use a sequence of three numbers, both on the chart and on the Written Standard Procedure; for example:

01:02:04.

The first two digits represent the form number: *01*, in this case, represents the sales order, while the second set of digits, *02*, refers to the copy in the set, and the third set of digits, *04*, refers to the step in the procedure. The two first digits find a useful place in the organization as an index number for forms, and they should be printed on the forms. The paper-flow chart should be numbered so that the standard operations are keyed to it for ready reference. A skeleton form of the Written Standard Procedure is shown in Figure 11–3.

Figure 11–3

Written Standard Procedure

Sales Order 01

Form 01 Sales Order, Copy 01

01:01:01	Write up sales order
:02	Move to file
:03	File in numerical order

Form 01 Sales Order, Copy 02

01:02:01	Write up sales order
:02	Move sales order to accounting department
:03	Check sales order with credit manual
:04	Fill in accounting information
:05	Move second copy of sales order to billing department
:06	Remove information for invoice
:07	Move to files
:08	File

Form 02, Invoice Copy 01

02:01:01	Write up Invoice from sales order
:02	Move to shipping department
:03	Fill order
:04	Move to file
:05	File

All the procedures should be kept in manuals, which are distributed to responsible people in the organization. The procedures should be reviewed periodically, and the revisions distributed.

This step-by-step method of squeezing profits out of paper work is one that can be successful for anyone, and with very little practice. One thing that can't be taught is how to acquire an inquisitive mind; this you *must* have, and this, used with the tools discussed here, will pay big dividends. There are many other approaches to the procedure analysis which will give good results. The symbols given should serve you well, but remember that the objective is to communicate with people. If they understand another set of symbols, then by all means use them.

Duplicating Equipment for Manual Systems

Communications is the one word which best describes the production control function of a factory, and paramount is the communication of the written word. So important is this today that practically every plant, be it large or small, contains a miniature printing plant for the production of the many forms needed in the course of today's business. Some member of the factory must take the responsibility for knowing something about the methods of printing. Because it is such an important function it is desirable for all factory management personnel to have some general knowledge of the important duplicating processes. It is probably sufficient if they have some knowledge of the following duplicating techniques:

Raised-type printing	Offset printing
Hectograph printing	Lensless copying
Stencil printing	Xerography

RAISED-TYPE REPRODUCTION

Among the raised-type methods, the typewriter is by far the most common for plant work. In fact, it is so well known to the average person that it is unnecessary to spend time describing it, but this does not mean that it should be overlooked: it is an important way of inexpensively producing a number of copies. It is of further importance as the method of originating the master for many of the long-run duplicating processes. The typewriter, in effect, does the typesetting and printing all at the same time.

The two most common forms of type are the *elite,* which is spaced 12 letters to the inch, and the *pica,* which is larger, spaced 10 letters to the inch. There are many styles of letters available, and on some of the bigger electric machines some of the letters can be exchanged for mathematical and other symbols. For a "near print" appearance there are typewriters especially designed to permit the alignment, or "justification," of the right-hand margin. This is done by adjusting either the space between the letters or the space between the words.

The electric typewriter brings some important advantages to the art of duplication. The work is less strenuous to the typist because both the keys and the carriage are electrically driven. In addition, the quality of the work is greatly improved since the force with which the keys hit the paper can be kept constant, which helps produce uniform copies. The attribute of the electric typewriter, which is of the greatest importance in the production control procedure, is the heavy force that can be applied by the typebars on the platen. If carbon paper is used, 20 copies can be produced. This is important when the alternative might be a time-consuming second operation on a duplicating machine.

With any typewriter, either manual or electric, additional copies can be made by using carbon paper. These can be separate sheets of carbon paper or ingeniously designed snap-out forms. The number of copies that can be made with carbon paper depends upon how legible the copies must be, how heavy the paper is, how hard the platen is, and how hard the keys are struck. In ordinary typing, three to five copies can be expected, but, if onionskin paper is used, as many as a dozen copies can be obtained. The difficulty and cost of making corrections on the carbon copies, however, puts a limit upon the number of copies it is economical to make.

For other raised-print methods, reference is limited here to the embossed-plate addressing machines which find their place in manufacturing control for the production of tags, addressed envelopes, and similar items. The embossing plate is made of thin ductile material which is placed in a special machine—similar to a typewriter, which embosses the desired printing on the plate. The metal plates are used in a printing Addressograph machine, which will produce tags at a rapid rate. The printing machines are designed to eject unwanted plates in any stack.

HECTOGRAPH

Also important are the gelatin and the spirit type hectographs. The gelatin type of hectograph probably came into its own in the little red schoolhouse where copies had to be made for art work and for similar projects. In its simplest form it consists of a flat pan filled with a rubbery pad of a mixture of gelatin and glycerin. The master is prepared by using ordinary paper and a special dye which comes in the form of typewriter ribbons, pencils, or ink. This master is placed face-down on the moistened gelatin surface for a short time, so that the ink is absorbed. The master is removed, and copies are made by simply placing an absorbent paper on the dampened impregnated surface.

The number of copies that can be made by this hectograph process depends upon how much ink is placed on the gelatin and how fast it is picked up by the copies being made. The process is comparatively slow and of poor quality, but it is suitable for internal communications of short runs, of about 10 to 50 copies.

The spirit hectograph (Figure 11–4) has found an important place in plant communications. The schematic, Figure 11–5, shows how the master is fastened around the drum.

Figure 11–4

Spirit Duplicating Machine

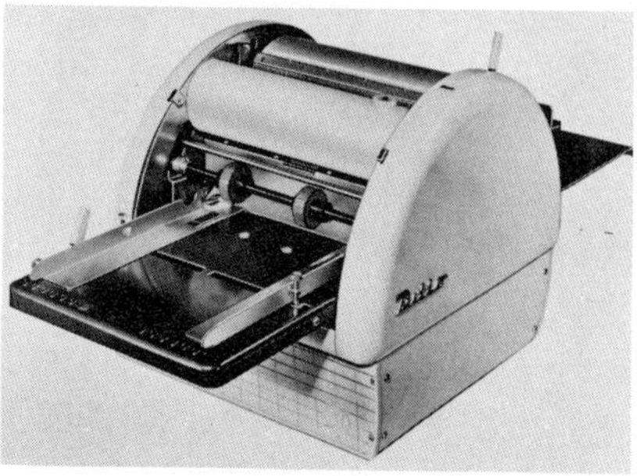

Courtesy of Ditto, Incorporated

The master is a hard-surfaced paper which comes packed with a carbon paper and a light, removable insert to keep the carbon from smudging. When an impression is made on the master with a typewriter, pencil, or similar method, the ink is picked up from the carbon paper in a thick layer by the master sheet. This produces a reversed, or mirror, image on the back of the master sheet. The carbon paper is removed and destroyed before the master is placed in the machine.

Figure 11–5

Spirit Hectograph Schematic

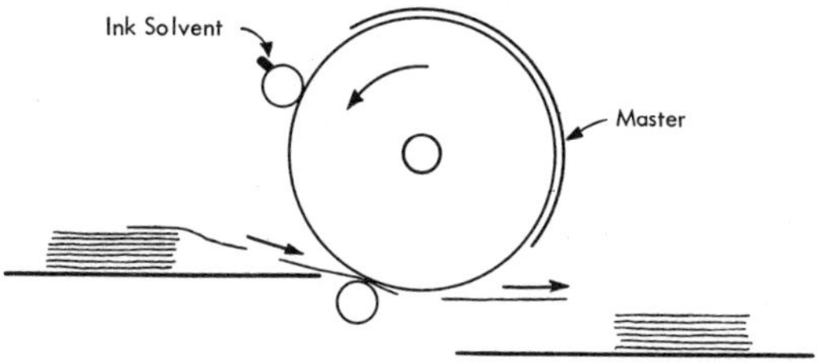

As the cylinder is revolved, the master comes in contact with a roller that is slightly moistened with an ink solvent. This loosens just enough of the ink to make a proper impression on the paper as it is rolled in contact with the master. The master produces a mirror image of itself on the copy paper, which gives a readable form.

The life of the master depends upon how much carbon is placed on it by the impression of the typewriter—as well as how fast the material is removed by the fluid. A common estimate of the number of good copies is 500, but this depends upon how dim the copies can be before they become worthless for your application.

The versatility of the spirit hectograph has been expanded for manufacturing control purposes by several techniques. One improvement is a method of blocking out areas or replacing portions with a variable master. Shingled slips (Figure 11–6) also add to the ease of producing manufactur-

Figure 11–6

Shingled Slips

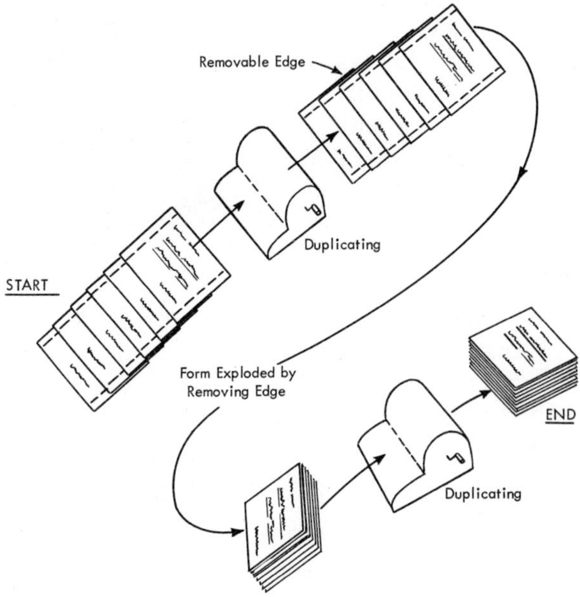

ing forms. These come bound on the edge so that they can all go through the machine at one pass, picking up the specific information from the master. They are then "exploded" and passed through the machine to pick up the common information for the heading. This is an important time-saving device in the preparation of instruction cards and time tickets.

The azograph resembles the spirit hectograph, both in appearance and method, except that the transfer sheet is covered with a layer of golden brown wax. When the wax has been moistened with a colorless fluid it leaves a blue image on the paper. This process has the advantage over the spirit hectograph in that it does not use staining aniline dyes, which are difficult to clean off.

STENCIL COPYING

The stencil copying machine, as can be seen in the schematic, Figure 11–7, is similar to the spirit duplicating machine, with one exception. The ink is not picked up from the master but is forced through from the back side. This is possible because the master is made of a fibrous paper covered with an impervious plastic coating which permits ink to flow through only where the plastic has been cut by type or a stylus. Since a quantity of the ink is squeezed through the master, it is desirable that the copy paper should be fairly porous, which would in general rule out slick card stock.

Figure 11–7

Stencil-Copying Schematic

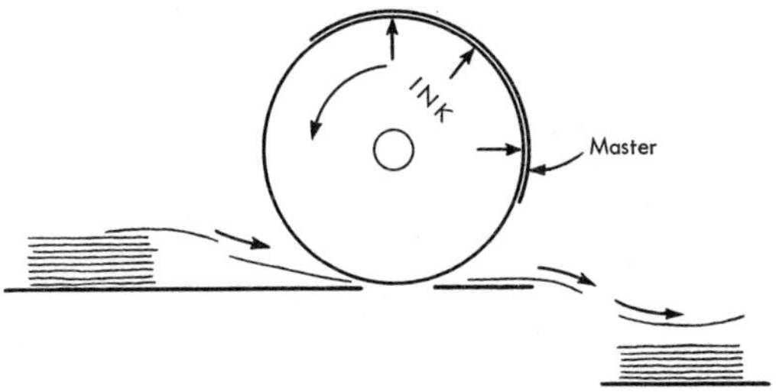

The master can be prepared by any skilled typist, but the quality of the final copy is dependent upon how well the original is prepared, and an electric typewriter with its uniform stroke is an important aid. If the stencil masters are thoroughly cleaned they can be used over and over, with only a slight decrease in the quality. These stencil machines also come equipped with attachments which make multiple-copy work for production control easier to handle.

OFFSET PRINTING

Offset printing, like many other products, has taken on the tradename of the manufacturers, which makes recognition of the process difficult. The key to the offset process is the aversion that water and oil have for each other. The ink, which is oily, will not adhere to a dampened surface but will be attracted to surfaces which are also oily.

The offset method is "flat printing," which means that it does not have the raised print of a typewriter or the "set-up" type used in publishing books. In the earliest form of flat printing—lithography—a special stone was used as a master and the part that was not covered with ink was treated to accept only water. Repeated applications of ink would be picked up only by the inked portion to be transferred to the copy paper.

Figure 11–8

Offset Duplicating Machine

Courtesy of Ditto, Incorporated

In the modern offset press the stone is replaced by metal or paper plates fastened to a drum, as shown in Figure 11–8 and Figure 11–9. The plate does not roll in direct contact with the paper as in lithography, but is in contact with a rubberized

Figure 11–9

Offset Printing Schematic

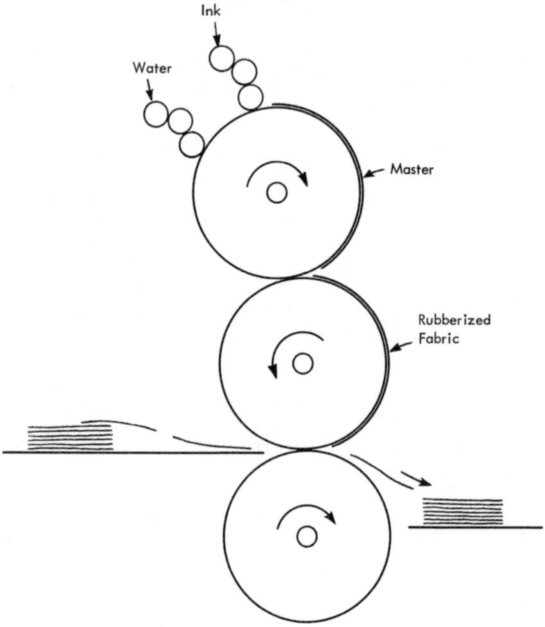

fabric on a drum which "offsets" the printing to the copy paper. It is this last cylinder which actually does the printing on the offset press. The third cylinder presses the paper against the rubber surface. These three cylinders are basic to nearly all offset presses.

The other components of the press run in gear with the main cylinder. The ink rollers apply the ink to the master. To get a uniform application, the ink is squeezed between several rollers, which are reciprocated as they turn. The water rollers, which are ahead of the ink rollers, apply the moisture to the portions not inked so that the ink will not be picked up. Naturally, there is considerable art in adjusting the quantity of ink and water to give the best results.

The master sheets used in offset printing are made of fiber, zinc, or aluminum, with perforations at the ends for fastening in the press. The printing surface of the metal sheets is finely grained and can be typewritten on directly, if a special ribbon is used. For drawings, a special ink must be used, and for photographs and transparencies, special light-sensitive sheets are necessary.

The advantage of the offset technique, as compared with direct printing of lithography, is that the quality of printing is improved considerably and that the master is protected because it does not come in contact with the printed paper. The output of the offset press is about 3,000 to 6,000 copies per hour. Ordinary office help can produce typewritten masters, but beyond this the skill necessary to make photographed masters increases rapidly. The number of copies that can be produced from one master for office use is practically unlimited.

LENSLESS COPYING

This method of making copies has had tremendous growth in the last few years so that now it is one of the most bewildering areas in which management has to make decisions. The lensless copying method requires the original document to be placed in close contact with a sensitive material while the exposure is made. There are two basic ways of exposing the sensitized paper. The light either passes through the master to expose the paper (as shown in Figure 11–10*a*) the "print-through" method; or the light is reflected from the master (Figure 11–10*b*), with the "reflex" technique.

Figure 11–10

Lensless Copying

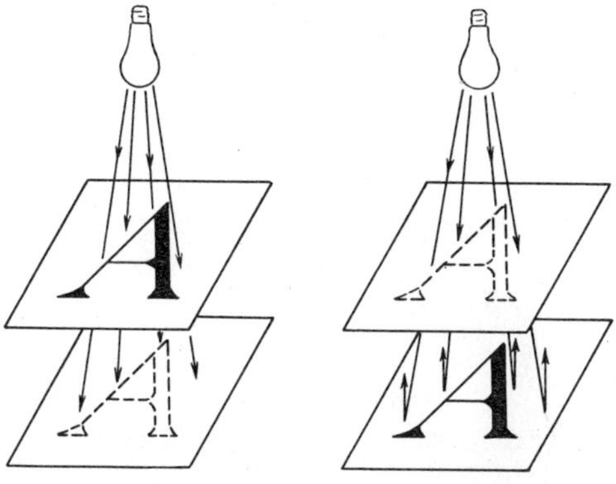

PRINT THROUGH METHOD (A)

REFLEX METHOD (B)

Of the print-through methods, the one used in the production of engineering drawings is probably the best known. The copying paper is covered with a light-sensitive material which can be destroyed by the light in the glass cylinder (Figure 11–11*a* and *b*). The remaining chemical turns to a dye when developed by either liquid or ammonia fumes within the machine.

This type of machine produces in dye the undestroyed area under letters and lines. The result is a copy practically identical with the original without any intermediate steps. Because of this, and because of its relatively low cost, it has found an important place in the production of materials for manufacturing control and other purposes.

Familiar to many is the blueprint machine, which, at a fairly low cost, produces copies in volume from translucent originals. The image is produced

Figure 11–11a

A Common Print-through Method

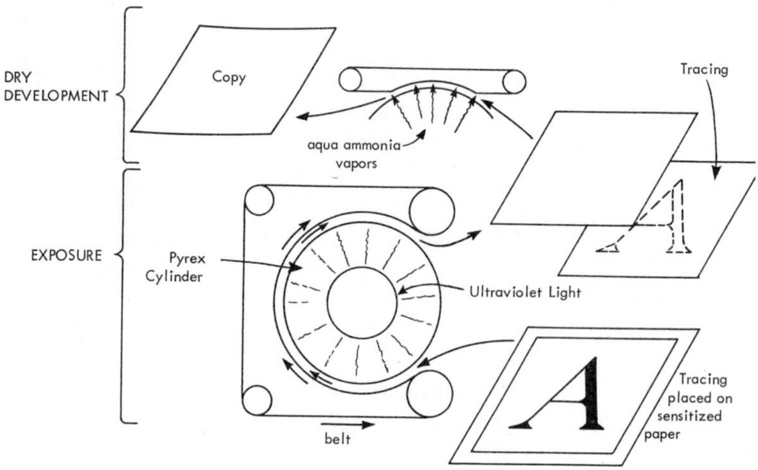

Figure 11–11b

A Print-through Process

Courtesy of Charles Bruning Co., Inc.

by passing a strong light through the translucent master, which is in direct contact with the copying paper. The light causes a chemical change on the copying paper, which is later brought out by a wet chemical bath to the characteristically blue color of the blueprint. Dark lines of the original show up as white lines against the blue overall background.

One common type of lensless copying machine is a modification of the familiar photographic process which uses a silver sensitized paper. This paper is placed in contact with the original and is exposed to a strong light. The sensitized paper is "developed," which brings out the image, and it is then placed in a "hypo" which washes away the undeveloped silver compound. This method produces a copy which has opposite tones to the original; thus it is necessary to use this copy as a master and repeat the process.

An improvement of the above process is the dry technique, to which is added a "receiving paper" (Figures 11–12 and 11–13). The negative, which

Figure 11–12

Lensless Copying Machine Schematic

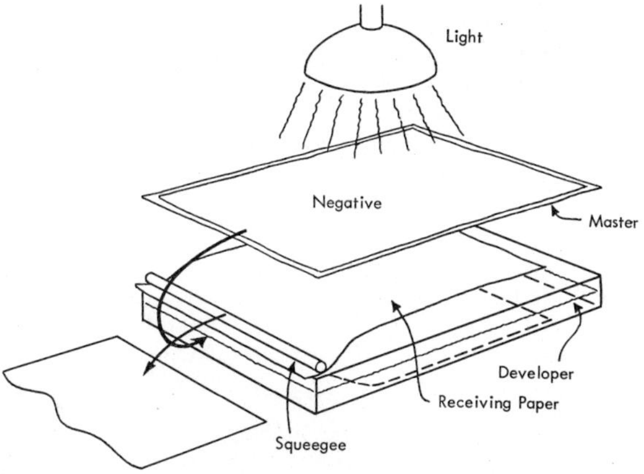

is photographed in direct contact with the master by the reflex method, is placed in a solution of developer and then placed in contact with the receiving sheet. The negative and receiving sheets are passed through a squeegee, which not only dries the copy but also transfers the image from the negative to the special receiving paper.

At least one reproduction machine, the Thermo-Fax, shown in Figure 11–14, makes use of radiant energy rather than light. A controlled beam from a tungsten filament lamp is used as the activating source. This source sends rays through the copy paper to the typewritten original. The dark areas of the original absorb the energy and convert it into a pattern of differential temperatures. This pattern acts on the temperature-sensitive

Figure 11–13

Lensless Copying Machine

Courtesy of Eastman Kodak Company

Figure 11–14

Thermo-Fax

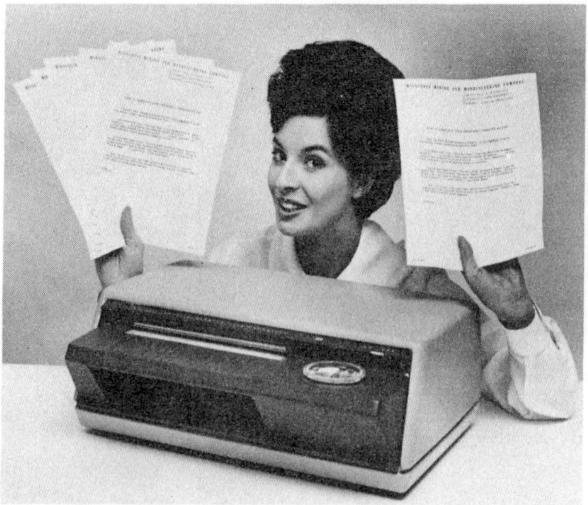

Courtesy of Thermo-Fax, Minnesota Mining and Manufacturing Co.

Thermo-Fax copy paper to reproduce the original. All this occurs in a fraction of a second, since the total time to copy an $8\frac{1}{2}$ x 11 sheet is four seconds. The process behind this product is an instantaneous one-step method of making copies of typewritten letters and other pieces of business communication.

Copies may be made from opaque or translucent originals, printed on one or both sides, since this is basically a reflex process. Copy papers are also available for direct-through copying techniques.

XEROGRAPHY

Xerography is a printing-like process basic to a variety of copying and reproducing equipment. The secret of this process is that an electrically charged plate, when exposed to light, will lose its charge and will not attract the printing medium of the opposite charge in the exposed areas. For a more detailed description of how this machine works, a step-by-step procedure will be outlined for the basic "flat-plate" machine (Figure 11–15). The four essential steps of the process are: 1. photographing, 2. developing, 3. printing, and 4. fixing.

Figure 11–15

Essential Steps of Xerography

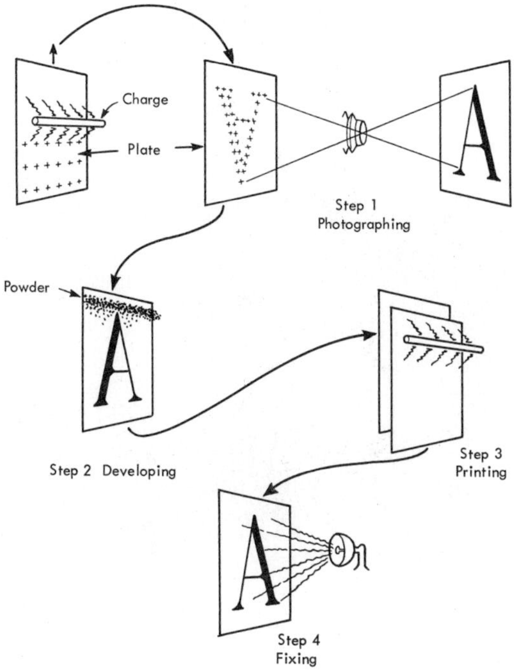

1. Photographing

A special xerographic plate is charged electrostatically, and shielded from light until it is placed in the camera. Exposure discharges the plate where light is transmitted through the lens of the camera, leaving the image area charged. The light shield is then placed over the plate and removed from the camera for developing.

2. Developing

A developing powder of an opposite charge to that charge placed on the plate is tumbled over the plate and attracted by the remaining charged portions to form the image. The plate now contains the mirror image of the picture photographed.

3. Printing

The image may be transferred to paper, vellum, or to an offset master. The transfer sheet is placed face-down on the Xerox plate in contact with the image. Then both are exposed to the same electrical charge of the photographic processor. When the paper is peeled from the plate, most of the powder stays with the paper, causing a good image to remain.

4. Fixing

The last step consists of putting the paper or master in a fuser, which heats and fuses the resinous developing powder.

Figure 11–16

Xerography Machine

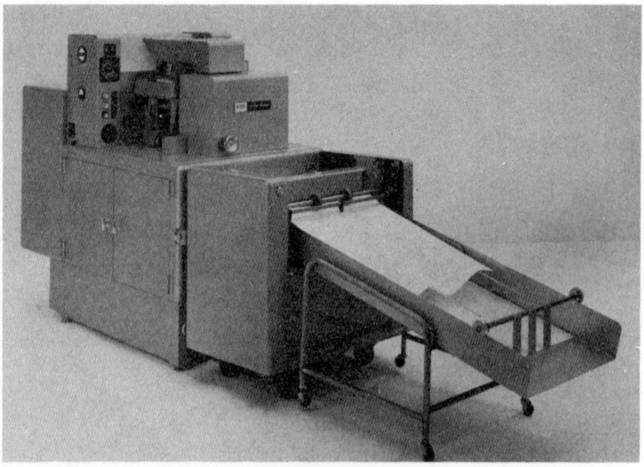

Figure 11–16 shows a Xerox machine which produces copies at a high rate in a continuous process, rather than in the step-by-step procedure. This

type of machine produces—from microfilm images—such things as engineering drawings and other large documents. The xerography family also contains efficient and compact office models.

SUMMARY

Many thousands of organizations use manual control systems which can be analyzed and improved by the techniques discussed in this chapter. For a complete analysis, the following steps should be performed:

1. A complete flow chart of the present system should be made which can be studied to reveal any inefficiencies in the system. After the original flow chart is studied, an improved flow chart should be made showing the system as it is to function.
2. All the forms in the system should be analyzed and redesigned for greater efficiency.
3. Finally, the improved flow chart is "frozen" in a Written Standard Procedure. This Written Standard Procedure has many uses in the organization besides serving as a written statement of the flow chart. It can be used for instruction and to discipline personnel, as well as to improve the general efficiency of an organization.

The manual method must lean heavily upon the duplicating methods available. The methods discussed are the most important to be found in today's businesses. What the future holds is difficult to anticipate. It has been said that in 1900 only two out of every one hundred employees handled paper; today it is sixteen out of one hundred. The copying business, a $60 million infant in 1950, will surpass $500 million today. Such a thriving business cannot help but have some influence on our industries.

Questions

1. Discuss the relative importance of the three steps of the systems analysis for manual methods.
2. What advantage does the paper-flow chart have over the procedures manual when considering a change in the system?
3. Show how the three steps of the manual method could be applied to some simple procedure, such as checking out books in a library.
4. Redesign the system discussed in the previous question, using the System Design Checklist.
5. Redesign some business or government agency form, such as the Bureau of Internal Revenue's form for income taxes. Use the Form Design Checklist.
6. As a new employee of a company, would you consider the Written Standard Procedure important or not? Explain your answer in full.
7. Which duplicating technique would you choose for:
   a) Engineering prints?
   b) Producing 10,000 blank operation sheets?

c) Producing five completed operation sheets?
d) Making one copy of a sales order?

8. Often the master of a form (such as the operation sheet) is retained in the files for many years and is used only occasionally for producing a few copies. Which duplicating processes would be suitable for this application? Explain your choice.
9. Often the master requires frequent but minor revisions. Which duplicating process would you choose to meet this requirement?
10. Why has a knowledge of duplicating techniques become more important in recent years?

References

AMERICAN MANAGEMENT ASSOCIATION, OFFICE MANAGEMENT DIVISION. *Organizing for Effective Systems Planning and Control.* New York, 1956.

FAIRBANKS, RALPH W. *Successful Office Automation.* Englewood Cliffs, N.J.: Prentice-Hall, Inc., 1956.

GREENE, JAMES H. "How to Squeeze Profits from Paper Work." *Manufacturing and Industrial Engineering.* Vol. 36, No. 5 (May, 1958).

HERRMANN, IRVIN A. *Manual of Office Reproductions.* New York: Office Publications Co., 1956.

LAZZARO, VICTOR. *Systems and Procedures.* Englewood Cliffs, N.J.: Prentice-Hall, Inc., 1959.

LEVIN, HOWARD S. *Office Work and Automation.* New York: John Wiley & Sons, Inc., 1956.

LITTLEFIELD, C. L., and PETERSON, R. L. *Modern Office Management.* Englewood Cliffs, N.J.: Prentice-Hall, Inc., 1956.

MACDONALD, JOHN H. *Office Management.* Englewood Cliffs, N.J.: Prentice-Hall, Inc., 1943.

MUNDEL, MARVIN E. *Motion and Time Study: Principles and Practice.* Englewood Cliffs, N.J.: Prentice-Hall, Inc., 1960.

NEUSCHEL, RICHARD F. *Management by System.* 2d ed. New York: McGraw-Hill Book Co., Inc., 1960.

NEUNER, JOHN J. W., and HAYNES, BENJAMIN R. *Office Management Principles and Practices.* 3rd ed. Cincinnati: South Western Publishing Co., 1953.

TERRY, GEORGE R. *Office Management and Control.* 3rd ed. Homewood, Ill.: Richard D. Irwin, Inc., 1958.

SENATE COMMITTEE ON GOVERNMENT OPERATIONS. *Documentation, Indexing, and Retrieval of Scientific Information.* Washington, D.C.: U.S. Government Printing Office, 1961.

VERRY, H. R. *Document Copying and Reproduction Processes.* London: Fountain Press, 1960.

CHAPTER 12

Card-Data Processing

Probably the most important innovation in production control and system design has been card-data processing. Information with which to make decisions and take action is essential in any kind of control system. Frequently, this information is kept in the mind of the individual, but as the systems become more complex it is imperative to have information recorded and available for a number of people with different needs. Writing, reading, and filing all the information needed is a time-consuming, costly operation. It is because of this that the idea of recording information by holes in cards was developed. Once the information takes the form of holes in a card, it can be sorted, filed, manipulated, and reproduced without error.

The cards are often used as instructions to human operators, but they can also be used to control machines directly, without any intervening operator. In fact, the first use of punched cards was probably to give weaving machines instructions directly. Today we find weaving machines being instructed by a set of cards, fastened together in a belt, so that the machine can continue for hours with little or no attention from the human operator.

Often the novice confuses card-data processing with computer data processing. This is understandable since computers often use cards as the input-output medium, and, at least in the past, the card-data processing equipment was used as peripheral equipment for the computer. In this chapter and the next, the computer which uses data and instructions stored in its memory will be excluded, and only card-data processing will be discussed.

It is difficult to have an understanding of system designing for card-data processing without first having a preview of the equipment. You will be given a look at not only the elementary edge-notched card and equipment, but also the higher speed and more sophisticated machine-punched card and equipment (as represented by the Remington Rand and International Business Machines systems). After the preview of the hardware, the techniques for system designing will be discussed.

Hand-Sorted Edge-Notched Cards

The edge-notched cards (Figure 12–1) are sorted by the presence or absence of a notch on the edge of the data card, as shown. The cards are supplied with prepunched holes around the periphery, to which information can be assigned. By merely notching or not notching the hole to the edge, as shown, a "yes" or "no" condition can prevail. When a needle-like tool is passed through any particular hole in a stack of cards, those which are notched will shake free from those being held by the needle.

Figure 12–1

Sorting Hand-sorted Cards

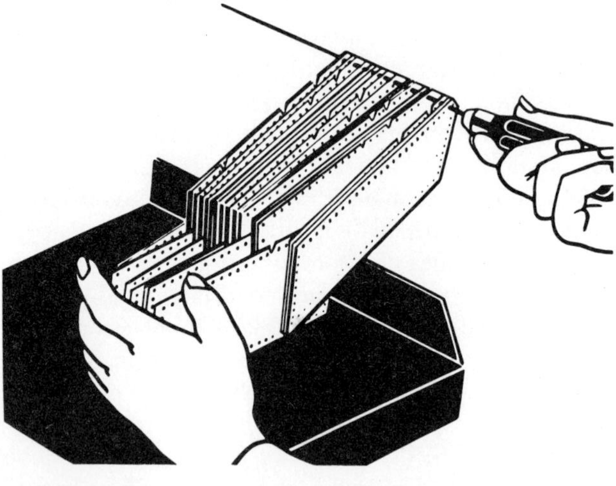

The cards are available in various sizes, but the one that is the most popular for production purposes conforms to the card used in other card-data processing systems. Since the center of the card is not used in the sorting process, it can be used for a written record, and standard information can be printed on the card according to what is required. Master cards for spirit duplicating are also available, so that cards with common information can be reproduced at one time.

CODING

The marginal holes on the hand-sorted card are known as "code positions" when assigned to a letter, number, or word. One or more code positions relating to a single subject is a "code field," and a "code section" is one or more fields relating to the same subject.

Figure 12–2
Yes–No Condition

Direct coding is used when a specific classification, such as a first or second work shift, is assigned to a hole position.

Numerical coding is not usually done directly. To save time and space a special numerical code system is in common use. Only four holes are used for each set of numbers 0 through 9. These four hole positions are assigned the values of 7, 4, 2, and 1, as shown in Figure 12–3. By notching either a single number or the combination of two numbers, any digit from 1 through 9 may be expressed. Zeros are not notched. A number such as 653 would require three four-hole fields, one field for each of the numbers 6, 5, and 3. It is possible to increase the coding capacity of the four-hole field to include numbers from 10 to 14, if desired.

Figure 12–3
Code System for Hand-sorted Cards

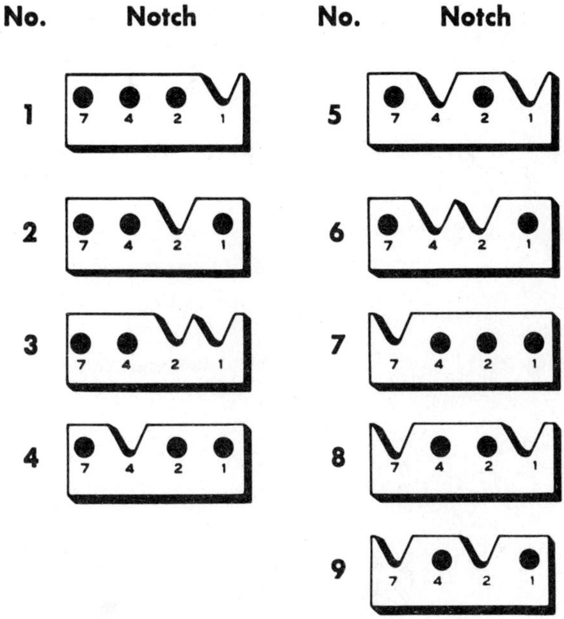

Courtesy of Royal McBee Corp.

To code the alphabet, each letter is numbered, but since there are more than 14 letters, the alphabet must be divided into two parts, A to M and N to Z. Each part is indicated by a separate punch position, as shown in Figure 12–4. If a letter from A to M is being punched, then the separate punch position is not notched. However, if the letter is between N to Z, the extra position is notched as shown.

Figure 12–4

Alphabetical Coding

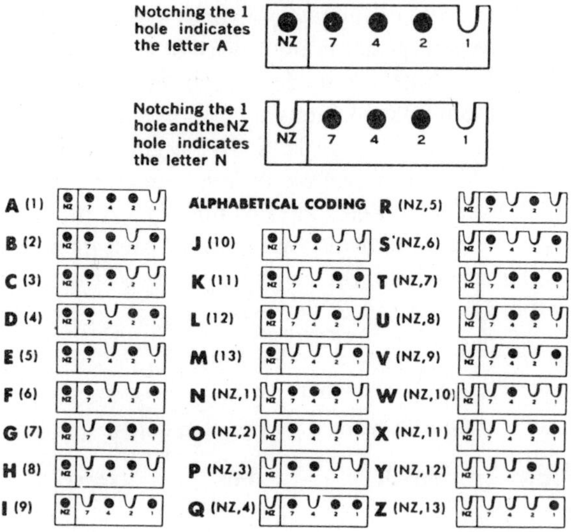

EQUIPMENT USED WITH EDGE-NOTCHED CARDS

Notching

A simple hand-operated paper-punch is available for notching the cards. This would be suitable where the volume of cards being processed is small and speed is not important, or for making occasional corrections in other, more rapid processes.

The card groover (Figure 12–5) is a high-speed device for notching com-

Figure 12–5

Card Groover

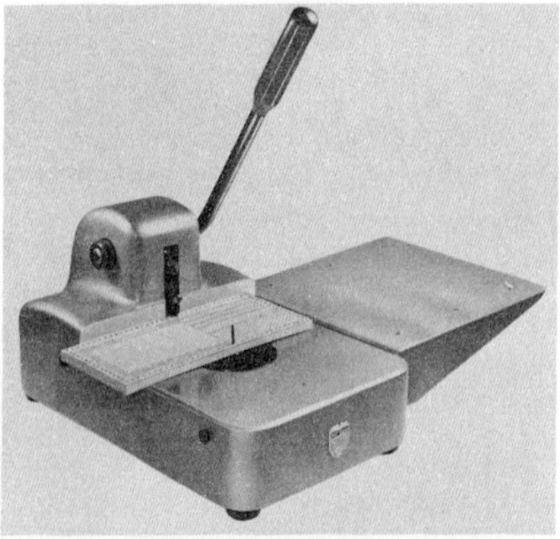

Courtesy of Royal McBee Corp.

mon information in a stack of cards. As many as 50 cards can be positioned in the machine and notched simultaneously.

For high-speed notching, the keyboard keypunch (shown in Figure 12–6) is available. This machine will notch one edge of a card at a time. This keypunch can be set to repeat any columns desired, while the unset keys will be restored to their original position after each operation.

Figure 12–6

Keyboard Keypunch

Courtesy of Royal McBee Corp.

The machine illustrated in Figure 12–7, the data punch, performs two operations simultaneously. It will print from an embossed plate and notch

Figure 12–7

Data Punch

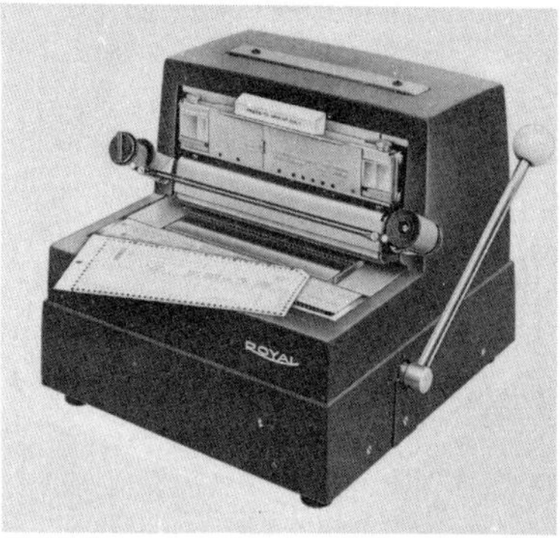

Courtesy of Royal McBee Corp.

the edge of the card with a single pull of the lever. Such a machine is ideally suited to the production of operation tickets or time cards (Figure 12–8) at the work location. It assures a legible, accurate, and clean card for data

Figure 12–8

Operation Ticket

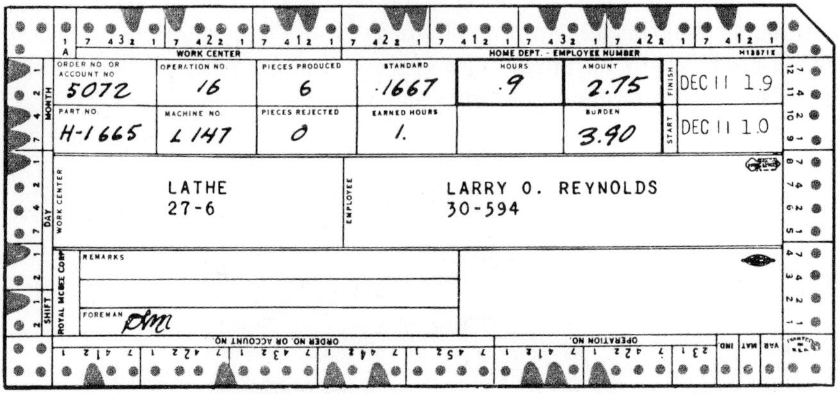

Courtesy of Royal McBee Corp.

processing. As illustrated, a production ticket is produced with interchangeable plates for employees and work centers.

Figure 12–9

Sorting Method

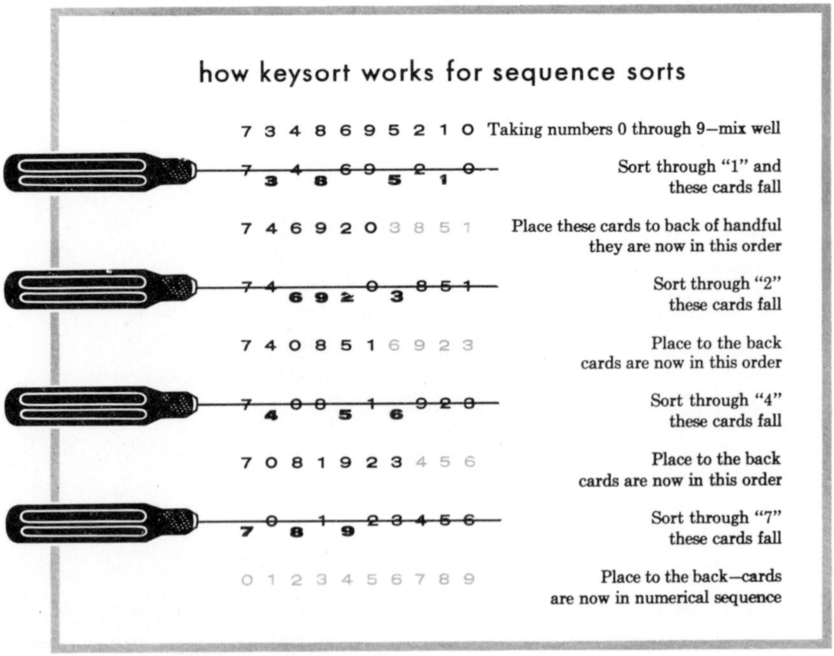

Sorting

The basic tool for sorting the edge-notched cards is the sorting needle (Figure 12–9). This is frequently used in conjunction with an *alignment block*, which increases the speed and ease of sorting. There are a number of useful hints for sorting efficiently, but the illustration shows the basic method of sequence sorting.

Tabulating

The tabulating machine (Figure 12–10), basically an adding machine with a tape print-out and facilities for printing and reading cards, extends the versatility of the edge-notched card. For *punching and tabulating*, the card is fed in and figures are—simultaneously—punched into the card, printed on the tape, and accumulated in the register. Then the card is automatically ejected and stacked.

For *reading and tabulating*, the sorted cards are fed through the sensing track; the machine automatically reads the cards and simultaneously accumulates the figures in the register and prints out on the tape. A summary card can be placed in the punching track, and the total is automatically punched into the card and printed on the tape.

Figure 12–10

Tabulating Machine

Courtesy of Royal McBee Corp.

Application of the Edge-notched Cards

The edge-notched cards find many applications wherever records are kept. They are suitable for production control in both small and large firms, depending upon the type of product and other conditions. Companies using extensive machine-processed card systems have found edge-punched cards suitable for certain applications, such as maintenance records and tool control.

Machine-Punched Cards

Herman Hollerith is given credit for developing the first punched-card systems. This he did shortly before the turn of the century, while working for the United States Census Bureau. The machines at first were crude, using many mechanical linkages and manual operations. They were far removed from the fast, electronic, dependable machines to be found in many of today's modern factories.

Since there are two common machine-card systems in use today, it will be necessary to make this division in the discussion of the material. Room does not permit an extensive discussion of both systems, so we will, of necessity, have to concentrate on only one group of machines.

THE CARD AS AN INFORMATION MEDIUM

The card is made of high-quality card stock of uniform thickness. It is about 3¼ inches wide by 7⅜ inches long. One corner is cut off for convenience in filing. Any card not in the correct position can be found readily because its corner will protrude.

International Business Machine Punched Cards

The IBM general-purpose card has 80 vertical columns, as shown in Figure 12–11. In each column there are 12 punching positions. The 0

Figure 12–11

International Business Machines General-Purpose Card

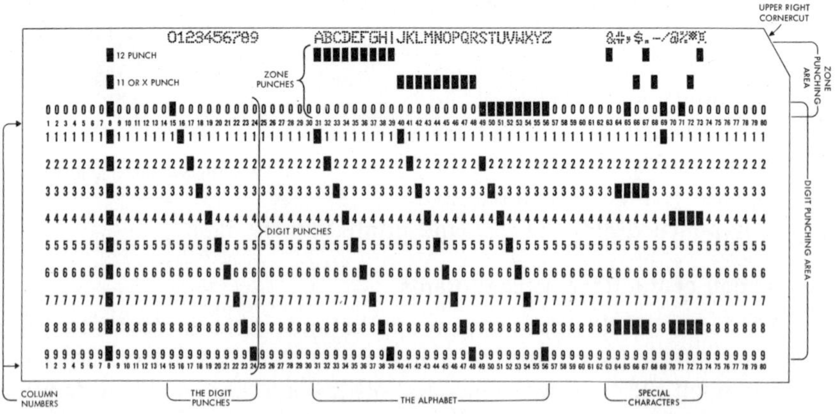

Courtesy of IBM Corp.

through 9 holes can be used to represent any number. In addition, there are two positions at the top of the card, called the 12 and 11 (or the Y and X) positions, which are used for coding the alphabet, indicating the sign of a number, or for controlling the machine. Seldom would the 12 and 11 positions be used for the numbers 12 and 11. The 12 and 11 and 0 are called *zone* punches, and are used along with the numbers to indicate letters in the alphabet.

The code used for the alphabet is shown on the card. The letters of the alphabet are automatically coded and punched in the columns. The reader is cautioned to remember that it takes only one column for each letter, not three, as it might appear.

There are other ways of coding cards, but this is the accepted way for the usual card-data processing applications. Mark-sensed cards find some applications, especially in manufacturing. A graphite pencil is used to make short marks directly on the cards to represent data. This card can then be passed through a machine which interprets the marks and punches holes in the card.

Remington-Rand Cards

The Remington Rand card has the same physical appearance as the IBM card, but the information is coded in a different fashion, as shown in Figure 12–12. The card is divided into upper and lower sections, with

Figure 12–12

Remington Rand Data Card

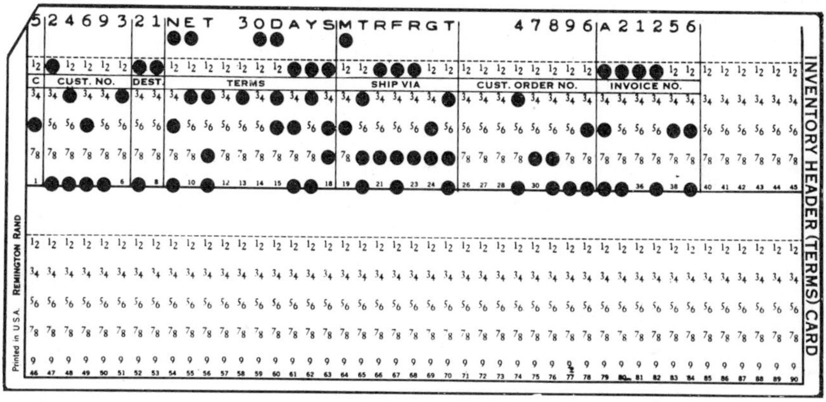

Courtesy of Univac Division of Sperry Rand Corp.

45 columns of six rows in each section, making a total of 90 columns. Each column of the card is headed by 0, with five positions vertically beneath representing (1,2), (3,4), (5,6), (7,8), and (9). The odd numbers are represented by one hole in the column and the even numbers are represented by two holes, one in the desired number and another in the 9 position. The alphabet is represented by one, two, or three holes punched in a column.

Card Layout

For any particular application, the card must be laid out into fields. A block of one or more columns having a specific meaning is called a "field."

Figure 12–13

Typical Card Layout

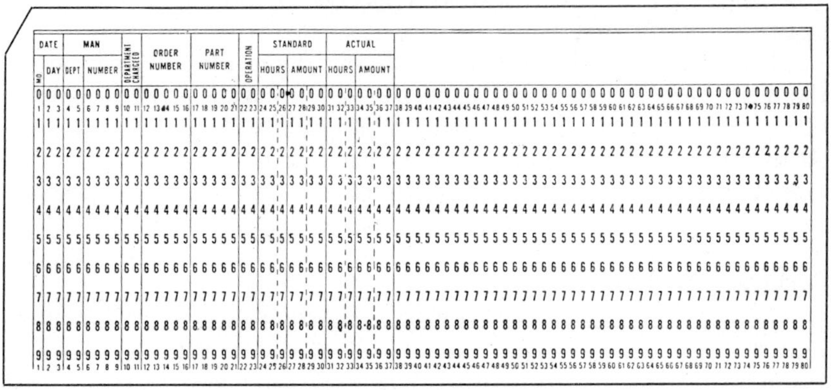

For example, the labor distribution card shown in Figure 12–13 has one column reserved for the month of the year, two for the day in the month, two for the department, etc. The order number field runs from column 12 to column 16. This task of laying out the fields must be done with care and forethought, for frequently the space must be used efficiently to record all the information desired.

OVERALL VIEW OF CARD-DATA PROCESSING MACHINES AND THEIR FUNCTIONS

Before going into details concerning the operations of the card-data processing (CDP) machines, let us take a brief overall view of some of the common machines and the tasks they perform.

Card Punch Machines

Card punches are used for translating written documents into punched-card form. Cards are fed into the machine automatically and are moved forward, column by column, under 12 punches which can be actuated either by a keyboard or by brushes (which are sensing the preceding card). The card is moved forward either by the manual control or by a programmed card which tells the machine to skip fields, repeat what was in the previous card, or shift to alphabetical coding from numerical coding.

Verifiers

Verifiers are used for checking the information which has been punched by the card punches. The verifier, which looks and operates much like the card-punch machine, merely senses the holes in the cards—to see if they are punched correctly—as an operator types the information for the second time.

Sorters

Sorters arrange cards by the information available in the punched columns. One of the purposes of putting data on punched cards is to make sorting easier. Consequently, it is possible to obtain more information from them.

Reproducers

Reproducers perform a number of functions besides that of reproducing a "deck" of cards. In addition, they can perform the important function of gang punching, which means taking part or all of the information from one card and punching it into all of the cards which follow. This machine will also do certain checking operations on the cards directly.

Collators

Collators, used in many operations, are more versatile than sorters. This machine is capable of comparing and selecting cards on the basis of sequence. It can also merge, in sequence, two decks of cards, or compare two decks to determine whether or not they match.

Interpreters

Interpreters translate the punched-hole information on the card to a readable, printed form. This machine prints this information on the card, which it "reads" from the punched holes in the same card; otherwise it would be difficult for an individual to interpret the meaning of the array of holes.

Accounting Machines

Accounting machines are capable of performing addition and subtraction by totals, subtotals, and sub-subtotals, with information read from a stack of cards. The results are printed out at a rapid rate on a continuous form.

Summary Punches

Summary punches are auxiliary machines which, when associated with other equipment (such as the accounting machine), will produce a new set of cards as a result of the operations going on in the other machine.

Transceivers

Transceivers are devices for transmitting data between two remote points, usually by commercial telegraph or telephone lines.

Time Clocks

Time clocks record time directly on a punched card for such applications as job tickets.

Techniques for Designing the Card-Data Processing System

The techniques of system design, as associated with the flow of paper work, are well established and can be found in various method-study books, industrial engineering handbooks, and office procedure manuals; but those system design techniques which are used in card-data processing are not readily available except in the manufacturers' manuals. In the latter, however, the emphasis is on a specific system rather than on the techniques of design. Consequently, they are useful primarily to those who wish to make an intensive study of the subject. The objective here is to put the information concerning the design of card-data processing systems in such a form that it can be understood by all who need some working knowledge of the subject.

The Language of System Design

System designs that include card-data processing are generally best illustrated by flow charts. These particular flow charts differ from others in that they use a unique set of symbols and are put together in a distinctive way. The symbols not only include those which depict the particular form, but also those which illustrate a particular machine operation. There is no attempt to show the spatial or time relationships between the operations, as is frequently done on other flow charting techniques, because timing is achieved after flow charting by calculating workloads for the various machines.

It is convenient to group the various symbols (Figure 12–14) into those used to illustrate forms, machine operations, clerical functions, source documents, and miscellaneous.

With these basic symbols we can now develop flow diagrams for various functions within the factory as they will be executed by card-data processing equipment. There is no better way of doing this than to illustrate a typical system. The ones included here are part of the production control function. The illustration shows the form or operation, and directly adjacent is an explanation. The first chart shows the system for determining the material requirements for a group of orders. Before going into that, it would be desirable to review some of the basic information which must be fed into such a system.

Into any control system must go the basic data on which the system operates. In the example given here, the basic data—which will be referred to later as master files or master cards—are:

Bill of Material Forms
Order Forms
Process Design Forms

The bill of material form goes hand-in-hand with the blueprints or prod-

Figure 12–14

Symbols for Card-Data Processing

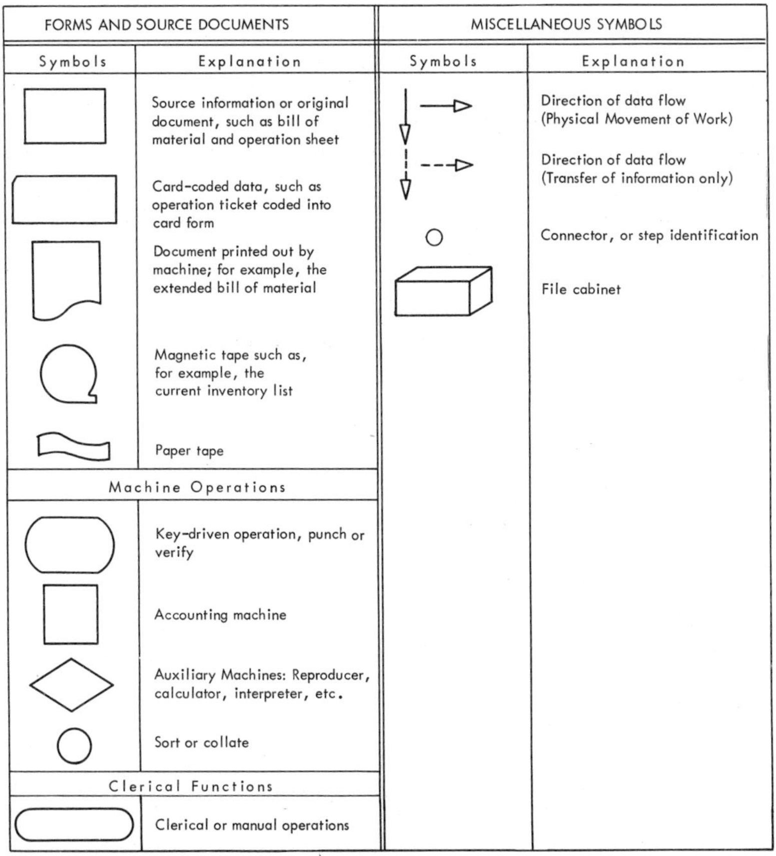

uct description, and contains a listing of all the material that goes into a specific product. From this original list, individual cards are made for each item on the list. These cards may eventually be grouped by final assembly, by accessory groupings, or by any other convenient arrangement. Each card would bear such information as part name, part number, and quantity. Order forms may either originate with the customer's order, or within the company's inventory control, when a balance drops below the order point. This form is the order to produce, and contains such information as order quantity, name of customer, time needed, etc.

The process design form goes by such names as process sheet, instruction sheet, route sheet, and others. This form supplements the blueprint by giving operation-by-operation instructions of how the product is to be produced to conform to the engineering requirements shown on the print. This form contains information concerning work to be included at each work station, machines to be used, standards of performance, and, of course, the part name, number, material used, and any other pertinent information.

From these basic control-data forms, which are usually handwritten or typed, punch cards are produced. For example, for each part on the bill of materials a corresponding card would be made; for each operation on the processing form, a card would be made; and the order-form information would also be reproduced in card form. All this is shown in two illustrations. Figure 12–15 shows how the material requirements are determined by card-data processing, while Figure 12–16 shows how the labor requirements are calculated.

These two flow charts are typical of those used in manufacturing industries. A little familiarization with the symbols and their meanings should

Figure 12–15

Material Requirements Flow Chart

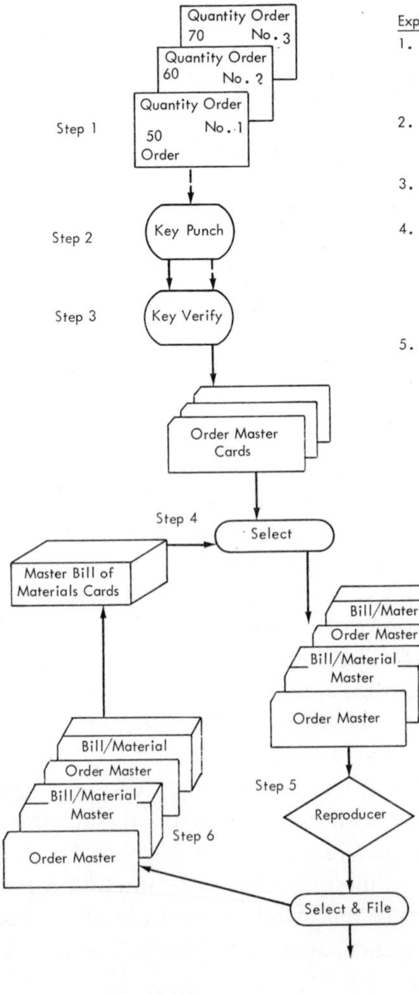

Explanation of Steps

1. The order forms, Nos. 1, 2, and 3 are received either from the customer or from the inventory control section.
2. From the order forms, individual order master cards are produced for each individual product.
3. Order master cards are key-verified. Order forms are filed.
4. At this point, the master B/M cards are manually selected from the master B/M card file. The order master card is placed in front of its corresponding master B/M card deck.
5. The combined cards are placed in a reproducing punch and a duplicate set of cards (requirement cards) are reproduced. In addition, information in the order master card is gang punched into the new requirement cards.

Figure 12–15 (continued)

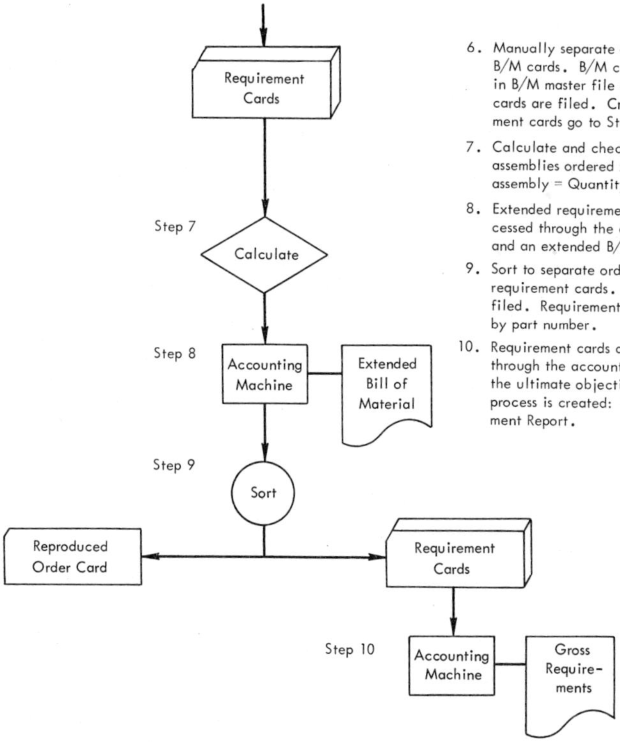

6. Manually separate order master and B/M cards. B/M cards are refiled in B/M master file and order master cards are filed. Created requirement cards go to Step 7.
7. Calculate and check: Number of assemblies ordered x Parts per assembly = Quantity required.
8. Extended requirement cards are processed through the accounting machine, and an extended B/M list is prepared.
9. Sort to separate order master and requirement cards. Order masters are filed. Requirement cards are sorted by part number.
10. Requirement cards are processed through the accounting machine and the ultimate objective of our entire process is created: the Gross Requirement Report.

make it possible to follow the diagrams and the verbal explanations. The next step is to take a company's routines and follow them, or, better still, try to design (and eventually improve) a system. Only by this procedure can you become completely fluent with the card-data processing language.

SUMMARY

Several card systems are used in industry. One, which has holes punched along the edge of the card, is used primarily in small systems where time and cost of handling the data are not of great importance. These systems, while not as fast as others, do have a place in industry, such as in tool control, inventory control, and similar applications.

Machine-processed cards require an extensive investment in equipment, but in many situations it is the only way that information for decision making can be obtained in the time permitted. The machines have only been introduced in this chapter, but in the next chapter you will become fully acquainted with how the machines are programmed.

These machines should not be confused with computers. Computers have a "memory" within which data and instructions are stored. This is not true of the card-data processing equipment, which will be discussed first.

Figure 12–16

Labor Requirements

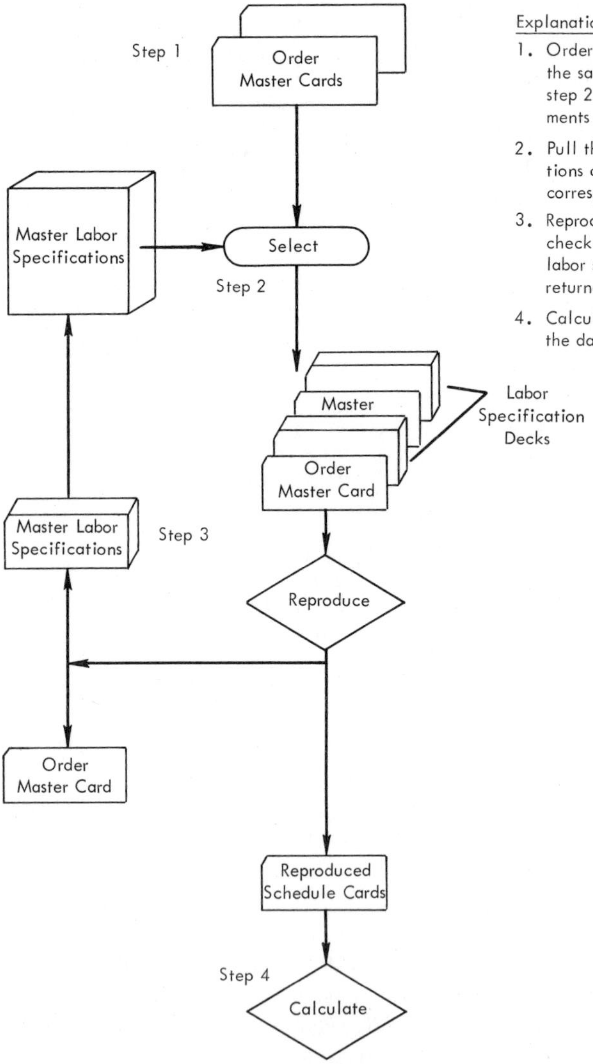

Explanation of Steps

1. Order master cards. These are the same cards as developed in step 2 of the Material Requirements.
2. Pull the master labor specifications and file them behind the corresponding order master cards.
3. Reproduce, gang punch, and check a "work deck." The master labor specification cards are then returned to their file.
4. Calculate the hours of load and the date the job should be started.

Questions

1. Explain why card-data processing has become important recently.
2. Why is the 7–4–2–1 method of coding used with edge-notched cards? Can you explain why this code is favored over the 8–4–2–1 code used with computers?
3. Give an example of where edge-notched cards are used. What has been the advantage of using edge-notched cards in this situation?
4. Define the following terms, as used with machine-punched cards: (*a*) column, (*b*) zone punch, (*c*) field.

Figure 12–16 (continued)

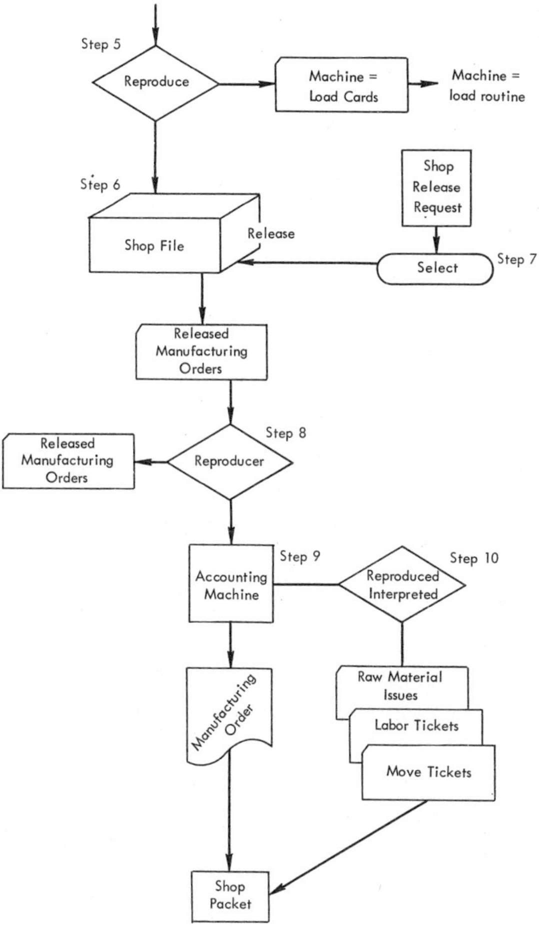

5. Reproduce the cards needed for use in machine loading.
6. The work deck is then placed in the shop release file awaiting further use.
7. When authorization to release the work deck is received, the work deck is removed and sent to the reproducer.
8. From the released manufacturing order a card is reproduced to indicate that the order has been released. This card is used in the progress routine.
9. The manufacturing order is printed out on the accounting machine and placed in the shop packet.
10. The various forms required for manufacturing are reproduced, interpreted, and placed in the shop packet.

From this routine all the essential material for the shop packet and for the progress and load routine is quickly and accurately produced.

5. Draw a facsimile of an IBM card and lay out the fields for an inventory card.
6. Show on the IBM facsimile card how your name and birth date would appear.
7. Select the IBM equipment you would need for an inventory records system (or other similar system). Explain why you have chosen this equipment.
8. Draw a flow chart showing the process in the previous question.
9. You could expect some organizational changes when going from manual to machine-punched cards. What changes would you anticipate, and how would you initiate these changes with a minimum amount of disturbance?
10. Compare the advantages and disadvantages of the edge-notched card and the IBM card.

References

(See end of Chapter 13)

CHAPTER 13

Card-Data Equipment

In the previous chapter you were introduced to card-data processing equipment and how it is used in a system. This would be sufficient if you were satisfied with only a superficial knowledge or had no need for further information.

There are, in fact, some who insist that an extensive knowledge of how the machines function is not necessary, and who even imply that such knowledge is undesirable. This chapter, however, should not be avoided if you wish to understand the whole production control function in depth, and wish to prepare for the opportunities available to those who understand the rapidly expanding field of system designing for card-data processing.

SOME GENERAL CHARACTERISTICS OF CDP MACHINES

Before discussing each machine, it will be more efficient to discuss the components which are common to many of the machines. This will give you a better understanding of the processes, and then, when each machine is discussed, it will not be necessary to delay progress while digressing into some detailed function of a part.

Card Reading

The card, previously described, passes between an electrically charged brush and roller, as shown in Figure 13–1. The card, being made of paper, serves as an insulator *except* where the holes have been punched. Where the brush drops into a hole and makes contact with the roller, a flow of current or "impulse" occurs, which in turn actuates some function of the machine.

The machine recognizes the number punched in the card by the elapsed time between the instant the leading edge passes the brush until the hole is sensed. In the machines to be discussed, we find a machine which has just one brush, and this is moved from column to column by the operator. In other machines there are 80 brushes, so that all columns may be read at the same time.

Machines developed in recent years scan the cards by means of electric eyes, which avoids the mechanical wear and consequent failure of mechanical brushes.

Figure 13–1

Card Reading

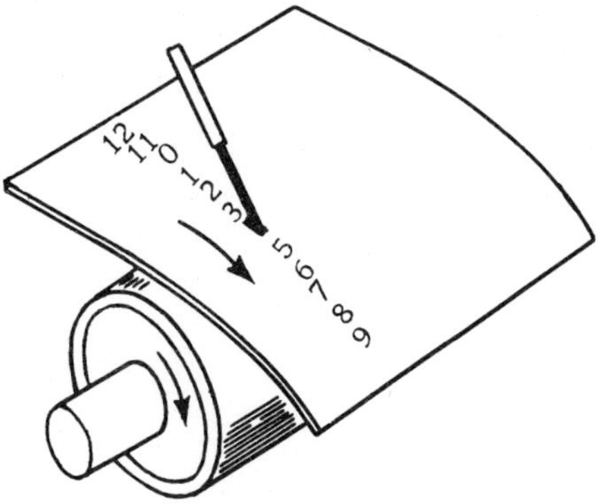

The Control Panel

In most cases the machines are not permanently wired for just one task but are designed so the operator can have some choice as to how they will perform. This choice is often exercised through a control panel, as shown in Figure 13–2. The control panel is similar to a telephone switch board since circuits may be directed in many ways. Wires from the brushes and other functional components of the machine are brought out to rows of

Figure 13–2

The Control Panel

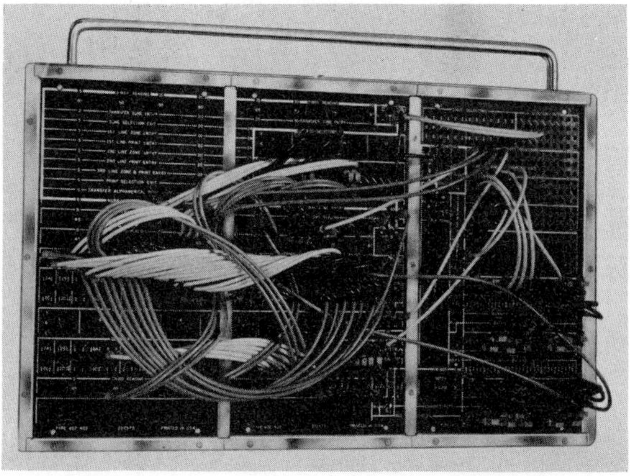

Courtesy of IBM Corp.

jacks. The panel board itself is a separate unit and can be replaced in the machine at will. This affords a great deal of flexibility because a number of control panels for different applications are quickly available when desired.

Control Panel Diagrams

Since it is not always convenient to work directly with the control panels when planning the circuitry, charts are available which represent the panel. A typical chart is the one shown in Figure 13–3. One should not be dis-

Figure 13–3

Control Panel Diagram

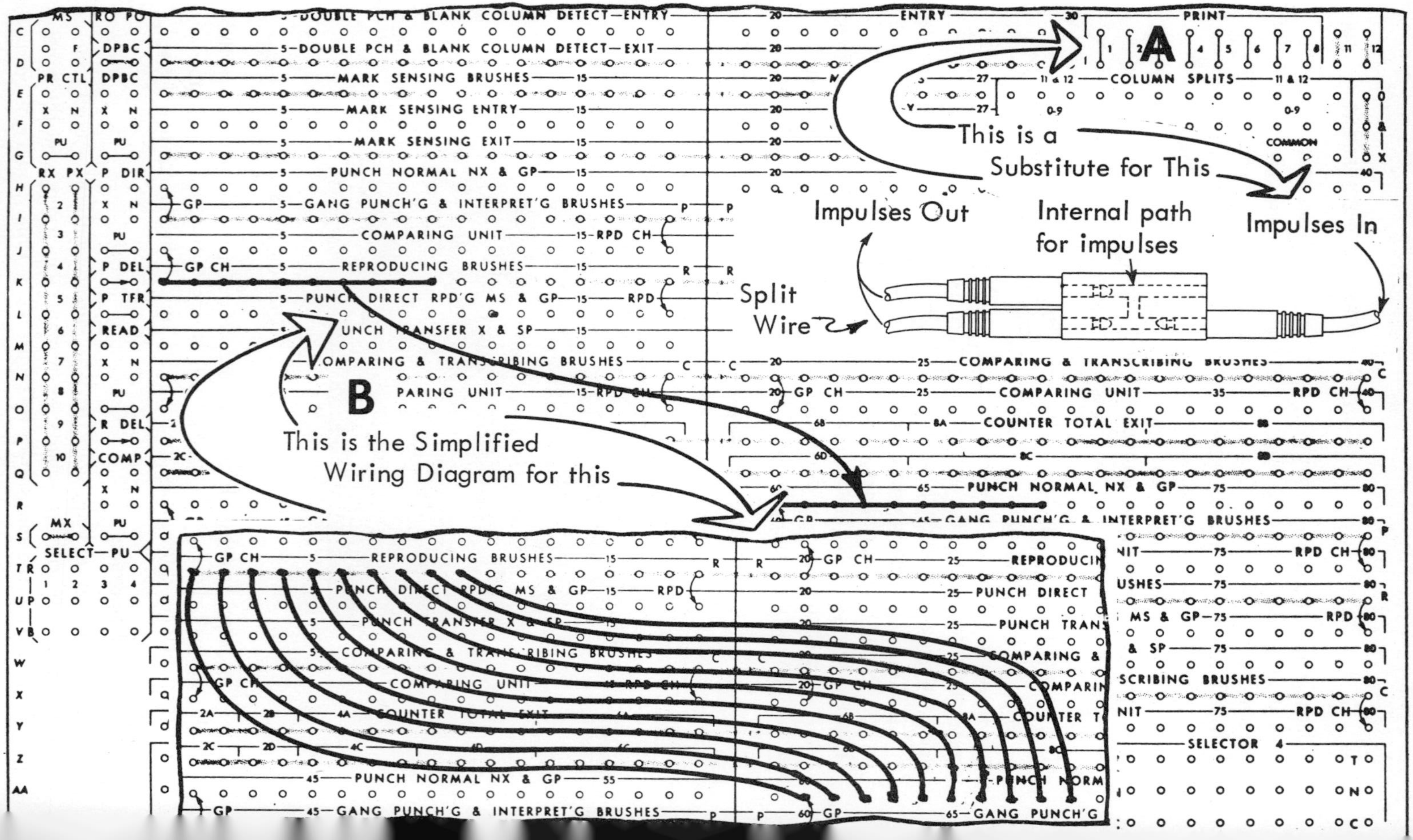

mayed by the number of *hubs* (terminals on the panel) because many of them are merely a repeat—80 times—of the same function. The hubs which will accept electric impulses are called *entries*, and those which emit impulses are called *exits*. Frequently it is desirable to have more than one exit or entry to save joining two wires together externally. This internal wiring is shown on the panel, as at A, and is referred to as *common hubs*. Several hubs hooked together internally are referred to as *bus hubs* and are merely for convenience in wiring where several wires are to be brought together. Another way of bringing connections together is the *split wire*, which is an external multiple-jack arrangement.

In laying out the panel it would be confusing if each wire were to be drawn in place. Instead, a simplified method is used, as shown in *B*. The section of hubs under consideration is joined by a straight line with the two end hubs (filled in solid). For example, if the reproducing brushes, 1 to 10, were to be connected with the punches, 60 to 69, a straight horizontal line would be drawn between 1 and 10 and between 60 and 69. These are then connected at their midpoint by one line, which indicates that actually there are wires from 1 to 60, 2 to 61, etc. If wires are to cross, the conventional bridge used in electrical circuitry is used.

Punching

As we know, the information on a machine-processed card is shown by holes. These holes are punched in the cards by magnet-actuated punches (illustrated in Figure 13–4). Some machines, such as the card punch, have these punches lined up so they punch column by column, while in other machines they are lined up to punch row by row (Figure 13–5).

Figure 13–4

Magnet-actuated Punches

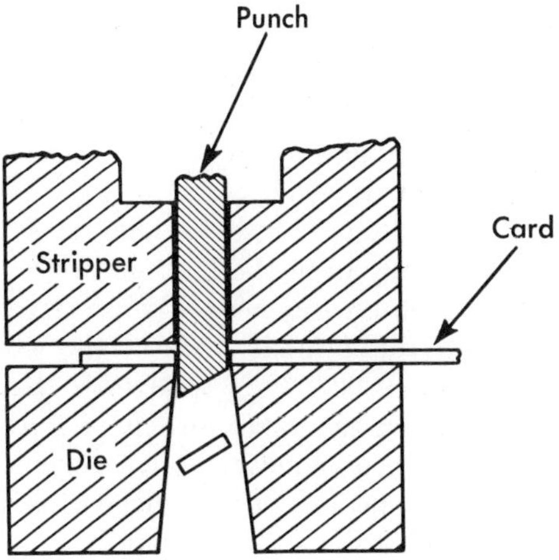

Figure 13–5

Methods of Punching

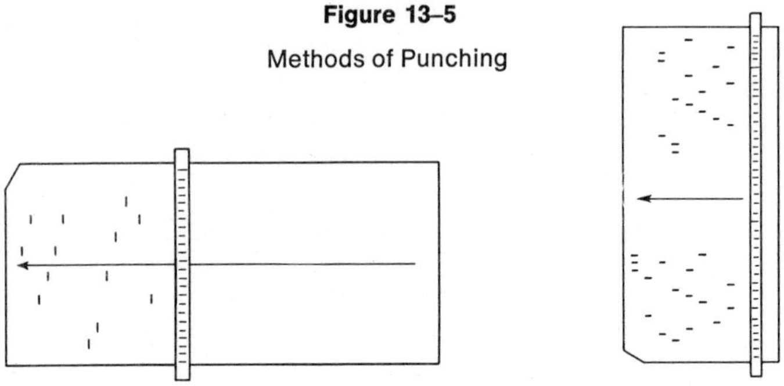

Timing

It is important to consider the timing of the card-data processing machines if one is to understand how they function. There is not a constant flow of current available through the brush contacts, rather, the current is available in 12 bursts, corresponding with the number and zone positions on the card. For example, when the 8 hole passes under a brush, it is referred to as the 8 *time* in the machine, and because of this the machine punches or prints an 8.

The machine cycle—the time it takes for a machine to complete the processing of a card—consists of the time it takes to process the card, plus the time for feeding, printing, and punching. Each type of machine has its own predetermined machine-cycle time, and in each machine there is a timing dial which the service engineer can compare with a timing chart in the service manuals to determine how each component is to function. This is analogous to the timing of an automobile.

Emitting

Often it is desirable to place information on a card, either in the printed form or punched-hole form (which is not available in the cards being fed into the machine). For example, a deck of cards may need a manufacturing order number inserted. This is done by one of two different devices, the *digit emitter* or the *digit selector*, which are identical except that the first receives an impulse internally from the machine while the latter has the source wired through a hub on the control panel. The function of these two devices can be more readily understood by the schematics in Figure 13–6.

Both of these devices serve as a rotary switch, producing an impulse for each position on the card. These impulses are available on the control panel, and, when wired to other functions of the machines, have the same effect as if they came from a card. It should be obvious that the digit selector may act the same as the digit emitter if the common hub is connected to a constant source of impulses on the panel, called a *digit impulse hub*. It also

Figure 13–6

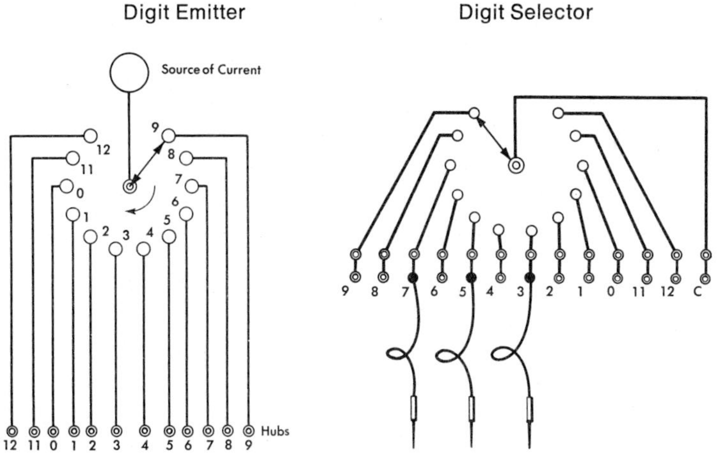

offers additional flexibility since it can be connected to a reading brush. Alphabetic information can be emitted and punched by wiring both a zone and a digit impulse to the same punching position. However, precautions must be taken to prevent *back circuits,* which will cause incorrect punching. The *column split,* to be discussed later, is a means of preventing back circuits.

Comparing

Comparing is checking two things to see if they are alike or different, and this is an important function of card-data processing machines. This ability of a machine serves a very important purpose in the verification and control of the machine. Verification is the process of testing to see if the holes have been punched correctly, while control is directing the machine to perform specific operations, such as making the machine stop when cards are out of sequence or forcing the machine to print out totals when different account numbers are recognized.

The cards to be compared are fed under two sets of brushes, as shown in Figure 13–7. The cards are synchronized so the left-hand brush is reading the same hole position as the right-hand brush. The impulses from these two brushes are fed to two *comparing magnets,* as illustrated. The armature will remain in the neutral position if no impulse is fed to the magnets or if they both receive an impulse at the same time.

For example, assume the conditions shown in the illustration. In the first figure, both magnets get the same signal at the same instant, so the magnets are unaffected. In the other two examples, the signals are out of phase, and the magnets are affected. Moving the armature back and forth is not important unless it actuates something else in the machine. It does this by switching a circuit, which stops the machine or causes some other action to take place in the machine.

Figure 13–7

Comparing

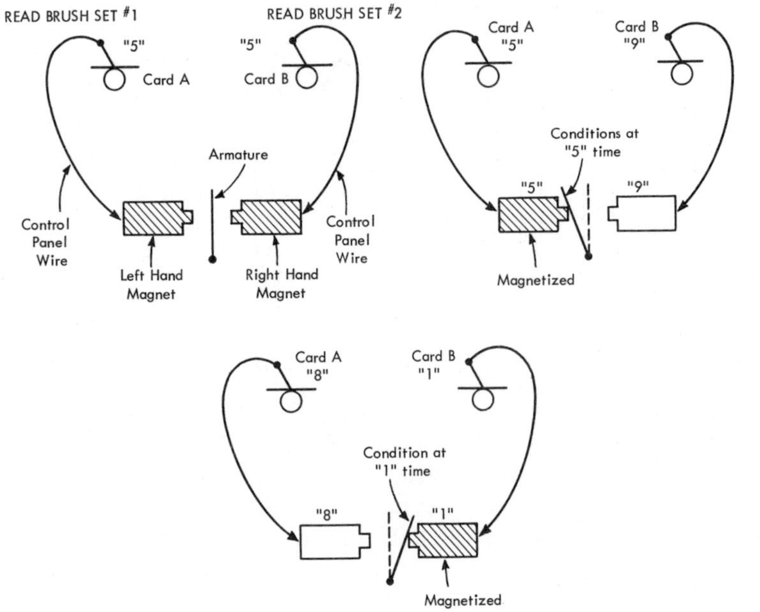

Sequence Checking

Closely related to the comparing magnets, the sequence-checking magnets (Figure 13–8) determine the order of a deck of cards. It is obvious that there are three orders in which cards might be: they can all be equal, they might increase in order, or they might decrease in order. The three conditions are shown with an example of the order. To the right is a schematic of the sequence-checking device in the position it would take for the particular condition illustrated. By checking the dark heavy line, the flow of the current is quite apparent.

Column Splits

Before exploring the need for the column-split mechanism, it is best that we see what it is. *Splitting* the column is separating the 0–9 punches from the 11 and 12 punches. The column-split mechanism consists of a magnet, armature, and switch, as shown in Figure 13–9. The magnet, which is impulsed only during the 11–12 time, lets the current flow from the common hub on the panel through the 11–12 hub. This is referred to as being *transferred*, while, during the 0–9 portion of the cycle, the armature is *dropped out*, and the current can flow from C (common) through the 0–9 hub. These two conditions are illustrated in the diagram.

Figure 13–8

Sequence Checking

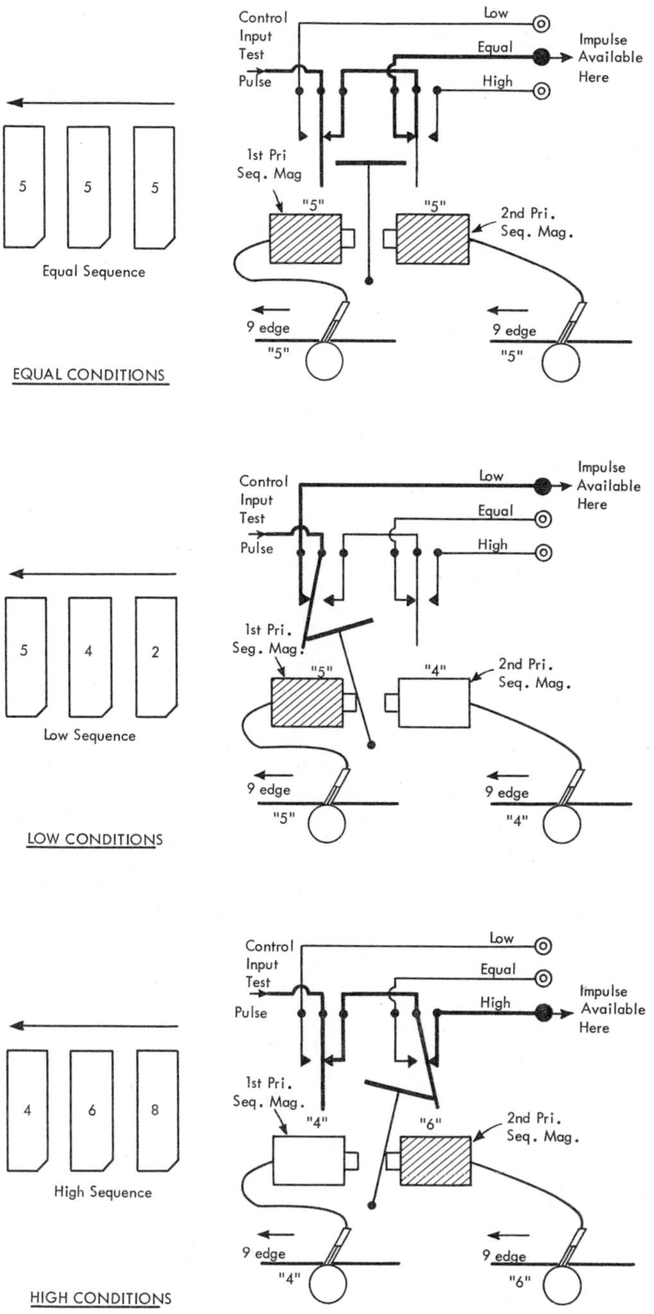

Figure 13–9

Column Split

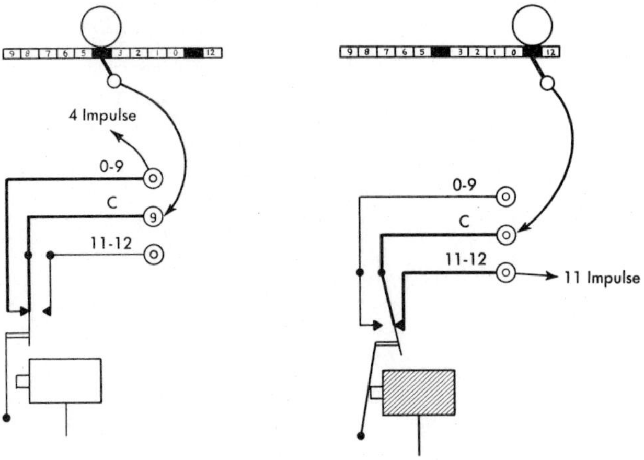

Let us now turn to how this device is used. Whenever there are two holes in a column, one might normally expect this to be a letter, if one hole is a zone punch, but it could be a number with an X-punch for some control purpose. If the machine isn't "told" differently, it will proceed to print a letter, and here is where the column split comes into play. The reading brush impulse is wired through the common of the column split, with the 0–9 exit wired to the punch (or whatever is to be actuated). When the card passes through the machine the number impulse will be sent to its proper place. The 11–12 impulses can be channeled to actuate an adder or other component.

The column split is also useful in preventing back circuits during *emitting*. Consider Figure 13–10, which shows an example of two letters using the same zone punch (such as J, which is 11 and 1; and M, which is 11 and 4). By tracing out the circuits on the diagram on the left it will be observed that each column will be punched with an 11, 1, and 4 hole. By inserting the

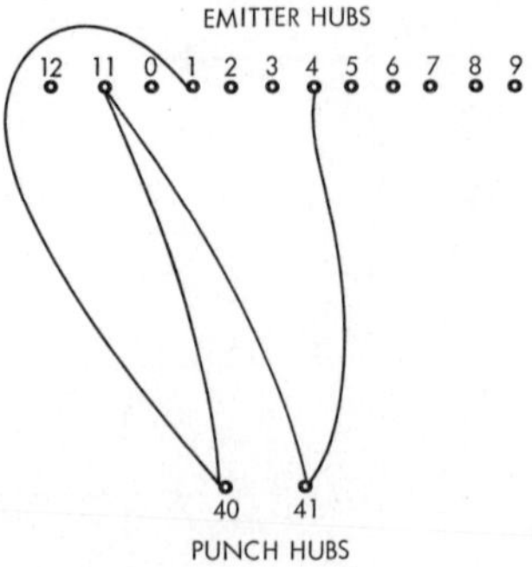

Figure 13–10

Emitter Wired for Back-Circuits

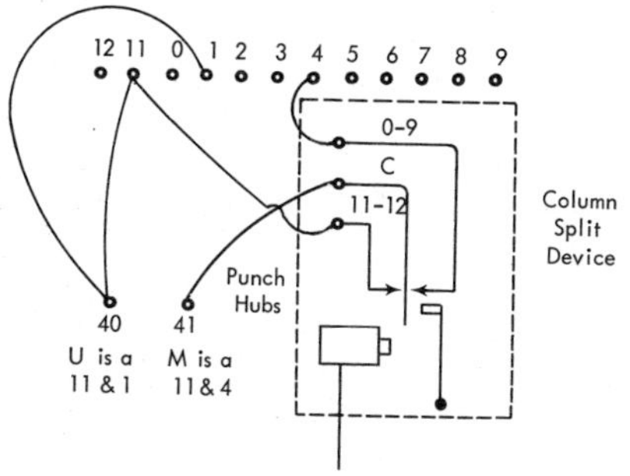

Figure 13–11

Emitter Wired with Column Split to Prevent Back-Circuits

column split in the circuit—shown on the right, in Figure 13–11—no back-circuit can exist. Incidentally, another name for the column split is X *eliminator,* which is a very descriptive name.

Selectors

The selector is basically the same as a column split, with one exception; the magnet is not energized directly and automatically from an internal circuit but is wired to an external hub on the panel where it may be wired or "picked up" from several sources. For example, the selector can be actuated on all impulses—on X impulses, or used to transfer immediately. The labeling of these hubs varies from machine to machine, but this should cause little difficulty if the operation is fully understood.

Printing

The card-data processing machines not only produce information in the form of holes but will also interpret the holes and print out the information. These printing facilities, when on a machine, are available through entry hubs on the control panel.

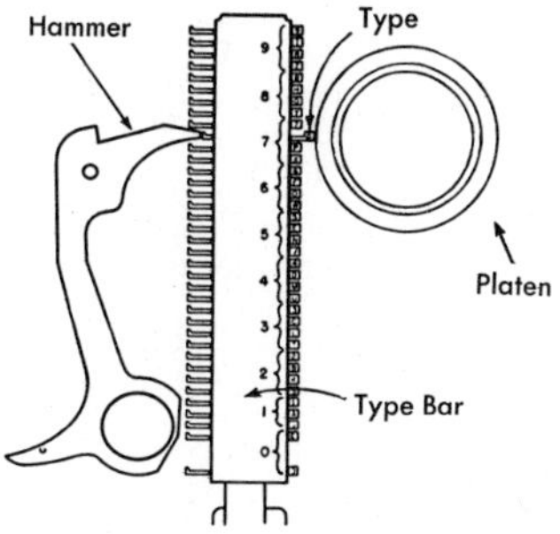

Figure 13–12

Printing Bars

A printing unit is shown in Figure 13–12. The paper is passed under a ribbon and around the platen, the same as in a typewriter, but the printing mechanism is entirely different. There is a bank of type bars, one for each printing position on the paper, so it is not necessary for the carriage to be moved back and forth as in the conventional typewriter. It should be apparent that this way of printing is much faster than the conventional typewriter's, which must peck out letter by letter, and it is one reason why automatic data processing is supplanting manual card-processing techniques. Other, and faster, printers will be discussed more fully in the computer section.

From the schematic of the type bar you can notice that the letters are grouped by number position, so it is necessary for the brushes to first determine the position and then determine the zone, which means that the card must be read 12-edge-last. Not all printing bars contain the *alphamerical* (numbers and alphabet) array shown. Some have numbers only, and these bars are usually placed on the right-hand margin (where it is common to place numerical values in any tabulation).

Figure 13–13

Print Wheel

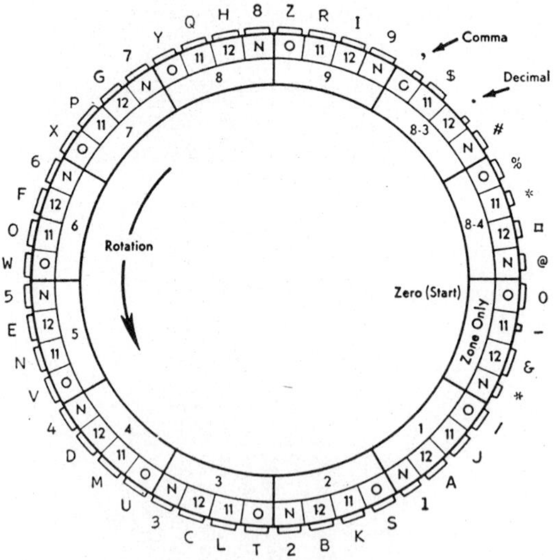

LOWER PUNCH	ZONE 12	11	O	N
1	A	J	/	1
2	B	K	S	2
3	C	L	T	3
4	D	M	U	4
5	E	N	V	5
6	F	O	W	6
7	G	P	X	7
8	H	Q	Y	8
9	I	R	Z	9
8–3	.	$	,	#
8–4	⌑	[1]*	%	@
	&	–	0	[2]*

1. Total Symbol 2. Check Protection

Another method of printing (Figure 13–13) uses a wheel, with type on the periphery, which is pressed on the paper after the wheel has been properly indexed. The wheel is first indexed to the proper number segment and then positioned according to the zone. Depending upon the design of the machine, the paper is either pressed against the wheel or the wheel is pressed against the paper.

Adding

There is a close analogy between the way a card-data processing machine "adds" and the way a *person* makes an addition on a calculating machine.

To make it easier to understand, this analogy is set up in table form:

	Adding Machine		*Card-Data Processing*
READ	Press keys to enter information.	READ	Data read by brushes from cards and sent by control panel to counters.
ADD	Pull handle to add.	ADD IMPULSE	Computer is told to add by an "add" impulse.
PRINT	Print out individual amounts.	PRINT IMPULSE	Counters and type mechanism are connected so all that is needed is a "print" impulse.
TOTAL	Press total key and pull handle.	TOTAL IMPULSE	Counters must receive a "total" impulse at the end of a card sequence.

More than one type of mechanism is used for adding, but the one discussed here is relatively simple and easy to understand. The counter uses wheels with 0–9 digits, as shown. Two or more of these work together in a *counter group*, each accounting machine having a number of these groups. A two-position counter can add to 99, a four-position counter can add to 9999, etc., so care must be taken that the counters do not *overflow*. Provisions are available for connecting several counter groups together to make adding large numbers possible.

Figure 13–14

Method of Adding

The way the counter operates is explained in Figure 13–14. The cards move through the machine 9-edge-first, as shown on the left. The wheel is at the zero position, where it remains until an impulse is felt; for example, at 3. The wheel then begins to turn in step with the card so that they stay in step, as shown.

The wheels start when the impulse is received and stop automatically at 0. On a print impulse, the information is read out of the counters.

	Card Position	*Counter Position*
No impulse	4	0
Impulse received	3	0
" "	2	1
" "	1	2
" "	0	3
Counter automatically stops		

This concludes the discussion of the components, which was essential if you are to understand the various machines. Should you become confused or forget how these parts function, turn back and reread parts of this section.

THE CARD-DATA PROCESSING MACHINES

Card Punch

The punched cards are produced by the card punch from the original written documents. It is the basic machine in the card-data processing system and the accuracy of this operation is the key to the accuracy of all subsequent operations. The card punch is a versatile machine on which information can be punched into cards by operating a keyboard, or the information can be punched from one card to a succeeding card in a *gang-punching* operation. An important part of the machine's versatility is the programming of such operations as skipping fields and the gang-punching operation just mentioned.

An illustration of the machine is shown in Figure 13–15, and an accompanying schematic in Figure 13–16. The path of the card, as shown on the schematic, is from right to left, passing under the twelve punches, the twelve reading brushes, and eventually to the card stacker. The function of each important part will be discussed in detail.

Figure 13–15
Card Punch

Courtesy of IBM Corp.

Figure 13–16

Schematic of Card Punch

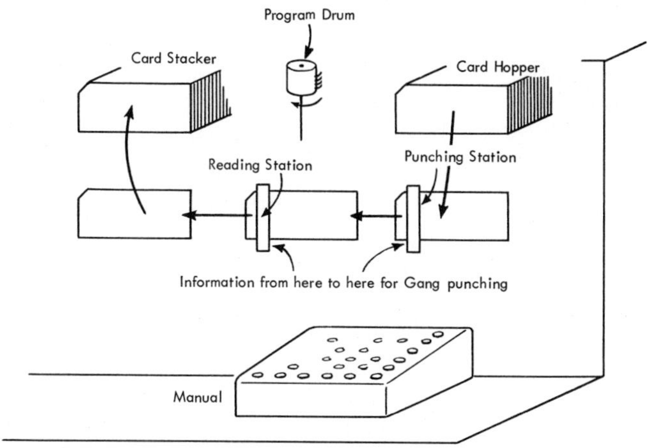

Keyboard. Several different keyboards are available, depending upon the capabilities of the machine. The machines are designed for punching numeric and alphanumeric information, and for typing out the information as it is punched.

Punching Station. The cards are fed from the card hopper, either automatically or by depressing a feed key. The card, controlled by the program card or the keyboard, then passes under the twelve punches.

Reading Station. A set of twelve reading brushes are located about a card's length ahead of the punching station so that two cards may move in step through both and so the information on the leading card can be fed back to the following card in a gang-punching operation. The completed cards are placed in the card stacker in their original sequence.

Programming. Some of the operations of the machine are controlled by a prepared program. This consists of a punched card that is wrapped around a cylinder which rotates in step with the card being punched. The four functions which can be programmed are readily summarized with their appropriate punching positions:

Code	*Function*
12	*Field Definition* tells the machine how long the following functions (11, 0, and 1) should be performed.
11	*Start Automatic Skip* carries over a field which (for some sufficient reason) is not to be punched at this time.
0	*Start Automatic Duplication* actuates the machine for gang-punching information. The 0 code starts this operation and the 12 code keeps it going by defining the field.

1 *Alphabetic Shift* makes it unnecessary for the operator to shift from numbers to alphabet on the keyboard—something he might easily forget to do.

As in other machines, there are a number of adaptations of the basic machine for specialized purposes. For example, one machine prints the information at the top of the card, as it is punched, while another machine has an extra drum upon which a card can be placed for programming common information. Interspersed gang-punching, and many other devices, are available for those special applications.

Verifier

After the cards have been punched it is usually desirable to check them in some way to be sure that they have been punched correctly. This can be done visually, but it is much faster and more convenient to place the cards in a machine which will automatically check the information as it is typed out again, preferably by another operator.

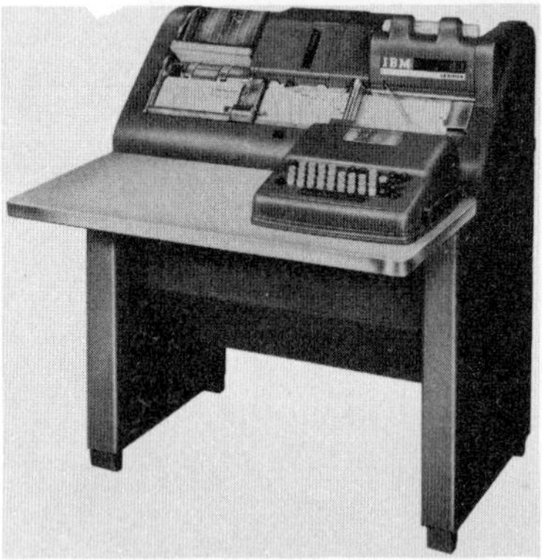

Figure 13–17
Card Verifier

Courtesy of IBM Corp.

The verifying machine (Figure 13–17) looks very much like the key punch, except that it has a verifying station (which is a set of brushes) instead of a punching station. The operator verifies information by depressing the keys, as in the original operation, and also verifies the gang-punching operations executed under the automatic control of a programming card. Any error is detected by a discrepancy between the digit punched and the key depressed, or between the digit punched and the digit in the preceding card. Provisions are made for three trials, so if the verifier operator makes an error there are two more opportunities to make the correction. If the third attempt to punch the correct information in the card fails, the card is "error notched" in the column where the error occurs. When the cards pass through "correct," a notch is made on the end of the card to indicate that it has been verified.

Sorter

One of the major purposes of punching information into cards is to make the information available for sorting and classifying, and for this reason the sorter is one of the most important machines in card-data processing.

The sorting operation is relatively simple. The cards are placed in the feed hopper, shown on the far right of the machine illustrated in Figure 13–18. A brush, shown in the schematic of Figure 13–19, is adjusted over

Figure 13–18
Sorter

Courtesy of IBM Corp.

Figure 13–19
Sorter Schematic

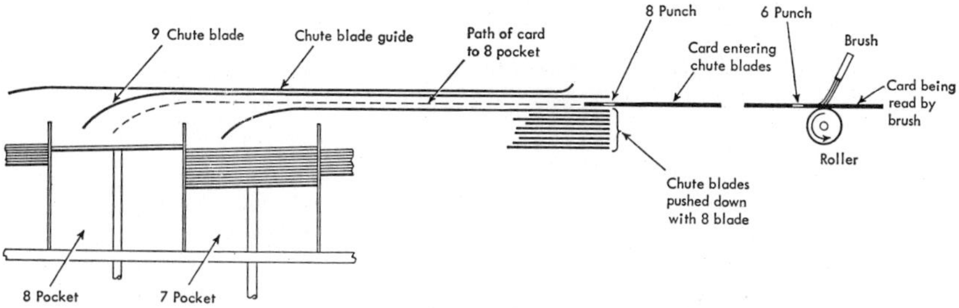

the column being sorted to detect the impulse and actuate the sorting mechanism. There are thirteen pockets into which the cards are sorted, one for each position in a column, plus one additional pocket for rejects. Sorting is done at the incredible speed of 2,000 cards per minute.

The card is conveyed over the pockets by rollers, but the guiding of the cards into the proper pocket is done by chute blades, as shown. The card is fed 9-edge-first and, when the hole is sensed, the magnet is actuated to pull down the corresponding blade. For example, in the illustration the 8 punch is detected, which causes the magnet to pull down the 8-chute blade (and, incidentally, all those before it: 7, 6, 5, 4, 3, 2, 1, 0, 11, and 12), leaving a gap between the 8 and 9 through which the card can pass and be guided to its proper bin. The alphabet, of course, requires two sorting operations.

There are several acceptable methods of sorting numbered cards, but the most common is to first sort on the units column, stack the cards out of the pocket so they are in ascending order, and then sort on the 10's column. This process is repeated for the 100's column, and so on. As with many other machines, special attachments can be added, such as counters and large feeding bins.

Reproducers

The reproducer is one of the most versatile of all card-data processing machines. It can reproduce and gang-punch decks of cards, and also check the work as it goes along. It works at the rate of 100 cards a minute. The numerous functions are listed below:

Reproducing is sensing any or all of the information in one deck of cards and punching it into another deck of cards (see Figure 13–20).

Figure 13–20

Reproducing

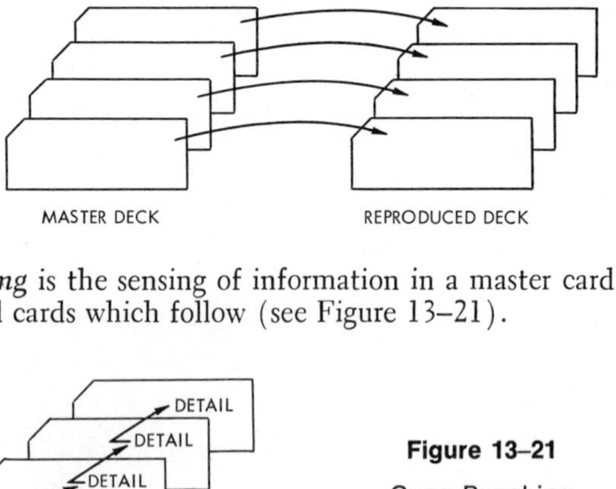

Gang-punching is the sensing of information in a master card and punching it into the detail cards which follow (see Figure 13–21).

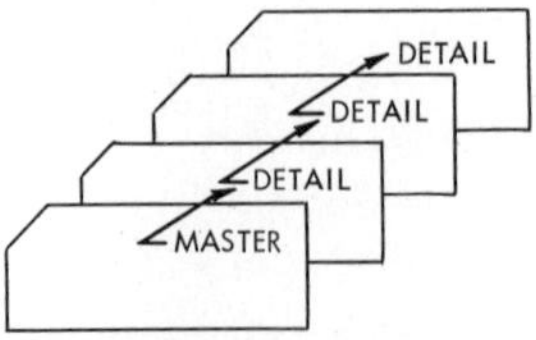

Figure 13–21

Gang-Punching

Comparing is done to check the agreement between the source and the resulting punched holes.

End printing features permit the printing of up to 16 numbers across the end of a card, such as might be done with time tickets that are stored in pockets with just the number showing.

Double-punch blank-column detection can be done (if this special device is installed on the machine).

Mark-sensing, also a special device, translates into punched holes the information which is placed on the card in the form of a pencil mark (Figure 13–22).

Summary punching can be done with this machine when it is properly

Figure 13–22

Mark-sensed Card

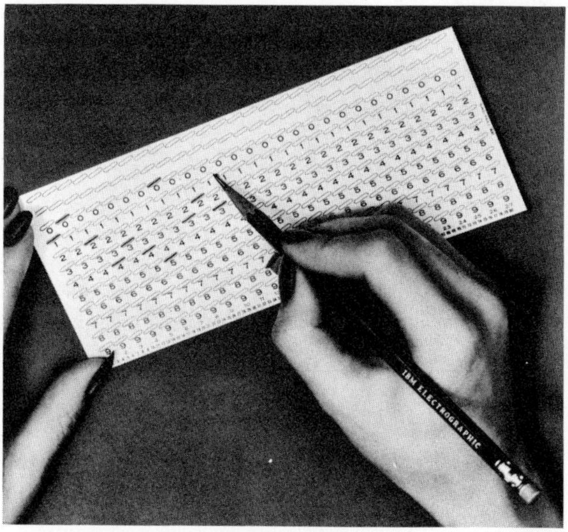

equipped. This means that it can take the information prepared by some other machine, such as an accounting machine, and punch it out on cards.

The Operation of the Reproducer. The reproducer is illustrated in Figure 13–23, and Figure 13–24 shows how it operates. Notice the agreement between the two; for example, the two card hoppers and the two card stackers.

Figure 13–23

Reproducer

Courtesy of IBM Corp.

On the front of the machine is the control panel, which is illustrated in more detail in Figure 13–25.

Figure 13–24

Schematic of the Reproducer

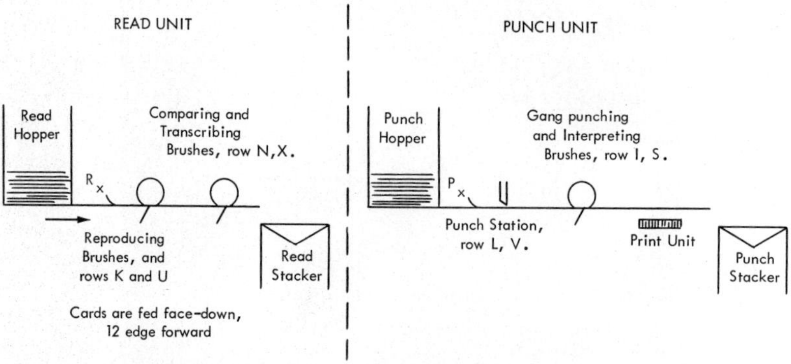

Figure 13–25

Control Panel for the Reproducer

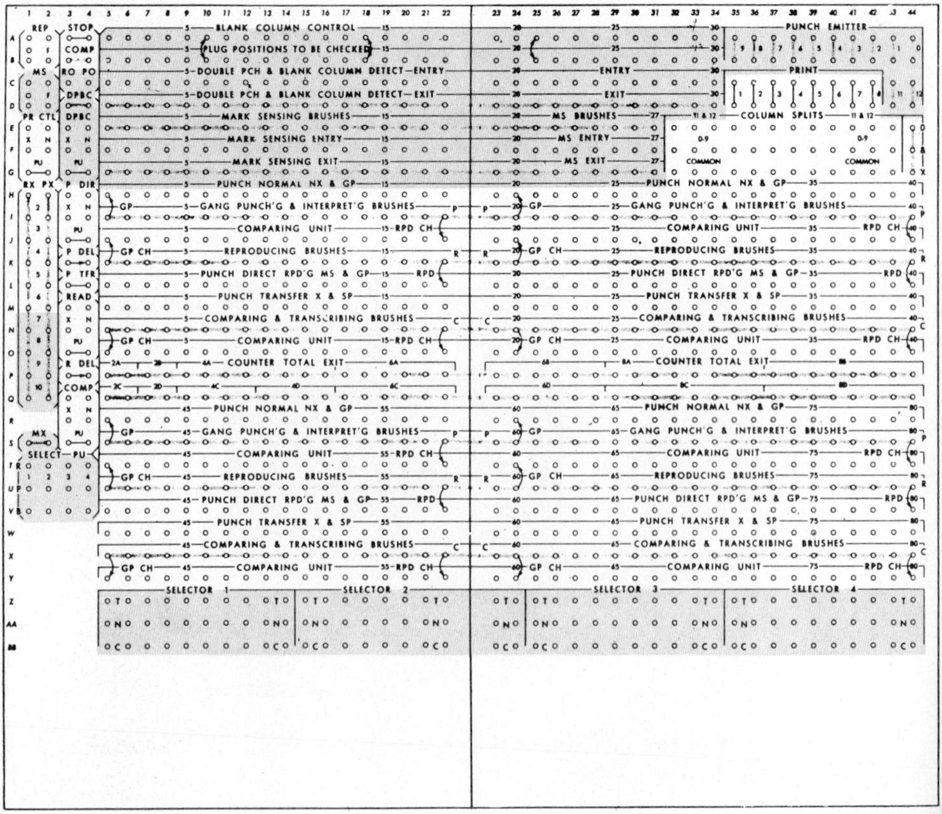

Those areas which are shaded are the hubs for the more uncommon devices which can be added, but we will restrict our discussion to the unshaded areas. On the schematic you will find letters (adjacent to the brushes and punches) which indicate in which rows on the control panel the hubs are to be found. You should not have any qualms about the complexity of the panel for many of the hubs are repeated 80 times, once for each column on the card. Also notice that the first 40 hubs are placed in the top half of the panel and the second 40 are in the bottom half, so that rows H and R perform the same function with different columns.

As is obvious from the schematic, the reproducer has two distinct units, the read unit and the punch unit. The feeds of these two units may operate separately or they may function together by jack-plugging the "reproducer on" at A–B under 1 on the panel.

In the read unit are three sets of brushes: the read–X brushes, the reproducing brushes, and the comparing and transcribing brushes, all of which have quite naturally been named for the function they perform. The read–X brushes are for detecting X punches, used to control the machine. Six such brushes (Figure 13–26) are standard and can be shifted from column to column, with some physical limitations as to how close the adjacent columns can be. It should be noted that the X panel is wired internally to the control panel; and the number on the control panel under RX, column 1, indicates

Figure 13–26

Brushes for Detecting X Punches

Reprinted, by permission, from IBM Corp. Reference Manual: Operator's Guide, Form No. A-24-1010.

which lead is brought out and does not indicate the column being read, which is determined by adjusting the brushes.

The reproducing brushes and the comparing and transcribing brushes consist of 80 brushes (the full width of the card) which can detect the holes punched in each column.

The punch unit, on the right, also has a set of X punch detecting brushes similar to the read–X brushes. At the punch station are 80 punch units, one for each column in the card. There are also 80 gang-punching and interpreting brushes, which can detect holes in any column of the card.

The leads to the punches terminate in the punch direct hubs, but frequently it is necessary to suspend punching momentarily. To do this there are 80 punch transfer magnets, illustrated in Figure 13–27. When the mag-

Figure 13–27

Punch Transfer Magnets

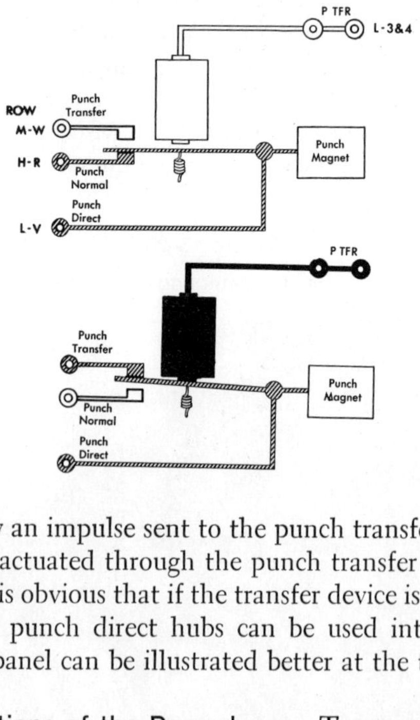

nets are actuated by an impulse sent to the punch transfer *magnet* hub, the punch can only be actuated through the punch transfer hubs, rows M and W on the panel. It is obvious that if the transfer device is not being used the punch normal and punch direct hubs can be used interchangeably. The other hubs on the panel can be illustrated better at the time of their application.

Typical Applications of the Reproducer. To reproduce all or part of the information in one deck of cards into another deck of cards is the problem of *reproducing*. We should also like to take advantage of the machine at the same time to determine whether or not the reproducing has been done correctly. This operation can be seen on the schematic, Figure 13–28, and on the control panel, Figure 13–29, for reproducing columns 5 through 11. The original information file is placed in the read unit on the

Figure 13–28

Reproducing and Comparing

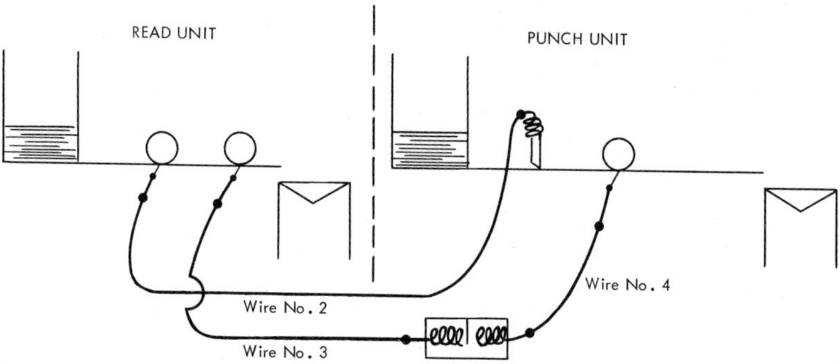

(Wire 1, which makes the read and punch units work together, cannot be shown on the schematic.)

left while the deck to be produced is placed in the punch unit on the right. The cards will move in step through both units if the reproducer-on hubs are jack-plugged (wire 1).

The reproducing brushes and the punch direct hubs are connected (wire 2) on both the schematic and control panel to do the punching operation. To check the cards, the comparing and transcribing brushes are connected to one side of a comparing unit (wire 3) while the other side of the comparing unit is connected to the gang-punch and interpreting brushes (wire 4). Notice that it doesn't particularly make any difference which comparing units are used, but naturally both hubs of any one unit must be used. It will make some difference when one interprets information on the comparing indicator, Figure 13–30, which tells the operator in which column an error in comparing occurred. This can also be seen on the front of the machine illustrated.

Occasionally the information to be reproduced comes from one field on some cards and from another field on other cards, and it is necessary for the machine to select the fields, as illustrated in Figure 13–31.

One set of cards must have a distinctive X punch to direct the machine. This operation is performed by the punch transfer magnets which have been discussed. Looking at the control panel—Figure 13–32 (wired for this operation)—we can see that the units must operate together, and the appropriate hubs are jack-plugged (wire 1). The punch X brush is wired to the punch transfer hub to actuate the magnets when X cards are read (wire 2). When cards without an X punch pass through the machine, information read in columns 5 to 15 is punched into 5 to 15 (wire 3), but when an X card passes the read–X brush, information in 50 to 60 is read and punched into 5 to 15 (wire 4). For checking, the information has to be transferred by means of a set of selector units located at the bottom of the control

Figure 13–29

Reproducer Panel Wired for Reproducing and Comparing

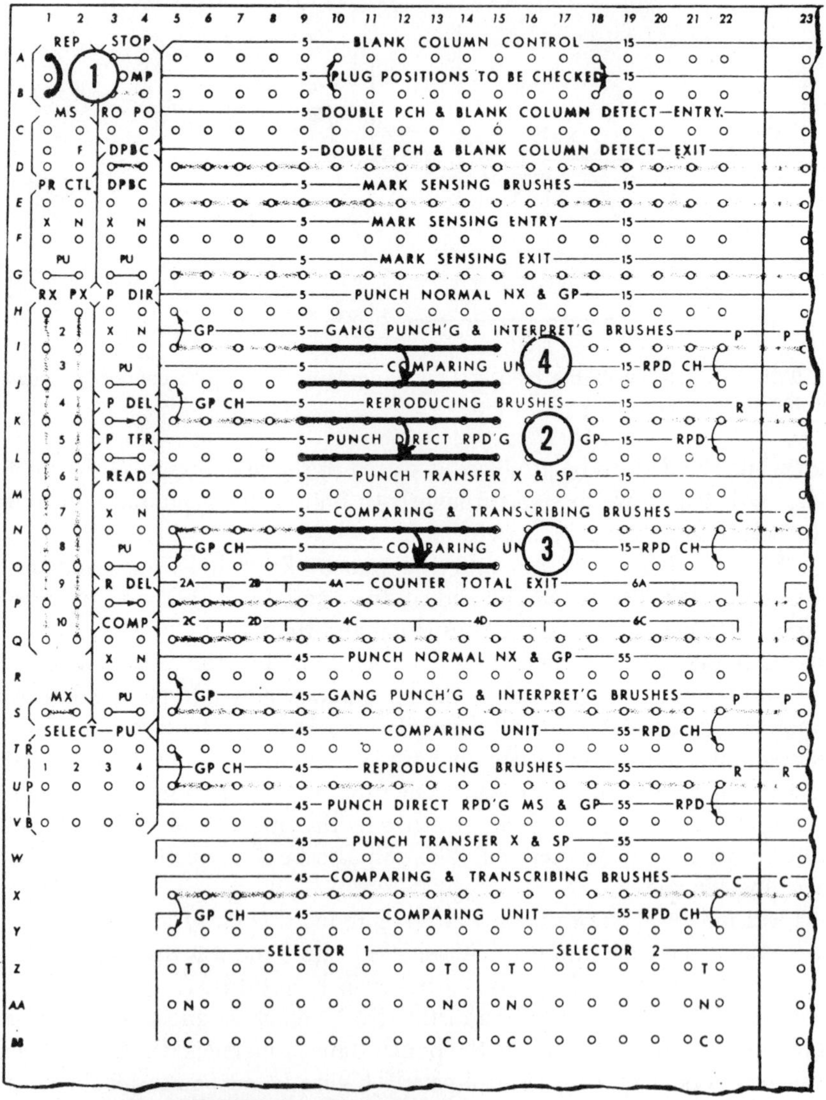

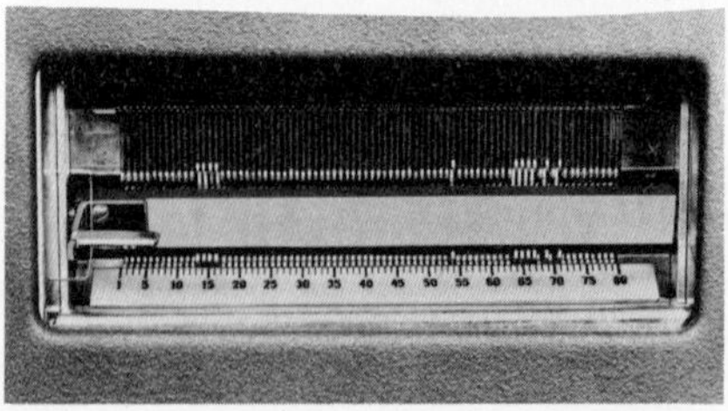

Figure 13–30

Indicators on the Reproducer

Courtesy of IBM Corp.

Figure 13–31

Shifting Fields

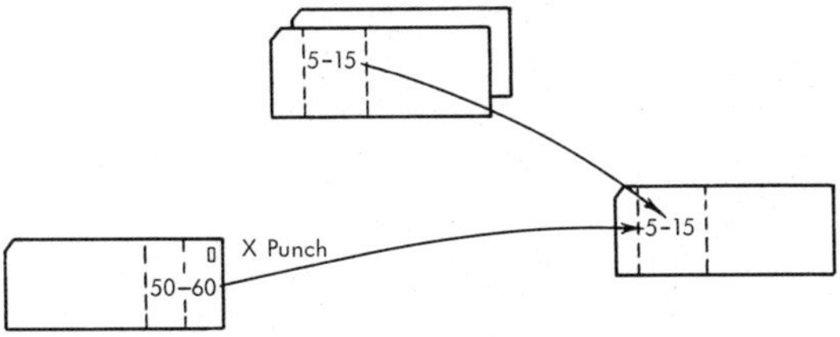

Figure 13–32

Shifting Fields: Field Selection

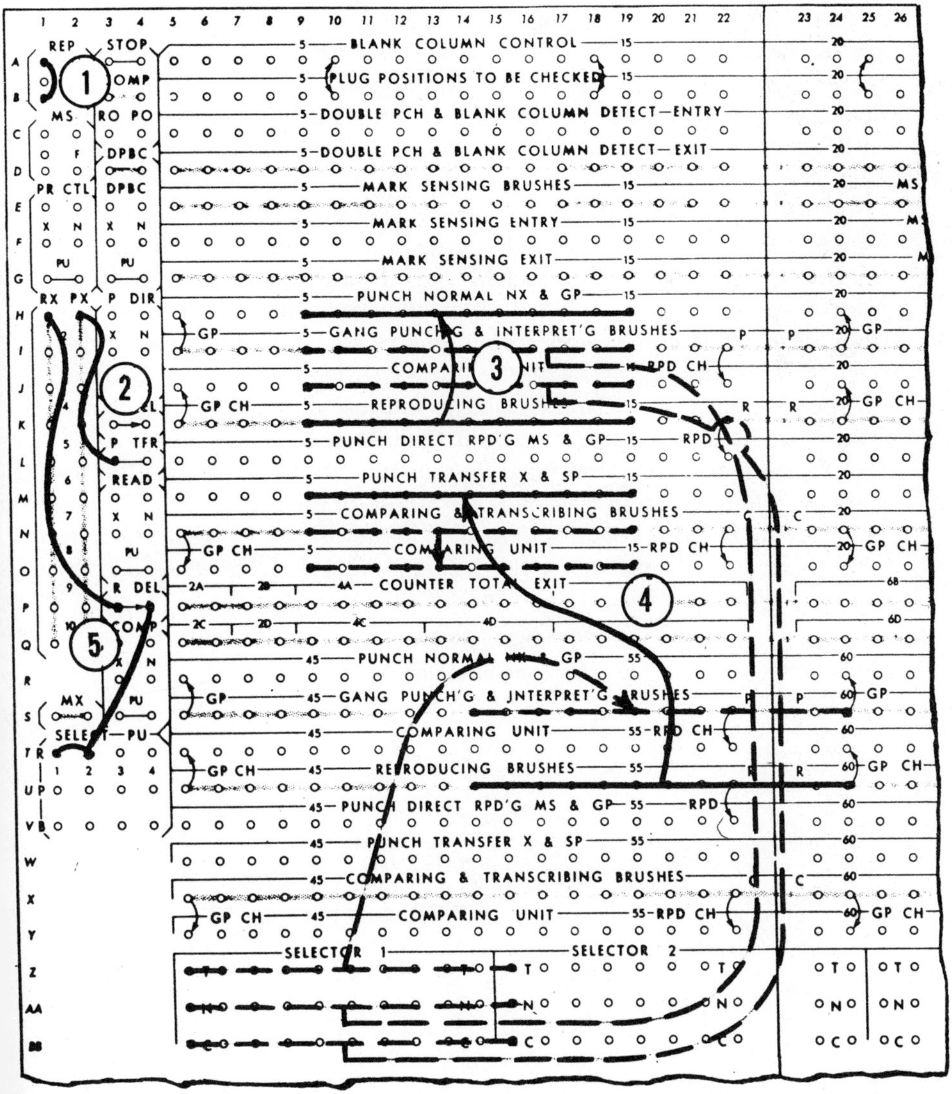

panel. The wiring for the checking operation is shown by dotted lines on the diagram, and it is apparent that the selectors have to be actuated through the read delay hub, which transfers the selector just before the X card passes the comparing brushes (wire 5).

Gang-punching is accomplished by wiring the machine, as shown in Figure 13–33. The cards to be gang-punched are placed in the right-hand punch unit and the impulses read by the gang-punching and interpreting brushes are fed back to the punch station. This is illustrated on the control panel, Figure 13–34, by wire 1. The cards are compared by placing them in the read unit after they have been punched. The read unit is wired (as shown by the dotted lines on the schematic and the accompanying panel diagram).

Since we are gang-punching cards which have the master card interspersed in the detail cards, it is necessary to suspend punching when the master card goes under the punch (otherwise information in the previous detail card will be punched in the master card, which of course we do not wish). The same problem arises on the read unit side. This difficulty is overcome by identifying either the master or detail cards with an X punch in one of the columns. These are detected by the punch–X and read–X brushes, which cause punching and reading to be suspended by jack-plugging the correct hubs at H–I, 3–4, and M–N, 3–4 on the control panel. If the X hubs are jack-plugged, only X cards are punched, and if the NX hubs are jack-plugged, only non-X cards are punched. This same suspension process can be done more selectively with the punch transfer feature of the machine. The punch transfer must be used when a suspension of punching is desired in only certain fields or when the printing feature is used.

Offset gang-punching also makes use of the punch transfer feature. In this situation information from certain columns in the master cards is gang-punched into different columns in the detail card, Figure 13–35. The wiring for this operation is shown on the accompanying diagram as solid lines,

Figure 13–33
Gang-punching

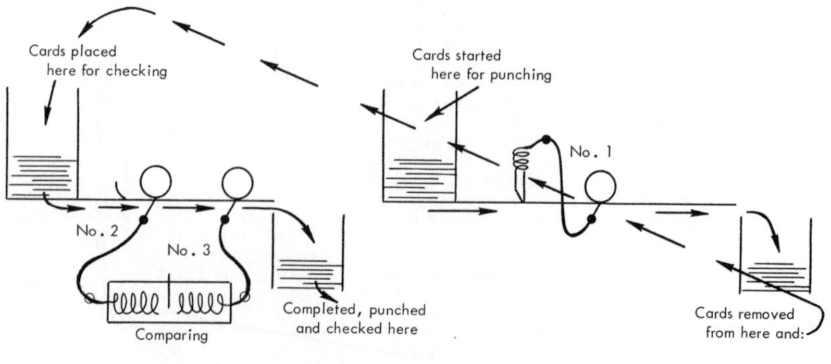

Figure 13–34

Gang-punching

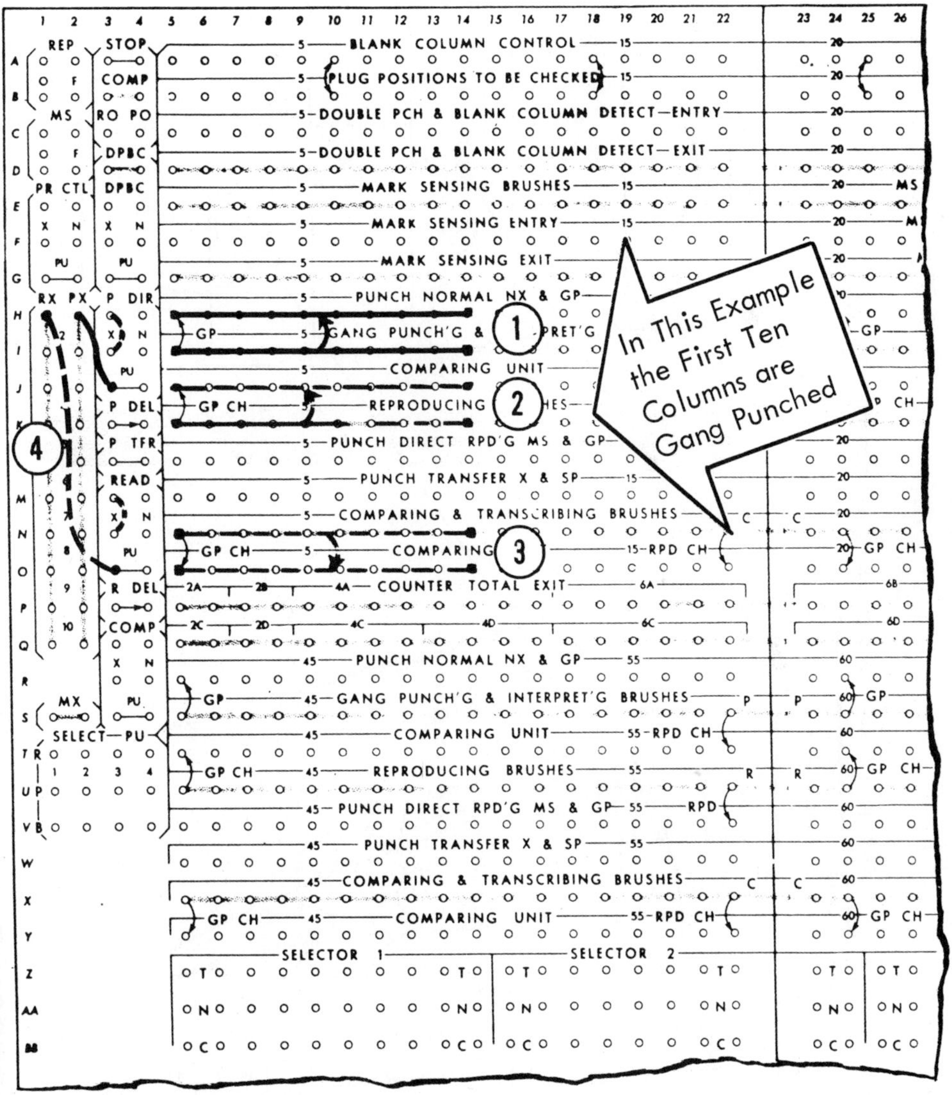

while comparing (shown by the dotted lines) follows the same wiring logic as the punching, but the selector unit replaces the punch transfer unit.

These few, simple examples should give you the logic of the reproducer. You should now be able to adapt this information to other situations. The reproducer can combine the operations of reproducing and gang-punching, and reproducing, gang-punching, and end printing—plus several other operations.

Figure 13–35

Example of Offset Gang-punching, with Schematic

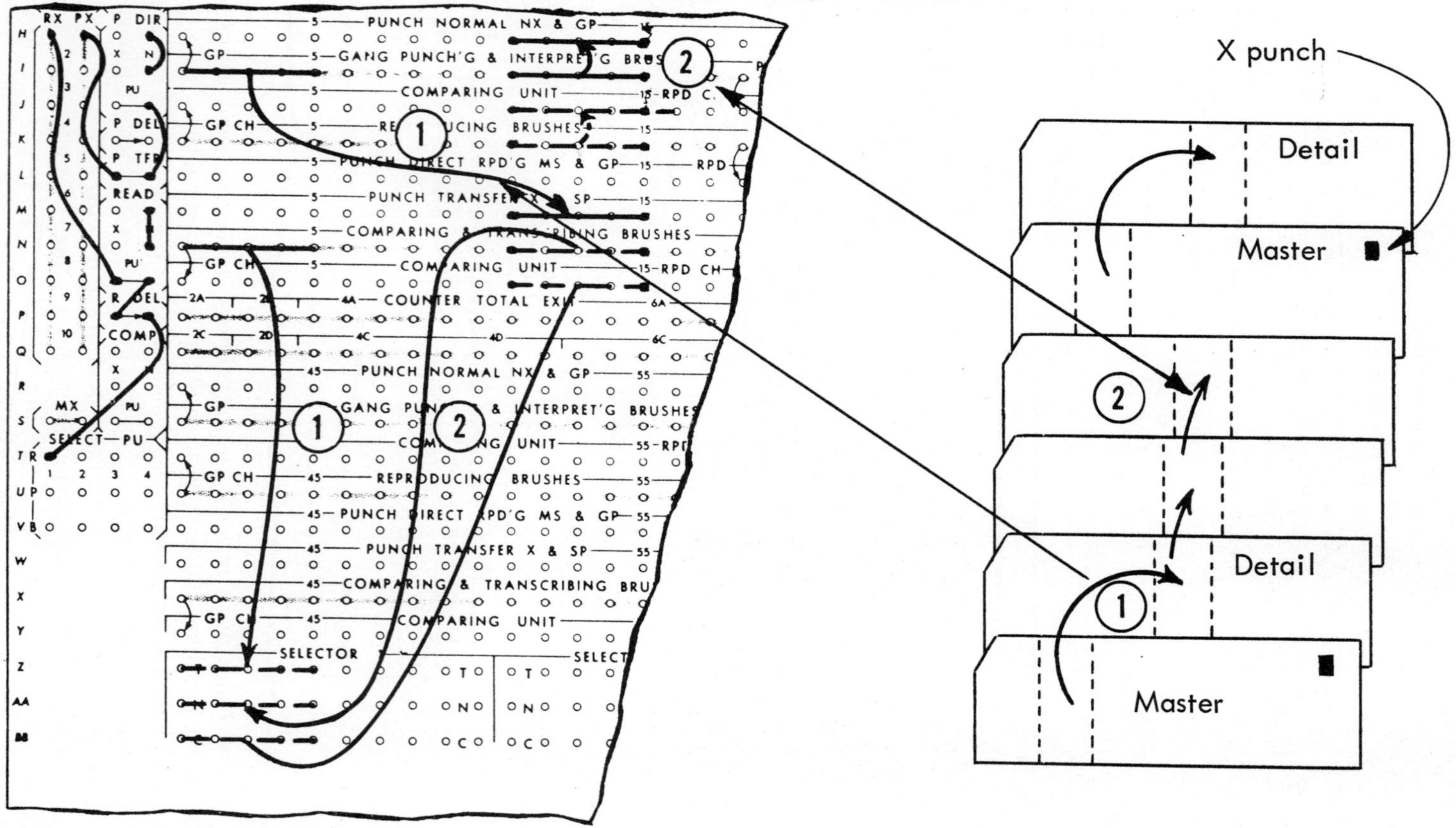

Collator

There are many sorting operations for which the sorter is not as suitable as the more versatile collator. This machine is capable of performing the many operations described here.

Card Selection. The control panel of the machine can be wired to select X cards, select non-X cards, the first card in a group, the last card in a group, a single card group, a zero balance card, a card with a particular number, or a card out of sequence.

Checking Sequence. The control panel of the machine can be wired to determine if cards are in proper numerical sequence.

Merging. If two decks of cards are in the same sequence order, they can be merged into one deck with all cards in the proper sequence.

Matching. The control panel can be wired to compare two decks of cards so that for each card in one deck there is a card in the other deck.

Editing. The cards in a deck can be checked for accuracy of punching. A double-punch or blank column can cause the machine to stop.

You will notice the agreement between the configuration of the collator in Figure 13–36 and the schematic shown below it in Figure 13–37. The

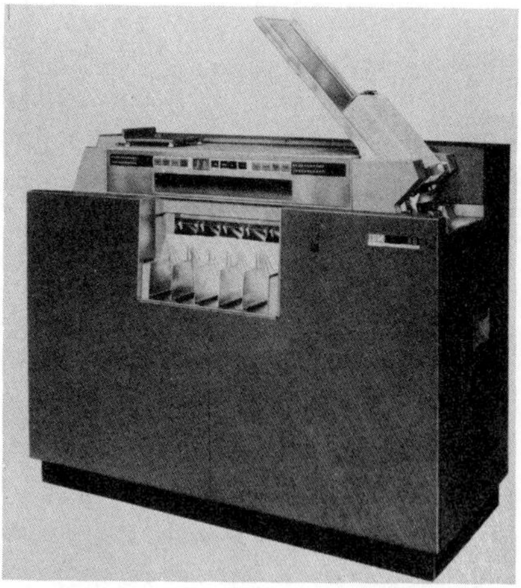

Figure 13–36

Collator

Figure 13–37

Collator Schematic

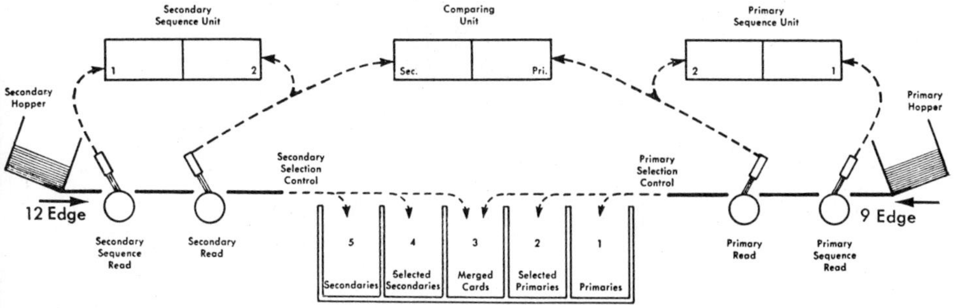

Figure 13–38

Collator Control Panel

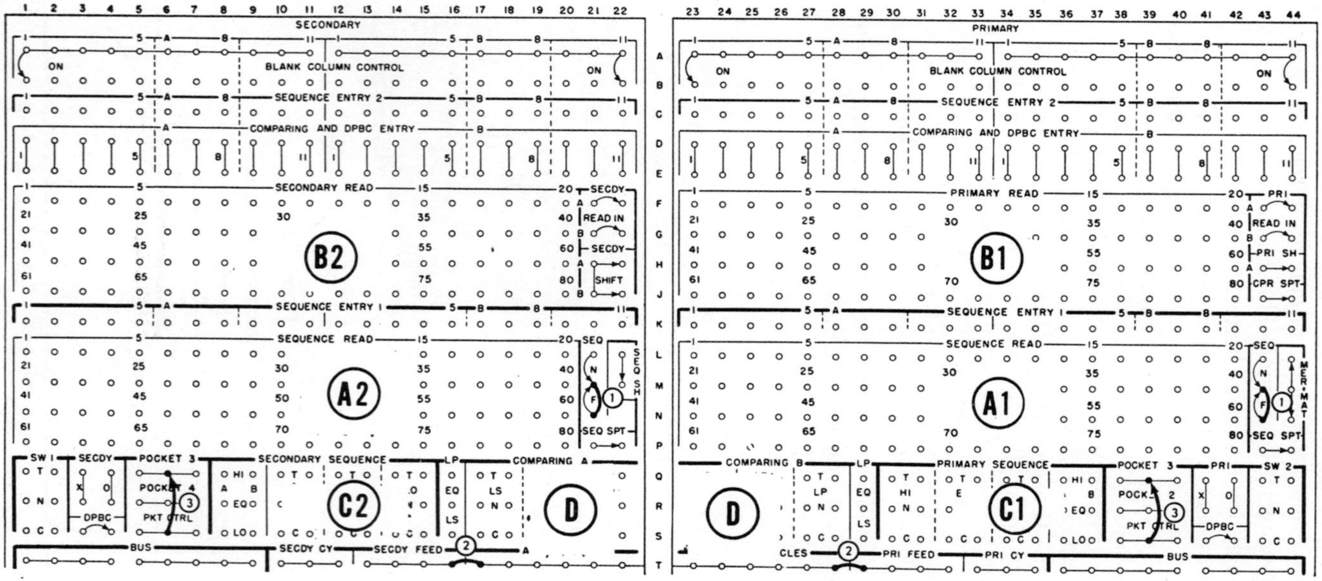

cards to be processed are placed either in the left- or right-hand hopper of the machine and are fed toward the center, under two sets of brushes, where the choice of receiving bins is made. All cards may be dumped into bin 3, with each feed having two additional options (as shown by the dotted lines).

Each feed operates at the rate of 650 cards a minute; the combined rate is 1300 cards per minute. This is a maximum rate, which is dependent upon the operation performed. Since the feeds are similar, we can concentrate our attention on one.

The cards pass under 80 sequence brushes and 80 read brushes. These contacts are brought out on the control panel, Figure 13–38, at A and B. Each machine is equipped with a number of sequence checking units, which function as described earlier. These units are shown on the schematic as primary and secondary sequence units. The two sides of the sequence magnets come out on the control panel at C. The comparing unit serves a similar function, and the two sides of these units come out on the control panel at D. The function of the three units are the same, but, because of the way the cards are fed, they are not entirely interchangeable.

Typical Applications of the Collator. It is impossible to discuss all the details of the machine in this limited space, and it is also impossible to discuss all the applications of the machine, but enough can be covered to give the reader some feeling of familiarity.

Frequently it is desirable to merge two decks of cards of different colors, which have yet to be punched. Such a case might be the tool orders and operations tickets for a manufacturing packet. This is easily accomplished by wiring the panel of the collator (as shown in Figure 13–38). Because the cards are unpunched, we cannot use holes to instruct the machine. One deck of cards is placed in one feed and the other deck in the other feed, so that, as long as the machine is running, the cards are being alternately merged in pocket 3. Each wire on the control panel is explained here:

Wire Number	*Explanation*
1	This causes the machine to feed. "Sequence off" means that the operation is not concerned with the sequence order of any numbers punched on the card.
2	The "all cycles" hub furnishes an impulse every machine cycle, which, when fed to the feeding mechanisms, causes the machine to feed cards.
3	The "pocket control" hub emits an impulse on every cycle to actuate the pocket "gates." In this case, all the cards are dumped in the center pocket.

Sequence Checking. Cards will normally be in ascending order, which means that each card will be followed by a card of equal or higher value. One of lower value is out of order, and this is what we wish to detect in this operation. The panel is wired—as shown in Figure 13–39, which illustrates

Figure 13–39

Sequence Checking

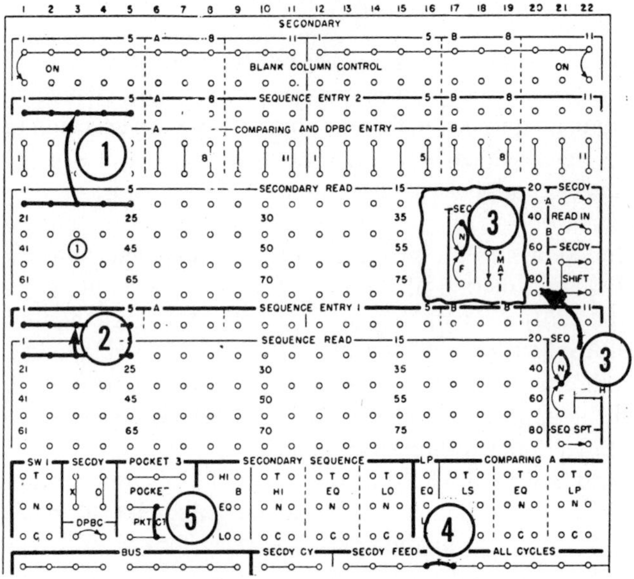

just one feed—but both feeds can be used simultaneously, or sequence checking can be done in conjunction with some other operation. Each wire on the control panel is explained here:

Wire Number	*Explanation*
1	Since we are checking the sequence in columns 1 to 5, we wish to wire these sequence brushes to one side of the comparing magnets in the sequence unit.
2	From the other side of the sequence magnets, the wire must go to the primary read brushes for columns 1 to 5.
3	The "sequence on" hub, 21–N, emits every machine cycle except when the sequence unit recognizes a low-sequence condition. The hub above it must receive an impulse every machine cycle to cause card feeding, so if there is a low condition there is no impulse, and consequently the machine stops feeding.

4 To feed a card every machine cycle, wire "all cycles" to the feed.

5 The wire from "pocket control" to pocket 4 causes all cards to drop into that pocket.

The merging operation consists of combining two files of cards, which are already in sequence, into one file which will still be in sequence. To do this, one file is placed in the primary feed of the collator and the other file is placed in the secondary feed. The machine is designed so that the primary feeds first. Primary and secondary sequence units are used, as well as the comparing unit, to detect the five different conditions which can exist as the cards pass through the collator, and to cause the machine to function properly. The panel wiring is a bit complex for the beginner to follow, so let us observe what happens by following a series of diagrams showing the position of the cards (Figure 13–40).

Figure 13–40

Merging

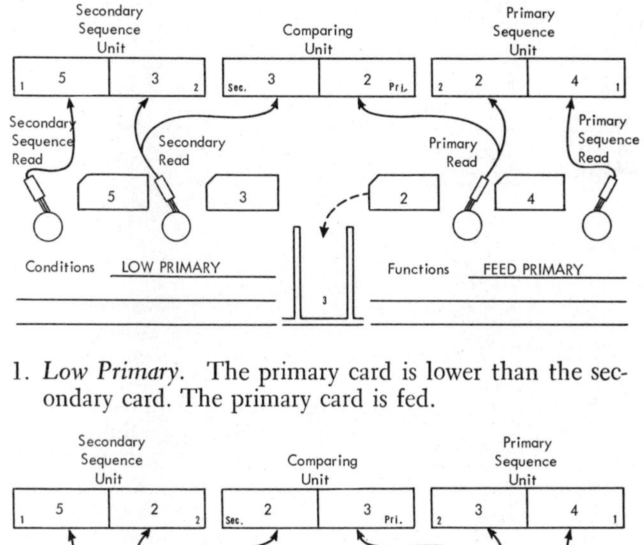

1. *Low Primary.* The primary card is lower than the secondary card. The primary card is fed.

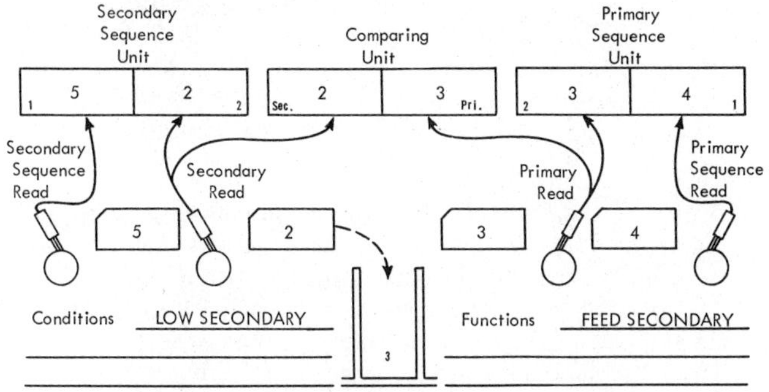

2. *Low Secondary.* The secondary card is lower than the primary card. The secondary card is fed.

Figure 13–40 (cont.)

Merging

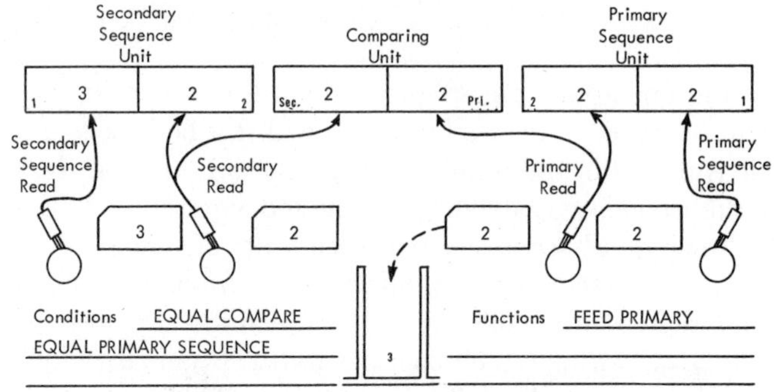

3. *Equal Comparing and Equal Primary Sequence.* The primary card is equal to the secondary card and to the primary sequence card. The primary card is fed because all primaries are normally filed ahead of the secondaries when there are several cards with the same control number in both files.

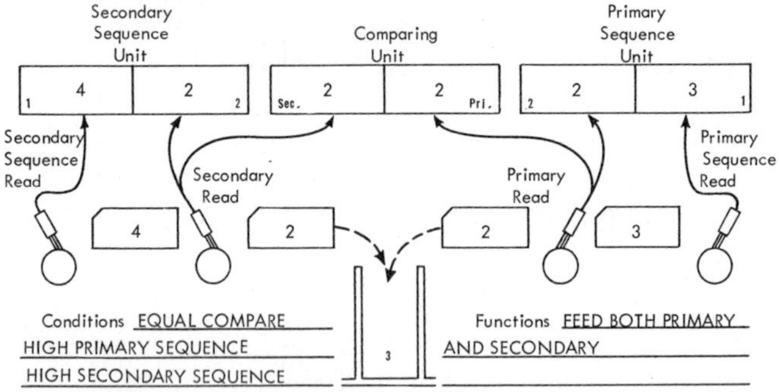

4. *Equal Comparing and High Primary Sequence.* The primary card is equal to the secondary card; the primary sequence card is higher than the primary card. Both the primary and secondary cards are fed. Thus, the last card of a group in the primary file and the first card of the same group in the secondary are fed simultaneously.

5. *Equal Comparing, High Primary Sequence, and Equal Secondary Sequence.* The primary card is equal to the secondary card; the primary sequence card is higher than the primary card; the secondary sequence card is equal to the secondary card. Both the primary and secondary cards are fed. Thus, as in condition 4, the last card of the primary group and the first card of the same group in the secondary are fed simultaneously. In addition, the equal secondary sequence condition interlocks the pri-

Figure 13–40 (cont.)

Merging

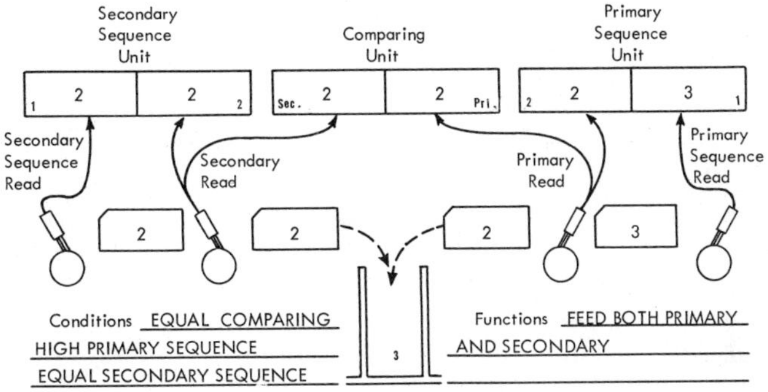

mary to provide continuous feeding of multiple secondaries on an equal comparison, until a high secondary sequence occurs. If this were not done, additional secondaries of an equal group (2) would be compared with the next primary card (3), and fed and erroneously selected as low secondaries in a merging-with-selection operation.

These examples will give the reader an insight to the operations of the collator—without going into all the detail found in operations manuals. For further information, he would do well to refer to these detailed descriptions of the operations.

Other Collators. You are apt to run into another model of a collator and some description of this machine may be useful. The configuration of the machine is as shown in Figure 13–41, which conforms to the schematic shown in Figure 13–42.

Figure 13–41

Collator

Figure 13–42

Collator Schematic

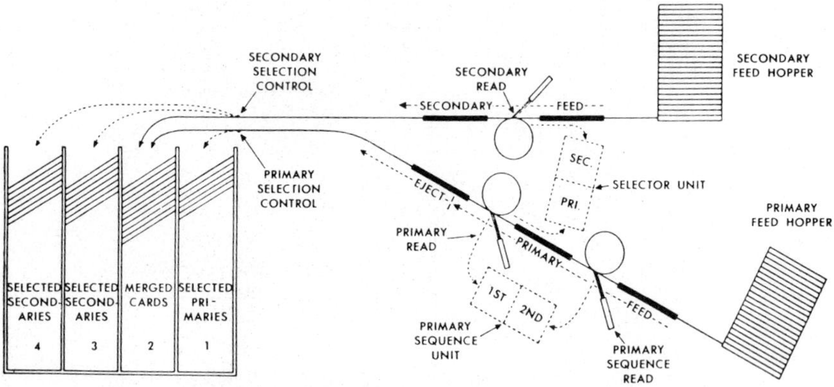

The primary is read by two sets of brushes, the primary sequence read brushes and the primary read brushes, which can be connected with sequence-comparing magnets as in the previous machine. The cards in the primary will normally go to the second pocket unless directed otherwise by the control panel. The secondary feed has only one set of brushes, the secondary read brushes. These can be used with comparing units, in conjunction with the primary read brushes (as shown). The secondary also feeds its cards to pocket 2 for merging cards from both feeds, but it can also be directed by control panel wiring to pockets 3 and 4. This machine is capable of selecting cards, checking sequence, and merging and matching cards, as was true of the previous machine, but this older design operates at a considerably lower speed and is less versatile.

Accounting Machine

The accounting machine is a versatile machine, having the basic function of printing out information from punched cards, but it can also perform the elementary arithmetic operations of addition, multiplication by multiple cycling, and subtraction. Other convenient operations can be performed by this machine, such as consecutive numbering for checks. The machine processes 150 cards per minute, printing out the information at some 18,000 characters a minute.

The illustration, Figure 13–43, can be compared with the schematic of Figure 13–44 and the close-up of the paper carriage shown in Figure 13–45. The card-feeding mechanism is to the far left of the machine and the paper carriage is in the middle, while the control panel can be seen on the right end of the machine.

The feeding and spacing of the print-out form is under the control of a paper tape, illustrated by Figure 13–46. Punched holes in the narrow paper

Figure 13–43
Accounting Machine

Figure 13–44
Reading Mechanism in Accounting Machine

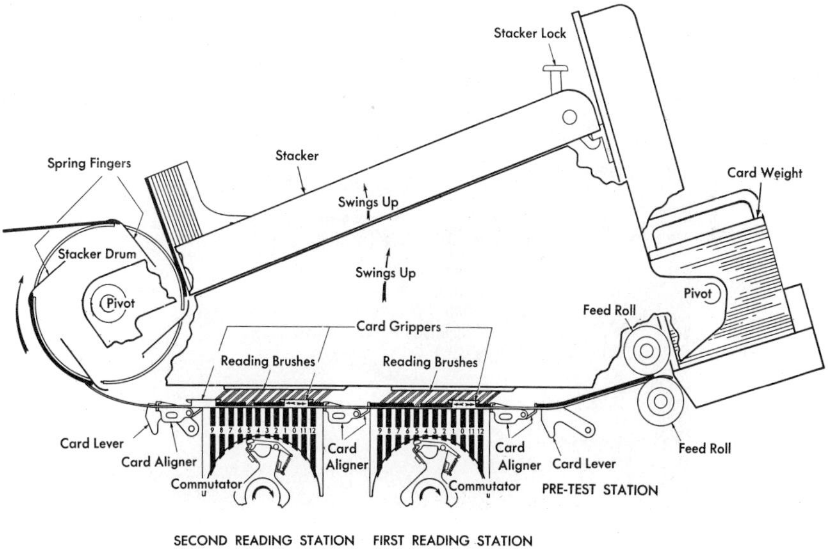

tape cause the form to skip, or to stop, when it reaches any predetermined position.

Cards are fed from right to left under the brushes, as illustrated in the schematic. They do not move continuously but are positioned under 960 brushes, where they are read by the commutator any given number of cycles. These two sets of brushes terminate on the control panel at A and B (Figure 13–47). If necessary, these can easily be connected to comparing units at C.

To list information taken from the cards it is only necessary to wire the second reading brushes to normal print entry (wire 1), as illustrated on the panel diagram.

Figure 13–45

Paper Carriage for Accounting Machine

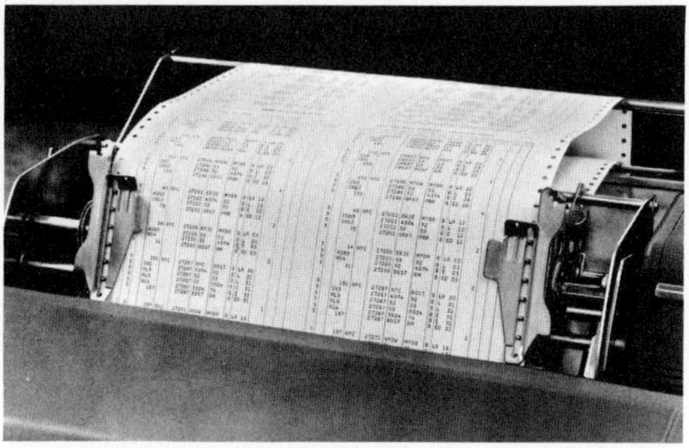

Reprinted, by permission, from IBM Reference Manual: Operator's Guide, Form No. A–24–1010.

Figure 13–46

Tape Control for Accounting Machine

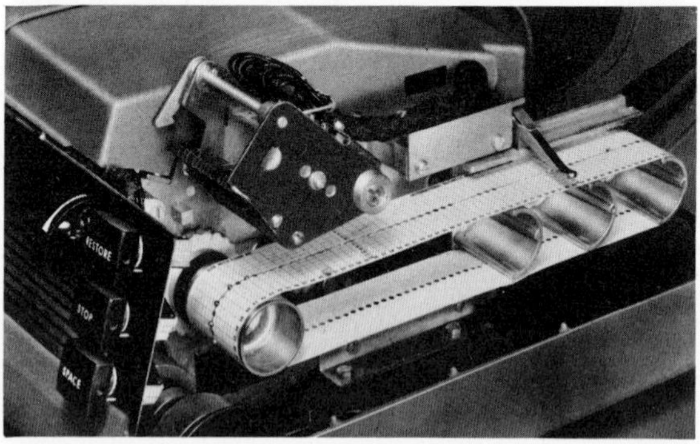

Reprinted, by permission, from IBM Reference Manual: Operator's Guide, Form No. A–24–1010.

Addition follows the steps of read, add, print, and total, which have been discussed earlier.

Read: The second reading brush impulses are taken to the counter entries, D, by wire 2. Care must be taken that the low-order position of the field in the card is taken to the low-order position of the counter.

Add: The counters, D, are told to add by an instruction impulse from card cycles to counter controls (wire 3).

Print and Total: This is taken care of by a wire from the counter exit to counter-controlled print (wire 4). The final total is accomplished by connecting read out and reset to final total (wire 5). Because of a characteristic of the counters on this particular machine, it is essential to also connect wire 6.

If you will look over the control panel you will see many hubs with which you are already acquainted, such as selectors, column splits, and emitters, which can be used as discussed earlier. In addition, a "consecutive printing" function can be used to number checks and similar forms.

Space does not permit the full development of all the accounting machine's many capabilities, but it is hardly necessary, for you have already been introduced (through the other machines) to many of the functions of this machine.

Interpreter

The basic purpose of the interpreter is to sense the holes punched in a card and translate this information into print which can be read. However, additional features on the machine can make it a versatile servant that is capable of doing many other tasks.

With the basic unit it is possible to print out information on any of 25 lines across the card, suppressing zero printing if desired. Column splits and selectors are available for controlling the machine, such as suppressing printing when cards have an X mark. Using special features, the machine can do card-to-card comparisons, select cards and stack them in one of four stacks, find and post the next line on a card, plus a number of other useful operations. The appearance of the machine, with only one stacker, can be seen in Figure 13–48, while Figure 13–49 shows the schematic of the machine.

The control panel for a typical operation is shown in Figure 13–50. Only a few comments will be made concerning the wiring of this machine since you are already acquainted with the various components. The wires marked 1 lead to the print entries, while 2 assures that all zeros will be printed. Number 3 is wired from the 80 column to detect an X, while 4 prevents the printing of all cards containing the X punch in column 80.

Data Transmission

In organizations with widespread activities it may be faster and more convenient and economical to centralize such activities as inventory control, production control, and payroll. A centralized data system requires transmission from many localities to a central organization.

Several systems are available which can be used in conjunction with

Figure 13–47 Control Panel for Accounting Machine

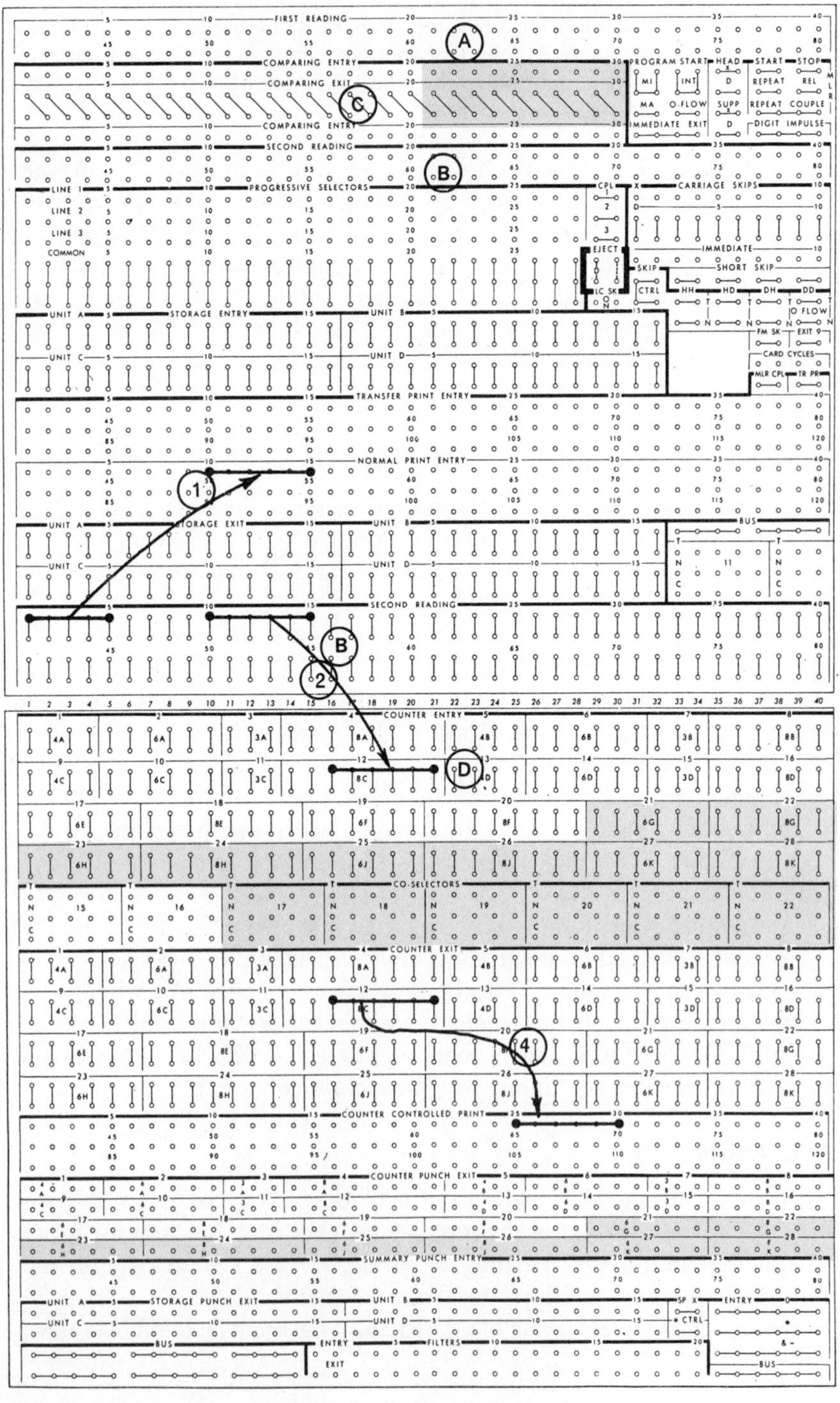

Figure 13–47 (continued)

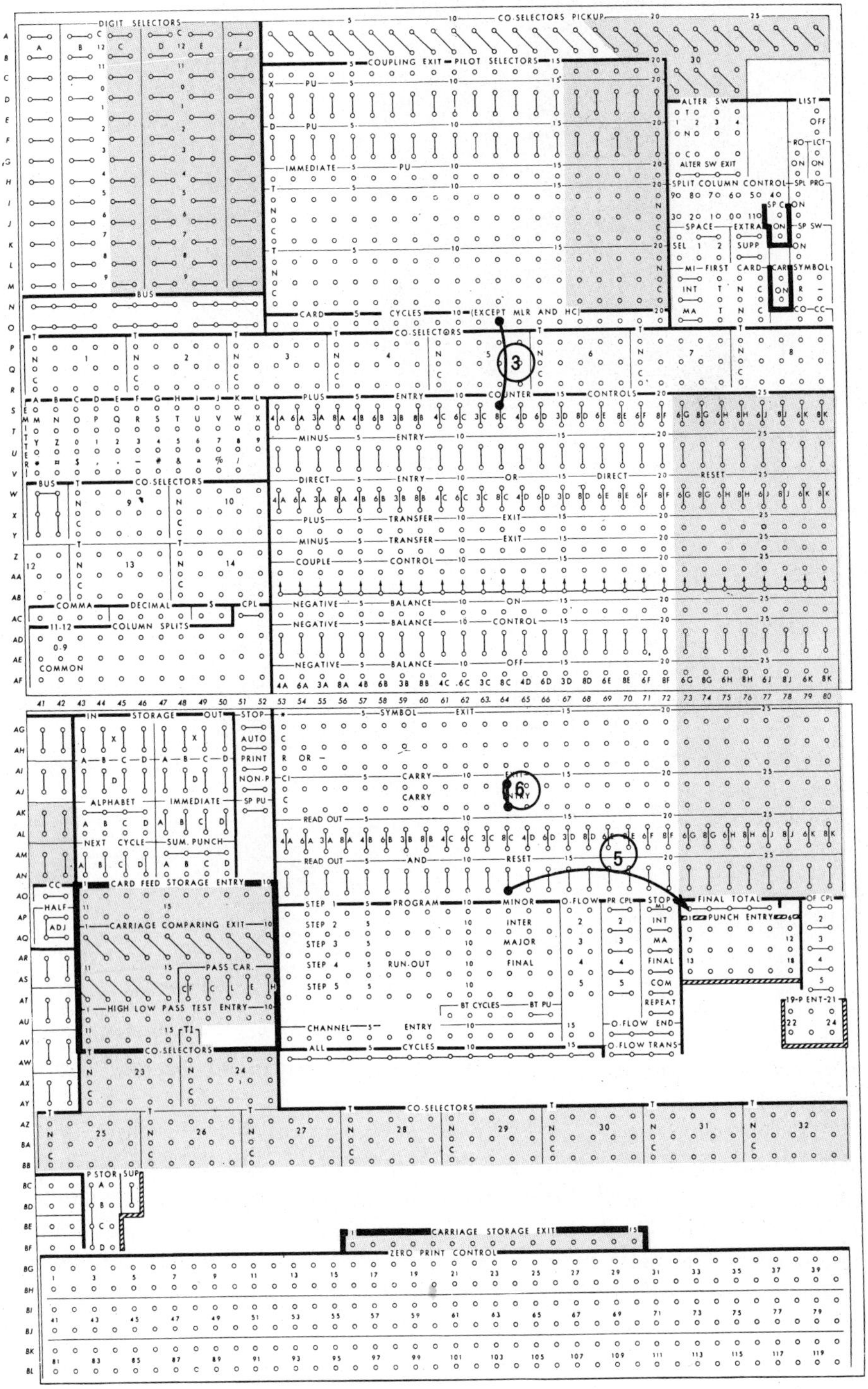

Courtesy of IBM Corp.

Figure 13–48

Interpreter

Figure 13–49

Feed Mechanism for Interpreter

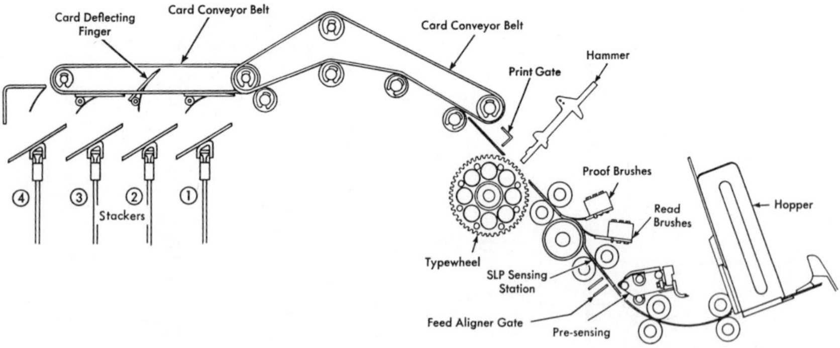

commercial telephone and telegraph lines and with microwave and short-wave radio circuits.

The schematic in Figure 13–51 shows the typical flow of information. The transmitting and receiving units, Figure 13–52, are identical, so only one machine is required at each end of the line. Output for such a machine is in the neighborhood of three to ten cards per minute, but up to four independent transmissions can be made at the same time over the same telephone lines, quadrupling the number of cards which can be sent per minute on any given line.

Figure 13–50

Interpreter Control Panel

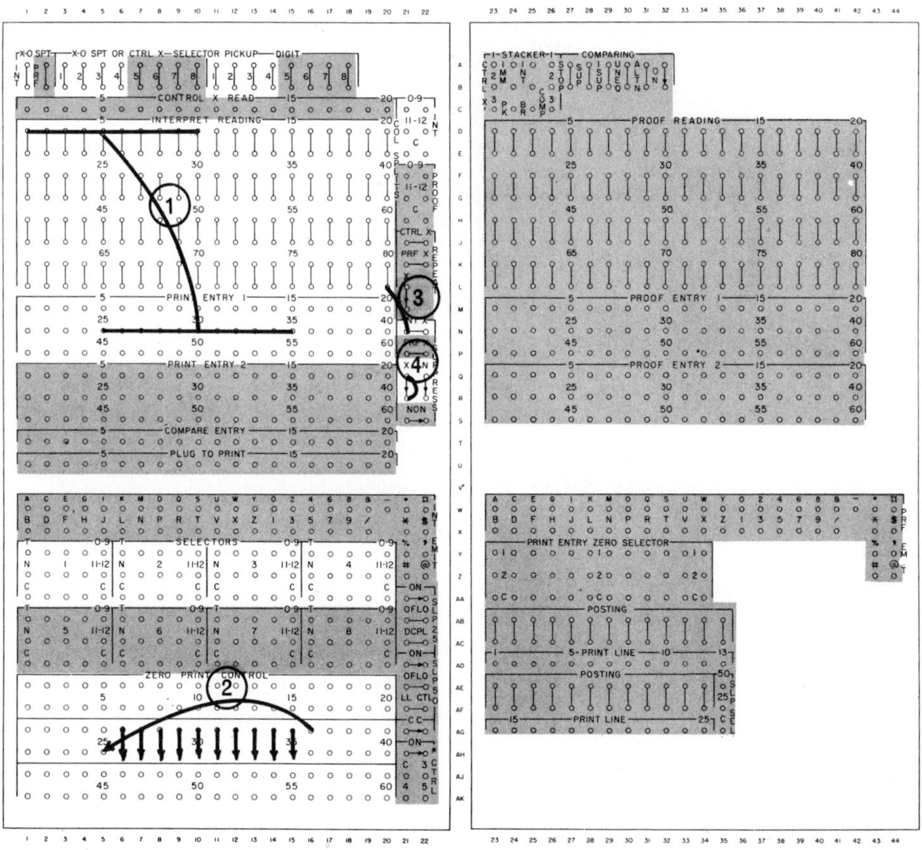

Figure 13–51

Schematic of Flow of Information

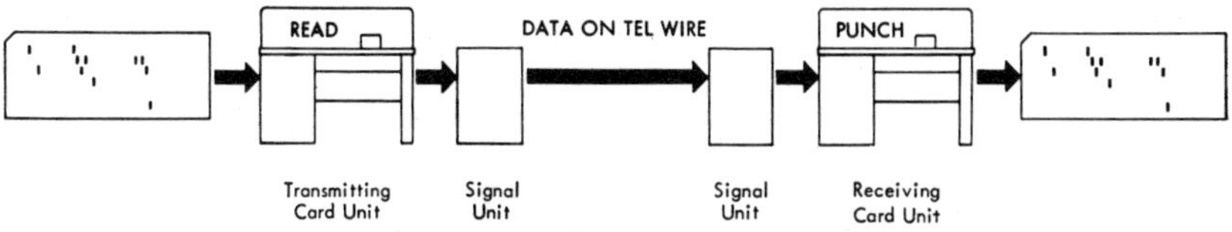

Further applications of data transmission include remote inquiry stations, on-line with computers, so that inquiries can be directed to—and answered by—a typewriter. Refinements include data transmission units

Figure 13–52
Data Transmission Unit

connecting two or more computers. Other common data transmission methods use paper tape, so that cards are converted to tape, and transmitted, and then converted back to cards.

SUMMARY

You should now have a broad comprehension of the card-data processing coding method, the machines, and the components which go into the machines. You should be able to discuss intelligently the applications of the various machines, and, in fact, to wire them to perform their functions. It was necessary and desirable to leave out all the detail material, such as location of switches and similar information, which may change from machine to machine—and which you would not retain anyway. The information included in this chapter is basic information, and you should be able to remember, or review it quickly, if the occasion arises. (How these machines are used in a system was discussed in the previous chapter.) You will be able to use these machines intelligently in designing a system because you know how they operate.

Questions

1. How are card-data processing machines instructed to perform their operations?
2. Define the following:
   a) Common hubs
   b) Bus hubs
   c) Emitting
   d) Read X

3. Is it possible that column 7 on a card could be compared with column 31? Explain.
4. How does the sequence-checking unit differ from the comparing unit?
5. Explain the purpose of the column split. Give an example of how it is used.
6. The accounting machine uses a printing bar. Explain why this is better than the mechanism used in an electric typewriter.
7. Is the information on the program card in the card punch machine, printed on the card being processed?
8. What are the uses of the programming card used with the card punch?
9. Why is the verifier needed? Would you have the same operator do the key punching and verifying for a particular deck of cards?
10. Why are sorters designed to sort just one column at a time?
11. Select the machines needed for a complete system to process students' grades. Explain your choice of equipment.
12. Give an application of reproducing and an application of gang-punching.
13. Select the machines for the following tasks:
    a) Merge two decks of cards which are in numerical sequence.
    b) Place the cards in numerical sequence before they are merged.
    c) Print information on the cards which are already punched.

References

Casey, Robert S., and Perry, James W. *Punched Cards, Their Applications to Science and Industry.* New York: Reinhold Publishing Co., 1951.

Doss, Milburn P. *Information Processing Equipment.* New York: Reinhold Publishing Co., 1955.

Fairbanks, Ralph W. *Successful Office Automation.* Englewood Cliffs, N.J.: Prentice-Hall Inc., 1956.

Fisher, Harrison. *Today's Business Machines.* Chicago: American Technical Society, 1959.

Friedman, Burton Dean. *Punched Card Primer.* Chicago: Public Administration Service, 1955.

IBM Personal Study Program. *Punched Card Data Processing Principles.* Endicott, N.Y.: International Business Machines Co., 1961.

McGill, Donald A. *Punched Cards: Data Processing for Profit Improvement.* New York: McGraw-Hill Book Co., Inc., 1962.

Rice, Donald E. *Introduction to Data Processing.* Dayton, Ohio: Otterbein Press, 1962.

Salmon, Lawrence J. *IBM Machine Operation and Wiring.* Belmont, Calif.: Wadsworth, 1962.

VanNess, Robert G. *Principles of Punched Card Data Processing.* Elmhurst, Ill.: Business Press, 1962.

CHAPTER **14**

Computer Equipment

A computer is a device which carries out logical and mathematical operations either mechanically or electrically.

There are two distinct types of computers, the *analog* and the *digital,* which have become important tools in science and industry. In the analog computer numbers are represented by a continuously variable physical quantity, such as an electrical voltage, a change in shaft rotation, and so forth. The answer is obtained as a measure of these physical quantities. The digital computer, on the other hand, deals directly with the digital form or with discrete items, such as counting the number of teeth on a gear or the number of electric pulses in a circuit.

Neither type of computer can be said to be superior to the other. Each type has its place, and occasionally one complements the other. Some idea of the qualifications of each can be obtained from the following:

Digital	*Analog*
Precision is somewhat limited by size of the computer.	Precision and accuracy limited by the quality of components.
Cost is relatively high for the basic unit, regardless of accuracy.	Cost depends upon quality of the units. Cost for 1 percent accuracy is relatively low, but for higher accuracy cost is high.
Easy to program for design problems, with the parameters easily adjustable. Answers are available immediately.	Programming for design problems is more complex and more time is required for obtaining answers to a number of parameter conditions.

Since digital computers are far more useful in manufacturing applications, this is where the emphasis will be placed. Analog computers have been used in some preliminary studies of simulation, but for the immediate future the emphasis will be on digital computers in the operation of manufacturing enterprises. Since all large digital computers of any consequence are electronic, this term will not be stressed in the definitions.

There are other ways of classifying computers, such as *general purpose,* or *special purpose.* Airlines are using special-purpose computers to keep an account of their space reservations. In fact, many airplanes have special-purpose computers built into navigation and gunnery controls, but here we are concerned with the general-purpose computer which can be adapted to many tasks.

Perhaps somewhere the reader has detected another classification of computers, those used for scientific purposes and those used for business purposes? It is true that, in some instances, there are differences, but many times one digital computer is used for both tasks. Several companies in recent years have put out an engineering computer which is relatively small and is characterized by its small memory and relative ease in programming the engineering type of problem. The computer used in business and manufacturing control, as we shall see, must and does have an extensive memory to keep track of the many accounts or items in an inventory. This distinction between the business and the engineering use of computers should be kept in mind.

DEVELOPMENT OF COMPUTERS

Anyone working with computers and data processing should have some appreciation of the rapid development of these remarkable devices which are making such radical changes in science and industry. Figure 14–1 presents some highlights of their history with approximate dates.

Figure 14–1

Development of Computers

Time	*Event*
?	Man's earliest attempts to devise a computer go back to the abacus. The first evidence of this important tool in commerce can be found in ancient Egyptian history. It is very common throughout the Orient, and improved models can be found in the Chinese laundry around the corner. This simple device uses beads to represent "place," such as units, tens, hundreds, etc. In the hands of a competent operator, this primitive device can compete very favorably with a modern desk calculator.
1642	Blaise Pascal, of France, invented the first calculating machine along modern lines, using numbered wheels.
1671	Gottfried Leibnitz, in Germany, developed the stepped cylinder calculator.
1812–30	Charles Babbage, in England, designed (but was unable to build) a computer which is said to be the forerunner of the modern digital computer.
1880–90	Dr. Herman Hollerith, in the United States, working for the Census Bureau, devised the punched card, which was to be the

start of our modern punched-card processes. This development was prompted by the fact that the census was becoming a huge task beyond the ability of the conventional methods.

1884 Dorr Felt, in the United States, designed the calculator, which is the predecessor of the present-day "comptometer."

1944 Harvard University and International Business Machines Corporation cooperated, under the direction of Howard Aiken, to build a general-purpose machine, the Mark I. Cards were used to feed the information to the machine, while relays were used in the computing process.

1947 The Moore School of Engineering, University of Pennsylvania, completed an all-electronic digital computer, the ENIAC: Electronic Numerical Integrator and Automatic Computer.

1949 Maurice Wilkes, in England, developed the first stored-program computer.

1949 International Business Machines Corporation made available the first automatic computer type of machine, the CPC.

1951 Remington Rand Company made available the UNIVAC I, which was the first large-scale automatic computer available commercially.

1952 Princeton University's Institute for Advanced Studies developed the IAS computer. This computer, designed by John von Neumann, A. W. Burks, and H. H. Goldstine, has been the basis of many other computers because of its simplicity and speed.

1955 International Business Machines Corporation developed the first commercially available automatic computer with variable word lengths.

It is impossible to record in this space all the recent innovations in *hardware*. *Software*, the programming techniques which have led to the broader use of the computers in industry and science, has also advanced rapidly. The trend is definitely towards solid-state computers, with the vacuum tube machines being taken out of service.

Organization of the Digital Computer

The casual reader of computer literature is frequently overawed by the science-fiction implication that computers are magic brains. In order that you do not become one of these overly impressed readers, the description of the computer will start with a very basic analogy.

The computers you see shrouded in slick, metal cases, purring away in air-conditioned rooms, can be readily compared to a student working at his desk with his slide rule. If you understand this analogy, you will be a long way on the road to understanding the mysteries of the computer. Five major sections of the computer are shown in Figure 14–2. Notice that the heavy lines show the paths for numerical or logical information flow. This flow of information is controlled by the *control unit*, through "gates," as indicated

Figure 14–2

Computer Organization

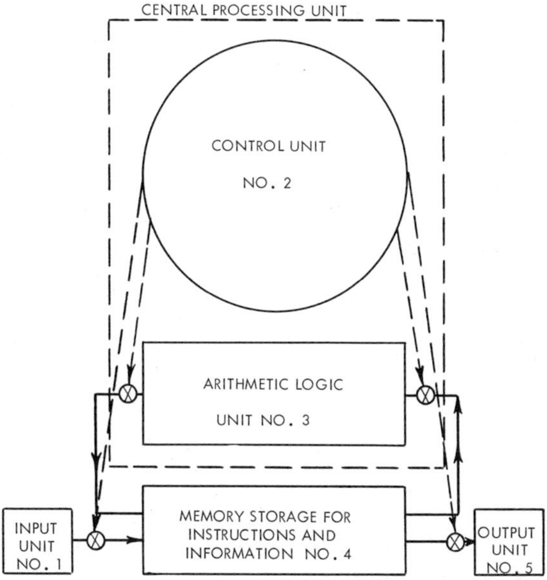

No. on Figure	Slide Rule Calculations	Computer Calculations
1	Input from work sheet	Input from cards
2	You, the human operator	Control unit
3	The calculator or slide rule	Arithmetic unit
4	Your memory or work sheet	Memory storage
5	Output onto work sheet	Output: cards, print-out device, etc.

by the circled X's. Each unit is, of course, a very complex organization of electrical and mechanical components, but, for our purpose of the moment, the boxes can serve.

In the desk calculator, you, the human control, replace the control unit of the computer. The calculator, or slide rule, is the arithmetic unit. Your work sheet, where you jot down information, or your memory is the memory storage. The input is the problem information taken from the work sheet, and the output is the problem information placed on the work sheet. The analogy is more readily followed by the table at the bottom of the illustration.

Computer Language

Before discussing the computer in detail, it is necessary to have some knowledge of the internal language used by the computer to communicate among the various components. These are primarily internal languages because the operator addresses today's modern computer using the conventional number and alphabet system.

BINARY NUMBERING SYSTEM

It is not difficult—although perhaps somewhat fanciful—to imagine that our timeworn, ten-digit numbering system began with some caveman sitting by his fire, counting wolf pelts (or wives) and, finding the customary pebbles out of reach, or too hot, started counting on his toes. Having ten of them, it was natural that he should use this as the basis of his counting system. The mathematician would say that this system, with its base of ten, had a *radix* of ten. There are other systems with other radices; but the one discussed here has a radix of two.

What is wrong with the old ten-radix system? After all, we have lived with it for many years. The trouble is that an electronic computer finds it difficult to recognize each of the ten different conditions or states required for a ten-radix number. This is easy to understand when we remember that, because of the electronic age, we are living more and more in a "two-condition" world. Either things are on, or they aren't.

For example, the furnace is on or off, the lights are on or off; and this is extended to the paper tapes and data cards for computers: there are holes or there are no holes. It is difficult for the modern machine to work with shades of meaning: everything must be either black or white, and this calls for a new numbering system, one with only two numbers. In referring to a two-number system, the *one* state is referred to as a *bit*. This two-number idea is about as disquieting, on first thought, as the mirror room in a house of horrors; it isn't bad, however, when one gets used to it.

There is a standard form by which any numbering system can be expressed. This is a series which has the general form:

$$A \times r^0 + B \times r^1 + C \times r^2 + D \times r^3 \ldots$$

or, for the ten-radix system:

$$A(10)^0 + B(10)^1 + C(10)^2 + D(10)^3 \ldots$$

For example, consider the number 1978:

$$\begin{aligned} A \times 10^0 &= 8 \times 1 = 8 \\ B \times 10^1 &= 7 \times 10 = 70 \\ C \times 10^2 &= 9 \times 100 = 900 \\ D \times 10^3 &= 1 \times 1000 = \underline{1000} \\ & \qquad\qquad\qquad 1978 \end{aligned}$$

It is obvious that the numbers 1, 9, 7 and 8 are the coefficients *D*, *C*, *B* and A.

Now that the system is apparent in our customary ten-digit numbering systems, see how the binary system can be developed. The series can be written:

$$A(2)^0 + B(2)^1 + C(2)^2 + D(2)^3 \ldots$$

$$\begin{aligned}
A \times (2)^0 &= 0 \times 1 = 0\\
B \times (2)^1 &= 1 \times 2 = 2\\
C \times (2)^2 &= 0 \times 4 = 0\\
D \times (2)^3 &= 1 \times 8 = 8\\
E \times (2)^4 &= 1 \times 16 = 16\\
F \times (2)^5 &= 1 \times 32 = 32\\
G \times (2)^6 &= 0 \times 64 = 00\\
H \times (2)^7 &= 1 \times 128 = 128\\
I \times (2)^8 &= 1 \times 256 = 256\\
J \times (2)^9 &= 1 \times 512 = 512\\
K \times (2)^{10} &= 1 \times 1024 = 1024
\end{aligned}$$

The number (in binary) 11110111010 = $\overline{1978}$
(the-bottom-to-top sequence of column 3).

If the number had not been a whole number, for example, 19.5 (with a decimal point between 9 and 5), no particular trouble would have been encountered.

$$\begin{aligned}
a(2)^{-1} &= 1 \times 2^{-1} = .5\\
A(2)^0 &= 1 \times 2^0 = 1.0\\
B(2)^1 &= 1 \times 2^1 = 2.0\\
C(2)^2 &= 0 \times 2^2 = 0.0\\
D(2)^3 &= 0 \times 2^3 = 0.0\\
E(2)^4 &= 1 \times 2^4 = 16.0
\end{aligned}$$

The binary number 10011.1 = $\overline{19.5}$ in decimal form.

The arithmetic of adding, subtracting, multiplying and dividing can be carried out in the binary system the same as in the ten-digit system. For convenience in checking results, the conversion table is inserted first:

Conversion Table

Ten	*Binary*	*Ten*	*Binary*	*Ten*	*Binary*
0	0	10	1010	20	10100
1	1	11	1011	21	10101
2	10	12	1100	22	10110
3	11	13	1101	23	10111
4	100	14	1110	24	11000
5	101	15	1111	25	11001
6	110	16	10000	26	11010
7	111	17	10001	27	11011
8	1000	18	10010	28	11100
9	1001	19	10011	29	11101
				30	11110

Examples

Addition

$$\begin{array}{rr} 9 & 1001\\ +6 & 110\\ \hline 15 = & 1111 \end{array}$$

Subtraction

$$\begin{array}{rr} 9 & 1001\\ -6 & 110\\ \hline 3 = & 11 \end{array}$$

Multiplication

$$\begin{array}{rr} 6 & 110\\ \times 3 & 11\\ \hline & 110\\ & 110\\ \hline 18 = & 10010 \end{array}$$

Division

$$6/3 = 2, \quad \frac{110}{11} = 10$$

The scheme is obvious when it is observed that $1 + 1 = 2$, but, in the binary system, $1 + 1 = 10$. The number to the left is carried as in the conventional system.

Not only is the electronic computer a near-illiterate with its "bi-syllable" language, it is also unsophisticated in arithmetic, for all it can do is add. So, if the computer wishes to do any of the other grade-school exercises, such as subtracting, multiplying or dividing, it must do them—in a roundabout fashion—by addition. The computer's secret of success is that it can add extremely fast.

Addition and Subtraction

The computer does not add a series of numbers at one crack, as we might do by longhand, but rather step-by-step. For instance, $6 + 7 + 3$ would be added (6) 110 + (7) 111 = (13) 1101, and then (13) 1101 + (3) 11 = (16) 10000. This method would be slow and long by hand operations, but not for the computer's quick electronic "thinking."

Subtraction, strangely enough, is also done by addition, addition of the complement of the number to be subtracted (subtrahend) to the number from which it is to be subtracted (minuend). The place farthest to the left is then ignored. As an example:

$$9 - 6 = 3 \quad \text{or} \quad 9 + 4 = \not{1}3$$

In the binary system, the complement is easily determined by changing 1's to 0's and 0's to 1's, and by adding a 1 in the least significant position. The complement of (6) 0110 is 1001 + 0001 = 1010, which, when added to (9) 1001, gives the correct answer.

$$\begin{array}{lr} (9) & 1001 \\ & 1010 \\ \hline (3) & \not{1}0011 \end{array}$$

Multiplication and Division

The process of multiplication is nothing but an extension of addition:

$$\begin{array}{rrl} (4) & 100 & \text{multiplicand} \\ \times\ (7) & 111 & \text{multiplier} \\ \hline & 100 & \\ & 100 & \\ & 100 & \\ \hline (28) & 11100 & \text{product} \end{array}$$

While this has been done in one step, the machine would actually take as many steps as there are numbers in the multiplier, and add each one.

Division, as could be expected, is a series of subtractions, and you will recall that subtraction is done by adding complements. It will be easier to show here if subtractions are used, realizing, of course, that the machine does it by adding complements:

$$\text{Division:}\quad 1000\ (8)\ \begin{array}{r} 11 \\ \sqrt{11100} \\ 1000 \\ \hline 1100 \\ 1000 \\ \hline 100 \end{array}\ (28)$$

(Dividend $= 11\frac{100}{1000}$ [quotient] in binary, or $3\frac{4}{8}$ in the decimal system, as can be seen by the Conversion Table.)

The machine does this by making a series of subtractions until the remainder changes sign from plus to minus, the answer being one less than the number of subtractions. For example:

$$1000\ (8)\ \begin{array}{r} \sqrt{11100} \\ 1000 \\ \hline 10100 \\ 1000 \\ \hline 1100 \\ 1000 \\ \hline 100 \\ 1000 \\ \hline -100 \end{array}\ (28)\quad \left.\begin{array}{c} 1 \\ \\ 1 \\ \\ 1 \\ \\ 1 \end{array}\right\} = 4,\ 4 - 1 = 3,\ \text{which is 11 in binary; the answer then is: } 11\frac{100}{1000},\ \text{or } 3\tfrac{1}{2},\ \text{as shown before.}$$

And so it is that computers can work in a realm of two numbers. It should be pointed out that some computers work directly with the binary form while others code the information in some more convenient form.

BINARY CODING OF DECIMAL DIGITS

The necessity and mystery of a two-state numbering system should be acceptable now, but an obvious drawback to this system should have attracted your attention. How can a person be expected to become familiar with this system? The memory of man seems quite capable of remembering long decimal numbers, but binary numbers—of any length—are quite meaningless. To overcome this, each decimal number may be coded into a group of binary *bits,* which are easily remembered. The computer then operates on this group of bits which represents the decimal digit. To become aware of how this system works, consider the most direct way of coding the decimal digits for the number 532, using the corresponding binary for each digit:

$$\overbrace{0101}^{5}\qquad \overbrace{0011}^{3}\qquad \overbrace{0010}^{2}$$

As can be seen, this is much easier to understand and to remember than 532 represented directly by the binary 10001010.

This illustrated numbering system is not a common one because it lacks many of the advantages of other codes. Not only should a code be easy to visualize, it should also take a minimum amount of space in the computer's memory and should lend itself to rapid manipulation within the machine. There is the problem of "complementing," which must be done within the design characteristics of the computer. In addition, the codes used today incorporate self-checking methods to insure accuracy. The characters are checked when they enter the computer to determine whether or not they are *valid* for the machine. Even-bit characters are forced to assume an odd number of bits when they enter by the addition of a *check bit*. Each character is frequently given a *parity check* during the process to determine if it has an odd number of bits.

Although many codes have been developed for computers, only the two which are to be found in the most common machine will be discussed. These are illustrated in Figure 14–3, and, as you will notice, a bit is represented by

					Biquinary						
Decimal Digit	8	4	2	1	5	0	4	3	2	1	0
0	0	0	0	0	0	●	0	0	0	0	●
1	0	0	0	●	0	●	0	0	0	●	0
2	0	0	●	0	0	●	0	0	●	0	0
3	0	0	●	●	0	●	0	●	0	0	0
4	0	●	0	0	0	●	●	0	0	0	0
5	0	●	0	●	●	0	0	0	0	0	●
6	0	●	●	0	●	0	0	0	0	●	0
7	0	●	●	●	●	0	0	0	●	0	0
8	●	0	0	0	●	0	0	●	0	0	0
9	●	0	0	●	●	0	●	0	0	0	0

Figure 14–3
Computer Codes

a black dot, which might represent a magnetized spot on a tape, a hole in a card, or other media using a two-state system. These two codes are referred to as weighted decimal codes because each place in the code is assigned a weighted value, and the decimal value is determined by adding these weights.

Biquinary Code

This is the code used on the IBM 650 control panel because it is easy to read, as is illustrated in Figure 14–4. It is not the code, however, which is used for the internal operations of the machine.

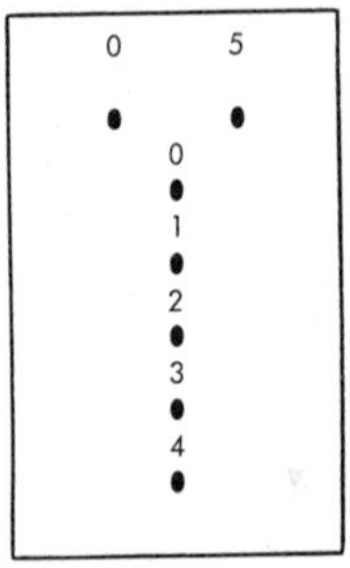

Figure 14–4
Biquinary Display

8-4-2-1 Code

This code is not unlike the one used for hand-punched cards illustrated in Chapter 12. It is the basis of other codes which are frequently used in computer designs. For example, the code for the IBM 1401 uses the 8–4–2–1 code with two additional places, A and B, for coding the alphabet. This is illustrated in Figure 14–5, and you will notice an additional position, C, is

Figure 14–5

1401 Code

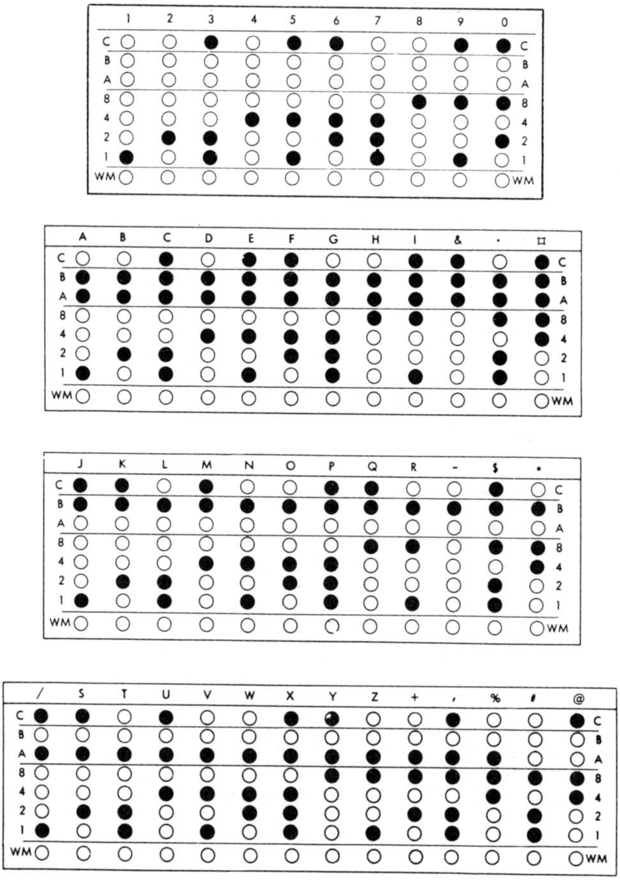

added for *parity checking*. This last feature requires that all characters have an odd bit count; a *check bit* is added to C when there is an even number of bits in a column.

COMPUTER WORDS

A group of characters treated by the computer as a unit is called a *word*. The word may be a piece of information, *data*, or an *instruction*. There is no way of telling one from the other except by the storage position, for in the computer the instructions are stored along with the data.

Fixed Word Length

The analogy has been made between the post office box system and the memory of computers, for it is essential not only to know what is in the box but also to know where the box is located. In a fixed-word-length computer there is a limit to the length of a word that can be placed in the box or *cell:* the computer memory is designed for only so much information, and no more can be placed in the cell. For example, a word length might be ten characters plus a sign. For data, this might look like Figure 14–6*a*, while the same block representing an instruction might look like Figure 14–6*b*.

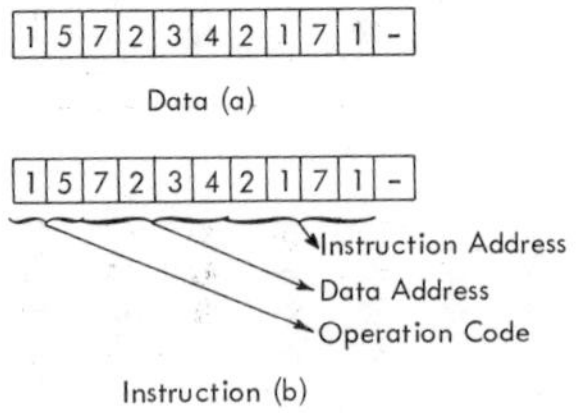

Figure 14–6
Fixed Word Length

(The use of the instruction word will be more fully developed at the point where it is going to be used.)

Variable Word Length

In the computers designed for variable word lengths, there are no cells designated, but the memory is subdivided into individual character positions. Words are stored in successive character positions, with an *end of word* mark placed at the end of the series. The mechanics of this process will be illustrated in the discussion of computer memories.

Computer System Input-Output Components

Before discussing the processing unit of the computer, it is desirable to take a look at the input and output units. There are a number of different devices which can be used for either the input or output units, and can also be used as part of the processing unit. The devices we will discuss are:

Input	*Output*
Punched cards	Punched cards
Punched tape	Magnetic tape
Magnetic tape	Printers
Magnetic character readers	Display units

It would be highly desirable if the input media could be the by-product of some operation, such as typing a document or billing a customer. Often this is impossible, and the information for the computer must be produced by card-punch machines from handwritten documents. However, producing the input as a by-product is a goal for which to strive, and it is being done successfully by means of special time clocks, scales which have a card output, and cash registers which have paper tape output.

If the information is transmitted to the computer as it is produced, it is said to be an *on-line* operation. It is more common to feed the information into the computer through an auxiliary operation.

PUNCHED CARD INPUT AND OUTPUT

The punched card (described in Chapter 12) is the most common form of computer input. The discussion in this text will be restricted to the conventional layout, but others—as dictated by the machine and the program—are also in use.

The cards are read by machines which operate on the same principles as those discussed in the earlier chapter. In fact, some of these machines can be attached to computers to function as the reading, punching, and print-out units.

A special read-punch unit is shown in Figure 14–7*a* and its schematic in Figure 14–7*b*. This unit has two card feeds. The read side operates at a

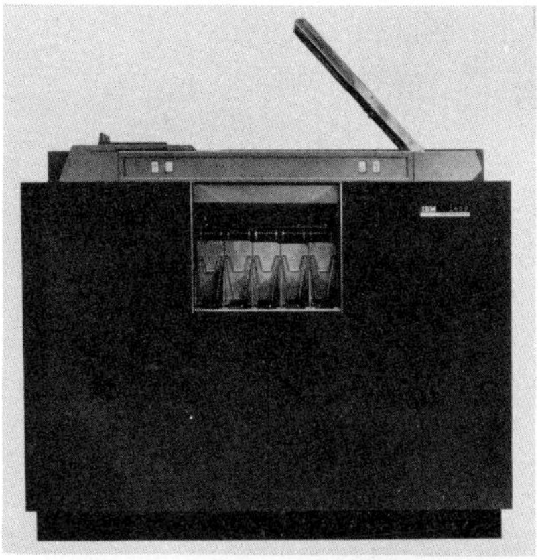

Figure 14–7*a*

Card Read-Punch

Figure 14–7*b*

Card Read-Punch Schematic

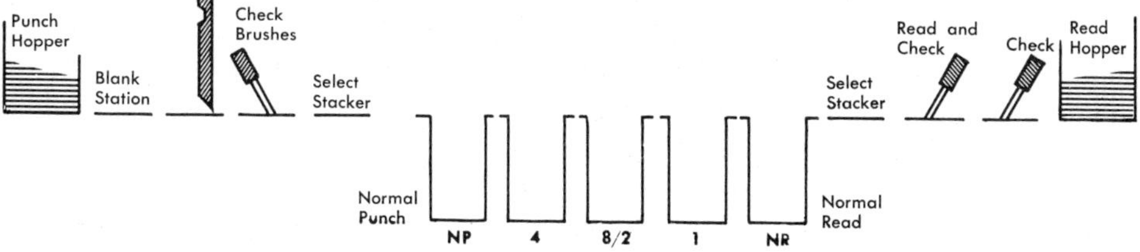

maximum speed of 800 cards a minute, passing the card under two sets of brushes. The hole count is checked between the two sets and the data are then directed to the processing unit. The punch side operates at 250 cards per minute, and also provides for a hole count check. Normally the cards will be stacked in the pocket nearest their feed hopper, but they can be directed to the two adjacent pockets (similar to the collator) as well.

The feed hoppers on this machine are of large capacity, and the stackers have a radial design which makes it possible to remove the cards with ease without stopping the machine. Since there are no electrical connections between the read and punch side of the machine, all information must pass through the processor.

MAGNETIC TAPE INPUT, OUTPUT, AND MEMORY

Magnetic tape serves the multiple purpose of input, output or memory, but, regardless of its application, the equipment and tape are the same.

The tape itself is usually plastic, coated with a magnetic substance, and is similar to the tapes used in home recording machines. Various widths of tapes have been used, from a fraction of an inch to several inches, but the most common width is one-half inch. The tape is purchased on $10\frac{1}{2}$-inch reels that hold 2,400 feet.

Information is recorded on the tape as magnetized spots, or bits, by magnetic read-write heads (Figure 14–8). The information is recorded in chan-

Figure 14–8

Magnetic Read-Write Heads

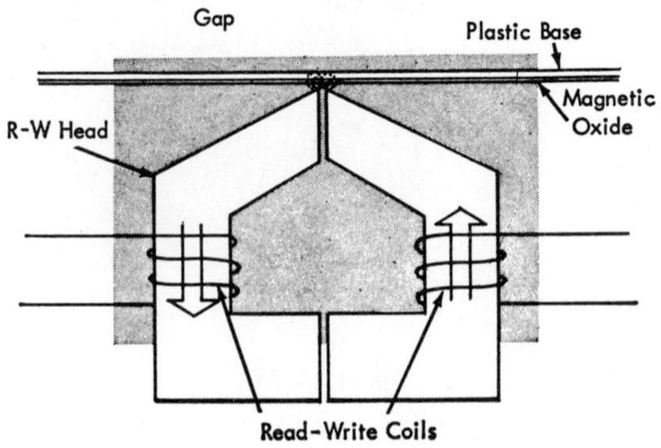

nels, as shown in Figure 14–9*a*. The code illustrated conforms to the one discussed previously, and, as you might expect, other coding systems can also be used. Information is usually recorded in blocks (Figure 14–9*b*). The size of the recorded blocks can be fixed or variable, depending upon the characteristics of the machine. The tape comes to rest with the magnetic head in

Figure 14–9*a*

Coded Magnetic Tape

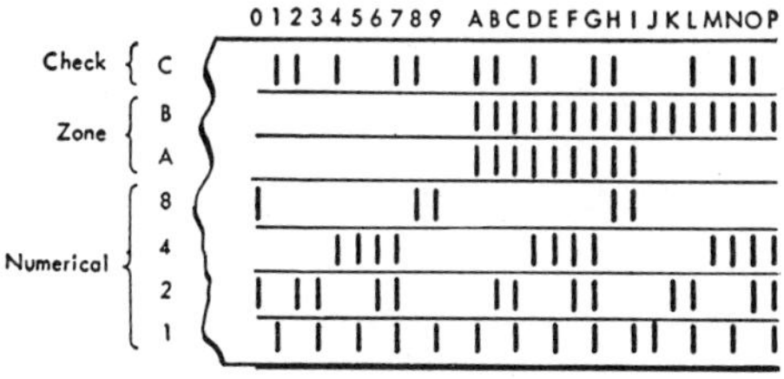

Figure 14–9*b*

Record Blocks

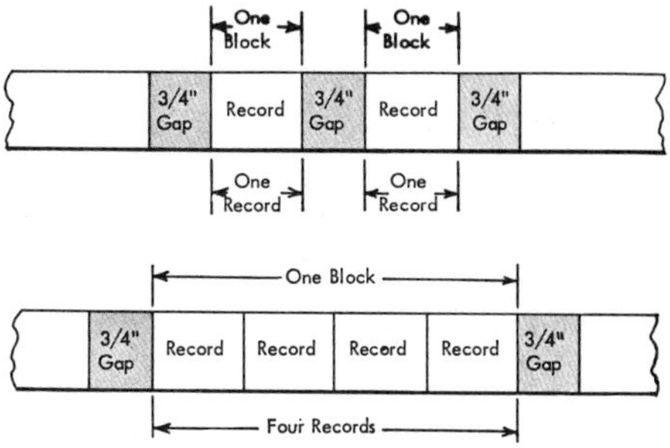

the middle of the "gap." The gap is essential for the acceleration and deceleration of the tape and for the proper functioning of the machine.

The reading process is nondestructive, so the information remains indefinitely. Writing, of course, destroys the previous information. To prevent accidental writing, which would destroy records, reels are equipped with a safety ring. Only when the ring is in place can writing occur.

Figure 14–10*a* shows a typical magnetic tape unit, and the schematic is shown in Figure 14–10*b*. The tape feed mechanism is complicated by the

Figure 14–10*a*

Typical Magnetic Tape Unit

Figure 14–10*b*

Schematic of Tape Unit

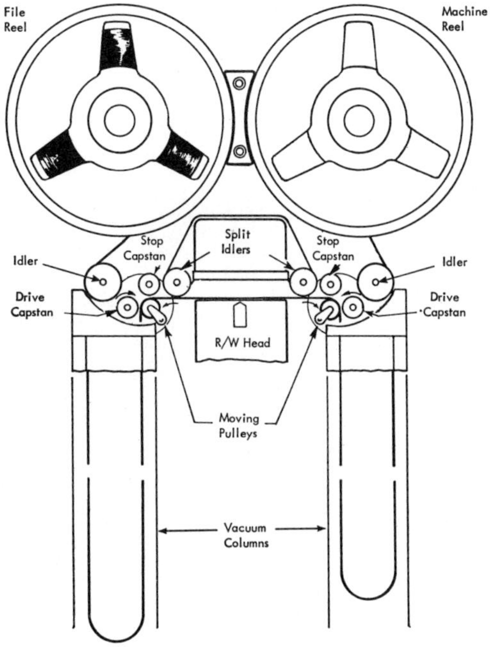

Courtesy of IBM Corp.

need to move the tape from reel to reel rapidly and to stop it quickly. This is made more difficult because of the inertia of the reels and the fragility of the tapes. The tape is moved across the magnetic heads when forced against a rotating drive capstan, and is stopped when it is forced against a stop capstan. The loops of tape which are stored in the vacuum columns act as buffers between the movement of the reels and the sensitive movement of the tape over the magnetic head.

Magnetic tape has become a well accepted form of storage and input-output media because of its large storage capacity, which can be added to easily by using more reels. A number of magnetic tape units can be under the command of one processing unit, extending the storage capacity and contributing to the versatility of the installation.

The major disadvantage of tape is its long access time. Since the information is placed on the reel in sequential order, it requires a long time to search along the length of tape to find the required information. In addition, it is difficult to update records when they need to be changed.

PAPER TAPE INPUT

Paper tape, which was originally applied to transmitting messages over telegraph wires, has been extended to include computer applications. Not only is it used to communicate between data processing units in remote locations, it is also used as a main input or auxiliary input for computers (Figure 14–11).

Figure 14–11

Paper Tape Punch and Read Units

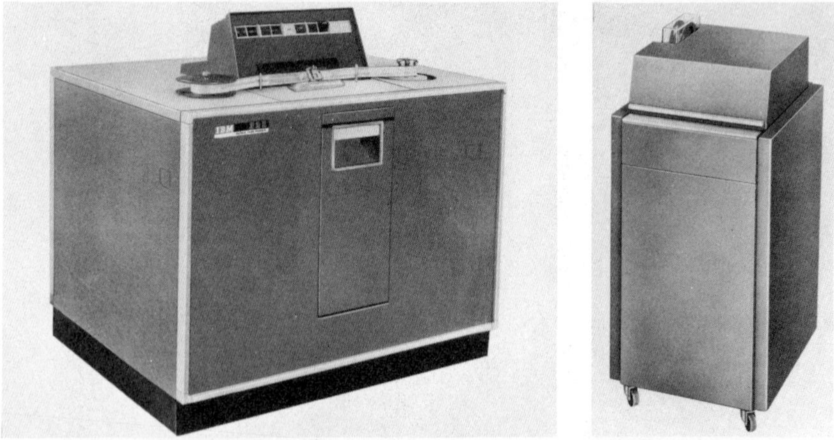

Courtesy of IBM Corp.

The tape is either partially perforated, with the advantage of being "chadless," or, as is more common with computers, completely perforated. Tapes vary in width, depending upon the application, but are generally about one inch wide. The tape is driven by a sprocket wheel which engages a series of small holes running the length of the tape. The information is recorded as holes spaced ten to the inch. The reading speed of the tape varies between 20 characters per second to a couple of thousand per second, depending upon how it is being used and the reading method. Electromechanical methods of reading are slow, compared with the much faster photoelectric reading methods. Punching the tape is an even slower process.

One method for long-distance transmission of information converts data from punched cards to paper tape, and sends the information over telephone and telegraph lines to produce a duplicate tape at the other end of the line, where it is converted back to punched cards. Paper tape records can be produced as a product, or by-product, of typewriters, calculators, bookkeeping machines, or cash registers, as well as special telephone and telegraph instruments.

Telegraph companies have used five-channel tapes, but there are other systems which use six, seven, or eight channels. Two of the most popular methods of coding tape are described here.

Five-Channel Code

Figure 14–12 illustrates the five-channel code as used for numbers and the alphabet. A brief explanation of the abbreviations should make the code easier to understand. Since there is a limited number of possible combina-

Figure 14–12

Five-Channel Code

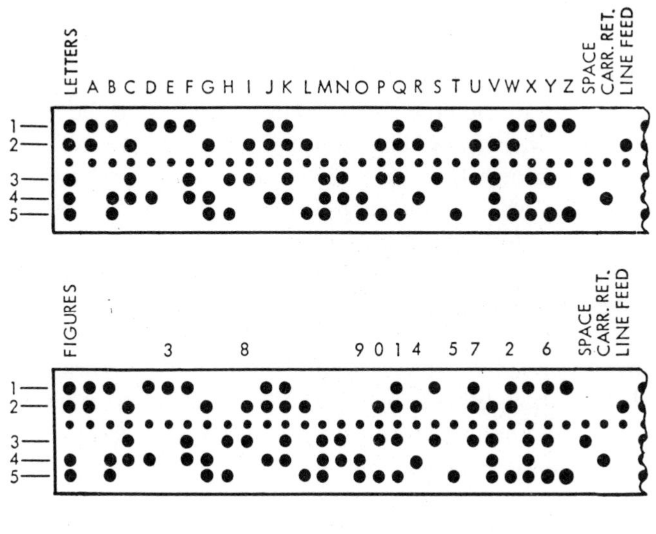

tions with this code, it is necessary to use a shift system. When the numbers are coded, a code letter precedes the section of the tape with the numbers. However, when the "letters code" precedes a section it means that the characters represent letters of the alphabet. In addition, there are code letters which control the operations of the receiving device. Such instructions as carriage return, line feed, and spacing can be conveyed.

Eight-Channel Code

The method of coding the eight-channel tape (Figure 14–13) is similar to the binary coded decimal system previously discussed. The lower four channels of the tape are used to represent the numbers by a combination, one or more, of the 1, 2, 4 and 8 channels. The X and 0 punches are similar

Figure 14–13

Eight-Channel Code

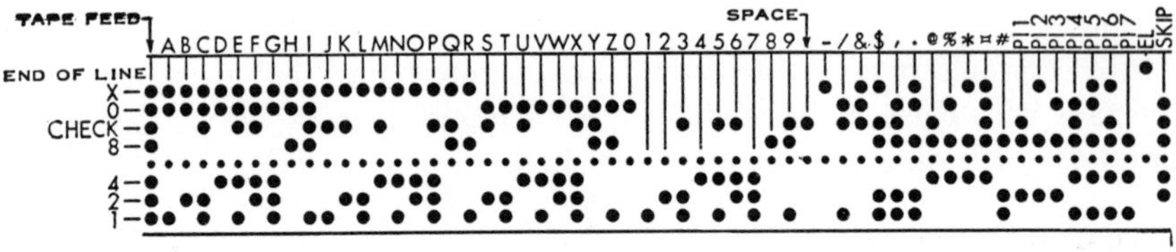

to the zone punches on an IBM card. These channels are combined with the number channels to record the alphabet, as shown. And a parity check column is designated by the word "check."

In addition to the special characters coded (as shown), there are instructions that are coded for the machine. The "end of line" channel is used to indicate the end of the record on the tape. The "tape feed code" is used to indicate blank character positions and instructs the reader to automatically skip over these areas.

Passkey Code

Any deficiencies in the tape codes discussed promise to be eliminated in a new standard code, *Passkey*. This code contains seven positions, which will yield 128 bits of information, or four times as many combinations as will five positions. This will be more than enough to satisfy the demand for the alphabet, numbers, and special characters.

Until recently, the codes in common use had their origin in the printing-telegraph codes developed before the turn of the century. Since that time, the demand on such coding systems has outgrown the vision of the originator. Passkey derived its name from the Proposed American Standard Code for Information Interchange, PASCII. It has already been accepted by many users, and undoubtedly all the others will soon fall in line, thereby endorsing universal acceptance.

MAGNETIC-INK CHARACTER READERS: INPUT

Another means of input which is of growing interest, especially in the field of commercial banking, is the magnetic-ink character, which can be read both by man and machine. Figure 14–14 shows a typical application

Figure 14–14

Example of Magnetic Characters

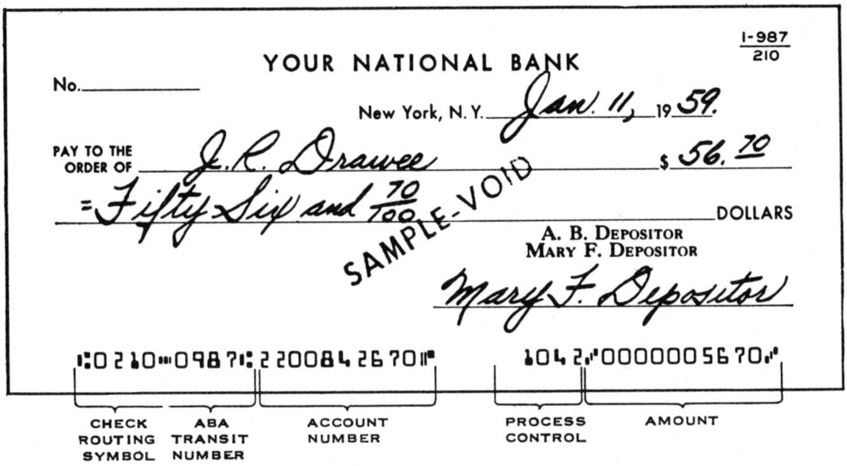

of the magnetic ink, with the figures at the bottom inscribed by a special electric typewriter. Later, these forms may be handled directly by a sorter, converted to magnetic tape, or fed on-line directly to a computer.

PRINTERS: OUTPUT

The electric typewriter is often used as an input-output device, especially in computers for engineering applications. Because of the single action of each individual key, the typewriter is a relatively slow output device.

Several line-at-a-time printers are capable of printing much faster than the typewriter, and one which uses a series of type bars raised to the correct position before imprinting was discussed in the card-data processing section. This device, however, is too slow for modern applications.

The chain printer (Figure 14–15) can print up to 132 positions on a line at the rate of 600 lines per minute. This printer uses engraved type assembled in a chain which travels horizontally (Figure 14–16). The paper is pressed against one piece of type in the moving chain by a magnetically actuated hammer.

The wire matrix printer prints the characters as an array of dots formed by a rectangle of 5 dots by 7 dots (illustrated in Figure 14–17). The dots are

Figure 14–15
Chain Printer

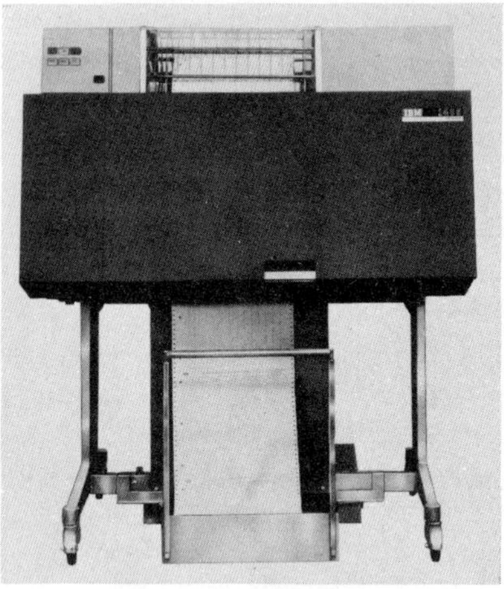

Figure 14–16
Print Chain

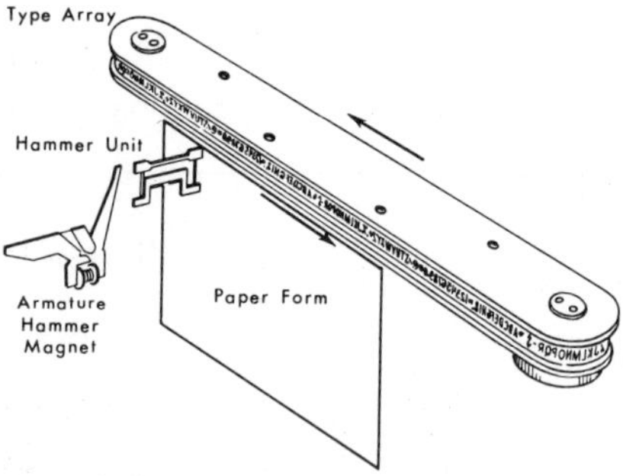

Figure 14–17
Wire Matrix Print

formed by the ends of wires, extended to form the proper patterns, which are pressed against an ink ribbon in contact with the paper. The characters can be printed 120 to the line at a rate of 500 or 1,000 lines per minute.

DISPLAY UNITS

There are a number of nonmechanical printers on the market. Because these devices do not have to contend with the inertia of heavy parts, they are capable of printing at unbelievable speeds. The IBM 2250 Display Unit has a cathode-ray tube as its principal component, on which alphanumeric, or graphic information is displayed at high speed to provide visual communication between a computer and its user. These units may be located some distance from the computer, but the user may key-in instructions or identifications from the display keyboard.

Central Processing Unit

The central processing unit supervises and controls the whole computer system, performing the arithmetic, editing, logic, and control necessary. Regrettably, it is impossible to discuss this part of the computer comprehensively in the short space available. However, the student, especially the engineering and science student, should enjoy further explorations into the subject. Several of the references in the bibliography should make rewarding reading excursions.

Computers, like other electronic devices, have gone through the evolutionary change with the transition to the transistor. The first computers used electrical relays for switching, but hundreds of relays with their electrical and mechanical weaknesses made a very unreliable computer. The next and very natural step was to the vacuum tube, which is an effective switch as it "gates" the flow of electrons in a circuit. The trouble with the vacuum tube, however, is that it requires much useless power, which is dissipated as undesirable heat. This, in turn, requires additional air-conditioning machinery, which in turn adds to the cost of a computer installation. Tubes also require space, are fragile, and are not too reliable.

The transistorizing of computer designs has been nearly completed. This, along with the innovations of improved circuits and miniaturization, promises to make the computer an even more important tool for engineers and industrialists.

Although there are hundreds and thousands of circuits in the digital computer, many of them are identical, merely being repeated time after time. Actually, there are only some 40 or 50 different types of circuits, and of these just a few make up the bulk of the computer circuitry, the rest being clocking circuits, power supplies, and other auxiliary circuits. Such "redundancy" of circuit components has simplified the design, manufacturing,

Figure 14–18

Replaceable Units of the Modern Computer

Courtesy of Computer Control Company, Inc.

and servicing of computers. Computers today are manufactured with quickly replaceable units, as shown in Figure 14–18.

A computer is designed in two stages, the logic design and the electrical design. One stage cannot be treated to the exclusion of the other, for the logic designer and the circuit designer must work hand in hand in a cooperative spirit. The logic designer may make certain requests, such as driving-power requirements, time for performance of the circuit, reliability, and so forth. The circuit designer will try to design a unit to fit this demand, but if it is impossible to do so, without incurring excessive costs, there must be some compromise.

Earlier it was pointed out that the computer works with binary numbers and that computers are composed of several circuits which are repeated time after time. Figure 14–19 will give you some understanding of how four

Figure 14–19

Common Computer Circuits

	Block Symbols for Computer Design	Circuit Functions	Relay Equivalent
AND Gate	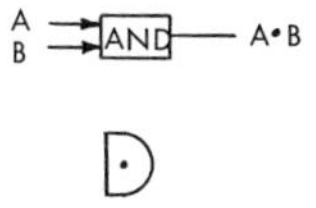	A B C 0 0 0 0 + 0 + 0 0 + + +	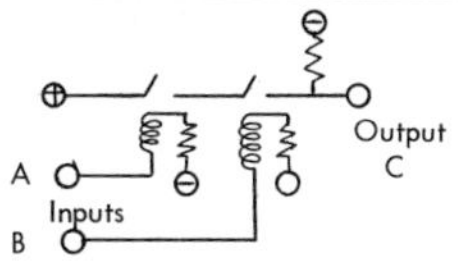
OR Gate	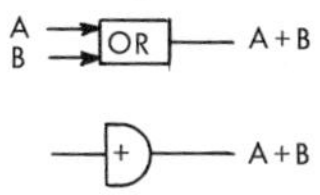	A B C 0 0 0 0 + + + 0 + + + +	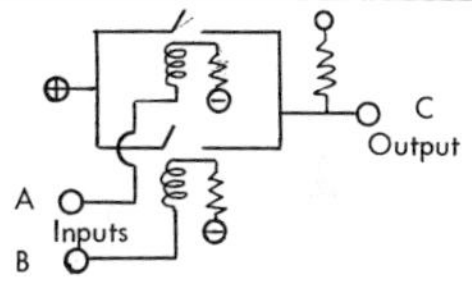
NOT Gate	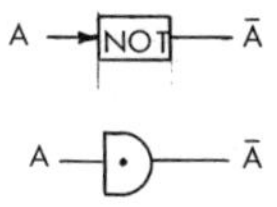	A C 0 + + 0	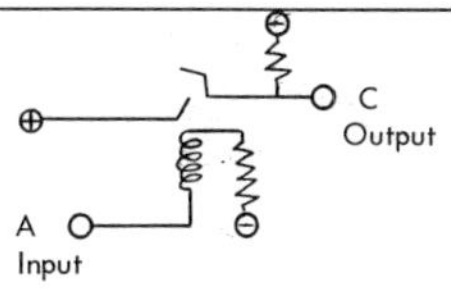
Flip-flop Circuit	———	———	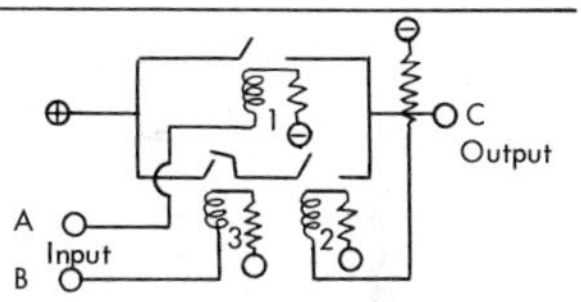

of the more common circuits function. The first column shows the decision which is made in the circuit, while the second column shows the block symbols which are used by the logic designers. The third column summarizes the decision process of the circuit. Column four shows how the circuit might be designed, using relays. The relays will be easier to use in tracing the function of the circuit.

A brief word of explanation will help us understand the circuits:

AND Gate: To raise the output voltage, C, it is essential for an input to be imposed on both A *and* B.

OR Gate: There is an output at C when there is an input at A *and/or* B.

NOT Gate: Only when current is *not* flowing in the relay will current flow at C.

The *flip-flop* circuit, which is the last one shown on the diagram, can store one *bit* of information, and is therefore a form of memory; but it is far too expensive for general storage and is restricted to applications such as *registers*, which are relatively small memories for temporary storage of information. The flip-flop circuit is a bi-stable device which will assume either stable state, depending upon its previous state at the time it receives a new impulse. The following is a brief explanation of the relay circuit, but more extensive explanations of vacuum tube and transistor circuits are to be found in the references.

Impulse A: *Relay 1* closes, which in turn closes *relay* 2. The current is maintained through *relay* 2, so the voltage is available at point *C*.

Impulse B: *Relay* 3 opens and the current is not maintained through the circuit, so the voltage at *point* C drops.

Computer Storage, or Memory

One of the important aspects of modern computers, especially those used in industry, is their ability to store, or "remember," large quantities of information. The *memory* or *storage* may be either internal, a magnetic core memory, or an external auxiliary unit, such as a magnetic tape reader. Remember that the magnetic tape cannot be considered only as a memory; it is also an input-output unit, and can serve either or both functions.

One important way of classifying memory units is by whether they have a linear, cycle, or random access.

Linear memories, such as magnetic tape, have the information distributed along the length. The tape must be searched from end to end for the information needed, so the access time depends upon the distance and the speed of the tape. A stack of cards being read can also be considered as a linear memory.

Cycle memories have storage locations which become accessible during a certain fixed time. Typical of this type of memory, as we shall see, is the magnetic drum. The information is impressed upon a certain position on the drum and is available only when that position passes under the reading head.

Random access memory is so described because every individual word, or bit of information, is equally accessible. The time is independent of the location. It does not mean that the information is selected by chance.

In the course of developing the electronic computer numerous devices have also been developed and tried as storage devices. These include such designs as ultrasonic delay lines, composed of cylinders of mercury in which vibrations are cycled until needed. Those discussed here are the ones which have survived the developmental stage and are actually in modern computers.

MAGNETIC DRUM STORAGE

The *magnetic storage drum* (Figure 14–20) is a cylinder made of brass, or bronze, or steel encased in a copper shell. It is machined to a very high degree of accuracy and is mounted in bearings that permit constant rotation at a high speed. The drum is coated by plating, or by spraying on iron oxide or a similar material.

Information is stored on the drum's magnetic surface in the form of small magnetized spots, as if thousands of small magnets were imbedded

Figure 14–20

Magnetic Storage Drum

Courtesy of The Teleregister Corp.

in the surface of the drum. The two states of the binary digits are represented by the polarity of the magnetized spots. This polarity is retained indefinitely, or until the polarity is deliberately changed by the controls of the machine.

To read and write the magnetic spots on the drum, a magnetic head is located extremely close to the surface. There are various designs of read-write heads, but the typical head consists of an electrically energized magnetic core close to the surface of the drum. If a current is passed through the coil, a magnetic field is built up across the gap, and some of the lines of force pass through the surface of the drum and magnetize the small spot that is to represent the bit. The magnetic heads are rigidly positioned—within 0.001 to 0.002 of an inch from the drum—because the efficiency drops off markedly as the space is increased.

Usually the same magnetic head is used for reading and writing. In reading, the lines of force of the magnetized bit induce an electrical current in the coil in much the same way that electricity is generated in a magneto.

It is obvious that the movement of the drum is essential to the production of a signal.

The surface of the drum is divided into imaginary strips called tracks or bands. Each track has a read-write head rigidly mounted adjacent to it. The tracks are, in turn, divided into sectors, so there are hundreds of addressable sectors—which might be considered as analogous to files where information is kept. These locations are systematically numbered and can be selected instantaneously by the computer.

The IBM 650 storage drum (Figure 14–21) has 40 circular bands and each band contains 50 ten-digit words, making a total of 2,000 words which can be placed on the drum. The addresses of these word locations are assigned four-digit numbers, from 0000 to 1999. As illustrated, the numbers on the first band run from 0000 to 0049; the second from 0050 to 0099, and so forth. (The section on Programming indicates the significance of these addresses.) Any address may be used for either data or an instruction.

Figure 14–21

Magnetic Storage Drum Addresses

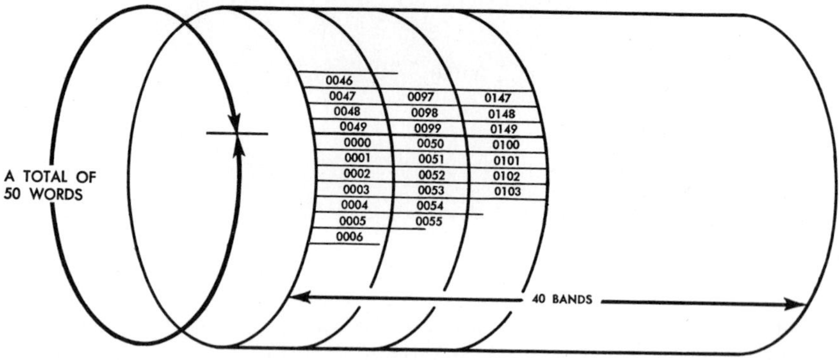

The time that it takes one word location to pass a magnetic head is called a *word time,* a basic timing unit in the computer. The maximum time that it takes to find any word on this drum is 50 word times and the average access time is 25 word times. The drum is 3.98 inches in diameter by 16 inches long, and rotates at 12,500 rpm, which is one revolution every 4.8 milliseconds, so the average access time is 2.4 milliseconds. One word time is 0.096 milliseconds, which will give you some concept of how fast the digital computer operates. Though this seems amazingly fast, computer designers have designed even much faster machines.

MAGNETIC DISK STORAGE

The magnetic disk storage (Figure 14–22) uses thin metal disks, approximately two feet in diameter, which are coated on both sides with ferrous

Figure 14–22

Magnetic Disk Storage

Courtesy of IBM Corp.

oxide. These two surfaces serve the same purpose as the outside surface of the drum. Fifty of these disks are spaced on a vertical shaft which rotates at some 1,200 rpm. Each disk has a storage capacity of 120,000 digits.

Forked reading arms traverse the disks to magnetically print and retrieve the information. Because these thin disks are bound to wobble as they rotate, the surfaces must be protected from being marred by the writing heads. This is done by air jets at the point of contact which produce an air-float, resulting in a small but relatively constant space between the disk and the magnetic head.

These storage units are *random access* units, with all information readily available. One should not get the impression that because access is random it is by chance. The one or more reading arms are traversed at the command of the processor to select the disk, after which the arm moves inward to select the proper track and information. This form of memory has been found suitable for manufacturing control applications because of the large quantity of information which is accessible.

An extension of the disk memory is the *disk pack* (Figure 14–23). A number of disks is packaged as a unit and the unit can be added to or removed from the computer system. This means that disk packs can be treated as separate account categories, such as accounts receivable, inventory items,

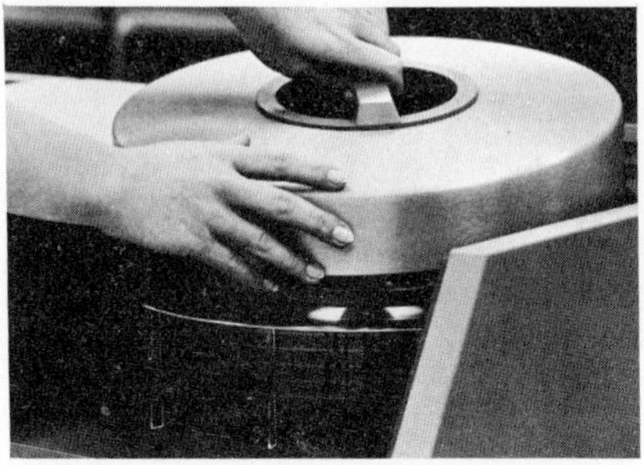

Figure 14–23
Disk Pack

and so forth. This adds considerably to the versatility of the computer, especially when it is used in the retailing and banking businesses.

MAGNETIC CORE MEMORIES

The magnetic core memory appeared in the first machines in the early 1950s. Although it is expensive to construct, it offers the advantages of being a nonmechanical, reliable memory that occupies a small space and consumes little power.

The heart of the core memory is a small toroid- or doughnut-shaped magnet, 30 to 50 thousandths of an inch in diameter, pressed out of ferric oxide powder and other materials and then sintered at a high temperature. The memory depends upon the two stable states of the magnet induced by a grid or matrix of wires upon which the magnets are strung like so many tiny beads (Figure 14–24*a*). When a current of sufficient magnitude is passed in one direction through the core, it is magnetized in one direction (Figure 14–24*b*). When the current is reversed, and is of sufficient magnitude, the magnetism of the core is in the opposite direction (as shown). It

Figure 14–24
Magnetic Core Memory

(a) **(b)**

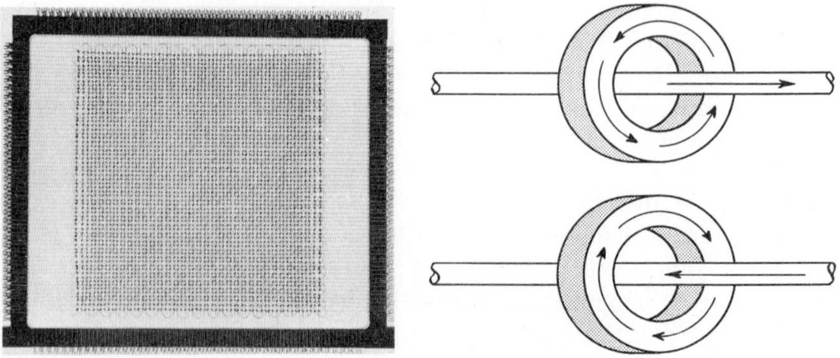

is apparent that there are two states available which can represent the binary numbering system.

Since the magnet must have two definable states which must be retained indefinitely, the magnetic material must be chosen with care. Illustrated in Figure 14–25*a* is the ideal hysteresis loop for a magnetic core. The magnetic flux is shown on the vertical axis, plotted against the flow of current in the wire. Notice that in the ideal magnet the direction of the flux does not shift until nearly all the total current is flowing (*path* A). As the current is reversed, the magnetism does not change again until nearly all the total current is flowing (as shown in *path B*).

Figure 14–25

(a) Hysteresis Loop

(b) Magnetic Cores

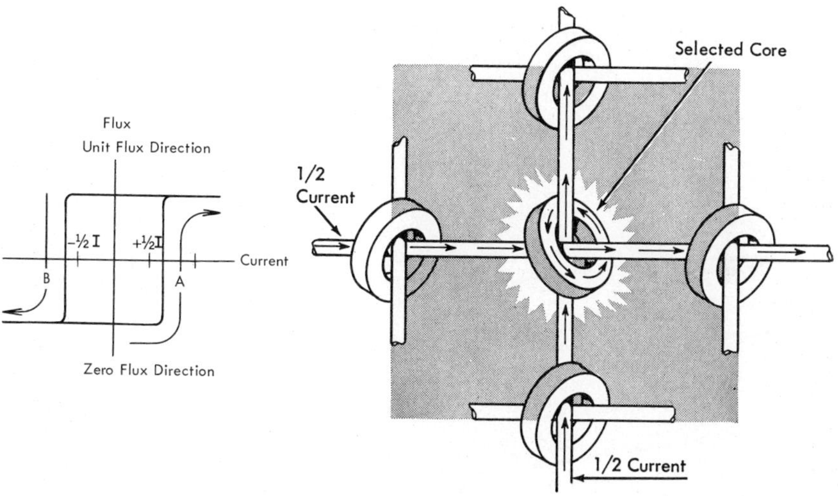

These cores are strung in a coordinate system (Figure 14–25*b*), with the address of any bit of information being the intersection of two wires. Each of the wires, which intersect at the address, will carry only a fraction of the current required to make the core change its magnetic direction, but the two wires intersecting at this point will carry, when combined, enough current to change the direction of the polarity. Since one wire alone does not carry enough current to change the polarity of the magnet, only the one at the intersection will be changed.

The cores in their stacked matrices form a three-coordinate system. The X and Y coordinates represent the address of the character, while the Z coordinate represents the character. A single column of cores, all with the same X and Y coordinates, represents a single character in the memory (shown in Figure 14–26*a*). Notice how the matrix presents a coded binary system, as discussed before. For variable word lengths there is an additional matrix for *end of word* designations.

Now that we see how information is read into a core memory, let us observe how this information may be read out. The matrix is laced by another wire (Figure 14–26*b*) called the sense wire. If the coordinate wires are impulsed, in turn, with a negative impulse, the core magnets which are zero with a negative state will not be influenced. Consequently, there will be no signal imposed upon the sense wire. But if a core magnet had a "one" of positive state when it received the impulse, it would "flip" to the zero state. This change in the magnetic field around the sense wire would induce a voltage which would be read out of the memory.

Figure 14–26

(a)
Stacked Matrices

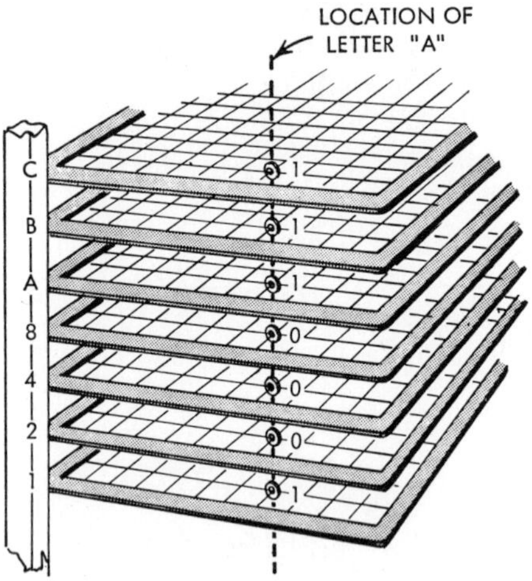

(b)
Read-Out Method

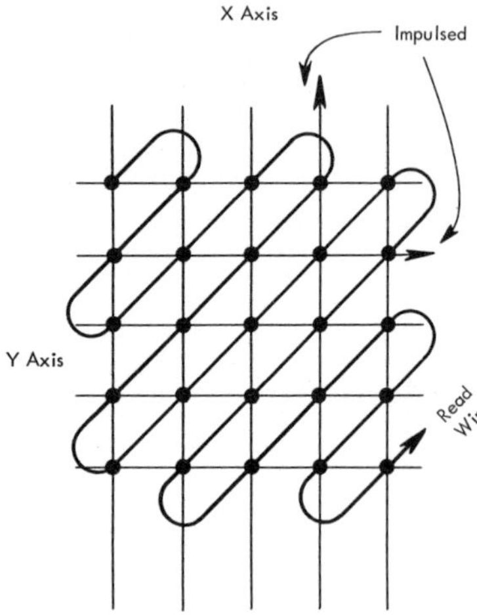

This process of reading obviously destroys the information in the memory, and it is essential to regenerate the information and return it to the storage. This is done electronically, as is the switching required for the matrix. Magnetic core memories are ideally suited for parallel arithmetic operations, which makes them especially desirable for high-speed operations.

REGISTER

A register is a small memory unit which is capable of receiving, holding, and transferring information as directed by the control circuits. These registers may be composed of vacuum tubes, transistors, or magnetic cores.

The register in the machine is named for the function it performs. If it is to hold the information regarding the location of data, it is called an *address register*; and an *instruction register* holds the instructions while they are being executed. For the more important registers, there are small lights on the control panel that indicate the register's contents so the operator can make a check any time he desires. The register is a versatile device and will enter into the discussion again when we examine how a computer is instructed.

SUMMARY

The history of the modern computer has been short and the developments fantastically rapid. It has been marked by the birth and consolidation of many companies, as is evidenced by the stock market reports of companies in this industry. If you have learned the principles of computer hardware you will have a strong background upon which to build in the future.

The software has also been punctuated by many historical bench marks. These you will also understand better if you have absorbed the principles of how a computer functions: the way it counts, and the way you can converse with it.

Above all, do not become overawed by this high-paid servant—even if it is "being paid" more per hour than you.

Questions

1. In what important respect is the computer different from the machines which are used with card-data processing?
2. What effect will the installation of a computer have upon the organizational structure?
3. Suggest an application of the analog computer in industry.
4. What is meant by a *fixed word length* computer? What is meant by a *variable word length* computer? What are the advantages of each?
5. What are the advantages and disadvantages of the various computer inputs?
6. Classify the memory devices as linear, cycle, or random types. Give the advantages of each.
7. What has been done to increase the print-out speeds of computers?
8. Why has the digital computer become more important in industrial applications than the analog computer?
9. What important contributions did the following men make in the history of the computer: Hollerith? Aiken? Wilkes?
10. Why is the binary system important in the design of computers?
11. Write your birth date in binary coding of decimal digits.

References

(See end of Chapter 15)

CHAPTER 15

Computer Systems

Designing systems for computers requires the knowledge of both *hardware* and *software*. Since you now have a background of how the hardware functions in the computer we can move on to making the computer our willing servant by the appropriate software.

The subject of system designing for computers will progress in three stages. First you will be introduced to flow charting for computer systems; next the "machine language" of the computer, which is used to address the machine directly; and finally the more sophisticated interpretative languages.

FLOW CHARTING

Many programmers will avoid a verbal statement of the problem, feeling that the flow diagram is statement enough. This *may* suffice, but it is often necessary to accumulate and list the information which must be conveyed. This stage may consist of collecting the forms which are presently used and of listing the source of the information and where it is needed. It may even consist of a flow chart using the techniques which have been previously described.

It would be a most talented person who could go directly to coding a problem without any intermediate steps. Quite often it is necessary to produce a *work-flow chart* showing *what* documents are being processed, followed by a detailed *block diagram* showing exactly *how* the problem is to be solved. The block diagram then becomes the basis for coding into the particular language.

Flow charts, as you have discovered, are just a method of distilling and conveying ideas. There is nothing sacred about the form of the chart or the symbols which are used. Consequently, programmers have improvised methods which reflect their ingenuity and analytical abilities. Any set of symbols can be used for these flow charts, but there is something to be said for a universal language understood by all. Attempts have been made to standardize the symbols, as illustrated in the template shown in Figure 15–1 (and which is available from one of the large computer manufacturers).

Figure 15–1

Flow-Chart Template

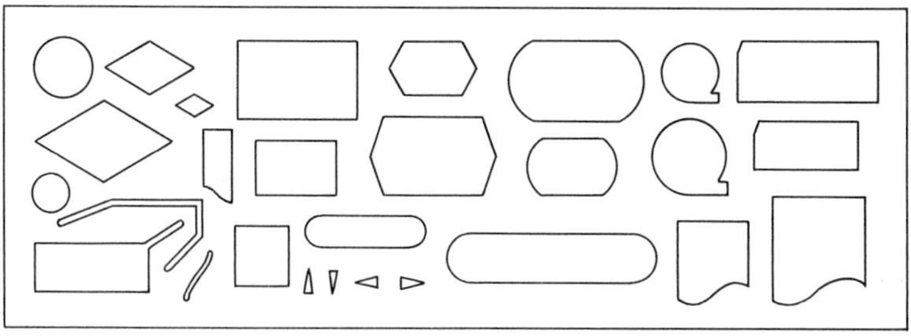

All the various charting techniques should be considered as being on a continuum of increasing refinements and one should choose the method which will fit the requirements. Two way-stations on the continuum are the work-flow chart and the block diagram.

The work-flow chart is merely a graphic representation of the data-flow network. It shows what is to be accomplished, with primary emphasis on the documents and less emphasis upon the work stations. It is used in the preliminary thinking stage of programming, and the symbols which seem to be the most useful for this phase are illustrated in Figure 15–2, along with an example of an inventory problem for which a work-flow chart has been made. This set of symbols is not restrictive and you should feel free to call on any others you may wish to use.

The block diagram, a refinement of the work-flow chart, shows in detail how the data are processed within a system. In this technique the emphasis is on the operations and the decisions necessary to complete the process. A work-flow chart shows *what* is to be done while the block diagram shows *how* the work is to be done. Again, there is a set of symbols which is used for this technique and which is illustrated in Figure 15–3 (with a brief description and a typical flow chart for part of an inventory control system).

Some people may be able to go directly to the coding stage without the block diagram but it should be pointed out that the block diagrams can serve several purposes:

1. The block diagram can be used in the development of programs, helping eliminate many errors which might otherwise occur.
2. The block diagram serves as an ideal means of communication among interested parties.
3. The block diagram serves as a guide while coding.
4. Finally, the block diagram serves as an excellent documentation of the code.

Figure 15–2

Work-Flow Chart and Symbols

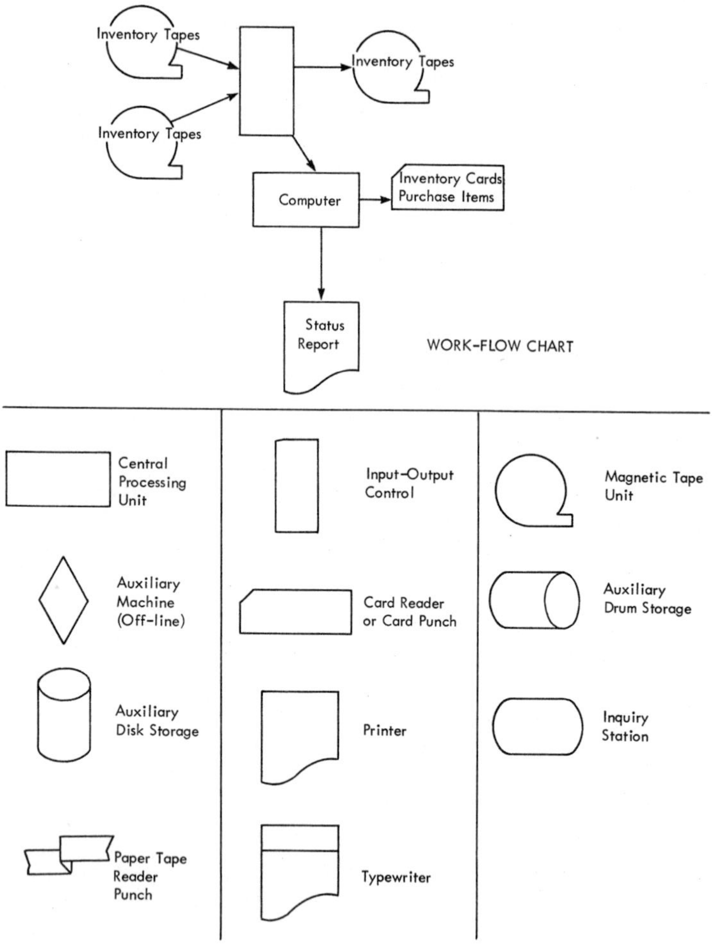

After the system is developed it is necessary to put it in a form for the computer to digest. This can be done by automatic programming, or directly in the computer language.

How the Computer Functions with Machine Language

If we wished to add elegance to this section we would say we are going to discuss *programming*. For the time being, this word will be avoided (but will appear later) and for the moment we will say only that we are going to learn how to tell the computer what to do.

Figure 15–3

Block Diagram and Symbols

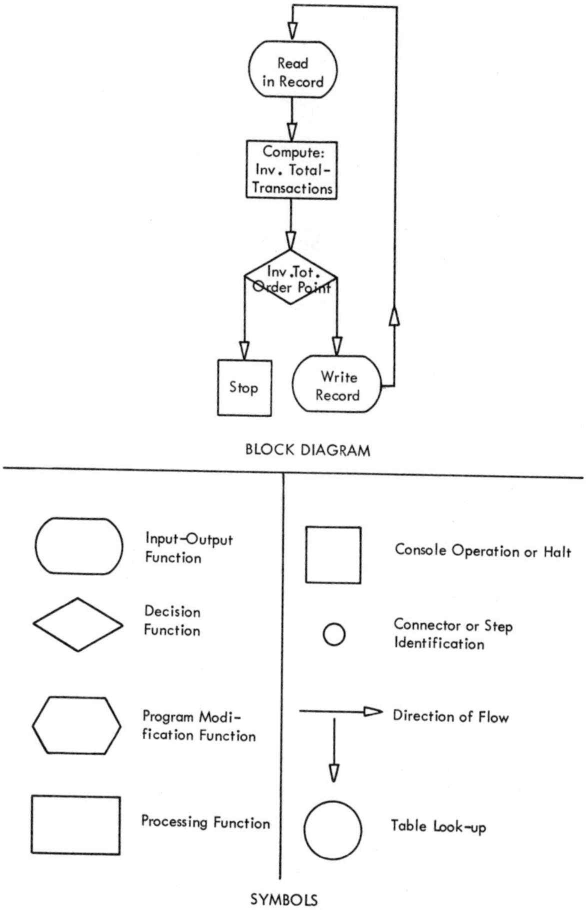

The situation is not unlike finding oneself in some primitive society with a house full of servants who can understand nothing but their village dialect of an obscure tongue. There is nothing to do but to learn enough of their language to permit communication. Undoubtedly, the rules of grammar differ from yours, but you don't impose your rules—you adopt theirs. Keep this in mind: you are the bright one, willing to accommodate yourself to the situation; the computer is the dull, inflexible servant.

It is well to know a little about any prospective servant, his likes and dislikes, to what he takes offense, and other characteristics. The same is true of your servant, the computer. For our purpose, a relatively primitive computer will be used as this makes it easier to see what is going on. Later a more sophisticated model will be considered. By seeing both you will gain a broader understanding.

Figure 15–4
IBM 650

Courtesy of IBM Corp.

The examples illustrated here are based on the IBM 650 (Figure 15–4), a drum type, fixed-word-length computer which has enjoyed considerable popularity, although it is being replaced by more sophisticated core-memory machines.

FORM OF INSTRUCTIONS

To talk to the computer in its own language, and without the aid of an interpreter, the sentences must be phrased in a certain way; nothing else is acceptable. Figure 15–5 is the form that an instruction for this particular computer must take. The field layout for the computer card is shown in Figure 15–6.

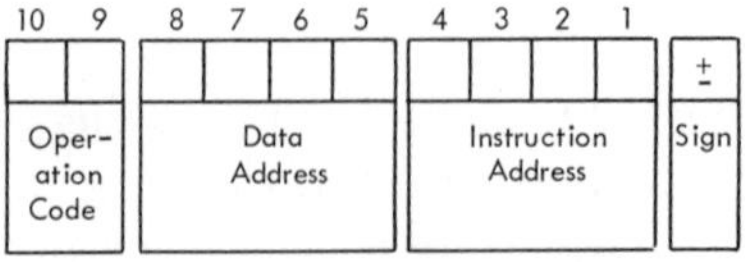

Figure 15–5
Form of Instruction for IBM 650

This instruction consists of 10 decimal digits and the sign. These 10 digits are divided into three groups, as shown, and are explained in greater detail here:

1. *Operation code:* The 10 and 9 positions indicate the operation to be performed by the computer. The computer operates on a set of commands established by the designer. This code is the language that the computer understands and is unique to this machine. Code 15 means to add, code 14 to divide, and so forth. This code, as listed in Figure 15–7, is of necessity brief; for a fuller treatment of any particular machine code the reader should refer to the manufacturer's manual.

Figure 15–6

Field Layout for Computer Card

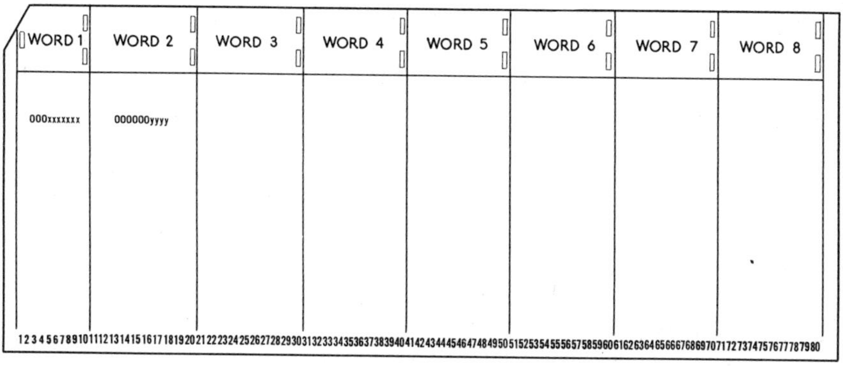

2. *Data Address:* Digit positions 8 through 5, referred to as *D*, tell where the information is which will be used in the operation. Remember that each storage position has an address number similar to a post office box, and it is this we are referring to—not to the information within the box. Depending upon the operation code, the data address may have one of several meanings:
   a) Storage location from which information comes.
   b) Storage location where information goes.
   c) The number of positions to shift information.
   d) Storage location where information is transferred from the input device.
   e) Storage locations to which information is transferred in the output device.
   f) Storage location of an alternate instruction.
   g) Storage location of the beginning of a table.
3. *Instruction Address:* The group of digit positions 4 through 1 is normally the storage location of the next instruction in the program. It is referred to as *I*.
4. *Sign:* The sign of the instruction is not used in the analysis and execution of the instruction, but it must be present to satisfy other control requirements of the system.

Figure 15–7

Abridged Computer Code

IBM 650 MACHINE LANGUAGE

READ-WRITE CODES

Code No.	*Mnemonic Code*	*Title*	*Description*
70	RD1	Read	Cause computer to read a card: Step 1. Contents of buffer are transferred to designated data address of instruction.

IBM 650 MACHINE LANGUAGE—*Cont.*

Code No.	*Mnemonic Code*	*Title*	*Description*
			Step 2. Next card is read into buffer. (The storage locations ending in 01 to 10 and 51 to 60 are valid read-in addresses.)
71	WR1	Write	Causes computer to punch a card. Step 1. Contents of designated address are transferred to buffer. Step 2. Card is punched from information in buffer. (The storage locations ending in 27 to 36 or 77 to 86 are valid punch addresses.)
		ARITHMETIC CODES	
Lower Accumulator			
15	ALO	Add to lower	Contents of the data address location are added to *lower* accumulator. (Carries from the high order of the lower accumulator will go into the upper accumulator.)
65	RAL	Reset and add to lower	1. Resets entire 20 positions of accumulator to zero. 2. Adds contents of data address location to lower accumulator—automatically assumes positive sign.
Upper Accumulator			
10	AUP	Add to upper	Similar to 15 ALO except the upper accumulator is used.
60	RAU	Reset and add to upper	Similar to 65 RAL except the upper accumulator is used.
		SUBTRACTION CODES	
Lower Accumulator			
16	SLO	Subtract from lower	With the exception of sign analysis, this code functions the same as 15 ALO.
66	RSL	Reset and subtract from lower	With the exception of sign analysis, this code functions the same as 10 AUP.
Upper Accumulator			
11	SUP	Subtract from upper	With the exception of sign analysis, this code functions the same as 10 AUP.
61	RSU	Reset and subtract from upper	With the exception of sign analysis, this code functions the same as 60 RAU.
		MULTIPLICATION CODES	
19	MPY	Multiply	Upper accumulator × contents of data address. Multiplier (10 digits) × Multiplicand (10 digits) = Product (20 digits). *Before using code:* Multiplier must be placed in upper accumulator. *When code is executed:* Multiplicand is placed in distributor where sign analysis is made before multiplication starts.

IBM 650 MACHINE LANGUAGE—*Cont.*

Code No.	Mnemonic Code	Title	Description
			After using code: Product is in accumulator. Multiplicand is still in distributor. Multiplier is lost.
		DIVIDE CODES	
14	DIV	Divide	Entire accumulator ÷ contents of data address. Dividend (20 digits) ÷ Divisor (10 digits) = Quotient (10 digits) + Remainder (10 digits). Quotient is in lower accumulator. Remainder is in upper accumulator. Dividend is lost.
64	DVR	Divide and reset upper	Same as 14 DIV except remainder is discarded.
		STORE CODES	
			The operation code determines what register, upper accumulator, lower accumulator, or distributor is to be stored. Information from one of these registers is sent to receiving address. Receiving register's contents change; sending register remains unchanged. Data address designates where the information is to go (0000–1999 are the only permissible locations).
20	STL	Store lower accumulator	Contents of lower accumulator with sign is placed in general storage.
21	STU	Store upper accumulator	Stores information that is in the upper accumulator. A. Normally sign is of entire accumulator. B. If 21 STU follows a 14 DIV so the upper accumulator contains a remainder, the sign is for the remainder and not the sign of the quotient.
22	SDA	Store data address of lower accumulator	Used for instruction modification. Position 8–5 of lower accumulator replaces contents of distributor. Contents of distributor are moved to storage.
23	SIA	Store instruction address of lower accumulator	1. Position 4–1 of lower accumulator replaces 4–1 in distributor. 2. Entire contents of distributor are then placed in storage.
24	STD	Store distributor	Entire contents of distributor with sign are placed in storage specified by *data* address.

IBM 650 MACHINE LANGUAGE—*Cont.*

Code No.	*Mnemonic Code*	*Title*	*Description*
			SHIFT CODES
			1. All shifting operations are accomplished in the accumulator. 2. Contents of both halves of the accumulator are shifted right or left as indicated by the code. 3. All positions which are made vacant by the shift are filled with zeros. 4. Sign is not affected by a shift. 5. The distributor is not affected by a shift. 6. Operation code indicates direction of shift. 7. *Units position* indicates number of positions to be shifted—maximum of 9 positions.
30	SRT	Shift right	Contents of entire accumulator are shifted right. All numbers shifted off right end are lost. Left-hand positions are filled with zeros as shift takes place.
31	SRD	Shift right and round	Same as 30 SRT except at the completion of a shift a 5 is added to the last digit shifted out of the accumulator. 1 to 9 in data address will cause a shift of 1 to 9. 0 in data address will shift 10 with rounding of the last figure.
35	SLT	Shift left	Causes the contents of the entire accumulator to be shifted left. Numbers shifted out the left end are lost. Places on the right are filled with zeros.
			BRANCHING CODES
			Branching codes are used for logical decisions. In effect ask question which can be answered yes or no. The answer determines where the next instruction is located.
44	NZV	Branch on non-zero in accumulator	Asks: Is there any significant digit in upper accumulator? Yes: Execute next instruction in D address. No: Execute next instruction in I address. Sign of accumulator is ignored.
45	NZE	Branch on non-zero accumulator	Asks: Is there any significant digit in entire accumulator? Yes: Execute next instruction in data address. No: Execute next instruction in instruction address. Sign of accumulator is ignored.

IBM 650 MACHINE LANGUAGE—*Cont.*

Code No.	*Mnemonic Code*	*Title*	*Description*
46	BMI	Branch on minus accumulator	Asks: Is sign of accumulator minus? Yes: Execute next instruction in data address. No (i.e., positive sign): Execute next instruction in instruction address. (When used after a 14 DIV the sign of the quotient and not remainder is tested.)
47	BOV	Branch on overflow	Effective only when machine is set to *sense*; when set to *stop* machine stops on every overflow. Asks: Has a verifiable overflow occurred in accumulator? Verifiable may result from arithmetic operations. Nonverifiable, which will stop the machine, can result from division if the machine tries to develop a quotient of more than 10 digits. Yes: Execute next instruction in data address. No: Execute next instruction in instruction address.
90–99	BD 0–9	Branch on digit 8 in a distributor position	Code causes machine to examine a particular position of the distributor for the presence of an 8 or 9. 91–99 tests positions 1–9 of distributor. 90 tests position 10. 8 present, location of next instruction is specified by data address. 9 present, location of next instruction is specified by instruction address. The absence of an 8 or 9 causes machine to stop.
		MISCELLANEOUS CODES	
00	NOP	No operation	Data address is bypassed (must be valid) and machine automatically goes to the instruction address.
01	HLT	Stop–halt	This code depends upon the PROGRAMMED switch on console. Status of PROGRAMMED Switch ↓ STOP: This code, 01, stops program execution ↓ RUN: This code, 01, is treated like 00–NOP
69	LDD	Load distributor	Contents of data address are placed in the distributor. This code, used with 24 STD *store distributor*, is used for transferring information from one general location to another.
84	TLU	Table lookup	This code is used to perform an automatic table lookup.

THE COMPUTER IN OPERATION

Figure 15–8 is a composite illustration showing—at the top—the components of the computer and—below—how they are affected by the steps of the instruction. The schematic of the machine shows the memory and

Figure 15–8

Computer Schematic (IBM 650) and Examples

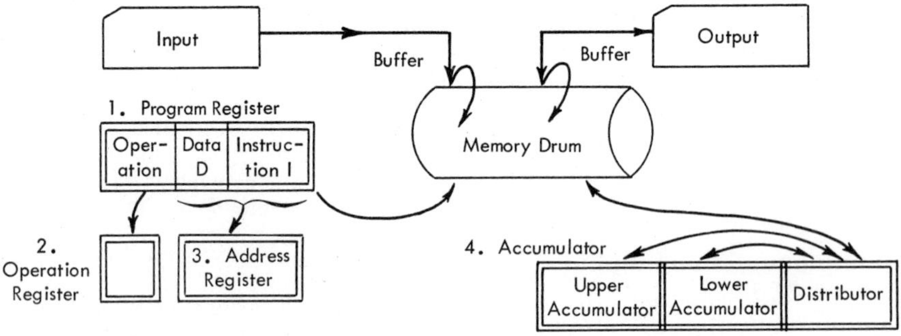

PLANNING SHEET

Step	Location	Operation	Data	Instruction	Upper Accumulator	Lower Accumulator	Distribution
Example 1. Addition:							
1	0600	70 RD1*	1501	0610	-----		
2	0610	65 RAL	1501	0620		29	29
3	0620	15 ALO	1502	0630	-----	52	52
4	0630	20 STL	1577	0640	-----	52	52
5	0640	71 WR1	1577	0600	-----	52	52
Example 2. Multiplication:							
1	0800	70 RD1	1701	0810	-----		
2	0810	60 RAU	1702	0820	1.23	+	1.23+
3	0820	19 MPY	1701	0830		10.1352 +	8.24+
4	0830	31 SRD	0002	0840		10.14+	8.24+
5	0840	20 STL	1936	0850		10.14+	8.24+
6	0850	71 WRI	1936	0810			
Example 3. Branching:							
1	0911	70 RD1	1801	0912			
2	0912	69 LDD	1801	0913			573+
3	0913	24 STD	1961	0914			573+
4	0914	69 LDD	1802	0915			3.2+
5	0915	24 STD	1962	0916			3.2+
6	0916	70 RD1	1801	0917			3.2
7	0917	65 RAL	1801	0918		573+	573+
8	0918	16 SLO	1961	0919	Go to Step 6	000+	573+
9	0919	45 NZE	(0923)	0920			573+
10	0920	65 RAL	1962	0921	Go to Step 1	3.2+	3.2+
11	0921	15 ALO	1802	0922		8.5+	5.3+
12	0922	20 STL	1962	(0916)		8.5+	8.5+
13	(0923)	WR1	1962	(0911)			

*These numbers agree with the code numbers in Figure 15-7.

registers connected by flow lines. Below the schematic is a program planning sheet with several examples, just as it would be used in writing instructions for a machine. The composite shows the registers in the machine and—below them, in the planning sheet—what will be found in each register at the completion of the instruction.

A short discussion of the function of each component will be helpful before starting with the planning sheet. Information is fed to and from the card through suitable buffering circuits to the drum storage. The buffers are secondary storages used to transfer data between internal and external storage when input and output speeds are not synchronized.

The various registers serve the particular functions described here:

1. *Program register* is a 10-digit register which acts as a temporary storage or memory for each instruction of the program as it is being analyzed and executed.
2. *Operation register* receives the operation code and analyzes it to determine the operation to be performed.
3. *Address register* receives the address portion of the instruction. The operation and address registers, together, control the execution of the analyzed instruction.
4. *Accumulator* is also an electronic storage unit but has a capacity of two words (20 digits) and an algebraic sign. This unit serves as a temporary storage for the results of arithmetic operations. Shifting of the information, either right or left, is also done here. Since the machine operates with 10-digit words and since some operations can result in 20-digit words, the accumulator is divided into two halves, called the *lower accumulator* and the *upper accumulator*.

Arithmetic operations are performed by combining the contents of the distributor with the contents of the accumulator and storing the results in the accumulator. The arithmetic operations are performed in the arithmetic unit. The accumulator can be tested for sign, all zeros in upper accumulator, all zeros in the lower accumulator, and for overflow to determine if the number is too large.

The instructions given on the *planning sheet* are in the same format as would be used in writing a program. Three examples are given: one for addition, the second for multiplication, and the third for branching when a decision is made. The addresses are chosen arbitrarily—except for the read-in and write-out ones, which are restricted to a particular block of the memory drum.

The explanation of each set of instructions is given below and you will find each step keyed to the planning sheet. Such a set of instructions would be added in an abbreviated form to the right margin of the planning sheet. The symbols for the simple flow charts and how they are connected should be obvious. This aspect of programming will be dealt with more extensively later.

Example 1, Additions

The problem is to add two quantities, A and B, together and punch out their total on a card. The flow diagram for this is shown in Figure 15–9.

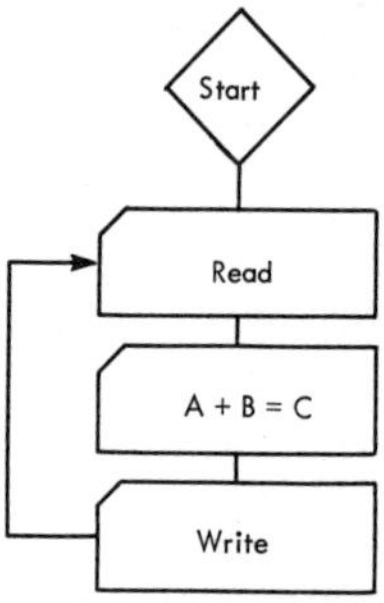

Figure 15–9

Flow Chart for Adding

For this problem, assume the cards have two 10-digit words in the first 20 columns. Following the planning sheet, this is an explanation of each step:

Step 1. In storage space 0600 there is the instruction 70 RD1 1501 0610, which tells the machine to read the first two words on the card into location 1501 and 1502.

Step 2. Clear the entire accumulator. Add A in 1501 to the lower accumulator. Assume for this card that the value of A is 29, which is now in both the lower accumulator and the distributor.

Step 3. The content of drum storage location 1502 is added to the lower accumulator. This is B, which for this card is assumed to have a value of 23.

Step 4. It is impossible to punch directly from the distributor, so the total, C, must be transferred to the drum. Only certain spaces (see code) are available for this purpose. The address, 1577, was chosen.

Step 5. Information is punched on cards. The next instruction in this step will be the same as for No. 1, to start the cycle over again. Further instructions will be needed to prevent cycling.

Example 2, Multiplication

The problem is to multiply two quantities, A and B, round off the answer, and punch it on a card. This is shown by the flow chart in Figure 15–10. For the example, the two quantities, A and B, equal 8.24 and 1.23, respectively.

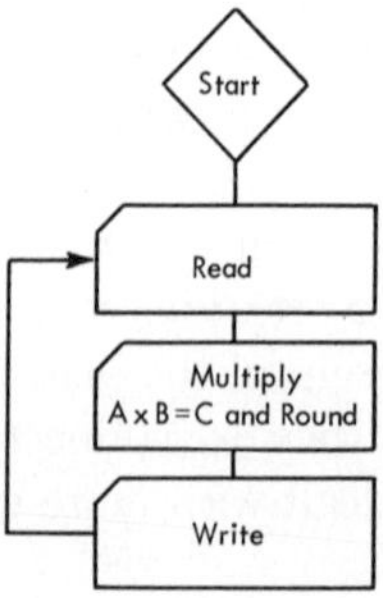

Figure 15–10

Flow Chart for Multiplying and Rounding

Step 1. In storage space 0800 there is an instruction, 70 RD1 1701 0810, which tells the machine to read the first two words on the card into memory locations 1701 and 1702.

Step 2. The upper accumulator is cleared and the content of 1702, which is 1.23, is entered.

Step 3. Multiply the content of the upper accumulator by the content of 1701, which is 8.24.

Step 4. Shift right and round. A equals 8.24, which has X.XX places, and *B* equals 1.23, which has X.XX places.

Only two places right of the decimal point are to be retained. The maximum number of figures in a product is the sum of the maximum number of figures that appear in each of the factors (X.XX × X.XX = XX.XXXX). To round off the answer with just two positions to the right of the decimal point it is necessary to shift two positions. The value in the data part of the instruction tells how far to the right the number is shifted.

Step 5. The content of the lower accumulator is placed in storage, 1936.

Step 6. Punch information into card. Further information would be needed to prevent cycling.

Example 3, Branching

Assume a deck of payroll cards which have been sorted in sequence by labor-force clock number. The problem is to accumulate the pay entered in each card and punch out the total. The clock number is in word position No. 1 and the amount is in word position No. 2.

The difficult part of this problem is making sure that the amount for a particular clock is accumulated and none is missed. This is accomplished by subtracting each successive clock number from the preceding one. If the difference is zero, the next card is tested for a zero difference. If the difference is not zero, the total is printed out. Just how this is done is shown on the Figure 15–11 flow chart.

An explanation of the steps of Example 3, Branching, follows:

Step 1. Read the card and store the first word, which is the clock number, into address 1801. The amount is stored in address 1802.

Step 2. Read information from storage 1801 into the distributor.

Step 3. Store information which is in the distributor in memory position 1961. (These three steps are a means of taking information from the card and placing it into storage.)

Step 4. Read information from memory position 1802 (the hours worked) into the distributor.

Step 5. Store the information which is in the distributor in the memory position 1962.

Step 6. Read the next card and store the first word (clock number) in address 1801. This destroys the old information in address 1801.

Step 7. Reset accumulator to zero and add information which is in memory 1801 into the accumulator.

Step 8. Subtract information in 1961 from lower accumulator.

Step 9. Test to see if the clock number has changed. In other words, test the accumulator to see if it is zero. If it has not changed (and reads zero) go to next *instruction* address. If it has changed, go to *data* address.

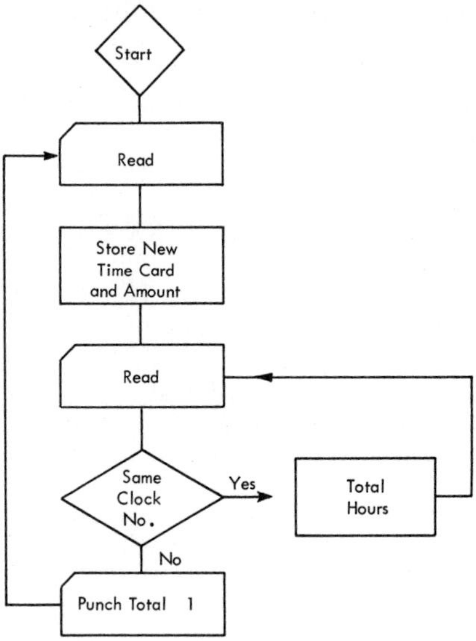

Figure 15–11

Flow Chart for Branching

Step 10. If the clock number has not changed, reset the accumulator and add the content of address 1962 to the lower accumulator.

Step 11. Add the content of 1802, the information on the second card (which is 5.3), to the accumulator.

Step 12. Store the information which is in the accumulator into 1962 to be used again.

Step 13. If in Step 9 a change in card is shown, print out the value in 1962 and go to Step 1 and start over. To prevent infinite looping, an appropriate halt instruction must be added.

You have just taken the beginning step in programming. It is not difficult, is it? Since you know how a computer functions, you are prepared to move on and learn ways of programming more efficiently. The machine-language programming just discussed has many obvious shortcomings:

1. The logic of the entire program is the responsibility of the programmer.
2. The programmer must have an extensive knowledge of the computer being programmed.
3. It is necessary for the programmer to keep an account of all storage areas.
4. It is difficult for the programmer to compensate for any omissions in the program.
5. Some machine languages are nearly impossible for the programmer to learn (especially those which use binary language).
6. The programmer must learn the language for each computer being used.

With these numerous obstacles in machine-language programming it is little wonder that better methods were sought.

Automatic Programming

The objective of programming is a series of coded instructions which guide the operations of the computer to the completion of the assigned task. For the early computers it was necessary to have a good working knowledge of the machines, how the registers function, how the storage areas are laid out, and in addition be conversant in binary language. This made programming an extremely tedious task, which hardly seemed worth the effort, until some ingenious person asked why the computer itself couldn't serve as the translator to change near-English into the computer's language. This is the revolution which has been taking place in the software of the computer industry and has resulted in numerous translating systems under such names as SOAP, MAD, FORTRAN, and COBOL. Some of these translators are original systems while others have been merely refinements of previous systems.

One suspects, at times, that computer and computer language name-dropping is a status symbol of our time. The languages listed here, with their area of application, should supplement your knowledge of computer software.

Name	*Meaning*	*Application*
ALGOL	ALGebraic Oriented Language	Science and Engineering
FORTRAN	FORmula TRANslator	" "
FAP	Fortran Assembly Program	" "
SAP	Symbolic Assembly Program	" "
SOAP	Symbolic Optimum Assembly Program	" "
MAD	Michigan Algorithmic Decoder	" "
COBOL	COmmon Business Oriented Language	Business data processing

Figure 15–12 illustrates the difference between using machine-language and automatic programming. At first glance, automatic programming would appear to consume more time, but this is not true. Automatic programming can usually reduce preparation time considerably.

In the illustration of automatic programming it should be pointed out that three programs are involved:

1. *Source program:* This is the set of basic instructions, written by the programmer, which follows the rules of the specific programming method used.
2. *Processor program:* This (also called the *translator* or *compiler*) consists of a list of instructions which tells the machine what to do with the source program to produce the *object program.* The processor programs are supplied by the manufacturers of the computers.
3. *Object program:* This is a machine-language program developed by the computer from instructions given by the source program and the processor program. It is the one used to read the data, process it, and produce the answer.

When one speaks of COBOL, FORTRAN, or other translating systems he means both the source program and the processor program. The fact is

Figure 15–12

Automatic Programming

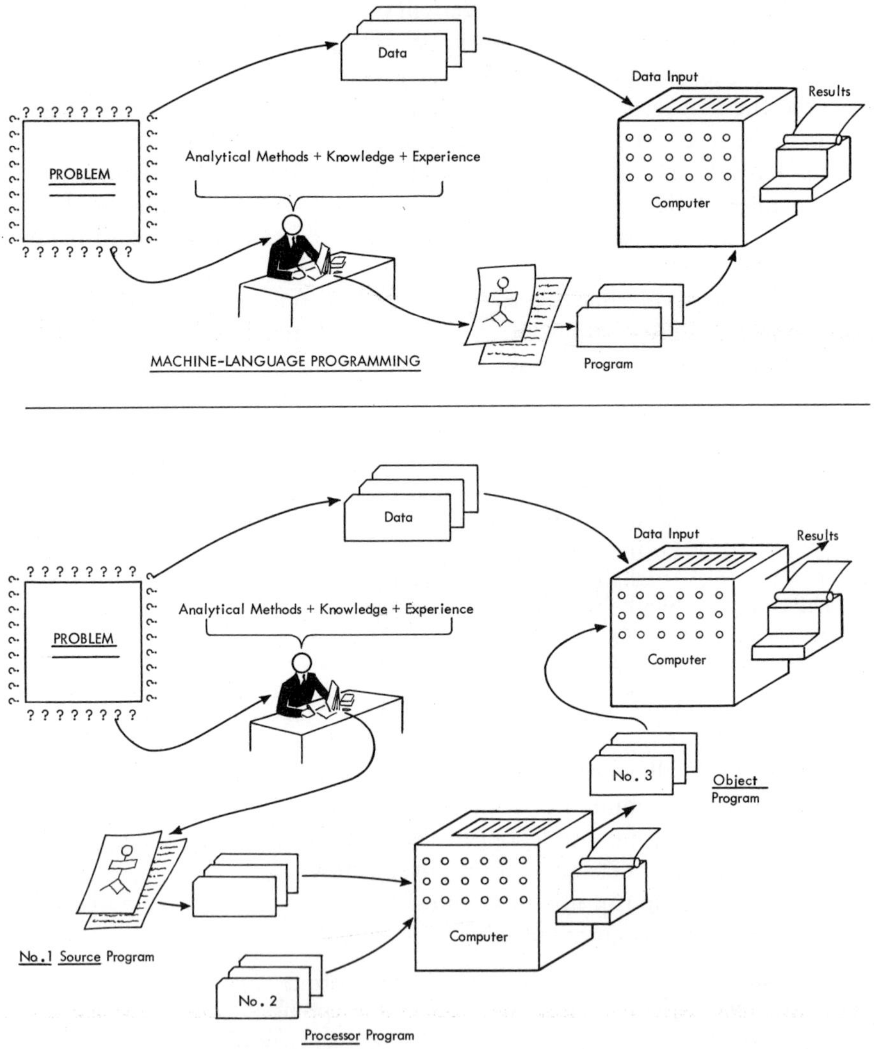

Note: Usually the same computer would be used; two are used to illustrate the steps.

that the source program must be written to a set of rules so that the processor program can make the necessary translation.

DEVELOPMENT OF COBOL AUTOMATIC PROGRAMMING

COBOL automatic programming is the first large-scale effort to design a single computer language which permits writing programs adaptable to many computers. It is designed for maximum compatability among the many different computers on the market.

The proliferation of innumerable automatic programming systems caused alarm in both industry and government as there was little opportunity to transfer knowledge among the languages of different computers. Consequently the Conference on Data Systems Languages (CODASYL) was called at the Pentagon in 1959. This committee, representing computer users in government and industry (as well as computer manufacturers), set in motion several subcommittees which had as their final objective a COmmon *B*usiness *O*riented *L*anguage for computers. This, shortened to COBOL,[1] was published by the Government Printing Office in 1960 with plans to publish revisions annually. The COBOL manual is the authoritative reference and the contents of this chapter are intended only as an introduction.

The philosophy of the COBOL system is easier to grasp when you see that it has four distinct divisions, three of which are independent of the computer being used.

1. The IDENTIFICATION DIVISION names the source program, the date the program was written, individuals involved, and other pertinent information.
2. The ENVIRONMENT DIVISION outlines the equipment used for compiling and running the object program.
3. The DATA DIVISION gives the file and record descriptions of data which the object program is to use. The data are described in terms of a standard data format which makes this section nearly independent of the computer being used.
4. The PROCEDURE DIVISION specifies the steps that the computer must take in solving the problem. The procedure is given in near-English and is independent of the computer.

These divisions, with the exception of the ENVIRONMENT DIVISION, are independent—or nearly independent—of the computer used. Only in this division is the program dependent upon the computer. So, theoretically at least, a universal program may be written and used on many common computers by merely changing the ENVIRONMENT DIVISION.

REFERENCE FORMAT

COBOL has a standard reference format which takes precedence over all other rules. The sequence of the program divisions must be IDENTIFICATION, ENVIRONMENT, DATA, and PROCEDURE DIVISIONS.

The COBOL *Coding Sheet* is illustrated in Figure 15–13. Pause now and explore the layout of this sheet and the explanations concerning the sequence numbers, margins, and other information given on the form.

It will help you understand the COBOL logic if you are aware that it is somewhat analogous to outlining. Figure 15–14 shows the COBOL outline with the four major divisions in their proper sequence. Under each

[1] See Acknowledgment at end of chapter.

Figure 15–13

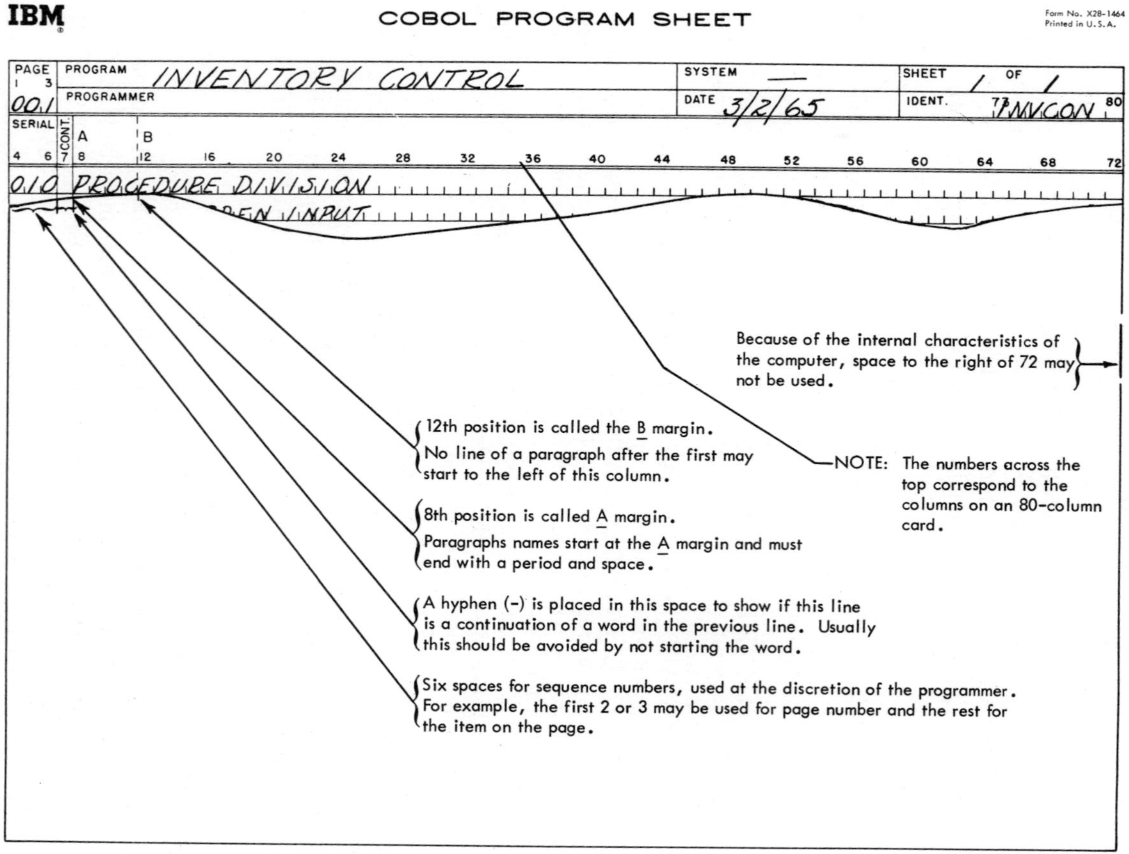
IBM
COBOL PROGRAM SHEET
Form No. X28-1464
Printed in U.S.A.
PAGE
1 3
001
PROGRAM INVENTORY CONTROL
PROGRAMMER
SYSTEM —
DATE 3/2/65
SHEET 1 OF 1
IDENT. 73 INVCON 80
SERIAL
4 6
CONT.
7
A
8
B
12
16
20
24
28
32
36
40
44
48
52
56
60
64
68
72
010 PROCEDURE DIVISION
OPEN INPUT
Because of the internal characteristics of the computer, space to the right of 72 may not be used.
12th position is called the B margin.
No line of a paragraph after the first may start to the left of this column.
NOTE: The numbers across the top correspond to the columns on an 80-column card.
8th position is called A margin.
Paragraphs names start at the A margin and must end with a period and space.
A hyphen (-) is placed in this space to show if this line is a continuation of a word in the previous line. Usually this should be avoided by not starting the word.
Six spaces for sequence numbers, used at the discretion of the programmer. For example, the first 2 or 3 may be used for page number and the rest for the item on the page.

Figure 15–14

Outline of COBOL Structure

	L	A B	
Identification Division	001010	IDENTIFICATION DIVISION PROGRAM-ID. (Inventory Control) AUTHOR (TIM) DATE-WRITTEN (Jan 10 196–) DATE-COMPILED (Jan 20 196–) REMARKS	
Environment Division		ENVIRONMENT DIVISION. CONFIGURATION SECTION. SOURCE-COMPUTER. OBJECT-COMPUTER. SPECIAL-NAMES. INPUT-OUTPUT SECTION. FILE-CONTROL. I-O-CONTROL.	

Data Division		DATA DIVISION.
		FILE SECTION.
		FD XXXXXXXXXXXXXXXXXX
		01 XXXXXXXXXXXXXXX
		    02 XXXXX
		        03 XXXXXX
		
		WORKING-STORAGE-SECTION.
		
		77 XXXX
		
		CONSTANT-SECTION.
		
		    XXX
			Note: This is a general form using indentation. Indenting is optional but if used each step must be set over four spaces.

Procedure Division		PROCEDURE DIVISION. XXXXXXXX (paragraph name) XXXXX (sentences)	

division heading you will see subheadings for information which may or may not be added. Each of these divisions, with the detailed sub- and sub-sub-headings, will be discussed in turn.

Before going too far in the discussion of COBOL, you deserve an explanation about some slight changes in the writing style in this part of the chapter. All words which are *reserved* for precise meaning in COBOL programming (listed in Figure 15–15) are in capital letters. In the instruction

Figure 15–15

Reserved COBOL Words

ABOUT	DOLLAR	MEMORY	REPLACING
ACCEPT	ELSE	MEMORY-DUMP	RERUN
ADD	END	MEMORY-DUMP-	RESERVE
ADDRESS	ENDING	KEY	REVERSED
ADVANCING	ENDING-FILE-	MINUS	REWIND
AFTER	LABEL	MODE	RIGHT
ALL	ENDING-TAPE-	MODULES	ROUNDED
ALPHABETIC	LABEL	MOVE	RUN
ALPHANUMERIC	END-OF-FILE	MULTIPLE	SAME
ALTER	END-OF-TAPE	MULTIPLIED	SECTION
ALTERNATE	ENTER	MULTIPLY	SELECT
AN	ENVIRONMENT	NEGATIVE	SENTENCE
AND	EQUAL	NEXT	SENTINEL
APPLY	EQUALS	NO	SEQUENCED
ARE	ERROR	NO-MEMORY-	SIGN
AREA	EVERY	DUMP	SIGNED
AREAS	EXAMINE	NOT	SIZE
AS	EXCEEDS	NOTE	SOURCE-
ASSIGN	EXIT	NUMERIC	COMPUTER
AT	EXPONENTIATED	OBJECT-	SPACE
BEFORE	FD	COMPUTER	SPACES
BEGINNING	FOR	OBJECT-	SPECIAL-NAMES
BEGINNING-FILE-	FILE	PROGRAM	STANDARD
LABEL	FILE-CONTROL	OCCURS	STATUS
BEGINNING-TAPE-	FILLER	OF	STOP
LABEL	FILLING	OFF	SUBTRACT
BIT	FIRST	OMITTED	SUPERVISOR
BITS	FLOAT	ON	SUPPRESS
BLANK	FORMAT	OPEN	SYNCHRONIZED
BLOCK	FROM	OPTIONAL	TALLY
BLOCK-COUNT	GIVING	OR	TALLYING
BY	GO	OTHERWISE	TAPE
CHARACTER	GREATER	OUTPUT	TEST-PATTERN
CHARACTERS	HASHED	PERFORM	THAN
CHECK	HIGH-VALUE	PICTURE	THEN
CLASS	HIGH-VALUES	PLACES	THROUGH } Equiva-
CLOCK-UNITS	I-O-CONTROL	PLUS	THRU } lent
CLOSE	IF	POINT	TIMES
COBOL	IN	POSITION	TO
COMPUTATIONAL	INCLUDE	POSITIVE	TYPE
COMPUTE	INPUT	PREPARED	UNEQUAL
CONSTANT	INPUT-OUTPUT	PRIORITY	UPPER-BOUND
CONFIGURATION	INTO	PROCEDURE	UPPER-BOUNDS
CONTAINS	IS	PROCEED	UNTIL
CONTROL	JUSTIFIED	PROTECT	UPON
COPY	LABEL	PROTECTION	USAGE
CORRESPONDING	LEADING	PURGE-DATE	USE
DATA	LEAVING	QUOTE	VALUE
DATE-WRITTEN	LEFT	RANGE	VARYING
DECLARATIVES	LESS	READ	WHEN
DEFINE	LIBRARY	RECORD	WITH
DEPENDING	LINES	RECORD-COUNT	WORDS
DIGIT	LOCATION	RECORDING	WORKING-
DIGITS	LOCK	RECORDS	STORAGE
DISPLAY	LOW-VALUE	REDEFINES	WRITE
DIVIDE	LOW-VALUES	REEL	ZERO
DIVIDED	LOWER-BOUND	REEL-NUMBER	ZEROES
DIVISION	LOWER-BOUNDS	RENAMING	ZERO

format, those uppercase words which are underlined are required, while those which are not are optional—optional only in the sense that they may be deleted. (Misspelling of an optional word, or replacement by another word of any kind, is not permitted.) This writing style has been used in the government COBOL manual, as well as in a number of textbooks, so you should not find it difficult to refer to them if you wish.

Incidentally, this short chapter cannot include all the many detailed facets included in the COBOL programming, and you are urged to supplement your knowledge with one of the excellent references listed. The objective is to familiarize you with the system and not to make you an expert programmer. This would probably require far more space and time than is available here. While an effort has been made to give a complete coverage of the system, it is impossible to guard against all the exceptions. This doesn't matter, however, for if you are going to do programming you will want to obtain the excellent, detailed government manual. The material presented here is intended to bridge the gap between having no knowledge of programming and becoming an experienced programmer.

SYNTAX

To understand a language one must know something about the sentence structure. This is called syntax, but the meaning will be stretched slightly to include the whole language structure. In COBOL, as in any language, we start with characters, the basic building blocks, and go on to the more complex words, statements, sentences, paragraphs, sections, and other combinations.

Characters

These are the basic elements of the COBOL language. Not all characters are used to form words, they are also used for punctuation and logical operations. The COBOL characters, with their uses, are illustrated in this resumé:

COBOL CHARACTERS

Used in Relations:

- > Greater than
- < Less than
- = Equal to

Used in Editing:

- $ Dollar sign
- * Check protection symbol
- , Comma
- . Decimal point

Used for Words:

0 through 9
A through Z
and the hyphen, or minus sign.

Used for Punctuation:

- " Quotation mark
- (Left parenthesis
-) Right parenthesis
- Space or blank
- . Period
- , Comma
- ; Semicolon

Used in Formulas:

- + Addition
- – Subtraction
- * Multiplication (**Exponentiation)
- / Division
- = Equality

Words

Words are composed of a combination of not more than 30 characters taken from the set of 37 *Used for Words* just given. Words must end with a space. For example, INVENTORY REPORT is two words, but INVENTORY-REPORT is considered as one word.

For convenience, words may be classified in the COBOL language as *nouns* or *verbs*. The nouns in turn may be classified as:

Data names: A word with at least one alphabetic character which designates any data specified in the data description, or the area which contains the data reference.

Condition names: The name assigned to a specific value in a set or range of values.

Procedure names: These are either a paragraph name or a section name. This permits one procedure to refer to another procedure.

Literals: A literal is an item of data, the value of which is identical to those characters comprising the item. There are two kinds of literals:

Numeric literal: Composed only of characters, 0 through 9, plus and minus, and the decimal point.

Nonnumeric literal: Composed of the allowable characters—with the exception of the quotation mark. The nonnumeric literal must be enclosed in quotation marks.

Figurative constants: These are items which have been assigned fixed data-names. Fixed data-names include ZERO, SPACE, UPPER-BOUND, LOWER-BOUND, QUOTE, and others to be found in the COBOL manual. The singular and plural of these forms are equivalent and they must not be enclosed in quotation marks.

Special registers: These are used to refer to special registers, such as TALLY, which is used to hold information.

Special names: Special names are used to refer to hardware, such as switches.

Verbs are single words, appearing in the PROCEDURE DIVISION, which specify an action such as ADD, SUBTRACT, MOVE, etc., and they will be discussed extensively when we dig deeper into the PROCEDURE DIVISION.

The *reserved* words have been listed earlier and are an important part of the COBOL system. These words must not be used for any other purpose than that specified. Users should avoid these words for data or procedure names.

Statement

After the word, the next classification is the statement. The statements in the PROCEDURE DIVISION which require action are of three types: imperative statements, conditional statements, and compiler directing statements.

Sentences

Superior to the statement is the sentence, which consists of a sequence of one or more statements. There is a parallel between the classification of statements and sentences for there are also imperative, conditional, and compiler directing sentences. The sentence must be terminated by a period. Separators may be used between statements within the sentence, to improve the readability, but their use is optional. The allowable separators are the semicolon and THEN. Of course, one separator cannot follow another. Other rules for the use of the separator in the conditional statement are to be found in the COBOL manual.

Paragraphs

Paragraphs have been included in COBOL so that the source programmer may group several sentences to convey one idea in a procedure. The paragraph begins with a name and is the smallest grouping in the PROCEDURE DIVISION which requires a name.

Section

A section consists of one or more successive paragraphs, and, when designated, must be named. The name is followed by the word SECTION. Section divisions are not essential for the operation of a program.

Procedure

The procedure is the largest grouping.

For a moment, review the structure of the COBOL language. Characters are used in words, words are used in statements, statements are used in sentences, which in turn are used in paragraphs, and these make up the sections which are included in the procedure. Most of the emphasis on programming logic is in the PROCEDURE DIVISION, and it is here that the higher classifications, statements, and sentences are most meaningful.

QUALIFIERS AND SUBSCRIPTS

In the COBOL source program names must be unique either because of spelling or because the name exists within a hierarchy of names such that the name can be made unique by mentioning one or more of the higher levels of the hierarchy. The qualifiers appear in ascending order and are appended by using the prepositional phrase containing IN or OF, depending upon the readability. As an example, DAY OF LAST-TRANSACTION-DATE OF MASTER would refer to the labeled transaction in the following list:

```
1 MASTER . . . . .
   2 CURRENT-DATE . . . . .
      3 MONTH . . . . .
      3 DAY . . . . .
      3 YEAR . . . . .
   2 LAST-TRANSACTION-DATE . . . . .
      3 MONTH . . . . .
    →3 DAY . . . . .
      3 YEAR . . . . .
```

There is a distinct difference between qualifiers (just mentioned) and subscripting. Qualification is necessary when the same data-name is used for several different items of data, and subscripting is necessary when some of the elements of a table or list have not been assigned individual names.

A subscript is an integer whose value determines which element is being referred to within a table or list of like elements. The subscripts may be represented either by a literal, which is an integer such as 40, or by a data-name, such as AGE, which has an integral value. The subscript represented by a date-name must be described by a Record Description entry in the DATA division. In both cases the subscript is enclosed in parentheses which appear immediately after the terminal space of the name of the element referenced, such as RATE (40).

The maximum number of levels which can be subscripted in a table is three. Multilevel subscripts are always written in the order: major, intermediate, minor. For example, a three-level subscript might appear as: RATE (REGION, STATE, CITY).

RULES OF PUNCTUATION

Splitting Words, Literals, and Paragraphs

Any paragraph occupying more than one line is split by starting the second line under *B* on the format. Any word or numeric literal can be split by placing a hyphen in the seventh-column position on the second line. A nonnumeric literal may be split, but any spaces appearing at the end of the line are considered as part of the literal. Continuation of nonnumeric literals must be preceded by a quotation mark.

Spacing

There must be at least one space between words, except in nonnumeric literals. Two or more spaces are treated as one space. The arithmetic operators *, –, /, ** must be preceded by and followed by a space.

Periods

Division titles are ended by a period and nothing else appears beyond the period on that line. Paragraph names and sentences must end with a period, followed by a space.

Commas and AND

Commas and AND may be used in the PROCEDURE DIVISION to clarify meaning in a series of operands.

Parentheses

Parentheses are used where needed in arithmetic and conditional statements to make the meaning clear.

DETAILED DISCUSSION OF DIVISIONS

Now that you have had some introduction to the COBOL format, rules of syntax, and punctuation you are ready for a more extensive explanation of each division. In the discussion of the divisions, a particular notation will be introduced which is used universally throughout COBOL references. It is this:

a) All underlined uppercase words are required when the functions of which they are a part are used.
b) All uppercase words not underlined are used for readability only. They may or may not be present.
c) All lowercase words represent generic terms which must be supplied by the user.
d) Material enclosed in braces { } indicates that a choice from the contents must be made.
e) Material enclosed in square brackets [ ] represents an option and may be included or omitted.
f) When two or more nouns are written in a series, commas are shown as connectives. Where a comma is shown in the format it may be omitted or replaced by either AND or ,AND .

IDENTIFICATION DIVISION

The purpose of the IDENTIFICATION DIVISION is to identify the source program and the outputs of a compilation. In addition, the user may include such information as the date the program was written, date of compilation, and other pertinent facts.

Fixed paragraph names are used as keys in this division to identify the information contained in the paragraph. The program name must be given in the first paragraph which is PROGRAM-ID. Other paragraphs which may be included in this division are author, installation, date-written, date compiled, security, and remarks.

ENVIRONMENT DIVISION

This division must be written every time the program is run on a different computer for the ENVIRONMENT DIVISION provides the link between the logical concepts of data and records and the physical aspects of the files on which they are stored. It is the division where all the computer-dependent information is centralized. The ENVIRONMENT DIVISION is divided into two sections.

CONFIGURATION SECTION: This section deals with the overall specifications of the computer or computers and, in turn, is divided into three paragraphs:

1. SOURCE-COMPUTER: This paragraph defines the computer on which the COBOL compiler is to run.
2. OBJECT-COMPUTER: This paragraph defines the computer on which the program produced by the compiler is to run.
3. SPECIAL-NAMES: This paragraph relates the actual names of the hardware used by the COBOL compiler to the names used in the program.

INPUT-OUTPUT SECTION: This section deals with the most efficient handling between the media and the object program and it consists of two paragraphs:

1. I-O-CONTROL which defines special input-output techniques.
2. FILE-CONTROL which names and associates the files with external media.

DATA DIVISION

COBOL makes the distinction between the *what* of processing and the *how* of processing. The what is included in the DATA DIVISION and the how is included in the PROCEDURE DIVISION. Although these two divisions are separate, they are interrelated. This separation is an important attribute of COBOL for it makes it possible to change from computer to computer without drastic revisions in the program. This is not true of many other computer languages.

The DATA DIVISION describes the files of data that are to be manipulated by the object program. Since a standard data format is used, the DATA DIVISION is to a large extent computer independent. Careful planning of the DATA DIVISION will permit the same data descriptions, with but minor modifications, to apply to more than one computer. Each item of data in the PROCEDURE DIVISION must be mentioned in the DATA DIVISION.

The DATA DIVISION is structured in three sections:

1. FILE section
2. WORKING-STORAGE section
3. CONSTANT section

Each of these will be discussed in turn, but first it should be mentioned that this division does not follow the paragraph, sentence, statement structure used in the PROCEDURE, ENVIRONMENT, and IDENTIFICATION DIVISIONS.

The basic unit in the DATA DIVISION is the entry. The entry consists of a level number, a data-name, and a series of independent clauses which may be separated by semicolons. The entry is terminated by a period. The section consists of a series of related or unrelated entries. A *File Description* consists of a single entry while the *Record Description* consists of one or more entries.

Level numbers for entries deserve extensive discussion at this point. Assigning level numbers is analogous to the outlining you have been exposed to in grammar school; it is inherent in any logical record system and comes from the need to identify subdivisions of records. To observe this analogy:

Outlining	*Programming*
I. Major topic	FD. Topic
A. Minor topic	01. First subtopic
1. First subtopic	02. First sub-subtopic
a. First sub-subtopic	03. First sub-sub-subtopic
b. Second sub-subtopic	03. Second sub-sub-subtopic
2. Second subtopic	02. Second sub-subtopic
a. First sub-subtopic	03. First sub-sub-subtopic
b. Second sub-subtopic	03. Second sub-sub-subtopic
c. Third sub-subtopic	03. Third sub-sub-subtopic

In COBOL, the various levels are indicated by a two-digit number, but the FD, standing for the File Description, does not have a number. Rather than follow the conventional numbering system, observe that all items on the same level have the same number. One level is contained within another if the second item has a higher level item and follows the first item; and there are no level numbers lower than the second number in between the first and second.

Indenting the topics, as shown, is optional, but if it is used the indentation must always be four spaces between levels. Forty-nine is the highest level number which may be used, but it is more than sufficient for any application. There are special level numbers which will be used later.

With this explanation of level numbers, which are used in the whole DATA DIVISION, it is time to look at each individual section.

The FILE section contains two elements, File Descriptions and Record Descriptions, of both label records (tapes) and data records:

1. The File Description refers to the physical aspect of the file.
2. The Record Description must follow the File Description for any particular file and refers to the conceptual characteristics of the data contained in the file.

The formats of the File Description and Record Description are shown in Figures 15–16 and 15–17, and explanations are given below the format for each.

The word PICTURE, appearing in the Record Description, is worthy of more discussion. It is used to dictate a detailed picture in the Standard

Figure 15–16

File Description

```
Option 1: FD file-name COPY library-name.
          This option is used when the COBOL library contains the entire File Description entry.

Option 2: (a) FD file-name   (b) [; RECORDING MODE IS mode]   (c) [; FILE CONTAINS ABOUT integer-1 RECORDS]

          (d) [; BLOCK CONTAINS [integer-2 TO] integer-3 {RECORDS   }]
                                                         {CHARACTERS}

          (e) [; RECORD CONTAINS [integer-4 TO] integer-5 CHARACTE RS]   (f) ; LABEL {RECORDS ARE}
                                                                                     {RECORD IS  }
          {STANDARD                    }
          {OMITTED                     } [, {data-name-2               }]
          {data-name-1                 }    {library-name-2 IN LIBRARY}
          {library-name-1 IN LIBRARY   }

          (g) [; VALUE OF data-name-3 IS {data-name-4 [HASHED]} [data-name-5 IS . . .]]
                                         {literal             }

          (h) ; DATA {RECORD IS  } data-name-6 [, data-name-7 . . .]
                     {RECORDS ARE}

          (i) [; SEQUENCED ON data-name-8 [, data-name-9 . . .]]
```

Note: The letters ( ) are not part of the program but a key to the explanations given below:

(*a*) File description.
(*b*) Specifies the format or organization of data on external media. When computer has only one mode this clause is not needed.
(*c*) Indicates the approximate number of logical records in a file and serves as an aid to optimization of the object program.
(*d*) Specifies the size of a physical record, that is, the block size.
(*e*) Specifies the size of data records.
(*f*) Used to cross-reference the descriptions of label records with their associated files.
(*g*) Particularizes the description of an item in the label records associated with a file.
(*h*) To cross-reference the description of data records with their associated files.
(*i*) Indicates keys on which data records are sequenced.

Figure 15–17

Record Descriptions

Option 1: level-number data-name [; REDEFINES]; COPY . . .

Option 2: (*a*) level-number {data-name / FILLER} (*b*) [; REDEFINES . . .] (*c*) [; SIZE . . .] (*d*) [; USAGE . . .] (*e*) [; OCCURS . . .]

(*f*) [; SIGN . . .] (*g*) [; SYNCHRONIZED . . .] (*h*) ; [POINT . . .] (*i*) [; CLASS . . .] (*j*) [; PICTURE . . .]

(*k*) [; JUSTIFIED . . .] (*l*) [; RANGE . . .] (*m*) [; editing clauses . . .] (*n*) [; VALUE . . .]

Note: The letters ( ) are not part of the program but a key to the explanations given below:
(*a*) Shows the hierarchy of data written in a logical record.
(*b*) To allow the same computer storage area to contain different data items.
(*c*) To specify, in terms of the number of standard data format characters, the size of an item.
(*d*) To specify the dominant use of a data item.
(*e*) To eliminate the need for separate entries for repeated data and to supply information required in the application of subscripts.
(*f**) To specify the operational sign of an elementary item.
(*g**) To specify positioning of an elementary item within a computer word or words.
(*h**) To define an assumed decimal point or binary point.
(*i*) To indicate the type of data being discussed: alphabetic, numeric, or alphanumeric.
(*j**) To show a detailed picture of the standard data format of an elementary item.
(*k**) To align, either right or left.
(*l**) To specify the potential range of the value of an item.
(*m**) The edit clause permits suppression of nonsignificant zeros and commas; permits floating dollar signs and blanking of zeros.
(*n*) To define value of constants.
* SIGN, SYNCHRONIZED, POINT, PICTURE, JUSTIFIED, and RANGE, as well as the editing clauses, must not be specified except at the elementary item level.

Data Format of an elementary item. This is done by symbols listed below, and the general structure of the PICTURE clause is:

```
[PICTURE IS { any allowable combination of the characters and symbols described below. }] [DEPENDING ON data-name]
```

Data characters:

9 represents a numeric character. For example, PICTURE 999 or PICTURE 9 (3) indicates three positions set aside for numbers.

A represents an alphabetic character. For example, PICTURE AAAA or PICTURE A (4) indicates that four positions have been set aside for the alphabetic characters.

X, in the same way, represents an ALPHANUMERIC character.

There are other characters available for zero suppression, for insertions—such as dollar signs—and for operation symbols.

The FILE section of the DATA DIVISION, just discussed, dealt with the requirements for the storage of each record of the files. The WORKING-STORAGE section of this same division has to do with that part of the computer memory set aside for the intermediate processing of data.

The WORKING-STORAGE section is different from the FILE section because it has only Record Descriptions rather than a File Description *and* a Record Description. Therefore it begins with a section-header, followed by a period, which in turn is followed by Record Description entries.

Items in WORKING-STORAGE which have no relationship to each other (noncontiguous) need not be grouped into records, provided they need no further subdivisions. Instead, they are classified and defined as noncontiguous items and each is given a separate Record Description which begins with the special level-number 77. Level-number, data-name, and CLASS or PICTURE, or SIZE (when PICTURE is not specified) are required in each entry.

Data elements in the WORKING-STORAGE section which bear a definite relationship to each other follow the general rules of the DATA DIVISION—as discussed for Record Descriptions.

The CONSTANT section of the DATA DIVISION is organized in the same way as the WORKING-STORAGE section. The concept of literals and figuratives permits the programmer to specify the value of a constant by writing its actual value. Often it is desirable to name the value and then refer to it by name. For example, a $2.25 per hour wage rate may be named WAGE-RATE and then referred to by its name WAGE-RATE and not by its value.

In review, the DATA DIVISION describes the files of data which are to be manipulated by the object program. It consists of the FILE section, WORKING-STORAGE section and the CONSTANT section. In the FILE section there are the File Description of the physical files and the

Record Description of the conceptual files. In the WORKING-STORAGE and the CONSTANT section only the Record Description exists.

PROCEDURE DIVISION

The PROCEDURE DIVISION contains those instructions needed to solve a given problem. It follows the syntax rules given earlier in that statements form sentences, which are combined to form paragraphs, which in turn may be combined to form sections. Recall that in the discussion of syntax it was also noted that at the statement level there are three different classifications:

Imperative statements, which consist of a verb (excluding compiler-directing verbs) and its operands.

Conditional statements, which may take the form:

$$\underline{\text{IF}}\ \text{condition}\ \left\{\begin{matrix}\text{statement-1}\\ \underline{\text{NEXT SENTENCE}}\end{matrix}\right\} \left\{\begin{matrix}\underline{\text{OTHERWISE}}\\ \underline{\text{ELSE}}\end{matrix}\right\} \left\{\begin{matrix}\text{statement-2}\\ \underline{\text{NEXT SENTENCE}}\end{matrix}\right\}$$

Compiler-Directing statements, which consist of a compiler-directing verb and its operands.

Recall that a statement or series of statements terminated by a period becomes a sentence, so there are imperative sentences, conditional sentences, and compiler sentences. In COBOL, imperative and conditional sentences describe the procedure to be accomplished. The sentences are written successively, according to the rules of the reference format, and establish the sequence in which the object program is to execute the procedure.

In the PROCEDURE DIVISION names are used so that one procedure can refer to another. In this way the sequence in which the object program is to be executed may be varied simply by transferring to a named procedure. The name consists of a noun, which is followed by a period, preceding the procedure it names.

In executing procedures, control is transferred only to the beginning of a paragraph. Control is passed to a sentence within a paragraph only from the sentence written immediately preceding it. If a procedure is named, control can be passed to it from the sentence immediately preceding it, or can be transferred to it from any sentence which contains a GO TO or PERFORM, followed by the name of the procedure to which control is to be transferred.

Conditional procedures, mentioned above, add immeasurably to the versatility of the computer program. COBOL conditionals generally contain the key word IF, followed by the conditions to be examined, followed by the operations to be performed. The flow chart for a simple conditional is shown at the right.

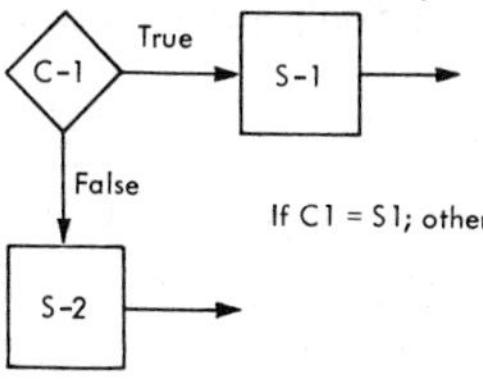

If C1 = S1; otherwise S2

Conditionals are classified as simple for two alternatives—or compound, consisting of two or more simple conditions which are interrelated. Simple conditionals have been classified as:

Relation tests: for numeric information to determine whether the value of one item is equal to, less, or greater than another.

Class tests: for determining whether the content of the item is numeric, alphabetic, or alphanumeric.

Conditional variable test: to determine whether or not one of the values associated with a condition name is present.

Switch status tests: to determine the ON or OFF status of a switch. The switch must be named in the SPECIAL-NAMES paragraph of the ENVIRONMENT DIVISION.

Writing compound conditionals is complicated, but it may be simplified by the following table:

A	B	NOT A	A AND B	A OR B
True	True	False	True	True
False	True	True	False	True
True	False	False	False	True
False	False	True	False	False

The simple conditions are combined with logical operators, as shown in the table, to form the compound conditions. For example, the first line of the table states that if A is TRUE, then A OR B and A AND B are TRUE, and not that A is FALSE.

DECLARATIVES are procedures which consist of compiler-directing sentences and their associated procedures. DECLARATIVES, if present, must be preceded by the key word DECLARATIVE and must be followed by the key words END DECLARATIVES. The DECLARATIVES must be grouped together at the beginning of the PROCEDURE DIVISION. The common DECLARATIVES and their meanings are:

DEFINE DECLARATIVE: Specifies the format and model of a new verb.

USE DECLARATIVE: Used to specify procedures which are to supplement the standard procedures provided by the input-output system.

INCLUDE DECLARATIVE: Used to incorporate a DECLARATIVE library routine in the source program, which is either a DEFINE DECLARATIVE or USE DECLARATIVE.

Formula Operations

Before writing a program that includes algebraic expressions it is necessary to understand how they are manipulated in the program.

1. Exponentiation is done first;
2. Multiplication and division are done next;
3. Addition and subtraction follow.

Parentheses are used to eliminate ambiguities, and the computer operates from the innermost set outward. For any one precedence level, and if no parentheses are present, the operations occur from left to right.

Subscripts are integers whose values determine which element is being referenced in a table. The tables may have a maximum of three levels, such as this example of sales information:

An Outline Form	*Computer Language*
District	01 SALES-TABLE USAGE IS COMPUTATIONAL
State	02 DISTRICT SALES OCCUR 8 TIMES
City	03 STATE SALES OCCUR 5 TIMES
City	04 CITY SALES OCCUR 25
⋮	TIMES; PICTURE IS 99999 99
City	
State	
City	
⋮	
City	
State	
⋮	
District	

In working with tables, two things are needed: a specification of size in the DATA DIVISION, and a means of referencing a specific item in the table—which is done with subscripts in the PROCEDURE DIVISION. The entries in the DATA DIVISION are shown on the right. In referring to the table, a reference such as SALES (2, Georgia, Macon) would refer to the entry in the DATA DIVISION.

Verbs

The detailed discussion of the verbs, which make up the important part of the PROCEDURE DIVISION, is long overdue and will be taken up immediately. The verbs, remember, are single words, appearing in the PROCEDURE DIVISION, which specify an action. They are listed by categories and are given below. To discuss each one in detail would take more space than is available, but the important ones will be shown in their proper format in the sequence.

Arithmetic Verbs:	ADD SUBTRACT MULTIPLY DIVIDE COMPUTE	Data Movement: Ending:	MOVE EXAMINE STOP
Input-Output:	READ WRITE OPEN CLOSE ACCEPT DISPLAY	Compiler Directing Verbs:	ENTER EXIT INCLUDE NOTE
Procedure Branching:	GO ALTER PERFORM	Compiler-Directing Declaratives:	DEFINE USE INCLUDE

Arithmetic Verbs. All of the arithmetic verbs follow similar forms and will be discussed at one time.

The ADD verb has several forms, but two common ones are:

$$\underline{\text{ADD}} \left\{ \begin{matrix} \text{data-name-1} \\ \text{literal-1} \end{matrix} \right\} \underline{\text{TO}} \text{ data-name-2}$$

$$\underline{\text{ADD}} \left\{ \begin{matrix} \text{data-name-1} \\ \text{literal-1} \end{matrix} \right\} \left\{ \begin{matrix} \text{data-name-2} \\ \text{literal-2} \end{matrix} \right\} \underline{\text{GIVING}} \text{ data-name-3}$$

The first form is used when the answer is to replace data-name-2 and the second form is used when the answer is to replace a data-name other than 1 or 2.

In the other arithmetic operations, ADD and TO are replaced with SUBTRACT and FROM, MULTIPLY and BY, or DIVIDE and INTO. The GIVING option is also applicable in these other arithmetic operations.

If the arithmetic operation produces an answer with a decimal larger than the allotted space, the answer will be truncated unless the word ROUNDED is added. For example, .279 would be stored in a two-decimal position as .27 (truncated) unless the ROUNDED command is given, in which case the answer would be .28.

On the other hand, the answer may extend too far to the left of the decimal point, overflowing the storage space. Overflow may be tested by an ON $\underline{\text{SIZE}}$ $\underline{\text{ERROR}}$ following the arithmetic statement. Ordinarily a GO TO statement will follow this, telling how the condition should be handled.

The COMPUTE verb permits the use of formulas:

$$\underline{\text{COMPUTE}} \text{ data-name-1 } [\underline{\text{ROUNDED}}] \left\{ \begin{matrix} \underline{\text{FROM}} \\ \underline{=} \\ \underline{\text{EQUALS}} \end{matrix} \right\} \left\{ \begin{matrix} \text{data-name-2} \\ \text{formula} \end{matrix} \right\}$$

$$[\text{; ON } \underline{\text{SIZE}} \ \underline{\text{ERROR}} \text{ any imperative statement}]$$

Input-Output. The READ verb is used to make the next logical record available from an input file. A common form of the sentence is:

$$\underline{\text{READ}} \text{ file-name RECORD } [\underline{\text{INTO}} \text{ data-name}] \text{ [; AT } \underline{\text{END}} \text{ any imperative statement]}$$

The OPEN statement for the file must be executed prior to the execution of the first READ for that file. The INTO option is the equivalent of a READ followed by a MOVED for the entire record. The AT END and an imperative statement dictates the routine in case an "end of reel" signal is obtained. If the AT END and imperative statement is written only once, the compiler will automatically assume that it goes with all other READS pertaining to the file.

The WRITE verb is used to release a logical record for an output file and to allow for vertical positioning if the output medium is an on-line printer. Its form is:

```
                                              ┌ ┌BEFORE┐            ┐
WRITE record-name [FROM data-name-1]          │ ┤      ├ADVANCING   │
                                              │ └AFTER ┘            │
                         ┌data-name-2 LINES┐                        │
                         ┤integer LINES    ├                        │
                         └mnemonic-name    ┘                        ┘
```

The OPEN verb is used to indicate the processing of both input and output files. Its general form is:

```
      ┌ [INPUT file-name-1  [REVERSED]  [, file-name-2 . . .] ┐
OPEN  ┤                                                       ├
      └ [OUTPUT file-name-3  [, file-name-4]  . . .]          ┘
```

The verb OPEN must be applied to all files and must be executed prior to the first READ or WRITE for a file. A second OPEN of a file cannot be executed prior to the execution of a CLOSE of the file.

The CLOSE verb terminates the processing of input and output reels and files, with optional rewind and/or lock:

```
                           ┌      ┌NO REWIND┐┐
CLOSE file-name-1 [REEL]   │WITH  ┤         ├│ [, file-name-2 . . .]
                           └      └LOCK     ┘┘
```

The ACCEPT verb makes it possible to receive low-volume data from an available hardware device:

```
ACCEPT data-name [FROM mnemonic-name]
```

The DISPLAY verb, on the other hand, makes it possible to display low-volume data on an available hardware device:

```
        ┌literal-1  ┐ ┌  ┌literal-2  ┐       ┐
DISPLAY ┤           ├ │, ┤           ├ . . . │ [UPON mnemonic-name]
        └data-name-1┘ └  └data-name-2┘       ┘
```

Procedure Branching. The GO verb is used to depart from the normal sequence of procedures and can be very simply stated:

```
GO TO [procedure-name-1]
```

ALTER is for modifying a predetermined sequence of operations:

```
ALTER procedure-name-1  TO PROCEED TO procedure-name-2
```

The PERFORM verb is used to depart from the normal sequence of procedures in order to execute a statement or series of statements a specified number of times or until a condition is satisfied. Then a means is provided for returning to the normal sequence. It is an important procedure-branching verb and is called into play when a subroutine is used repeatedly. Using subroutines repeatedly is one of the ways the computers are coaxed into operating more efficiently. The subroutine "loops" may be executed one or a number of times, as determined by a variety of controls. In its simplest form, the PERFORM statement looks like this:

```
PERFORM procedure-name-1 [THRU procedure-name-2]
```

It can be much more complicated than this, too.

Data Movement. The MOVE verb is used to transfer data, in accordance with the rules of editing, to one or more data areas:

```
MOVE { [CORRESPONDING] data-name-1 }
     { literal                     }
TO data-name-2 [, data-name-3 . . .]
```

The EXAMINE verb is used to replace and/or count the number of occurrences of a given character in a data item:

```
                          { UNTIL FIRST }
         { TALLYING       { ALL         } literal-1                          }
         {                { LEADING     }                                     }
EXAMINE  {                               [REPLACING BY literal-2]            }
data-name{                { ALL          }                                    }
         { REPLACING      { LEADING      } literal-3 BY literal-4            }
                          { [UNTIL] FIRST}
```

Ending. The STOP verb is used to halt the object program either pernently or temporarily, and it takes the form:

```
STOP { literal }
     { RUN     }
```

The "STOP literal" could indicate an error condition, and the computer must be told to continue while the STOP RUN terminates the running of the object program.

Compiler-Directing Verbs. ENTER provides a means of allowing the use of more than one language in the same program:

```
ENTER language-name [routine-name]
```

EXIT furnishes an end point for a loop when this is required. It is used in conjunction with procedures referenced by either the PERFORM or the USE verb. It is stated very simply: EXIT.

INCLUDE is used to incorporate library routines into the source program. A library routine is a COBOL procedure which has been stored in a library. The routine is composed of either one COBOL paragraph or one COBOL section. The routine is copied from the library during the compilation, and the results are the same as if it were part of the source program. Its form:

INCLUDE procedure-name

[REPLACING {routine-word-1 / data-name-1} BY {word-1 / data-name-2}]

NOTE is used to allow the programmer to write explanatory statements in the PROCEDURE DIVISION of his program, which will be produced on the listing but not compiled. Its form is very simply: NOTE . . .

Compiler-Directing Declaratives. DEFINE allows new verbs to be defined in the terms of standard COBOL verbs, thus maintaining both an open end and compatability:

DEFINE verb-name WITH FORMAT verb-name

USE specifies the procedures for any computer input-output error and for label-handling, both of which are in addition to the standard procedures supplied by the input-output system. One example of how this verb is used is:

USE AFTER STANDARD ERROR PROCEDURE ON {file-name / INPUT / OUTPUT}

APPLICATION OF COBOL

You are probably not an expert programmer now—at least not from the knowledge you have gained from this short introduction to COBOL. Hopefully, you have some feel for the subject and are able to understand a prepared program when you read it. To check this understanding, read through the example program which is presented in Figure 15–18.

COBOL IN REVIEW

It is impossible to cover, within these few pages, all the many details of COBOL included in the extensive government manuals and other programming books which deal exclusively with the subject. You have obtained a mountain-top view of COBOL logic, and you have been properly impressed, so that when the time comes for you to discuss programming—or even write a program—you will have a structure upon which to build.

The straightforward logic of COBOL is evident in its standard format. Its versatility is enhanced by the four IDENTIFICATION, ENVIRONMENT, DATA, and PROCEDURE divisions, of which only the ENVIRONMENT division is computer-dependent. It is this feature which makes COBOL one of the most important events in computer history.

Figure 15–18

COBOL Example

```
       PROG.1                      JOB 326                    DATE 01/22/65           TIME 03.029       PAGE  1

REPLICA CF THE SOURCE PROGRAM AUGMENTED BY THE EQUIVALENT NAMES AND CARD NUMBERS ASSIGNED BY THE COMPILER.

            0000 $IBCBC PRCG.1.

            0001        ICENTIFICATION DIVISION.
            0002        PRCGRAM-ID. PAYROLL-MASTER-FILE. PROG.1. FOR CS 580.
            0003        AUTHORS. H.M. SETHNA + D. WATANAPCNGSE.
            0004        DATE-WRITTEN. JAN 1C,1965.
            0005        REMARKS. CESIGNED FOR WEEKLY PAYROLL COMPUTATION.
            0006        ENVIRONMENT DIVISION.
            0007        CONFIGURATION SECTICN.
            0008        SOLRCE-COMPUTER. IBM-7094.
            0009        OBJECT-COMPUTER. IBM-7094.
            0010        INPUT-OUTPUT SECTION.
     EN0224 0011        FILE-CONTROL.  SELECT INPUT-FILE ASSIGN TO SYSIN1.
     EN0228 0012                       SELECT OUTPUT-FILE ASSIGN TO SYSOU1.
            0013        DATA DIVISION.
            0014        FILE SECTION.
            0015        FD  INPUT-FILE
     ENC234(0015)
            0016            LABEL RECORDS ARE OMITTED
            0017            DATA RECORD IS DATA-CARD.
            0018        01  DATA-CARD.
     ENC235(0018)
     EN0237 0019            02 NAME            PICTURE X(30).
     EN0238 0020            02 PAY-RATE        PICTURE 99V999.
```

Figure 15–18—Cont.

```
ENO239 0021          02 FILLER            SIZE 5.
ENO240 0022          02 HRS-WORKED          PICTURE 99V99.
       0023      FD  OUTPUT-FILE
ENO241(0023)
       0024          LABEL RECORDS ARE OMITTED
       0025          DATA RECORD IS OUTPUT-RECORD.
ENO242 0026      01  OUTPUT-RECORD      PICTURE X(132).
       0027      WORKING-STORAGE SECTION.
ENO245 0028      77  TEMP-1             PICTURE 999V99.
ENO246 0029      77  TEMP-2             PICTURE 999V99.
       0030      01  PAY-TABLE.
ENO247(0030)
ENO248 0031          02 FILLER          PICTURE 9         VALUE 0.
ENO249 0032          02 NAME            PICTURE X(30).
ENO250 0033          02 PAY-RATE        PICTURE $$.999.
ENO251 0034          02 FILLER          PICTURE A(7)      VALUE SPACE.
ENO252 0035          02 HRS-WORKED      PICTURE Z9.99.
ENO253 0036          02 FILLER          PICTURE A(10)     VALUE SPACE.
ENO254 0037          02 GROSS-PAY       PICTURE $$$.99.
ENO255 0038          02 FILLER          PICTURE A(8)      VALUE SPACE.
ENO256 0039          02 FICATAX         PICTURE $$$.99.
ENO257 0040          02 FILLER          PICTURE A(6)      VALUE SPACE.
ENO258 0041          02 NET-PAY         PICTURE $$$.99.
ENO259 0042          02 FILLER          PICTURE A(41)     VALUE SPACE.
       0043      01  HEADING.
ENO260(0043)
ENO261 0044          02 FILLER          SIZE 1        VALUE 1.
ENO262 0045          02 FILLER          SIZE  4       VALUE 'NAME'.
ENO263 0046          02 FILLER          SIZE 26       VALUE SPACE.
ENO264 0047          02 FILLER          SIZE  8       VALUE 'PAY-RATE'.
```

The syntax of COBOL is well organized, with characters building words, words statements, etc. The only difficulty you will encounter is adhering to the detailed rules. The list of reserved words, with their strict interpretation, is typical of one of the sets of rules you must learn to live by.

COBOL's near-English statements, its universal acceptance by most computers, and its logical structure make it the computer language which promises to take a prominent place in industrial applications.

SUMMARY

As you might expect, system designing is more complicated for computers than it is for either manual methods or card-data processing. Making an efficient computer program requires sufficient knowledge of computer hardware as well as software. As in solving any problem, there is a logical approach, and this can be summarized in the following steps:

1. Make a statement of the problem.
2. State the problem with a flow chart:
   a) A work-flow chart to show what is to be done.
   b) A detailed block diagram to show how the work is to be done.
3. Code the block diagram in the language of the computer program.
4. Convert the source program when necessary.
5. Debug the program when necessary.
6. Place the program and data in the computer and solve.

Figure 15–18—Cont.

```
   PROG.1                        JOB 326                       DATE 01/22/65              TIME 03.029      PAGE  2

EN0265 0048            02 FILLER        SIZE  5     VALUE SPACE.
ENC266 0049            02 FILLER        SIZE 10     VALUE 'HRS-WORKED'.
EN0267 0050            02 FILLER        SIZE  5     VALUE SPACE.
EN0268 0051            02 FILLER        SIZE  9     VALUE 'GROSS-PAY'.
EN0269 0052            02 FILLER        SIZE  5     VALUE SPACE.
EN0270 0053            02 FILLER        SIZE  7     VALUE 'FICATAX'.
EN0271 0054            02 FILLER        SIZE  5     VALUE SPACE.
EN0272 0055            02 FILLER        SIZE  7     VALUE 'NET-PAY'.
EN0273 0056            02 FILLER        SIZE 40     VALUE SPACE.
       0057        CONSTANT SECTION.
EN0275 0058        77  FICATAX-RATE  PICTURE 99V99      VALUE .18.
       0059        PRCCEDURE DIVISION.
       0060        BECIN.
ENC278(0060)
       0061            OPEN INPUT INPUT-FILE OUTPUT OUTPUT-FILE.
       0062            WRITE OUTPUT-RECORD FROM HEADING.
       0063        REAC-DATA-CARC.
ENC279(0063)
       0064            READ INPUT-FILE RECORD
       0065                AT END GO TC END-OF-JOB.
       0066            MOVE CORRESPONDING DATA-CARD TO PAY-TABLE.
       0067            COMPUTE TEMP-2 ROUNDED = PAY-RATE OF CATA-CARD * HRS-W
       0068      -     ORKED OF CATA-CARD.
       0069            MULTIPLY TEMP-2 BY FICATAX-RATE GIVING TEMP-1 ROUNDED.
       0070            COMPUTE NET-PAY ROUNDED = TEMP-2 - TEMP-1.
       0071            COMPUTE FICATAX EQUALS TEMP-1.
       0072            COMPUTE GROSS-PAY EQUALS TEMP-2.
       0073            WRITE OUTPUT-RECORD FROM PAY-TABLE.
       0074            GO TO REAC-DATA-CARD.
       0075        ENC-OF-JOB.
EN0280(0075)
       0076            CLOSE INPUT-FILE   OUTPUT-FILE.
       0077            STOP RUN.
       0078 $CBEND
```

Usually the initial step is to make a flow chart which expresses your interpretation of how the system should function. This flow chart may show only the gross steps, but eventually it will be refined to a block diagram showing (in detail) the steps which must be taken in the program.

After diagramming the flow of information, the information is coded. This can either be done directly with machine language or by putting it in a form suitable for translation to machine language by one of the various translators, such as COBOL.

You now have a basic knowledge of computer hardware and software, but don't let this lull you into inactivity. Knowledge is expanding in this area and new equipment and techniques are being introduced daily. Form the habit of keeping up with these innovations.

Acknowledgment (for COBOL-61 Manual)

This publication is based on the COBOL System developed in 1959 by a committee composed of government users and computer manufacturers. The organizations participating in the original development were: Air Materiel Command, United States Air Force; Bureau of Standards, Department of Commerce; David Taylor Model Basin, Bureau of Ships, United States Navy; Electronic Data Processing Division, Minneapolis-Honeywell Regulator Company; Burroughs Corporation; International Business Machines Corporation; Radio Corporation of America; Sylvania Electric Products, Inc.; Univac Division of Sperry-Rand Corporation.

In addition to the organizations listed above, the following other organizations participated in the work of the Maintenance Group: Allstate Insurance Company; Bendix Corporation, Computer Division; Control Data Corporation; DuPont Corporation; General Electric Company; General Motors Corporation; Lockheed Aircraft Corporation; National Cash Register Company; Philco Corporation; Standard Oil Company (New Jersey); United States Steel Corporation.

This COBOL-61 manual is the result of contributions made by all of the abovementioned organizations. No warranty, expressed or implied, is made by any contributor or by the committee as to the accuracy and functioning of the programming system and language. Moreover, no responsibility is assumed by any contributor, or by the committee, in connection therewith.

It is reasonable to assume that a number of improvements and additions will be made to COBOL. Every effort will be made to insure that the improvements and corrections will be made in an orderly fashion, with due recognition of existing users' investments in programming. However, this protection can be positively assured only by individual implementors.

Procedures have been established for the maintenance of COBOL. Inquiries concerning the procedures and the methods for proposing changes should be directed to the Executive Committee of the Conference on Data Systems Languages.

The authors and copyright holders of the copyrighted material used herein, FLOW-MATIC (Trademark of Sperry-Rand Corporation), Programming for the UNIVAC® I and II, Data Automation Systems © 1958, 1959, Sperry-Rand Corporation; IBM Commercial Translator, Form No. F 28-8013, copyrighted 1959 by IBM; FACT, DSI 27A5260-2760, copyrighted 1960 by Minneapolis-Honeywell, have specifically authorized the use of this material, in whole or in part, in the COBOL specification. Such authorization extends to the reproduction and use of COBOL specifications in programming manuals or similar publications.

Any organization interested in reproducing the COBOL report and initial specifications in whole or in part, using ideas taken from this report or utilizing this report as the basis for an instruction manual or any other purpose, is free to do so. However, all such organizations are requested to reproduce this section as part of the introduction to the document. Those using a short passage, as in a book review, are requested to mention "COBOL" in acknowledgment of the source, but need not quote this entire section.

Questions

1. What advantages are there in *flow charting* computer operations?
2. Flow-chart some simple system with which you are acquainted, such as the one used to check out books in a library or supplies from the chemistry storeroom.
3. Computers have been referred to as "*magic brains*." To what extent is this true?
4. Compare the advantages and disadvantages of machine language and automatic programming.
5. What is the purpose of the *buffer* in the computer?
6. To what extent is the form of the instruction for machine language left to the discretion of the programmer?
7. Define: (*a*) branching, (*b*) register, and (*c*) block diagram.
8. Draw a simplified flow chart of the operations required for programming in machine-language and automatic programming.
9. What advantages does COBOL have over other automatic programming systems?
10. What is the sequence of the program divisions? Briefly explain the purpose of each division.

References

BECKER, JOSEPH, and HAYES, ROBERT M. *Information Storage and Retrieval: Tools, Elements, Theories*. New York: John Wiley & Sons, Inc., 1964.

BROOKS, FREDERICK PHILLIPS, JR., and IVERSON, KENNETH E. *Automatic Data Processing*. New York: John Wiley & Sons, Inc., 1963.

CANNING, RICHARD G. *Electronic Data Processing for Business and Industry*. New York: John Wiley & Sons, Inc., 1956.

———. *Installing Electronic Data-Processing Systems*. New York: John Wiley & Sons, Inc., 1957.

CHAPIN, NED. *Programming Computers for Business Applications*. New York: McGraw-Hill Book Co., Inc., 1961.

DEPARTMENT OF DEFENSE, SUPERINTENDENT OF DOCUMENTS, U.S. GOVERNMENT PRINTING OFFICE. *COBOL—1961*. Washington, D.C.

DESMONDE, WILLIAM H. *Computers and Their Uses*. Englewood Cliffs, N.J.: Prentice-Hall, Inc., 1964.

ELLIOTT, C. O., and WASLEY, ROBERT S. *Business Information Processing Systems*. Homewood, Ill.: Richard D. Irwin, Inc., 1965.

FISHER, F. PETER, and SWINDLE, GEORGE F. *Computer Programming Systems*. New York: Holt, Rinehart & Winston, Inc., 1964.

GALLER, BERNARD A. *The Language of Computers*. New York: McGraw-Hill Book Co., Inc., 1962.

GREENE, JAMES H. "Computer Integration for Small Industy." *Systems Magazine*, Vol. XXII, No. 2 (March-April 1958).

GREGORY, ROBERT H., and VAN HORN, RICHARD L. *Automatic Data-Processing Systems*. San Francisco, Calif.: Wadsworth, 1960.

GRUENBERGER, FRED J., and McCRACKEN, D. D. *Introduction to Electronic Computers*. New York: John Wiley & Sons, Inc., 1963.

IRWIN, WAYNE C. *Digital Computer Principles*. Princeton, N.J.: D. Van Nostrand Co., Inc, 1960.

LADEN, H. N., and GILDERSLEEVE, T. R. *System Design for Computer Applications*. New York: John Wiley & Sons, Inc., 1964.

LAUBACH, PETER B. *Company Investigations of Automatic Data Processing*. Boston: Graduate School of Business Administration, Harvard University, 1957.

LEDLEY, ROBERT S., and WILSON, JAMES B. *Programming and Utilizing Digital Computers*. New York: McGraw-Hill Book Co., Inc., 1962.

LEESON, DANIEL N., and DIMITRY, DONALD L. *Basic Programming Concepts and the IBM 1620 Computer*. New York: Holt, Rinehart & Winston, Inc., 1962.

MANDL, MATTHEW. *Fundamentals of Digital Computers*. Englewood Cliffs, N.J.: Prentice-Hall, Inc., 1960.

MARTIN, E. W., JR. *Electronic Data Processing*. Rev. ed. Homewood, Ill.: Richard D. Irwin, Inc., 1965.

McCRACKEN, DANIEL D. *A Guide to COBOL Programming*. New York: John Wiley & Sons, Inc., 1963.

———. *A Guide to FORTRAN Programming*. New York: John Wiley & Sons, Inc., 1962.

———. *A Guide to IBM 1401 Programming*. New York: John Wiley & Sons, Inc., 1963.

———. *Digital Computer Programming*. New York: John Wiley & Sons, Inc., 1957.

———; WEISS, HAROLD; and LEE, TSAI-HWA. *Programming Business Computers*. New York: John Wiley & Sons, Inc., 1962.

MEACHAM, ALAN D., and THOMPSON, VAN B. *Total Systems*. Detroit: American Data Processing, 1962.

OAKFORD, ROBERT V. *Introduction to Electronic Data Processing Equipment*. New York: McGraw-Hill Book Co., Inc., 1962.

O'NEAL, LEELAND R. *Electronic Data Processing Systems: A Self-Instructional Programmed Manual*. Englewood Cliffs, N.J.: Prentice-Hall, Inc., 1964.

ORGANICK, ELLIOTT I. *A Primer for Programming with the FORTRAN Language*. Houston, Texas: University of Houston Computing and Data Processing Center, 1961.

RICHARDS, RICHARD KOHLER. *Digital Computer Components and Circuits*. Princeton, N.J.: D. Van Nostrand Co., Inc., 1959.

SAXON, JAMES A. *COBOL, A Self-Instructional Manual*. Englewood Cliffs, N.J.: Prentice-Hall, Inc., 1963.

SCHMIDT, RICHARD N., and MEYERS, WILLIAM E. *Electronic Business Data Processing*. New York: Holt, Rinehart & Winston, Inc., 1963.

SHERMAN, PHILIP M. *Programming and Coding Digital Computers*. New York: John Wiley & Sons, Inc., 1963.

SIEGEL, PAUL. *Understanding Digital Computers*. New York: John Wiley & Sons, Inc., 1961.

SMITH, J. SANDFORD. *The Management Approach to Electronic Digital Computers*. London: Macdonald & Evans, 1957.

SPRAGUE, RICHARD E. *Electronic Business Systems*. New York: Ronald Press Co., 1962.

WALLACE, EDWARD L. *Management Influence on the Design of Data Processing Systems, A Case Study*. Boston: Graduate School of Business Administration, Harvard University, 1961.

WRUBEL, MARSHAL H. *A Primer of Programming for Digital Computers*. New York: McGraw-Hill Book Co., Inc., 1959.

SECTION FOUR

Decision Making

CHAPTER 16

Graphical Scheduling

To schedule is to make a timetable for activities which are using certain facilities. In this case the interest is in making a timetable for manufacturing orders using the production facilities in the plant. The problems, however, are not a great deal different than those encountered in setting up railroad schedules, athletic-event schedules, or class schedules. The time for each activity must be predicted by methods similar to those discussed in Chapter 9, *Scheduling Information*. The activities must be coordinated to optimize investments, transportation, payrolls, or any other desired criteria.

This chapter is devoted primarily to graphical decision-making techniques, but some of them can be extended to the applications of computers. The emphasis here will be placed upon the principles, but many of these principles are applied to commercial appliances, such as the Produc-trol Board and Sched-U-Graph, which are readily available on the market. These appliances, or hardware, will be discussed separately in Chapter 18.

The examples given here will be just extensive enough to make the principles clear. Nothing will put a student in shock quicker than studying elaborate scheduling charts. Before presenting the scheduling techniques, it is desirable to clarify some of the things that scheduling is not.

MASTER SCHEDULE

The Master Schedule (Figure 16–1), like the Production Order, is an authority to manufacture. It is issued periodically by management to let the factory know how much of each product is to be produced in each of several time periods. The Master Schedule is used primarily in high production industries making a limited number of products. This important production form also goes under such names as the Manufacturing Master Schedule, Release, Manufacturing Release, and by others.

Figure 16–1

Master Schedule

ZEPHYR MANUFACTURING COMPANY
MASTER SCHEDULE

Date Aug. 1st
By T.I.M.

Model Number	Date	8/9	8/16	8/23	8/30	
65 - A - 732	7-18	50	50	50	50	
65 - A - 791	7-20	80	80	30	0	
65 - A - 891 L	7-21	120	120	120	120	
65 - A - 891 S	7-28	60	60	60	60	
65 - A - 890	7-28	90	90	90	90	
66 - A - 791	8-2	3	3	40	80	

The Master Schedule is an order and is related to the problems of scheduling. However, it is not as intimately related to the problem which we will be discussing: that of fitting the available facilities to the requirements.

LOADING

The schedule pertains to *when* an activity is to take place, and the load has to do with the *amount* of work to be done. The *work load* is the anticipated activity for a machine, department, or factory. The load is usually stated as being so many hours of work. A typical load chart is shown in Figure 16–2. Notice that the chart does not indicate when a task is to be performed but only how much work is ahead of each machine.

Figure 16–2

Load Chart

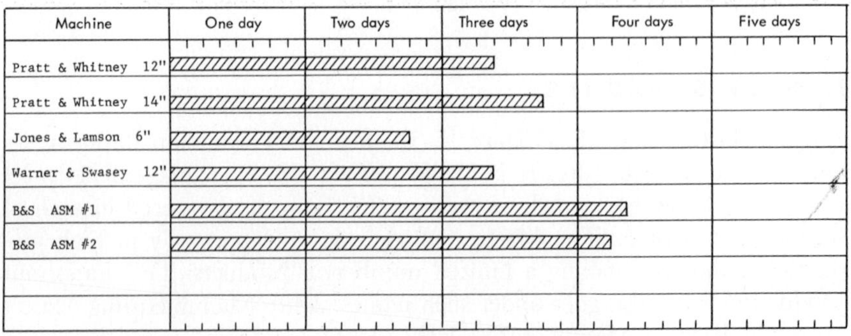

Calculating the load for a load chart is an extensive problem which is more easily understood if put as a series of steps:

Step 1. Determine the number of product assemblies to be produced, either from the master schedule or from the accumulation of manufacturing orders.
Step 2. Adjust this quantity by any excess or shortage in finished inventory.
Step 3. Determine the number of parts needed for each assembly by *product explosion* or similar technique (see Chapter 8).
Step 4. Multiply the quantity of assemblies required by the number of parts required per assembly: Step 2 × Step 3 = Step 4.
Step 5. Multiply, if necessary, by a scrap factor. If 100 is needed, and there is a loss of 15 percent in the process, then the order must be placed for at least 118: Assemblies started − 15% of assemblies started = 100.
Step 6. Adjust the number of parts by any excess or shortage in the parts inventory.
Step 7. Determine from the time-standards records the standard time for each operation for each part. Multiply this by the number of parts found in Step 6.
Step 8. Accumulate the time for each machine, department, or other breakdown desired.
Step 9. Adjust the times values, found in Step 8, by an efficiency factor. This is the work load: Accumulated time/efficiency = work load.

The order of the steps listed above can be altered slightly and still produce the correct answer. The work load is usually shown in some graphical method, such as the bar chart. If a work load is excessive, then other arrangements will have to be made—such as shifting the work to another machine or department, or perhaps even subcontracting the work to other shops.

By proper loading, those facilities which are not active will be revealed. This permits shifting of personnel, planning vacations, scheduling maintenance, and other activities. From the information obtained by loading it is possible to make the necessary labor budgets for hiring and laying off personnel.

The efficiency factor mentioned in the last step should be determined for each department. A common efficiency factor is 80 percent, although often this is not substantiated by facts. Some factories find that the slack in the standard time just compensates for the factory inefficiencies.

SCHEDULING REQUIRES FEEDBACK

In the second chapter, the need for feedback in a system with varying output was discussed. If the output is as planned, without any variation, there is no need for feedback, but this would seldom be the case because there are many unpredictable secondary inputs which are constantly changing the output from what has been planned.

The scheduling process is dynamic because conditions are changing constantly. In any good scheduling system the actual production is being constantly compared with the proposed, and necessary steps are taken to compensate for the error. This means that a feedback link is necessary to show what the actual production is.

More than one scheduling system has been devised without adequate feedback links, and the systems were soon abandoned. In the production control system the feedback link may consist of production tickets returned by the operators, showing the completion of a task; the move order, showing that the process is completed and the product has been moved; or a time card, showing that so much of the product is completed. Even a verbal report of the work completed might be suitable—if not as desirable as a written record. Some more elaborate systems have electric counters in the scheduling room which are attached directly to the machine, making a production count available every minute of the day. In some situations these counters have been tied directly to on-line computers which update the schedule constantly.

Often an employee feels that once a schedule is made it should not be tampered with. Nothing could be further from the truth. The schedule must be made to reflect reality or it is worthless, and this means that it must be adjusted periodically. How often it should be adjusted is a question of economics. Too-frequent adjustment may be wasteful, while too-infrequent adjustments may not present the information when wanted. To do scheduling efficiently requires certain kinds of personality characteristics not to be found in every individual.

SELECTING SCHEDULING PERSONNEL

Frequently, education is the predominant criterion for selecting people to do scheduling. While this is important, it should not be the only consideration. Some of the desirable attributes for scheduling personnel are:

1. A proficiency in working with details.
2. A knowledge of factory activities. They can frequently detect errors or propose alternate processes if they have a knowledge of the factory.
3. A good memory is useful, as is an ability to solve the "puzzles" of scheduling.
4. Involvement in their work is important; frequently they may be called on to work overtime.
5. Since they are in contact with many of the factory workers, and even customers at times, it is desirable that they have good personal habits and get along well with people.

It is probably impossible to find personnel with all these attributes, but if they are found they contribute immeasurably to the efficient operation of a factory.

Techniques for Scheduling

Here are a number of scheduling techniques. Some are not new but have proven themselves useful over the years; others are new, and appear to be important, but require further trial. As you will observe, some are very closely related while others are not.

1. Gantt Chart
2. Critical Path Method
3. PERT Scheduling
4. PERT/COST Scheduling
5. Line of Balance Scheduling

GANTT CHART

"Plan your work and work your plan" has long been a byword in industry, and for many years one of the best tools for doing this has been the Gantt Chart. The Gantt Chart is a simple way of showing graphically both the anticipated and completed production on the horizontal axis of a chart.

Henry L. Gantt developed this charting technique as one of his many contributions to the scientific management movement, and it is probably one of the most successful devices of this type ever invented. Some modification of the Gantt Chart is to be found in practically every production office, so the basic concepts of the technique should be understood by everyone in manufacturing management.

So much has been said and written about this method of planning and controlling production that the basic principles are frequently lost in a clutter of details. However, there are some real advantages in this technique which can be found in no others:

1. It forces a plan to be made, which in itself is a big step toward more efficient operations.
2. Work planned and work accomplished are easily compared; there is no need to remember a wealth of information for comparison purposes.
3. Gantt Charts are compact; one chart can replace file drawers full of information.
4. Anyone can produce a Gantt Chart with paper, pencil, and rule.
5. These charts are dynamic, showing a moving picture of plant activities.

Charts, you must realize, use a shorthand form of language and, to be effective, everyone using them must know the symbols. Many symbols have been used and there is nothing wrong if a company wishes to develop its own. There are some which are frequently used and a few of them (as shown in Figure 16–3) are given here to make the rest of the discussion understandable.

Just to show how this technique works, look at the example in Figure 16–4 for charting the manufacturing orders.

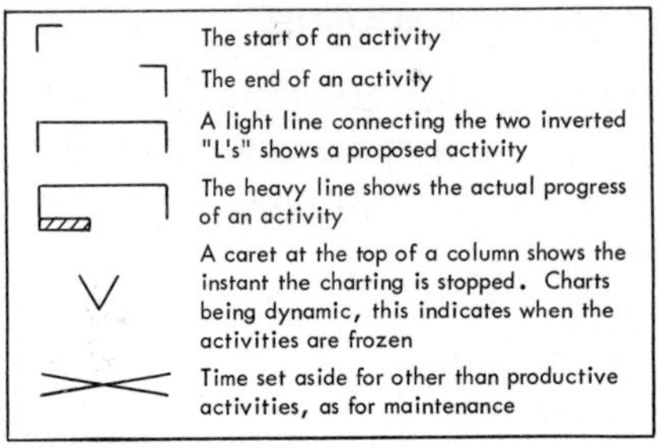

Figure 16–3

Gantt-Chart Symbols

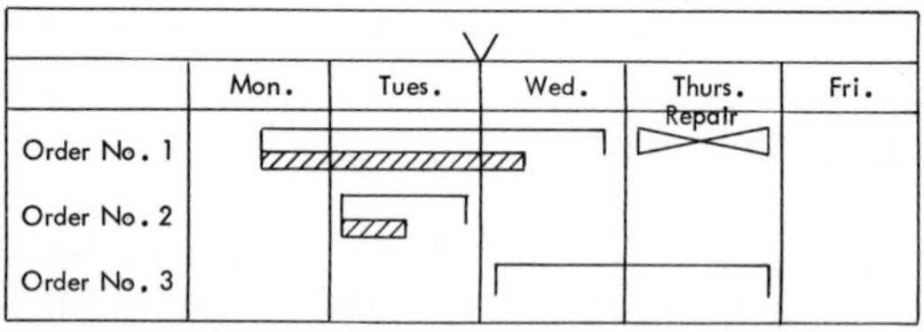

Figure 16–4

Example of a Gantt Chart

The chart was brought up to date Tuesday night, as shown by the caret, V. Order No. 1 was started Monday noon and is to be completed Wednesday night, as shown by the light line. The heavy line, which extends beyond the present time, shows that the order is ahead of schedule. By the same reasoning, order No. 2 is behind schedule and order No. 3 has not been started.

There are a few basic principles that must be understood before successful Gantt charting can be made. The first is that distances along the horizontal axis represent either time or production. For example, one can say that a space between two vertical lines on the charts represents one hour in which 15 parts are produced, or the space represents 15 parts which take one hour to produce. It doesn't matter which way you say it for it comes out the same. Again it should be pointed out that if production standards are in use they will have to be modified by the plant-efficiency factor to make them realistic.

Parallel to the light line, representing the proposed production, is a heavy line that shows the actual progress of production. The difference between the two lines shows how near the production is to completion.

A vertical line drawn through the caret at the top of the chart represents the instant the charting is stopped. The difference between the heavy-black progress line and the vertical line through the caret shows how far ahead or behind schedule the production is. This can be easily understood by referring to the example.

The Two Basic Charts

Although there are many confusing variations of the Gantt Chart, it is possible to classify them into two basic types. For want of better names these might be called *forward* and *backward* charts. The first one is frequently called a Schedule Chart and the work is scheduled from the present date forward to determine the completion date. The backward chart, which is often called a Project Chart, is used when a completion date is known and it is desired to work backwards to find a starting date.

A simple analogy might make the distinction between these charts easier to see. Take, for example, the planning of a trip by two alternatives, either train or car. The train, as you know, goes at a certain instant, and if you are not there it goes without you. In this case it is essential to start the planning from the instant the train leaves and work backwards to fit everything into the schedule. This kind of chart would be a backward or project type of chart.

On the other hand, if you can leave by car at any time, and it doesn't matter exactly when, then you can plan your work ahead from this present moment and leave at any time you wish; and for this you need a forward or schedule chart.

Another way of saying this is that for a forward, or schedule, chart you start at the left-hand side and work to the right for the completion date. On the backward or project chart you start with the completion date on the right-hand side and work to the left. Of course, in this latter case, you would start at the bottom and work upwards so that when you read it you will be following the conventional method. Backward and forward charting are two viewpoints and both are often used on one chart.

Often the question comes up as to what to chart. Chart whatever is worthwhile charting and for which data are available. Companies are now planning and controlling workers, work centers, machines, departments, plants, parts, work orders, operations, and assemblies by this very simple device. The earlier example showed how this technique could be used for keeping track of orders, but observe here (Figure 16–5) how it might be used for scheduling machines, and also an assembly (Figure 16–6).

Figure 16–5

Machine Scheduling Chart

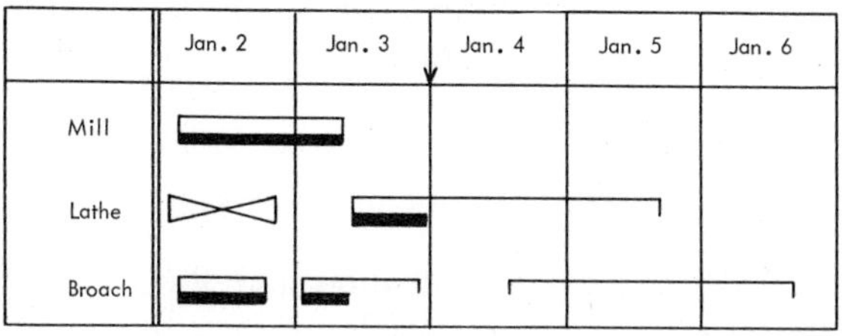

Note that this first example is usually a forward chart, for the objective is to keep the machines always loaded. Blank spaces are to be avoided for this shows when the machines are not productive. The chart should be self-explanatory if the previous symbols are understood.

Figure 16–6 is a good example of a backward or project chart. In this case it is desired not to finish before a certain date because of inventory costs and space limitations. It is easier to keep track of the necessary parts for the final assembly, and to be sure they are brought together in the final assembly on the required date, if a backward chart is used.

Figure 16–6

Project Chart

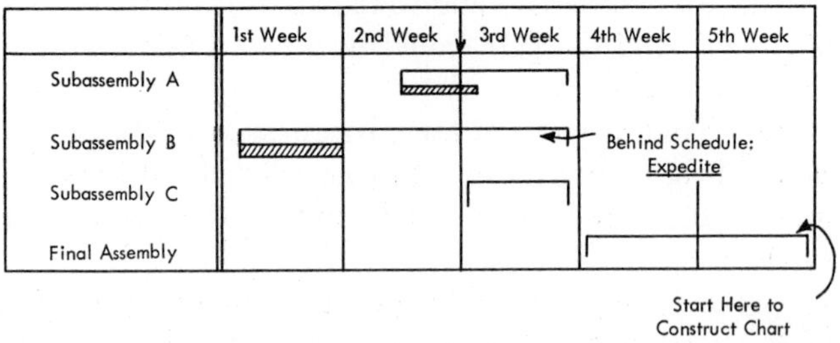

The methods proposed here can be used on any piece of ruled paper with the proper scale. Lines can be drawn in with pencil, crayon, or ink—although an erasable substance is preferred. One technique is to represent the lines with colored masking tape cut to length. A plastic overlay on a piece of coordinate paper makes an easily erased surface.

Several commercial applications of the Gantt Chart, discussed in Chapter 18, are available and should be explored before an installation is made. One common device, the Produc-trol Board, uses spring-loaded strings to represent the bars. Another popular application of the Gantt Chart is the Sched-U-Graph, a series of plastic-edged flaps mounted so that they overlap, showing a clear plastic edge. In the plastic edge can be placed cards cut to length to represent the bars. Both of the above systems have vertical dividers and methods of representing the caret.

Whatever system is used, a piece of cheap ruled paper or an elaborate commercial product, be sure the basic principles of the Gantt Chart apply. One should be cautious in accepting some standard plan proposed by the vendor of a commercial product. Rather, design the method to suit the problem.

Critical Path Method

CPM and PERT (Program Evaluation and Review Technique) are just two of the newer techniques which depict activities by a network. Usually these techniques have a limited use in production but are particularly useful for projects with one terminating event. RAMP (Review Analysis of Multiple Projects) is useful for guiding the activities of several projects at one time, but it has been slow in gaining acceptance.

As in the Gantt Chart, the CPM uses a set of shorthand symbols with which one must become familiar before using the method successfully. These symbols are shown in Figure 16–7.

Figure 16–7

Critical Path Symbols

Symbol	*Term*	*Comments*
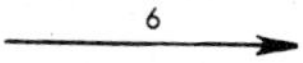	Activities	Shows an activity. No attempt is made to scale the arrow to represent time. A number over the arrow shows the time in units of hours, days, months, or other increments.
	Node, Event	An event or node is the end of an activity.
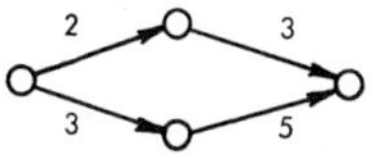	Network	Networks are composed of activities and events.
	Critical Path	The longest time path through the network.
	Float	Difference between the earliest and latest time a task can be completed and still stay on schedule. Also called "slack."
	Anchor Point	Latest time on the critical path.
	Latest Time	Start with Anchor Point and subtract each of the activity times.
	Earliest Time	Sum of activity times leading to an event.

There are several phases of the CPM and one has a choice of how far to carry it. How far to go is, of course, an economic decision and refinements should be included only on the promise of a payoff. Projects with hundreds of individual activities have been planned and scheduled by a computer. Some of the advantages of the Critical Path Method are:

1. It requires the selection of specific and well defined *events* which occur along the network of activities.
2. The events are linked with activities which show the interdependencies among events.
3. The development of a CPM chart requires an estimation of the time for all activities.
4. The critical aspects of each event are signaled well in advance of the occurrences.
5. Trade-offs between two activities may be calculated in terms of dollars, which makes it possible to decide which activities should or should not be expedited.

The Critical Path Method is easier to comprehend if it is approached in a step-by-step procedure.

Step 1. Planning: The first step is to list all the jobs, as shown on the left of the table in Figure 16–8, in the order of their precedence. From this, an *arrow diagram* is produced as shown. Each task is indicated by an arrow, with the direction of the arrow showing the sequence of the task. The length of the arrows has no significance. The jobs are placed on the diagram one by one, keeping in mind what precedes and follows each job as well as what jobs can be done simultaneously.

Figure 16–8

Critical Path Calculations

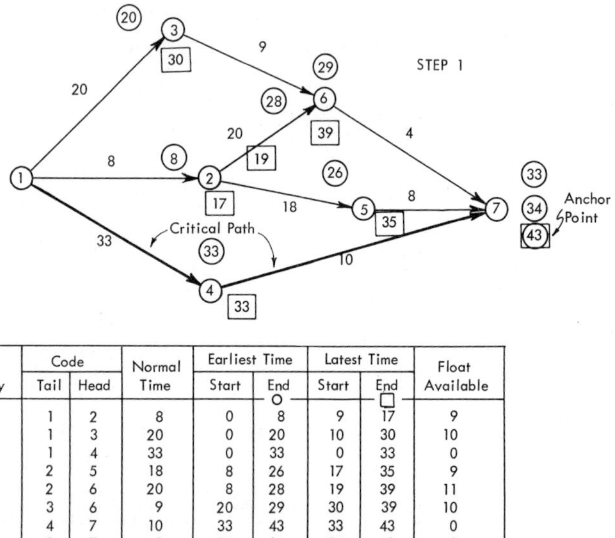

Activity	Code: Tail	Code: Head	Normal Time	Earliest Time: Start	Earliest Time: End ○	Latest Time: Start	Latest Time: End □	Float Available
List all activities here	1	2	8	0	8	9	17	9
	1	3	20	0	20	10	30	10
	1	4	33	0	33	0	33	0
	2	5	18	8	26	17	35	9
	2	6	20	8	28	19	39	11
	3	6	9	20	29	30	39	10
	4	7	10	33	43	33	43	0
	5	7	8	26	34	35	43	9
	6	7	4	29	33	39	43	10

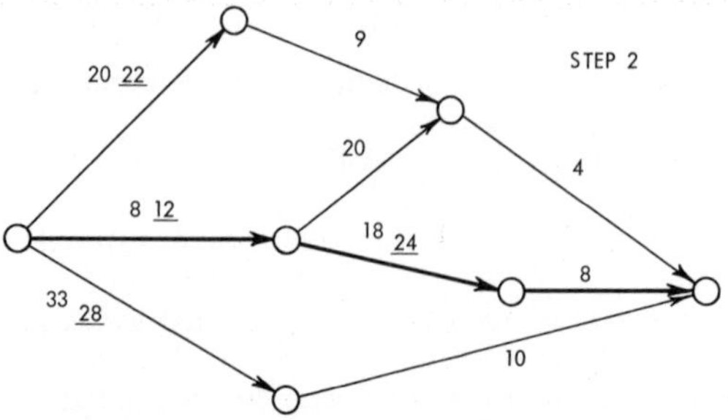

Step 2. *Scheduling:* The task times are considered to be deterministic if there is no great variation observable in the completion times. These time elements, shown adjacent to each arrow, are determined as accurately as possible and should reflect the normal times for each job, taking into consideration the usual delivery times and applying the typical work force.

The longest time path through the network is the *critical path,* shown by the dark line on the example. Every activity on this path must be completed on time or the schedule will fall behind. But what about the other paths? Each of the other paths has some slack time (which is also termed "float"). The method of determining this slack is shown in the table. It is first necessary to calculate the earliest possible time for each event. These are the circled figures on the diagram. Then, working backwards from the longest time—determined by the critical path—find the latest possible time. These latest times are shown by the figures in the squares. The difference between the earliest and latest time, for each node, is the slack.

It is apparent that there is no slack on the critical path. In fact, one way of defining the critical path is to say it is a path with no slack. Often two or more activities lead to one node, such as 6 on the diagram. You will notice that the latest time, 29, was used in making the forward calculations.

The advantage of CPM, up to this point, has been that all critical jobs are pinpointed and the amount of slack available on all noncritical legs of the network is readily obtained. This gives one the opportunity of trading off facilities between critical and noncritical jobs.

Step 3. *Cost Analysis:* The CPM cost analysis step makes it possible to determine the advantage or disadvantage of making any changes in the schedule. If it is necessary to compress a schedule, it is possible to determine in advance just how costly this step will be. Before looking at the application of this step, let us be sure the theory upon which it is based is understood.

In many situations management has some flexibility in determining the completion date of a task by merely adding more men and equipment. The relationship between the cost of adding facilities and the duration of a job can be illustrated by a cost-time curve similar to the one in Figure 16–9. The lowest point on the curve would be the *normal time,* T_n, and the management will undoubtedly try to work as close to this level as possible. It wouldn't be reasonable to schedule the job for any longer than the normal time—and thus increase the cost.

By adding extra facilities, the duration of the job is reduced and the cost is increased. The ultimate in applying extra facilities is indicated on the curve by the *crash time,* T_c. The curve between T_c and T_n can be approximated by a straight line, as shown. The slope of this line is referred to as the *cost slope* and is expressed as so many dollars per unit of time, such as $20 per day.

Figure 16–9

Critical Path Cost Information

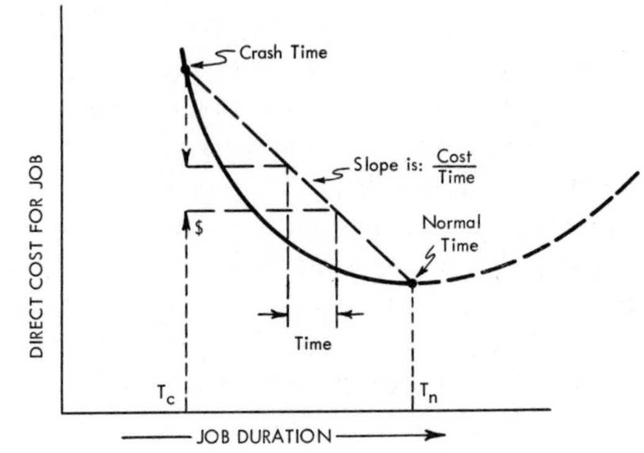

CPM COSTS

Activity	Normal Days	Normal Dollars	Crash Days	Crash Dollars	Cost Slope Dollars/Day
1-2	8	80.00	7	100.00	20.00
1-3	20	150.00	18	180.00	15.00
1-4	33	400.00	30	490.00	30.00
2-5	18	250.00	16	350.00	50.00
2-6	20	400.00	20	400.00	- - -
3-6	9	120.00	9	120.00	- - -
4-7	10	150.00	8	220.00	35.00
5-7	8	160.00	6	280.00	60.00
6-7	4	120.00	3	190.00	70.00
Total	130	Total	117		

Example for Job 1-2

Cost Slope, \$/Day =

$$\frac{\text{Crash cost} - \text{Normal cost}}{\text{Normal time} - \text{Crash time}} =$$

$$\frac{\$100.00 - \$80.00}{8 \text{ days} - 7 \text{ days}} = \$20.00/\text{Day}$$

Now to return to the application of this information to the network. The normal time and the crash time for each job are determined as well as the costs for these two conditions. From this can be determined the cost per unit time, as shown in the table. Now management has a tool and the information by which to make some reasonable decisions. If the cost for delaying the project is available, a comparison can be made between the cost of expediting the project and the cost of delay.

Step 4. Monitoring: Like all scheduling charts, the CPM is dynamic and is always subject to changes. The changes are dictated by a constant feedback of information. The source of the information depends upon the type of activity and could come from shipping orders, work orders, time cards, or other business forms.

If you will refer back to the second step of the Critical Path Diagram

(Figure 16–8) you can observe the changes caused by activities being ahead and behind schedule. The times for the completed activities are shown adjacent to the arrow by an underlined number. As you will observe, some of the activities were completed ahead of schedule while others fell behind. Consequently, the critical path has changed and management must turn its attention to finding ways of channeling the resources to complete the project on time. How the resources are allocated will depend upon what is a feasible schedule, as well as upon the economics of the situation as determined by the cost analysis of Step 3.

THE PERT METHOD OF SCHEDULING

PERT is an abbreviation for Program Evaluation and Review Technique, a technique which gained acceptability in government and industry after meeting with unusual success in the Polaris ballistic missile program. In such a program innumerable parts must be brought together at the right time to produce an extremely complex product. PERT is an ideal tool for scheduling such activities.

The objective of PERT is to put planning and evaluation on an orderly and consistent basis, and also to provide an automatic device to identify potential trouble spots. The PERT technique allows some degree of simulation as well, without requiring actual changes in the project schedule.

The important points of the PERT scheduling network can be summarized as follows:

1. PERT, like CPM, requires the selection of specific and well-defined "events" that occur along the network of activities.
2. The events are linked with activities which show the interdependencies among events.
3. The development of a PERT chart requires an estimation of the time for all activities and reveals the uncertainty involved.
4. Like CPM, the critical aspects of each event are signaled well in advance of the occurrence.
5. The probability of meeting a contract date is provided.

PERT is a management-by-exception tool which is uniquely suitable for preplanning extremely involved problems where time data are not readily available, as in a research program. It is closely related to the Gantt Charts, but it shows more distinctly the interrelationships of combined activities and also introduces the concept of probability by which better decisions can be made.

The PERT diagram is similar to the CPM diagram except that it will contain more information. The development of PERT will parallel CPM until the probabilistic reasoning is added. PERT is used for predicting and scheduling progress as well as for measuring compliance to plan. Sister techniques are being developed for the measurement and prediction of cost and reliability.

Figure 16–10

PERT Glossary of Symbols

Term	*Symbol*	*Comments*
PERT		Abbreviation for Program Evaluation and Review Technique.
Event		Events are shown as squares or circles and indicate what has gone before. Therefore events are phrased in the past tense. Events are "check-points" and show that work has been accomplished up to this point.
Activity	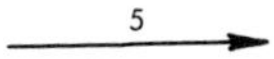	Activity lines represent the work needed to accomplish an event. An event is completed when the activity is accomplished. No work can start on the next activity until the preceding event is completed. The activity lines are not scaled, but the numbers over the line indicate time required.
Network (sequential flow diagram)	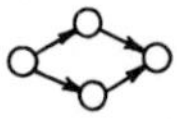	A web of events and activities with one starting event and one objective event.
Time Estimates		Discussed more fully in text.
Optimistic Time	t_o	There is very little chance that the activity can be done in less time than t_o.
Most Likely Time	t_m	The best guess of the time required. If only one time were available, this would be it. This is the "mode" of the distribution.
Pessimistic Time	t_p	There is little chance that the task would take longer than t_p.
Expected Time	t_e	There is a 50% probability that the activity completed will take less time—and 50% probability, of course, that it will take more time. $t_e = \left[\frac{t_o + 4t_m + t_p}{6}\right]$
Earliest Expected Time	T_e	The summation of all times, t_e, up to an event, staying with a single path from start to finish. When two paths lead to an event, use the one with the greatest time. For example: 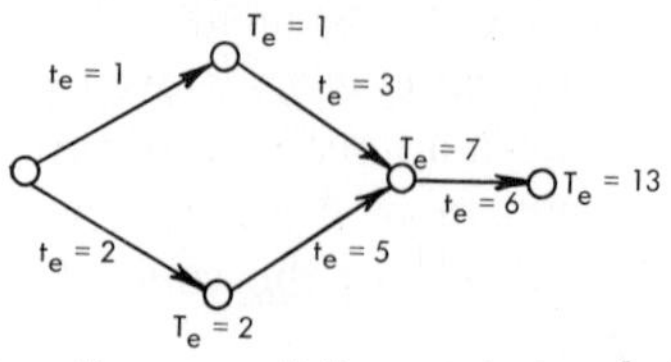
Latest Allowable Time	T_L	The latest time an activity can start and stay on schedule.
Completion Time	T_c	The instant in time that the project is scheduled for completion.
Critical Path		The longest time path through the network. Any delay in the critical path will cause delay in the final event.
Slack	T_s	Difference between latest allowable time and earliest expected time: $T_L - T_e$.

As with the Gantt Chart—and any other similar charting techniques—it is important to understand the symbols used. Figure 16–10 presents them in table form for your convenience.

Assumptions for Times Estimates

The opportunity to determine the probability of completing a project by a certain time is a unique feature of PERT. This, however, requires a knowledge of the mean time and variance for each activity. In turn, this means that the activity supervisors must furnish three pieces of information rather than one:

1. Optimstic time, t_o: there is very little chance the activity can be completed before this time.
2. Pessimistic time, t_p: at the opposite extreme of t_o is t_p. There is very little likelihood that the task would take a longer time than this.
3. Most likely time, t_m: this is the best guess of the time needed. If only one time were available, this would be it.

How well t_o, t_p, and t_m are determined depends upon the skill and experience of the person furnishing the estimate. The probability distribution of the time involved in performing the activity might be characterized by

Figure 16–11
Typical Distribution for PERT

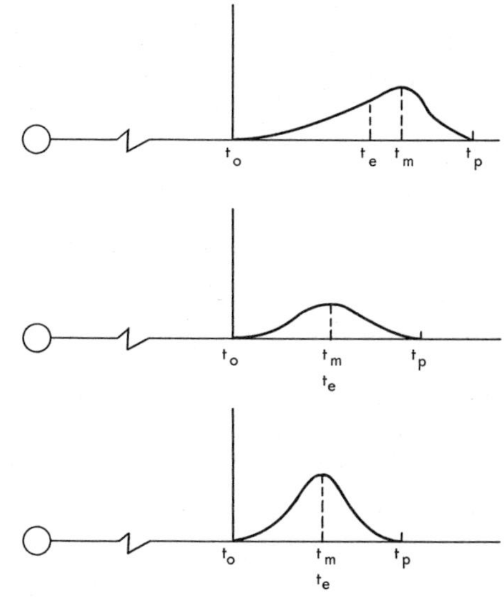

any one of the curves illustrated in Figure 16–11. It is assumed that the distribution is unimodal and the peak will represent the value of t_m, the most probable time for completing the activity. There is very little chance that the task can be completed before t_o or after t_p. The point, t_m, is free to move between these two, depending upon the estimator's judgment.

From these three values it is necessary to derive the expected value, t_e, commonly referred to as the average or mean. This is accomplished by an approximation developed by the originators of PERT.[1]

$$t_e = \left[\frac{t_o + 4t_m + t_p}{6}\right]$$

Another assumption made concerning the distribution is that, for unimodal distributions, the standard deviation can be estimated roughly as one-sixth of the range:

$$\sigma = \frac{t_p - t_o}{6} \text{ and, of course, } \sigma^2 = \left(\frac{t_p - t_o}{6}\right)^2$$

From these assumptions and approximations we can proceed to discuss an example of a PERT network.

PERT NETWORK EXAMPLE

Figure 16–12 shows a very simple network, similar to one discussed with CPM. The starting point is at 1 with three paths showing activities required to reach objective 5. Above each activity is the previously calculated expected time, t_e. The concept of earliest expected time, latest allowable time, slack, and critical path can best be illustrated by this simple example.

The first thing we wish to learn is the earliest expected time, T_e, for each event. This is shown for each event following each path. Event 5, of course, has three time values, depending upon which path is followed. The path taking the greatest time will give the latest expected time, T_e. In our example it is obvious that this is path 1, 3, 5, which gives a total time of ten hours.

Everything up to this point must be delayed for the activities which occur on the longest path. This longest time path, as in CPM, is called the critical path.

The latest time, T_L, is the latest time a job can start and is calculated by using the latest event as an anchor point and working backwards. The earliest expected time, T_e, for the last event on the critical path became the anchor point or latest allowable time, T_L.

---

[1] *PERT Summary Report, Phase 1*, Department of the Navy, Bureau of Naval Weapons Special Projects Office, Washington, D.C., 1961.

Figure 16–12

PERT Example

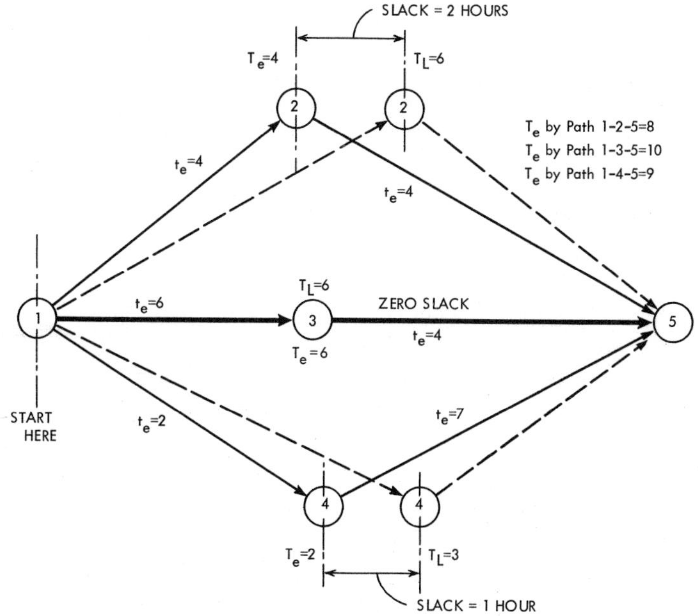

The T_L for event 2, 3, and 4 can be calculated by subtracting t_e for the various events from the T_L for 5.

$$\begin{aligned} T_L \text{ for } 2 \text{ is } T_L - t_e &= 10 - 4 = 6 \\ 3 \qquad\quad &= 10 - 4 = 6 \\ 4 \qquad\quad &= 10 - 7 = 3 \end{aligned}$$

Probability of Meeting the Contract Date

With PERT it is possible to determine the probability of completing a contract on schedule. For example, the expected time to complete a con-

Figure 16–13

Probability of Completing on Schedule

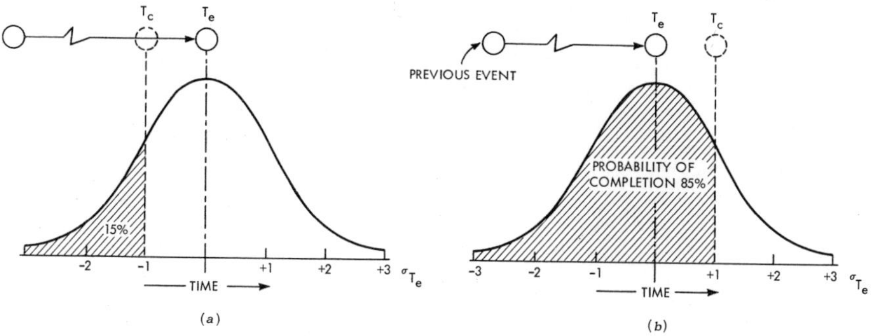

tract is shown by T_e in Figure 16–13, but we know that only seldom will it be completed exactly as expected. We can expect to get a distribution of possible completion dates as represented by the normal curve illustrated.

The standard deviation, σ_{T_e}, of this distribution can be determined by obtaining the square root of the sum of all the variances of the activities leading up to the event under consideration:

$$\sigma_{T_e} = \sqrt{\sigma_{t_{e_1}}^{\ 2} + \sigma_{t_{e_2}}^{\ 2} + \sigma_{t_{e3}}^{\ 2} + \sigma_{t_{e4}}^{\ 2} + \ldots . + \sigma_{t_{e_n}}^{\ 2}}$$

Once this is obtained we can resort to the normal statistical tables to determine the probabilities—if we know the number of standard deviations that the completion date, T_c, is from the expected date, T_e.

The probability of a task being completed at any particular time is shown on the curve by the shaded area. In Figure 16–13*a* the probability of meeting the scheduled date is about 15 percent, while in *b* it is about 85 percent.

If the contract time is T_c, as shown in Figure 16–13*a*, the chances of completing the contract on time are probably too slight, while too much safety is built into a situation where the contract time is represented by anything to the far right. If T_e is equal to T_c, the probability of completing the schedule on time is 50 percent.

As in CPM, the difference between the time when an activity *can* start and when it *has* to start is referred to as the slack or float. Slack, in terms of the symbols already developed, is:

$$T_L - T_e = \text{Slack}$$

This, so far, has been an attempt to define the terms used in the PERT technique. It is now time to see an application.

Figure 16–14

PERT Example

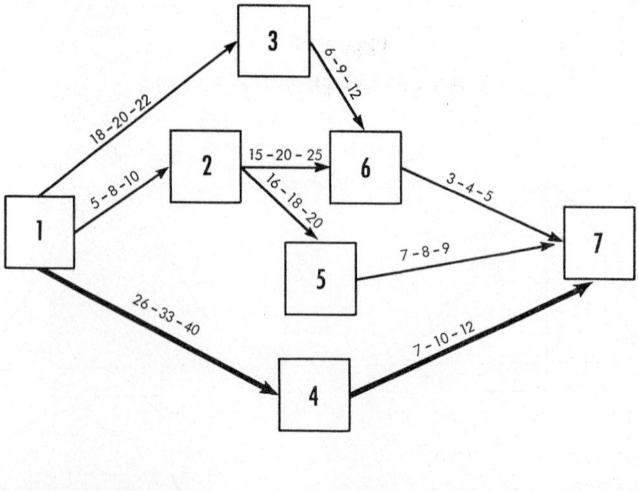

A PERT Problem

The PERT techniques are best discussed by means of an example, such as is shown in Figure 16–14. The boxes indicate the events, and the activity lines between them have three numbers above them showing t_o, t_m, and t_p.

The calculations are most readily handled if they are put in a tabular form, as shown in Figure 16–15. Each column in the table will be explained in turn.

Figure 16–15

Example of PERT Calculations

1	2	3	4	5	6	7	8	9	10	11	12	13
Event	Previous Event	t_o	t_m	t_p	t_e	σ^2	T_e	T_L	T_s	T_c	D	P
7	6	3	4	5	4.0	0.111				41.5		
	5	7	8	9	8.0	0.111						
	4	7	10	12	9.8	0.694	42.8	(42.8)	0.00		.52	30%
6	3	6	9	12	9.0	1.000	29.0	38.8	9.8			
	2	15	20	25	20.0	2.78						
5	2	16	18	20	18.0	0.443	25.8	34.8	9.0			
4	1	26	33	40	33.0	5.429	33.0	33.0	0.0			
3	1	18	20	22	20.0	0.444	20.0	29.8	9.8			
2	1	5	8	10	7.8	0.694	7.8	16.8	9.0			

T_c is 41.5 weeks

$$D = \frac{41.5 - 42.8}{\sqrt{5.429 + 0.694}} = 0.52 \text{ deviations}$$

Area under normal curve for 0.52 is about 30%

Column 1. Each event is listed, starting from the last (or objective) and working downward to the start.

Column 2. Previous events: all of the events that have gone before the event listed in column 1 are listed.

Column 3. The optimistic time, t_o, for an activity as determined by someone who is practiced in estimating, such as a foreman or industrial engineer.

Column 4. The most likely time, t_m.

Column 5. The pessimistic time, t_p.

Column 6. The expected time, t_e, as calculated from the three previous times:

$$t_e = \left[\frac{t_o + 4t_m + t_p}{6}\right]$$

Column 7. The variance, σ^2, for the activities calculated on the following basis:

$$\sigma^2 = \left[\frac{t_p - t_o}{6}\right]^2$$

Column 8. The earliest expected time for each event. Sum the total expected times for all activities leading to the event. When more than one activity leads to an event, the greatest T_e is chosen. For example, times leading to the event 6 from 3 and 2 are $20 + 9 = 29.0$ and $7.8 + 20 = 27.8$. Since we wish to choose the largest, T_e is 29.0 for 6.

Column 9. The latest time is calculated in the following manner: Start with the T_L for the last event as equal to T_e (see circled figures on Figure 16–15). Now for each path work backwards, subtracting the t_e for each activity link.

Column 10. The slack time is the difference between the latest allowable time and the earliest expected time:

$$T_s = T_L - T_e$$

The critical path may now be determined by finding the path with zero slack. This is shown by dark lines on the activity chart. Those paths with considerable slack can now be scrutinized for "trade offs" between facilities to reduce the overall time of the critical path. The most efficient program is the one with the greatest number of events having the least possible slack.

Column 11. T_c is the original contract time for the completion of an activity. We are now concerned with the probability of meeting the contract, and therefore go through the following sequence of activities.

Column 12. D indicates the distance in standard deviations that T_c is from T_e.

$$D = \frac{T_c - T_e}{\sigma_{T_e}}$$

Column 13. The probability, P, of an event occurring at the proposed completion date can be obtained by entering a probability table (see Chapter 6) with the value of D.

This has been a relatively easy problem to solve, but you can imagine the difficulties that would be encountered if there were hundreds of different activities. These more complex problems have been programmed on a computer, but even then there are limits to the size of the problem which can be handled.

PERT/COST

An extension of PERT has been the development of PERT/COST, which not only keeps time under surveillance but also costs. Superimposed upon the usual PERT network is a cost network (Figure 16–16) consisting of cost estimates for each activity. After this planning stage is completed, control is exercised when it is discovered from the feedback of information that costs are exceeding the predictions. One way of reporting the differences between the planned and actual is shown in the PERT Time and Cost Status Report illustrated below the network. This is just one of the many reporting forms designed to keep management informed of a project's status. Of those available, the Cost Outlook Report and the Schedule Outlook Report (Figure 16–17) are the most easily understood.

Figure 16–16

PERT Time and Cost Status Report

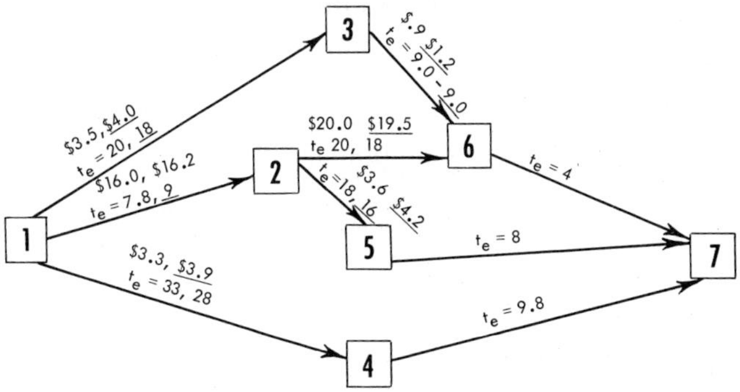

PERT/Cost Network

PERT Time = Cost Status Report

1st Summary Report for 8/8653 Project for 7/8

Identification			Time Status					Cost Status			
Begin Event No.	End Event No.	Account No.	Expected Elapsed Time t_e	Scheduled Elapsed Time t_s	Scheduled Completion Date	Latest Allowable Completion Date T_L	Activity Slack $T_L - T_S$	Cost Estimate ($ Thousand)	Actual Cost	Over or Under	Comments
1	3	A-160	20.0	20.0	2/22	3/3	9.8	3.5	4.00	+.5	
1	2	A-183	7.8	7.8	2/10	2/19	9.0	16.0	16.2	+.2	
1	4	A- 68	33.0	33.0	3/7	3/7	0.0	3.3	3.9	+.6	
2	5	A- 51	18.0	18.0	2/28	3/9	9.0	20.0	19.5	-.5	
2											

Figure 16–17

Cost and Schedule Outlook Reports

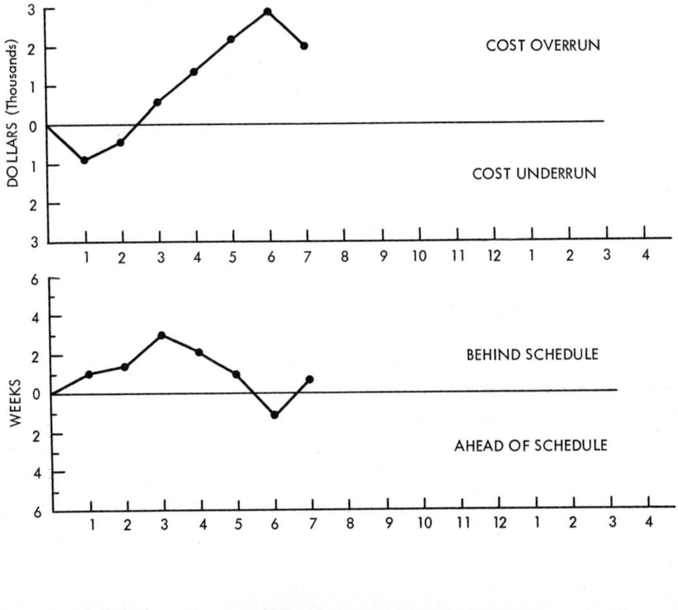

Out of PERT came a diversity of conflicting cost analysis techniques which required standardization before they could become universally acceptable. Two of these supplements to PERT/COST are discussed here:

Time-Cost Option

Most proposals require that only one cost estimate be prepared for each activity. This does not permit determining:

1. The amount of time that could be saved by spending more money;
2. The amount of money that might be saved by extending the completion date.

The Time-Cost option, illustrated in Figure 16–18, permits the management to make decisions on the basis of technical risks, costs, and time.

Figure 16–18

Time-Cost Option Chart

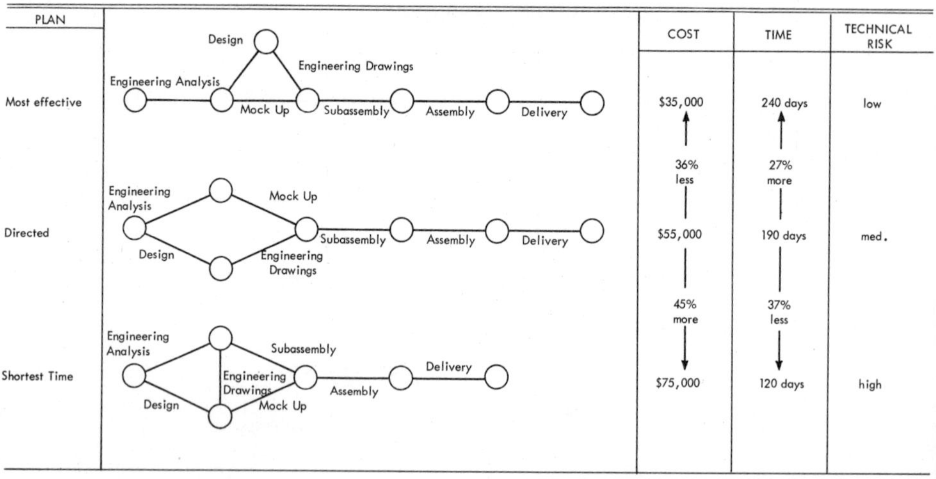

Resource Allocation

This technique is, in general, the equivalent of the cost analysis step of CPM discussed earlier. It can be explained by the series of steps:

1. The PERT/COST network is constructed as is partially illustrated in Figure 16–19.
2. Obtain alternative cost and time estimates for each activity. The number of alternatives for each activity will depend upon the nature of the activity as well as upon the available resources.
3. Select the lowest cost with its associated time for each activity.
4. Calculate the time for the critical path. If the critical path is longer than the scheduled time, recalculate a critical path using other available estimates, and making note of the time saved and the cost increase for each succeeding alternative.

Figure 16–19
Resource Allocation Supplement

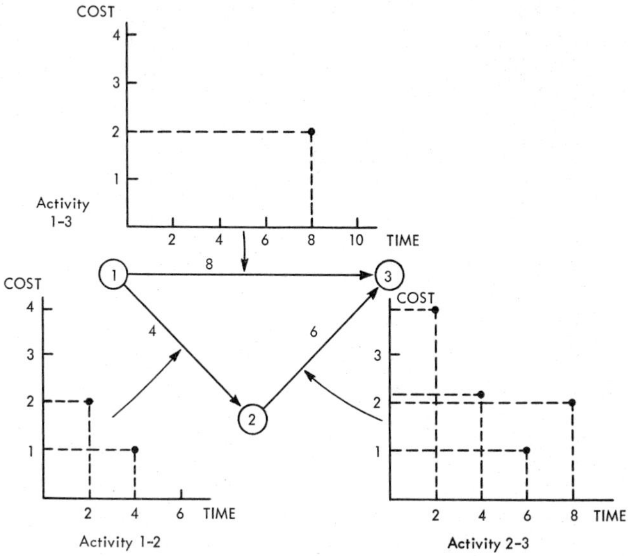

5. If the critical path is less or equal to the permitted time, print-out the time and cost as a possible solution.
6. If the critical path is longer than the time permitted, review the activities along the critical path and select the one with the lowest cost slope. Change this activity to a shorter time.
7. Calculate a new critical path and continue with Step 6 until the critical path is less than the permitted time.
8. After the critical path has been established by Step 7, consider all of the paths with slack time. Shift activities with slack to longer time and lower cost points whenever possible. The slack points with the steepest cost-time slope should be considered first in revising the schedule.

PERT and PERT/COST have been two important developments for planning and controlling the many activities of large projects. Needless to say, only projects of a relatively small size could be handled conveniently by hand, but this difficulty can be overcome because special PERT programs are available for those companies having computer time available.

LINE-OF-BALANCE TECHNIQUE

This is another method of planning and scheduling production developed by the armed forces to monitor large projects, but it is equally suitable for job shop scheduling of complex assemblies. The line-of-balance incorporates some of the Gantt charting methods, and, like it, tells how far a project has progressed as compared with where it should be. It is a management-by-exception tool which promises to find even greater use in the future.

The line-of-balance technique consists of three charts: the planning chart, the objective chart, and the progress chart. Each is a useful planning and scheduling device, but, when used together, they yield much more information than when used alone—and with little more labor. These three charts will be described independently, and then will be combined to illustrate their maximum utilization.

Figure 16–20

Line-of-Balance Chart

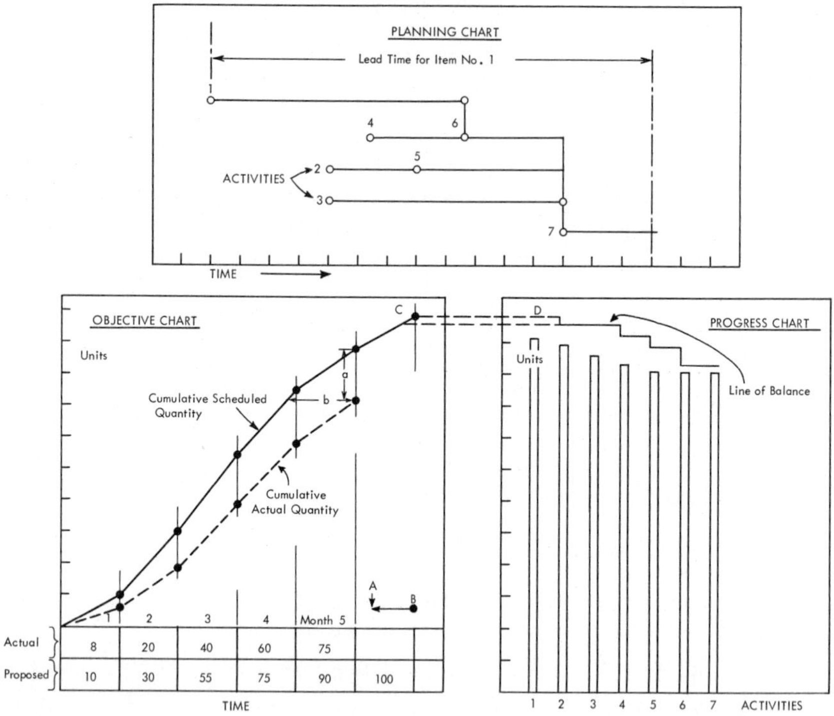

Planning Chart

The planning chart is the first step in the application of the line-of-balance procedure. The chart in Figure 16–20 is closely related to the Gantt Project Chart and, as before, the horizontal scale is in units of time with the completion date shown on the right end. Each phase of a project is shown as a scaled horizontal bar which is interconnected with the others by vertical lines to form a network. Any activity can be charted, and, if necessary, can be subdivided to form monitoring points. The extent to which it is desirable to subdivide the work should be decided upon an economic basis. The jobs are numbered starting with the one which extends to the left with the earliest starting date. If two activities have the same starting date, they are numbered in order, starting with the top one first.

The Objective Chart

This chart has quantity scaled on the vertical axis and time on the horizontal axis. But, in addition, it shows—below the time scale—the quantities scheduled to be delivered in each time period. At the end of each period the quantities delivered are also recorded. It should be pointed out that both of these are cumulative figures.

In plotting the curves the cumulative scheduled quantity is plotted immediately and the cumulative actual deliveries are plotted as the information is obtained. From these curves several pieces of important information are available:

1. The vertical distance between the two curves, *a*, at any instant shows what the production gap is between the actual and proposed production.
2. The horizontal distance between the two curves, *b*, shows how far off the schedule is in terms of time.
3. The slopes of the lines are indicative of the production rates and the differences in slopes give some indication of whether production will eventually catch up or continue to lag behind.

The Progress Chart

Adjacent to the objective chart is the progress chart. As you will observe, the vertical axes of each are scaled the same. However, on the progress chart the events are listed from left to right. On this chart we plot two types of information. First we shall plot the progress by showing the cumulative number of units completed to date. This is done by a vertical bar, as is shown on the chart. Those units which are nearly completed might also be shown as a phantom bar to give a little clearer picture of the progress. The second step is to draw a *line of balance* on the progress chart, which can be illustrated best by a series of steps:

1. The "study date" is determined for the example at A on the objective chart. This is the instant when all activities are frozen and is equivalent to the caret symbol on the Gantt Chart.
2. From the planning chart the lead time for the first activity is obtained and its time span laid off on the objective chart from the caret, as shown by the line *A–B*.
3. From the end of the lead time a line is extended vertically to intersect the schedule line at *C*.
4. Point *C* is extended horizontally to the progress chart to intersect the projection of the event bar, as shown at *D*.

This procedure is repeated for each activity and is shown by the dashed line in the example. This produces a series of lines which, when connected, comprise a stair-step—*line of balance*—on the progress chart.

The line of balance shows where the activities should be if the project is on schedule. If the line coincides with the bar, the activity is right on schedule. If the bar is below the line, that activity is behind schedule and should be expedited. If the bar extends above the line, it indicates that the activity is ahead of schedule.

By means of this technique it is possible to get an overview of a project and tell exactly where any delays might occur and what corrective action will be necessary to bring the project back on schedule.

All the scheduling techniques described here have found their places in industry. One thing should be kept in mind, however: conditions change from factory to factory and even from department to department. You will be wise to learn the principles and you should feel free to adapt them to any conditions you encounter.

DISPATCHING

Dispatching is the process of issuing the necessary orders for production at the scheduled time. In the classical approach dispatching is considered as a subject separate from scheduling. In actuality, dispatching and scheduling are bound together so that it is difficult to treat them separately, for as an order is issued a worker is told *what* work to do as well as *when*.

In the evolution of a factory, dispatching and scheduling were combined in the early stage. The owner-manager verbally told each worker what he was to do and when. The next step was probably to have a clerk issue written orders made up in advance. It is not difficult to imagine this system, with the foreman carrying these written orders around in his vest pocket. In fact, this is probably the reason why the vest became a status symbol for supervisors in the earlier days. It was probably the time that the vest remained at home with an overindulgent foreman that a more formal system of dispatching became essential. The more formal system probably consisted of filing the orders in a cigar box or perhaps in a more elegant wire basket. Even today one can find production tickets filed in this fashion in some out-of-the-way nook in the factory, but to which all employees have access for picking and choosing their jobs.

A more formal system, and one found in common practice, involves a *dispatch board*. This can take various forms, depending upon the ingenuity of the company's handyman or upon the funds available in the treasury. Some of the commercial boards are described in Chapter 18, but the principles will be illustrated here.

The typical dispatch board consists of a piece of plywood fastened to the wall at some convenient location in the factory. The board is equipped with a number of equally spaced hooks. Each set of three, as shown in Figure 16–21, represents one work station. It is on these hooks that the production forms, such as the operation ticket or time ticket, is filed. Each hook position for each work station has a significant meaning:

For machine: The bottom hook in each set of three hooks is used to file all the operation tickets for work that is to be performed at this work station.

Figure 16–21

Dispatch Procedure

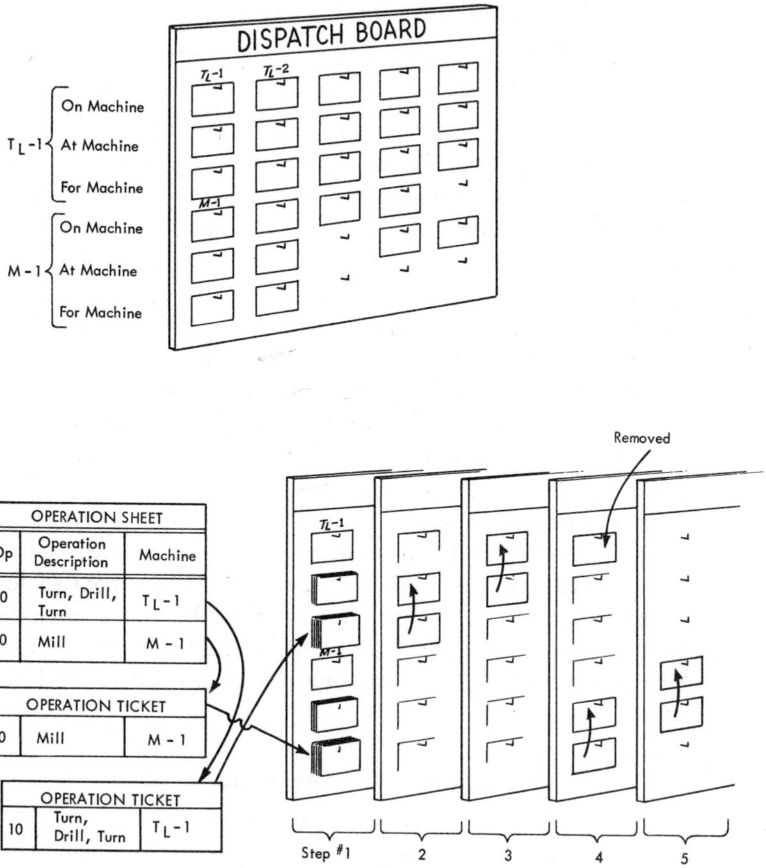

At machine: When the work has been moved to the work station, the ticket is moved up to the *at-machine* position.

On machine: When the work is actually placed on the machine, the ticket is moved from the *at-machine* position to the *on-machine* position.

When the tickets are on the *for-machine* hook, work can be rescheduled if there are machines available. It is more difficult to reschedule when the work has been moved to the work station.

Just how the board functions will be shown by following one order through the procedure.

Step 1. When orders are released to the factory, the operation tickets are placed on their proper *for-machine* hook, as shown.

Step 2. When the material is sent from the stores to the first operation, the operation ticket is moved to the *at-machine* position.

Step 3. Eventually, when the jobs ahead of this one are completed, the operator is told to do this one, and the ticket is moved up to the *on-machine* position.

Step 4. When the work is completed, it is moved to the second operation, and the second operation ticket for the milling machine work station is moved to the *at-machine* position.

Step 5. As before, the card is moved from the *at-machine* position to the *on-machine* position. If there had been more operations they would have followed similar sequences until the whole order was completed.

This has been just one simple order with two operations. Imagine the complexity of having several hundred jobs going through the factory, each with a number of operations. It is obvious that to make all these jobs dovetail, so that the machines are running near full capacity, is a difficult undertaking requiring a great deal of skill.

The dispatch board can show information other than production conditions. For example, a red ticket on the board might indicate that the machine is not manned, or an orange ticket might indicate the machine is down for repair. At a glance, it is possible to obtain a complete picture of the plant. A visual display may not seem important, but it is not unusual to have a machine out of production for a number of hours before it comes to the attention of the supervisor so he can take action.

The dispatch board is frequently used as a substitute for a load chart. By looking at the thickness of the stack of cards it is possible to get some idea of the load of work ahead of each machine. If the jobs have drastically different durations it may be necessary to scan the length of time needed for each job. At times the scheduling board (Figure 16–22) is used for dispatch-

Figure 16–22

Scheduling and Dispatch Board

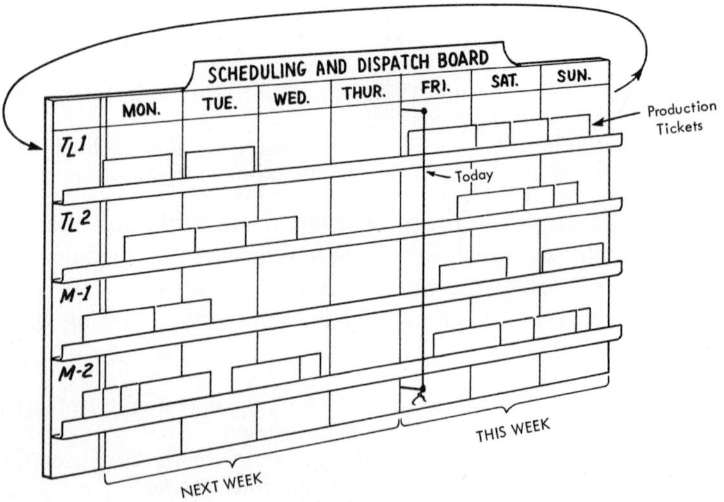

ing as well. The cards are lined up on the board to represent the bar of a Gantt Chart, and, as the jobs are completed, they are removed. Rescheduling can be done conveniently by shifting the cards around.

The location of the dispatching function is an important policy decision for management. In some situations it may be desirable to maintain a highly centralized control while in other situations this may not be desirable.

Centralized Dispatching

Some companies have followed the practice of having a highly centralized dispatching system. This can be objectionable because the supervisors are not permitted to exercise control over the area for which they are responsible. The supervisors are not given the flexibility necessary to keep their departments operating at a high level of efficiency. Communication delays can also contribute to inefficiencies.

Decentralized Dispatching

This puts the responsibility upon the supervisors to run a tight ship. They are given freedom to schedule the jobs—within rather broad limits—to get the greatest efficiency out of their part of the factory. Often the supervisors are incapable of coping with the clerical facets of dispatching.

Centralized–Decentralized Dispatching

In this system the centralized dispatching is combined with scheduling to establish the overall operations of the factory. The supervisors, on the other hand, are given freedom to meet their departments' objectives. Because of this they can schedule machines more efficiently and take advantage of such work-saving techniques as scheduling two jobs back-to-back when the machine set-ups are similar. When centralized–decentralized dispatching is used it is necessary to maintain a close liaison between the two groups. This is often done by a once-a-day meeting of all supervisors and control personnel. It may be costly from a time viewpoint, but it may create better communications and understanding among departments.

The feedback of information is important to the efficient operation of a dispatch board. In the decentralized system this is not important because the supervisor can maintain a close contact with the machine operator. In some situations the work tickets for the task being performed are displayed at the work stations on a convenient clip board. When this is done, it may replace the form shown on the dispatch board for *on-machine*. Usually, when the operator completes his job, he returns to the dispatcher where he turns in the card for the work completed and picks up another; so the problem of feedback is not difficult.

SUMMARY

There are several important things to consider before attempting to chart any activity. The first thing to ask is: Is it worthwhile? It costs money to prepare charts and keep them up to date. The information given on a chart must be important and not just busy work.

Another thing to ask is: Is the information available? If the information cannot be obtained, is inaccurate, or so out of date that action cannot be taken, then it is worthless to consider the establishment of charts.

A consideration often forgotten when setting up charts is whether the right type of personnel is available. Choose a person who likes to work with details and is not overburdened with larger problems. To keep the charts going day after day requires someone not given to boredom and negligence. Frequently, a clerk or secretary is the person best suited for the job.

A chart is "dynamic" and must be constantly fed information. If the information is not available, then the chart cannot work. This is sometimes referred to as feedback. Once the course of a chart is set, it can never be corrected without the feedback of information. This information may take the form of job tickets, time cards, move cards, material requisitions, etc., which will be useful in bringing a chart up to date.

Since charts are dynamic, it does little good to establish systems without tolerating changes. The system should be pliable, allowing charts to be brought up to date frequently without any hesitation or mourning over past events.

Questions

1. What is the purpose of the master schedule? In what type of industry would it be used?
2. What qualifications would you look for when selecting someone to work in the scheduling department?
3. Often people feel that a schedule should never be changed once it is made. Why is this true? Should it be true?
4. Draw a Gantt Chart for your activities during a day. Would this be a useful chart? Why is it difficult to draw?
5. Cite two factory functions which could use the Gantt Charts to schedule their activities. What difficulties would you expect them to encounter in applying this technique?
6. Should an extremely expensive product be scheduled on a forward, or backward, Gantt Chart? Explain why.
7. Evaluate the comparative advantages of the Gantt Chart, PERT, and Critical Path techniques.
8. Draw a Critical Path network for some activity such as building a house.
9. Compare the Line-of-Balance technique with the Gantt Chart. What advantages does the Line of Balance have?

10. What are the advantages of centralized dispatching? What effect will it have on the efficiency of the operations? In what type of industry would it prevail?
11. The horizontal bars on a Gantt Chart might represent work centers or machines. What would be the advantage of one over the other?
12. What is essential if the various scheduling techniques are to work?

References

AMERICAN MANAGEMENT ASSOCIATION (GABRIEL N. STILIAN, *et al.*, eds.). *PERT, A New Management Planning and Control Technique, Report No. 74*. New York, 1962.

BATTERSBY, ALBERT. *Network Analysis for Planning and Scheduling*. New York: Saint Martin's Press, Inc., 1965.

BRUCE, ROBERT T.; CHANDRUC, JEAN; and HORNBRUCH, FREDERICK W. *Practical Planning and Scheduling*. New London, Conn.: National Foremans' Institute, 1950.

CLARK, WALLACE. *The Gantt Chart, A Working Tool of Management*. 3rd ed. London: Pitman, 1952.

EVARTS, HARRY F. *Introduction to PERT*. Boston: Allyn & Bacon, Inc., 1964.

FORD, LESTER R., and FULKERSON, D. R. *Flows in Networks*. Princeton, N.J.: Princeton University Press, 1962.

GREENE, JAMES H. "Control Charts—Key to Efficiency." *The Tool Engineer*, Vol. 43, No. 3 (September, 1959).

GUIDA, J. V., and BRUDER, K. A. *PERT—A Management Control System*. Great Neck, N.Y: Sperry Gyroscope Co, Division of Sperry Rand Corporation.

HARTUNG, LEONARD P. *PERT—A Dynamic Project Control Method*. Oswego, N.Y.: International Business Machines, Inc., Space Guidance Center, 1962.

KNOEPPEL, C. E. *Graphic Production Control*. New York: The Engineering Magazine Co., 1920.

MILLER, ROBERT WALLACE. *Schedule, Cost and Profit Control with PERT*. New York: McGraw-Hill Book Co., Inc., 1963.

MODER, JOSEPH J. *Project Management with CPM and PERT*. New York: Reinhold Publishing Co., 1964.

MUTH, JOHN F., and THOMPSON, GERALD L. *Industrial Scheduling*. Englewood Cliffs, N.J.: Prentice-Hall, Inc., 1963.

NATIONAL AERONAUTICS AND SPACE ADMINISTRATION, OFFICE OF THE SECRETARY OF DEFENSE. *DOD and NASA PERT COST, Systems Design*. Washington, D.C.: U.S. Government Printing Office, June, 1962.

PERT COORDINATING GROUP. *Supplement No. 1 to DOD and NASA Guide PERT COST—Output Reports*. Washington, D.C.: Superintendent of Documents, U.S. Government Printing Office, March, 1963.

———. *PERT Guide for Management Use*. Washington, D.C. U.S. Government Printing Office, June, 1963.

PHILLIPS, CECIL R., and MODER, JOSEPH J. *Manual of Critical Path Theory and Practice*. 2nd ed. Silver Springs, Md.: Operations Research, Inc., 1962.

RICE, WILLIAM B. *Control Charts in Factory Management*. New York: John Wiley & Sons, Inc., 1947.

Special Projects Office, Department of the Navy, Bureau of Naval Weapons. *PERT Summary Report, Phase 1*. Washington, D.C.: U.S. Government Printing Office, 1958.

———. *PERT Summary Report, Phase 2*. Washington, D.C., U.S. Government Printing Office, 1958.

———. *An Introduction to the PERT/COST System for Integrated Project Management*. Washington, D.C., U.S. Government Printing Office, 1961.

Stires, David M., and Murphy, Maurice M. *Modern Management Methods PERT & CPM*. Boston: Materials Management Institute, 1963.

———, and Wenig, Raymond P. *PERT/COST*. Boston: Industrial Education Institute, 1964.

CHAPTER 17

Linear Programming

Matrices, which were introduced into mathematics near the middle of the nineteenth century by Cayley,[1] provide a compact method of dealing with a number of linear equations. Matrix algebra has become an important tool of the modern engineer and has found many applications in physics as well as in all of the important fields of engineering.

One of the reasons why matrix algebra is of growing importance is because it is the basis upon which linear programming is built. Linear programming is one of the several tools which has grown out of the operations research movement. Although many books have been written concerning the application of linear programming as a "cook book" technique, no one should be satisfied with this approach but should look behind the technique for the reasoning. It is impossible to have an understanding of this tool without some basic knowledge of matrix algebra.

Linear programming would be reason enough for a person to master some of the elementary concepts of matrix algebra, but there is another good reason. This is the advent of the digital computer and the numerous standard programs which are available. Computer programmers have constructed routines for manipulating the matrices and industrial people have been quick to interpret their problems as matrix problems so that they can be placed on the computer with the advantage of much shorter processing time. Not only has industry discovered the advantage of processing data in this way, it also has found the advantage of thinking about problems in terms of matrix algebra.

Matrix Algebra

A matrix is a rectangular array of elements (often numbers) arranged in horizontal rows (m) and vertical columns (n). The position of each element is denoted by a set of subscripts. The first letter in the subscript indi-

[1] E. F. Beckenbach, *Modern Mathematics for the Engineer* (New York: McGraw-Hill Book Co., Inc., 1961).

cates the row it is in, while the second indicates the column, such as a_{ij}. It is quite common to call the last row in a matrix the mth row and the last column the nth column. The term i is often used to indicate the general row subscript, and the term j is often used to indicate any column subscript. At times, the notation a^i_j is used, the upper letter indicating the row and the lower letter the column. The array of numbers is usually enclosed in a set of brackets: [ ].

Copying the entire matrix is tedious, so a shorthand system has been adopted. The matrix is frequently represented by a bold face letter such as **A, B, I.**

TYPES OF MATRICES

Square Matrix

The number of rows, m, is equal to the number of columns, n. The array on the left is referred to as a 2 × 2 matrix and the middle one is said to be a 5 × 5 matrix. The one on the right is *not* a square matrix but is a 5 × 6 *rectangular* matrix.

$$m \text{ rows} \left\{ \overbrace{\begin{bmatrix} a_{11} & a_{12} \\ a_{21} & a_{22} \end{bmatrix}}^{n \text{ columns}} \right. \qquad \begin{bmatrix} a_{11} & a_{12} & a_{13} & a_{14} & a_{15} \\ a_{21} & a_{22} & a_{23} & a_{24} & a_{25} \\ a_{31} & a_{32} & a_{33} & a_{34} & a_{35} \\ a_{41} & a_{42} & a_{43} & a_{44} & a_{45} \\ a_{51} & a_{52} & a_{53} & a_{54} & a_{55} \end{bmatrix} \qquad \begin{bmatrix} a_{11} & a_{12} & a_{13} & a_{14} & a_{15} & a_{16} \\ a_{21} & a_{22} & a_{23} & a_{24} & a_{25} & a_{26} \\ a_{31} & a_{32} & a_{33} & a_{34} & a_{35} & a_{36} \\ a_{41} & a_{42} & a_{43} & a_{44} & a_{45} & a_{46} \\ a_{51} & a_{52} & a_{53} & a_{54} & a_{55} & a_{56} \end{bmatrix}$$

Diagonal Matrix

This is a square matrix with all off-diagonal elements equal to zero. The diagonal elements can equal any value except zero. The matrix shown is a diagonal matrix.

$$\begin{bmatrix} 3 & 0 & 0 \\ 0 & 5 & 0 \\ 0 & 0 & 4 \end{bmatrix}$$

Unit or Identity Matrix

This is a *diagonal square* matrix with each of the diagonal elements having the value of one. This matrix is important enough, as we will see, to have a special designation, **I**, which stands for *identity*.

$$\begin{bmatrix} 1 & 0 & 0 \\ 0 & 1 & 0 \\ 0 & 0 & 1 \end{bmatrix}$$

Inverse Matrix

A matrix is the inverse of a square matrix if the product of the two is equal to an identity matrix. Symbolically, $\mathbf{A}^{-1}$ is used to denote the inverse of a matrix **A**, so this relationship can be stated as:

$$\mathbf{A}^{-1}\mathbf{A} = \mathbf{A}\mathbf{A}^{-1} = \mathbf{I}$$

The importance of this relationship will be brought out when discussing the inverse technique for evaluating a vector.

One might well ask, at this point, why all the concern about the use of matrices? Therefore, it might be well to illustrate the economy of using matrix notation. Given below is a set of linear equations, in (*a*). The matrix of the coefficients is given just below it (*b*), and the whole set of equations is given just below this (*c*). The shorthand designation of a matrix is a boldface capital letter. A vector is a boldface small letter, as shown just below (in *d*, which represents in matrix notation the set of equations in *a*).

$$\begin{aligned} 15x_1 + 6x_2 &= 4320 \\ 9x_1 + 10x_2 &= 3240 \\ 4x_1 + 10x_2 &= 4800 \end{aligned} \qquad (a)$$

$$\mathbf{A} = \begin{bmatrix} 15 & 6 \\ 9 & 10 \\ 4 & 10 \end{bmatrix} \qquad (b)$$

$$\begin{bmatrix} 15 & 6 \\ 9 & 10 \\ 4 & 10 \end{bmatrix} \begin{bmatrix} x_1 \\ x_2 \end{bmatrix} = \begin{bmatrix} 4320 \\ 3240 \\ 4800 \end{bmatrix} \qquad (c)$$

$$\mathbf{Ax} = \mathbf{b} \qquad (d)$$

Vectors

We may locate points in space either by giving the coordinates of the point or by giving the direction and the distance. For example, if you were trying to tell someone where a certain sand trap is located on a golf course (Figure 17–1) you could say that it is 40 yards north and 30 yards

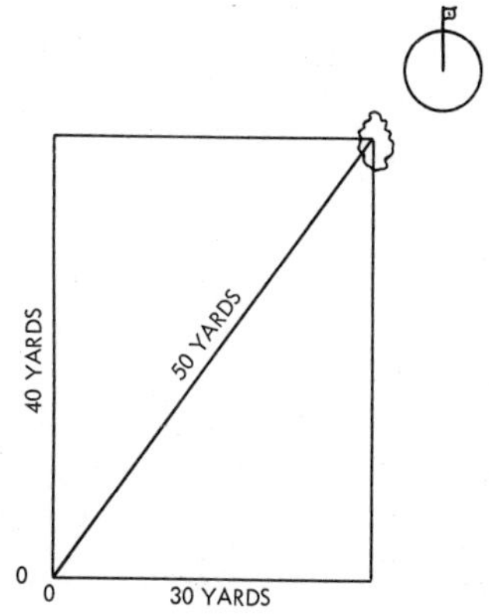

Figure 17–1
Vectors

east; or you could say that it is 50 yards in that direction, as you point to the northeast. This latter description can be considered as a *vector*, which is a translation of the origin, 0, 0, by the amounts of 30 yards and 40 yards. Either method of designating a point can be used and used interchangeably. A *scalar* is a quantity possessing only magnitude, as compared with a vector which also has direction. Vectors can be multiplied by scalars such as $\alpha\mathbf{U}$.

Matrix (b), above, can be written as a set of vectors. The array on the left, below, shows the matrix as row vectors, and the array on the right shows the same matrix as column vectors. The matrix on the right is said to be a transpose of the matrix on the left—the transpose of a column vector is a row vector and vice versa.

$$\begin{bmatrix} 15 & 6 \\ 9 & 10 \\ 4 & 10 \end{bmatrix} \qquad \begin{bmatrix} 15 & 9 & 4 \\ 6 & 10 & 10 \end{bmatrix}$$

Now, how do the vector and matrix tie together? A column vector is a matrix with only one column while the row vector is a matrix with only one row. An $m \times n$ matrix can be considered as a collection of m row vectors or as a collection of n column vectors.

ARITHMETICAL OPERATIONS WITH MATRICES

Now that we have a general idea of what matrices and vectors are and some of the forms they take, let us proceed to see how they can be manipulated in the conventional arithmetical operations of addition, subtraction, multiplication, and division. Each one of these methods of operation will be described briefly and then a simple application example shown. By this means the reader should get not only a good idea of how the equations are manipulated but should also have some concept of how they can be used.

Addition

To add two matrices, they must both have the same number of rows and columns. Corresponding elements are added. This procedure is shown below:

$$\mathbf{A} + \mathbf{B} = \mathbf{C}$$

$$\begin{bmatrix} 2 & 5 \\ 3 & 1 \end{bmatrix} + \begin{bmatrix} 7 & 8 \\ 6 & 2 \end{bmatrix} = \begin{bmatrix} 9 & 13 \\ 9 & 3 \end{bmatrix}$$

Example: Table A is the shipping schedule for the first quarter of the year for Plant A, manufacturing pumps. Table B is the shipping schedule for Plant B. To determine the quantity shipped by both plants, the problem can be stated in matrix form:

	Shipping Schedule for Plant A			*Shipping Schedule for Plant B*		
	small	*medium*	*large*	*small*	*medium*	*large*
January	300	800	600	100	500	0
February	200	1000	500	90	700	0
March	300	850	500	120	600	0

$$\overset{\mathbf{A}}{\begin{bmatrix} 300 & 800 & 600 \\ 200 & 1000 & 500 \\ 300 & 850 & 500 \end{bmatrix}} + \overset{\mathbf{B}}{\begin{bmatrix} 100 & 500 & 0 \\ 90 & 700 & 0 \\ 120 & 600 & 0 \end{bmatrix}} = \overset{\mathbf{C}}{\begin{bmatrix} 400 & 1300 & 600 \\ 290 & 1700 & 500 \\ 420 & 1450 & 500 \end{bmatrix}}$$

Subtraction

Two matrices must have the same number of rows and columns if they are to be subtracted. Corresponding elements are subtracted. As you might expect, this is very similar to the rules for addition. To keep the examples consistent, observe the following example of matrix subtraction:

$$\overset{\mathbf{A}}{\begin{bmatrix} \textcircled{8} & 7 \\ 6 & 2 \end{bmatrix}} - \overset{\mathbf{B}}{\begin{bmatrix} \textcircled{2} & 9 \\ 4 & 1 \end{bmatrix}} = \overset{\mathbf{C}}{\begin{bmatrix} \textcircled{6} & -2 \\ 2 & 1 \end{bmatrix}}$$

Example: The pump manufacturer referred to before may have a shipping schedule for the first quarter designated by the matrix **S**. Plant A's production is shown by matrix **A**, and it is necessary to find out what Plant B will have to ship. This can be easily done:

$$\overset{\mathbf{S}}{\begin{bmatrix} 400 & 1300 & 600 \\ 290 & 1700 & 500 \\ 420 & 1450 & 500 \end{bmatrix}} - \overset{\mathbf{A}}{\begin{bmatrix} 300 & 800 & 600 \\ 200 & 1000 & 500 \\ 300 & 850 & 500 \end{bmatrix}} = \overset{\mathbf{B}}{\begin{bmatrix} 100 & 500 & 0 \\ 90 & 700 & 0 \\ 120 & 600 & 0 \end{bmatrix}}$$

Multiplication (Scalar)

First let us consider multiplying matrices by constants or scalars. Each element of the matrix is multiplied by the constant or scalar to form a new matrix.

Example: Assume the company producing pumps expects to double its output in the next year. This is easily determined by:

$$2 \times \mathbf{S} = 2 \times \begin{bmatrix} 400 & 1300 & 600 \\ 290 & 1700 & 500 \\ 420 & 1450 & 500 \end{bmatrix} = \begin{bmatrix} 800 & 2600 & 1200 \\ 580 & 3400 & 1000 \\ 840 & 2900 & 1000 \end{bmatrix}$$

Multiplication (Matrix)

Next let us consider the multiplication of a matrix by a matrix. Multiplication of matrices is only permissible when the number of columns of the first matrix is equal to the number of rows of the second. Matrices that satisfy this condition are said to be "conformable."

Each of the ij^{th} elements of the product matrix is the sum of the products obtained by multiplying the elements in the ith row of the first matrix by the elements in the jth column of the second matrix. The result of this mutiplication is a matrix with the number of rows equal to the number of rows in the first matrix, and the number of columns equal to the number of columns in the second matrix. This can be expressed symbolically:

$$\mathbf{A}_{mp} \times \mathbf{B}_{pn} = \mathbf{C}_{mn}$$
$$(m, p) \times (p, n) = (m, n)$$

or perhaps it will be easier to see in this form:

Number of columns p in first = Number of rows p in second & Results in a matrix with m rows and n columns

$$m\left\{\underbrace{\begin{matrix} 0 & 0 \\ 0 & 0 \\ 0 & 0 \end{matrix}}_{p}\right. \qquad p\left\{\underbrace{\begin{matrix} 0 & 0 & 0 \\ 0 & 0 & 0 \end{matrix}}_{n}\right. \qquad m\left\{\underbrace{\begin{matrix} 0 & 0 & 0 \\ 0 & 0 & 0 \\ 0 & 0 & 0 \end{matrix}}_{n}\right.$$

The actual multiplication procedure can best be described by an illustration:

$$\mathbf{AB} = \mathbf{C}$$

$$\begin{bmatrix} a_{11} & a_{12} & a_{13} \\ a_{21} & a_{22} & a_{23} \end{bmatrix} \times \begin{bmatrix} b_{11} & b_{12} \\ b_{21} & b_{22} \\ b_{31} & b_{32} \end{bmatrix} = \begin{bmatrix} c_{11} & c_{12} \\ c_{21} & c_{22} \end{bmatrix}$$

The c_{ij} element $= a_{i1}\, b_{1j} + a_{i2}\, b_{2j} + a_{i3}\, b_{3j}$, so $c_{11} = a_{11}b_{11} + a_{12}b_{21} + a_{13}b_{31}$

Example: The usefulness of matrix multiplication can be cited. A manufacturer of paints wishes to determine his material needs for the next two months and has developed the following manufacturing schedule:

	Product		
	No. 1	*No. 2*	*No. 3*
Production for 1st month	5	7	10 lots
Production for 2nd month	10	8	3

The material requirements for each of these lots are given in the following table:

Product 1:	5 drums of A	3 drums of B	1 drum of C
Product 2:	7 drums of A	2 drums of B	2 drums of C
Product 3:	1 drum of A	4 drums of B	6 drums of C

Putting this information into matrix form:

$$\begin{bmatrix} 5 \text{ lots} & 7 & 10 \\ 10 & 8 & 3 \end{bmatrix} \times \begin{bmatrix} 5 \text{ drums/lot} & 3 & 1 \\ 7 & 2 & 2 \\ 1 & 4 & 6 \end{bmatrix} = \begin{bmatrix} 84 \text{ drums} & 69 & 79 \\ 109 & 58 & 44 \end{bmatrix}$$

The detailed method of determining the answer can be seen by the following:

$(5 \times 5) + (7 \times 7) + (10 \times 1) = 84$ | $(5 \times 3) + (7 \times 2) + (10 \times 4) = 69$ | $(5 \times 1) + (7 \times 2) + (10 \times 6) = 79$
$(10 \times 5) + (8 \times 7) + (3 \times 1) = 109$ | $(10 \times 3) + (8 \times 2) + (3 \times 4) = 58$ | $(10 \times 1) + (8 \times 2) + (3 \times 6) = 44$

Interpreting the answer is straightforward:

$$(5 \text{ lots} \times 5 \text{ drums/lot}) + (7 \text{ lots} \times 7 \text{ drums/lot})$$
$$(10 \text{ lots} \times 1 \text{ drum/lot}) = 84 \text{ drums.}$$

Matrix Division (The Inverse Matrix)

The division of matrices is not a straightforward process and it requires some review of our previous definitions. We described the matrix form in a shorthand language:

$$\mathbf{Ax} = \mathbf{b}$$

where:

$\mathbf{A}$ = an $m \times n$ matrix of the coefficients of the unknowns,
$\mathbf{x}$ = a column vector of n unknowns,
$\mathbf{b}$ = a column vector of m constants.

The problem is to determine the unknown $\mathbf{x}$ quantities. To start, we might consider dividing both sides of the equation by $\mathbf{A}$, but, since division has not been defined, let us search for another method. Here is the place where the inverse of a matrix defined earlier can be called into play. Let us see what happens if we multiply both sides of the previous equation by $\mathbf{A}^{-1}$.

$$\mathbf{A}^{-1}\mathbf{Ax} = \mathbf{A}^{-1}\mathbf{b}$$

Since $\mathbf{A}^{-1}\mathbf{A}$ is the identity matrix, $\mathbf{I}$, $\mathbf{Ix} = \mathbf{A}^{-1}\mathbf{b}$. The $\mathbf{I}$ washes out as we see:

$$\begin{bmatrix} 1 & 0 \\ 0 & 1 \end{bmatrix} \times \begin{bmatrix} x_1 \\ x_2 \end{bmatrix} = \begin{bmatrix} x_1 \\ x_2 \end{bmatrix}$$

So it seems that we can solve for the value of x_1 and x_2, if we know the value of the inverse, $\mathbf{A}^{-1}$.

Let us digress a moment here to see how to obtain the inverse matrix.

Matrix Inversion

There are a number of methods for finding the inverse of a nonsingular[2] square matrix but they are all tedious and time consuming. This is the reason why the digital computer has made industrialists take a new interest in matrix algebra.

The method, discussed briefly here, consists of writing an identity matrix to the right of the matrix $\mathbf{A}$. The next problem is to reduce the matrix $\mathbf{A}$ to an identity and at the same time perform the same operations on the identity matrix on the right. The row operations which may be performed on the matrices, and not alter their mathematical equivalence, are:

1. Any two rows may be interchanged;
2. Any row may be multiplied by a non-zero number (scalar);
3. Any multiple of a row may be added to another.

[2] The square matrix, $\mathbf{A}$, is said to be singular if $|\mathbf{A}| = 0$, nonsingular if $|\mathbf{A}| \neq 0$, where $|\mathbf{A}|$ denotes the determinant of $\mathbf{A}$.

By using these rules, the appearance of the matrices will change but the mathematical equivalence will remain. In other words, the solution of a modified matrix is the same as the original. The process of inverting the matrix, step by step, is illustrated:

$$\overbrace{\begin{matrix} x_1 & x_2 \end{matrix}}^{\mathbf{A}} \quad \overbrace{}^{\mathbf{I}}$$

$$\left[\begin{array}{cc|cc} 1 & 3 & 1 & 0 \\ 2 & 3 & 0 & 1 \end{array}\right]$$ Start with this.

$$\left[\begin{array}{cc|cc} 1 & 3 & 1 & 0 \\ 0 & -3 & -2 & 1 \end{array}\right]$$ Rule 3: Add the product: (—2) (row 1) to row 2. Remember row 1 is not altered.

$$\left[\begin{array}{cc|cc} 1 & 0 & -1 & 1 \\ 0 & -3 & -2 & 1 \end{array}\right]$$ Rule 3: Add the product: (1) (row 2) to row 1.

$$\underbrace{\left[\begin{array}{cc} 1 & 0 \\ 0 & 1 \end{array}\right.}_{\mathbf{I}}\underbrace{\left|\begin{array}{cc} -1 & 1 \\ 2/3 & -1/3 \end{array}\right]}_{\mathbf{A}^{-1}}$$ Rule 2: Multiply row 2 by —⅓.

(Only those rules were used which quickly reduced matrix **A** to an identity. Rule 1 was not needed.)

A check on the inversion process may be made if we recall $\mathbf{AA}^{-1} = \mathbf{I}$:

$$\begin{bmatrix} 1 & 3 \\ 2 & 3 \end{bmatrix} \times \begin{bmatrix} -1 & 1 \\ 2/3 & -1/3 \end{bmatrix} = \mathbf{I}$$

Multiplying as described earlier:

$$\begin{aligned} (1)(-1) + (3)(2/3) &= 1 \\ (2)(-1) + (3)(2/3) &= 0 \\ (1)(1) + (3)(-1/3) &= 0 \\ (2)(1) + (3)(-1/3) &= 1 \end{aligned}$$

which is an identity: $\begin{bmatrix} 1 & 0 \\ 0 & 1 \end{bmatrix}$

Before passing on to other subjects, let us look at a real-life problem using matrix division. This will be another example taken from the paint industry, but not the same problem described before. The problem is this: The paint manufacturer has 40 drums of material A and 60 drums of material B, and he wishes to make it all up into products 1 and 2, knowing the relationships of the quantities used. This can be written into mathematical form as shown here:

$$\begin{aligned} 1x_1 + 3x_2 &= 40 \\ 2x_1 + 3x_2 &= 60 \end{aligned}$$

A problem this size can be hastily solved by simultaneous equations with little difficulty, and $x_1 = 20$, $x_2 = 20/3$.

Solving this by means of the inverted matrix gives the same answers:

$$\begin{aligned} \mathbf{Ax} &= \mathbf{c} \\ \mathbf{A}^{-1}\mathbf{Ax} &= \mathbf{A}^{-1}\mathbf{c} \\ \mathbf{Ix} &= \mathbf{A}^{-1}\mathbf{c} \\ \mathbf{x} &= \mathbf{A}^{-1}\mathbf{c} \end{aligned}$$

The matrix we inverted is the one associated with this problem; thus the problem can be stated:

$$\begin{bmatrix} x_1 \\ x_2 \end{bmatrix} = \begin{bmatrix} -1 & +1 \\ +2/3 & -1/3 \end{bmatrix} \times \begin{bmatrix} 40 \\ 60 \end{bmatrix} = \begin{bmatrix} -40 & +60 \\ 2/3\,40 & -1/3\,60 \end{bmatrix}$$

$$x_1 = 20$$
$$x_2 = 20/3$$

which is exactly as we expected from the simultaneous equations solution.

By these simple examples, it has been shown that matrix algebra is a practical tool for industrial personnel to use. Bigger problems are suitable for digital computers.

Linear Programming

So far we have learned something about linear algebra and have become aware that the simple arithmetic of this discipline has some meaning and potential for the industrialist. The real interest in this area of knowledge has come about because of improved methods of solving linear equations, which, with the advent of the digital computer, has opened up a whole new frontier of decision making.

The term *linear programming* refers to a number of related techniques under the names of Simplex method, Transportation or Distribution method, Assignment method, and a number of others. These names of special methods should not be taken literally. For example, the Transportation method can be used for problems with no physical transportation involved. Similarly, the Assignment method can be used for problems other than those involving the assignment of people to tasks. In the development of the special cases the type of problem was essentially the same as the name implied, but in recent years the methods have been applied to a variety of problems.

Linear programming is a systematic, mathematical approach to a given problem to arrive at an optimal or best solution. It involves a linear objective equation and a set of linear restrictions or constraints. The objective equation of a problem may be to minimize some function, such as time, cost, or materials, or to maximize some function, such as profits. The restrictions may be due to machine capacities, available time, available raw materials, available capital for investment, and other limiting factors.

Typical of the linear programming problem is a large number of alternative choices. Initially, the problem is formulated mathematically into a set of equalities, or inequalities, with more variables present than the number of equations.

SOME USES FOR LINEAR PROGRAMMING

Linear programming has been found useful in several types of problems which are common to many industries. To this long list of applications, new ones are being added. A brief comment about a few of these applications will give you a greater appreciation of the techniques:

Optimization of Production

Such an example will be used as an illustration in this chapter for the simplex technique. Given production time and process limitations in a linear form, along with the profit for each part, we can maximize the overall profit or minimize costs.

Product Mix or Diet Problem

Here the linear programming technique is used to determine the right mix of such ingredients as vitamins, gasolines, alloys, etc., to produce a product of the required specifications at a minimum cost.

Transportation and Allocation

Typical of this problem is a supply of material available at various points (warehouses) which is to be distributed to other points. Linear programming can help decide this question on a minimum cost basis.

Job and Salary Evaluation

Job evaluation has been criticized for many years because of the subjective approach of its practitioners. Linear programming has been found to be a useful tool for assigning weights to the factors in a job evaluation system.

THE SIMPLEX METHOD OF LINEAR PROGRAMMING

The *simplex method* of solving simultaneous equations, devised by G. B. Dantzig, is one of the most powerful tools developed in recent years for analyzing economic, business, and manufacturing data. It has contributed greatly to the impetus of scientific decision making which has taken hold of manufacturing engineering during recent years.

At the outset, the reader should be cautioned that the word *simplex* is not a catch word for *simple*. On the contrary, it is one of the most complicated forms of linear programming, but it is worthy of consideration because of background and the fact that it is the most general and universal method of solving the linear programming problems. *Simplex* is a mathematical term and refers, in its geometric interpretation, to an n-dimensional convex polyhedron having exactly $n + 1$ vertices. The linear programming model, in its geometric interpretation, is a simplex. Don't let this alarm you, but don't approach the simplex in the wrong frame of mind; it is not simple. On the other hand, it is not beyond the comprehension of anyone who has been exposed to algebra.

The simplex method will be developed with the idea of making each step understandable and logical. This is a middle ground between the two common presentations—one in which little attempt is made to make the procedure appear logical, and the other in which the procedure is bound by rigorous mathematical proofs that delay the comprehension of the simplex method. The proofs of the underlying theorems are highly desirable for one who has gained a good grasp of the technique, and it is hoped that students will learn the theory given in the reference texts.

There are several ways of approaching the simplex procedure but here we will first present a typical small-scale problem which can be manipulated as a problem in geometry. After you get some feeling of this—and more important, faith in the procedure—we will move on to a mathematical *algorithm*, which is a particular method of solving a problem.

EXAMPLE PROBLEM

The problem with which we are starting is too simple for linear programming, but it will best serve our purpose now because it is not so large that you will lose track of what we are doing.

A company is producing two aluminum forgings for the aircraft industry at a plant on the eastern seaboard. This is a small plant and has more work than it can handle, so the management has decided to produce as much as possible at this plant and to make as much profit as possible. The balance of the work will be sent to a "captive plant" in the midwest. They have decided to concentrate on two parts at the eastern plant and wish to determine how much of each they should make to maximize the profits. Part 1 is a heavy part, requiring considerable prework but very little straightening. Part 2 is

OPERATION SHEET

		Part No.:	1
		Part Name:	*heavy forging*
Operation No.	*Operation Description*	*Department*	*Time*
10	Upset	U	15 min./part
20	Press	P	9 min./part
30	Heat Treat and Straighten	S	4 min./part

OPERATION SHEET

		Part No.:	2
		Part Name:	*light forging*
Operation No.	*Operation Description*	*Department*	*Time*
10	Upset	U	6 min./part
20	Press	P	10 min./part
30	Heat Treat and Straighten	S	20 min./part

a light and intricate part which requires little prework but considerable straightening. The operation sheets for these two parts furnish us with the information we need.

This company, because of overtime costs and maintenance, has the following limitations on each of the three departments used for the forgings:

Operation	*Department*	*Maximum Time*
Upset Press	U	72 hours/week
Press	P	54 hours/week
Heat Treat and Straightening	S	80 hours/week

From the operation sheets, and the available time in each department, we can see that the time used for prework in the upset press for product 1 and product 2 must be equal to, or less than, the time available on the upset press. This can be said more easily in this form where x_1 and x_2 refer to the unknown quantities of parts 1 and 2.

Dept. U: $15 \text{ min./part} \times x_1 \text{ parts} + 6 \text{ min./part} \times x_2 \text{ parts} \leq 72 \text{ hrs.} \times 60 \text{ min./hr.} \leq 4320 \text{ min.}$

Dept. P: $9 \text{ min./part} \times x_1 \text{ parts} + 10 \text{ min./part} \times x_2 \text{ parts} \leq 3240 \text{ min.}$

Dept. S: $4 \text{ min./part} \times x_1 \text{ parts} + 20 \text{ min./part} \times x_2 \text{ parts} \leq 4800 \text{ min.}$

The subscript on the x's is used to represent the various products—rather than such terms as X and Y—because we will soon be considering other products and would run out of suitable letters.

MATHEMATICAL INTERPRETATION OF PROBLEM

Let us digress for a moment and get a feeling for these equations and what they mean when represented geometrically. Referring to Figure 17–2, equation U, representing the upset department, is shown in two dimensions. What this means is if all the available time is used on the upset press, we can make any ratio of part 1 and part 2 which lies on the boundary represented by the line. For example, we can make no part 1s ($x_1 = 0$) and 720 parts 2s, or no part 2s ($x_2 = 0$) and 288 part 1s—or any proportion of parts 1 and 2 which is represented by the line. If we wish, we could make 220 part 2s and have enough time left to produce 200 part 1s (as shown at point a on the diagram). This upset process line divides the space into areas of permissible and unpermissible answers. Answers in the half-space below the line are permissible while those above are not.

We know from the restrictions of the problem that we cannot use the upset press for more than 72 hours. If, however, we should extend this limitation by adding overtime of perhaps 8 hours (for a total of 80 hours), the line would shift to the right (as shown by the dashed line). This, then, becomes another problem.

Figure 17–2
Production for Dept. U

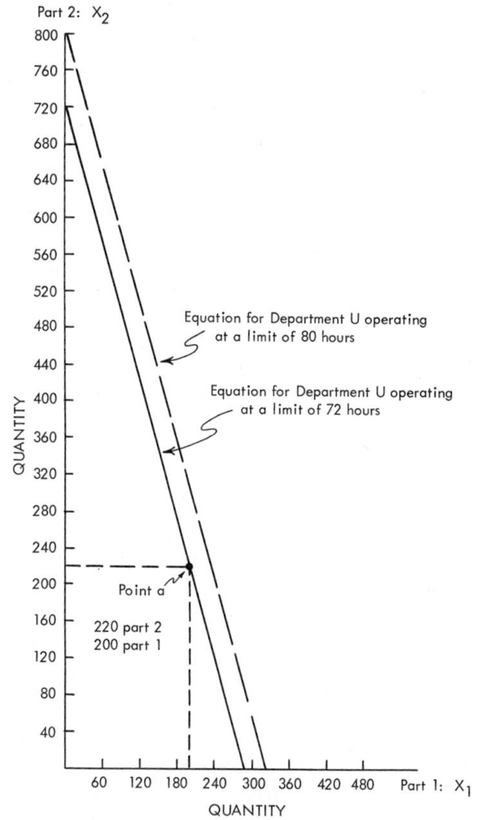

The lines for the equations *P* and *S*, representing the production in Departments P and S, can also be shown on the diagram (as in Figure 17–3). The limit has been set on the operations at 72 hours, 54 hours, and 80 hours; but, to optimize the profit, it may be desirable for at least some department to operate at less than maximum. In fact, it may be impossible to operate all departments at their maximums.

The answer then is to the left of the lines and might be any point, such as *a*, where part 1 is 90 and part 2 is 120. The area of possible solutions is bounded by the lines as indicated by the arrows. Therefore we are not considering an equation as represented by the equal sign (=) but inequations represented by the "less than" (<) and the "more than" (>) signs. Since the departments will not exceed their limits, the problem is correct as stated before:

U: 15 min./part $\times$ x_1 parts + 6 min./part $\times$ x_2 parts $\leq$ 4320 min.
P: 9 min./part $\times$ x_1 parts + 10 min./part $\times$ x_2 parts $\leq$ 3240 min.
S: 4 min./part $\times$ x_1 parts + 20 min./part $\times$ x_2 parts $\leq$ 4800 min.

Figure 17–3

Production for Three Departments

It is worthwhile to insert a word or two about the meaning of the inequality signs. These symbols represent such restrictions as "pay no more than," "produce no more than," "stock no less than," etc. In solving a problem containing mixed inequalities, that is, with some < and some >, it is essential to make the system consistent. For example, if we had a set of inequalities:

$$x_1 + x_2 \geqq Y$$
$$x_1 + x_2 \leqq Z$$

we can make them consistent by multiplying one of the equations by -1. The equation choice depends upon whether we wish to maximize the problem or minimize the problem:

$$-x_1 - x_2 \leqq -Y \qquad\qquad x_1 + x_2 \geqq Y$$
$$x_1 + x_2 \leqq Z \qquad\qquad -x_1 - x_2 \geqq -Z$$

(You should recognize that the equations on the left represent the area below the line and the equations to the right represent the area above the line.)

Returning now to our set of equations, and the way they are represented on the diagram, it is apparent that the lines for the equations bound the area containing the answers, but there might be some question about certain portions of the diagram. Let us look at one particular point on the last figure which might be confusing. Assume that 208 part 1s and 198 part 2s are made, as represented by point *b*. How does this affect equation *P*?

$$9 \text{ min./part} \times 208 \text{ part } 1 + 10 \text{ min./part} \times 198 \text{ part } 2 = 64.2 \text{ hrs.}$$

This exceeds the quantity of time available by more than 10 hours, so it is apparent that the equation for *P*, with its 54-hour limitation, helps form the boundary of feasible solutions within the space A, D, J, H, E, A.

This is a good place to pause for a moment and insert some of the language which prevails in the literature of linear programming to make the introduction of more complicated discussions a little easier.

A *point* is a certain position in space such as A, D, J, etc., and a collection of such points is said to be a *set*. A straight line joining two points, such as A–D, D–J, and the others, is called a *segment*. Then a *convex set* is a collection of points such that a segment joining any two points will be within the collection of points. The solution boundaries—A, D, J, H, E—are shown on the left in Figure 17–4. We can see that it is a convex set because any two connected points, such as *a* and *b*, will be within the collection. The diagram on the right is not a convex set.

Figure 17–4

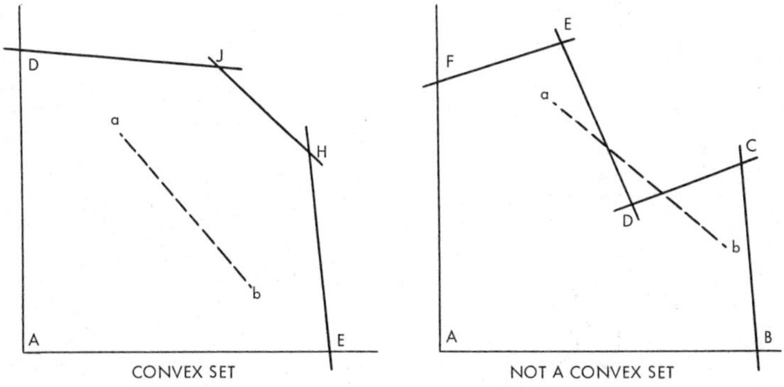

The *vertex* is an extreme point in a convex set. It is a point in the convex set which does not lie on a segment joining two other points. A, D, J, H, E are vertices, but *no* other points are.

It is apparent, although we have not proved it, that the answer to our problem is one of the vertices. These extreme points are feasible solutions, but we are searching for the *best* feasible solution. We are searching not for any answer but for the best answer. Not only does our answer have to satisfy the restraints given, it must also maximize the profit. The profit on each part, as furnished by the cost accounting department, is:

Part 1: \$10/part
Part 2: \$40/part

So the total profit, Z, can be expressed:

$$\$10/\text{part} \times x_1 \text{ parts} + \$40/\text{part} \times x_2 \text{ parts} = Z \text{ dollars profit}$$

We can illustrate, by a number of lines, a series of profit values—as in Figure 17–5. Slide the line from left to right in your mind to obtain increas-

Figure 17–5

Production for Three Departments and Profit Curve

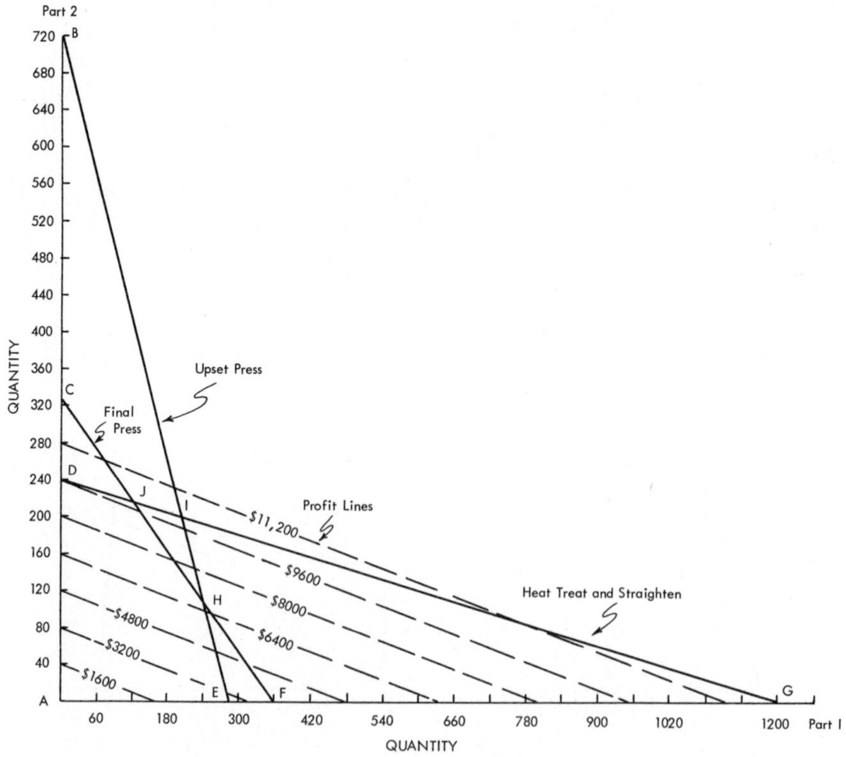

ing values of Z. We can start with producing little or no product, and make little or no profit with the line to the far left. We can keep shifting the line to the right until it intersects *E* to produce more profit; still farther, and the profit increases until point *H* is reached. Try going beyond this, and point *J* is reached. You cannot continue any farther without going beyond the feasible solution, as represented by the boundary of A, D, *J*, *H*, *E*.

Up to this point we have purposefully used a two-dimensional example because the concepts can be easily grasped. It would be a little more difficult to consider a three-dimensional problem. Instead of working with lines and intersections, we would be working with planes and the intersections of planes. We cannot extend our visual concepts beyond the three dimensions, but this does not mean that linear programming is limited to two or even three dimensions. A rigorous mathematical proof is available for the multidimensional problems which cannot be readily seen graphically.

THE ALGORITHM OF THE SIMPLEX

Linear programming is unlike many problems in which you close in on a solution in a predictable number of steps. It requires an unpredictable number of steps or *iterations*. Because of the sequence of steps and the number of iterations, an explanation becomes quite involved, for it is difficult to remember in which part of the cycle we are. To help overcome this difficulty a flow chart (Figure 17–6) is given here. Each step is numbered on the

Figure 17–6

Flow Chart for the Simplex Algorithm

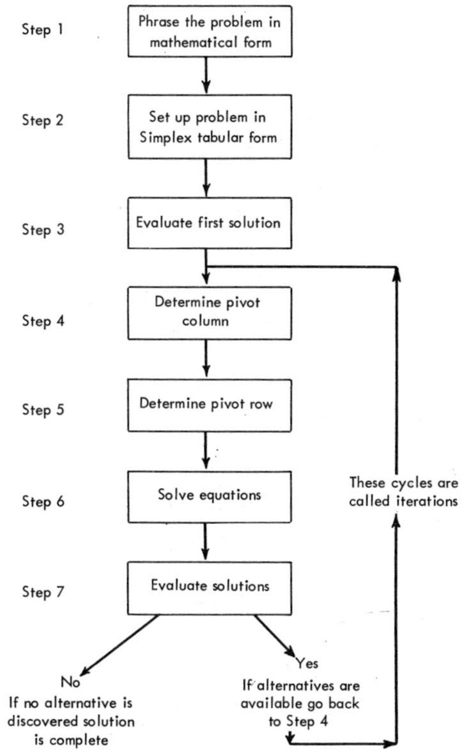

left side, and each step will be discussed in turn. Remember that this initial solution will appear long and drawn out, but this is because each step is accompanied by explanations. Subsequent solutions would, of course, be much more abbreviated as you gain confidence in what you are doing. Check back to the flow chart and occasionally see where you are, for it is there to help you. The steps will be keyed to the chart numbers.

Step 1. Phrasing the problem in mathematical form is the most difficult part of the problem. Often, trained clerical help or a computer can handle the calculations, but the real skill lies in this first step of phrasing the problem correctly.

Step 2. Since numerous calculations are required in each iteration, it is essential that the equations be set up in a form which makes the calculations as convenient as possible. There has been a good, systematic method developed for solving the problems, which will be illustrated.

Step 3. The simplex is an iterative or cycling procedure in which new factors are added while others are removed and evaluations made at each step. The evaluation of the problem, as it is first proposed, occurs.

Step 4. In this step the new factor is selected.

Step 5. The factor to remove is selected in this step.

Step 6. The problem is actually solved here.

Step 7. The solution is evaluated to determine whether the cycling is concluded or whether it should be continued by going back to Step 4 and starting over.

It may not be apparent in the flow chart and the explanations, but there are three really distinct steps in the problem which can be repeated over and over again. The first of these is finding the *pivot column*, the second is finding the *pivot row*, and the third is to *solve the simultaneous equations*. You should keep these in mind and not run them all together. Let us now start working through the steps of the algorithm.

STEP 1: PHRASE PROBLEM IN MATHEMATICAL FORM[3]

Reviewing the previous example, you will observe that the problem has two distinct parts:

Constraints: The set of equations expressing the quantity of material which could be produced in the given time.

Objective function: The equation which expresses the profit.

One additional condition was implied but not expressed. This is the *nonnegative condition*, which means that the value of the quantities of production, x_1, x_2, etc., must be equal to or greater than zero.

In a general mathematical form the problem could take the shape of a tableau (table or matrix), as has been referred to previously, and of the additional *objective function* and *nonnegative condition*.

[3] In the first part of the discussion "degeneracy" will not be considered.

Constraints

$$\begin{cases} a_{11}x_1 + a_{12}x_2 + a_{13}x_3 + \ldots + a_{1j}x_j + \ldots + a_{1n}x_n = b_1 \\ a_{21}x_1 + a_{22}x_2 + a_{23}x_3 + \ldots + a_{2j}x_j + \ldots + a_{2n}x_n = b_2 \\ \cdots\cdots\cdots\cdots\cdots\cdots\cdots\cdots\cdots\cdots\cdots\cdots \\ a_{i1}x_1 + a_{i2}x_2 + a_{i3}x_3 + \ldots + a_{ij}x_j + \ldots + a_{in}x_n = b_i \\ \cdots\cdots\cdots\cdots\cdots\cdots\cdots\cdots\cdots\cdots\cdots\cdots \\ a_{m1}x_1 + a_{m2}x_2 + a_{m3}x_3 + \ldots + a_{mj}x_j + \ldots + a_{mn}x_n = b_m \end{cases}$$

Objective function

$$c_1x_1 + c_2x_2 + \ldots + c_jx_j + \ldots + c_nx_n = Z$$

Nonnegative condition

$$x_j \geqq 0$$

Following the same notation used in matrix operations, the first number of the subscript gives the row and the second number gives the column. Any general a is referred to as a_{ij}. The tableau is said to be an $m \times n$ tableau, meaning that it has m rows and n columns. The *c*s refer to profit per unit.

Since you have been introduced to the subject of matrices and vectors, either here or elsewhere, you should recognize that this tableau is a matrix, or vector problem, which could be stated:

1. Find a vector $(x_1, x_2, \ldots, x_j, \ldots, x_n)$ which maximizes the *objective function,*
2. Subject to the linear *constraints,*
3. Subject to $x_j \geqq 0$.

The original example will now be restated for convenience:

Constraints:

U: 15 min./part × x_1 parts + 6 min./part × x_2 parts ≦ 4320 min.
P: 9 min./part × x_1 parts + 10 min./part × x_2 parts ≦ 3240 min.
S: 4 min./part × x_1 parts + 20 min./part × x_2 parts ≦ 4800 min.

Objective function:

4. \$10/part × x_1 parts + \$40/part × x_2 parts = Z dollars

Nonnegative condition:

5. $x \geqq 0$ for all x_j.

Before completing this step, let us consider one more aspect of the problem, that of the inequalities. The inequalities, less than (<) and greater than (>), might be disturbing, but this need not be so as we can easily make these inequalities into equalities by taking out some *slack*. These nonnegative variables, which are added as slack variables, form slack vectors which you will recognize as an identity matrix.

U: 15 min./part × x_1 parts + 6 min./part × x_2 parts + x_3 parts = 4320 min.
P: 9 min./part × x_1 parts + 10 min./part × x_2 parts + x_4 parts = 3240 min.
S: 4 min./part × x_1 parts + 20 min./part × x_2 parts + x_5 parts = 4800 min.

The slack variables have meaning in real life and can be represented by an imaginary product with no profit. These products, which we do not produce, cause no wear on the machine, no labor costs, and use no material. Slack vectors are sometimes called *giveaway vectors* or *disposal activities.* As has been pointed out, these slack vectors form an identity or unit matrix which provides an initial *basis,* a basis being m variables which are not set equal to zero.

If the constraints are set up in the form of equalities, and an identity is not available, artificial variables can be used to provide a basis. In this case, maximizing the objective function requires associating with the artificial variables large negative "profit" values, which need not be specified, to insure that the vector does not come into the optimal solution.

Another use of the artificial variable appears when an equation contains a negative value. For example, if x_4 were preceded by a negative sign, this would be interpreted as $x_4 = -3240$, which would make a problem impossible to solve. An initial solution of the correct form can be forced by adding an artificial variable to the second constraint. This artificial variable, x_6, will be assigned a large negative profit.

One other point should be brought up while discussing the mathematical phrasing of the problem. So far it is assumed that we are maximizing the functional, but there are also situations in which the functional should be minimized. Switching from one situation to another is easily done by merely changing the signs. For example:

$$c_1x_1 + c_2x_2 + \ldots + c_nx_n = \text{max.}$$

is the same as:

$$-c_1x_1 - c_2x_2 - \ldots - c_nx_n = \text{min.}$$

Up to this point we have discussed a typical problem and how it can be put into mathematical form, but for the repeated operations a compact form is desirable.

STEP 2: SET UP PROBLEM IN TABULAR FORM

The simplex technique requires repeated solutions, or iterations. This means that the problem must be stated and written down time after time. This is tedious, so the problem is to simplify the mechanics of displaying the equations.

First, there is no point of stating—let alone repeating—the dimensions or the variables. As long as all like entries are placed one under the other, we can merely designate the column. Also, it is more convenient to reverse the equations and change the order slightly to put them into the conventional simplex form.

c_j					$10.00	$40.00
	P_0	P_3	P_4	P_5	P_1	P_2
	4320	1			15	6
	3240		1		9	10
	4800			1	4	20

The vertical double lines replace the equal signs, the single line replaces the plus signs, and blank spaces represent zeros. Notice that the factors for the objective function are placed above their respective P columns in the c_j row. Here is displayed, in a highly abbreviated form, all the information contained in the original equations.

It will be even more convenient to give names to the various parts of the tableau and these we will add. Some parts will be added at this point which won't make much sense but which will be explained later. You should become acquainted with these terms before you go much further.

	c_j						\$10.00	\$40.00	Objective Row
Θ	C_i 1		P_0	P_3	P_4	P_5	P_1	P_2	Variable Designations
	0	P_3	4320	1			15	6	Constraints
	0	P_4	3240		1		9	10	Constraints
	0	P_5	4800			1	4	20	Constraints
		z							
		$z_j - c_j$							
Minimum Ratio Column	Objective Column	Basis Variable	Constant Column	Identity (Initial Basis)			Body		
	Stub								

STEP 3: EVALUATE FIRST SOLUTION

It is fortunate that in the way the problem is originally set up there is an initial solution. Without explaining why at this point, we set the columns P_1 and P_2 equal to zero. Thus they contribute nothing to our solution. The solution can be interpreted as producing 4320 P_3s, 3240 P_4s, and 4800 P_5s. We should recall that the profit values for P_3, P_4 and P_5 are zero. The fact that these Ps are the ones used in the solution is indicated by placing the appropriate Ps in the Basis Variable column. The profit values for the products P_3, P_4, P_5 are placed for convenience in the Objective column. The total profit for this solution is given by $(4320 \times 0) + (3240 \times 0) + (4800 \times 0) = Z$, which is, of course, nothing at all.

Thus what we are doing is starting with a "trivial" solution, which is point A of Figure 17–3, if interpreted in terms of the geometric presentation.

STEP 4: DETERMINE (FIRST) PIVOT COLUMN

Since this initial solution produces no profit, it is desirable to move on to a combination which would be profitable. The question is, which combination would be the best? For a start, it would seem wise to produce the most profitable item, and, by scanning the Objective row values, it can be seen that P_2 with $40 profit is the best.

Our initial Tableau A below shows what vector is to be taken out of the body and placed where it can count in the basis. The question is, which vector, P_1 or P_2, shall replace P_3, P_4, or P_5 in the variable column? (This is to be answered in Step 5.) At the end of Step 4 the tableau looks like this:

(Tableau A)

c_j						$10.00	$40.00
c_i		P_0	P_3	P_4	P_5	P_1	P_2
0	P_3	4320	1			15	6
0	P_4	3240		1		9	10
0	P_5	4800			1	4	20
	z						
	$z_j - c_j$						

STEP 5: DETERMINE PIVOT ROW

The decision must be made concerning which P to replace in the Objective column. The answer to this can be simply stated: Produce as many parts as possible without exceeding the time available. The number of parts which can be produced is found by dividing the time available in each department by the piece rate.

$$\text{From equation } U: \quad \frac{4320 \text{ min.}}{6 \text{ min./part}} = 720 \text{ parts}$$

$$\text{From equation } P: \quad \frac{3240 \text{ min.}}{10 \text{ min./part}} = 324 \text{ parts}$$

$$\text{From equation } S: \quad \frac{4800 \text{ min.}}{20 \text{ min./part}} = 240 \text{ parts}$$

If 720 parts were produced, the time in Departments P and S would be exceeded, and if 324 parts were produced, the time in Department S would be exceeded. Therefore it seems obvious that 240 parts is the maximum that can be produced. All the time in Department S will be used, and a surplus of time will be left in Departments U and P.

The row to replace is apparently the one with the minimum positive ratio, which, incidentally, is frequently referred to as *theta* (Θ). *Theta* can be appended to the left side of the tableau for convenience.

The old tableau, with the Pivot row and the Pivot column encircled, is shown below. The intersection of the Pivot row and Pivot column is called the *pivot*. The Θ value, for the ratio of the available time and the Pivot column, is shown at the far left.

(Tableau A)

	c_j						\$10.00	\$40.00 (Pivot Column)
Θ	c_i		P_0	P_3	P_4	P_5	P_1	P_2
$\frac{4320}{6} = 720$	0	P_3	4320	1			15	6
$\frac{3240}{10} = 324$	0	P_4	3240		1		9	10
$\frac{4800}{20} = 240$	0	P_5	4800			1	4	20 (Pivot) — Pivot Row
		z						
		$z_j - c_j$						

STEP 6: SOLVE EQUATIONS

It is now essential to lay a little groundwork because this part of the problem becomes quite involved. A discussion of solving simultaneous equations will be presented, and from this a systematic and rapid way of solving the equations in the simplex algorithm will be developed.

There has been at least some indication that the feasible solutions to the problems are at the vertices where two lines cross in our two-dimensional model. While we cannot take time to prove it here, the set of all feasible solutions is a convex set and the objective function assumes its minimum or maximum at an extreme point of the convex set.

The first problem here is to solve the equations and thus find the extreme points. Later we will see how to find the optimum extreme point. Refer again to the graphical illustration of the problem, Figures 17–3 and 17–5, and take into consideration all of the lines that intersect. The lines represented by the two ordinates and the equations for U, P, and S create a boundary to the feasible solution. The vertices can be obtained by solving two of the equations involved, simultaneously. A table showing these solutions is given below. The letters refer to the intersections on the diagram. The ones enclosing the solutions are encircled.

Vertices	(A)	B	C	(D)	(E)	F	G	(H)	I	(J)
x_1	0	0	0	0	288	360	1200	247.50	208.70	120.0
x_2	0	720	324	240	0	0	0	101.25	198.26	216.0

The next thing to consider is the five-dimensional problem, which has been revised to include the slack variables.

There are three equations with five unknowns, which we know from high school algebra cannot be solved simultaneously. Fortunately, there is an out. A theorem exists which states that there can be no more positive x values in a solution than there are rows. A *basic feasible* solution is a feasible solution with no more than m positive x_i.[4] This is an important theorem for our simplex procedure. We can then take the next step and set any $n - m$ coefficients equal to zero, and solve for the remaining m coefficients. These solutions are given below in table form.

$$\begin{aligned}
\text{Eq. } U:&\quad 15x_1 + 6x_2 + 1x_3 + 0x_4 + 0x_5 = 4320\\
\text{Eq. } P:&\quad 9x_1 + 10x_2 + 0x_3 + 1x_4 + 0x_5 = 3240\\
\text{Eq. } S:&\quad 4x_1 + 20x_2 + 0x_3 + 0x_4 + 1x_5 = 4800
\end{aligned}$$

Vertices	(A)	B	C	(D)	(E)	F	G	(H)	I	(J)
x_1	0	0	0	0	288	360	1200	247.5	208.70	120
x_2	0	720	324	240	0	0	0	101.25	198.26	216
x_3	4320	0	2376	2880	0	−1080	−13680	0	0	1224
x_4	3240	−3960	0	840	648	0	−7560	0	620.81	0
x_5	4800	−9600	−1680	0	3648	3360	0	1785	0	0

The vertices which are encircled at the top of the table are the ones which are feasible solutions, forming the convex set A, *D*, *E*, *H*, *J*.

This pattern, with two zeros in each column, would lead one to believe that all solutions to the problem have two axes which are zero. In other words, $n - m$ of the factors is zero, and this is true. This is a fundamental theorem of linear programming which will be of help in creating solutions.

The linear programming technique is a method of searching the basic feasible solutions in an efficient way to find the optimum. It is a technique for modifying a basic solution step by step so that an optimum solution is obtained.

Now a method of obtaining feasible solutions with less energy will be developed. Start with Tableau A of the algorithm, and following it, place a revised tableau which will be called Tableau B.

(Tableau A)

	c_j						$10.00	$40.00	
Θ	c_i		P_0	P_3	P_4	P_5	P_1	P_2	Check
	0	P_3	4320	1			15	6	
	0	P_4	3240		1		9	10	
	0	P_5	4800			1	4	20	
		z							
		$z_j - c_j$							

[4] Saul I. Gass, *Linear Programming Methods and Applications* (2d ed.; New York: McGraw-Hill Book Co., Inc., 1964), p. 38.

(Tableau B)

		P_3	2880	1		−3/10	13 4/5	0	
		P_4	840		1	−1/2	7	0	
	40.00	P_2	240			1/20	4/20	1	

The first step, shown in Tableau B, is to bring into the basis P_2 and take out another. We will want to bring in the limiting P_2 quantity of 240 parts, so that in effect we must divide both sides of equation P_5 by 20. The elements in the basis are placed on the left side under the Basis Variable column, so we can keep track of which variables are in the solution.

Notice the pattern of this first solution. There is an identity matrix and the body matrix. One of the columns will be reduced to a 1, to form a new identity matrix, while one of the 1s will take its place in the body matrix. Also notice how the dimensions of the entries change as we go from one matrix to another. Row P_5 is expressed in units of *time* in Tableau A, but when it is divided by minutes per part it is restated in number of *parts* in Tableau B.

$$240 \text{ parts} = \tfrac{1}{20}x_5 + \tfrac{1}{5}x_1 + 1x_2$$

The next problem is to remove the x_2 from the other equations:

$$\begin{aligned} 240 \text{ parts} &= 0x_3 + 0x_4 + \tfrac{1}{20}x_5 + \tfrac{1}{5}x_1 + 1x_2 \\ 1x_2 &= -0x_3 - 0x_4 - \tfrac{1}{20}x_5 - \tfrac{1}{5}x_1 + 240 \end{aligned}$$

$$\begin{aligned} 3240 \text{ min.} &= 0x_3 + 1x_4 + 0x_5 + 9x_1 + 10x_2 \\ 3240 \text{ min.} &= 0x_3 + 1x_4 + 0x_5 + 9x_1 + 10(-0x_3 - 0x_4 - \tfrac{1}{20}x_5 - \tfrac{1}{5}x_1 + 240) \end{aligned}$$

$$840 \text{ parts} = 1x_4 + 7x_1 - \tfrac{1}{2}x_5$$

$$\begin{aligned} 4320 \text{ min.} &= 1x_3 + 0x_4 + 0x_5 + 15x_1 + 6x_2 \\ 4320 \text{ min.} &= 1x_3 + 0x_4 + 0x_5 + 15x_1 + 6(-0x_3 - 0x_4 - \tfrac{1}{20}x_5 - \tfrac{1}{5}x_1 + 240) \\ 4320 \text{ min.} &= 1x_3 + 0x_4 + 0x_5 + 15x_1 - 0x_3 - 0x_4 - \tfrac{6}{20}x_5 - \tfrac{6}{5}x_1 + 1440 \\ 2880 \text{ parts} &= 1x_3 + 0x_4 - \tfrac{3}{10}x_5 + \tfrac{69}{5}x_1 \end{aligned}$$

We can see that this solution gives point *D*. In other words, the solution calls for 2880 part 3s and 840 part 4s (both being fictitious products) and 240 parts 2s—which is a real product.

The profit has been improved, as will be seen. The profit value, *c*, is placed on the left side in column c_i for convenience in multiplying. The Z value, or total profit, is:

$$Z = \sum_{i=1}^{5} c_i x_i$$

What we have just developed leads us into a quick and simple method of solving the equations. As stated before, the row that is being replaced is called the *pivot row* and the column that is being replaced will be called a *pivot column*. The point at which these two intersect will be called the *pivot*.

Continuing the process which has been developed, we notice that the pivot, regardless of its original value, is changed to a 1. All the rest of the column values are zero. From this we can develop an algorithm.

Step I. Reduce the pivot position to 1 by dividing the old row equation by the number in the pivot:

	P_0	P_3	P_4	P_5	P_1	P_2
(Tableau A—Old)	4800			1	4	20
÷ 20						
(Tableau B—New)	240			1/20	4/20	1

The generalized statement for this is: The revised row is the pivot row divided by the pivot number. Notice that the revised row replaces the pivot row and has the same identical position.

Step II. This part of the algorithm modifies all the other rows besides the pivot row, which has just been changed in Step I. First we will show how to do it, and then we will show how this agrees with the previous method of modifying the equations.

$$\text{New number } (a_{ij}) = \text{Old number } (a_{ij}) - \frac{\text{Corresponding old number in pivot row} \times \text{Corresponding old number in pivot column}}{\text{Pivot number}}$$

Let us now transform the first matrix by this method to see if it works.

(Old Tableau)

	P_0	P_3	P_4	P_5	P_1	P_2
P_3	4320	1			15	6
P_4	3240		1		9	10
P_5	4800			1	4	20

$$2880 \text{ min.} = 4320 \text{ min.} - \frac{4800 \text{ min.} \times 6 \text{ min./part}}{20 \text{ min./part}}$$

(New Tableau)

	P_0	P_3	P_4	P_5	P_1	P_2
P_3	2880	1		−3/10	13 4/5	0
P_4	840		1	−1/2	7	0
P_2	240			1/20	1/5	1

Finishing this row, P_3, we have the following values:

$$\text{Under } P_3\text{:} \quad 1 - \frac{0 \times 6}{20} = 1$$

$$P_4\text{:} \quad 0 - \frac{0 \times 6}{20} = 0$$

$$P_5\text{:} \quad 0 - \frac{1 \times 6}{20} = -\tfrac{3}{10}$$

$$P_2\text{:} \quad 6 - \frac{20 \times 6}{20} = 0$$

$$P_1\text{:} \quad 15 - \frac{4 \times 6}{20} = 13\tfrac{4}{5}$$

Calculations for row P_4:

$$\text{Under } P_0\text{: } 3240 - \frac{4800 \times 10}{20} = 840$$
$$P_3\text{: } 0 - \frac{0 \times 10}{20} = 0$$
$$P_4\text{: } 1 - \frac{0 \times 10}{20} = 1$$
$$P_5\text{: } 0 - \frac{1 \times 10}{20} = -\tfrac{1}{2}$$
$$P_1\text{: } 9 - \frac{4 \times 10}{20} = 7$$
$$P_2\text{: } 10 - \frac{20 \times 10}{20} = 0$$

Now to see how this agrees with the original method of solving equations, as developed in the earlier method:

Original Method:

$$3240 = 0x_3 + 1x_4 + 0x_5 + 9x_1 + 10(-0x_3 - 0x_4 - \tfrac{1}{20}x_5 - \tfrac{1}{5}x_1 + 240)$$
$$\mathbf{840} = \mathbf{0}x_3 + \mathbf{1}x_4 - \mathbf{\tfrac{1}{2}}x_5 + \mathbf{7}x_1 + \mathbf{0}x_2$$

Improved Method:

$$3240 = \frac{4800 \times 10}{20} = \mathbf{840}$$
$$0 - \frac{0 \times 10}{20} = \mathbf{0}$$
$$1 - \frac{0 \times 10}{20} = \mathbf{1}$$
$$0 - \frac{1 \times 10}{20} = \mathbf{-\tfrac{1}{2}}$$
$$9 - \frac{4 \times 10}{20} = \mathbf{7}$$
$$10 - \frac{20 \times 10}{20} = \mathbf{0}$$

STEP 7: EVALUATE OTHER ALTERNATIVES

The problem here is to determine which product should be chosen for the program. In other words, what column should be used for the pivot column? This was not a difficult decision in the simple example since all we had to do was to choose the most profitable product first, which is certainly logical. Then we had only one product left, and thus there was no choice but to put it into our solution. The decision would not have been as easy if this problem had been longer and had more choices. Therefore a method of evaluating other alternatives is needed.

Let us review what has been done up to this point. The first solution, Tableau A, indicated that no products should be made, and this would satisfy the constraints (but with a zero profit). The second solution, Tableau B, indicates that we can do $9,600 better if we make 240 light castings, P_2.

You will recall that row P_5 is expressed in units of time in Tableau A, but when it is divided by minutes per part it is restated in number of parts (Tableau B). The other rows did not change their dimensions. It is obvious that P_3 and P_4 will neither contribute nor take anything away because the coefficients are zero. Producing more of P_5 will reduce the profits by $2 a part. On the other hand, producing P_1 will improve the profits by $2 a unit. It seems obvious that it would be a good idea to bring P_1 into the production for the next program. This procedure should be continued until all difference coefficients are either zero or positive, for this is the best program that can be produced.

(Tableau A)

	c_j						$10	$40
Θ	c_i		P_0	P_3	P_4	P_5	P_1	P_2
	z_j							
	$z_j - c_j$		0				−$10	−$40

(Tableau B)

	$40	P_2	$240			1/20	1/5	1
	z_j		$9600			$2	$8	$40
	$z_j - c_j$		$9600			$2	−$2*	$00

* Promises the greatest improvement.

The rule for the algorithm is to program the product which shows the greatest opportunity for profit, that is, the product with the greatest negative $z_j - c_j$ difference. In Tableau A this is −$40 for product P_2 and in Tableau B is it −$2 for product P_1. Notice that we are searching for the largest negative number in the $z_j - c_j$ row as we are trying to maximize the profit. If costs, rather than profits, had been under consideration, and c had represented costs rather than profits, we would have been searching for the largest positive value—assuming, of course, that we desire to minimize costs.

This concludes the seventh step of the algorithm flow chart and we have seen how the No–Yes decision is made. If there is a negative number in the $z_j - c_j$ row in this maximization problem, we return to Step 4 and continue the cycles until this condition does not exist.

In order for you to have a better picture of this process, the entire set of tableaus is given here and you can trace through step by step to see how the final answer is obtained.

A *check column* has been added to the tables for convenience. The entry in Tableau A for the check column is the total of the respective rows. This total is treated as another entry in the row, and, if the calculations are correct, the total of each row will equal the entry in the check column. (The check column would never be used as the pivot column.)

(A)

	c_j						\$10.00	\$40.00	Check
Θ	c_i	Basis	P_0	P_3	P_4	P_5	P_1	P_2	
$\frac{4320}{6} = 720$	0	P_3	4320	1			15	6	4342
$\frac{3240}{10} = 324$	0	P_4	3240		1		9	10	3260
$\frac{4800}{20} = 240$	0	P_5	4800			1	4	20	4825
		z_j	0						
		$z_j - c_j$					−10.00	−40.00*	

(B)

$\frac{2880}{13\frac{4}{5}} = 208\frac{16}{23}$	0	P_3	2880	1		$-\frac{3}{10}$	$13\frac{4}{5}$	0	$2894\frac{1}{2}$
$\frac{840}{7} = 120$	0	P_4	840		1	$-\frac{1}{2}$	7	0	$847\frac{1}{2}$
	40.00	P_2	240			$\frac{1}{20}$	$\frac{1}{5}$	1	$241\frac{5}{20}$
		z_j	9600			2.00	8.00	40.00	
		$z_j - c_j$	9600			2.00	−2.00*	00.00	

(C)

	0	P_3	1224	1	$-1\frac{34}{35}$	$\frac{24}{35}$	0	0	$1223\frac{25}{35}$
	10.00	P_1	120	0	$\frac{1}{7}$	$-\frac{1}{14}$	1	0	$121\frac{1}{14}$
	40.00	P_2	216	0	$-\frac{1}{35}$	$\frac{9}{140}$	0	1	$217\frac{1}{28}$
		z_j	9840		$+\frac{10}{35}$	$+1\frac{12}{14}$	+10.00	+40.00	
		$z_j - c_j$	9840		$+\frac{10}{35}$	$+1\frac{12}{14}$	00.00	00.00	

It is evident that this solution is point *J* on the graphical solution, as of course it should be. The optimum production is 120 P_1's and 216 P_2's.

DEGENERACY IN THE SIMPLEX PROBLEM

In Step 5 of the simplex algorithm we selected the pivot row by determining the minimum Θ value. But what if there had been a tie between two Θ values? Occasionally a tie will occur at this stage, between rows, signalling a *degenerate* condition. The wrong choice at this step could result in a solution which would cycle without reaching an optimum solution. The method proposed to resolve the tie follows:

1. Divide each element in the tied rows by the value in the pivot column for that row.
2. Compare the resulting ratios, column by column, from left to right, in the original identity, until the tie is broken. The first unequal ratio breaks the tie.
3. Select as the key row the row which had the smallest algebraic ratio.
4. Continue with Step 6 of the simplex flow chart.

THE DUAL PROBLEM

Because of the dual theorem there is a choice of two problems to solve instead of just one. The linear program has two forms, the *primal* and the *dual*.

Consider, for example, a problem similar to the one just discussed. It is desired to maximize:

$$3x_1 + 1x_2 = Z$$

subject to:

$$\begin{aligned} 0x_1 + 1x_2 &\leq 8 \\ 1x_1 + 0x_2 &\leq 6 \\ 1x_1 + 1x_2 &\leq 10 \end{aligned}$$

As before, we can write these equations in this form:

	x_1	x_2	
	0	1	$\leq$ 8
	1	0	$\leq$ 6
	1	1	$\leq$ 10
Max $Z = \Sigma c_j x_j$	3	1	

Suppose now that new variables, *m*, are assigned to the rows and the *x*s are crossed out:

	x_1	x_2	
m_1	0	1	$\leq$ 8
m_2	1	0	$\leq$ 6
m_3	1	1	$\leq$ 10
Max $Z = \Sigma c_j x_j$	3	1	

These new equations are stated more conveniently if the tableau is rotated 90 degrees:

	m_1	m_2	m_3	
	0	1	1	≥ 3
	1	0	1	≥ 1
Min $R = \Sigma g_i m_i$	8	6	10	

The primal and dual problems are stated graphically in Figure 17–7. As is apparent in the tableau and in the diagram, we are searching for the maximum in the primal and the minimum in the dual. The situation could have been reversed, of course.

You will obtain a better grasp of the problem, and the solution, if you understand the dimensions of the equations. In the first tableau we are attempting to maximize the value of Z, the profits, while in the second we would like to minimize the value of R, the cost of the resources.

Figure 17–7

Dual Problem: The Solution to One Is the Solution to the Other

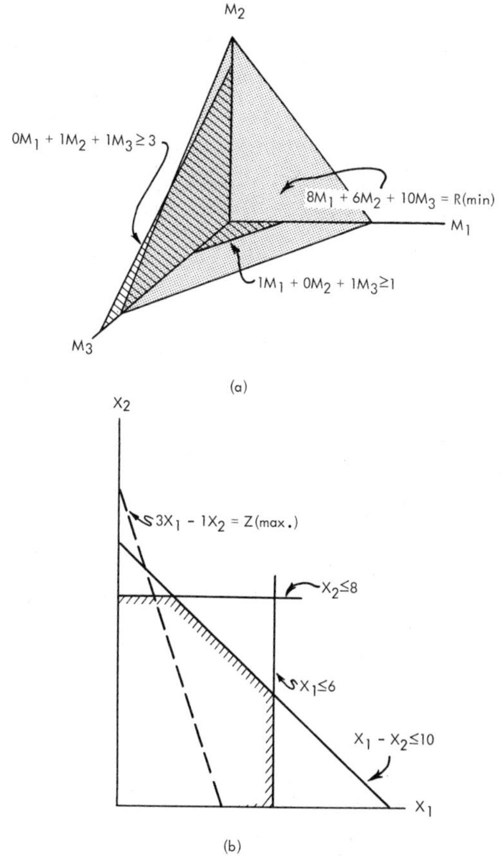

Max $Z = \Sigma c_j x_j$ where:

Z is the profit of all products,
c represents the profit per unit of product,
x represents the units of product.

Min $R = \Sigma g_i m_i$ where:

R is the cost of all resources,
m represents the cost per resource,
g represents units of resources.

Because of the dual problem, one can choose which one to solve. It is possible that a judicious choice between the two forms will reduce the time expended for a solution.

THE TRANSPORTATION TECHNIQUE OF LINEAR PROGRAMMING

A special family of linear programming problems, the *transportation technique*, is derived from the simplex procedure already discussed. The word *transportation* is used because this technique is especially suitable for solving problems of minimizing transportation distances and costs, but this technique is equally suitable for other problems which fit the general terms of the transportation model.

As before, the discussion will start with an example which will give some meaning as to what we are saying, and also give some assurance of the practical use of the technique. Again, the model will be kept small and simple so that you won't get lost in the details and miss the all-important overview of the problem. As before, we shall plot our course by means of a flow chart (shown in Figure 17–8).

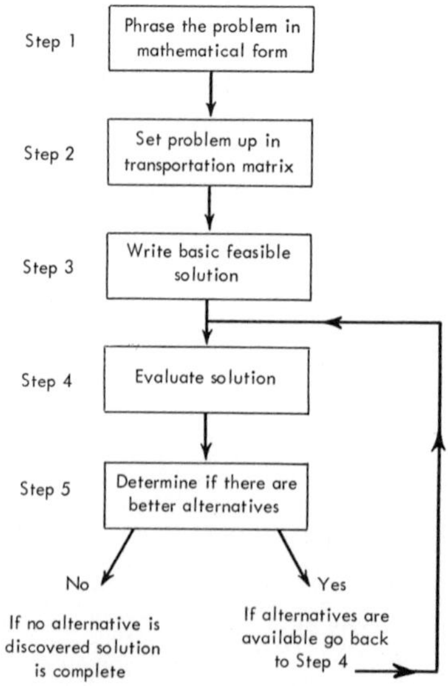

Figure 17–8

Flow Chart for Transportation Technique

STEP 1: PHRASE THE PROBLEM IN MATHEMATICAL FORM

Assume that a meat packer has three packing plants, P_1, P_2, P_3, within a statewide area—as shown on the map in Figure 17–9. Each plant buys

Figure 17–9

Transportation System

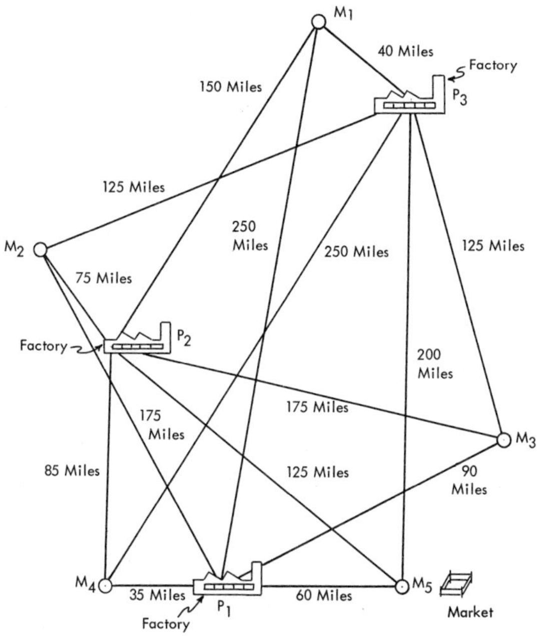

hogs in the city in which it is located, but also buys from five auction markets, M_1, M_2, M_3, M_4, and M_5 (as shown). The distances between markets and plants are given on the map, but are also tabulated in the matrix below.

	M_1	M_2	M_3	M_4	M_5
P_1	250	175	90	35	60 (miles)
P_2	150	75	175	85	125
P_3	40	125	125	250	200

The problem is to move the hogs purchased in each market to the packing plants, according to the needs, at a minimum cost.

The type of hog being purchased on one day averaged 240 pounds. The weight loss in the hog and the transportation costs average one cent a mile per hundredweight. The mileage matrix can easily be changed to a cost matrix for 240-pound hogs.

$$\text{For } M_5 \text{ to } P_1\text{: } \frac{240 \text{ lbs./hog}}{100 \text{ lbs.}} \times \frac{1¢ \times 60 \text{ miles}}{1 \text{ mile}} = \$1.44/\text{hog}$$

	M_1	M_2	M_3	M_4	M_5
P_1	6.00	4.20	2.16	.84	1.44
P_2	3.60	1.80	4.20	2.04	3.00
P_3	.96	3.00	3.00	6.00	4.80

The matrix shows the cost of moving a hog from a market, *M*, to a plant, *P*.

On the day under consideration the company's buyers were able to buy the following number of hogs at each of the various markets:

Market:	M_1	M_2	M_3	M_4	M_5
Number of hogs:	140	180	220	250	200

Each of the plants, for the following day, accepted the following quantities:

Plant:	P_1	P_2	P_3
Number of hogs:	180	320	490

You will notice that all the hogs purchased in the markets are to be processed. This is a condition of "balance," which does not need to exist—as we will see later.

STEP 2: SET UP PROBLEM IN TRANSPORTATION MATRIX

All the conditions of the problem can be stated very simply in one tableau:

	M_1	M_2	M_3	M_4	M_5	Receivables
P_1	x_{11} −6.00	x_{12} −4.20	x_{13} −2.16	x_{14} − .84	x_{15} −1.44	180
P_2	x_{21} −3.60	x_{22} −1.80	x_{23} −4.20	x_{24} −2.04	x_{25} −3.00	320
P_3	x_{31} − .96	x_{32} −3.00	x_{33} −3.00	x_{34} −6.00	x_{35} −4.80	490
Shipables	140	180	220	250	200	990

The costs are placed in the small corner boxes and the total quantities (*shipables*) to be moved from the markets are shown in the bottom "rim," while the *receivables* are placed in the right "rim." The xs for the unknown quantities have been placed in each box to indicate that we don't know yet what these values should be. Notice that the subscripts indicate the plant (in rows) and the markets are in the columns.

It should be noted here that costs are assigned negative signs (−) and profits are assigned positive signs (+). In the solution of the problem the mathematics will remain the same, whether maximizing profits or minimizing costs.

This is the problem, stated in simple form, and we will develop an algorithm for solving it. You might want to try estimating the answer before we go on to obtain a systematic method for solving the problem.

THE GENERAL FORM OF THE TRANSPORTATION PROBLEM

Now that we have discussed, but not solved, a typical transportation problem, let us outline briefly what the general form of this problem is so that you will recognize situations which fall into the transportation pattern, for this, after all, is the purpose of studying this technique.

There are markets, M_1, M_2, M_3, etc., each having a certain amount of homogeneous products available, s_1, s_2, s_3, for shipping.

There are plants, P_1, P_2, P_3, etc., each with a certain amount of material that it can receive, r_1, r_2, r_3, etc.

The quantity of material which moves between a market and a factory is x_{ij}, where i designates the plant and j the market.

The cost for the product to move between a market and plant is c_{ij}. The ijs have the same meaning as those associated with the xs.

One of the conditions set up in the problem was that all that is received is to be shipped. We can overcome this condition—as will be shown eventually—but for the moment the following statement holds:

$$\sum_{i=1}^{m} r_i = \sum_{j=1}^{n} s_j$$

where m indicates all the rows, P, and n indicates all the columns, M. This restriction is reasonable for this example because holding the animals for processing would be costly and risky. This is not an essential requirement for solving the problem, however.

The transportation problem takes the following form:

Minimize:

$$\sum_{j=1,}^{n} \sum_{i=1}^{m} c_{ij} \cdot x_{ij}$$

Subject to:

$$\sum_{j=1}^{n} x_{ij} = r_i \qquad i = 1, 2, 3, \ldots, m$$

$$\sum_{i=1}^{m} x_{ij} = s_j \qquad j = 1, 2, 3, \ldots, n$$

$$x_{ij} \geqq 0$$

Figure 17–10

Transportation Problem in Algebraic Form

Minimize

$$6.00x_{11} \quad 4.20x_{12} \quad 2.16x_{13} \quad .84x_{14} \quad 1.44x_{15} \quad 3.60x_{21} \quad 1.80x_{22} \quad 4.20x_{23} \quad 2.04x_{24} \quad 3.00x_{25} \quad .96x_{31} \quad 3.00x_{32} \quad 3.00x_{33} \quad 6.00x_{34} \quad 4.80x_{35}$$

Subject to

m equations

$$x_{11} \quad x_{12} \quad x_{13} \quad x_{14} \quad x_{15} = 180$$

$$x_{21} \quad x_{22} \quad x_{23} \quad x_{24} \quad x_{25} = 320$$

$$x_{31} \quad x_{32} \quad x_{33} \quad x_{34} \quad x_{35} = 490$$

n equations

$$x_{11} \quad x_{21} \quad x_{31} = 140$$

$$x_{12} \quad x_{22} \quad x_{32} = 180$$

$$x_{13} \quad x_{23} \quad x_{33} = 220$$

$$x_{14} \quad x_{24} \quad x_{34} = 250$$

$$x_{15} \quad x_{25} \quad x_{35} = 200$$

x_{ij} 0

$x_{ij} \geq 0$

If a problem can be written in this form, it is possible to use the transportation technique. It would be interesting now to cast our example problem into an algebraic form and notice some of the aspects which are peculiar to the transportation problem (See Figure 17–10).

This is an interesting set of equations from several viewpoints. First, all the multiples of x are either $+1$ or 0, as a negative value would have no logical interpretation. This fact, that a is either $+1$ or 0, makes the transportation equations much simpler to handle than the simplex equations. Another interesting point is that each variable appears only once in each of the m equations and once in the n equations.

If n_1, n_2, n_3, n_4, n_5 equations are added, and equations m_2, m_3 are subtracted, we will have m_1 left, which means that one equation is redundant and can be stated in terms of the others. There are then $m + n - 1$ equations in $m \times n$ unknowns.

STEP 3: WRITE A BASIC SOLUTION

From the matrix form of the problem it is possible to derive the initial basic solution, which you will remember was our first step in solving the simplex algorithm.

	M_1		M_2		M_3		M_4		M_5		Receivables
P_1	140	−6.00	40	−4.20		−2.16		−.84		−1.44	180
P_2		−3.60	140	−1.80	180	−4.20		−2.04		−3.00	320
P_3		−.96		−3.00	40	−3.00	250	−6.00	200	−4.80	490
Shipables	140		180		220		250		200		990

It is apparent that each column must have at least one value in it to satisfy the bottom rim conditions. The same is true of the rows; at least one value must be placed in each row to satisfy the right-hand rim condition. This is a backward way of saying that the conditions of the problem will not be satisfied if we leave a column or row blank. For example, if column M_1 and row P_1 were left blank, the shipping conditions of 140 hogs and the receiving conditions of 180 would not exist.

On the other hand, all the blanks cannot be filled in; there cannot be an x value for each position in the matrix. As has been learned from the simplex model, the basic feasible solution has, at most, as many x_{ij} values as there are rows. So we have as a limit $m + n - 1$ positive x_{ij}s.

A popular method for obtaining the first basic solution is the *northwest corner rule*, which leads automatically to $m + n - 1$ positive x values in the matrix—and also at least one value in each row and in each column. The logic of the northwest corner rule is easier to follow if it is presented as a series of stages (see previous tableau).

Stage 1. Start in the upper left-hand corner, x_{11}—which is the northwest corner of the conventional map and the reason we borrowed the name. P_1 has a need for 180, and M_1 can deliver 140. All of M_1's supply will be used and 40 more from M_2.

Stage 2. The 140 left over at M_2 are used to partially satisfy P_2's need, along with 180 from M_3.

Stage 3. The balance of M_3's supply, 40, is sent to P_3, and all of M_4's and M_5's supply is sent to P_3.

Notice there is at least one x in each column and row, and also that we have $m + n - 1 = (3 + 5 - 1)$ positive x's, which is our assurance of a basic solution.

This method of solving the transportation problem has become known as the "stepping stone" method. Each of the x's forms stepping stones across the "water area," where no stones exist. We will be less facetious and refer to the matrix squares as being filled or not filled.

STEP 4: EVALUATE SOLUTION

This initial solution, of course, gives us one solution, which is: the product of the x's of the filled square and the cost factors shown in the small square:

Box 1–1	140 hogs ×	\$6.00/hog =	\$ 840.00
1–2	40	4.20	168.00
2–2	140	1.80	252.00
2–3	180	4.20	756.00
3–3	40	3.00	120.00
3–4	250	6.00	1500.00
3–5	200	4.80	960.00
			\$ 4596.00

Up to this stage we have produced an initial basic solution somewhat similar to the simplex solution, and we could continue the solution along the lines of the simplex form illustrated; however, there is a more common way of looking at the problem, which seems to be favored, and we will use it.

STEP 5: DETERMINE IF THERE ARE BETTER ALTERNATIVES

The problem is to check each of the blank squares to determine if a quantity shipped from that M to the corresponding P would be more favorable than the solution of Step 3. You can memorize a procedure for this, but we prefer to present a logical method of changing the tableau. Let us start out by checking the blank square, P_2, M_1, which we will refer to as 2–1, and, for convenience, reproduce the initial solution here:

	M_1	M_2	M_3	M_4	M_5	
P_1	140 − 1	40 + 1				180
P_2	+1	140 − 1	180			320
P_3			40	250	200	490
	140	180	220	250	200	990

The method is to add one unit at 2–1 and see what happens. If the rim conditions are to be maintained, we cannot add one at 2–1 without making an adjustment in column M_1 and in row P_2 to compensate for the gain. Adding one at 2–1, we will move to the right and deduct one from 140 at 2–2. This will throw column M_2 out of balance, and we will have to add one to 40 at 1–2. This, in turn, will require an adjustment to the 140 at 1–1, which closes the circuit. This makes an interesting pattern with plus signs, indicating the addition of a unit at two opposite corners and negatives at the other two.

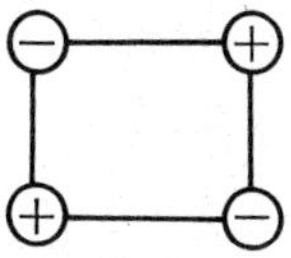

Now see what adding and subtracting these units has done to the solution:

	Costs Added		*Costs Removed*
2–1	−\$3.60	1–1	+\$6.00
1–2	− 4.20	2–2	+ 1.80
	−\$7.80		+\$7.80

It is obvious that there is no advantage in adding one at 2–1, but this may not be true for all unfilled squares. The procedure for checking the other squares is to form the shortest closed loops from the unfilled square back to the unfilled square. Right-angle turns are permitted only at the filled squares, and it is possible to skip over any filled squares to produce the loop. The costs are alternately added and subtracted. The value for each square is placed in the upper right-hand corner of the block, as you will notice.

Be mindful of how the signs are being used. Costs have a negative sign (−) and profits a positive sign (+), so that the costs added and subtracted (as shown in the diagram) will have the negative values for costs added and positive signs for costs removed. Since the difference between the two values will bear the sign of the larger, the alternatives with negative signs are not as good as the original solution. The alternatives with positive signs are better. The largest positive number is, of course, the best alternative.

The largest positive number is found by finding the advantage or disadvantage of bringing into the solution all of the blank squares. The calculation for each of these squares is shown below Tableau I and it would be advisable to calculate these values on your own to be sure you understand the procedure.

(Tableau I)

	M_1		M_2		M_3		M_4		M_5		
P_1	140	 −6.00	40	 −4.20		+4.44 −2.16		+8.76 − .84		+6.96 −1.44	180
P_2		00 −3.60	140	 −1.80	180	 −4.20		+5.16 −2.04		+3.00 −3.00	320
P_3		+1.44 − .96		−2.40 −3.00	40	 −3.00	250	 −6.00	200	 −4.80	490
	140		180		220		250		200		990

2–1 −3.60 + 1.80 − 4.20 + 6.00 = .00
3–1 − .96 + 3.00 − 4.20 + 1.80 − 4.20 + 6.00 = +1.44
3–2 −3.00 + 3.00 − 4.20 + 1.80 = −2.40
1–3 −2.16 + 4.20 − 1.80 + 4.20 = +4.44
1–4 − .84 + 4.20 − 1.80 + 4.20 − 3.00 + 6.00 = **+8.76**
2–4 −2.04 + 4.20 − 3.00 + 6.00 = +5.16
1–5 −1.44 + 4.20 − 1.80 + 4.20 − 3.00 + 4.80 = +6.96
2–5 −3.00 + 4.20 − 3.00 + 4.80 = +3.00

The next question is: How shall we alter this initial solution to give us a better answer? First, it would seem logical to change the problem in favor of the most profitable change, which is $8.76 (in position 1–4). If we add one unit of this box to the solution, the answer is improved by $8.76, and if we add two, it is improved by $17.52. But how far can we go in this direction? Let us retrace our path to see if this gives us any clue:

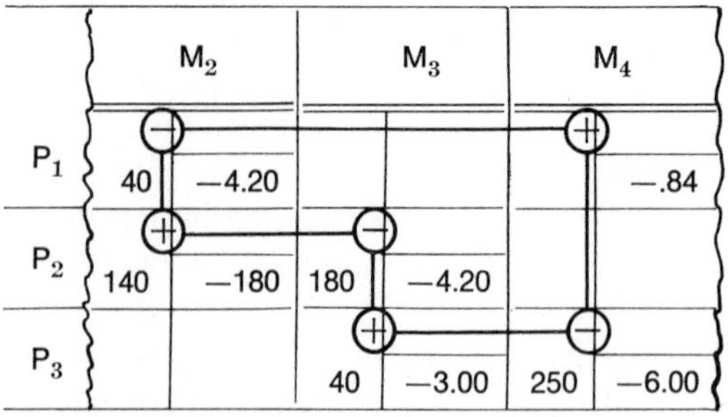

The smallest quantity at a negative spot limits the change that can be made. In this example, the 40 at 1–2 is the limiting number, for, if we changed it any more, this number would become negative, creating the impossible (if amusing) situation of the hogs going from the packing plant to the markets.

Adding 40 to 1–4 and removing 40 from 1–2 will result in the rim conditions not being satisfied. It is necessary to retrace the path, adding and subtracting quantities until the rim conditions are satisfied. After each iteration it is essential to scrutinize each unfilled block to see if there is a better solution, as indicated by plus signs.

The improved solutions are shown in the following tableaus. (There is no need to rewrite the tableau each time, but it will be easier to follow the changes if we do.) It is obvious that the second solution to the tableau gives a better solution than the first. How do these answers compare with your early estimate?

(Tableau II: $4245.00)

	M_1	M_2	M_3	M_4	M_5	
P_1	140 −6.00	−8.76 −4.20	−4.32 −2.16	40 − .84	−1.80 −1.44	180
P_2	+8.76 −3.60	180 −1.80	140 −4.20	+5.16 −2.04	+3.00 −3.00	320
P_3	+10.20 − .96	−2.40 −3.00	80 −3.00	210 −6.00	200 −4.80	490
	140	180	220	250	200	990

(Tableau III: $2817.60)

	M_1	M_2	M_3	M_4	M_5	
P_1	— −6.00	— −4.20	— −2.16	180 − .84	— −1.44	180
P_2	— −3.60	180 −1.80	140 −4.20	+5.16 −2.04	+3.00 −3.00	320
P_3	140 − .96	— −3.00	80 −3.00	70 −6.00	200 −4.80	490
	140	180	220	250	200	990

(Tableau IV: $2456.40)

	M_1	M_2	M_3	M_4	M_5	
P_1	— −6.00	— −4.20	+ .84 −2.16	180 − .84	+3.36 −1.44	180
P_2	— −3.60	180 −1.80	70 −4.20	70 −2.04	+3.00 −3.00	320
P_3	140 − .96	— −3.00	150 −3.00	— −6.00	200 −4.80	490
	140	180	220	250	200	990

(Tableau V: $2221.20)

	M_1		M_2		M_3		M_4		M_5		
P_1		— / −6.00		— / −4.20		— / −2.16	110	−.84	70	−1.44	180
P_2		— / −3.60	180	−1.80		— / −4.20	140	−2.04		— / −3.00	320
P_3	140	−.96		+ .96 / −3.00	220	−3.00		— / −6.00	130	−4.80	490
	140		180		220		250		200		990

(Tableau VI: $2115.60)

	M_1		M_2		M_3		M_4		M_5		
P_1		— / −6.00		— / −4.20		— / −2.16	0	— / −.84	180	−1.44	180
P_2		— / −3.60	70	−1.80		— / −4.20	250	−2.04		+ .60 / −3.00	320
P_3	140	−.96	110	−3.00	220	−3.00		— / −6.00	20	−4.80	490
	140		180		220		250		200		990

(Tableau VII: $2103.60)

	M_1		M_2		M_3		M_4		M_5		
P_1		— / −6.00		— / −4.20		— / −2.16		— / −.84	180	−1.44	180
P_2		— / −3.60	50	−1.80		— / −4.20	250	−2.04	20	−3.00	320
P_3	140	−.96	130	−3.00	220	−3.00		— / −6.00		— / −4.80	490
	140		180		220		250		200		990

ZERO EVALUATIONS IN OPTIMUM SOLUTION

In the example just given, all the evaluation figures in the final optimum tableau turned out to be negative numbers. It is possible, however, that some of the evaluation numbers might have turned out to be zero, in which case there are alternative solutions. This is something that the management must be aware of, for it gives an opportunity to make decisions by criteria other than those given in the requirements of the problem.

The only change in our procedure is that zeros which appear in the optimal solution are treated just the same as the most positive value—that is, in the same way as the square which will make the greatest contribution. The next solution is worked out accordingly.

UNEQUAL SUPPLY AND DEMAND

Our example was neater than could possibly be expected in an actual situation for it is doubtful that the supply and demand would ever be equal. Unequal supply and demand is not difficult to overcome if we are willing to insert fictitious plants or markets in the tableau.

First let us see what would have occurred if the supply had been less than the demand:

	M_1	M_2	M_3	M_4	M_5	
P_1	130	50				180
P_2		130	190			320
P_3			30	250	200	Not equal to 490
Supply	130	180	220	250	200	

It is apparent that the northwest corner rule, which was used for the initial solution, works on a first-come-first-served basis—so that P_1 and P_2 get all they want in this solution, but P_3 is shorted. We can't make up the shortage out of thin air, but, on the other hand, it may not be profitable to always short the same factory. There is a way of letting the mathematics decide to which plant it is best to ship. This is done by including in the problem a mythical *dummy* market which ships at higher but equal costs to all than any other market. These shipments would be the last to enter the solution, and their transportation cost can be subtracted from the total. This technique has been used in the following initial solution.

By following the technique for obtaining improved solutions, the shortage is distributed to the plants by cost, which is as it should be. It is worth observing that this makes it possible to stay within the requirements of the rim conditions. In this example the demand was greater than the supply. Should the supply be greater than the demand, the procedure is altered and a dummy factory (instead of a dummy market) is added.

	M_1	M_2	M_3	M_4	M_5	M_{Dummy}	
P_1	130	50					180
P_2		130	190				320
P_3			30	250	200	10	490
	130	180	220	250	200	10	990

This has been the complete transportation solution, using the northwest corner rule to obtain an initial solution. If you have followed the solution in detail, you have probably been impressed by the number of calculations needed. An easier solution is needed.

THE VOGEL APPROXIMATION METHOD

The northwest corner rule leads to an initial feasible solution but usually does not yield the optimum solution since no consideration is given to costs. A technique for obtaining a better initial solution was developed by Vogel, and is referred to as the Vogel Approximation Method—or VAM.[5] The stages for this initial solution are given along with a tableau illustrating each stage for the example problem:

Stage 1: Consider each row and each column separately, and for each one compute the difference between the two lowest cost values. These are shown adjacent to the tableau.

Stage 2: Select the row or column with the greatest *difference* value (see circled figure on the tableau marked Stage 2).

Stage 3: Determine the lowest cost in the row or column selected in Stage 2.

Stage 4: Assign as much as possible to the square determined in Stage 3.

Stage 5: Whenever a row or column rim condition is satisfied, fill in the remaining squares in that row or column with crosses.

Stage 6: Return to Stage 1 and repeat the sequence of stages until all squares are filled with either an assignment or cross.

In the example, the difference values for each iteration are shown. It is not necessary to repeat them time after time, for, as you will notice, some remain the same. If a column has the highest difference value, then the other columns will remain the same for the next iteration; and if a row has the highest difference value, the other row values will remain the same for the next iteration. Knowing this should save you some unnecessary work. Ties between two difference values may be broken by making a random choice. This may not give the most efficient solution but an error in choice will be rectified in the steps to come.

This has been the *initial* solution, but we must move on to Step 4 to evaluate the solution, and to Step No. 5 to determine if there are better alternatives. The results of Step 4 are shown on the tableau and the negative

[5] See Nyles V. Reinfeld and William R. Vogel, *Mathematical Programming* (Englewood Cliffs, N.J.: Prentice-Hall, Inc., 1958).

Step 3: The VAM Method for Obtaining the Initial Solution

		M₁	M₂	M₃	M₄	M₅							
													5
			1.20	1.20								4	
			1.20	1.20		(1.80)					3		
				1.20	(3.96)	1.80				2			
		Stage 2	1.20	.84	1.20	(1.56)			1				
		(2.64)	1.20	.84	1.20	1.56		0	Stage 1				
Stage 5		M₁	M₂	M₃	M₄	M₅							
	P₁	x — −6.00	x — −4.20	x — −2.16	x — −.84	180 −1.44	180	.60	.60				
Stage 4	P₂	x — −3.60	50 −1.80	x — −4.20	250 −2.04	20 −3.00	320	.24	.24	.24	1.20	(2.40)	
	P₃	140 −.96	130 −3.00	220 −3.00	x — −6.00	x — −4.80	490	2.04	00	00	00	00	00
		140	180	220	250	200	990						

Stage 3

Step 4: $2103.60.
Step 5: See upper right-hand corner of each box.

signs in the upper right corner of each square show that an optimum solution has been found.

Fortunately—or unfortunately—in this example the initial solution turned out to be the optimum solution. This, of course, doesn't always occur, and the problem solution could have continued through a number of iterations before the optimum solution was obtained. However, this rapid converging upon the solution points up the superior efficiency of the VAM technique over the northwest corner rule.

DEGENERACY IN THE TRANSPORTATION MODEL

Degeneracy can occur in the transportation model just as it can in the simplex model. If less than $m + n - 1$ positive values occur in the tableau, the problem becomes *degenerate* and the common method of solving for the optimum solution won't work. If more than $m + n - 1$ values occur, there has been an error.

Of course, degeneracy can occur because an error has been made in the calculations, and a quick check back through the tableaus should be made to be sure that this is not the case. If there is no error, techniques for overcoming degeneracy should be used. The method discussed here involves *perturbing*, or adding a small amount in the square which is causing the difficulty. When we add a small amount to one square it will affect some of the others, and one must account for this. Let us discuss a particular situation: One of the shipping and receiving schedules for the packing plant looks like this:

	M_1	M_2	M_3	M_4	M_5	
P_1	70	(90)	(+1)			160
P_2		(+?)	(120)			120
P_3			50	40	80	170
	70	90	170	40	80	450

Look for a moment at 1–3 and 2–2. There is no way of closing the path in the usual way of determining a better alternative. If, however, a small amount is added to each market (even though we recognize we can't add a fraction of an animal), the usual approach can be made. When the solution is concluded, these small amounts may be disposed of by simply rounding off all the answers, as we know they must be integers.

	M_1	M_2	M_3	M_4	M_5	
P_1	70 + .1	90 − .1				160.0
P_2		+ .2	120 − .2			120.0
P_3			50 + .3	40 + .1	80 + .1	170.5
	70 + .1	90 + .1	170 + .1	40 + .1	80 + .1	450 + .5

The Assignment Method

The assignment method is used to distribute n things to n requirements. The "things" may be jobs to machines, trailers to shippers, people to machines, or similar distributions.

Each requirement can be satisfied by any of the facilities available, but not more than one facility can be assigned to a requirement. This becomes apparent when one studies the *assignment matrix* illustrated in Figure 17–11. A facility assigned to a requirement is indicated by a 1 appearing at the intersection of a row and column, as at 3–*D*.

Figure 17–11

The Assignment Method

Machines (Facilities)

Jobs (Requirements)	A	B	C	D
1	1			
2			1	
3				1
4		1		

Assignment Matrix

Machines (Facilities)

Jobs (Requirements)	A	B	C	D
1	30	40	50	80
2	40	70	20	60
3	50	40	30	20
4	60	40	80	50

Cost Matrix

	A	B	C	D
1	00	10	20	50
2	20	50	00	40

Step 1

Since each requirement must be satisfied with one facility, no more than one figure may appear in any row or column in the assignment matrix. All others will appear blank in the final solution.

This is an $n \times n$ matrix. When $x_{ij} = 1$, the ith requirement is being met by the jth facility. Said in equation form this is:

$$\sum_{i=1}^{n} x_{ij} = 1 \qquad j = 1, 2, \ldots, n$$

$$\sum_{j=1}^{n} x_{ij} = 1 \qquad i = 1, 2, \ldots, n$$

Next, consider the cost relationships between the facilities and requirements. While any facility may be used to satisfy a requirement, the cost might vary considerably from assignment to assignment. A *cost matrix* is shown just below the assignment matrix.

The cost for any assignment, c_{ij}, is shown at the intersection of i and j. The problem is to minimize the total cost, C.

$$C = \sum_{i=1}^{n} \sum_{j=1}^{n} c_{ij} x_{ij}$$

Solving this problem follows basic investigations made by König; and one solution technique, the *Hungarian method*, bears the name of his na-

Figure 17–12

Flow Chart for the Assignment Method

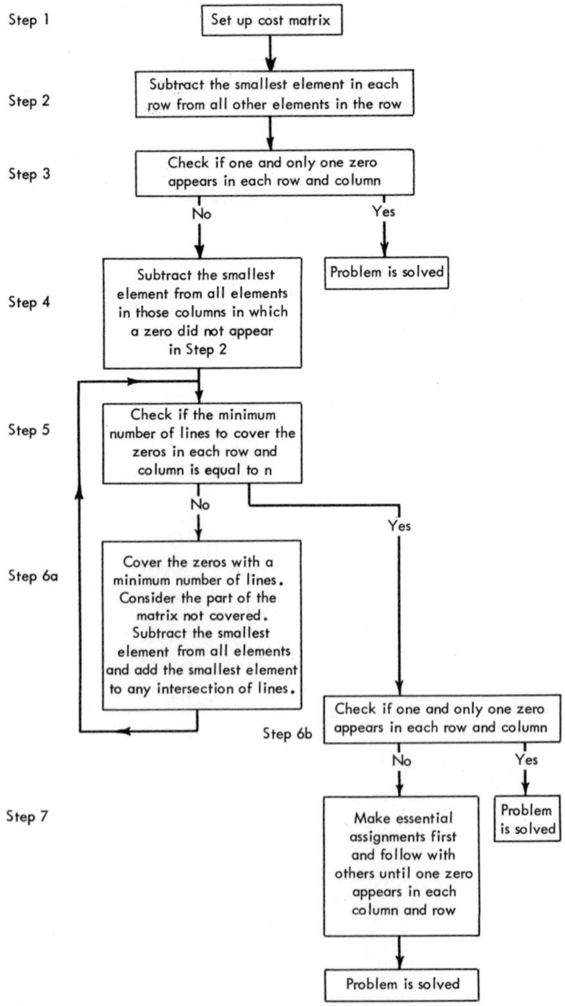

Figure 17–13

Three Examples of the Assignment Method

EXAMPLE I

	A	B	C	D	E
1	30	60	70	80	90
2	40	70	20	60	80
3	50	60	40	20	60
4	60	40	80	50	70
5	110	80	90	100	70

Step 1

↓	↓	↓	↓	↓
00	30	40	50	60
20	50	00	40	60
30	40	20	00	40
20	00	40	10	30
40	10	20	30	00

Step 2

00				
		00		
			00	
	00			
				00

1				
		1		
			1	
	1			
				1

Assignment

EXAMPLE II

	A	B	C	D	E
1	30	60	70	80	90
2	20*	70	40*	60	80
3	50	60	40	20	60
4	60	40	80	50	70
5	110	80	90	100	70

Step 1

↓	↓		↓	↓
00	30	40	50	60
00	50	20	40	60
30	40	20	00	40
20	00	40	10	30
40	10	20	30	00

Step 2

↓	↓	↓	↓	↓
00	30	20	50	60
00	50	00	40	60
30	40	00	00	40
20	00	20	10	30
40	10	00	30	00

Step 3

↓	↓	↓	↓	↓
(00)				
~~00~~		(00)		
		~~00~~	(00)	
	(00)			
		~~00~~		(00)

Steps 5, 6 & 7

1				
		1		
			1	
	1			
				1

Assignment

EXAMPLE III

	A	B	C	D	E
1	30	60	70	80	90
2	20	70	80*	60	80
3	50	60	40	20	60
4	60	40	50*	50	70
5	110	80	90	100	70

Step 1

↓	↓		↓	↓
00	30	40	50	60
00	50	60	40	60
30	40	20	00	40
20	00	10	10	30
40	10	20	30	00

Steps 2 & 3

↓			↓	↓	
00	30	30	50	60	
00	50	50	40	60	
30	40	10	00	40	
20	00	00	10	30	←
40	10	10	30	00	

Steps 4 & 5

↓					
00	20	20	50	60	
00	40	40	40	60	
~~30~~	~~30~~	~~00~~	~~00~~	~~40~~	←
~~30~~	~~00~~	~~00~~	~~20~~	~~40~~	←
~~40~~	~~00~~	~~00~~	~~30~~	~~00~~	←

Step 6a

↓	↓				
00	00	00	30	40	
00	20	20	20	40	
50	30	00	00	40	←
40	00	00	20	40	←
60	00	00	30	00	←

Steps 5 & 6b

~~00~~	(00)	~~00~~		
(00)				
		~~00~~	(00)	
	~~00~~	(00)		
	~~00~~	~~00~~		(00)

Step 7

	1			
1				
			1	
		1		
				1

Assignment

tionality. If a constant is added or subtracted from all elements in a row or a column of the cost matrix, the optimal solution remains the same as the optimal solution for the original matrix (Step 1, Fig. 17–11).

To make an optimum assignment, it makes sense to first assign the lowest cost facility, A, to requirement 1. This is illustrated by subtracting $30 from all elements in the first row. The row values change to $00, $10, $20, and $50. Zero in the *A–1* position means that an assignment has been made. This is the equivalent of the 1 appearing in the assignment matrix. So now it appears that one and only one zero must appear in each column and row in the final solution. Verification of an optimal solution can be determined by observing the matrix, but an easier accounting method is to *cover* all the zeros with the minimum number of lines drawn through the rows and columns. If the number of lines is equal to n, an optimal solution has been obtained. (Rows and columns having lines are shown by arrows.)

While the solution is optimal when there are n lines, there may be a choice of two or more assignments available in a row or column. This problem is overcome by first assigning those facilities for which there can be no other choice, and then continuing this process until each row and column has one and only one assignment.

A flow chart for the assignment algorithm is given in Figure 17–12, and three different example problems are illustrated in Figure 17–13. The reason three different examples are given is to illustrate what happens when a problem terminates at one of the various intermediate steps. The initial matrices shown are similar (with the exception of the numbers marked with asterisks).

It is not necessary to elaborate upon the numerous applications suitable for the assignment model. It is a technique which can be used with hand calculations or can be adapted to computer operations.

SUMMARY

This has been only an introduction to linear programming, an introduction which has attempted to teach the logic rather than to demand an acceptance on faith.

Only some of the common forms of linear programming problems have been discussed, but the knowledge is expanding rapidly and you should become acquainted with some of the excellent references and the professional journals on the subject.

In general, theory of linear programming has outdistanced practice. This is probably as it should be; but soon, people like you will have the knowledge to apply the methods. Probably no technique has held out such great opportunities to improve the decision-making processes.

Many attempts to put linear programming into practice have failed because the problem was not fully understood at the outset. Just as often, the necessary information for the linear programming model was not available, or the method was too complicated for a clerk to use. In this latter case, the results of the linear programming model might have been tabulated or put in nomograph form. In any event, one must always ask: Is the information costing more than it is worth?

Questions

1. Define the following:
   a) Matrix
   b) Row and column
   c) Scalar
   d) Vector
   e) Iteration
2. Perform the following matrix operations:

$$\begin{bmatrix} 3 & 9 \\ 2 & 5 \end{bmatrix} + \begin{bmatrix} 6 & 2 \\ 8 & 1 \end{bmatrix} = \qquad \begin{bmatrix} 4 & 2 \\ 6 & 1 \end{bmatrix} \times \begin{bmatrix} 8 & 9 \\ 7 & 2 \end{bmatrix} =$$

$$\begin{bmatrix} 9 & 6 \\ 8 & 2 \end{bmatrix} - \begin{bmatrix} 3 & 1 \\ 4 & 1 \end{bmatrix} =$$

3. Give an example of each of the following:
   a) Square matrix
   b) Rectangular matrix
   c) Diagonal matrix
   d) Identity matrix
4. What is the *objective equation*? What is the *set of linear restrictions*? Give an example of each.
5. Suggest some industrial applications of the linear programming technique.
6. What is a *set*, a *convex set*, a *point*, and a *vertex*?
7. Describe, in your own words, and with a sketch if necessary, how the linear programming technique works.
8. What is an *alogrithm*? Give an example of one.
9. What is the purpose of the *dummy* in the Transportation model?
10. What advantage does the VAM technique have over the Northwest Corner rule?
11. What requirements have to be filled when using the Assignment method?
12. What should you consider before making an application of one of the other linear programming techniques?

References

AITKEN, ALEXANDER CRAIG. *Determinants and Matrices*. 9th ed. Edinburgh: Oliver & Boyd; New York: Interscience Publishers, 1956.

BAER, ROBERT M., and KRUHE, L. (A translation from the Russian author, TRAKHTENBROT, B. A.). *Algorithms and the Machine Decision Problem*. Lafayette, Ind.: Purdue University, 1957.

BAUMOL, WILLIAM J. *Economic Theory and Operations Analysis*. Englewood Cliffs, N.J.: Prentice-Hall, Inc., 1961.

BECKENBACH, EDWIN. *Modern Mathematics for Engineers.* New York: McGraw-Hill Book Co., Inc., 1956.

BELLMAN, RICHARD ERNEST, and DREYFUS, STUART. *Applied Dynamic Programming.* Princeton, N.J.: Princeton University Press, 1962.

BELLMAN, RICHARD ERNEST. *Introduction to Matrix Analysis.* New York: McGraw-Hill Book Co., Inc., 1960.

BIERMAN, HAROLD, JR.; BONINI, CHARLES P.; FOURAKER, LAWRENCE E.; and JAEDICKE, ROBERT K. *Quantitative Analysis for Business Decisions.* Rev. ed. Homewood, Ill.: Richard D. Irwin, Inc., 1965.

BOWMAN, EDWARD H. *Analysis for Production Management.* Homewood, Ill.: Richard D. Irwin, Inc., 1957.

———, and FETTER, ROBERT B. *Analyses of Industrial Operations.* Homewood, Ill.: Richard D. Irwin, Inc., 1959.

BUFFA, ELWOOD SPENCER. *Models for Production and Operations Management.* New York: John Wiley & Sons, Inc., 1963.

———. *Modern Production Management.* New York: John Wiley & Sons, Inc., 1961.

CARR, CHARLES R., and HOWE, CHARLES W. *Quantitative Decision Procedures in Management and Economics.* New York: McGraw-Hill Book Co., Inc., 1964.

CHARNES, ABRAHAM, and COOPER, W. W. *Management Models and Industrial Applications of Linear Programming.* New York: John Wiley & Sons, Inc., 1961.

CHURCHMAN, CHARLES WEST; ACKOFF, RUSSELL L.; and ARNOFF, E. LEONARD. *Introduction to Operations Research.* New York: John Wiley & Sons, Inc., 1957.

CHATTO, KENNETH A. "An Application of Operations Research Methods to the Selection of a Processing Plan in a Meat Packing Plant." Unpublished thesis, M.S., I.E. Lafayette, Ind.: Purdue University, 1955.

COOPER, WILLIAM WAGER; HENDERSON, A.; and CHARNES, ABRAHAM. *An Introduction to Linear Programming.* New York: John Wiley & Sons, Inc., 1953.

DANTZIG, GEORGE BERNARD. *Linear Programming and Extensions.* Princeton, N.J.: Princeton University Press, 1963.

DEAN BURTON, V.; SASIENI, MAURICE W.; and GUPTA, SHIV K. *Mathematics for the Modern Management.* New York: John Wiley & Sons, Inc., 1963.

DORFMAN, ROBERT. *Application of Linear Programming to the Theory of the Firm.* Berkeley, Calif.: University of California Press, 1951.

———; SAMUELSON, PAUL A.; and SOLOW, ROBERT M. *Linear Programming and Economic Analysis.* New York: McGraw-Hill Book Co., Inc., 1958.

DOTY, WILLIAM K. "An Introduction to the Application of Linear Programming to Industrial Engineering." Unpublished thesis, M.S., I.E. Lafayette, Ind.: Purdue University, 1954.

FERGUSON, ROBERT O., and SARGENT, LAUREN F. *Linear Programming: Fundamentals and Applications.* New York: McGraw-Hill Book Co., Inc., 1958.

GALE, DAVID. *The Theory of Linear Economic Models.* New York: McGraw-Hill Book Co., Inc., 1960.

GASS, SAUL I. *Linear Programming Methods and Applications.* 2d ed. New York: McGraw-Hill Book Co., Inc., 1964.

GRAVES, ROBERT L., and WOLFE, PHILIP. *Recent Advances in Mathematical Programming.* New York: McGraw-Hill Book Co., Inc., 1963.

GREENE, JAMES H.; CHATTO, K.; HICKS, C. R.; and COX, C. B. "Linear Programming in the Packing Industry." *Journal of Industrial Engineering.* Vol. X, No. 5 (September-October, 1959).

GREENWALD, DAKOTA ULRICH. *Linear Programming, an Explanation of the Simplex Algorithm.* New York: Ronald Press Co., 1957.

HADLEY, GEORGE. *Linear Programming.* Reading, Mass.: Addison-Wesley Publishing Co., 1963.

HOLZMAN, ALBERT G.; SCHAEFER, H. H.; and GLASER, R. *Matrices and Mathematical Programming: Mathematical Bases for Management Decision Making.* Chicago: Encyclopaedia Britannica Press, 1962.

KEMENY, JOHN G.; SCHLEIFER, ARTHUR, JR.; SNELL, LAURIE J.; and THOMPSON, GERALD L. *Finite Mathematics with Business Applications.* Englewood Cliffs, N.J.: Prentice-Hall, Inc., 1962.

LLEWELLYN, ROBERT W. *Linear Programming.* New York: Holt, Rinehart & Winston, Inc., 1964.

LOOMBA, N. PAUL. *Linear Programming, an Introductory Analysis.* New York: McGraw-Hill Book Co., Inc., 1964.

METZGER, ROBERT W. *Elementary Mathematical Programming.* New York: John Wiley & Sons, Inc., 1958.

MILLER, DAVID W., and STARR, MARTIN K. *Executive Decisions and Operations Research.* Englewood Cliffs, N.J.: Prentice-Hall, Inc., 1960.

PEDOE, DANIEL. *A Geometric Introduction to Linear Algebra.* New York: John Wiley & Sons, Inc., 1963.

REINFELD, NYLES V., and VOGEL, WILLIAM R. *Mathematical Programming.* Englewood Cliffs, N.J.: Prentice-Hall, Inc., 1958.

RILEY, VERA, and GASS, SAUL I. *Linear Programming and Associated Techniques.* Baltimore: Johns Hopkins Press, 1958.

SASIENI, MAURICE; YASPAN, ARTHUR; and FRIEDMAN, LAWRENCE. *Operations Research—Methods and Problems.* New York: John Wiley & Sons, Inc., 1959.

SCHWARTZ, JACOB T. *Introduction to Matrices and Vectors.* New York: McGraw-Hill Book Co., Inc., 1961.

STOCKTON, ROBERT STANSBURY. *Introduction to Linear Programming.* 2d ed. Boston: Allyn & Bacon, Inc., 1963.

VAJDA, S. *An Introduction to Linear Programming and the Theory of Games.* London: Methuen; New York: John Wiley & Sons, Inc., 1960.

VAZSONYI, ANDREW. *Scientific Programming in Business and Industry.* New York: John Wiley & Sons, Inc., 1958.

CHAPTER 18

Mechanical Aids

The imagination used in the development of devices for the control of manufacturing systems has known no bounds. Some of these devices have been found useful and remain important adjuncts to systems. Others have had a relatively short life and have been discarded, often to be rediscovered periodically.

These mechanical contrivances have often been plagued by overselling as well as overbuying. Often the product has been sold without concern for the design of the system. There have been cases where extensive installations were sold without adequate product descriptions and time study data being available. Elaborate mechanical aids will not overcome these shortcomings. Management also has been remiss by acquiring such equipment with the hope that managerial incompetency will be obscured.

The urge to gain status, or to have a new plaything, has often been the basis for acquiring the mechanical aid. As soon as the newness wears off, the device loses its appeal, and the aid, no matter how well conceived, falls into disrepute.

Often these aids fail to function because of personnel who may lack understanding of the necessity for the system aid, or who may be temperamentally unsuited to operate the device. Maintaining a schedule board, for instance, requires a person who likes to work with details and accepts the challenge of an ever-changing situation.

The discussion of mechanical aids for control systems has been excluded from the other chapters in an effort to concentrate on the principles. The display boards used for Gantt charts could have been included in the chapter on Graphical Scheduling, but many people would have confused the principles with the mechanical aids. The mechanical aids discussed here are grouped according to their applications:

Visible Bar Chart Panels
Visible Display Panels
Visible Card Filing
Intraplant Communications
Miscellaneous Aids for Production

No attempt has been made to include all the mechanical aids, but only those which are representative.

Visible Bar Chart Panels

The panels discussed in this section are suitable for bar chart displays. They have been found especially suitable for displaying Gantt charts.

SCHED–U–GRAPH

The Sched–U–Graph (Figure 18–1) is the Remington Rand company's device for making the Gantt chart a more convenient tool. This charting device has many varied applications and can be adapted to a number of uses.

Figure 18–1

Sched–U–Graph

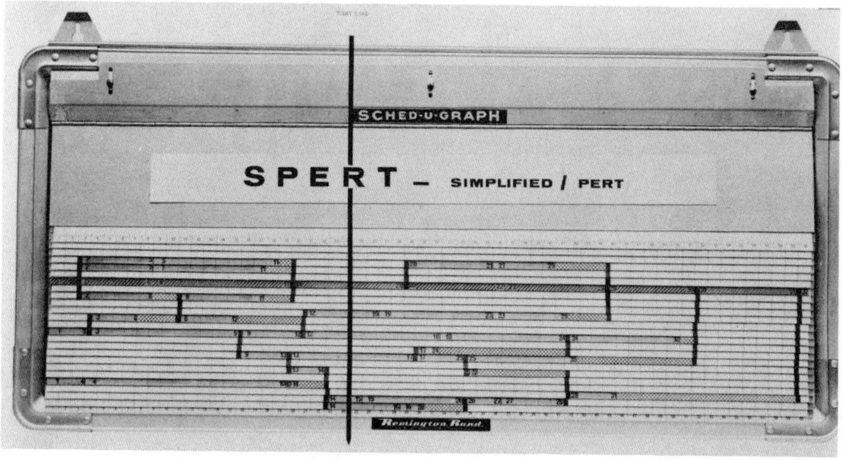

Courtesy of Remington Rand, Inc.

The Sched–U–Graph is actually the familiar visible card file enlarged to display-board size. This type of card file consists of a number of overlapping cardboard flaps (as shown in Figure 18–2). Each flap is bound with a plastic lip on the lower edge in which a card can be filed. The flap can be raised to expose the entire card, but in its normal position only the lower margin is exposed.

As in the Gantt chart, time or quantity is the common denominator; and in the application illustrated, a time scale—consisting of a folded date strip—is placed in the plastic pocket. The span card, which is placed behind the date strip (as shown), can be cut to any length desired, thus representing different periods of time. A colored plastic strip can be placed inside the

Figure 18–2

Details of Sched–U–Graph

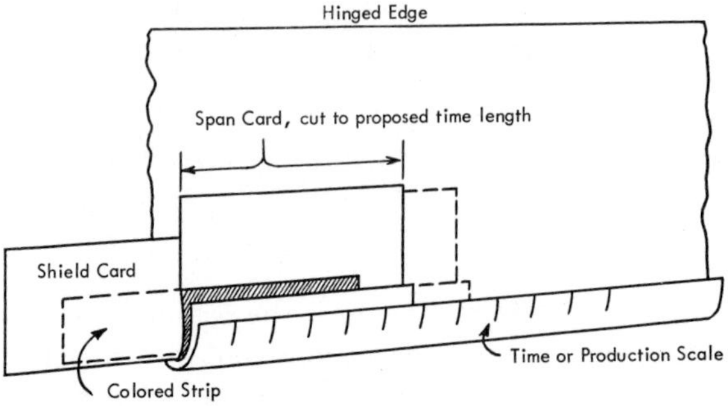

pocket of the span card, which can be hidden behind shield cards (as shown). Signals, consisting of movable colored plastic tabs, are available for the edge and can be slid along as desired.

Figure 18–3 shows the Sched–U–Graph used for machine loading and scheduling. On the left are cards representing and describing each work center, such as the radial drill and other machine tools. In the plastic slot for each work center is placed the operation record cards for the various orders presently being manufactured. Each operation record card is cut to the proper length to represent the time it should take to complete the job. A folded "day-strip" is placed in each slot so that the dark edge of the operation record card, when placed in the slot, will appear as a bar. The white spaces indicate free time. The "today-line" is represented by the vertical tab, while progress is indicated by tabs on each plastic strip.

One obvious advantage of the Sched–U–Graph is the ease with which schedule changes can be made; it is only necessary to reshuffle the cards. This is probably one of the most practical devices for charting and it is quite readily applied to production scheduling, graphical inventory control, and similar applications.

PRODUC-TROL BOARD

The Produc-trol Board (Figure 18–4) is also suitable for Gantt charting and other bar chart applications. On the left side of the illustration is shown a removable card filing system. The flaps are bound on the lower edge to hold such forms as inventory cards, operation sheets, or other manufacturing records. Filing information can be placed at the bottom of the form in order to be easily seen. The information on the records, as well as the records themselves, can be simply changed.

Adjacent to the card file is a board which resembles a king-size punch board. For each card in the file there are two rows of holes that extend across the board. One row is equipped with an elastic string which can be

Figure 18–3

Machine Loading and Scheduling

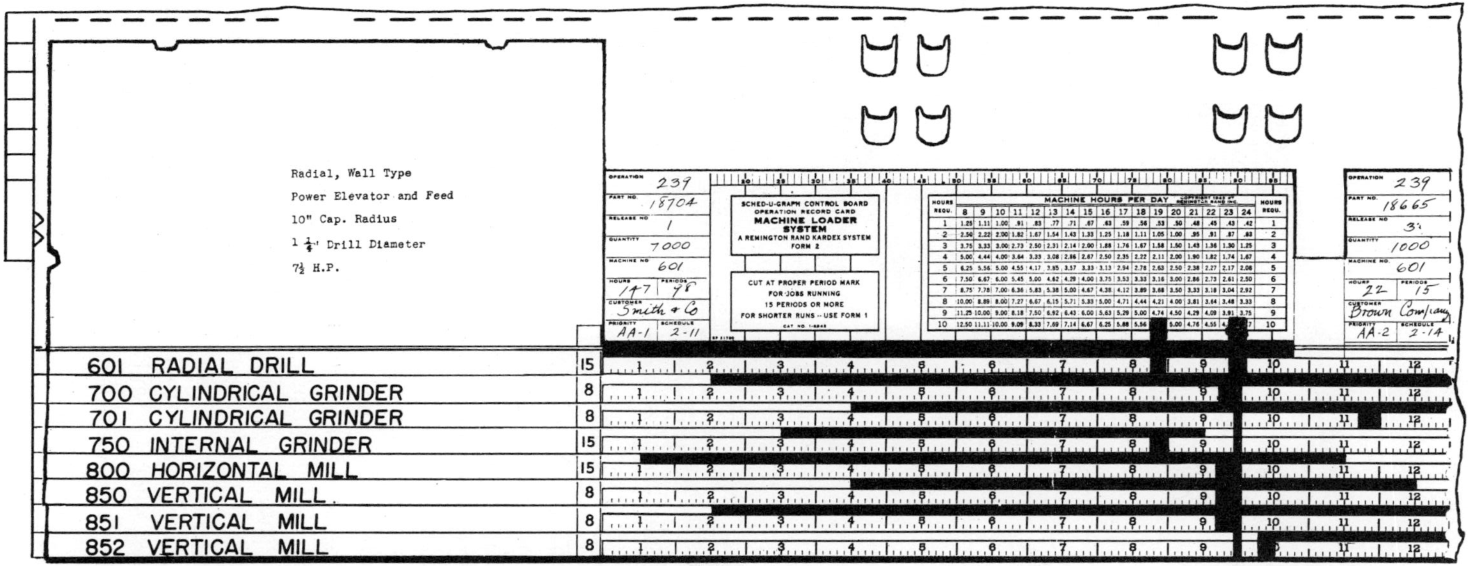

Courtesy of Remington Rand, Inc.

Figure 18–4

Product-trol Board

Courtesy of Wassell Organization, Inc.

stretched across the board to form a bar. The other row of holes has a colored peg which marks off a span of holes representing time or quantity. Across the top of the board is a clip in which a paper strip can be placed, imprinted to represent time, quantity, or other desired information. A vertical, spring-loaded string can be used to indicate a today-line or, in the case of inventory applications, a reorder point.

This control panel can be used to maintain machine schedules, as previously discussed, or the individual work orders can be placed in the file card holders. When this method is used the horizontal distance across the board represents the expected and actual time for each activity. The pegs show when each individual operation will be completed, and the solid horizontal string shows what has been actually performed. A vertical string, which is moved from day to day, represents the today-line. If the horizontal strings representing the work orders are to the left of the today-line, the work is behind schedule; if they are to the right, the orders are ahead of schedule.

The board is also suitable for inventory control applications. The inventory record card can be placed in the file section where it is available for posting. The horizontal string represents the quantity on hand, while the vertical string indicates reorder and other control points. Care must be taken in selecting the units to display on the board. For example, a manufacturer of prefabricated houses would wish to reduce the component requirements to terms of houses; otherwise the record for bundles of shingles would extend off the board to the right while front doors would be hardly noticeable.

ROL-A-CHART

The Rol-a-Chart (Figure 18–5) offers the advantage of a continuous charting surface in the form of a plastic belt which can be moved horizontally under a vertical, elastic, today-line. The plastic is transparent and is backed up by a permanently gridded surface which may be used to represent time or quantity units.

On the left side of the chart is a stationary section on which can be placed the items to be charted, such as work orders, work centers, and inventory

Figure 18–5

Rol-a-Chart

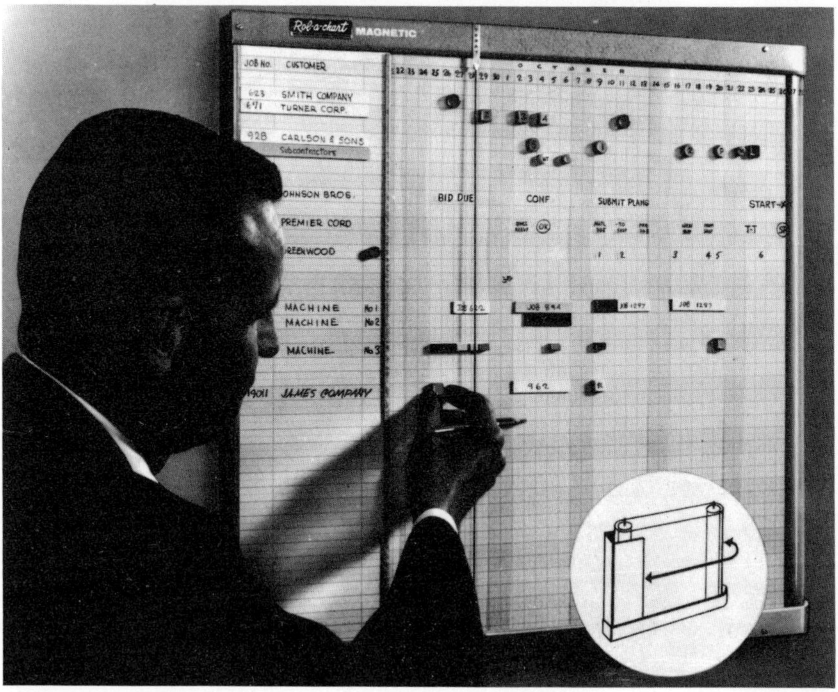

Courtesy of Wm. A. Steward Co., Rol-a-Chart Division

items. The surface of the board accepts grease pencil markings (which are easy to erase). Eighty items can be listed vertically on this chart while the one-half-inch blocks make it possible to record 168 units on the horizontal axis. A special feature of this board allows the use of magnetic ceramic blocks and plastic strips which are also acceptable for grease pencil use. This chart is adaptable to the Gantt and other charting techniques which have been discussed.

ACME VISIBLE CHART

Another versatile charting device is shown in Figure 18–6. The horizontal bars consist of plastic strips. Inserts for the plastic strips can be printed to specification and exposed to permit hand posting. Colored signals, interior and over-riding styles, snap on and off or slide freely, bypassing one another. The panels are available in various sizes.

Figure 18–6

Visible Charts

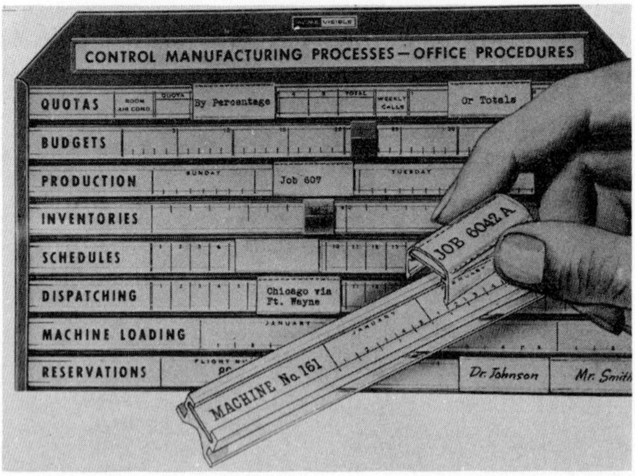

Courtesy of Acme Visible

UNIGRAPH

Another ingenious charting device is shown in Figure 18–7. It consists of rows of plastic discs held between two engraved plastic scales. Each disc can be rotated, and consists of five colored segments, including white. By using a combination of colors it is possible to have ten color choices. The separators between discs have holes in which plastic plugs or metal card holders can be placed. These charts come in various sizes and have much the same versatility as the charts previously described.

Figure 18–7

Unigraph Control Chart

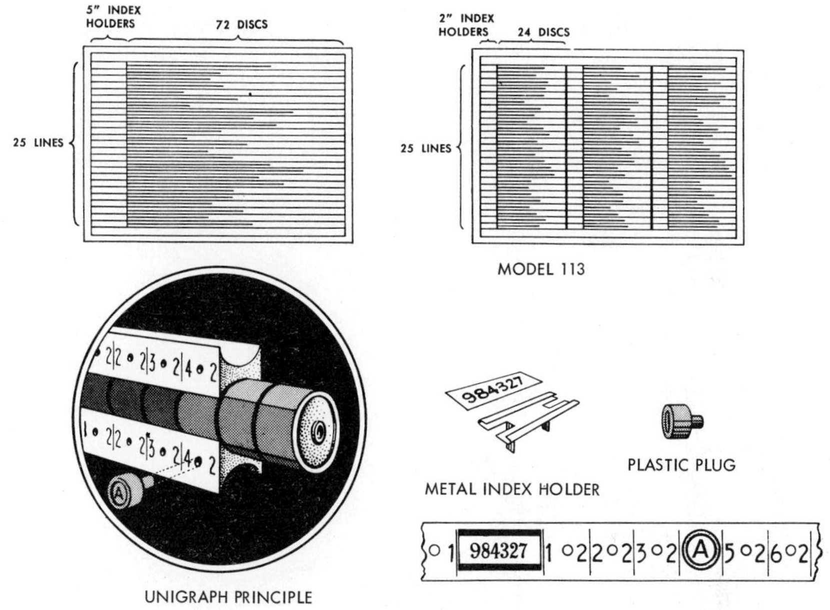

Visible Display Panels

Display panels may be nothing more exotic than a piece of plywood mounted in some strategic position in the factory to display production information. Refinements might consist only of gridded boards or cork-surfaced panels to accept thumb tacks. A display panel made by the factory carpenter might turn the trick, but, if not, numerous commercial devices are available.

The Boardmaster (Figure 18–8) is typical of the appliances available. Cards are posted on the board by snapping them in four corner holders. Cards are available in a number of colors, plain or preprinted, with information or symbols. Cards come in a snap-out form, which makes typing more convenient. Large cards which span several spaces are also available.

The panel can be used as a Gantt chart. Plastic clips can be added to the cards for signals, and today-lines are readily added by applying a ribbon held by scotch tape. These boards also come with hinged vertical edges for mounting on the wall where wall space is limited.

Figure 18–8

Visible Display Panel

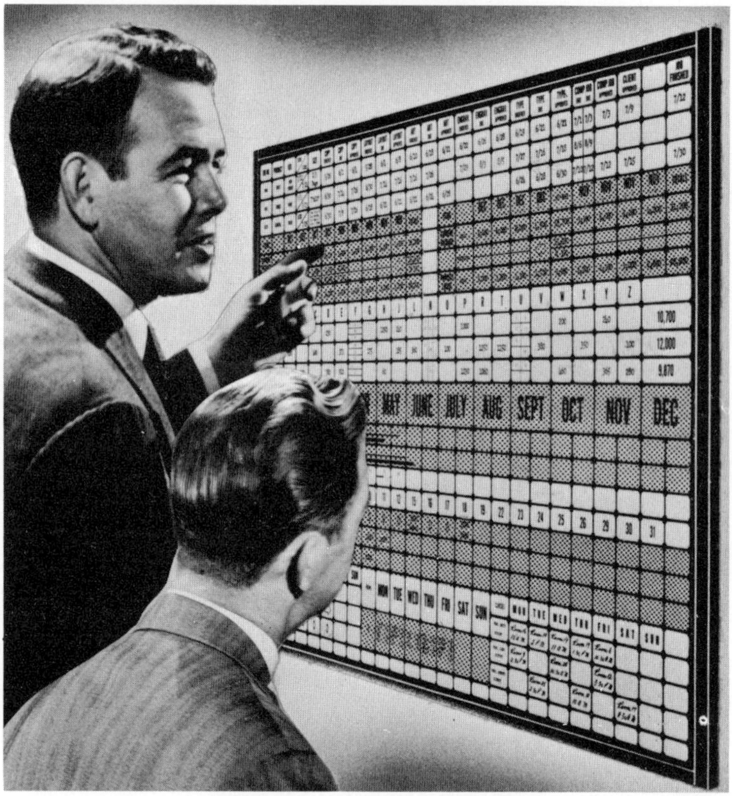

Courtesy of Graphic Systems

Spring clips for holding various manufacturing forms are characteristic of the display board illustrated in Figure 18–9. Behind the surface might be one or more pockets for filing forms pertaining to the one posted under the clip.

These display boards are frequently used with specially designed systems and duplicating processes which minimize the amount of writing and posting. They have been used satisfactorily in a number of applications, such as tool control, project control, and inventory control—as well as in production control. A typical production control application is shown in Figure 18–10.

The work order for the job, along with the material requisition, is filed in the far left position. To the right, posted by operation sequence, are the productive time tickets. Either the time ticket or the move order can be used as feedback to update the productive time ticket, as shown in the bottom portion of the card.

Figure 18–9

Industrial Control Panel

Courtesy of Victor Comptometer Corp.

The Flexoline display (Figure 18–11) consists of a panel which holds plastic strips. Reference material can be printed or typed directly on the plastic material, which comes in one piece (as shown in Figure 18–12) and in a variety of colors. To remove a strip it is only necessary to break it loose along a serration. The stand illustrated is only one of several designs for specific purposes.

Visible Card Filing

The innumerable transactions that occur in production planning and control systems have made the development of rapid record handling imperative. The ones illustrated will give you some idea of the diversity of products available.

VERTICAL VISIBLE FILE

Figure 18–13 shows a vertical visible card file that has many applications in industry. The merit of such a system is that the cards are readily removed for posting. The card number is always visible on the mitered edge and any one that is missing is indicated by the "flag" of the card underneath. The type of file equipment which can be used with this system is illustrated in Figure 18–14.

Figure 18–10

Application of Visible Control System

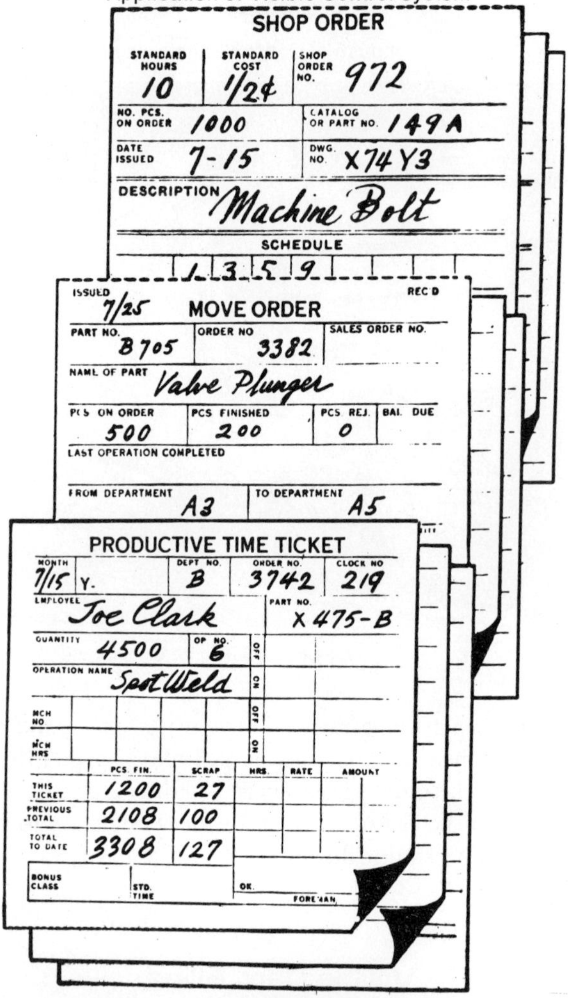

Courtesy of Victor Comptometer Corp.

Figure 18–11

Display Panel

Courtesy of Acme Visible

Figure 18–12

Typing Display Inserts

Courtesy of Acme Visible

Figure 18–13

Vertical Visible File

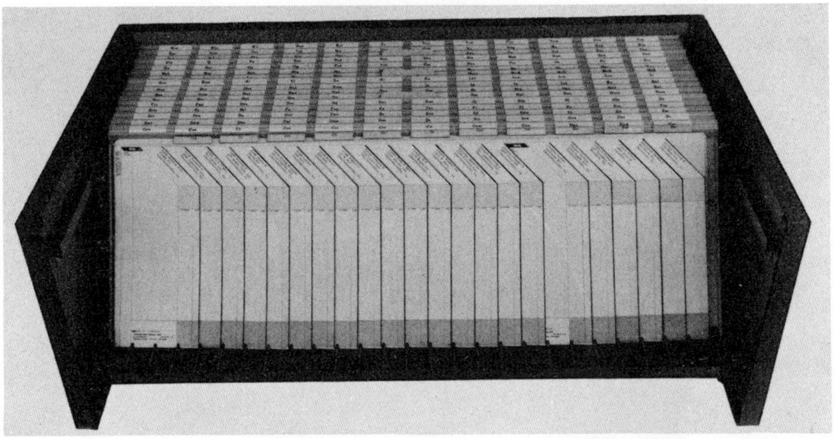

Courtesy of Acme Visible

Figure 18–14

Vertical File System

Courtesy of Acme Visible

EXPOSED BOTTOM MARGIN FILE

A typical file system, which exposes the pertinent filing information on the bottom edge of the card, is illustrated in Figure 18–15. The cards lie flat in the tray (Figure 18–16), taking up very little room. They are hinged at the top edge to be easily exposed for changing or modifying. The card trays can be removed from the cabinet and the files can be worked on with ease. The edge of the card, besides holding the important filing information, can also be used as a bar chart to indicate quantities or time. Signal flags are available which slide along the edge of the card to indicate these values.

Figure 18–15

Exposed Bottom Margin File

Courtesy of Acme Visible

Intraplant Communication

Communications prevail in all facets of production control, so it is little wonder that a number of ingenious systems have been developed. Discussed here are some modern computer-orientated systems, as well as some older ones which have been proven by time.

Figure 18–16

Exposed Bottom Margin File Cabinet

Courtesy of Acme Visible

PNEUMATIC TUBE COMMUNICATIONS

The pneumatic tube is an excellent way of communicating between remote points in a factory or even between buildings in a factory complex. It is especially useful when it is necessary to move papers, such as production orders, or even small parts required for quality control checks.

This system, which you see in large metropolitan department stores, carrying sales slips and cash to a centralized accounting office, can serve an important function in industry as well. The carrier consists of a capsule-like device (Figure 18–17) which moves through the tube by a difference in air pressure. Where a number of lines are used it is quite common to have a centralized dispatcher, but there is a system which makes it possible to dial the destination on the capsule and send it directly without further handling or delay.

TRANSACTER

The Stromberg Transacter System is an automatic data collection and transmission system which is suitable for the internal communications encountered in production control. In its basic form it consists of a transmitting unit, the transacter, and the receiving unit, called a compiler.

As many as 36 transmitting units can be connected to one compiler, which means that transmitting units can be located throughout the plant wherever data are being generated. The compiler, on the other hand, is located at the nerve center of operations, and will frequently be found in the data processing center.

Figure 18–17

Pneumatic Tube

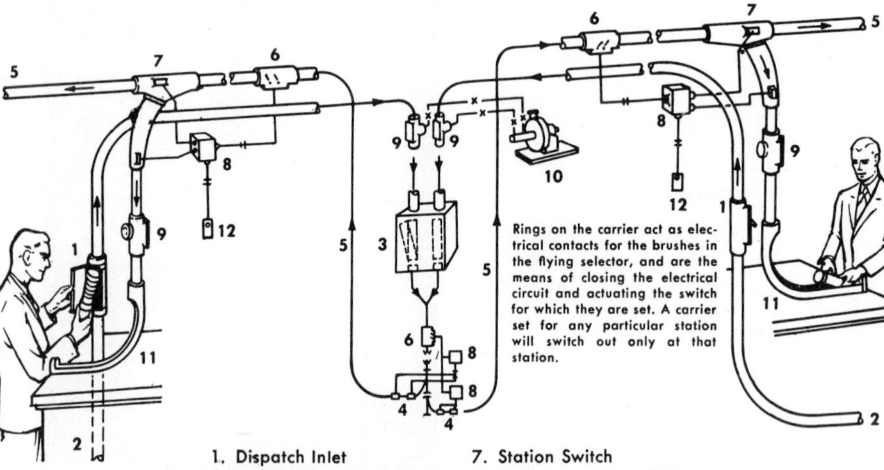

1. Dispatch Inlet
2. Sending Tube
3. Carrier Spacing Device
4. Line Selector Switch
5. Receiving Tube
6. Flying Selector
7. Station Switch
8. Elektrigger Power Unit
9. Terminal
10. Exhauster (Blower)
11. Delivery Chute
12. Power Outlet

The input unit, or transacter, is illustrated in Figure 18–18. Fixed information is entered by punched cards placed in the slot on the top of the console. This slot will accommodate several cards at one time. For example, the employee card, job card, and a prepunched variable card can be placed in the slot together, and all the related information will be conveyed at one time to the compiler where it is punched into paper tape. For variable

Figure 18–18

Transmitting Unit

Courtesy of General Time Corporation, Stromberg Division

Figure 18–19

Receiving Unit

Courtesy of General Time Corporation, Stromberg Division

information, the transactor has dials which can be set. Location codes and programming instructions are contributed by the transacter's self-contained plug board.

The compiler (Figure 18–19) has built-in checking circuits to insure that the message received is what has been sent. These messages are punched in paper tape at the rate of 60 characters per second. The tape can then be used with tape-to-punched-card converters, automatic typewriters, tape-to-tape converters, and for direct input into computers.

The versatility of the transacter system is extended by additional pieces of equipment, and one is an automatic badge reader (Figure 18–20). This is an automatic time clock which uses the employee's badge as a time card. The card or badge, with prepunched information, is inserted in the clock and the information is instantaneously transmitted to the compiler, where

Figure 18–20
Time Clock

Courtesy of General Time Corporation, Stromberg Division

the exact time and code number are punched into data processing tape. This information is entered into the data processing system to complete the payroll, thus eliminating all human operations and errors. These badge readers can also be used for other applications, such as document control. Also available with the transacter equipment is a high-speed read-out unit which can be used for listing information.

The transacter system eliminates many handwritten documents and presents information in a ready-to-use form to data processing systems. It is applicable to scheduling, payroll, quality control, inventory control, and other systems in a factory where high-speed communications are important.

TELECONTROL

Telecontrol is another means of communicating between the activities on the factory floor and a central control point. All production information can be fed into the centralized control from remote stations, reducing the paper work involved in timekeeping, scheduling and rescheduling, dispatching, and other activities which are primarily communications.

This system has a control box (Figure 18–21) located at each production machine and work station. These boxes are linked electrically to a control panel (Figure 18–22) in a central control room. An actuator at the work station, consisting of a switch, is connected from the production activity, through the control box, and to the centralized control panel, where production is counted automatically. The control box at the machine is also equipped with switches, signal lights, and a phone jack which are connected with the central control panel.

In the control room there is an individual display on a panel for each control box. The display has a holder for the job card and red and green lights which correspond to those on the control box, as well as time clocks and counters. The time clocks will register elapsed productive time and downtime. The counters record the units produced and the balance. In addition, there is a jack in which an operator key is placed which closes the circuit between the control box and the control panel so that production will be registered.

Figure 18–21

Control Box

Courtesy of Hancock Telecontrol Corp.

Figure 18–22

Control Panel

Courtesy of Hancock Telecontrol Corp.

A green light on these control units indicates that production is progressing, while a flashing green light shows that the production order is nearing the end. A toggle switch on the control box turns on a flashing red light which warns the central dispatcher of trouble. He, in turn, can call the foreman by means of a public address system. The foreman carries a phone headset with him at all times and can communicate with the dispatcher through a phone jack on the control box. If the foreman authorizes downtime, he places a key in the lock switch for that machine, which immediately turns on the red light in the control panel and starts the downtime clock. A reset button on the control box is used to stop the recording of downtime and to clear the red light.

We have described only one manufacturer's version of this type of communications system, but other versions have also been widely accepted.

TELautograph

Perhaps you have stood around a railroad station schedule board and watched a small machine pen information regarding the arrival of trains. This machine, the TELautograph (Figure 18–23) obeys perfectly the hand writing that is taking place on another machine in some remote location. The sender writes with an attached pen on a flat, horizontal surface, and the message is conveyed to the receiver where the information is written automatically on the horizontal surface of the receiving board. It not only conveys the message but develops a permanent record. The problems of scheduling both trains and production are similar, and so it is natural that the TELautograph has been applied to production control tasks.

Figure 18–23

TELautograph

Courtesy of TELautograph Corp.

MICROFILMING AND APERTURE CARDS

Miniaturization, which has had its effect upon many products in recent years, has also had an impact upon manufacturing planning and control systems. Many companies have found it profitable to reduce the bulk of their business and engineering files by placing them on microfilms. The sorting difficulties inherent in microfilming have brought forth another development, aperture cards (Figure 18–24), which are designed to hold the microfilm and are sorted by modified card-data processing equipment.

Figure 18–24
Aperture Card and Microfilm

Courtesy of Recordak Corp., subsidiary of Eastman Kodak

A typical application of the aperture card is found in many busy engineering departments. Their product drawings, which may amount to many thousands, are photographed and filed as cards. When the drawings are needed they are easily sorted out, and, if necessary, enlarged copies can be made. Often, however, the engineering and production people work directly from the microfilm by means of a special enlarger (as illustrated). These cards require considerably less space than the full-size drawings, and they last longer and are easier to send through the mail. The equipment required for the microfilming and embossing process has been highly developed and is virtually automatic.

FLEXOWRITER

The Flexowriter, an electric typewriter, is illustrated in Figure 18–25. In addition to the document that can be typed out in the usual manner, the machine will also produce a coded and punched paper tape. The tape can be run back through a Flexowriter to reproduce the document either in part or in whole. A tape reader is available which will control the input of two tapes so that fixed and variable information may be used as input to the Flexowriter as desired. The Flexowriter is one of the more versatile devices and can be used extensively in control systems.

Figure 18–25
Flexowriter

Courtesy of Friden, Inc.

TAG PRODUCTION

Some production and inventory control systems require innumerable tags for marking and controlling production. Chapter 11, which includes duplicating machines, discusses one which is used for making tags, but there are others you should also become acquainted with.

Figure 18–26 illustrates a versatile machine which will print tags or labels from continuous strips or rolls of stock. The machine prints a full line of alphabetical and numerical characters at the rate of 165 impressions per min-

Figure 18–26
Tag Machine

Courtesy of Dennison Manufacturing Company

ute. The characters in the line of print are easily set up by the dial shown on the machine. Later, if it is necessary, one or more of the characters can be changed without destroying the whole line. More than one line can be printed on the form by merely sending it through the machine again. A counter keeps track of the number of tags which have been printed and an automatic knife separates the tags as needed. For tags which are to be numbered consecutively, there is an automatic serial imprinting device.

An even more versatile tag imprinting machine is shown in Figure 18–27. Not only will this machine accomplish as much as the previous machine, it will imprint two lines of numbers and also punch holes in the card which can be interpreted for card-data and computer processing. The total maximum capacity of this card is 47 columns of printing, of which 25 columns can be punched.

Figure 18–27

Tag-Punch Machine

Courtesy of Dennison Manufacturing Company

These tag-punch machines are applied in diverse control systems. They are to be found in inventory control, production control, cost control, labor control, and quality control systems, as well as in many others.

TRAVELING SHOP-ORDER FOLDERS

Frequently it is desirable to circulate certain manufacturing forms through the factory where they will be handled numerous times, often by people whose hands may be soiled by cutting-oil and dirt. In these situations it is imperative that the documents be protected in some way. Plastic shop-order folders will protect the forms but will also leave the important information of where to move the order exposed.

SUMMARY

One of the most important parts of the production planning and control function is communication, and in any communications system we look for mechanical aids to store and convey information. The mechanical aids discussed in this section were designed for this purpose.

The economic considerations for selecting mechanical aids are important. No amount of money spent for these will overcome a poorly conceived system or one which lacks adequate input information.

Personnel available for the system is important. For some, the system may need to be detailed, but for others this would be frustrating. Some people are temperamentally suited for one system while others are suited for another. A good selection of equipment takes this into consideration.

Representative devices were discussed, but the system designer should watch for new and better developments which more nearly fit the needs.

Questions

1. Establish a procedure for using one of the commercially available panels as a Gantt chart.
2. Outline a method for selling management the idea that the present file drawer method of keeping records should be replaced by a visible control chart. What should be considered? Could you put a dollar value on all of these considerations? Can you justify the purchase of these visible control charts in terms of dollars?
3. Compare the various commercially available bar charts and choose the one which you think is the best for some particular application.
4. In what type of plant would you expect to find such an internal communications systems as the Transactor? Why? What would be the advantage of this system? What preparations would be necessary to install such a system?
5. List the advantages and disadvantages of microfilming engineering drawings.

References

Brush, William H., and Lazzaro, Victor. *Systems and Procedures: A Handbook for Business and Industry*. Englewood Cliffs, N.J.: Prentice-Hall, Inc., 1959.

Herrman, N. Irvin Albert. *Office Methods, Systems and Procedures*. New York: Ronald Press Co., 1950.

Hicks, Charles B. *Office Management*. 2d ed. Boston: Allyn & Bacon, Inc., 1962.

Littlefield, Cleatice L., and Rachel, Frank. *Office Administrative Management; Systems Analysis, Data Processing, and Office Services*. 2d ed. Englewood Cliffs, N.J.: Prentice-Hall, Inc., 1964.

Terry, George. *Office Management and Control; the Actions of Administrative Management*. 4th ed. Homewood, Ill.: Richard D. Irwin, Inc., 1962.

Wylie, Harry L. (ed.), and Harty, James G. (staff ed.). *Office Management Handbook*. 2d ed. New York: Ronald Press Co., 1958.

CHAPTER 19

Simulation and Heuristic Models

Simulation is a method of solving problems by designing, constructing, and manipulating a model of the real system. Solving problems by simulation is perhaps the one thing that has distinguished the engineering profession from others. Since their earliest history, system designers have devised analogies in an effort to obtain an insight and the eventual solution to their problems.

The models may take many forms. For instance, they may be no more than scaled versions of the real thing; or they may rely on the transformation from one system to another, such as an electrical analog of a hydraulic system. Most commonplace is the symbolic model which uses mathematical and logical symbols to represent a system. The particular simulation model of interest here is a symbolic model which requires repeated solutions from which the best is chosen. This particular type of simulation has been referred to as the heuristic model because it points the way to a better solution.

The reasons for resorting to simulation are numerous, but probably cost is the one which tops the list. The symbolic models are, of course, very efficient, and even three-dimensional models—such as those used in shipbuilding—are far cheaper than the real thing. Often, the symbolic model is unable to cope with the numerous interactions, so probably the only method is to work with two- or three-dimensional models. This occurs in aircraft designs when it is impossible to express mathematically all of the structural interrelationships, so a model is made and tested. The test flight of the prototype can even be considered as a full-scale model for simulation purposes.

The transformation technique, going from one system medium to another, is used both for teaching and for gaining a greater understanding. It is not uncommon to describe electrical systems by hydraulic systems, and often the mechanical system can be solved more easily and cheaply by means of an electrical system. This, in fact, is one reason for the use of the electrical analog computer. This transformation from one system to another is, in reality, a method of logic which has had a profound effect upon the scientist and engineer, making them efficient thinkers.

An extremely important aspect of simulation is that it often makes it possible to compress time. This means that costs can be reduced and decisions can be made available sooner.

INDUSTRIAL SIMULATION

Every schoolboy knows of the automobile mock-ups which are made during the development stage of new car models. This is just one form of simulation which the industrialist uses. He also uses flow charts of the factory system in his analysis, as well as elaborate two- and three-dimensional layouts. More recently, people in industry have become interested in simulating managerial systems for determining the best operating policies.

Simulation has also had considerable impetus from the interest in management games. In the management games, business systems are simulated so that the player may whet his managerial decision-making ability, making numerous decisions in a relatively short time. Management games have been designed for hand calculations, but many of them use the computer for rapid calculations. These management or business games have enjoyed an extensive popularity, and one can find them being played in the most remote parts of the world.

The industrial simulation models which are used to optimize a system generally have variable inputs which can be changed to study the overall effect. A particular type of model which has been found useful in factory simulation uses probabilistic (or stochastic) inputs and bears the name of the Monte Carlo Technique, after that renowned mecca on the Mediterranean.

We are interested in simulation as a method of obtaining decisions for production planning and control. Regrettably, there is probably no way of outlining a procedure for learning the simulation techniques. The simulation model must spring from the ingenuity and background of the designer. He must have a broad experience with the subject under consideration to evaluate all factors which might enter into the construction of the model and to discard those which have a trivial effect. Probably the best designer of the factory simulator is a person who has had consulting experience and has a flair for innovation. Since it is not possible to set forth steps for simulation, the next best is to observe a simulation model.

AN EXAMPLE OF A FACTORY SIMULATION[1]

A part of the cheese industry in the United States is characterized by many small plants located in rural communities. The supply of labor is drawn from the community and is relatively flexible.

---

[1] Material for this section is condensed from a Purdue University Agriculture Experiment Station research bulletin, No. 757, December 1962, by Aaron Glickstein, E. M. Babb, C. E. French, and J. H. Greene: *Simulation Procedures for Production Control in an Indiana Cheese Plant*. The author is especially indebted to Dr. Glickstein, for his Ph.D. dissertation was the basis for the above bulletin.

The milk for producing the cheese either comes from the farmer-producer or is surplus from the bottlers. Brokers and cooperatives also supply milk, but charge a slight premium. Not only is the quantity of milk variable, but so is the price. The problem is: At what level of production should the plant be operated, considering the fluctuating quantity and price of milk? (Government support prices established the price of cheese and therefore price did not enter into the problem as a variable; consequently, attention can be focused on costs.)

The problem is easier to visualize by a flow chart (Figure 19–1). The processing facilities, indicated on the model, consist of a manufacturing plant for the production of 12- to 15-pound Colby cheeses which are sold, without further processing, to distributors. Cheese making is a batch process, and in the particular plant under consideration there are seven 15,000-pound cheese vats and such auxiliary facilities as pasteurizers, storage tanks, hoops, and other necessary equipment.

Figure 19–1

Simulation Model of Cheese Plant

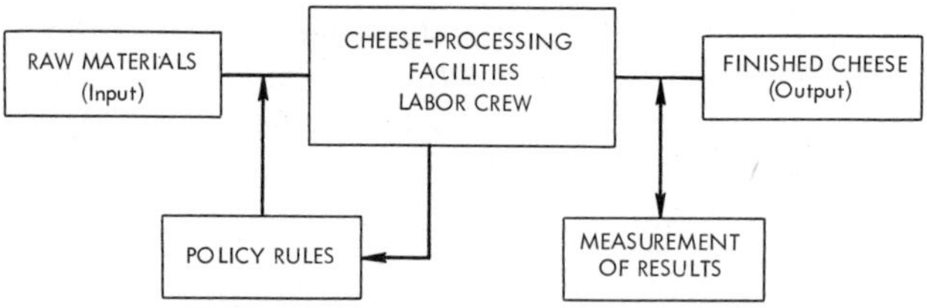

Cheese plants traditionally accept the milk as it is available from the farmer-producers. Milk, being perishable, and in spite of the improved technology for keeping it, must be manufactured into cheese in a relatively short time. This means that production is almost directly tied to the milk supply. On the average, for each 100 pounds of milk 10.7 pounds of Colby cheese is obtained.

The production level of the plant is dependent upon the supply of milk, so the quantity of labor tends to vary with the milk supply. Additional employees can be obtained during the production peaks to work for one-, two-, or three-month periods. The plant operates seven days a week, and employees work more than eight hours a day—and 40 hours a week when needed, without premium pay for overtime or for working on Saturday and Sunday. Nevertheless, efforts were made in the simulation model to limit the time for each worker to a 12-hour day.

The problem, as stated, is to determine the operating policy which will minimize the cost, considering the variations in the quantity and cost of raw materials. The first policy to be examined is the purchase of all milk available from the producers and none from the bottlers or other sources. To

Figure 19–2

Annual Fixed Costs

Plant depreciation	$ 2,207.00
Equipment	11,645.00
Interest on invested capital	6,179.00
Repair and maintenance of building	736.00
Repair and maintenance of equipment	8,373.00
Insurance	1,807.00
Taxes	4,448.00
Total	$35,395.00

determine this cost, and costs for other production policies, it is necessary to evaluate the cost factors which make up the total. Each cost factor is given below and will be discussed in the order given.

1. Fixed labor costs
2. Fixed plant and facilities costs
3. Fixed services and supplies costs
4. Material costs
5. Variable labor costs
6. Variable services and supply costs

1. *Fixed labor costs* include the labor used in receiving and warehousing the material as well as the labor in the office and management. These costs are assumed not to vary with the change in production. The fixed costs for the year under consideration were $45,995.

2. *Fixed plant and facilities costs* include depreciation, equipment, interest on capital, insurance, and repairs and maintenance on buildings and equipment. The sum of these costs is $35,395 (as shown in Figure 19–2).

3. *Fixed services and supplies* were difficult to separate from similar variable costs. Utilities and cleaning supplies were included in this classification and totaled $10,927.75 for the year.

4. *Material costs* for any year depend upon the purchasing policy which is being pursued. In the first policy, only the milk obtained from the farmer-producer was considered. The supply of milk from this source for each day is plotted for two different years in Figure 19–3.

To determine the milk input for the simulation model, it was necessary to consider two factors: the seasonal variation and the random day-to-day variation.

The seasonal effect for each day was predicted by fitting a regression line to the data illustrated (as discussed in Chapter 6). This equation turns out to be a fourth-order polinomial of the form:

$$Y = 74{,}192 + 10{,}372X - 1{,}077X^2 + 32X^3 - .294X^4$$

In this equation, April 15th coincides with the first day. By starting with this date, the value of Y is determined for any day in the year, and column 2 of Figure 19–4 shows this value, which was calculated for the first 30 days.

Figure 19–3

Milk Supply Available from Farmer–Producers for Two Years

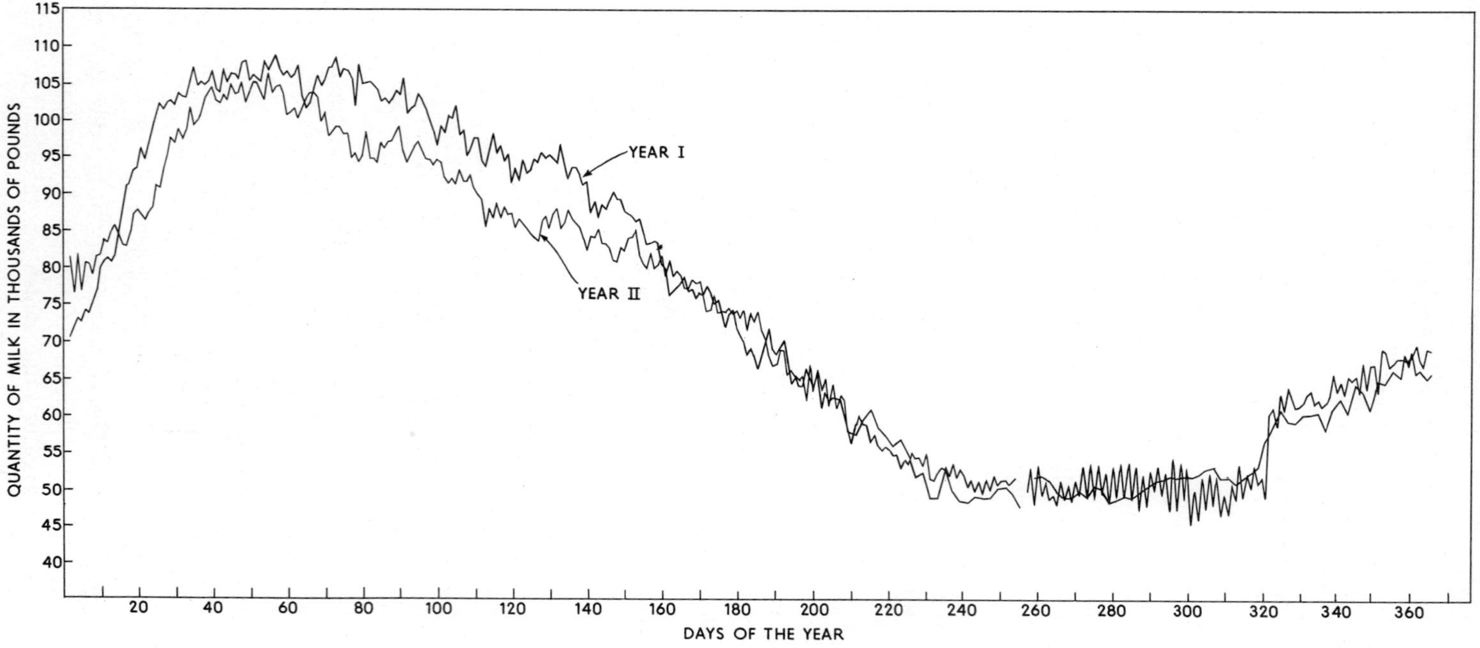

Figure 19–4

Quantity of Milk Received

(1) Day	(2) Y Value (Seasonal Milk Supply)	(3) Number from Random Digit Table	(4) Z Values (From Table 19–5)	(5) Z Value × Standard Error of Estimate	(6) Simulated Milk Arrivals (Col. 6 = Col. 2 + Col. 5)
				s = 3477	
1.	75,218	66,082	+ .45	+1565	76,783
2.	76,224	97,377	+1.95	+6780	83,004
3.	77,208	60,779	+ .25	+ 869	78,077
4.	78,171	63,537	+ .35	+1217	79,388
5.	79,114	65,496	+ .35	+1217	80,331
6.	80,036	69,571	+ .55	+1912	81,948
7.	80,937	12,609	−1.15	−3999	76,938
8.	81,819	20,688	− .85	−2955	78,864
9.	82,680	02,033	−2.05	−7128	75,552
10.	83,522	76,629	+ .75	+2608	86,130
11.	84,344	39,183	− .25	− 869	83,475
12.	85,146	40,747	− .25	− 869	84,277
13.	85,930	31,375	− .45	−1565	84,365
14.	86,694	21,365	− .75	−2608	84,086
15.	87,439	74,854	+ .65	+2260	89,699
16.	88,165	56,525	+ .15	+ 522	88,687
17.	88,874	48,434	− .05	− 174	88,700
18.	89,563	35,904	− .35	−1217	88,346
19.	90,235	80,246	+ .85	+2955	93,190
20.	90,888	17,440	− .95	−3303	87,585
21.	91,524	29,143	− .55	−1912	89,612
22.	92,142	33,118	− .45	−1565	90,577
23.	92,743	15,045	−1.05	−3651	89,092
24.	93,326	76,598	+ .75	+2608	95,934
25.	93,893	88,558	+1.25	+4346	98,239
26.	94,442	41,532	− .25	− 869	93,573
27.	94,975	38,276	− .25	− 869	94,106
28.	95,491	28,215	− .55	−1912	93,579
29.	95,991	02,782	−1.95	−6780	89,211
30.	96,474	39,416	− .25	− 869	95,605

The Y values obtained by regression must be adjusted for random daily variations, which are assumed to be distributed normally about the regression line. The procedure of doing this is followed easier if it is given step by step.

Step 1. With a table of areas of standard normal distribution for Z values (as shown in Chapter 6), a series of equal Z classes is established, as shown in the first column of Figure 19–5. These classes are assigned the mid-point value, as shown in column 2.

Step 2. In column 3, the probabilities below the Z boundaries are listed.

Step 3. For each day, a number is selected from a random number table. Looking in the column of probabilities, it is determined within which class the number fits.

Step 4. The mid-value of that class is then multiplied by the standard error of the estimate, 3,477 pounds (the standard error of the estimate was calculated as illustrated in Chapter 6). This product is then added to the value of Y, and the daily simulated milk arrivals are shown in column 6 of Figure 19–4.

Figure 19–5

Table for Determining *Z* Values

1 Lower class boundary of Z	2 Mid value of Z	3 Probability below class boundary	1 Lower class boundary of Z	2 Mid value of Z	3 Probability below class boundary	1 Lower class boundary of Z	2 Mid value of Z	3 Probability below class boundary
—4.00	—4.05		—1.50	—1.55	.06691	+1.10	+1.05	.86433
—3.90	—3.95	.00005	—1.40	—1.45	.08076	+1.20	+1.15	.88493
—3.80	—3.85	.00007	—1.30	—1.35	.09680	+1.30	+1.25	.90320
—3.70	—3.75	.00011	—1.20	—1.25	.11507	+1.40	+1.35	.91924
—3.60	—3.65	.00016	—1.10	—1.15	.13567	+1.50	+1.45	.93319
—3.50	—3.55	.00023	—1.00	—1.05	.15866	+1.60	+1.55	.94520
—3.40	—3.45	.00034	— .90	— .95	.18406	+1.70	+1.65	.95543
—3.30	—3.35	.00048	— .80	— .85	.21186	+1.80	+1.75	.96407
—3.20	—3.25	.00069	— .70	— .75	.24196	+1.90	+1.85	.97128
—3.10	—3.15	.00097	— .60	— .65	.27425	+2.00	+1.95	.97725
—3.00	—3.05	.00135	— .50	— .55	.30854	+2.10	+2.05	.98214
—2.90	—2.95	.00187	— .40	— .45	.34458	+2.20	+2.15	.98610
—2.80	—2.85	.00256	— .30	— .35	.38209	+2.30	+2.25	.98928
—2.70	—2.75	.00347	— .20	— .25	.42074	+2.40	+2.35	.99180
—2.60	—2.65	.00466	— .10	— .15	.46017	+2.50	+2.45	.99379
—2.50	—2.55	.00621	.00	— .05	.50000	+2.60	+2.55	.99534
—2.40	—2.45	.00820	+ .10	+ .05	.53983	+2.70	+2.65	.99653
—2.30	—2.35	.01072	+ .20	+ .15	.57926	+2.80	+2.75	.99744
—2.20	—2.25	.01390	+ .30	+ .25	.61791	+2.90	+2.85	.99813
—2.10	—2.15	.01786	+ .40	+ .35	.65542	+3.00	+2.95	.99865
—2.00	—2.05	.02275	+ .50	+ .45	.69146	+3.10	+3.05	.99903
—1.90	—1.95	.02872	+ .60	+ .55	.72575	+3.20	+3.15	.99931
—1.80	—1.85	.03593	+ .70	+ .65	.75804	+3.30	+3.25	.99952
—1.70	—1.75	.04457	+ .80	+ .75	.78814	+3.40	+3.35	.99966
—1.60	—1.65	.05480	+ .90	+ .85	.81594	+3.50	+3.45	.99977
			+1.00	+ .95	.84134	+3.60	+3.55	.99984
						+3.70	+3.65	.99989
						+3.80	+3.75	.99993
						+3.90	+3.85	.99995
						+4.00	+3.95	.99997
						+4.10	+4.05	.99999

The price of milk also varied with the season, as shown in Figure 19–6. From this data a regression line for prices was obtained:

$$Y = 3.16 - .010X + .023X^2$$

(where Y is the monthly milk price and X is the month of the year)

Figure 19–6
Seasonal Milk Prices

Month	Price in dollars 1953	1954	1955	1956	1957	1958
January	4.26	3.69	3.52	3.76	3.80	3.57
February	3.98	3.45	3.43	3.55	3.67	3.55
March	3.70	3.18	3.35	3.46	3.55	3.42
April	3.46	2.97	3.19	3.36	3.40	3.27
May	3.28	2.89	3.04	3.25	3.25	3.17
June	3.20	2.86	3.00	3.23	3.24	3.10
July	3.24	2.89	3.05	3.18	3.19	3.12
August	3.33	3.02	3.15	3.31	3.21	3.20
September	3.53	3.25	3.31	3.50	3.37	3.37
October	3.77	3.54	3.61	3.70	3.52	3.48
November	4.00	3.82	3.75	3.81	3.62	3.62
December	3.93	3.82	3.84	3.85	3.66	3.66

A summary of the milk costs for one year is shown in Figure 19–7. This table does not show the butter fat recovered from the process. This amounted to 0.5 pounds for each 100 pounds of milk received. The total quantity recovered for the period was 135,471 pounds, at 68¢ a pound, or $92,120.82. This, deducted from the cost of the milk, left a cost of $821,791.56. In ad-

Figure 19–7
Calculations of Milk Costs

Days (1)	Equivalent period (2)	Quantity of milk (3) Pounds	Price /100 lb. milk from Table 8 (4)	Cost (5) = (4) (3)
1- 16	April 15-31	1,311,604	$3.27	$ 42,889.45
17- 47	May	3,007,214	3.19	95,930.13
48- 77	June	3,121,838	3.16	98,650.09
78-108	July	3,125,515	3.17	99,078.83
109-139	August	2,824,580	3.23	91,233.93
140-169	September	2,423,819	3.34	80,955.55
170-200	October	2,093,816	3.49	73,074.18
201-230	November	1,761,685	3.65	64,301.50
231-261	December	1,631,453	3.93	64,116.10
262-292	January	1,557,040	3.75	58,389.00
293-323	February	1,463,171	3.57	52,235.20
324-351	March	1,841,273	3.40	62,603.28
352-365	April 1-14	931,350	3.27	30,455.14
Total		27,094,358		$913,912.38

Figure 19–8

Man–Machine Chart

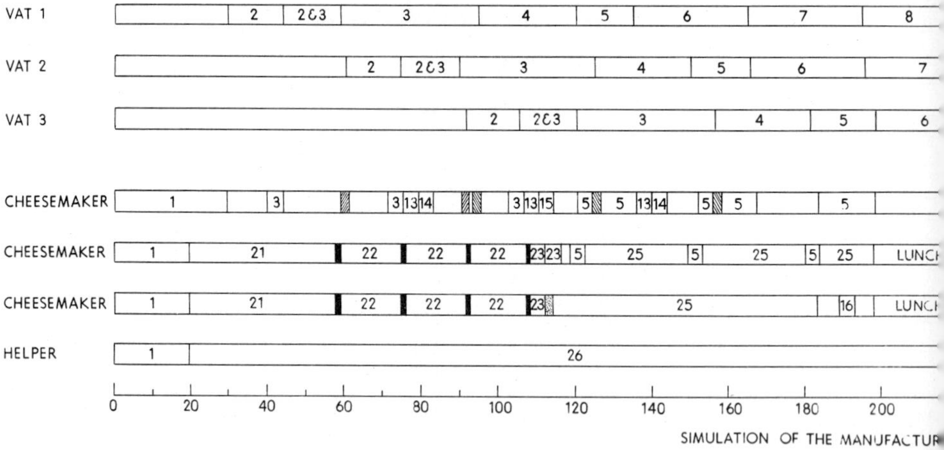

dition there was the cost of rennet, salt, starter, coloring, and packaging material, which was $41,183.19 for the quantity of milk processed. The total materials cost was $862,974.75.

5. *Variable labor costs,* involving the number of people required for a particular production level, was determined by simulating the plant activities with different size labor crews. But first it was necessary to obtain time study data to determine how long it takes to do each of the various activities. This information is tabulated in Figure 19–11, and the data were put together in man-machine charts (Figure 19–8) to simulate work crews of various

Figure 19–9

Crew Size and Labor Costs

No. vats per day (1)	Crew size (2)	Labor cost per day (3)	Dollars Cost per vat (4) Dollars
3	4	49.77	16.59
4	4	63.84	15.96
5	4	76.26	15.25
5	7	81.25	16.25
6	7	90.30	15.06
7	7	100.59	14.37
8	7	108.01	13.50
8	9	112.25	14.03
9	9	124.06	13.78
10	9	132.25	13.25

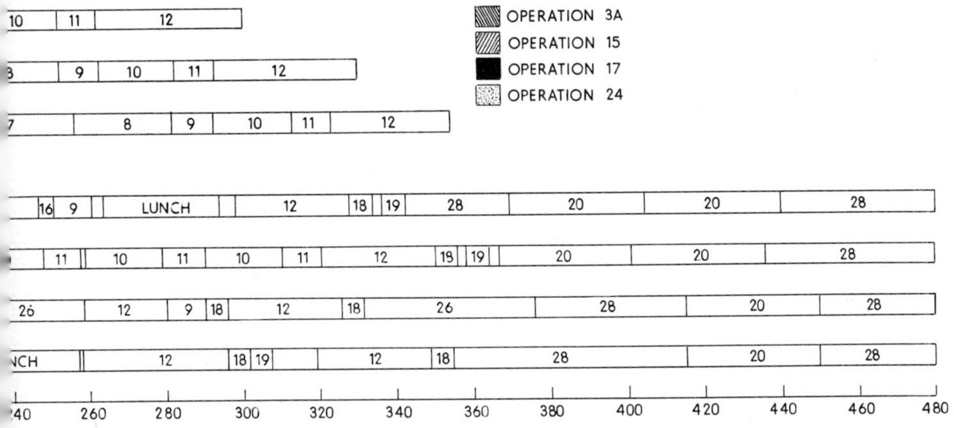

TS OF CHEESE USING A 4-MAN CREW

Figure 19–10

Milk Received and Vats Produced

Total milk receipts	Quantity manufactured	No. vats of cheese
Pounds	Pounds	
From:		
13,250 to 14,500	all	1
14,501 to 26,499	14,500	1
26,500 to 29,000	all	2
29,001 to 39,749	29,000	2
39,750 to 43,500	all	3
43,501 to 52,999	43,500	3
53,000 to 58,000	all	4
58,001 to 66,249	58,000	4
66,250 to 72,500	all	5
72,501 to 79,499	72,500	5
79,500 to 87,000	all	6
87,001 to 92,749	87,000	6
92,750 to 101,500	all	7
101,501 to 105,999	101,500	7
106,000 to 116,000	all	8
116,001 to 119,249	116,000	8
119,250 to 130,500	all	9
130,501 to 132,499	130,500	9
132,500 to 145,000	all	10
145,001 and up	145,000	10

sizes. The cost of operating the plant with different crew sizes is shown in Figure 19–9. Notice that five vats can be produced, either by a crew size of four or of seven. This is because the crew members can work longer than an eight-hour day when necessary.

The number of vats to be made each day depends upon the milk available. A schedule showing the number of vats to be produced for any quantity of milk received is illustrated in Figure 19–10.

Figure 19–11

Time Study Data

Operation	Operation description	Machine time Minutes	Labor requirements Minutes
1	Set up (pasteurizer, piping, vats, etc.)	90.0	90.0
2	Fill 14,500 lb. vat with milk	29.0	
3	Get starter, add to vat, ripen and agitate		4.0[a]
	Get rennet and add	51.0	2.0[b]
4	Set vat of cheese	25.0	—
5	Cut, scrape, agitate, turn steam on	15.0	15.0[c]
6	Cook curd, turn off steam	30.0	
7	Agitate while acidity and temperature are reached	30.0	
8	Drain whey	26.0	
9	Wash curd	10.0	10.0
10	Drain water, add salt	20.0	20.0
11	Break curd with fork, shovel to side	10.0	10.0
12	Fill hoops, place bandages and tops	60.0	60.0
13	Test vat for acidity	—	4.0
14	Add coloring	—	4.0
15	Stop filling one vat, adjust piping, start filling next vat	—	2.0
16	Prepare screen, attach piping in preparation for whey drainage	—	4.0
17	Move rack of cheese to storage (2 men) and return	—	1.0 each
18[d]	Take hoops from vat, place in cheese press, tighten press	—	12.0
19[d]	Tighten press, adjust for buckling	—	6.0
20[d]	Loosen press, dress horns, retighten press	—	60.0
21[d]	Loosen press, turn horns, remove lids and top bandage	—	26.0
22[d]	Log horns, rack cheese and aside horn	—	32.0
23	Wash the horns and the press with hose	—	4.0
24	Get bandage and return to press	—	2.0
25	Line horn with bandage per horn	—	.315
26	Wash horn lids and horns	—	.760
27[d]	Loosen press, remove horns to work bench	—	16.0
28	Clean up	—	240.0

[a] Get cans of starter and add to vat, start mechanical agitators.
[b] Stop agitators, add rennet.
[c] Cutting curd takes two men 4.0 minutes each.
[d] Per 125 horns.

Figure 19–12 shows the daily simulation for the cheese room labor costs. Column 2 indicates what has been carried over from the previous day, while column 3 shows what has been received. The total quantity available for manufacture is compared with the scheduling table to determine the number of vats which should be produced for that day.

As is apparent from the table, the number of vats for this period of time varied between five and seven. To take care of all arrivals during such a

Figure 19–12

Simulation of Milk Arrivals

(1) Day	(2) Quantity of Milk Carried Over from Previous Day	(3) Pounds of Milk Received from Farmers (Table 4)	(4) Pounds of Milk Received from Other Sources	(5) Total Quantity Available for Manufacturer	(6) Quantity Manufactured (Table 5)	(7) Quantity Carried Over to Next Day	(8) Number of Vats Manufactured
1.	—	76,783	0	76,783	72,500	4,383	5
2.	4,383	83,004	0	87,387	87,000	387	6
3.	387	78,077	0	78,464	72,500	5,964	5
4.	5,964	79,388	0	85,352	85,352	—	6
5.	—	80,331	0	80,331	80,331	—	6
6.	—	81,948	0	81,948	81,948	—	6
7.	—	76,938	0	76,938	72,500	4,438	5
8.	4,438	78,864	0	83,302	83,302	—	6
9.	—	75,552	0	75,552	72,500	3,052	5
10.	3,052	86,130	0	89,182	87,000	2,182	6
11.	2,182	83,475	0	85,657	85,657	—	6
12.	—	84,277	0	84,277	84,277	—	6
13.	—	84,365	0	84,365	84,365	—	6
14.	—	84,086	0	84,086	84,086	—	6
15.	—	89,699	0	89,699	87,000	2,699	6
16.	2,699	88,687	0	91,386	87,000	4,386	6
17.	4,386	88,700	0	93,086	93,086	—	7
18.	—	88,346	0	88,346	87,000	1,346	6
19.	1,346	93,190	0	94,536	94,536	—	7
20.	—	87,585	0	87,585	87,000	585	6
21.	585	89,612	0	90,197	87,000	3,197	6
22.	3,197	90,577	0	93,774	93,774	—	7
23.	—	89,092	0	89,092	87,000	2,092	6
24.	2,092	95,934	0	98,026	98,026	—	7
25.	—	98,239	0	98,239	98,239	—	7
26.	—	93,573	0	93,573	93,573	—	7
27.	—	94,106	0	94,106	94,106	—	7
28.	—	93,579	0	93,579	93,579	—	7
29.	—	89,211	0	89,211	87,000	2,211	6
30.	2,211	95,605	0	97,816	97,816	—	7
31.	—	96,073	0	96,073	96,073	—	7
32.	—	98,611	0	98,611	98,611	—	7
33.	—	100,785	0	100,785	100,785	—	7
34.	—	95,642	0	95,642	95,642	—	7
35.	—	100,567	0	100,567	100,567	—	7
36.	—	98,523	0	98,523	98,523	—	7
37.	—	104,809	0	104,809	101,500	3,309	7

period—and not vary the labor force from day to day—the crew size would be maintained at seven. An analysis of this sort was done for the whole year, and is summarized in Figure 19–13. The variable labor cost was $28,861.44.

Figure 19–13

Summary of Direct Labor Costs

No. vats cheese mfd. per day (1)	Frequency (no. days) (2)	Daily labor cost (Table 6) (3)	Cost (4) = (2) (3) (4)
		Dollars	Dollars
3	38	49.77	1,891.26
4	113	63.84	3,355.44
5	45	76.26	7,290.18
5	14	81.25	1,137.50
6	53	90.30	4,785.90
7	83	100.59	8,348.97
8	19	108.01	2,052.19
Total			28,861.44

6. *Variable services and supplies* includes office supplies, laboratory supplies, and laundry service. The total for the year under consideration was $5,160.34.

A summary of all the cost is given in the table in Figure 19–14. Each item has been explained, as you will notice; but this is only one policy, and there may be many others which could be evaluated. Some that were considered are:

Figure 19–14

Summary of All Costs for Policy 1

Item	Total Cost (Dollars)	Cost Per Pound of Cheese (Cents)
1. Fixed labor costs	45,995.00	1.58
2. Fixed plant and facilities costs	35,395.00	1.22
3. Fixed services and supplies costs	10,927.75	.38
4. Material costs	862,974.75	29.76
5. Variable labor costs	28,861.44	1.00
6. Variable services and supplies costs	5,160.34	.18
	989,314.28	34.12

Policy 1. Recall that this policy permitted the purchase of raw materials only from the producers.

Policy 2. Same as Policy 1, but, in addition, surplus milk was purchased from April 15 to August 31.

Policy 3. This was an attempt to iron out the seasonal problem of the milk sup-

Figure 19–15

Comparison of Six Operating Policies

Policy number	Total pounds cheese mfd.	F. labor cost/lb.	Var. labor cost/lb.	F. plant & facilities cost/lb.	F. serv. & supplies cost/lb.	Var. serv. & supplies cost/lb.	Material cost/lb.	Av. total cost/lb.
		cents	cents	cents	cents	cents	cents	cents
1	2,899,096	1.58	1.00	1.22	.38	.18	29.76	34.12
2	3,423,190	1.34	.96	1.10[a]	.32	.17	29.80	33.69
3	3,440,174	1.34	.98	1.03	.32	.18	30.48	34.33
4	3,440,174	1.34	.98	1.03	.32	.18	30.85	34.70
5	3,981,252	1.16	.94	.89	.27	.17	31.00	34.43
6	3,981,252	1.16	.94	.89	.27	.17	31.63	35.06

[a] Plant facilities had to be expanded for Policy No. 2.

ply. The milk was purchased from the producers at 25¢/hundredweight, and in addition 3000 gallons/day were purchased from an outside source during October 1 to April 14.

Policy 4. Same as Policy 3, except the premium was 50¢/hundredweight.

Policy 5. Same as Policy 3, except 51,600 pounds of milk were purchased from the outside.

Policy 6. Same as Policy 5, except the premium was 50¢/hundredweight.

Many other policies may be examined, but this will give you some idea of the procedure. A summary of costs for these various policies is shown in Figure 19–15.

SUMMARY

This has been only one example of how simulation can be applied to industrial problems. There are many more. For example, simulation has been used to solve inventory problems, scheduling problems, marketing problems, and many others.

Simulation is not new; it is only that it is being applied in new areas. As we have seen, industries are using this method to establish policies, but they are also using this technique (in the form of management games) to train executives and would-be executives. Simulation is just another method of solving problems.

Questions

1. Define *simulation* and *heuristics*.
2. What are the advantages and disadvantages of simulating industrial problems?
3. Give some examples of simulated models which are used in industry.
4. Discuss how simulation might be used as a method for selecting employees.
5. Cite two examples where simulation could be used to solve industrial problems at the top management level.

References

Blackwell, David Harold, and Girshick, M. A. *Theory of Games and Statistical Decisions*. New York: John Wiley & Sons, Inc., 1954.

Bonini, Charles P. *Simulation of Information and Decision Systems in the Firm*. Englewood Cliffs, N.J.: Prentice-Hall, Inc., 1964.

Burger, Ewald. *Introduction to the Theory of Games*. Englewood Cliffs, N.J.: Prentice-Hall, Inc., 1963.

Glickstein, Aaron; Babb, E. M.; French, C. E.; and Greene, J. H. "Simulate Your Way to Sound Decisions." *Food Engineering*, Vol. 35, No. 6 (June, 1963).

———; ———; ———; — ———. *Simulation Procedures for Production Control in an Indiana Cheese Plant.* Research Bulletin No. 757. Lafayette, Ind.: Purdue University Agriculture Experiment Station, 1962.

GREENLAW, PAUL STEPHEN; HERRON, LOWELL W.; and RAWDON, RICHARD H. *Business Simulation in Industrial and University Education.* Englewood Cliffs, N.J.: Prentice-Hall, Inc., 1962.

JENNESS, ROGER R. *Analog Computation and Simulation, Laboratory Approach.* Boston: Allyn & Bacon, Inc., 1965.

MALCOLM, D. G. *A Bibliography on the Use of Simulation in Management Analysis.* Santa Monica, Calif.: System Development Corp., 1959.

MARKOWITZ, HARRY M.; HAUSNER, BERNARD; and KARR, HERBERT W. *Simscript: A Simulation Programming Language.* Englewood Cliffs, N.J.: Prentice-Hall, Inc., 1963.

MARTIN, E. W. *Management Decision Simulation.* Homewood, Ill.: Richard D. Irwin, Inc., 1960.

SOROKA, WALTER W. *Analog Methods in Computation and Simulation.* New York: McGraw-Hill Book Co., Inc., 1954.

TOCHER, K. D. *The Art of Simulation.* Princeton, N.J.: D. Van Nostrand Co., Inc., 1963.

TONGE, FRED M. *A Heuristic Pattern for Assembly Line Balancing.* Englewood Cliffs, N.J.: Prentice-Hall, Inc., 1961.

VANCE, STANLEY. *Management Decision Simulation.* New York: McGraw-Hill Book Co., Inc., 1960.

SECTION FIVE

Systems in Practice

CHAPTER **20**

Presenting the System Design

Nothing can be more devastating to the ego of the system designer than to present a system improvement which goes unnoticed—unnoticed not because of faulty design but perhaps because it was not properly presented. It would be better not to initiate a system study than to let it fail in this final step.

The objective in the presentation of a new system is to transfer the idea in your mind to the audience with such ease that it will be accepted as a course of action. This type of persuasion is not an activity peculiar to the system designer; it is found in every profession where creative efforts exist. You will soon be using your persuasive abilities in industry, and undoubtedly your income will reflect, to some extent, your ability to persuade. Do not object to the extra effort necessary to prepare and present your ideas in a manner which will assure their acceptance.

ORGANIZING FOR SYSTEM DESIGNING

The impetus for a new or revised system may come from any number of sources. The system manager may sense the need for changes because of increases in production, replacement of personnel, or improved system equipment. He may have time to introduce these revisions himself, or he may resort to using a staff assistant.

Often the need for a change is recognized by someone who is in a higher position than the system manager. In this case the system manager may be directed to make the necessary revisions, or, if necessary, call in outside help.

For minor changes it is best that one man with the time and ability consult with others and implement the necessary revisions. For major system overhauls, probably the best plan is to establish a special committee representing all interested groups. For a production control system this would mean at least one representative each from product design, production, accounting, payroll, inventory control, and purchasing. In such a committee all interested parties have an opportunity to air their views and, hopefully, no one will dominate at the expense of the others.

No committee can function without strong leadership. This leadership may be exercised by someone from top management who sees the "big picture," or by someone appointed because of his outstanding performance on similar tasks. Frequently, the leadership will be exercised by an outside consultant who has been selected because of his wide experience. A full understanding of the methods of approaching the problem and of what information is needed are essential before the committee leader can perform satisfactorily.

SETTING THE STAGE FOR SYSTEM DESIGNING

Introducing the system design assumes that a logical sequence of activities has preceded the final report. This book is dedicated to those activities which can be used for the logical design of systems. So important are the steps of logic stated in Chapter 2, that it is worthwhile to review them briefly.

1. Become aware of the problem.
2. Define the problem.
3. Locate, evaluate, and organize information.
4. Discover relationships and formulate hypotheses.
5. Evaluate the hypotheses.
6. Apply the solution.

Assuming that the committee has become aware of the problem, and that the problem has been defined, it is then necessary to collect information which will help produce an optimum design. The following are examples of information which should be available to all members of the committee.

Product information: Is the product perishable or fragile? Does it require special handling? Is it a style product which is likely to be dated? Is it small or large? Does it require high quality workmanship? Has the product been standardized?

Raw material: What are the raw materials? What are their costs? Are there any substitutes? What are the sources? What is the nature of the markets for these products? Is the source of raw material monopolized by any one vendor?

Plant facilities and processes: Is the plant a job shop or production line? Is this going to change in the future? What are the plans for expansion? How are materials handled? Does the process require special-purpose tools? How old are the tools? What are the machine capacities?

Personnel: Is there an organizational chart? Should it be revised? Are the employees on incentive? Are they skilled or unskilled? What personality conflicts exist which might make it difficult to introduce a new system?

The present system: It is nearly impossible to consider a new system without knowing what has gone before. A complete picture of the present system should be produced. The decision must then be made to modify the present system or to abandon it and start anew. In either case the new system may be introduced piece by piece, ironing out the problems as they occur in each stage before going on to the next.

The timetable: A timetable for introducing the system should be established and adhered to (if possible). Schedules for intermediate steps and the final installation should be established in advance.

PRESENTING THE SYSTEM DESIGN BY MEANS OF A WRITTEN REPORT

Probably no stage in the life of a system design is as critical as its presentation to those who have the power to accept or reject it. It is probably also one of the most critical times in your career as a system designer: Your whole future may depend on how well the system is accepted. Often the written report is practically the only way of communicating with the people above and below you in the organizational structure, and it is therefore not surprising that many industrialists' careers have hinged on a well written report.

Before the report is written, the ideas should be clearly outlined and committed to paper. If, in the course of writing the report, you find you are using excessive explanations, it is probably because the ideas have not been clearly outlined. Do not let this delay you, for just putting ideas down on paper will help clear away the fog. Sometimes, if you let the report "jell" for a few days at this stage, the ideas will become clearer. Many people stumble at this initial stage; they can't put down the first word of the first paragraph. Start writing, even if it is in the middle of the report. You can always go back and fill in parts which are missing.

It is usually best if the report contains a single, main idea. This is true from an efficiency as well as a strategy viewpoint. One idea will get your reader's attention in the shortest possible time. He also is likely to accept ideas one at a time. More than one good idea has been lost because the reader took exception to some of the minor ideas included in a report.

In industry, brevity is important because "time is money." If you don't "sell" your idea in the first few minutes of reading, you probably won't sell it at all. This is a key point in the organization of the written report, as you will see in the following outline.

Typical Outline for the Written Report

The ideal written report is economical of the reader's time, clear as to meaning, precise in its recommendations, and unambiguous. The outline proposed here will help you meet these objectives.

Outline for the Written Report

1. Preface
   A. *Title page.* Contains the name of the report, and the authors; date; and any other information necessary to tie down the report subject in time and place.
   B. *Table of contents.* Here is a place to stir the interest of the prospective reader, for often he will turn to this section first. Do not kill his interest by having obscure, or too brief or too extensive titles. Make a good first impression here.
   C. *Letter of transmittal or forward.* This gives your report additional authority if it is used correctly.

2. Abstract. Should give enough information for a decision. Often the reader will go no further than the abstract. If he is to go further, you must get him involved here. He will want to read on if the idea you are conveying is important enough to become operational. Work this part over carefully, and make it *concise.*

3. Main Discussion
   A. *Background of study.* This part of the report should be treated with care for often there is a tendency to build volume regardless of the contribution to the report. Only pertinent background should be included.
   B. *Need for study.* Be sure your points will be meaningful to all. Your close association with the problem may make you tend to gloss over the need for the study. On the other hand, do not point out every trivial need or you will downgrade the importance of the report.
   C. *Procedure.* This section should outline, in detail, the procedure used in the study. It should be outlined in sufficient detail so that any experimental work could be repeated at some future date.
   D. *Important data and results.* The main emphasis in this section should be on the development of results. If the data do not lead directly to the results, but are important for a full understanding, it should appear in an appendix. Make specific recommendations in this section and be sure no questions are left unanswered.
   E. *Appendix.* Sections A through D should be kept to a moderate size; therefore much of the supporting material should be placed in appendices, where it can be referred to as needed.

This is an acceptable outline for a written report, but effective reports have been written which deviated from this form. Variation may be the very thing which will bring your report to the attention of your reader.

Principles of Report Writing

No number of principles of report writing will make you a good report writer without practice. However, a few good principles can well be kept in mind as you practice.

1. Write for your audience. If your audience has a technical vocabulary, you too may use a technical vocabulary. Remember, you are trying to convey

an idea which you wish to have accepted, so use examples which coincide with your reader's experience.

2. Use simple, familiar words. Some of the most effective writing of all time has been in simple words simply put.
3. Keep sentences short. Short sentences are easier to read, but vary their lengths or your report will appear choppy.
4. Discard unnecessary words. Everyone tends to use more words than he needs. If a word does not add meaning, discard it. Use a newspaper style.
5. Let your personality show through. Write the same way you talk, otherwise you will sound stilted and affected. It is no crime to let your personality show—as long as it is the *most favorable* side of your personality.
6. Make your writing live. Use active verbs. In many situations using the first person will add life to your writing. Don't hesitate to refer to people by name. Don't use terms or phrases which will "date" you.
7. Point the way. Make sure there is no doubt in the reader's mind about what you think is important. This can be assured if you work from an outline and give the most important points the most weight.
8. Create a good first impression. Be sure the report has a suitable cover, for this is your introduction to the reader. It is his invitation to read your ideas and be convinced.
9. Conform to style standards. Often the first draft of a report should be done by double-spacing the typewritten page. This permits editing. In the final draft single spacing is often preferred. Your typist can advise you about the style used in the company; listen to her.
10. Abbreviate and symbolize with care. Remember you are trying to convey ideas; don't lose your reader with abbreviations or symbols with which he may not be familiar. If there is any question, use a glossary of terms.
11. Paragraph with care. The first sentence should tell what is coming and be followed by several explanatory sentences. Cover only one idea per paragraph.
12. Be brief, but not so brief the reader misses the point.
13. Use visual aids. The old cliché about a picture being worth a thousand words is equally true in report writing. Use charts, diagrams, and pictures with care, and place them in the text where they will do the most good.
14. Be accurate. In an engineering or cost report accuracy is paramount. One error can discredit all your work. Check and double-check.
15. Write to express, not to impress. If you write to express your ideas, and to persuade people to use them, you won't have to try to impress them. They will be.

PRESENTING THE SYSTEM DESIGN BY THE CONFERENCE METHOD

When ideas are presented orally instead of by a written report, it is usually because two-way rather than unilateral communications are needed. The need for two-way communications may come about for several reasons. It may be necessary to get the group together to agree on something as simple as an appropriate time for action. The system designer might convene the members of the committee to obtain their ideas. Often there are faults in the proposed system that can only be brought to light by the members' focusing their attention on the problem as a group.

Of greatest importance, the conference offers the opportunity to obtain participation. Only by involvement will you be able to tap all the resources of the personnel, and only by involvement will they accept the system and make it work. If it is this objective of group involvement for which you are striving, you will have to become aware of—and practice—the art of conference leadership. This is an activity which has been given considerable attention in recent years, and you will be wise to supplement the conference outline below by exploring some of the references listed in the bibliography.

Typical Outline for the Conference Procedure

Like the written report, the conference also has an approved form; and, like the report outline, it is only a recognized guide, and one should feel free to deviate from it as necessary.

1. Advance Planning for the Conference
   - A. Decide what the objectives are.
   - B. Be sure the topic is suitable for a conference solution.
   - C. Prepare a conference agenda with time schedule and key questions.
   - D. Prepare visual aids and assemble any references and other information needed for the conference.
   - E. Be sure conferees are invited well in advance so they will have the opportunity to arrange their schedules.
   - F. The conferees should be told the subject of the conference well in advance.
   - G. Prepare the meeting place: Consider noise, temperature, seating, and other factors that affect the physical setting of the conference.
2. Opening the Conference
   - A. Start on time; this can set the tone for the entire conference.
   - B. Introduce conference members who are not known to all.
   - C. Establish a friendly atmosphere.
   - D. Review the background of the problem and relate it to the conference theme.
   - E. Present the conference theme in a way that will interest the conferees and so that they will wish to discuss and contribute.
   - F. Use illustrations to point up the importance of the problem and write the problem on the board.
3. Direct the Discussion
   - A. Direct the discussion to draw out the conferees' viewpoints. Ask key questions.
   - B. Encourage participation by directing questions to those who are not participating.
   - C. Do not make a practice of answering questions, but redirect them to conferees.
   - D. Write the pertinent decisions of the group on the board.
   - E. Keep the conference moving, but do not display a feeling of impatience.
   - F. Be alert and take advantage of every break in the conference.
4. Summarize
   - A. Obtain agreement upon points along the way.
   - B. Obtain final agreement and formulate a plan of action before the end of the conference.

5. Follow-up
   A. After the meeting, write up a brief report or minutes.
   B. Send each member a copy to help reinforce any action that was taken.

Twenty "Don'ts" for the Conference Leader

1. Don't discuss personalities.
2. Don't permit arguments.
3. Don't answer questions if you can redirect them to other conference members.
4. Don't let the conference drag; keep it on schedule. Quit when the work agenda is finished.
5. Don't let the discussion wander from its objective.
6. Don't be sarcastic or use a patronizing attitude.
7. Don't lose control of the conference.
8. Don't monopolize the conversation.
9. Don't let any member, or group of members, monopolize the conference time.
10. Don't play the role of an expert.
11. Don't let the shy conferee escape fielding a question; encourage involvement.
12. Don't let an important point of agreement go by without recording it.
13. Don't accept agreement on the basis of deference to authority. This will kill the voluntary contributions you want.
14. Don't dampen the enthusiasm of the conferees.
15. Don't forget to use visual aids when they can be effective.
16. Don't take credit when it can be given to someone else.
17. Don't let the meeting break up on an unfriendly note.
18. Don't forget to summarize.
19. Don't lose the confidence of the conferees.
20. Don't neglect to issue a report of minutes.

Visual Aids for the Conference

Often the entire tone of the conference can be set by the use of visual aids. If they are thoughtfully prepared and well done, the conferees will take the meeting seriously and put their minds to the objectives. Some of the various visual aids which can be found in a well run conference are discussed briefly here.

Blackboards are still one of the best devices for conferences. Be sure they are clean and you have plenty of space. Needless to say, there should be an ample supply of chalk and erasers. A little practice in drawing on the board will help. Develop your discussion by writing on the board from left to right just as you write on a page. Solving the problem of writing on the board while talking to the audience takes practice.

Flip Charts are large tablets hung on an easel. The charts may be prepared in advance or developed in a manner similar to the blackboard technique. Charts need not be prepared by an artist; they are quite effective even if crudely drawn. Develop one point per sheet, and don't forget the man in the back row who doesn't have 20/20 vision.

Flannel or magnetic boards are covered with cloth, such as outing-flannel, that has a nap. Cutouts, mounted on sandpaper, adhere to the nap. The cutouts may be words or illustrations which can be placed on the board during the development of the presentation. The magnetic board uses small magnets, instead of sandpaper, which adhere to an iron-surfaced board. Both techniques are effective, and impressive displays can be prepared by a resourceful conference leader. They are, however, expensive displays and should be used only when the cost is warranted.

Overhead projectors are used with slides or larger transparencies. The image is projected over the head of the conference leader onto a screen in back of him, but in full view of the audience. This permits the leader to face the audience as he discusses the material. An objection to this device is that the room must be slightly darkened.

Slides and moving picture films are useful for presenting some types of material. Films take some lead time and expense to prepare. Also, the room must be darkened and some members may be overcome by the urge to sleep.

Opaque projectors are excellent devices for presenting printed material to a small audience. The efficiency of the projectors is not great, so the print must be large and the picture must be shown on a good screen in a darkened room.

Printed handouts are convenient for developing discussions, but they must be used with caution. The members of the conference are apt to be distracted by reading ahead. The material should not be handed out before time of use. They do serve as excellent take-home material.

SUMMARY

Any presentation such as this concerning written reports and conference leadership is superficial, to say the least. The real effectiveness of these techniques depends upon you and who you are. This chapter cannot train you to be honest, to be courteous, to have insight to problems, and all the other numerous characteristics required for success. You must work on developing these attributes yourself, every day.

A system design is an idea or group of ideas. The idea should be acceptable to those who must use it. This means that persuasion must be employed. Today's system designer has numerous devices for persuasion. Some of these methods are the product of extensive research. Become acquainted with them and make the greatest possible use of them to insure your success.

Questions

1. Why should every system designer know the fundamentals of persuasion?
2. What are the advantages and disadvantages of having a committee responsible for a system design?

3. Outline the way you would approach and complete the task of redesigning a system.
4. Which principle for report writing do you consider the most important? In your own writing, which is the most difficult to master?
5. How can practice in report writing help you in presenting better oral reports?
6. Write a report on some selected industrial subject following the principles given.
7. Present an oral report of the above question and have the members of your class evaluate your presentation. Are you guilty of any "don'ts" for the conference leader?
8. Compare the advantages and disadvantages of the various visual aids which can be used in presenting a system.

References

ABELSON, HERBERT IRVING. *Persuasion: How Opinions and Attitudes are Changed*. New York: Springer Publishing Co., Inc., 1959.

BLICKLE, MARGARET D., and HOUP, KENNETH W. *Reports for Science and Industry*. Henry Holt & Co., 1958.

CADY, EDWIN LAIRD. *Creative Communication*. New York: Reinhold Publishing Corp., 1957.

CASEY, ROBERT S. *Oral Communication of Technical Information*. New York: Reinhold Publishing Co., 1958.

DOOHER, M. JOSEPH. *Effective Communication on the Job: A Guide to Employee Communications for Supervisors and Executives*. New York: American Management Association, 1956.

FISHER, WALDO E. *Conference Leader's Guide*. Pasadena, Calif.: California Institute of Technology, 1948.

HOVLAND, CARL I.; JANIS, IRVING L.; and KELLY, HAROLD H. *Communication and Persuasion*. New Haven, Conn.: Yale University Press, 1963.

KOSKY, THOMAS A. *How to Make and Use Flannel Boards*. San Francisco, Fearon Publishers, Inc., 1961.

LEBRETON, PRESTON P., and HENNING, DALE A. *Planning Theory*. Englewood Cliffs, N.J.: Prentice-Hall, Inc., 1961.

MILLER, CLYDE R. *The Process of Persuasion*. New York: Crown Publishers, Inc., 1946.

MINOR, EDWARD. *Preparing Visual Instruction Material*. New York: McGraw-Hill Book Co., Inc., 1962.

SHELLOW, SADIE MYERS, and HARMON, GLENN R. *Conference Manual for Training Foremen*. New York: Harper & Bros., 1935.

STRAUSS, BERT and FRANCES. *New Ways to Better Meetings*. New York: Viking Press, 1952.

SURLES, LYNN, and STANBURY, W. A. *The Art of Persuasive Talking*. New York: McGraw-Hill Book Co., Inc., 1960.

UMBACH, CLAYTON A., JR. *How to Prepare for Management Responsibilities*. Houston, Texas: Gulf Publishing Co., 1961.

WAGNER, RUSSELL, and ARNOLD, CARROLL C. *Handbook of Group Discussion*. Boston: Houghton Mifflin Co., 1944.

WINFREY, ROBLEY. *Technical and Business Report Preparation.* Ames, Iowa: Iowa State University Press, 1962.

WEAVER, G. G., and BOLLINGER, E. W. *Visual Aids.* Princeton, N.J.: D. Van Nostrand Co., 1959.

WITTLICH, WALTER W., and SCHULLER, CHARLES F. *Audio-Visual Materials.* New York: Harper & Bros., 1951.

WOLFF, JACK L. *The Production Conference.* Boston: Houghton Mifflin Co., 1944.

CHAPTER 21

Design and Redesign

In the first part of this chapter you will find applications of some of the system-designing techniques with which you became acquainted earlier. These real-world systems have been analyzed and redesigned in much the same way you will be expected to analyze and redesign a system.

As you would anticipate, these are improved designs, but not perfect designs; there is always the possibility of further improvement. In fact, you might look for ways of improving the systems presented. The possibility of improvement is what makes system designing so challenging.

Examples of System Designing

Since more than one system is to be presented, a word about the organization of the chapter should be helpful. Each system will be presented as a separate package, preceded by some general information about the company, the product, and whatever is necessary to give you an insight to the example. After the brief introduction, the system will be isolated and presented.

Not only will you obtain some insight to system analysis but you will also become familiar with some real systems which work. A methodical approach to designing a system will be used. It is a method you may wish to follow when you become involved in similar problems during your industrial experience. These steps are:

1. Record and analyze the structure of the organization. Often the organizational chart has not been drawn, and consequently the areas of authority and responsibility are not known.
2. Make a flow chart of the present system, for this is the only way to visualize it clearly. A chart helps to draw out conflicting viewpoints and gives an opportunity to obtain and record the information in a short time. You can then remove yourself from the distracting factory environment to consider any improvements.
3. Redesign the system and describe it with a revised flow chart. This is the "thinking" step. It gives the designer an opportunity to experiment with several designs. Don't forget that there will be other people who can contribute worthwhile ideas on how the system should be designed. Explore all possibilities, but give credit to all those who contribute.

Figure 21–1 Present and Revised System for Sales Order

Present System

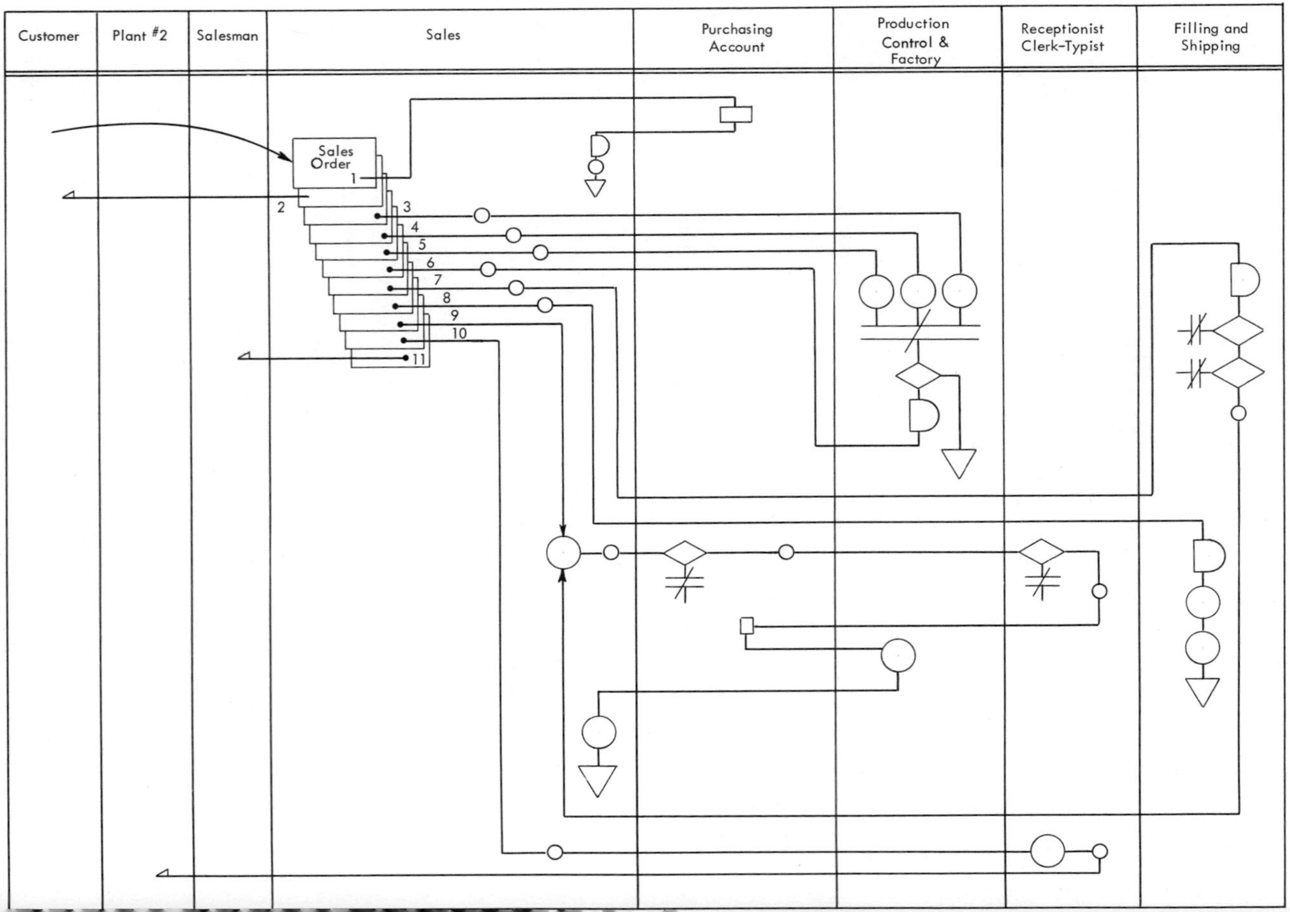

Revised System

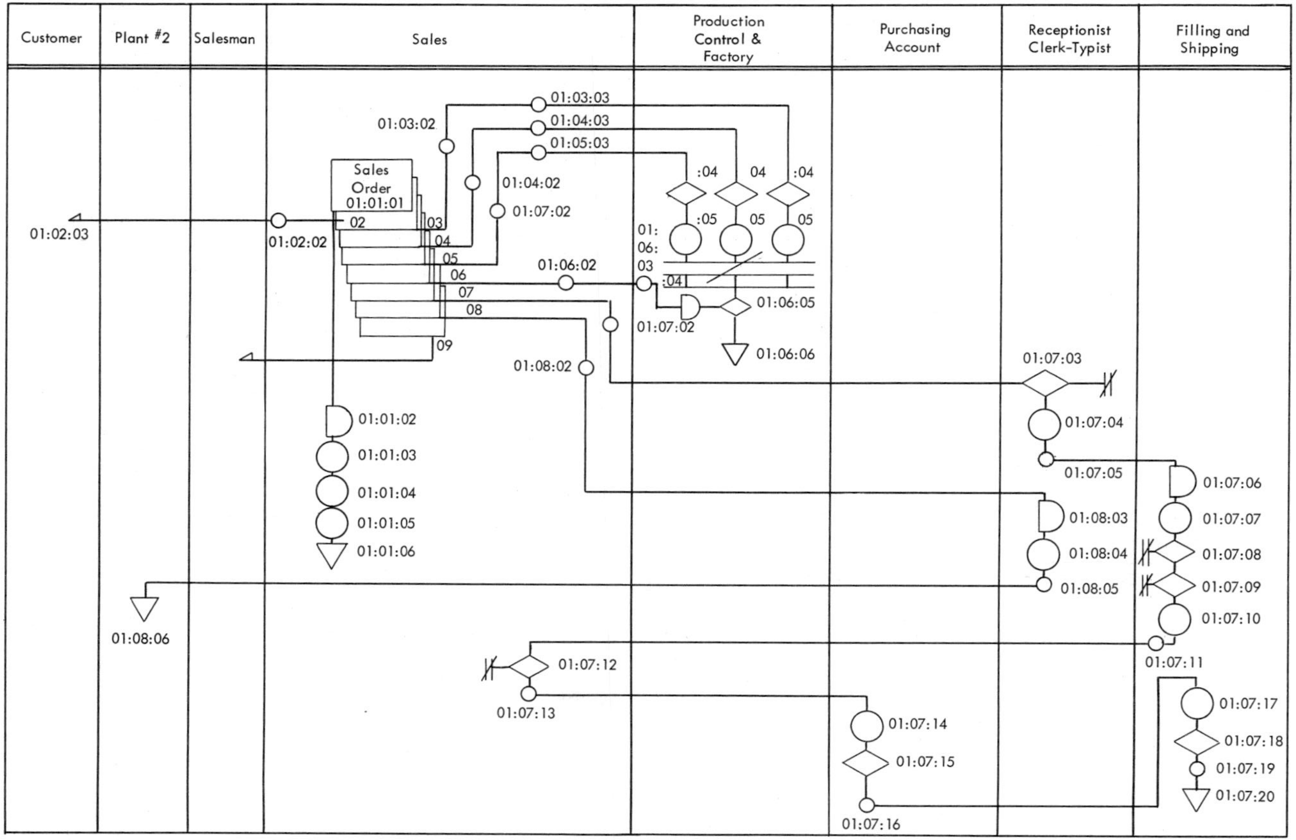

4. During and after the redesigning step the forms should be analyzed to determine their efficiency. The check list presented in Chapter 11 is useful in this step.
5. All of the work done in the previous steps culminates in the Standard Operating Procedure. This set of written instructions explains to each individual involved in the system what he must do to make the system function.

The redesigned system should be prepared and presented, either in a written or oral form, with all the persuasive skill available.

In a book such as this, a certain degree of poetic license must be exercised to delete repetitious material. Also, in many cases the identity of the company in the example cannot be divulged. Therefore, companies will be given fictitious names and conditions will be altered slightly.

One word of caution. Often students are shocked by the inefficiencies of some real-world systems. They will wonder why companies have overlooked obvious improvements. They should not forget that the companies have probably been successful and the management has been often too busy to keep the control systems up to date. The student should be prepared to cope

Figure 21–2

Present and Revised System for the Master Formula Card

Present System

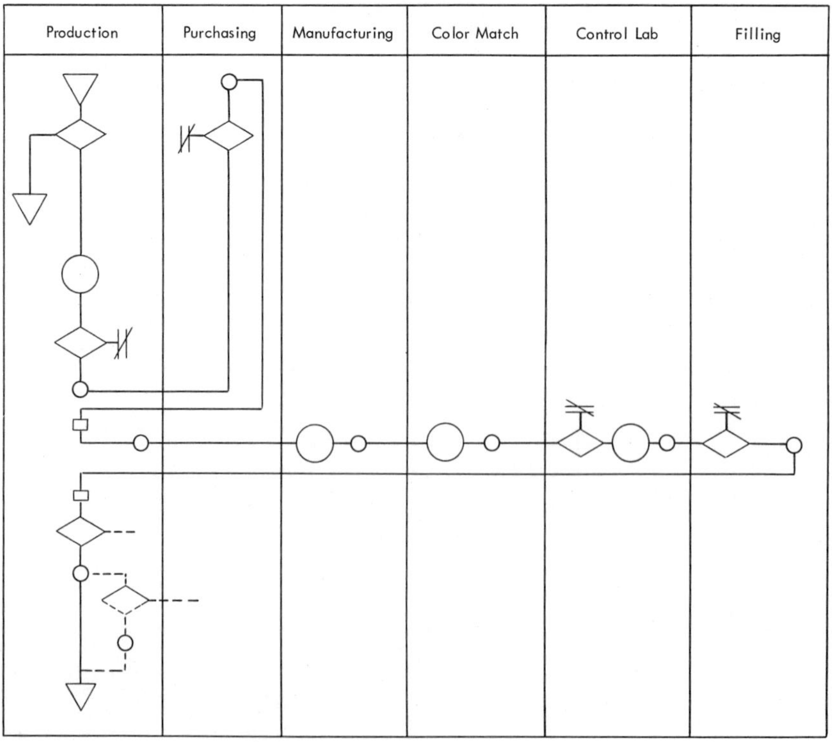

with introducing changes and not become too impatient if every one doesn't see what to him may seem obvious.

The first redesign example will show how a hand-processed system can be improved, while the second will be an example of converting a hand-data-processing system into a card-data processing system, and the third a computerized system. These will be followed by several illustrations of other systems of interest.

THE REDESIGN OF A HAND-DATA PROCESSING SYSTEM

Industrial finishes such as enamels, lacquers, and varnish are produced by the Alpha Paint Company for manufacturers of such varied products as

Figure 21–2 (cont.)

Revised System

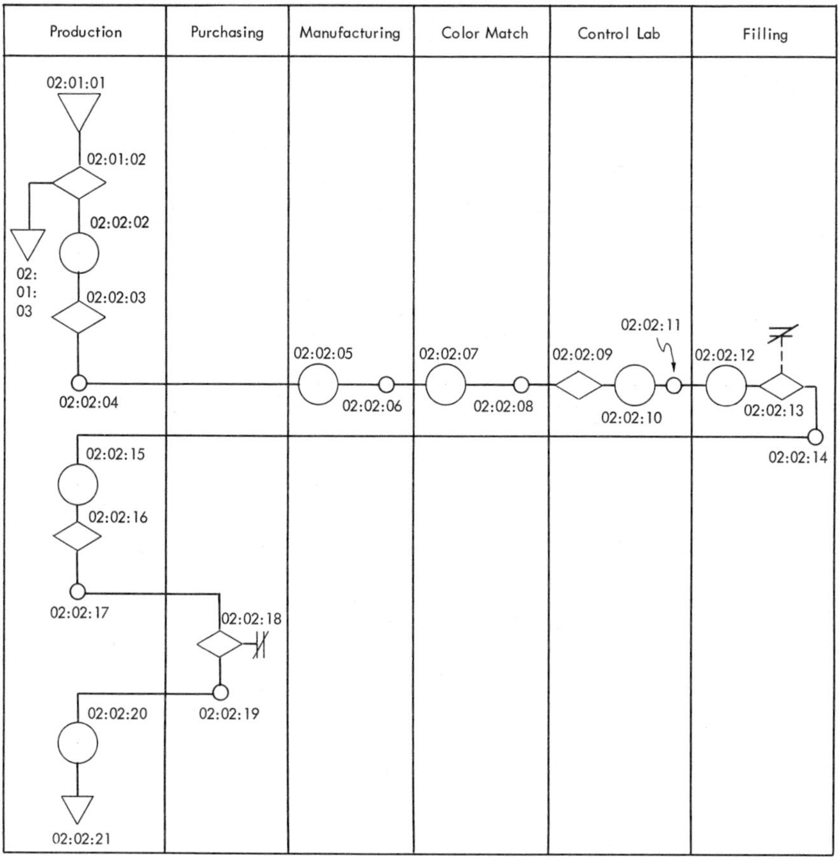

automobiles, Christmas tree ornaments, machine tools, and caskets. Alpha is a relatively small manufacturer of paint in a field dominated by giants. This has not been a deterrent to the company, however, because it has specialized in customer service.

The Alpha Paint Company maintains two manufacturing plants. One on the east coast serves that area while the other in the midwest serves the midwest and western part of the United States. Each plant operates independently and has its own sales force. The two plants exchange and store each other's paint formulas to safeguard against loss by fire.

The manufacturing in the midwest plant is done on a job-lot basis, with

Figure 21–3

Present and Revised System Design for the Invoice

Present System

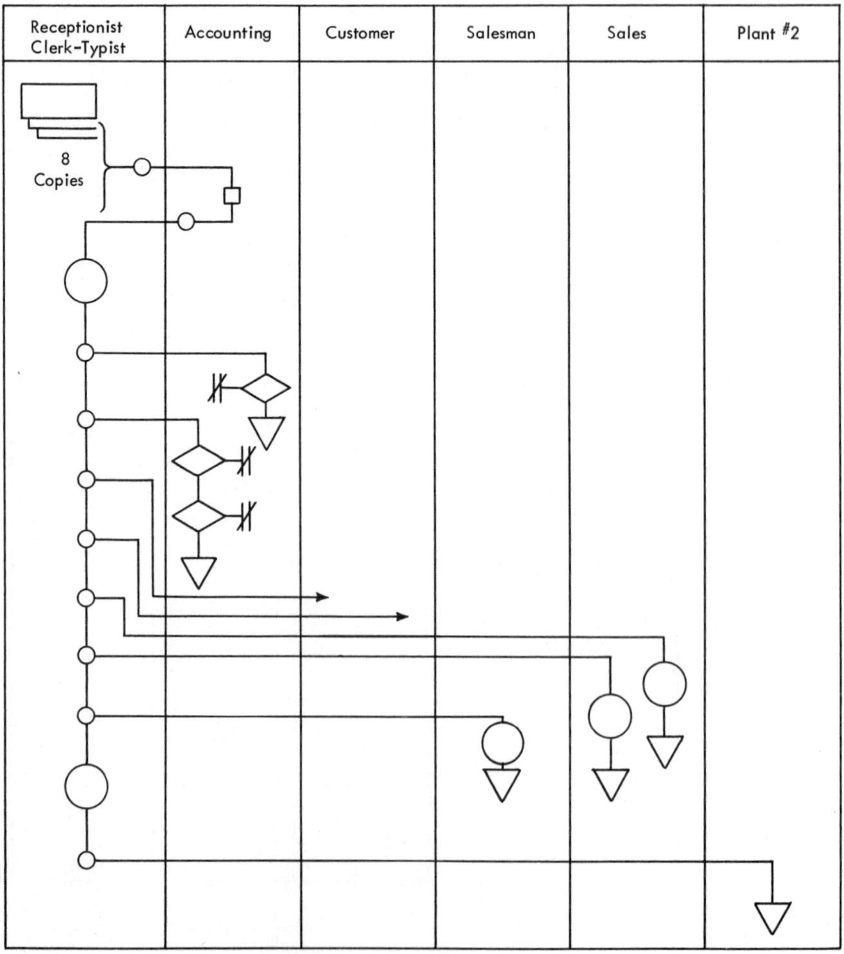

the minimum lot size being maintained at 30 gallons. Raw materials are purchased from vendors and are ground, blended, and packaged in this factory. The lots are manufactured to standard formulas or specifications presented by the customer. Specifications may be nothing more than a chip of paint from a used piece of machinery.

Excluding the sales staff, there are between 60 and 70 regular employees organized into purchasing and accounting, laboratory, production control, manufacturing, filling, and shipping.

The problem of interest here is the present production control system, which starts with the sales order and terminates with the invoice. It consists of the following forms:

Figure 21–3 (cont.)

Revised System

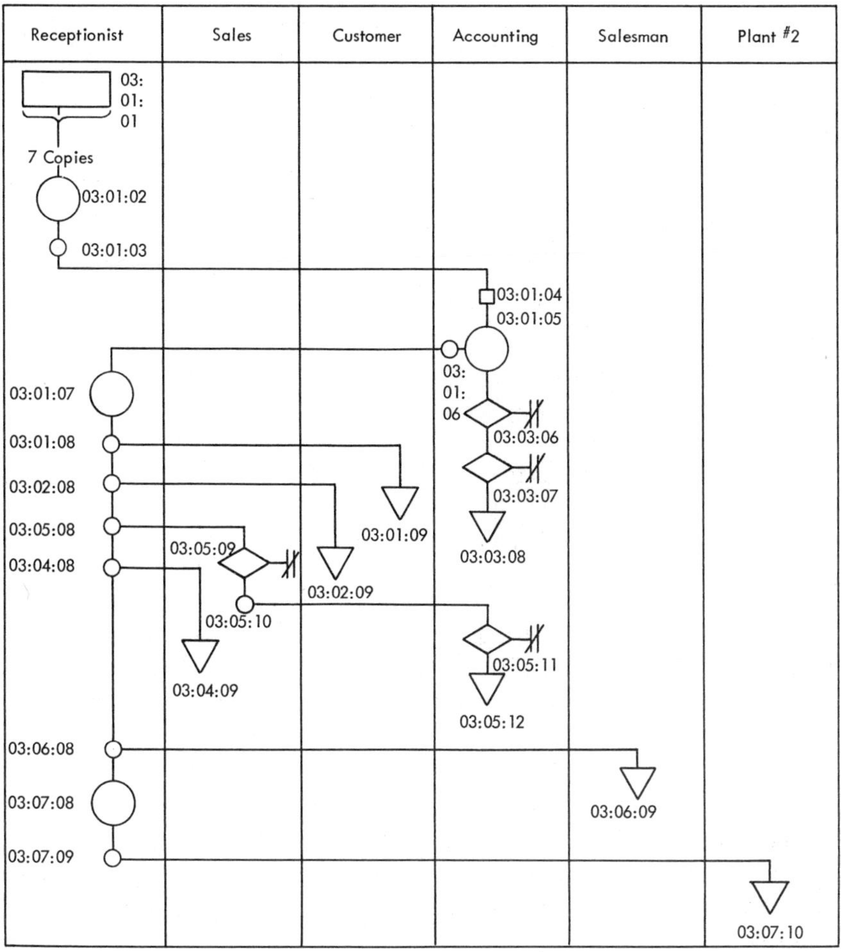

1. *Sales order:* This form initiates the sales transaction. It is a specially designed multiple-copy, multiple-colored form, typical of those used for this application.
2. *Master formula card:* This is used for processing information and instructions needed to produce a particular batch of material.
3. *Formula requirement sheet:* This denotes characteristics of the paint, such as luster, color, and method of application, as well as how it is to be used and tested in the laboratory. This form is used only with new orders.
4. *Invoice:* Like any invoice, this form serves notice that the material has been shipped, and it also states the terms of the sale.

The analysis of this system is given in the same series of steps discussed before, so you should have little difficulty following the developments.

Record and Analyze the Organizational Structure. This is a relatively small organization, which includes chemists and other highly specialized personnel. Consequently, there is little opportunity to improve upon the organizational structure.

Make a Flow Chart of the Present System. The flow chart could be drawn to show the entire system under consideration, but it would be too cluttered with details for practical purposes. Therefore it is divided into three separate flow charts, shown on pages 558–63.

1. Figure 21–1 shows the present and revised system for the sales order.
2. Figure 21–2 shows the present and revised system for the master formula card.
3. Figure 21–3 shows the present and revised system for the invoice.

(Notice that the formula requirement sheet has been combined with the sales order so that a flow chart is not needed.)

Redesign the System with a Revised Flow Chart. Following each of the original flow charts can be seen the redesigned system, also represented by a flow chart. Positioning the charts this way should make it easier to compare and study the changes which will be discussed.

Redesign of Forms. The forms were redesigned and will be discussed in detail. The checklist in Chapter 11 was used to make sure that all of the possible changes were included.

Record the New System in a Standard Operating Procedure. The Standard Operating Procedure for the new system is illustrated in Figure 21–4. You will notice that this follows the same general format discussed earlier in Chapter 11. A number of improvements were made to the system, which should be pointed out.

Changes Made in the Sales Order System

The information contained on the formula requirement sheet has been included in the lower portion of each filling copy of the sales order. This eliminates the formula requirement sheet and places the information where it can be used conveniently.

Figure 21–4

Standard Operation Procedure

:01 SALES ORDER

XX: XX: XX:

Form No. → first XX
Copy No. → second XX
Step No. → third XX

SALES DEPARTMENT

01:01:01 thru 01:09:01	Type multiple part form. Complete all items on the upper part of form except "Shipped To." Number each order consecutively. Pricing data is obtained from the Customer Record or will be computed if no information is available in customer record. Place no more than three (3) types of finish on any one order form.
01:01:02	Place form in tickler file by promised date.
:03	Remove form from file on promised date or upon receipt of completed Shipping Copy (01:07).
:04	Complete lower portion of form using data extracted from the Shipping Copy. If the order has not been shipped by promised date investigate cause of delay.
:05	Attach copy :03 of Bill of Lading and original customer order.
:06	File in Customer File alphabetically by name of customer.
01:02:02	Mail to customer.
01:03:02 *	Enter suggested basic formula information on lower portion of form.
:03 *	Send form to Production Department.
01:06:02	Send form to Production Department.
01:07:02	Send form to Receptionist (clerk-typist).
:12	Extract quantity shipped and date shipped and enter on lower portion of Sales Copy (01:01). Initial form to indicate posting.
:13	Send form to Receptionist.
01:08:02	Send form to Receptionist (clerk-typist).
01:09:02	Mail form to Salesman.

PRODUCTION

01:03:04 *	Extract formula data for the preparation of the Batch Data Sheet (02:02).
:05 *	Attach form to Batch Data Sheet.
:06 thru :23 *	Form accompanies Batch Data Sheet. See 02:02:03 thru 02:02:20.
:24 *	Attach form to Expedite Copy (01:06).
:25 *	File in Production Record File (see 01:06:06).
01:06:03	Extract order information and record in Order Log.
:04	Place form in tickler file by date promised.
:05	Remove from file on date promised or upon return of Filling Copies (01:03 thru 01:05). Attach Filling Copies. If Fill-

Figure 21–4 (cont.)

Standard Operation Procedure

	ing Copies not available by date promised, investigate cause of delay.
:06	File form plus attached Filling Copies in Production Record File for two years.
ACCOUNTING	
01:07:17	Verify information contained on Invoice (03).
:18	Extract cost data for Accounts Receivable.
:19	Detach Invoice and Copy :01 of Bill of Lading.
:20	Send form to Shipping Department.
SHIPPING	
01:07:06	Place form in tickler file by date promised.
:07	Upon receipt of order from Filling remove form from file. Attach Filling Tag(s) form 12 to form :07.
:08	Extract information from form and attached tags for preparation of Bill of Lading form L-9.
:09	Extract information from the form and attached tags for Gallonage Report entries.
:10	Attach copies :01 and :03 of Bill of Lading to form.
:11	Send form with attachments to Sales Department.
:21	Place form in Shipping File for two years.
CLERK-TYPIST	
01:07:03	Type labels from information extracted from form.
:04	Attach labels to form.
:05	Send form with attached labels to Shipping Department.
:14	Extract information from form and attached Bill of Lading for the preparation of Invoice (form 03).
:15	Attach completed invoice to form.
:16	Send form with attachments to Accounting Department.
01:08:03	Place in temporary file.
:04	Remove from file upon receipt of proofread invoice from Accounting. Attach Storage Copy of Invoice (03:07) and Copy 01 of Bill of Lading to form.
:05	Mail form with attachments to Plant No. 2 for file storage.

* Follow same procedure for 01:04 and 01:05.

Portions of the filling copy of the sales order are blocked out to prevent errors, and lines were added to assist in making out the form.

Blanks for certain shipping data were added to the lower portion of the sales copy, 01:01. The entry of data in this section assures that all the necessary information is contained in the customer's file without the necessity of filing the shipping copy, 01:07.

Two copies of the original sales order—the traffic and accounting copies—have been eliminated. The checking of the accounting copy is eliminated, although a spot check with the shipping or storage copies is possible when they are in the hands of the clerk-typist.

The sales department, in the revised system, will use the sales copy, 01:01, for its tickler file and also, with the shipping data added, this copy can be used for the permanent customer's file. Shipping will use the shipping copy, 01:07, for its tickler file and place it into a permanent file upon its return from the accounting department. This will eliminate the need for the traffic copy.

Formula Card

The important change on this form (Figure 21–5) is the way the information is grouped. The master formula data are separated from the batch data information. The worker now concentrates his attention on the lower portion of the card while the standard data are available for reference at the top of the card. Columns have also been added for the checks by the purchasing and manufacturing departments to avoid confusion. Other changes are self-explanatory.

Figure 21–5

Alpha Paint Company Revised Formula Card

CUSTOMER____________________ DATE__________

FORMULA REQUIREMENT SHEET

Suggested Basic Formula:

Match: Wet sample	( )	for Color:	( )	
Panel	( )	Gloss:	( )	
Other (see below)	( )	HP:	( )	
____________		Other:	( )	__________

Apply by: Surface:
Coats: Thinner: Reduction:
Type oven: Type heat:
Cure:
Article: To be used on:
Made of:

Exposure: Interior ( ) Exterior: ( ) Remarks________
Bleeder: Acceptable ( ) Not acceptable: ( )
Price: Inexpensive ( ) MAX. R.M.:____________
Special tests and/or remarks:______________

Invoice Form

The statements of the conditions of the sale appearing at the bottom of the form have been deleted from all copies except the customer's copy. In addition, copy titles such as sales copy, statistical copy, etc., have been moved from the top of the page to the lower margin where they can be easily seen.

The district sales manager's copy has been eliminated. This copy, which was formerly filed for income tax purposes, has been replaced by the statistical copy, 03:05. Information from the statistical copy is extracted by both the statistics clerk and the tax record clerk, but is filed in the income tax record file.

The Formula Requirement Form

This form is no longer necessary in the system, for, as you will recall, this was combined with the filling copy of the sales order.

Even though this is a relatively small company and the system is simple, some important and worthwhile improvements were made. These are typical rewards which can be gained by some elementary tools of system analysis.

THE REDESIGN OF A SYSTEM FOR CARD-DATA PROCESSING[2]

We will start with a manually operated system in this example and show how it can be redesigned for card-data processing. Since the system has already been established for the manual method, we will start with the flow charts, system forms, and the standard operating procedure. Consequently, the present manual system will be illustrated, followed by the card-data processing system.

The history of the Beta Gear Company extends back to near the turn of the century, when the automobile first became an important means of transportation. Since that time the company has manufactured special gears and has recently been shipping as many as 50,000 gear assemblies per month. These units are sold to the manufacturers of automobiles, trucks, military vehicles, and machines such as street cleaners, and materials-handling trucks. Since some of the larger automobile companies manufacture their own special gears, the Beta Gear Company generally deals with the smaller manufacturers.

The factory is organized on a modified job shop basis, and all the machining is done in the confines of one factory building where some 800 people are employed. The processing equipment consists of automatic screw machines, drill presses, punch presses, and standard and special gear cutting machinery. Assembly of the complex gear train is done on an assembly line. Special parts, such as bearings and most fasteners, are purchased from the outside, as are all of the castings.

Because of the complexity of the product and the customer service requirements, production control is an extensive function with 27 employees. It is the design of this production control system which is to be discussed here.

---

[2] Abstracted from an analysis by Stanley J. Domal.

Record and Analyze the Organizational Structure. The company has recently gone through an organizational study which resulted in a number of changes, so no other changes are warranted at this time. Eventually, when the card-data processing system is installed and the production control system is integrated with the others, changes within the organizational structure and new assignments will be made.

To begin with, a committee composed of representatives from the accounting, industrial engineering, production control, and sales departments was established. The person in the factory with the greatest card-data processing know-how was in the payroll department of the accounting office and was assigned to work with the head of production control. The committee reported once a week to the president or senior vice-president. The committee had the authority to discuss any possible changes with the factory personnel involved, and also the responsibility of keeping all factory employees informed of any changes which might affect them.

Make a Flow Chart of the Present System. The flow chart of the present system is illustrated in Figure 21–6. This system has been revised in the past and is an acceptable design for the manual system. The form numbers and the flow-chart symbols are given on the diagram for your convenience.

Sales orders are made in six copies, five of which are routed to the various departments in the company. Copy No. :05 is received in the production department and there receives a tentative date for production. It then goes to scheduling where a master schedule is compiled.

Production receives the master schedule from scheduling and a set of explosion cards (:04) from engineering for each order. (If the order is a repeat, explosion cards are already on file in production.) A breakdown is then made, and production schedules are written for the 12 departments in manufacturing.

One set of the departmental schedules are used, along with reports from storage and shipping, to maintain a perpetual inventory on all stocks, both finished and rough. By combining the figures, production informs purchasing what stock purchases must be made to maintain a working inventory.

Redesign the System with a Revised Flow Chart. The redesigned system for card-data processing is illustrated in Figure 21–7. Since this processing occurs primarily in the card-data processing section, the flow chart is all that is necessary, and a standard operating procedure is not usually included in the complete study.

The redesigned system would, of course, be prepared in a form suitable for presentation by the committee. Since space does not permit the entire presentation in a text, only some general comments about the changes are made here.

The system illustrated is designed to yield three reports, and all other information would remain in punched-card form unless a special need oc-

Figure 21–6

Flow Chart of Original System (Beta-Gear Company)

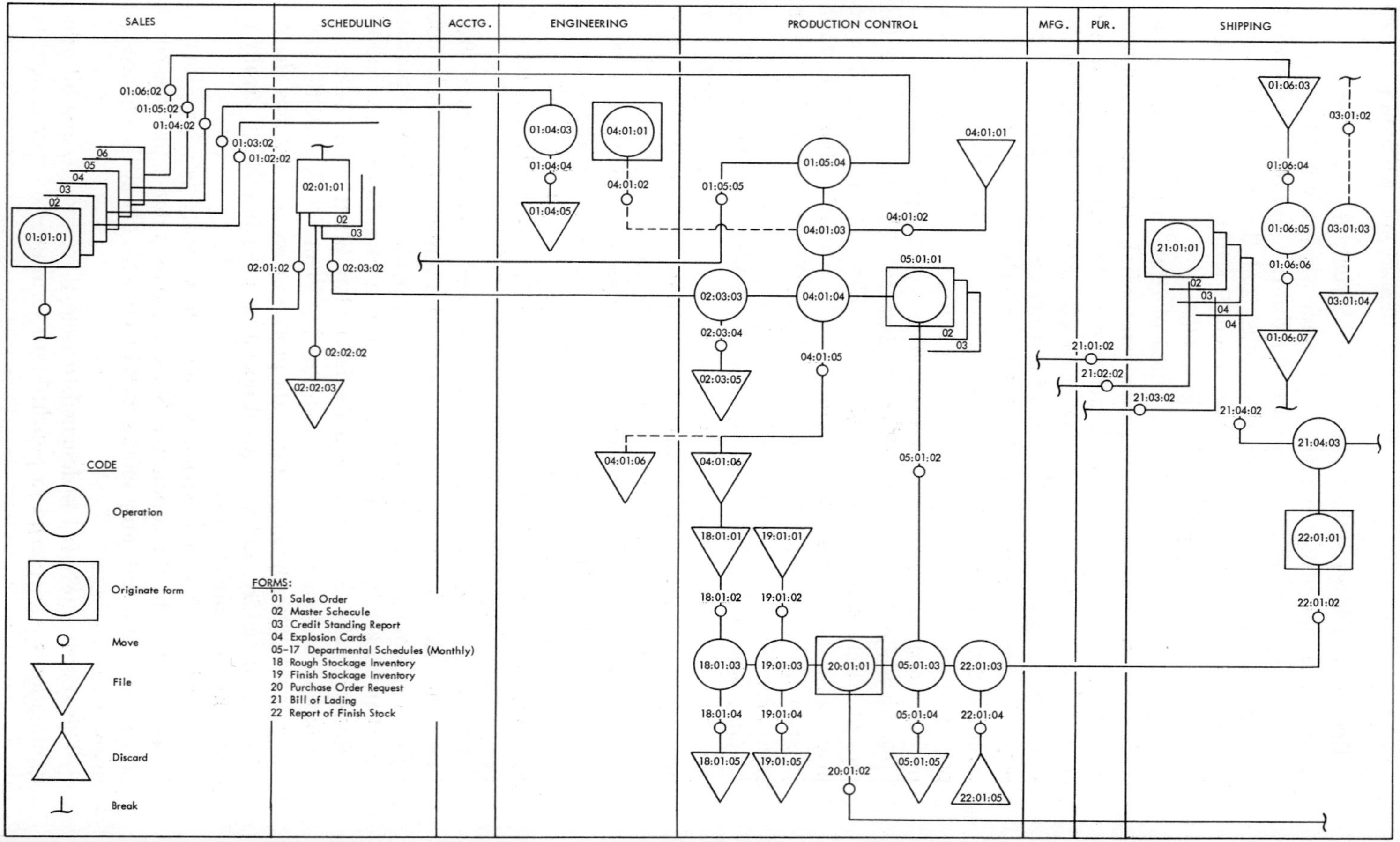

Figure 21–7

Card-Data Processing System for Beta Gear Company

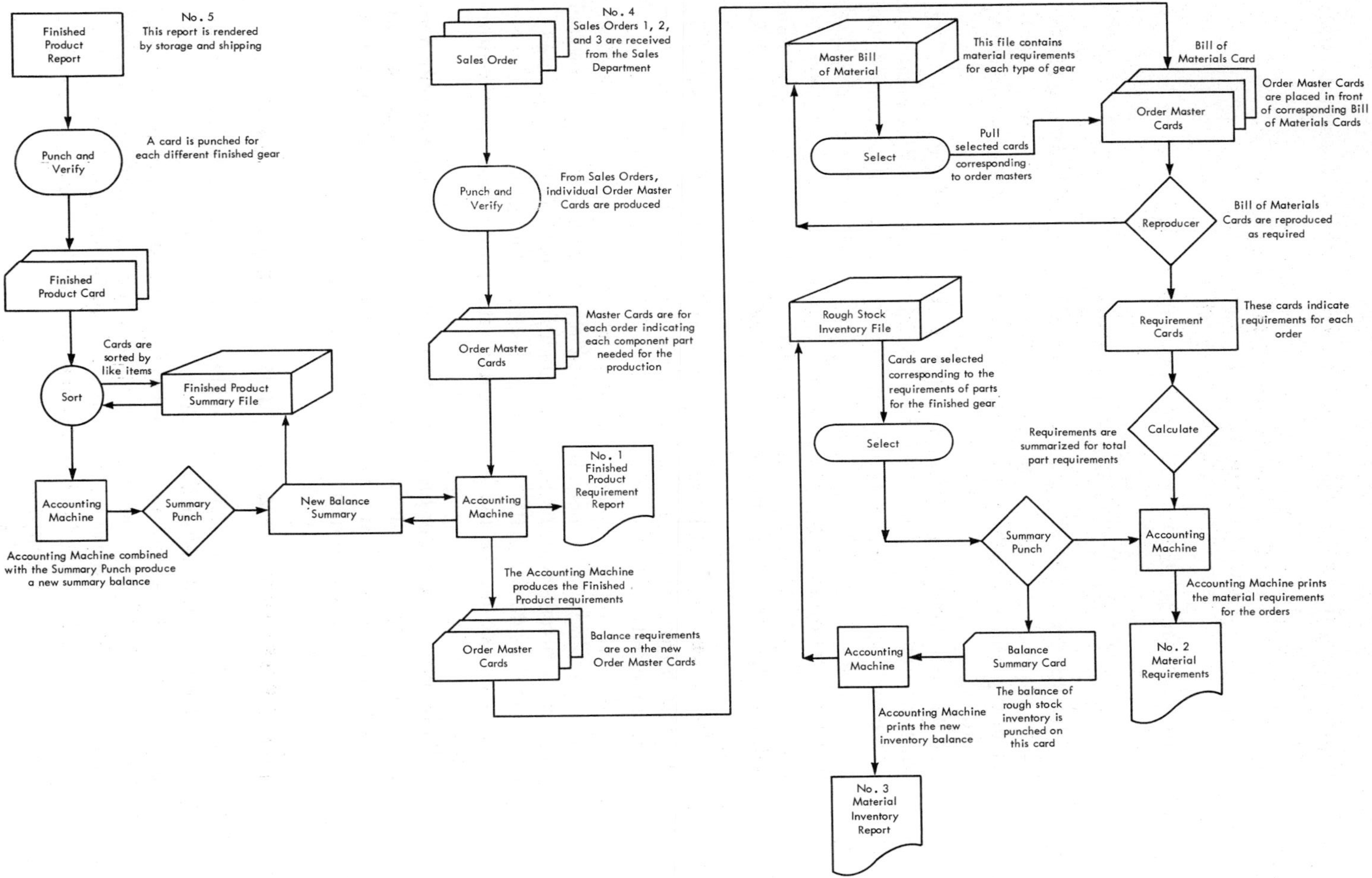

curred. These reports are shown on the flow chart and are numbered as shown below:

No. 1. Finished product requirement report,
No. 2. Materials requirement report,
No. 3. Materials inventory report.

Information is fed to the system in two forms:

No. 4. Sales orders,
No. 5. Finished product reports.

The only other time that information would be fed to the system is when bill of materials changes occur or when physical inventory counts indicate quantities which are different than those shown on the perpetual inventory record.

A finished product inventory is supplied to the production control department. These data, put in punch-card form, and sorted with the previous summary file, are summarized and put back into the finished product summary file as the new balance. Each new order, after being put into punched-data form, reduces the finished product inventory of the affected product—if any such inventory existed. The printed report produced at this point indicates the number and type of product that must be produced to fill the order.

The master order cards are then merged with the bill of materials cards and reproduced, yielding individual requirement cards for the various parts to be produced.

Total requirements are calculated and then the cards are run through the accounting machine to yield the printed report. Simultaneously, selected rough-stock inventory cards are run through a summary punch connected to the accounting machine. Balance summaries from this operation are also put through an accounting machine, yielding the printed balance inventory report.

This entire cycle is run for each order or group of orders. Not only does this system reduce the number of clerical employees used, it makes a more efficient organization, since pertinent information for decision making is obtained in a shorter time than was previously possible.

THE REDESIGN OF A SYSTEM FOR COMPUTERS

The Delta Farm Building Corporation is a large manufacturer of prefabricated farm and industrial buildings. This company, which had an unpretentious birth, is now one of the largest manufacturers of prefabricated farm and industrial buildings used for sheltering farm animals, grain, and implements. What started as primarily a farm building business has been extended to include small industrial buildings used for manufacturing, warehousing, and similar purposes.

To keep up with its growth, the company has found it necessary to keep improving its data-processing system. It first started with a manual system, went through the stage of elaborate control panels, and eventually graduated to card-data processing. From this, it was a natural step to go to a computer which could be used for payroll and accounting purposes—as well as for an extensive mortgage business. Consequently, it is impossible, within this book, to describe all of the evolutionary steps of a constantly changing system. However, Figure 21–8 illustrates the block diagram for one of the recent control systems.

The forms of particular interest in this system design are the sales order, interpreting sheet, shipping tally, bill of lading, picking tickets, invoice,

Figure 21–8

Simplified Block Diagram for Delta Farm Building Corporation

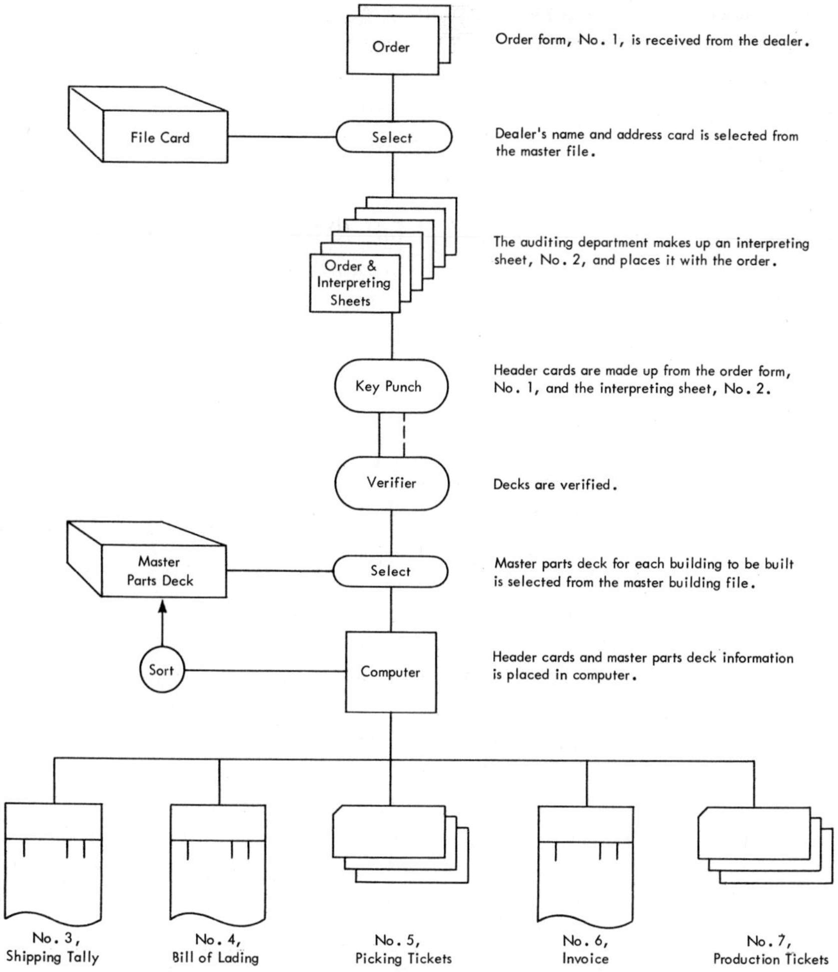

and production tickets. A brief description of these are listed below and you will find that the number of each agrees with the number on the flow chart:

1. Dealer's order: The customer's order is made up by the dealer in multiple copies. The first two are sent to the factory.
2. Interpreting sheet: The language on the order form is translated into data-processing language.
3. Shipping tally: This computer print-out is the bill of materials and is used to determine whether or not all the parts are available.
4. Bill of lading: This is the shipping manifest.
5. Picking tickets: These are attached to the parts of the building and are checked against the tally sheet when the parts of the buildings are loaded into trucks for transporting to the building site.
6. Invoice: Used for accounting purposes—one copy sent to dealer.
7. Production ticket: This is the usual authority to produce.

In addition, progress reports, which are used to set production schedules and to notify the dealer of the proposed delivery date, are printed out. As you can observe from the flow chart, a master file of dealers is kept. There is also a master parts deck for each one of the buildings listed in the advertising brochures.

The block diagram of the system just discussed was selected because of its simplicity. An improved and integrated data-processing system is illustrated in Figure 21–9. No attempt will be made to explain this elaborate chart in detail, but undoubtedly you will find it profitable to study it carefully.

Models for Designing Control Systems

Your success as a designer of control systems will depend, to a degree, upon your ingenuity in applying the right method to the right situation. Your ability to do this will reflect the scope of your experience. It is this broad knowledge that is the stock-in-trade of the consultant. As he moves from company to company he is constantly alert for new techniques which he can apply if the situation should arise. The old cliché, there is nothing new under the sun, is at least partially true. It is just a matter of obtaining broad experiences to realize that practically every idea has been tried at one time or another.

The purpose of the examples which follow is to broaden your viewpoint and let you see some ideas which have operated successfully in certain situations. These will be vignettes of control systems and no attempt will be made to give you the entire picture, but just enough to show you the unique application.

Figure 21–9

Integrated Data-Processing System for Delta Farm Building Corporation

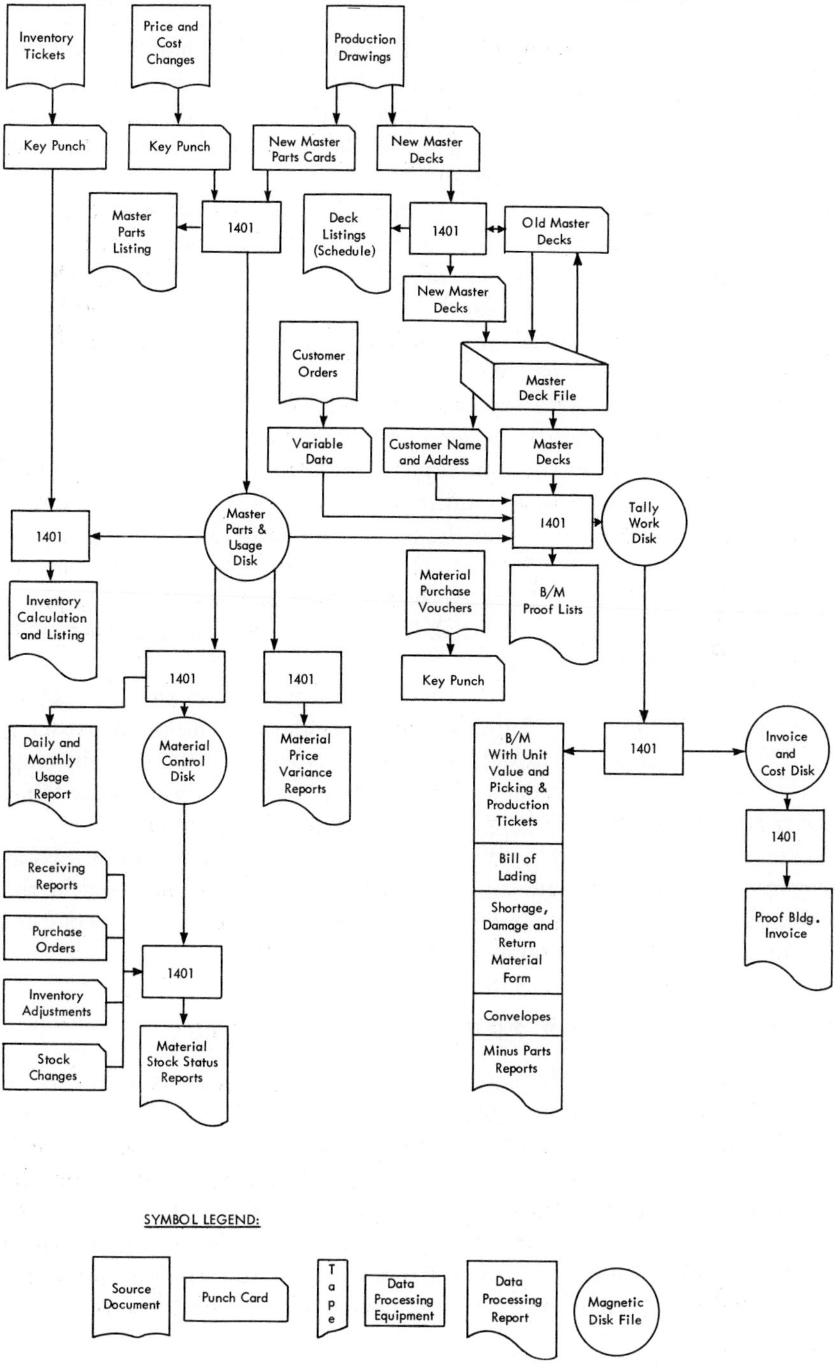

ORDER CONTROL FOR A NATIONWIDE FACTORY COMPLEX

The Aluminum Company of America coordinates its manufacturing facilities with a telephone and telegraph network which includes all the manufacturing facilities, as well as the many sales offices. All orders received by the field sales offices are relayed to the Pittsburgh office, where they are dispatched to the appropriate plant.

The procedure starts when the customer's order is written in the sales office. This order, along with the customer card and tape, are fed to the Flexowriter to obtain proof copies of the sales order, which are distributed as shown in the flow chart of Figure 21–10. As these copies are being typed, a tape is also being produced which will in turn be used to teletype the information to the Pittsburgh office.

At the Pittsburgh office the tape produced by the teletype is used to produce a four-part sales order. A serial number is assigned to the tape, which is stamped on it and on the four copies of the printed form. After certain checks for accuracy and an accounting for all orders are made, the production planning department assigns the order to a plant. The planning department retains one copy, sends one to the tabulating room, and the others to the Teletypewriter room. The tape is used to transmit the order to the plant. While the order is being transmitted, five copies of the order are being made for use in the Pittsburgh office.

At the plant the sales orders are received on tape, from which a six-part order is written. The orders are distributed as shown. The plant master is printed on master stock, backed by a black hectograph carbon for dittoing, so that many copies are available. The various production forms needed may either be obtained from the ditto process or typed from the tape.

This system took several years to develop, and although a committee was responsible for the ultimate installation, all of the people involved in the system were asked to contribute. It is a perfect example of how a complex organization can be tied together with a simple system.

A TAG SYSTEM FOR PRODUCTION CONTROL

The Perfect Circle Company, famous for its piston rings, uses tags to control production, reaping a $5,000 a year saving.

There are 14 steps in the production of the Perfect Circle piston ring—from the raw casting stores to the chrome-plating department—and the company wishes to keep track of and schedule the product through each of these steps. To do this, a printed 7- by 14-inch serrated tag (as shown in Figure 21–11) is printed by a multilith process. The information printed is the general routing data which do not change from order to order.

Figure 21–10

Flow Chart for Nationwide Control System

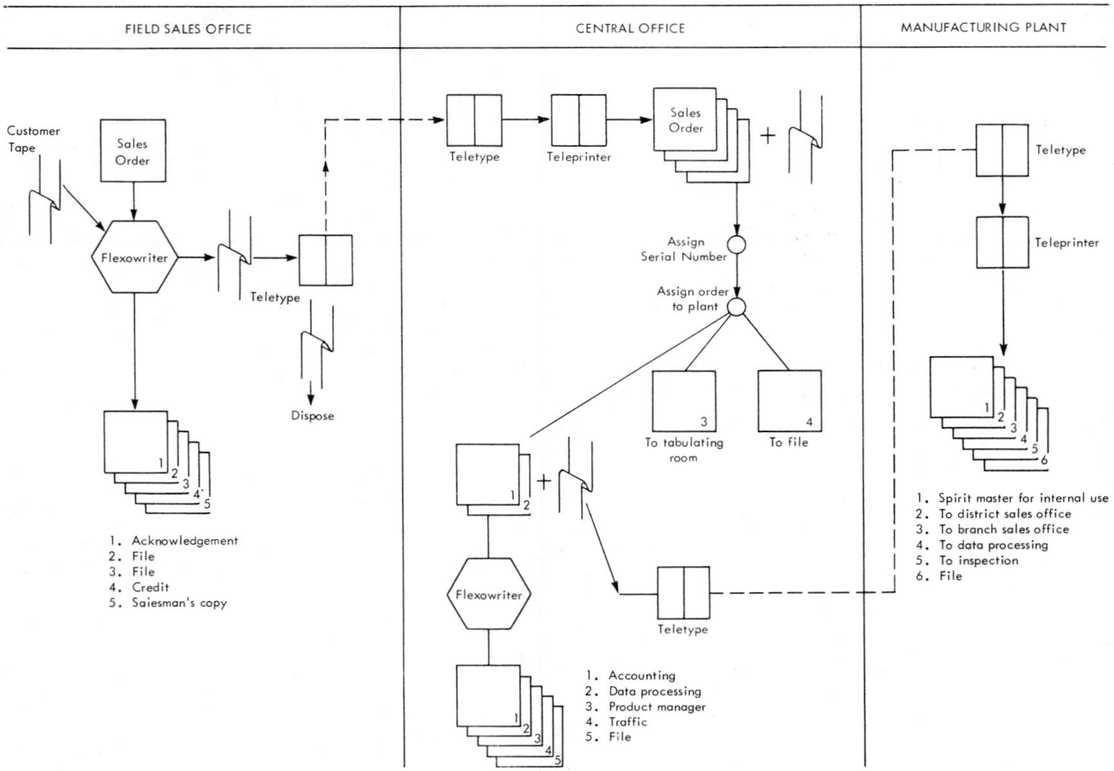

Courtesy of Aluminum Company of America

Figure 21–11

Tag Form Used at Perfect Circle Company

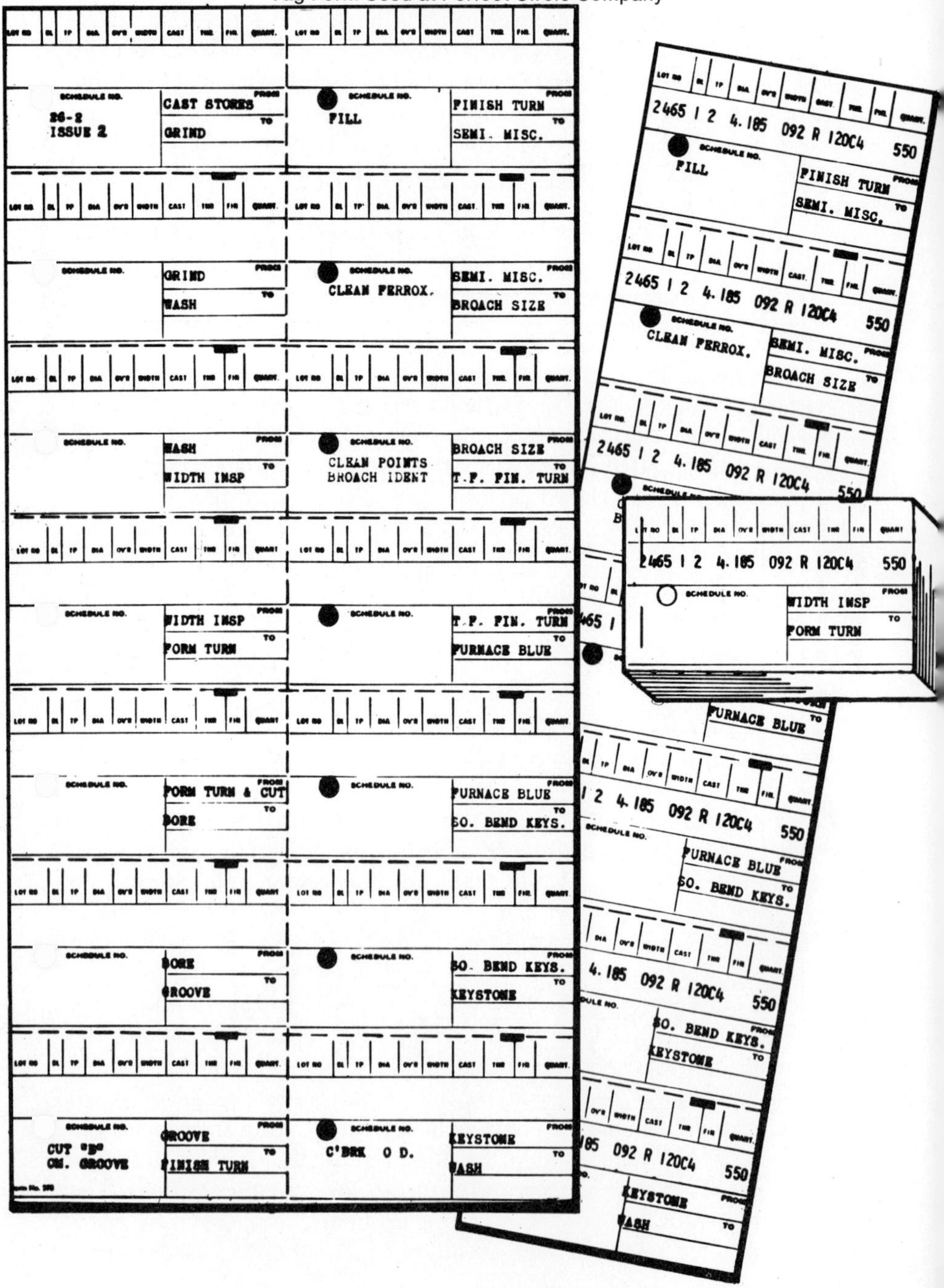

Courtesy of Dennison Manufacturing Company

After the cards are processed for general information they are separated into three strips, which are in turn run through a Dennison Dial-Set printer. Identical information is then printed on all the stubs before they are separated and stapled into a packet (as illustrated). This packet of stubs becomes part of the work order. The first stub is attached to the container of material to be processed through a first operation. When completed, the stub is sent to the scheduling department where the lot is recorded as having been completed for that stage. The second stub accompanies the material in the next operation and is eventually removed and sent to the scheduling department. By this means, the scheduling department always has a feedback of information telling where the product is. The routing stubs on the material guide the material to each subsequent operation.

PUNCHED TAGS FOR A CONTROL SYSTEM

A more sophisticated system than the one just illustrated might have used punched tags, which would have been converted to punched cards, which in turn would have been processed in the usual way to give information rapidly and on time. A slightly different application is shown in Figure 21–12 in which the punched tag is used for an inventory application. The advantages of this system should appear quite obvious.

A MAINTENANCE CONTROL SYSTEM USING EDGE-PUNCHED CARDS

Developing and operating a maintenance control system is often more difficult than designing a control system for production. The example illustrated in Figure 21–13 was developed by the Simonds Saw and Steel Company.

This company, which is engaged in the manufacture of cutting tools for use in wood working, metal working, pulp and paper, plastics, and the graphic art industries, was founded in 1832 and has a history of progressive modern management. The problem that prompted the development of the maintenance control system was an increasing backlog of maintenance work. If this backlog continued to grow it could seriously affect production and, consequently, the company's position in industry. The management was well aware that the system should not increase costs but should contribute to the profits. This was one reason they turned to edge-punched cards. The system illustrated was a first step in setting up an incentive system for workers, which resulted in income increases of 5 to 8 percent for each maintenance worker.

Figure 21–12

Punched-Tag System

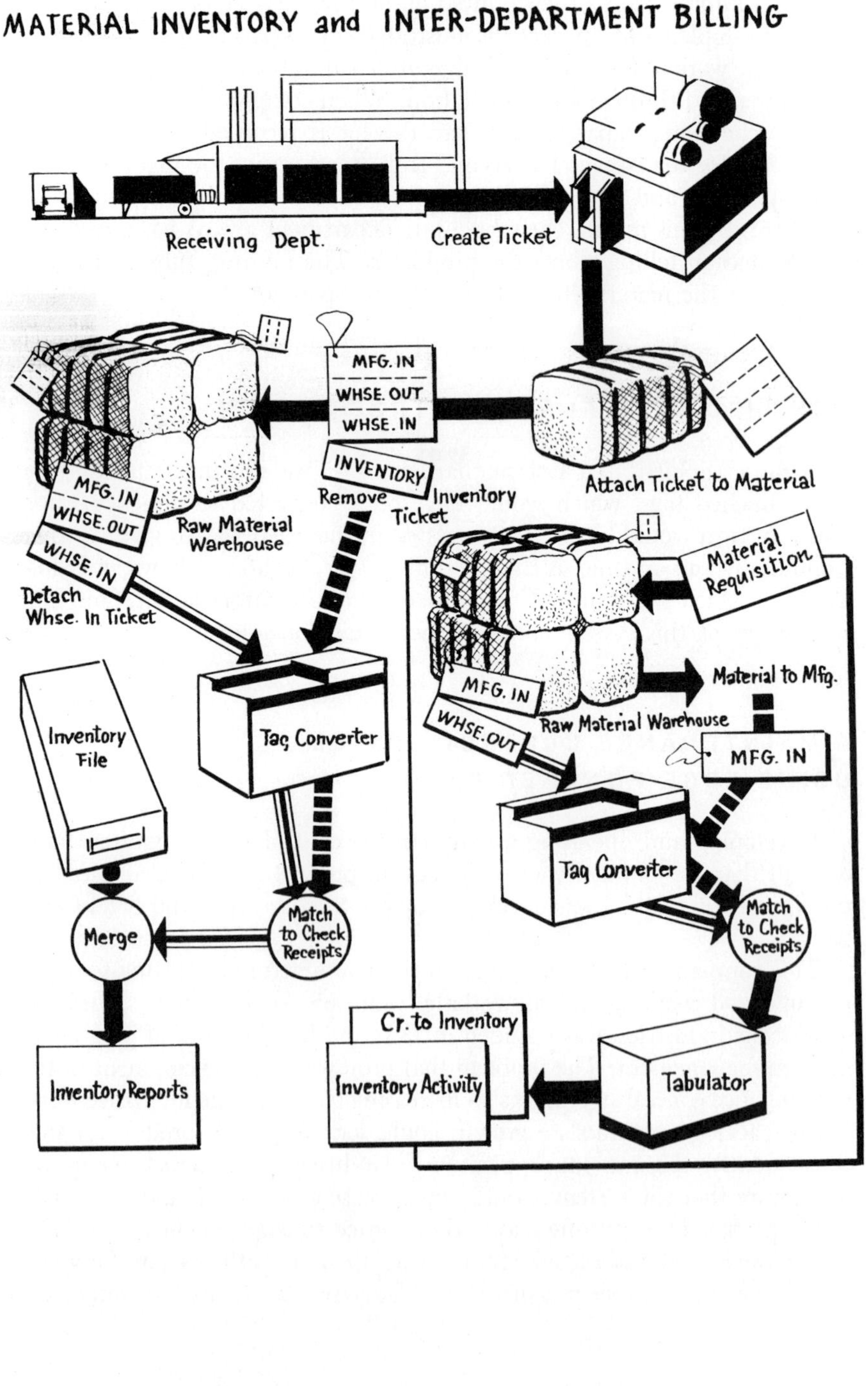

Figure 21–13

A Maintenance System Using Edge-Punched Cards

FLOW CHART SHOWING USE OF MAINTENANCE WORK ORDER FORMS AND TIME SLIPS

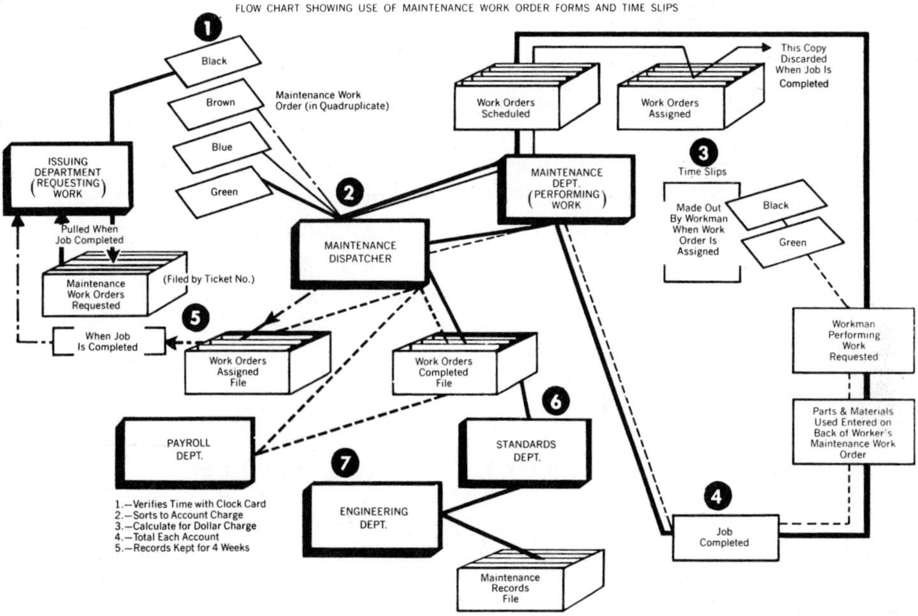

1. The nucleus of the system is the Maintenance Dispatcher, who receives maintenance requests from 40 to 50 sources, enters detail information and then distributes the orders to the various craft foreman. Approximately 1,500 Maintenance Work Orders are handled by the Maintenance Dispatcher every week.
2. The quadruplicate Maintenance Work Order form is initiated by the requesting department, giving a description of the work to be performed, time wanted, cause of trouble and other data. The issuing department then forwards three copies of the form to the Maintenance Dispatcher, keeping the top copy for its files.
3. As the orders come in, the Maintenance Dispatcher gives each one a number, using an electric numbering machine. Schedule date and priority are also entered before forwarding the order to the appropriate maintenance department. The dispatcher keeps one copy of the order in a "work order assigned" file.
4. Upon reaching the maintenance department, the orders are divided by the foreman into two groups—Emergency Jobs and Other Jobs. As each job is assigned to a workman, the date and employee clock number are entered on the order. The bottom (hard) copy of the Work Order is used by the workman as a work sheet, and is kept by him until the job is completed. The back of the Work Order is used to record issuance of parts and materials by the Stock Room.
5. The workman prepares a Time Slip for each job to which he is assigned. When the job is completed, the maintenance foreman returns the hard copy of the Work Order to the Maintenance Dispatcher, along with the workman's Time Slip (or Slips, if the job takes more than one day).
6. Information on the completed job is then sent back to the requesting department. The Time Slips and Work Orders are Keypunched simultaneously by craft and group. Then, the Time Slips are sent to the Payroll Department where further Keypunching is performed to give data for cost accounting and labor distribution, in addition to data for wage purposes.
7. The work copies of the Maintenance Work Orders (hard copies) are forwarded to the Standards Department weekly, where they are Keysorted by various factors such as department charges, work cause, maintenance craft, time groups, and delay codes. This information is used to keep the program running at the proper level.

After serving their purpose in Standards, the Work Orders are sent to Engineering. There, they are Keysorted by machine number and filed for periodic recapping of maintenance costs to each individual machine in the factory.

CENTRALIZED CONTROL PANEL FOR MONITORING PRODUCTION

If the internal control system is refined to its ultimate, it would be an example of "automation," a subject much discussed in recent years. In most cases complete automation is not economically feasible, and we find systems which are something less than automated. The centralized control panel, which monitors all work stations, is an example of such a system. Figure 21–14 shows how the Hancock Telecontrol equipment is integrated in a job shop production control system. The system parallels any other production control system up to the point where the manufacturing order and schedule are issued. The control of the factory facilities are then taken over by the centralized control system, resulting in increased efficiency and reduced costs.

CENTRALIZED INVENTORY CONTROL SYSTEM

A major manufacturer of rubber footwear produced more than 30,000 different styles at a rate exceeding 100,000 pairs a day. Before it automated its inventory control system it was possible to have more than 200,000 pairs of shoes which, because of the lag in the recording system, were not accounted for. The problem was complicated by the fact that the company maintained several large warehouses around the country to service its thousands of retail outlets. This problem was solved by Teleregister equipment, coupled with peripheral data processing equipment (as shown in Figure 21–15).

The Teleregister equipment is probably better known in the application of accounting and displaying stock market transactions, and transportation reservations; but our illustration, which is an oversimplification of the real system, shows that a tape is produced giving the stock number, size, and quantity of incoming footwear. The information on this tape is sent by wire to the main office, where it is entered as a transaction in the magnetic storage drum.

Orders, written on Flexowriters, simultaneously produce a typed copy of the shipping release and a tape which is used to record the withdrawal of material. The orders are released on a geographical basis to assure the efficient use of transportation. This planning is done by the order supervisor.

The order supervisor interrogates the memory when an order is received to determine whether or not the quantity is sufficient. The quantities available are displayed on a tote board so that decisions about filling the order can be made rapidly. If there is enough material available to fill the order, it is classified as an automatic release and the quantities are deducted from

Figure 21–14 The Use of Hancock Telecontrol in a Job Order Plant

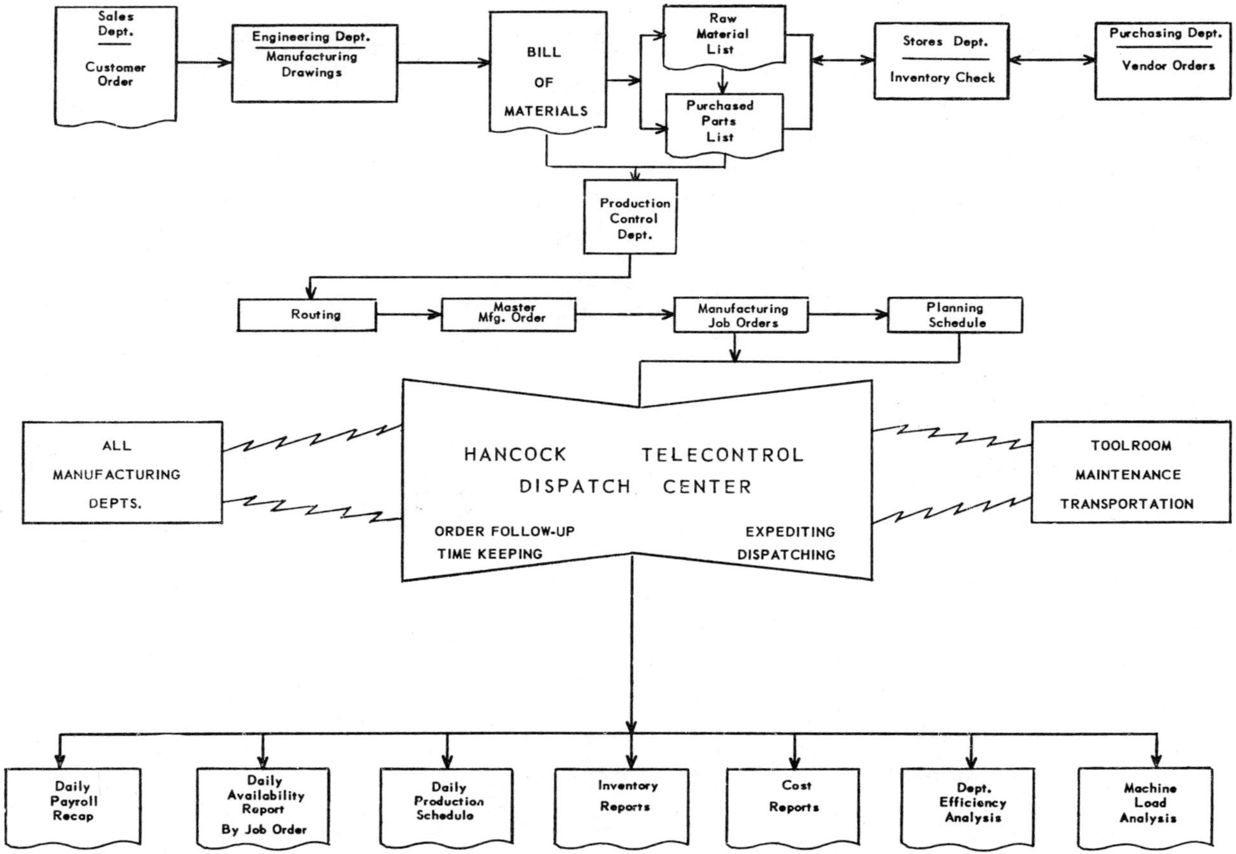

Courtesy of Hancock Telecontrol Corporation

Figure 21–15 Teleregister Magnetronic Inventory Control System

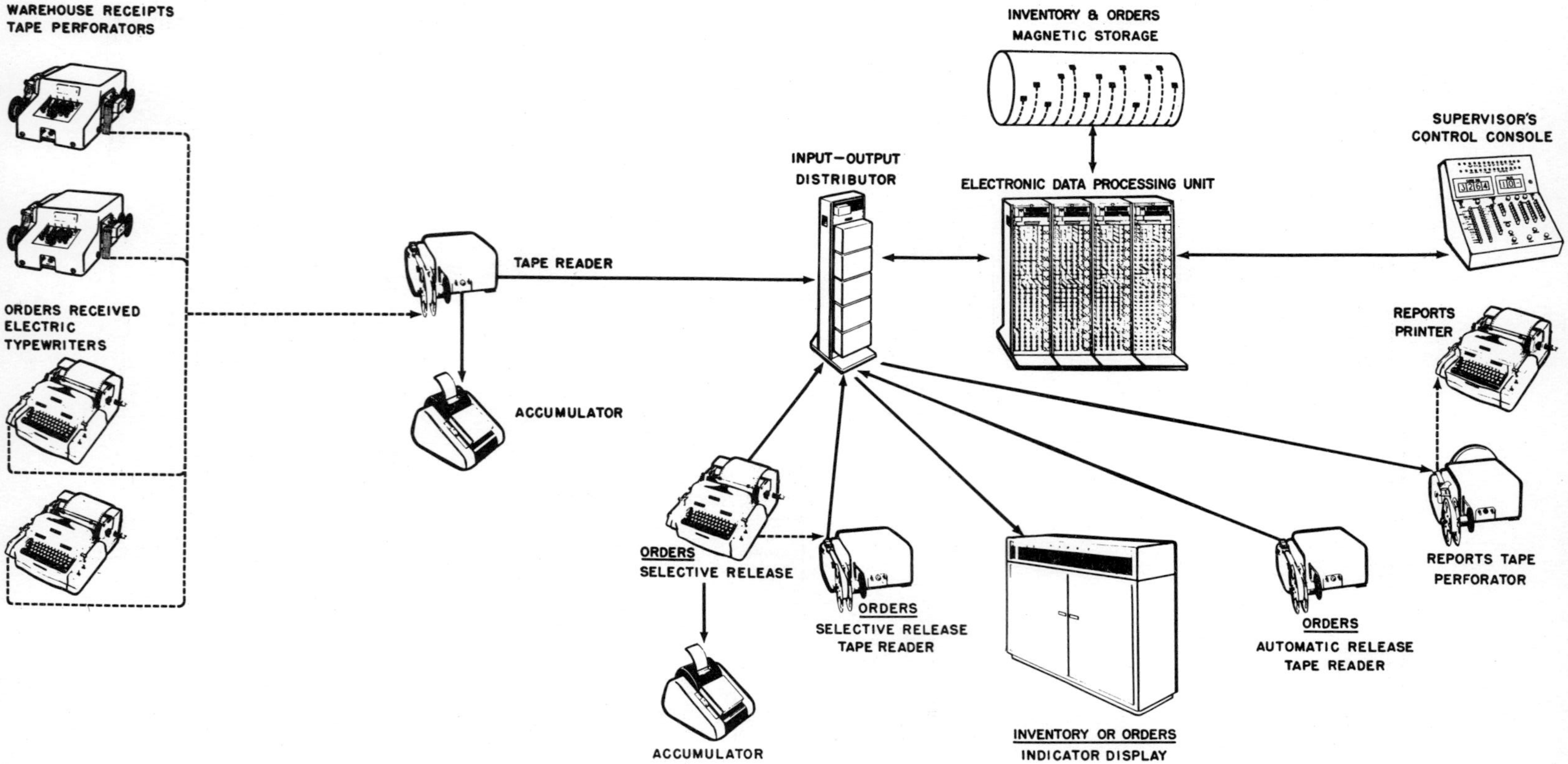

Courtesy of Bunker-Ramo Corporation

the inventory. If the quantity is not sufficient, the order is classified for selective release, in which case the order may be held, other sizes substituted, or some other line of action taken. If the product must be backordered, new release and backorder tapes must be made and processed. In addition, the system is tied to a card-processing system which makes the data available for analysis in forecasting and planning.

SUMMARY

This chapter has illustrated how the design techniques you have learned earlier can be put into action. It has also been an opportunity for you to observe some real-life systems. Regrettably, all the details of the case problem histories cannot be brought out for there is neither space nor time enough. Besides, it takes a very avid student of system designs to keep from being bored by the many details which are necessary to make the system complete.

You have had the opportunity of seeing how the system design is approached step by step. Some of these steps may be left out in certain situations, or at least pitched in a low key, but usually it is best to account for them as follows:

1. Record and analyze the organizational structure.
2. Make a flow chart of the present system.
3. Redesign the system with a revised flow chart.
4. Redesign the forms.
5. Write the standard operating procedure.
6. Introduce the system.

With a little practice, you should be able to perform these steps with skill. Don't hesitate to review (frequently) the techniques to be found in the early part of the text.

Your ability to design control systems will reflect your experience with different examples. Take every opportunity to observe and work with various systems if you wish to make a successful career in this area.

Questions

1. What are the steps in a complete system design?
2. Which steps would be of greatest importance when designing a new system?
3. Which steps would be of greatest importance when redesigning a system?
4. Evaluate the importance of the steps of system designing for hand-data processing, card-data processing, and computers.
5. What advantages are there in the tag system used at the Perfect Circle Company? In what other industry would the tag method be suitable?
6. Design a tag system using flow charts. Lay out the tags as they should be used.
7. What impact do you think a computer would have on the design of an organization?

CHAPTER 22

The Present and the Future

Production planning and control involves so many aspects of the factory operation that the study of it becomes the study of nearly the entire factory operation. From past experiences you must realize that factories vary through a broad spectrum, from inefficient operations to highly streamlined organizations doing their utmost to keep abreast of developments. Some factories have but a handful of employees while others have thousands. Some produce many different kinds of products while others produce only one standardized product. Some produce inferior products and others produce quality products. Some are under one roof while others are spread around the world, requiring a complex network of communications for coordination. As factories vary, so do the production planning and control systems vary. This means that it is impossible to generalize and say that this is the best system regardless of product, size of company, or other consideration.

It is always unnerving for the novice to discover that factories are not always the highly efficient organizations with well-developed production control departments which he has been led to expect. On the other hand, he is usually equally amazed to discover that the companies have been doing business a long time, and, what's more, are paying regular and adequate dividends.

Some factories don't use all the latest techniques for several reasons. Often the management is aware of other methods, and may have even tried these methods but discarded them because they could not be justified. It may be that the necessary personnel for making the changes have not been available. It is always possible that the management has not had time to catch up with some of the techniques. If this is true, you may be lucky enough to have the opportunity to install one or more yourself. Should this be the case, do it discreetly, with an awareness that others have spent many hours in developing what you are now applying.

Be aware of another aspect of development, too. Today, many of the papers being written about inventory control, scheduling, and other related subjects are the products of government-sponsored research or have been developed by graduate schools. More often than not these models have not been thoroughly tested in industry. If they have been tested, it has probably been in a situation where all the requirements have been met. Finding the situation where the model fits can often be as strenuous as the research itself. This does not mean these studies are valueless but it does mean that someone must take the next step and make the studies operational. There is a danger that the student reading these research studies will assume they are the "way of life" in the industrial world. Nothing could be further from the truth.

An author of a production planning and control book has a responsibility beyond relating case histories of production control systems as they are now; he should lead you into the frontiers of research and development. The student, on the other hand, has the responsibility of reading and weighing the ideas and placing them in a body of knowledge useful to himself. This body of knowledge should be in a constant state of flux as the student gains from further reading and actual experiences.

EXPANDING YOUR KNOWLEDGE

Many publications contain information about production planning and control. Some of these are commercial publications, sponsored by publishers for financial reasons. Often these articles will be of the how-to-do-it variety and will contain few if any sophisticated ideas. They will give you confidence in making applications.

Another important source of information is to be found in the publications of various professional societies. It would be difficult to classify these societies, or even to be sure of having an up-to-date listing, but look to groups representing these areas to publish useful information:

- Production and inventory control
- Accounting and cost accounting
- Management
- Economics
- Systems and procedures
- Operations research
- Industrial engineering

The publications put out by these groups will range all the way from how the Sew and Sew Garment Company redesigned its production forms to scheduling models which will require computer facilities more costly than the manufacturing facilities they are intended to schedule.

THE APICS REPORT

In recent years the American Production and Inventory Control Society[1] has been formed for those particularly interested in production and inventory control. It is undoubtedly the most active society, representing people who are actually involved in the day-to-day operations of these functions. To them we must express a debt of gratitude for cooperating with *Factory* magazine to produce a survey of common practices.[2]

Factory magazine sent the questionnaires for its survey to 1,500 members of the American Production and Inventory Control Society and received 453 replies, representing 387 plants in the United States. The typical respondent was a "production and control manager," from 30 to 40 years old, with a college education either in science or engineering. He reports to the plant or production manager, and his background is production, engineering, or sales. The size and type of industry that the respondent represents is shown in Figures 22–1 and 22–2. The results of this extensive survey are summarized in the following paragraphs.

Figure 22–1

Size of Plants in Survey

Size of Plants	*No. of Plants*	%
Under 200	48	12
200– 500	104	27
500–1000	101	26
1000–2000	46	12
2000–3000	30	8
3000–5000	20	5
Over 5000	9	3
Not identified	29	7
Total	387	100

Figure 22–2

Type of Plants in Survey

Type of Industries	*No. of Plants*	%
Heavy processing	26	7
Light processing	57	15
Heavy assembly	48	12
Light assembly	155	40
Benchwork assembly ..	36	9
Other fabrication	65	17
Total	387	100

Production and Inventory Control Organizations

Figure 22–3 shows how extensive the responsibilities of the production and inventory control departments are. It is interesting to notice what appear to be the basic responsibilities:

1. Establishing inventory levels
2. Scheduling production through the plant
3. Dispatching production orders
4. Some control over raw materials and inventories

[1] 330 South Wells Street, Chicago 6.

[2] Material is abstracted from an article, *Exclusive Survey of Production and Inventory Control*, Factory, April, 1961; reprinted by special permission of FACTORY, McGraw-Hill, Inc. The survey was conducted by the American Production and Inventory Control Society.

Figure 22–3

Major Responsibilities

What are major responsibilities of P&IC?

Activity	Responsible (%)	Others also responsible	(%)
Production planning			
Levels of production	77	Production manager	8
Plant capacity studies	50	Chief industrial engineer	15
Release new products for production	50	Chief product engineer	24
Participate in sales forecast	**35**	Sales manager	**36**
Authorize new product tooling	**18**	Chief industrial engineer	**24**
Levels of inventories for:			
Work in process	88	Plant manager	3
Production materials	81	Procurement	5
Finished goods	70	Sales manager	9
Decide to manufacture new products	**25**	Top management	11
Customer service			
Delivery schedules	76	Sales manager	10
Delivery promises	76	" "	11
Answers for customer follow-ups	**48**	" "	28
Order records	**46**	" "	26
Instructions to ship	**44**	" "	28
Shipping department			
Control of physical quantities of finished goods	**65**	Shipping foreman	5
Traffic			
Routing shipments	**27**	Traffic department	**36**
Routing purchased goods	**23**	Procurement	**32**
		Traffic	**26**
Production control			
Product routing	55	Chief industrial engineer	9
Make-or-buy decisions	**37**	Chief product engineer	11
Production orders			
Preparation and issue	91	Production manager	1
Order frequency (no. of runs)	90	Plant manager	1
Quantity determination	90	Sales manager	2
Scheduling product through factory	87	Plant manager	2
Estimating manufacturing lead time	87	Production manager	2
Machine loading scheduled products	77	" "	3
Scrap allowances	68	Chief product engineer	3
Dispatching			
Schedules and instructions	91	Production manager	2
Follow-up reporting	87	" "	2
Expediting in plant	87	" "	2
Control quantity of work-in-process	82	Plant manager	5
Intra-plant traffic	66	" "	3
Controlling raw material inventories			
Control quantity of production material	78	Procurement director	7
Placing purchase requisition	77	" "	11
Record keeping	75	" "	9
Determine item inventory level	75	" "	9
Determine order frequency	73	" "	14
Determine inventory reserves	71	" "	10
Determine order quantity	70	" "	16
Control operating supplies inventory	53	" "	10
" " " quanties	**48**	" "	11
Determine purchase lead time	**36**	" "	**51**

It is of further interest to observe how P&IC shares responsibilities with the other organizational functions. Routing of purchased goods is usually the responsibility of the traffic or purchasing department, but in 25 percent of the plants this was being done in production control.

In 37 percent of the plants the make-or-buy decision rested with the P&IC group. In 30 percent of the plants, P&IC did not have the responsibility for raw materials inventory, although it would seem to be one of its primary functions. This may have come about because 27 percent of the companies reported they did not have separate inventory control groups.

In as many as 21 percent of the companies there was no formal control organization, while 27 percent had no adequate job descriptions. Fifty-one percent of the companies had no formal training program for positions in the control department and 61 percent had no procedures manual.

A report of the number of people employed in P&IC is revealing (Figure 22–4). The range was between 1 and 10 percent of the total employed, with

Figure 22–4

People Needed for P&IC

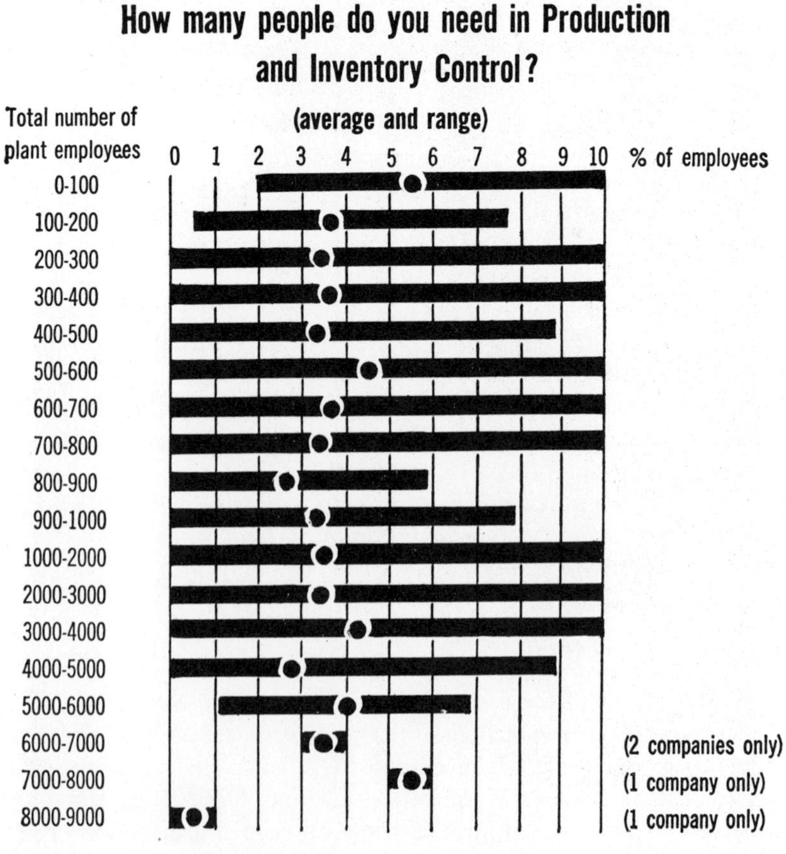

3½ percent being about average. As the plant size grows larger, apparently the percentage goes down.

Eighty percent of the plants measured effectiveness of inventory management, but 14 percent gave it no attention (Figure 22–5). Seventy-two percent measured the efficiency of production control by such means as comparing actual production with planned production, the overtime required for direct labor, and also the percentage of machine utilization.

Figure 22–5

Measuring Effectiveness

Are you measuring effectiveness of...		% of plants	How?	% using
inventory control?	Yes	80	Inventory turnover	86
	No	14	Dollar investment	89
	No answer	6	Return on investment	41
			Obsolescence	60
			Surplus	56
production control?	Yes	72	Actual vs. planned	90
	No	17	Overtime (hourly workers)	75
	No answer	11	Machine utilization	39

Sales Forecasting

Sales forecasting is still a seat-of-the-pants procedure in most companies (Figure 22–6). Most of the forecasting was limited to less than four months in advance, while about 40 percent tried to extend it to a year. A few, 17 percent, forecast as far as five years in advance.

Less than 20 percent of the companies placed any faith in the estimate of the customers. Most of them relied on sales department estimates, but the most surprising thing is that 80 percent of the P&IC groups adjusted this information in some manner before it went into the production figure. The number of companics using the statistical methods for forecasting was, as can be seen, surprisingly low.

The most important factor in planning production is the forecast, but it is not the only one. In a good many plants it is done by executive opinion, as shown in Figure 22–7. The basis for the decision is also revealed in this interesting table.

Inventory Control

Only 49 percent of the companies used the ABC method of classifying and controlling their raw materials inventories and supplies. In 70 percent of the plants, raw materials inventories were calculated by adjusting for abnormal use or deliveries during the lead time. Only 20 percent of the plants used a mathematical formula based on normal distribution of prob-

Figure 22–6

Methods of Sales Forecasting

How are sales forecasts developed?

	Number of plants	5-year	Annual	Quarterly	Monthly	Moving 12-month	Moving 3-month
By estimates from:							
Customers	81	6	63	27	38	15	27
Salesmen	118	15	96	50	45	20	25
Sales managers	186	49	163	71	70	31	34
Executives	150	65	135	42	51	20	32
Market analysis	119	61	104	36	35	21	26
Company's share of market	130	62	122	25	21	17	11
By statistical methods:							
Correlation with economic indicators	58	32	58	22	15	9	11
Trend and cycle analysis	69	27	49	22	33	24	20
Leading series	19	3	10	4	5	3	2
Charted control limits	34	17	17	11	23	7	16
By historical averages:							
Without adjustment	21	6	26	7	13	7	11
Adjusted for current demand of orders	104	10	51	50	73	19	39
Adjusted by latest sales information	138	21	84	66	91	26	36
Adjusted by statistical formula smoothing	33	5	23	13	16	19	15

ability. The methods used for calculating orders for raw materials are shown in Figure 22–8.

Scheduling and Loading

For short production runs, one operation completed before the next one is started was preferred three to one. For long production runs, 53 percent of the companies overlapped schedules.

For loading machines, time standards adjusted for incentive pace and downtime were used in 45 percent of the plants. Historical averages were used 22 percent of the time. Estimates from industrial engineers were used only 15 percent of the time, while those produced by production control were used 12 percent of the time. Some mathematical methods were used for loading by 30 percent of the respondents.

Scheduled dispatching was 70 percent centralized, with schedules being

Figure 22–7

Determining Production and Inventory Levels

What determines production output? ...and inventory levels?

This method	In these plants	Of raw materials	Of work in process	Of finished goods
Executive opinion	**171**	94	82	140
Over-all financial considerations	153	**164**	**116**	**172**
Employment level and seasonal fluctuations	156	44	82	109
Production plan related to:				
Over-all sales forecast	**191**	96	90	136
Details in sales forecast	160	100	**107**	140
Total plant load by applying re-order point on EOQ for each product	75	70	71	66
Optimum inventory calculation	63	69	50	64
Inventory turnover	83	**106**	80	117
Linear programing	23	13	16	13
Other calculations	12	7	8	8
Other methods	23	19	19	11

Figure 22–8

Determining Raw Material Quantities

What methods are used for calculating orders for raw materials?

(quantities and frequencies)

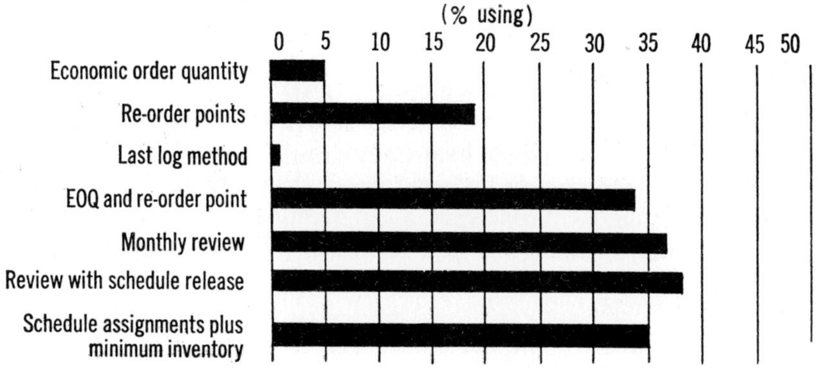

sent directly to the foreman. Only 27 percent of the companies used a chief dispatcher, who released work through departmental dispatchers.

The use of tabulating equipment and computers is very limited in scheduling.

Processing Data

In this study some companies reported that they had no way to process data (Figure 22–9). As could be expected, punched cards, next to manual

Figure 22–9

Information Processing

is information processed efficiently?

This information	...Is processed by this method (%) Manually	Control boards	Edge-notched cards	Punched card tab. equipment	Computer	No method
Customer delivery schedules and order backlog	58	7	2	27	10	4
Production order:						
Quantity and timing	66	8	1	15	11	1
Preparation	67	3	2	15	8	2
Detail schedules for production department	69	11	1	11	5	7
Follow-up reporting of progress on schedules	68	7	1	14	5	4
Inventory records:						
Finished goods	56	1	1	34	15	1
Work in process	59	3	3	24	9	5
Raw materials	67	1	1	23	10	1

processing, was the most prevalent method of processing. The punched cards were used primarily for inventory control and not for scheduling. Less than 10 percent of all the companies used computers for controlling production orders and schedules. It is of interest to note that only 62 percent of the companies reporting were concerned about meeting delivery dates—a situation that is surely to change in years to come.

Operations Research

Over three-fourths of the companies were not using the known OR techniques (Figure 22–10). Economic order quantities were used in less

Figure 22–10

Use of Operations Research

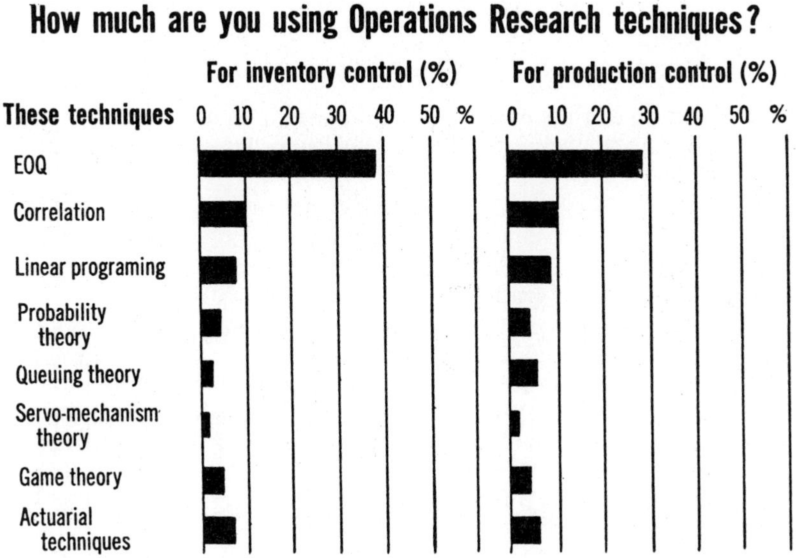

than 40 percent of the factories for inventory control. Less than 30 percent used economic order quantities for production control. There has been an increase in the use of OR over the previous survey in 1959, but the philosophy can probably be conveyed more directly by quoting from the report:

> Where then lies the reason for failing to use these tools? Partly with management. Only 23% have assigned someone the responsibility of using operations research in the plant, although some have assigned it to company headquarters.
>
> Solid reasons for not adopting OR techniques are recognized. One plant reports it could not afford to spend $4000 to gather the information it needed in order to set up an economic order quantity system. Besides, its existing order quantity system operates satisfactorily.
>
> Reluctance to adopt helpful new mathematical techniques stems from a feeling that this surrenders judgment to figures. But as anyone using these techniques knows, they are not a substitute but only a helpful guide when employed correctly.

SUMMARY

This *Factory–APICS Survey,* as you can see, is a most revealing study. It is obvious that most companies are not as advanced as one might expect. This should serve as a challenge to you, revealing as it does the uncovered potential in this field; but it should also give you pause—to wonder why more improvements have not been made. Perhaps it was the way the ideas were presented. Be sure your study of a system is complete, test your ideas, ask others for their opinions, hold your ideas up to the glare of an economic analysis, and then, if all looks well, put the change into effect with all the enthusiasm at your command.

Questions

1. What are some of the organizations interested in production, inventory control, and peripheral problems? Briefly describe the types of articles to be found in their publications.
2. Why is there a gap between the knowledge and application of control theory?
3. Why is forecasting, as practiced, unscientific?
4. Explain why the routing of purchased goods is in some situations the responsibility of production control.
5. What changes do you envision occurring in production and inventory control within the next ten years? Will these changes occur in all industries? Will these changes occur in plants of all sizes? Explain your answers.
6. The APICS report states that 80 percent of those production control departments using sales estimates make some adjustment of the information. Why do you think this is true?
7. According to the APICS report, 21 percent of the companies had no formal control system. Why is this true?
8. What is the future of Operations Research in inventory and production control?

Index

Index

This book has been set in 10 point Electra, leaded 2 points, and 9 point Electra, leaded 1 point. Section and chapter numbers are in 9 point Helvetica caps; section and chapter titles are in 24 point Small Univers Medium. The size of the type page is 27 by 46½ picas.